INTERNATIONAL LAW

VOLUME 2

THE LAW OF PEACE

PART I

INTERNATIONAL LAW IN GENERAL

INTERNATIONAL LAW

BEING THE COLLECTED PAPERS OF

HERSCH LAUTERPACHT

Q.C., LL.D., F.B.A.

SYSTEMATICALLY ARRANGED AND
EDITED BY

E. LAUTERPACHT, Q.C.

VOLUME 2

THE LAW OF PEACE

PART I

INTERNATIONAL LAW IN GENERAL

CAMBRIDGE UNIVERSITY PRESS

CAMBRIDGE

LONDON · NEW YORK · MELBOURNE

CAMBRIDGE UNIVERSITY PRESS
Cambridge, New York, Melbourne, Madrid, Cape Town, Singapore, São Paulo, Delhi

Cambridge University Press
The Edinburgh Building, Cambridge CB2 8RU, UK

Published in the United States of America by Cambridge University Press, New York

www.cambridge.org
Information on this title: www.cambridge.org/9780521107419

First published 1975
This digitally printed version 2009

A catalogue record for this publication is available from the British Library

Library of Congress Catalogue Card Number: 70-92250

ISBN 978-0-521-20480-4 hardback
ISBN 978-0-521-10741-9 paperback

CONTENTS

PREFACE

As Hersch Lauterpacht never wrote a comprehensive treatise reflecting the full range of his wide knowledge of international law, I have thought it appropriate in these *Collected Papers* to attempt to weave his many writings into some systematic form. However, it has been necessary to devote volume I of these papers to three general works which could not conveniently fit into such a scheme. Thus it is only in this volume that the systematic presentation of the separate writings can begin, in rough accord with a series of headings which Lauterpacht at one time prepared when contemplating the possibility of his own textbook.

The whole volume is devoted to a single Part which, as it contains the miscellaneous chapters normally forming the introductory portion of a textbook, has been called 'International Law in General'. But the titles of three of the sections refer to areas within which Lauterpacht wrote major monographic studies. Thus much of the subject matter of *The Function of Law in the International Community* falls within section I on 'International Law as Law'; the content of *Private Law Sources and Analogies of Public International Law* enters the area of section III on 'Sources'; while the material which appeared in *International Law and Human Rights* touches upon both section V, 'Subjects of International Law', and the section which will be included in a later volume on 'The Individual in International Law'.

In deciding on the proper relationship between Lauterpacht's monographs and the contents of the present volume, I have been faced first by the question of what to do with articles which were subsequently incorporated into these monographs. I have on the whole felt it better to omit these – though with occasional exceptions. 'The nature of international law and general jurisprudence' and 'The subjects of the Law of Nations' have been included in this volume, notwithstanding their later appearance in *The Function oj Law* and in *International Law and Human Rights* respectively, because they were of special importance in their time.

Another question has been occasioned by the existence of fragments of partial revisions of *Private Law Sources* and of *The Function of Law* While the former represents only a very small part of *Private Law Sources*, its relatively advanced state of preparation has led me to include it. But the changes in *The Function of Law* are too scattered and too minor to justify any attempt to incorporate them here.

Chapters 3, 4 and 7 have not previously been published. Chapter 2 was only circulated in mimeographed form. Chapter 8, as stated, contains the revision of part of chapter 1 of *Private Law Sources*. As to the latter and other published works, I am glad to be able to acknowledge with gratitude the permission to reprint them given on behalf of the copyright owners of the chapters identified below: George Allen and Unwin Limited – chapter 6; the American Society of International Law – chapter 11; the British Institute of International and Comparative Law – chapter 19; Cambridge University Press – chapter 5; Professor A. L. Goodhart, K.B.E., Editor-in-Chief of the *Law Quarterly Review* – chapter 18; Longman Group Limited – chapter 8; N. V. Martinus Nijhoff's Boekhandel en Uitgeversmaatschappij – chapter 9; Oxford University Press – chapters 15 and 16; and the Royal Institute of International Affairs, London – chapters 2, 10, 12, 13 and 17.

The copy for this volume was the object of much painstaking attention by Mr D. J. Driscoll, of Edinburgh University, and by the staff of Cambridge University Press. Dr Gillian White and Mrs Charity Hopkins gave great help with the proofs and prepared, respectively, the Index and the Table of Cases. I tender my warmest thanks to them – as I do also to my secretary, Mrs S. Rainbow, and to the production staff of Cambridge University Press.

E. LAUTERPACHT

Trinity College
Cambridge
October 1974

TABLE OF CASES

ABBREVIATIONS

OF TITLES OF BOOKS, ETC., QUOTED IN THIS VOLUME

The books referred to in the bibliographies and notes are, as a rule, quoted with their full titles and the date of their publication. But certain books and periodicals which are often referred to in this volume are quoted in an abbreviated form, as follows:

Accioly	Accioly, *Tratado de Direito internacional público*, 3 vols. (1933–5).
A.J.	*American Journal of International Law.*
Annuaire	*Annuaire de l'Institut de Droit International.*
Annual Digest	*Annual Digest and Reports of Public International Law Cases*: 1919–22, edited by Sir John Fischer Williams and H. Lauterpacht (1932); 1923–4, edited by the same (1933); 1925–6, edited by A. D. McNair and H. Lauterpacht (1929); 1927–8, edited by the same (1931); 1929–30 (1935); 1931–2 (1938); 1933–4 (1940); 1935–7 (1941); 1938–40 (1942); 1941–2 (1945); 1919–42 (supplementary volume) (1947); 1943–5 (1949); 1946 (1951); 1947 (1951); 1948 (1953); 1949 (1955) – all edited by H. Lauterpacht.
Anzilotti	Anzilotti, *Corso di diritto internazionale*, vol. I, 3rd ed. (1928), French translation by Gidel (1929); vol. III, part I (1915).
A.S. Proceedings	*Proceedings of the American Society of International Law.*
Balladore Pallieri	Balladore Pallieri, *Diritto internazionale pubblico* (1937).
Baty	Baty, *The Canons of International Law* (1930).
Bibliotheca Visseriana	*Bibliotheca Visseriana Dissertationum Jus Internationale Illustrantium.*
Bittner	Bittner, *Die Lehre von völkerrechtlichen Urkunden* (1924).
Bluntschli	Bluntschli, *Das moderne Völkerrecht der zivilisierten Staaten als Rechtsbuch dargestellt*, 3rd ed. (1878).
Borchard	Borchard, *The Diplomatic Protection of Citizens Abroad* (1915).
Br. and For. St. Papers	*British and Foreign State Papers* (Hertslet), vol. I (1841), continued up to date.
Brierly	Brierly, *The Law of Nations*, 5th ed. (1955).

Bustamante	Bustamante, *Derecho internacional público*, 3 vols. (1933–5).
B.Y.	*British Year Book of International Law.*
Calvo	Calvo, *Le Droit international théorique et pratique*, 5th ed., 6 vols. (1896).
Cavaglieri	Cavaglieri, *Lezioni di diritto internazationale* (general part, 1925).
Clunet	*Journal du droit international.*
Cruchaga	Cruchaga-Tocornal, *Nociones de Derecho internacional*, 3rd ed., 2 vols. (1923–5).
Dicey	Dicey, *Conflict of Laws*, 4th ed. (1927).
Dickinson, *Cases*	Dickinson, *Cases and Other Materials on International Law* (1950).
Documents	*Documents on International Affairs.*
Fauchille	Fauchille, *Traité de droit international public*, 8th ed. of Bonfils' *Manuel de droit international public*, vol. I, part I (1922), vol. I, part 2 (1925), vol. I, part 3 (1926), vol. II (1921).
Fenwick	Fenwick, *International Law*, 3rd ed. (1948).
Fiore	Fiore, *Nouveau droit international public.* French translation by Antoine from the 2nd Italian edition, 3 vols. (1885).
Fiore, *Code*	Fiore, *International Law Codified.* Translation by Borchard from the 5th Italian edition (1918).
Fischer Williams, *Chapters*	Fischer Williams, *Chapters on Current International Law and the League of Nations* (1929).
Fontes Juris Gentium	*Fontes Juris Gentium*, edited by V. Bruns.
Garner, *Developments*	Garner, *Recent developments in International Law* (1925).
Gemma	Gemma, *Appunti di diritto internazionale* (1923).
Genet	Genet, *Traité de diplomatie et de droit diplomatique*, 3 vols. (1931–2).
Gidel	Gidel, *Le droit international public de la mer, le temps de paix*: vol. I, *Introduction – La haute mer* (1932); vol. II, *Les eaux intérieures* (1932); vol. III, *La mer territoriale et la zone contiguë* (1934).
Grotius	Grotius, *De Jure Belli ac Pacis* (1625).
Grotius Annuaire	*Grotius Annuaire International.*
Grotius Society	*Transactions of the Grotius Society.*
Guggenheim	Guggenheim, *Lehrbuch des Völkerrechts*, Parts I and 2 (1947).
Guggenheim, *Traité*	Guggenheim, *Traité de Droit International Publique*, vol. I (1953); vol. II (1954).
Hackworth	Hackworth, *Digest of International Law*, 7 vols. (1940–3).

Hague Recueil	*Recueil des Cours, Académie de Droit International de La Haye.*
Hall	Hall, *A Treatise on International Law*, 8th ed. (1924), by A. Pearce Higgins.
Harvard Research	*Research in International Law*. Under the Auspices of the Harvard Law School. Draft Convention Prepared for the Codification of International Law. Directed by M. O. Hudson: (1929) I. *Nationality* (Reporter: Flournoy); II. *Responsibility of States* (Borchard); III. *Territorial Waters* (G. G. Wilson); (1932) I. *Diplomatic Privileges and Immunities* (Reeves); II. *Legal Position and Functions of Consuls* (Quincy Wright); III. *Competence of Courts in regard to Foreign States* (Jessup); IV. *Piracy* (Bingham): V. *A Collection of Piracy Laws of Various Countries* (Morrison); (1935) I. *Extradition* (Burdick); II. *Jurisdiction with respect to Crime* (Dickinson); III. *Treaties* (Garner).
Heffter	Heffter, *Das europäische Völkerrecht der Gegenwart*, 8th ed. by Geffcken (1888).
Heilborn, *System*	Heilborn, *Das System des Völkerrechts entwickelt aus den völkerrechtlichen Begriffen* (1896).
Hertslet's *Commercial Treaties*	Hertslet, *Collection of Treaties and Conventions between Great Britain and Other Powers, so far as they relate to Commerce and Navigation*, vol. I (1820), continued to date.
Higgins and Colombos	Higgins and Colombos, *The International Law of the Sea*, 2nd ed. (1951).
H.L.R.	*Harvard Law Review.*
Holland, *Lectures*	Holland, *Lectures on International Law*, edited by T. A. and W. L. Walker (1933).
Holland, *Studies*	Holland, *Studies in International Law* (1898).
Holtzendorff	Holtzendorff, *Handbuch des Völkerrechts*, 4 vols. (1885–9).
Hudson, *Cases*	Hudson, *Cases and Other Materials on International Law*, 3rd ed. (1951).
Hudson, *Legislation*	Hudson, *International Legislation*: vols. I–XI (1931–50).
Hyde	Hyde, *International Law, chiefly as interpreted and applied by the United States*, 2nd ed., 3 vols. (1945).
I.C.J.	*International Court of Justice.*
I.C.L.Q.	*International and Comparative Law Quarterly.*
I.L.R.	*International Law Reports*, being the continuation of *Annual Digest*, edited by H. Lauterpacht until volume 24 and thereafter by E. Lauterpacht.

J.C.L.	*Journal of Comparative Legislation and International Law.*
Keith's Wheaton	*Wheaton's Elements of International Law*, 6th English edition by A. Berriedale Keith, vol. I (1929); vol. II (7th ed., 1944).
Klüber	Klüber, *Europäisches Völkerrecht*, 2nd ed. by Morstadt (1851).
Lapradelle-Politis	Lapradelle-Politis, *Recueil des arbitrages internationaux*, vol. I (1905), vol. II (1924), vol. III (1954).
Lauterpacht, *Analogies*	Lauterpacht, *Private Law Sources and Analogies of International Law* (1927).
Lauterpacht, *The Function of Law*	Lauterpacht, *The Function of Law in the International Community* (1933).
Lawrence	Lawrence, *The Principles of International Law*, 7th ed., revised by P. H. Winfield (1923).
Lindley	Lindley, *The Acquisition and Government of Backward Territory in International Law* (1926).
Liszt	Liszt, *Das Völkerrecht*, 12th ed. by Fleischmann (1925).
L.N.O.J.	*League of Nations, Official Journal.*
L.N.T.S.	*League of Nations Treaty Series.* Publication of Treaties and International Engagements registered with the Secretariat of the League of Nations.
Lorimer	Lorimer, *The Institutes of International Law*, 2 vols. (1883–4).
De Louter	De Louter, *Le droit international public positif*, French translation from the Dutch original, 2 vols. (1920).
L.Q.R.	*Law Quarterly Review.*
McNair	McNair, *The Law of Treaties: British Practice and Opinions* (1938).
McNair, *Opinions*	McNair, *International Law Opinions* (1956).
Maine	Maine, *International Law*, 2nd ed. (1894).
Martens	Martens, *Völkerrecht*, German translation from the Russian original, 2 vols. (1883–6).
Martens, G. F.	G. F. Martens, *Précis du droit des gens moderne de l'Europe*, new edition by Vergé, 2 vols. (1858).
Martens, R. Martens, N. R. Martens, N. S. Martens, N. R. G. Martens, N. R. G., 2nd ser. Martens, N. R. G., 3rd ser.	These are the abbreviated quotations of the different parts of Martens, *Recueil de Traités*, which are in common use.
Martens, *Causes célèbres*	Martens, *Causes célèbres du droit des gens*, 2nd ed., 5 vols. (1858–61).

Mérignhac	Mérignhac, *Traité de droit public international*, vol. I (1905), vol. II (1907), vol. III (1912).
Möller	Möller, *International Law in Peace and War*, English translation from the Danish, vol. I (1931), vol. II (1935).
Moore	Moore, *A Digest of International Law*, 8 vols. (1906).
Moore, *International Arbitrations*	Moore, *History and Digest of the International Arbitrations to which the United States has been a Party*, 6 vols. (1898).
Nordisk T.A.	*Nordisk Tidskrift for International Ret. Acta scandinavica juris gentium.*
Nys	Nys, *Le droit international*, 2nd ed., 3 vols. (1912).
Off. J.	*Official Journal of the League of Nations.*
Oppenheim, I. II	Oppenheim, *International Law*, vol. I, 8th ed. (1955), by H. Lauterpacht; vol. II, 7th ed. (1952), by H. Lauterpacht.
O.Z.ö.R.	*Österreichische Zeitschrift für öffentliches Recht.*
P.C.I.J.	*Publications of the Permanent Court of International Justice*: Series A: Judgments. B: Advisory Opinions. A/B: Cumulative Collection of Judgments and Advisory Opinions given since 1931. C: Acts and Documents relating to Judgments and Advisory Opinions. D: Collection of Texts governing the Jurisdiction of the Court. E: Annual Reports.
Perels	Perels, *Das internationale öffentliche Seerecht der Gegenwart*, 2nd ed. (1903).
Phillimore	Phillimore, *Commentaries upon International Law*, 3rd ed., 4 vols. (1879–88).
Praag	Praag, *Jurisdiction et droit international public* (1915).
Praag, *Supplément*	Supplement to the above (1935).
Pradier-Fodéré	Pradier-Fodéré, *Traité de droit international public*, 8 vols. (1885–1906).
Pufendorf	Pufendorf, *De Jure Naturae et Gentium* (1672).
Ralston	Ralston, *The Law and Procedure of International Tribunals*, revised ed. (1926). Supplement (1936).
Ray, *Commentaire*	Ray, *Commentaire du Pacte* (1930).
Recueil T.A.M.	*Recueil des décisions des tribunaux arbitraux mixtes.*
Reddie, *Researches*	Reddie, *Researches, Historical and Critical, in Maritime International Law*, 2 vols. (1844).
Répertoire	Lapradelle et Niboyet, *Répertoire de droit international.* Founded by Darras in 1929.

R.G.	*Revue générale de droit international public.*
R.I.	*Revue de droit international et de législation comparée.*
R.I. (*Geneva*)	*Revue de droit international, de sciences diplomatiques, politiques et sociales.*
R.I. (*Paris*)	*Revue de droit international.*
R.I.F.	*Revue internationale français du droit des gens.*
Rivier	Rivier, *Principes du droit des gens*, 2 vols. (1896).
Rivista	*Rivista di diritto internazionale.*
Rousseau	Rousseau, *Principes généraux du droit international public*, vol. I (1944).
Satow	Satow, *A Guide to Diplomatic Practice*, 3rd ed. by Ritchie (1932).
Scelle	Scelle, *Précis de droit des gens*, vol. I (1932), vol. II (1934).
Schücking und Wehberg	Schücking und Wehberg, *Die Satzung des Völkerbundes*, 2nd ed. (1924).
Schwarzenberger	Schwarzenberger, *International Law as Applied by International Courts and Tribunals*, vol. I (1945).
Scott, *Hague Reports*	Scott, *Hague Court Reports* (1916).
Scott, *Hague Reports* (2nd)	Scott, *Hague Court Reports* (*Second Series*) (1932).
Sibert	Sibert, *Traité de droit international public*, 2 vols. (1951).
Sirey	*Recueil général des lois et des arrêts* (founded by Sirey).
Smith	Smith, *Great Britain and the Law of Nations, a Selection of Documents*, vol. I (1932), vol. II (1935).
Spiropoulos	Spiropoulos, *Traité théorique et pratique du droit international public* (1933).
Stowell	Stowell, *International Law. A Restatement of Principles in Conformity with Actual Practice* (1931).
Strupp, *Éléments*	Strupp, *Éléments du droit international public, universel, européen et américain*, 2nd ed., 3 vols. (1930).
Strupp, *Wört.*	*Wörterbuch des Völkerrechts und der Diplomatie*, ed. by Strupp (begun by Hatschek), 3 vols. (1924–9).
Suarez	Suarez, *Tratado de Derecho internacional público*, 2 vols. (1916).
Temperley	Temperley, *History of the Peace Conference of Paris*, 6 vols. (1920–4).
Testa	Testa, *Le droit public international maritime*, translation from the Portuguese by Boutiron (1886).
Toynbee, *Survey*	Toynbee, *Survey of International Affairs.*
Travers	Travers, *Le droit pénal international*, 5 vols. (1920–2).
Treaty Series	United Kingdom Treaty Series, vol. I, 1892, and a volume every year.

Twiss	Twiss, *The Law of Nations*, etc., 2 vols., 2nd ed., vol. I (Peace, 1884), vol. II (War, 1875).
U.N.R.I.A.A.	United Nations, *Reports of International Arbitral Awards*.
U.N.T.S.	*United Nations Treaty Series*.
Vattel	Vattel, *Le droit des gens*, 4 books in 2 vols., new edition (1773).
Verdross	Verdross, *Die Verfassung der Völkerrechtsgemeinschaft* (1926).
Walker	Walker, *A Manual of Public International Law* (1895).
Walker, *History*	Walker, *A History of the Law of Nations*, vol. I (1899).
Walker, *Science*	Walker, *The Science of International Law* (1893).
Westlake	Westlake, *International Law*, 2 vols., 2nd ed. (1910–13).
Westlake, *Chapters*	Westlake, *Chapters on the Principles of International Law* (1894).
Westlake, *Papers*	*The Collected Papers of John Westlake on Public International Law*, ed. by L. Oppenheim (1914).
Wharton	Wharton, *A Digest of the International Law of the United States*, 3 vols. (1886).
Wheaton	Wheaton, *Elements of International Law*, 8th American edition by Dana (1866).
Z.I.	*Zeitschrift für internationales Recht*.
Z.ö.R.	*Zeitschrift für öffentliches Recht*.
Z.ö.V.	*Zeitschrift für ausländisches öffentliches Recht und Völkerrecht*.
Z.V.	*Zeitschrift für Völkerrecht*.

I

INTERNATIONAL LAW AS LAW

CHAPTER I

THE NATURE OF INTERNATIONAL LAW AND GENERAL JURISPRUDENCE

Editor's note This chapter is reprinted from *Economica*, 12 (1932), 301–20. Most of the article was incorporated in *The Function of Law in the International Community* (first published in 1933 by the Oxford University Press and reprinted photographically in 1966 by Archon Books, Conn., U.S.A.), at pp. 420–3 and 432–8. Nonetheless, as explained in the Preface to volume I of these Papers, it has been thought appropriate to include this item in the systematic presentation of Lauterpacht's works.

I. THE DENIAL OF INTERNATIONAL LAW

A large and not the least important part of present-day international law is based on the assumption that what appears to the ordinary lawyer as incompatible with the conception and the purpose of law is not necessarily inconsistent with the body of rules called international law. This is so, it is said, because international law, far from being like any other law, is a 'specific' law. The purpose of this article is to examine the relevance of this view both to the question of the nature of international law and to the major question of the conception of law in general jurisprudence. In the first place we must inquire how far theories based on the independence of international law of the conception of law as developed in municipal jurisprudence can be regarded as consistent with the legal nature of international law. It will be submitted in this article that such theories, in so far as they have a definite meaning, amount to a negation of international law.

The number of writers who deny, without any qualifications, the existence of international law is comparatively small. In their view the relations of States are in effect governed by rules neither legal nor moral but by laws regulating the mutual relations of physical forces. Thus Hobbes found in the relations of States the historical demonstration of what, even in his own view, would otherwise have been a mere hypothesis, namely, of the existence among men of a pure state of nature[1] co-extensive with an entire absence of

[1] *Leviathan*, part I, ch. xiii: 'But though there had never been any time, wherein particular men were in a condition of war one against another; yet in all times, kings and

legal regulation. Spinoza followed him closely.[1] In the middle of the nineteenth century Lasson, a prominent German writer, gave clear expression to the same negative attitude towards international law.[2] He found followers both before and after the World War.[3] For some of these writers the negative attitude towards international law has been merely a link in the chain of an argument calculated to support their political theory of the State. This was notably the case with Hobbes and Spinoza. With others it is an expression and a justification of an attitude of nationalism and of a deliberate negation of the existence or of the practicability or of the need for an organized international community under the reign of law. With others still it is a denunciation of the predominant attitude of complacent disregard of realities and of the actual reign of force in an admit-

persons of sovereign authority, because of their independency, are in continual jealousies, and in the state and posture of gladiators; having their weapons pointing, and their eyes fixed on one another; that is their forts, garrisons, and guns upon the frontiers of their kingdomes; and continual spyes upon their neighbours; which is a posture of War.' This is the true meaning of Hobbes's identification of the law of nature with the Law of Nations: 'Concerning the offices of one sovereign to another, which are comprehended in that law, which is commonly called the *Law of Nations*, I need not say anything in this place; because the Law of Nations and the law of nature, is the same thing. . . . And the same law, that dictateth to men that have no civil government, what they ought to do, and what to avoid in regard to one another, dictateth the same to commonwealths, that is, to the consciences of sovereign princes, and sovereign assemblies' (*ibid.* part II, ch. XXX (*in fine*)). And see part II, ch. X (*in fine*) of his *De Corpore Politico* (1640) for a clear statement to the effect that 'that which is the law of nature between man and man before the constitution of commonwealth, it is the Law of Nations between sovereign and sovereign, after.' And see also the well-known Dedication to *Elementa philosophica de Cive* (1642) for the juxtaposition of the principles *homo homino deus* and *homo homini lupus*, the first obtaining within the State, the second in the relations of States.

[1] See Lauterpacht in *B.Y.* 8 (1927), 89 *et seq.* [printed below p. 366], and the literature there quoted; and Verdross in *Z.ö.R.* 7 (1927), 100 *et seq.*

[2] *Prinzip und Zukunft des Völkerrechts* (1871); *System der Rechtsphilosophie* (1882). He says, in the former work: 'Two States confront each other like two physical forces. It is true that they are persons endowed with intelligence enabling them to recognize what is advantageous to them and to act accordingly. But there is no other link between them than their common interests, and no form of moral will limits their attitude of selfishness' (at p. 56). And he says, in the latter work: 'International law lacks the quality of true law . . . not only provisionally and for the duration of a lower stage of civilization, but permanently' (at p. 402). Seydel, a distinguished German constitutional lawyer, gave expression to the same views in almost identical terms: *Grundzüge einer allgemeinen Staatslehre* (1873), pp. 31–2.

[3] See, for instance, Binder, *Philosophie des Rechts* (1925), pp. 550–93; Hold-Ferneck, *Lehrbuch des Völkerrechts* (1930). Hold-Ferneck doubts whether there is in the modern world any measure of cultural or legal unity to serve as a basis for international law (pp. 23–4). He is of the opinion that a true community of law between States is inconceivable (p. 86); that the relation between sovereign States is necessarily one of enmity, international law being merely the expression of a *modus vivendi* in the permanent state of latent warfare (pp. 86–8); that obligatory arbitration is inconsistent with the right of self-preservation and any large measure of acceptance of the commitments of obligatory arbitration constitutes a departure 'from the wide and clear paths dictated by the very nature of the State' (p. 151).

tedly transient stage in the development of the international society.[1]

Another group of writers, while not denying the obligatory force of the rules governing the relations between States, have denied to them the character of legal rules. Thus Austin regarded rules of international law – conceived as an independent system of law[2] – as 'positive moral rules which are laws improperly so-called', i.e., 'laws set or imposed by general opinion',[3] and pointed to 'the greatest logical error of all . . . committed by many continental jurists, who include in public law, not only the law of political conditions, of crimes, and of civil and criminal procedure, but also international law; which is not positive law at all, but a branch of positive morality.'[4] But he agreed that these rules were binding and that they were enforced by moral sanctions like fear of provoking general hostility and reprobation for the violation of maxims generally received and respected.[5] Recently, Felix Somló, an able representative of the Austinian method on the continent of Europe, without denying the binding force of the rules commonly referred to as international law, denied that they partake of the character of law.[6]

Both the denial of the existence of international law and the denial of its legal nature are, as mentioned, comparatively rare. The more usual approach is to maintain that it is either a 'necessarily weak law' or 'specific law'. It is maintained that international law is a law

[1] See Lundstedt, *Superstition or Rationality in Action for Peace? Arguments against Founding a World Peace on the Common Sense of Justice. A Criticism of Jurisprudence* (1925). See also Nelson, *Rechtswissenschaft ohne Recht* (1917). And see Fricker in *Zeitschrift für die gesamte Staatswissenschaft*, 28 (1872), 90 *et seq.* and 347 *et seq.*; *ibid.* 34 (1878), 368 *et seq.*

[2] *Lectures on Jurisprudence or the Philosophy of Positive Law* (5th ed., 1885), I, 182.

[3] *Ibid.* II, 754.

[4] The denial of the legal nature of international law conceived as an independent system of law is not incompatible, and must not be confused, with the affirmation of the legal character of some of its rules, namely, of those which are administered as legal rules expressly adopted by the State and its courts. Austin distinguished clearly between these two aspects of the question. He was pointing out repeatedly that 'although positive international morality (so-called international law) . . . has no force within one nation yet . . . a nation may adopt it and enforce it as positive law within itself': *Jurisprudence* (4th ed. by Campbell, 1873), II, 635. This point of view is clearly expressed in *Mortensen* v. *Peters* in the High Court of Justiciary of Scotland (8 Session Cases 93): 'It is a trite observation that there is no such thing as a standard of international law extraneous to the domestic law of a kingdom, to which appeal may be made. International law, so far as this court is concerned, is the body of doctrine regarding the international rights and duties of States which has been adopted and made part of the law of Scotland.' It is generally accepted by writers on English law in so far as they touch on international law. For a recent affirmation of international law as external constitutional law see Wenzel, *Juristische Grundprobleme* (1920). See also Akzin, *Les problèmes fondamentaux du droit international public* (1929).

[5] *Jurisprudence*, I, 226.

[6] *Juristische Grundlehre* (2nd ed., 1927), pp. 153–73.

analogous to that obtaining among primitive communities; that these undoubted shortcomings do not seriously imperil the legal nature of international law; that they are the necessary consequence of the existence of a community of sovereign States; and that to remedy them would in effect mean the termination of international law and its transformation into internal or federal law. This is a school of thought which is generally not regarded as unprogressive. It combines an idealistic defence of the legal nature of international law – conceived as weak law – with repeated assertions that its shortcomings are of a permanent nature as there 'is not and never will be a central authority above the several States'.[1] This view is held by writers as wide apart as Holland,[2] Zitelmann[3] and De Louter.[4] Some writers even go to the length of maintaining that although most of these permanent deficiencies constitute legal shortcomings, they contribute towards making international law a superior type of law from the moral and social point of view.[5]

[1] Oppenheim, *International Law* (4th ed., by McNair, 1928), I, 288. And see *ibid.* pp. 13–15, for an exposition of the legal character of international law notwithstanding its being a weak law. The view that there cannot and 'never will be' an organized *civitas maxima* exercising authority over States is a persistent feature of Oppenheim's treatise.

[2] *The Elements of Jurisprudence* (6th ed. 1893), p. 339. International law, he says, 'is the vanishing point of Jurisprudence: since it lacks any arbiter of disputed questions, save public opinion, beyond and above the disputant parties themselves, and since, in proportion as it tends to become assimilated to true law by the aggregation of States into a larger society, it ceases to be itself, and is transmitted into the public law of a federal government'.

[3] *Die Unvollkommenheit des Völkerrechts* (1919). After enumerating a series of shortcomings of international law, he expresses the opinion that these shortcomings are the necessary consequence of an international law as a law between sovereign States. The present shortcomings of international law, he says, could be removed by the League of Nations becoming the *civitas maxima* and exercising judicial and executive functions over the States. 'But then,' he says, 'this would no longer be international law seeing that the latter presupposes logically the existence of sovereign States' (at p. 53).

[4] De Louter, I, 59: 'Le droit international n'a pas de législateur, et, qui plus est, n'en aura jamais. Un pouvoir législatif ne saurait exister que *dans* un État. Dès que le droit international cesse d'être un droit *entre* des États souverains, pour devenir le droit d'un pouvoir qui leur est supérieur et auquel tous sont soumis, les États perdent leur souveraineté et le droit international se métamorphose en droit public d'un État mondial.'

[5] 'The Law of Nations is of a distinctly different character from municipal law. It may truly be affirmed that the *lex gentium* is of a more elevated nature. Applying as it does *inter gentes*, it does not appeal to the policeman; it appeals to reason itself, to the sense of equity, to a higher moral consciousness' (Philip Marshall Brown, *International Realities* (1917), at p. 104). See also Sauer, *Lehrbuch der Rechts- und Sozialphilosophie* (1929), at p. 290, to the effect that although international law is deficient *qua* law, it is a superior cultural phenomenon: 'From the cultural point of view international law transcends municipal law as based on compulsion. It aspires, from the limited domain of strict law, to an affirmation, as a matter of moral conviction, of the cultural community of mankind.' The historian of legal thought will note with interest that at a certain stage of the development of international law its notional attractiveness was regarded by some as a sufficient compensation for its substantial shortcomings.

The latter doctrine, although viewing the weaknesses of international law as necessarily and permanently connected with the existence of the international society of States, admits that they are shortcomings from the more general legal point of view. But according to another view, the so-called shortcomings of international law are merely the manifestation of its specific character. They are shortcomings, it is said, only so long as they are viewed from the narrow perspective of municipal law, whereas in fact they are a reminder of the existence of a wider conception of law of which municipal law is only a historical category. Thus we find Westlake suggesting that the controversy whether rules of international law are rules of law or of morality can be solved if we decline 'to treat the law of the land as the only proper kind of jural law, for then while keeping law distinct from morality, we shall not encourage an undue attribution to international law of the characters only appropriate to the law of the land'.[1] It is said that 'the orthodox concept of law is not sacrosanct'; that 'it is necessary to inquire whether it ought not to be adapted to the requirements of actual life' (actual life meaning for this purpose the existence of rules called international law);[2] and that the proper way to approach philosophy of law is international law 'through which one is in the position to follow the delicate problem of the creation and the development of law'.[3]

We thus arrive at the central problem in the question of the determination of the legal nature of international law. The answer to this question obviously depends upon the conception of law which we adopt as the basis of the investigation. To what conception of law must international law conform in order that it can accurately be described as law? Is it a conception of law deduced from the positive legal order within the State, i.e., a conception of law of general jurisprudence in modern society? Or is it a conception of law made so elastic as to embrace the body of rules regulating at present the mutual relations of modern States? Shall international law be guided, while admitting its own shortcomings, by the generally

[1] *Papers*, p. 14. However, Westlake himself saw the dangers of this method of approach, and admitted that 'if we give the name of law to anything which we so discover in a remote state of society before we have fixed in our minds what we mean by that name, we beg the question, and have no security that our language has any consistent, or therefore useful, sense' (*ibid.* p. 22). The whole trend of his work justifies the observation of Oppenheim that 'he belonged to the legal school of international jurists who, in contradistinction to the members of the diplomatic school, desire International Law to develop more or less on the lines of Municipal Law' (*ibid.* p. 10).

[2] Mayer in *Archiv des öffentlichen Rechts*, 38 (1918), 14.

[3] Sauer, *Grundlagen der Gesellschaft* (1924), p. 431.

accepted notion of law which few would venture to deny but for the necessity of defending the legal nature of international law? Or shall it broaden it and impart to it some of its elasticity? To put the question in a manner expressing the view of the present writer – Shall international law aim at improvement by trying to bring its rules within the compass of the generally accepted notion of law, or shall it disintegrate it and thus deprive itself of a concrete ideal of perfection? It will be noted that the question thus put transcends the limits of a problem of international law. It becomes a problem of general jurisprudence, a problem whether the general conception of law should be broadened by the inclusion of a generalized norm of conduct based on the relations of sovereign States as at present constituted. Before answering these questions it is necessary to consider the doctrine in which the theory of the specific character of international law has found its current expression. This is the so-called theory of international law as a law of co-ordinate entities or, shortly, as a 'law of co-ordination'.

2. INTERNATIONAL LAW AS A SO-CALLED LAW OF CO-ORDINATE ENTITIES

The notion of international law as a law of co-ordination has recently been increasingly adopted by writers, but there has been no attempt to elaborate it in detail.[1] In a recent text-book of

[1] See, for instance, Strupp, *Éléments*, I, 11 ('Les États étant égaux entre eux, le droit international public en tant droit entre les États est un droit de co-ordination et non un droit de subordination'); Liszt, p. 8 ('International law is based on a corporate not authoritarian principle'); Walz, *Das Wesen des Völkerrechts und die Kritik der Völkerrechtsleugner* (1930), pp. 252–61, also bases his construction of international law on the theory of co-ordination, but there is no attempt at a detailed exposition of what the law of co-ordination really means. Ultimately, the whole theory is reduced to a difference in the manner of the creation of rules of law. Walz does not deny that rules of international law, once established, bind States independently of their will. But he attaches decisive importance to the difference in the 'process of positivation' (i.e. of creation) of rules of law. There is no explanation why this should be a reason for regarding international law as 'a law of a specific character strongly differing from municipal law' (p. 295). See also Heller, *Die Souveränität* (1927), pp. 43–4, who regards international law as 'a non-authoritarian legal order based on contract' (*herrschaftsfreie Vertragsordnung*).

It seems that the insistence on the specific law of co-ordination on the part of German writers has recently assumed the form of a particularly German conception of international law grounded in the Teutonic as distinguished from the Romanistic tradition as embodied in some peculiarities of the political structure of German society in the Middle Ages and in the feudal period. See, for instance, Sternberg, *Einführung in die Rechtswissenschaft* (2nd ed. 1927), part I, p. 26. See also for an admirable survey with an extensive bibliography, Borchard in *Yale Law Journal*, 36 (1926–7), 1058–74. That the idea of the *societas inordinata* as the basis of political relations is necessarily bound up with the existence of a legal power above the *societas inordinata* is clearly pointed out by Binder, *Die Philosophie des Rechts* (1925), p. 572.

Hatschek[1] there is a restatement of the theory of co-ordination, but the attempt is not particularly illuminating. International law, he says, is a legal system based on co-ordination.[2] This, he explains, means that, unlike municipal law, which is based on subordination of persons to the legal rule, there is in international law no superior will which imposes the law. There is no super-State endowed with authority. He then proceeds to define the international law of co-ordination as a 'legal order based on the recognition of States as equal subjects of international law' – a somewhat inconclusive explanation seeing that municipal law, which is a law of 'subordination', is also based on the equality of individuals before the law. How are rules of international law created in such a system? They are created principally by parallel legislation or customary municipal rules in various countries, for instance, by that relating to the inviolability of envoys and foreign heads of States. These rules are binding upon States not as legal rules but as so-called social or conventional rules, i.e., rules which are not created by an authoritative source of law and whose sanction consists merely in social compulsion.[3] From these conventional rules there grows, as the result of their becoming part of the legal conviction of States, particular and, in the long run, general customary international law. We are not told what is the basis or the nature of the binding force of this customary international law. This somewhat slender basis serves as the foundation for Hatschek's exposition of international law. For a more satisfactory exposition of the law of co-ordination it is necessary to go back to earlier German writers, in particular to Jellinek and Triepel.

Jellinek was the first to construe international law as a specific law of co-ordination. He did it with the help of the theory of self-limitation,[4] a theory originally developed in order to demonstrate

[1] *Völkerrecht als System rechtlich bedeutsamer Staatsakte* (1923). An English translation by Manning of the abridged version of this book appeared in 1930.

[2] *Ibid.* p. 2.

[3] Hatschek instances the conventions and customs of the constitution in Great Britain as an example of conventional rules. On the whole the term 'conventional rules' as used by Hatschek and other German writers is identical with Austin's 'positive morality'.

[4] The theory was first formulated in Jellinek's *Die rechtliche Natur der Staatenverträge* (1880), and subsequently amplified and defended in his *Allgemeine Staatslehre* (1st ed. 1900). Of the latter a French translation by Fardis appeared in two editions under the title *L'État moderne et son droit* (2nd ed. in 1911 and 1913). The rudiments of the doctrine of self-limitation will be found in Ihering's *Der Zweck im Recht* (1880), I, 318, and possibly even in Rousseau's *Contrat Social* (Book I, chs. IV and VII). See Sukiennicki, *Essai sur la Souveraineté des États en Droit International Moderne* (1926), pp. 170–4. For examples of the adoption of the theory of self-limitation see Nippold, *Der völkerrechtliche Vertrag* (1894), pp. 19–22, and Zorn, *Grundzüge des Völkerrechts* (1903), p. 7. The doctrine has been accepted by some French writers, for instance, Mérignhac, I, 291 *et seq.*; Malberg, *Contribution à la théorie générale de l'État*, I (1920), 237 *et seq.*

the partial subjection of the State to law. In this act of self-limitation Jellinek recognizes also the source of such binding force as international law possesses. He sees no difference between international and municipal law except that, whereas the latter is a relation of subordination of the members of the community to law, the former is one of co-ordination of entities. International law is grounded in the will of the State, and ultimately it is this basis of international law which is decisive. Where international law and the existence of the State conflict, the former must yield, for international law exists for States and not States for international law. Legally, says Jellinek, the State is entitled to disengage itself at any time from an obligation deemed to be inconsistent with the interests of the State. This precarious nature of international obligations does not, in his view, deprive them of their legal nature, for in addition to the purely normative aspect there is a psychological foundation for law arising out of the fact that it is recognized as binding by the members of the society. Such obligations are not absolutely binding as a matter of strict law, but they possess a binding force grounded in the objective nature of international relations which from the point of view of their social necessity are comparable to those obtaining among individuals.[1] Thus, although as a matter of legal theory the will of the State is the origin and the basis of the obligation, that will is not an entirely irrational factor.

This juxtaposition of two conflicting methods of approach has led to some confusion as to the actual meaning of Jellinek's combination of the doctrine of self-limitation and the theory of a law of co-ordination. Whereas his treatment of international law is generally subjected to severe criticism and regarded as the very negation of law and a glorification of force, there are writers who draw attention to Jellinek's insistence on the objectively binding force of international law and express the opinion that there is no substantial difference between his approach and the more recent doctrines from Triepel to Kelsen and Verdross.[2] It may be doubted whether this is so. As a legal theory the doctrine of self-limitation cannot be interpreted otherwise than as a denial of the binding force of international law. As a sociological and psychological doctrine it amounts to a negation of the ultimate supremacy of the legally sovereign State and thus to an affirmation of the binding force of international law. This double method of approach Jellinek defended on the ground that the same

[1] *Die rechtliche Natur der Staatenverträge*, pp. 46–9.

[2] See, for instance, Spiropoulos, *Théorie générale du droit international* (1930), pp. 46–50.

object may form the subject-matter of various modes of cognition. Thus, he said, a symphony may be the subject-matter of physiology or aesthetics. In proceeding thus he laid himself open to the reproach that it is scientifically impossible to treat objects as the subject-matter of various modes of knowledge at the same time.[1] The fact that the juridical supremacy of the State is sociologically or morally limited by other considerations necessarily escapes juridical appreciation. In practice these considerations may or may not become operative; in practice political considerations may limit the State's freedom from the legal bond, but they need not when these very considerations dictate to the State the necessity of disregarding its obligations. The juridical theory of self-limitation leaves open that possibility. It makes the observance of rules of international law not a matter of legal obligation, but the result of a calculation—which may or may not take the long view – as to the compatibility of the observance of the obligation with the interests of the State. Jellinek himself admitted that as the result of a law of co-ordination thus conceived, 'the community of States is of a purely anarchical nature and international law, originating from an unorganized authority and possessing accordingly no overriding authority, may properly be described as an anarchical law'.[2] It is not surprising that he regarded war not only as a necessary factor but also as an element of progress in this anarchical society. This is in fact the attitude of most of the adherents to the doctrine of auto-limitation. Thus Bergbohm, one of the precursors of the doctrine, regarded the very idea of a permanent international court as incompatible with the modern conception of the State.[3] This was also the attitude of some of the followers of Jellinek.

Where, as the result of the adoption of a somewhat promiscuous method, a writer's opinion lends itself to two diametrically different interpretations, then that interpretation ought to be preferred – as being more accurate – which is most in accordance with the actual influence exercised by the doctrine.[4] It must be judged by its fruits.

[1] See for a vigorous criticism of this 'two-sides' theory Kelsen, *Der soziologische und der juristische Staatsbegriff* (1922), pp. 114–20. [2] *Allgemeine Staatslehre* (3rd ed. 1921), p. 379.

[3] *Staatsverträge und Gesetz als Quellen des Völkerrechts* (1877), p. 32. See also the same, *Jurisprudenz und Rechtsphilosophie* (1892).

[4] For a criticism of the doctrine of self-limitation see Triepel, *Völkerrecht und Landesrecht* (1899), pp. 77–81; Duguit in *H.L.R.* 31 (1917–18), 139–48; Kelsen, *Das Problem der Souveränität und die Theorie des Völkerrechts* (1920), pp. 168–74; Sukiennicki, *op. cit.*, pp. 174–222; Verdross, pp. 12–20, and in *Hague Recueil*, 16 (1927) (i), 262–74; Chklaver, *Le droit international dans ses rapports avec la philosophie du droit* (1929), pp. 179–87; Brierly, 'Le fondement du caractère obligatoire du droit international', *Hague Recueil*, 23 (1928) (iii), 482–4.

From this point of view there is little doubt as to the meaning and consequences of the theory of self-limitation as combined with the doctrine of co-ordination. It constitutes a negation – in all but words – of the binding force of international law. This can be clearly seen from Kaufmann's monograph on 'The Nature of International Law and the Clause *rebus sic stantibus*' – the only work in which an attempt has been made at a detailed exposition of the results of the doctrine of a law of co-ordination.[1]

According to Kaufmann, the basic principle of a law of co-ordination is to be found in the maxim 'Who can, may.'[2] That principle alone is a just and appropriate principle in regard to States which, being responsible for the preservation of the highest values, cannot be subordinated to any higher community and which, at the same time, have to justify their separate existence by their physical and moral power. The victorious war is the vehicle of the law: it alone decides which State is in the right. The consequences of the law of co-ordination thus conceived are various. It means, in the first instance, that legal relations between States are based only on express recognition. There are no imposed obligations. There does not exist an all-embracing community of interests; there are no collective interests unless they include the interests of the State concerned. Self-preservation and self-development are the overriding principles. In a law of co-ordination the subjective interests of individual members constitute objective rules of law. Accordingly, although international law owes its existence to a solidarity of international interests, it does not owe it to *the* solidarity of *the* international interests. There are no such interests. There is, apart from the domain regulated by expressly accepted international obligations, no international community. As these obligations exist only in the limited sphere of the expressly recognized partial community of interests, the individual interests of each State must always remain the guiding consideration. In a system of a law of co-ordination the will of the State is essential not only for the creation but also for the continuation of the obligation. As Hegel said, the relation of States is one of the independent entities which make promises but at the same time stand above their promises. Nothing done in the interest of the preservation of the State is illegal. The State may conclude treaties – including onerous treaties – to escape major evils, but it may legally abrogate them when circumstances have changed so that they cannot be kept

[1] *Das Wesen des Völkerrechts und die clausula rebus sic stantibus* (1911).
[2] *Ibid.* pp. 159 *et seq.*, 179–89 *et seq.*

without disadvantage to the interests of the State. There is, in a law of co-ordination, nothing higher than the interest of *each* of the parties. If the other party is unwilling to give in, then only war can decide whose interest is legally stronger. This is not the denial of law, but the only legal proof possible in a legal system of co-ordination.

Probably an apology is due to the reader for this detailed account of a doctrine propounded over twenty years ago and which may not entirely represent the present views of its author. But the references to the specific character of international law as a system of a law of co-ordination have recently been so frequent that it may be of advantage to see at close quarters what the 'law of co-ordination' really is. Writers will be less eager to base their theories on the 'specific character of international law' if they realize what is the meaning attached to it by its outspoken protagonists. It is true that Kaufmann has pressed the idea of a law of co-ordination to its extreme consequences, but it is doubtful whether he could have done anything else. There is no middle course between subjection to law and the negation of its binding force.

While that branch of the doctrine of co-ordination which is based on the theory of self-limitation has necessarily resulted in a clear denial of international law, the position is different in regard to the second principal theory, namely, Triepel's theory of international law based on the law-making 'agreement' (*Vereinbarung*).[1] Like Jellinek, Triepel adopts the doctrine that international law is a law of co-ordination. But the difference between him and Jellinek is fundamental. Unlike Jellinek, he recognizes the existence over and above States of a juridical norm whose continued validity is independent of the will of States. This is the norm that the law-making agreement is binding. The law-making 'agreement' derives its force from the common will resulting from a combination of wills, but ultimately independent of and superior to the wills of the individual States. The way is thus paved for an objective basis of international law which, upon analysis, proves tantamount to the abandonment of the 'law of co-ordination'. The transition from a purely contractual to an objective international law is slow, but the trend of development is clearly marked.

Cavaglieri,[2] too, rejects the view which bases the binding force of

[1] For a clear statement of the doctrine see his *Völkerrecht und Landesrecht* (1899), which is a powerful piece of juristic thinking. Triepel has restated his views on the subject in *Hague Recueil*, I (1923), 77–118.

[2] Cavaglieri, pp. 44 *et seq.*

international law on a *command* issued by a superior power. There remains, he says, only the possibility of conceiving international law as 'a system of promises between co-ordinated and juridically equal subjects'. He points out that 'recent studies in the general theory of law have shown that the legal rule need not necessarily assume the character of a command emanating from a superior authority, but that, in certain circumstances, it can have its origin in a promise'. Where, in the international sphere, lies the binding force of the promissory rule of conduct? This ultimate source of obligation Cavaglieri finds in the rule *pacta sunt servanda.* The slowness of the progress is marked by Cavaglieri's insistence that the principle *pacta sunt servanda* itself owes its existence to the practice of States.

Anzilotti goes a step further. He, too, starts from the proposition that the rules governing the relations of States are fundamentally different from those governing the relations of persons within the State.[1] Within the State, he says, which is governed by the relation of supremacy and subordination, the creation of legal rules is exclusively, or almost exclusively, left to organs exercising power over the people of the State so that the legal rule appears as a command issuing from above, whereas the legal rules among States cannot be anything else except agreements and promises between equals. But what is the foundation of this system of promises? The question, answers Anzilotti, of the *vis obligandi* of the common will of States is a problem which cannot be solved by purely empirical considerations and which requires therefore a solid juristic foundation. This foundation is the rule *pacta sunt servanda* conceived as a necessary *a priori* assumption of the international legal order which, although capable of proof by political or moral considerations, cannot itself be proved juridically, just as the legal force of the highest constitutional rule within the State cannot be proved as a juridical proposition. Within the State the rule *pacta sunt servanda* is one of the rules of law sanctioned by the legal order; in the international society it constitutes the highest, irreducible, final criterium. The basis of international law is thus finally divorced from the will of States as its ultimate and formal source.

3. THE INITIAL HYPOTHESIS IN INTERNATIONAL LAW

It has been shown that the doctrine of international law as a law of co-ordination amounts either to a negation of international law or

[1] Anzilotti, p. 46.

else, by recognizing the objectively binding force of international obligations, reveals itself as a typical 'law of subordination', i.e., the normal type of law as adopted in municipal society. For the school of writers from Triepel to Anzilotti and Cavaglieri the conception of 'co-ordination' consists not in the absolute absence of will or obligation overriding the will of the State, but merely in the rule that new obligations cannot be imposed upon a State against its will. Now the view that States are bound only by rules expressly accepted is, of course, the assertion of the extreme positivist view. However, it is not necessary here to refute that opinion. It has no reference to the question of subjection to existing law. It is not inconsistent with the assumption of the existence of a legal command, in the form of a basic legal hypothesis – even in its original form of the theory of the common will – to abide by obligations expressly or tacitly undertaken. So long as the binding force of this basic postulate is assumed, the view that international law is a 'system of promises' is of only secondary importance.[1] The rule *pacta sunt servanda* confronts States as an objective principle independent of their will. It is from this point of view of little importance whether we adopt the view put forward by Kelsen and accepted by Anzilotti that the rule *pacta sunt servanda* is an original hypothesis which cannot be proved juridically, or whether, like Cavaglieri, we see in it a rule which can be proved juridically by reference to the practice of States and to their conviction as to what is the law. For in each case the rule, in its actual operation, confronts the State independently of its will; the binding force of this ultimate principle, once established, is as objective as the corresponding rule within the State. It does not matter whether the rule *pacta sunt servanda* is juridical or not; whether it is imposed as a matter of juridical construction or as a clear generalization from the actual practice and legal convictions of States. The result is the same. It is therefore – it is submitted – impossible to follow those writers who, from the fact that individual obligations of international law owe their origin to the will of States, proceed to develop the view as to the essential differences between a law of co-ordination and a law of subordination. In both cases the basic rule constitutes a command, i.e., a rule existing independently of the will of the parties. It is of no consequence that in the international sphere the command does

[1] It is a fatal mistake on the part of the modern positivist school—a mistake which renders the doctrine largely unreal—that it attaches decisive importance to the freedom of States not to accept new obligations and that it disregards their subjection to rules undertaken either expressly or—and this applies to the bulk of international duties of the State—impliedly.

not issue from a political superior. Law may be a command without being the command of a concrete political authority. Only the antiquated view that law is the will of a real group entity will raise the query, How is a command possible without there being an authority issuing the command? Once it is recognized that for juristic perception the State is the law and that the juxtaposition or opposition of the two is only a convenient mode of expression, then there is no difficulty in accepting the view that the law may be a command merely by virtue of its external nature.

What is the explanation of the fact that the literature of international law – even in its more radical manifestations as expressed in the adoption of the 'initial hypothesis'[1] – failed to draw what seem to be the necessary conclusions from the assumption of the objectively binding force of international law? It is believed that one of these reasons is the form in which writers have clothed that fundamental premise. Its very form seems to suggest adherence to an attitude which has in fact been abandoned. The habits of a generation are not easily discarded, and the theory – abandoned by the adoption of the rule *pacta sunt servanda* as the fundamental rule – that the will of the States is the ultimate source of international law still continues to find partial adherence in the view that international law is not a command but a system of promises. The two views are, of course, irreconcilable. It is hardly permissible to speak in the same breath of international law as a system of promises and as a system governed by the objective rule *pacta sunt servanda*. *Pacta sunt servanda* is an external rule of conduct obliging States to abide by the rules of intertional law. The fact that the basic principle of international law as expressed in the rule *pacta sunt servanda* refers exclusively to agreements of States is responsible for the confusion that has arisen. Possibly the choice, for which Verdross and, following him, Kelsen, are

[1] As international lawyers in English-speaking countries are not always familiar with this term it may perhaps be useful to refer the reader to Salmond's *Jurisprudence* (8th ed. 1930), §48 ('Ultimate Legal Principles') for a most lucid exposition of the necessity of what some continental jurists have called the 'initial hypothesis' (*Ursprungsnorm*). He says: 'It is requisite that the law should postulate one or more first causes, whose operation is ultimate, and whose authority is underived. In other words there must be found in every legal system certain ultimate principles, from which all others are derived, but which are themselves self-existent. . . Whence comes the rule that Acts of Parliament have the force of law? This is legally ultimate; its source is historical only, not legal. . . No Statute lays it down. It is certainly recognized by many precedents, but no precedent can confer authority upon precedent. It must first possess authority before it can confer it. If we inquire as to the number of these ultimate principles, the answer is that a legal system is free to recognize any number of them, but it is not bound to recognize more than one. From any one ultimate legal source, it is possible for the whole law to be derived, but one such there must be' (p. 169).

responsible, of this particular formula is unfortunate inasmuch as, at least *prima facie*, it refers to *pacta*, i.e. contractual agreements evidencing the direct will of States. It is only by dint of the legal construction of custom as tacit agreement that it can bring within its purview the by far the most important part of international law. Only by an even more strained construction can the formula include such customary international law to which the State has consented impliedly by virtue of – another implied factor – its application for admission into the family of nations. And only by a further effort of legal reasoning can it be made to include those generally recognized principles of law to which States have only recently granted express recognition,[1] but which, quite apart from the constant practice of States, necessarily form part of international law, as indeed of any conceivable law.

The initial hypothesis in municipal law is that the will of the State must be obeyed; by way of a further explanation of this hypothesis it may be said that the will of the State consists of duly enacted statutes and custom as interpreted by courts. There is no reason why the original hypothesis in international law should not be that the will of the international community must be obeyed. By way of further explanation it could be said that, although in many cases the will of the international community must be deduced from the mere fact of its existence, i.e. from 'the reason of the thing', the organs of the formation of the will of the international community are, in default of an international legislature, States themselves, their consent being given by custom or treaty and being capable of impartial ascertainment and interpretation by international tribunals. An initial hypothesis expressed in the terms of *voluntas civitatis maximæ est servanda* would point, as the source of law, to the will of the international society expressing itself in contractual agreements between its constituent members, in their customs, and in the general principles of law which no civilized community can afford to ignore; it would refer to the *civitas maxima* as meaning that super-State of law which, through the recognition of the binding force of international law *qua* law, States have already recognized as existing over and above the national sovereignties; it would be compatible with the fact that the authority of that legal super-State extends so far not so much to the creation of new concrete rules as to the maintenance and respect of obligations already expressly or impliedly contracted.

[1] See Article 38(3) of the Statute of the Permanent Court of International Justice.

The hypothesis *pacta sunt servanda* has proved a beneficent transition from a doctrine of international law based on the will of sovereign States to a doctrine of the Law of Nations based on the law's impersonal sovereignty. But at present it contains both incongruous elements. It pays homage both to the will of States as the fountain of law and to the heteronomous command of the rule of law. The synthesis is only one of words; it is not, and cannot be, one of substance. A more satisfactory solution can be found in a hypothesis which, by courageously breaking with the traditions of a past period, incorporates the rational and ethical postulate, which is gradually becoming a fact, of an international community of interests and functions. That such a community exists is not only the view of the modern critics of State sovereignty. By the end of the nineteenth century it was given lucid expression by Westlake, who saw in the fact of the existence of the international community the true basis of international law. It was stated on the very threshold of international law by Grotius: 'hæc vero . . . societatis custodia, humano intellectui conveniens, fons est ejus juris, quod proprie tali nomine appellatur'.[1] It was expressed by Christian Wolff in the first scientific attempt to lay the legal foundations of the *civitas maxima*, when he referred to *jus gentium voluntarium* as being deduced not *ex factis gentium* but 'ex fine civitatis maximæ, quam perinde ac societatem inter omnes homines instituit ipsa natura, ut in jus istud consentire debeant gentes. . .'[2] If it is true that the initial hypothesis ought to be not a maxim with a purely formal content, but an approximation to social reality, then, indeed, the first postulated legal cause can fittingly be formulated by reference to the international community as such, and not to the will of individual States.[3]

The suggestion for a change in the formulation of the initial premise is not merely a matter of wording. The initial premise is to a large extent expressive of the nature of the legal system in question. It may influence that legal system so far as it is in the power of a legal theory to do so. This may be clearly seen from the fact that the initial premise embodied in the principle *pacta sunt servanda* could be held compatible not only with the spurious theory of an international law of co-ordination, but also with the affirmation of the view that it is

[1] Grotius, *Proleg.*, 8.

[2] *Jus gentium methodo scientifica pertractatum* (1749), *Praefatio.*

[3] On the question of the initial hypothesis in international law see Kelsen, *Das Problem der Souveränität und die Theorie des Völkerrechts* (1920), *passim*; Verdross, pp. 21–33; Cavaglieri, pp. 40–50; Ottolenghi, in *Rivista*, 17 (1925), 343–57; Kunz, *Völkerrechtswissenschaft und reine Rechtslehre* (1923), and in Strupp, *Wört.*, 1, 787 *et seq.*; Salvioli in *Rivista*, 14 (1921–2), 20–80; Merkl in *Z.ö.R.* 6 (1926), 497 *et seq.*; Heinrich, *ibid.* 308 *et seq.*

the essence of existing international law that a State can legally claim the right to remain judge in disputes with other States by the simple means of refusing to them the benefit of judicial settlement.

4. INTERNATIONAL LAW AND GENERAL JURISPRUDENCE

Once the doctrine of international law as a specific law of co-ordination has been reduced to its true proportions – i.e. either to a denial of international law or to a mere phrase devoid of legal consequences – the way is open to a consideration of the central problem of international law, which is at the same time one of the principal problems of the philosophy of law in general. Shall international law, by refusing to admit its present imperfections and by elevating them to the authority of legitimate and permanent manifestations of a 'specific' law, abdicate the task of raising itself above the level of a primitive law of a primitive community? Shall it follow that law or shall it claim independence of it? The answer, it is submitted, is that, as international law is, like any other law, a 'law of subordination', its future development is conditioned by its incorporation into the general principles and conception of law as developed by civilized communities without reference to the 'state of nature' existing among States. The more international law approaches the standards of municipal law, the more it approximates to those standards of morals and order which are the ultimate foundation of all law. The time-honoured repudiation and disparagement of the analogy with municipal – and, in particular, private – law is merely another aspect, or the consequences of the insistence on, the so-called specific character of international law.

It is better that international law should be regarded as incomplete and in a state of transition to the finite and attainable ideal of a society of States under the binding rule of law as generally recognized and practised by civilized communities within their borders than that, as the result of the well-meant desire to raise its formal authority *qua* law, it should be treated as the perfect and immutable species of a comprehensively diluted *genus proximum*.[1]

[1] This latter course is generally followed by international lawyers, and only in time of international crises disclosing the imperfections of the existing law does there reveal itself the tendency towards what we believe to be a more accurate approach. Liszt, the author of a well-known German text-book, was in ten editions of his treatise inculcating into the mind of the student the view that international law is based on agreement, that it is a law different from municipal law, and that the element of compulsion must necessarily be absent from it (10th ed., p. 10). But in the eleventh edition, prepared by Liszt himself in 1918, there is a radical change of attitude (p. 8). International law is there said to be

There is an obvious disadvantage attaching to the application, in the domain of jurisprudence, of the principle of the Gresham law in economics according to which bad currency drives out the good one. There is no good reason why primitive law, if law it be, should drive out developed law as the decisive factor in determining the conception of law. A departure from this path of juridical rectitude constitutes only an insignificant danger to municipal jurisprudence, where what has been called 'the normative force of social reality' automatically acts as a corrective to misguided legal theory. In international law the effects of such methods are more pernicious. They sanction its imperfections. They prevent its development. They tend to deprive it of an attainable ideal. It may be admitted that the conception of law is a historical category, subject to changes of time and space, but because it is a historical category it is inappropriate and inadmissible that the conception of law gained from the generalization of a practice in the rudimentary stage of legal development should determine that of a more advanced stage and disintegrate it in consequence.

It is submitted that the arguments usually adduced in support of the legal nature of international law conceived as a 'weak law'[1] may be plausible and even scientifically accurate, but that their cumulative effect is such as to explain it away to the point of extinction. It is possible by reference to the history of primitive communities to assert the existence of a legal order without a sovereign authority enacting laws; it is possible to think of a rudimentary legal order possessing no courts having obligatory jurisdiction in the matter of ascertaining disputed rights; it is possible to conceive of a system of law having no organs for its enforcement and relying for that purpose upon self-help. But it is permissible to ignore the vitiating consequences of any single defect only if other essential elements are present to neutralize the results of the shortcomings in one particular sphere. To assert the possibility of the existence of a legal system in which *all* these elements are lacking is to reduce the conception of law to a shadow of its own self or else to apply it in a meaning different from that usually attached to it.

The difficulty is not solved by dint of the assertion that primitive communities do offer a historical proof of the possibility of rudimentary systems of law existing notwithstanding these shortcomings.

of the same nature as the law of the State, and the introduction of the factor of compulsion is described as the necessary practical goal of its development if it is to maintain itself as law.

[1] See above, pp. 5–6.

For not only does the designation of the rules governing the conduct of its members as rules of law beg the question of their legal nature; and not only is a cumulation of these shortcomings unknown even to primitive society. The decisive factor is that modern States are *not* primitive communities and that there is a patent contradiction in any attempt to construe the relations between States of today as governed by the law of primitive peoples. Civilized States are *not* primitive tribes. Accordingly, lawyers who endeavour to explain by this method the perpetuation of the existing shortcomings of international law are engaged in a task which is as unscientific as it is unprogressive.[1] This reproach cannot effectively be met by the plea that there is nothing contradictory in the fact that States with a developed system of law within their borders are governed in their relations *inter se* by a deficient and almost illusory system of law. Only the current personification of the metaphysical State supported by the questionable doctrine of States as the sole subjects of international law enables writers to assert and justify the possibility of human beings – for States and Governments are human beings – adopting fundamentally differing standards of order and justice in different spheres of action.

The notion of law with the help of which the international lawyer gauges and determines the nature of the rules which form the subject-matter of his science is necessarily an *a priori* one. But this is an additional reason why it should be construed on the basis of what is best and most developed in legal experience – not on the basis of the emaciated, fragmentary and historically questionable experience of primitive communities in past ages. It is of the essence of the dignity of legal science – including the science of international law – to resist the temptation to lower the standard of law to the low level of an avowedly rudimentary practice.

[1] Professor Brierly (*The Law of Nations* (1st ed. 1928), p. 52), referring to the weakness of international law in regard to the imperfections of its law-creating machinery says—rightly, it is submitted—that such 'customary law can never be adequate to the needs of any but a most primitive society, and the international society of to-day is not, except in the matter of its law, at the primitive stage'.

CHAPTER 2

THE REALITY OF THE LAW OF NATIONS

Editor's note This chapter consists of a lecture given at a meeting at the Royal Institute of International Affairs, Chatham House, London, on 27 May 1941. The text was subsequently revised and enlarged by Lauterpacht and was circulated in mimeographed form amongst members of the Institute. It has not previously been printed. The summary of the discussion after the lecture is omitted.

Anyone who, in these days, chooses to speak of 'The Reality of the Law of Nations' lays himself open to the charge of untimely simplicity or even of audacity. For the reality of international law has become, for many, a byword; and mention of it has often been used as an occasion for recrimination. However, in this as in other matters, despondency or cynicism may be a cloak for facile thinking, and the time is perhaps ripe for facing the issue squarely on a not purely technical ground. Nor is it sufficient – although it may be legitimate and necessary to do so – to stress the fact that the sad plight of the world, which for a long time tolerated grievous violations of the Law of Nations, provides impressive evidence of its significance, or that the World War which began in 1939 is in itself a vindication of its vitality. The problem of international law and of its reality is, in essence, identical with the problem of world order in general and of the post-war World Order in particular. This being so, it is proper that a discussion of it should not be confined to a limited circle of experts.

I. THE REALITY OF INTERNATIONAL LAW AS A QUESTION OF TERMINOLOGY

Before the First World War the question of the reality and justification of international law as a legal discipline was not a subject of active inquiry by the ordinary citizen. It was, it is true, a matter of interest and discussion for jurists and political writers. Among them, the claim of international law to rank as a branch of law had been for generations a subject of dispute. The possibility and, indeed, the necessity of rules, legal or otherwise, regulating the conduct of States in a binding manner had been denied by philosophers and political theorists less notorious than Macchiavelli or Treitschke. We have only to think of such names as Spinoza and Bosanquet, one of the leading exponents of English idealistic philosophy. Thus Spinoza denied, by dint of a singularly unconvincing argument, that there operate in the mutual relations of States the same factors which impelled individuals to abandon the state of nature and to establish, by means of the social contract, a civil government for securing the reign of law. The State, he asserted, is self-sufficient in the matter of external defence; it is immune from the physical disabilities and limitations to which individuals are subject because of the infirmities of disease, of old age, of the need for sleep, and of other natural troubles which flesh is heir to.[1] Bosanquet used involved language in the same vein in order to show that a state of nature is the perpetual condition of international relations, for the reason that the State 'has no determined function in a larger community, but it is itself the supreme community; the guardian of a whole moral world, but not a factor within an organised world'.[2] He was emphatic that there can be no breach of law by the State on the ground that a State is not subject to the law of any other State. The possibility of a State being subject to a law other than that of a State was apparently dismissed as unworthy of argument.

These had been controveries in which the average person – the man in the street – showed but little interest. The catastrophe of the First World War and the establishment of the League of Nations in 1919 marked a radical change in this respect. The new international order set up by the Covenant symbolized, for the sceptic and the believer alike, the first organized attempt made by sovereign States to establish the rule of law – of international law – within the community of nations as the indispensable condition of the well-being of their citizens. This was the sentiment among large numbers of the population in many countries.[3] The period of retrogression which began with the successful invasion of Manchuria, which resulted in

[1] *Tractatus Politicus*, ch. iii, 11.

[2] *Philosophical Theory of the State* (4th ed. 1923), pp. 302–3. For scathing comment thereon see Hobhouse, *The Metaphysical Theory of the State* (1918), *passim*, and Carritt, *Morals and Politics* (1935), pp. 154–7.

[3] It has been suggested occasionally that one of the reasons for the failure of the League of Nations has been that when it was set up there was, among peoples, no general comprehension of its essential purpose of ensuring peace by force and of the obligations which that purpose involved. A study of the trend of public opinion on this matter in the concluding years of the First World War shows that that view is devoid of foundation.

the elimination of the League as an effective instrument of peace, and which culminated in the Second World War confirmed the disbelief of the cynic and disappointed the hopes of the faithful. But, once more, the experience of failure has made both conscious of the problem of the reality of international law as a permanent factor in the life of man and not merely as a topic of dialectical controversy in the domain of terminology and classification. The intensity of modern warfare and the horrors of aerial bombardment have had the same effect. The ordinary citizen is no longer in a mood to look at the matter as an object of doctrinal dispute. The subject has acquired a renewed vitality, both direct and urgent. It has been recently suggested by an American scholar that international lawyers must – as he put it in a homely phrase – learn to 'sell' international law to the public. Apart from the question of the propriety of international lawyers embarking on this kind of activity, it is clear that there are influences more potent than propaganda and persuasion which tend to impart that weighty lesson.

When we speak of the reality of the body of rules called international law we may mean two different things. In the first instance, without raising the problem of its efficacy or otherwise, we may question its reality as a body of law, as a body of legal rules. It is the very old question: Is international law really *law*? This line of attack has for long been a favourite pastime of lawyers and non-lawyers, especially the latter.[1] However, the resulting controversy has been to a large extent one of words and of a choice of premises. Its outcome has depended mainly on the definition of law chosen as the starting-point. For those wedded to the Austinian conception of law, which postulates a definite political superior with organs laying down the law by legislative action, ascertaining it through the normal judicial activity of tribunals endowed with obligatory jurisdiction, and habitually enforcing it by the organized and impartial might of the State – for those jurists, international law had no reality at all *qua* law. But there have been lawyers of no mean authority – Sir Henry Maine and Sir Frederick Pollock among them – who doubted whether we are justified in relying for the purpose on a conception

[1] International law has not been the only discipline whose existence as a subject of scientific exposition has been doubted. Thus, for instance, we find Thomas Hill Green intimating in the Introduction to his *Prolegomena to Ethics* that the writer on moral philosophy 'can scarcely be aware that Moral Philosophy is a name of somewhat equivocal repute; that it commands less respect among us than was probably the case a century ago; and that anyone who professes to teach or write upon a subject to which this name is in any proper or distinctive sense applicable, is looked upon with some suspicion'.

And note Renan's reference to the 'miniature science' of history.

of law confined to fully developed modern States. They have insisted that in framing our definition of law we are not entitled to restrict ourselves to a limited orbit of legal experience and to disregard the law of primitive communities, which know no lawgiver, no regular tribunals, and no superior enforcing agencies. These protagonists of the legal nature of international law have made the most of this type of argument – so much so that they had to be reminded occasionally that, after all, civilized States are not primitive communities – normally at least – except in their mutual relations. Thus, from this angle, the problem of the reality of international law *qua* law has tended to end in a deadlock.[1]

2. THE REALITY OF THE LAW OF NATIONS AND THE EXISTENCE OF AN INTERNATIONAL COMMUNITY

Neither have the defenders of the reality of international law been prepared to yield when confronted with the argument that international law is impossible, as would be any other law, on the ground that there is no international community in the true sense of the word – a community of moral sentiment, of fundamental standards of justice, and of an essential solidarity of interests. For in the view of the believer in the reality of the Law of Nations there is among the peoples of the modern world, in addition to the biological fact and the moral postulate of the unity of the human race, a true solidarity of interest – economic, cultural and scientific – deeper and more significant than the loudly proclaimed divergencies of conflicting claims and aspirations. The importance of the geographical factor making for isolation and self-sufficiency has tended to diminish. The advent of aircraft and radio communications and of broadcasting have caused not only a shrinkage of distances but a penetration of national frontiers. That comprehensive unity, it is true, is obscured, nay effectively suppressed, by the often short-sighted and often ruth-

1 The suggestion of some political writers to the effect that to a person trained in the English law tradition the notion of international law has been confusing and a source of despair – see e.g., the view of Sir Alfred Zimmern, Professor of International Relations at Oxford, *The League of Nations and the Rule of Law* (1936), p. 14 – invites the answer that this has not been the view of the great majority of English and American jurists or, even more so, of English and American judges. A former Professor of Jurisprudence at Oxford probably accurately summarizes the position: 'Few jurists would deny that the term "law" can properly be applied to International Law, or would insist, because of certain obvious deficiencies, on calling it mere "positive morality"' (Allen, *Law in the Making* (3rd ed. 1938), p. 149). See also, to the same effect, Goodhart in *Grotius Society*, 22 (1936), 32–4; Pollock in *Columbia Law Review*, 2 (1902), 511, 514; Vinogradoff, *Collected Papers*, II (1928), 365.

less assertions of national sovereignty, especially when wielded by dictatorships of persons or of classes. But it is nevertheless a fact ultimately more enduring than national isolation and conflicting claims of national interest. It is a fact brought about not only by external conditions but also by the growing consciousness of the increasing inter-dependence of States. As such it provides a sufficient basis for a beneficent system of the organized rule of law. The disunity of the modern world is a fact; but so, in a truer sense, is its unity.

This essential and manifold solidarity, coupled with the necessity of securing the rule of law and the elimination of war, constitutes a harmony of interest which has a basis more real and tangible than the illusions of the sentimentalist or the hypocrisy of those satisfied with the existing *status quo*. The ultimate harmony of interest which within the State finds expression in the elimination of private violence is not a misleading invention of nineteenth century liberalism. The assertion of that transcending harmony of interests is fully compatible with the admission that there exist constant and serious divergencies of national interests.[1] There is, in general, an ultimate and comprehensive harmony of interest among the citizens of the State notwithstanding any conflicts of particular or collective interests.

Similarly, prior to the advent of dictatorships wedded to the absolute glorification of the aggressive State and to the relegation of the individual human being to a mere instrument thereof, there was present among the nations of the world that community of fundamental moral standards and political notions without which any law must remain precarious and artificial. The restoration of that community, brutally assaulted and diverted from its natural channels, is admittedly a vital condition of the resumption of the progress of the Law of Nations.

These considerations supply the answer to the denial of the reality of international law on the ground of the absence of a true international community – an answer so conclusive that it is hardly worth while to indulge in jurisprudential controversies to which that objection gives rise. Thus, for instance, there is room for the view that the law – which normally means the State – far from being the product of an existing community of interest and sentiment, is the cause and the originator of an organically growing unity and solidarity of those subjected to its sway.

[1] For a cogent presentation of the contrary view, see Carr, *The Twenty Years' Crisis 1919–1939* (1939), pp. 54–80.

3. THE LIMITS OF THE OBSERVANCE OF THE LAW OF NATIONS

After the problem of the existence of an international community as a condition of the reality of the Law of Nations has been reduced to its true proportions, there remains the inescapable question of the reality of the Law of Nations viewed as a matter of actual observance. We may agree to treat as irrelevant the question of the nature of the rules passing by the name of international law. But, it is said, we cannot shut our eyes to the fact that, whatever it be in terms of scientific concepts, it has no reality in terms of actual conduct which it is supposed to govern. The dogmatic lawyer would reply that even this is not decisive seeing that the validity of a rule of law, unlike that of a scientific law, is not affected by occasional or even frequent departures from the norm. Such a reply might be open to challenge even by lawyers; it would certainly tend to exasperate the layman, who has shown some disposition to charge international lawyers not indeed with responsibility for the widespread violations of the law but with a dangerous complacency in assuming the existence of an imaginary international order.

There is, of course, a less dialectical and more convincing answer, namely, that violations of important political treaties,[1] aggressions against and annihilation of the independence of States, and disregard of the laws of war are only one side of the picture. For at this same time, it is urged, even in periods of lawlessness and widespread breaches of treaties, we witness a wide though not conspicuous measure of application of international law.[2] We see Government departments and foreign offices invoking, seeking counsel upon, and relying on international law in daily intercourse with other States, great or small. Anyone who has had the opportunity of studying, for instance, the files of the British Foreign Office on any particular

[1] It has been suggested (see, e.g., Carr, *Twenty Years' Crisis*, p. 232) that violations of important political treaties in the nature of international settlements like the provisions of the Treaty of Paris of 1856 relating to the Black Sea, or of the Treaty of Berlin concerning Bosnia-Herzegovina, or of the Treaty of Versailles, are not relevant to the question of the observance of international law for the reason that treaties, like contracts among private individuals, are not law in the proper sense of the word. The answer is that treaties, like contracts, *are* law in the full sense of the word. Both lay down rules of conduct binding upon the parties. Municipal courts apply private contracts more often than they apply Acts of Parliament. Treaties figure first in the list of the sources of the law which its Statute enjoins upon the Permanent Court of International Justice. Most of the Judgments and Advisory Opinions of the Permanent Court of International Justice have been concerned with the interpretation of treaties.

[2] Professor Jessup has recently stressed this aspect of the problem: see *Foreign Affairs*, 18 (1939–40), 244 *et seq.*

topic must be profoundly impressed by the care with which rules of international law and arguments drawn from its armoury are relied upon in controversies with small States against which a show of power or of mere displeasure might prove equally effective. We observe courts, national and international, rendering decisions based on international law. In particular, we find courts in Great Britain and in the United States administering for generations the Law of Nations as part of the law of the land – that Law of Nations without which, in the words of Blackstone and Maine, this country would cease to be part of the civilized world.[1]

This answer pointing to the normal observance and application in time of peace of rules of international law, such as they are, is weighty, but it is of limited persuasiveness. When Mr Moore, a former Judge of the Permanent Court of International Justice, says that 'international law is *on the whole*[2] as well observed as municipal law', it is difficult to dismiss the impression that that qualification is more substantial than appears at first sight. For that part of international law which is normally observed and enforced by national courts and agencies is of minor import as compared with that which is either violated or which is not violated but merely so for the reason that it leaves rigidly alone the most important spheres of the freedom of action of States either in the international field or in the internal sphere in so far as the latter affects international relations. From this point of view international law, even if fully observed, must, in the eyes of the observer, possess an exceptional degree of unreality. It lays down detailed, though often controversial, rules on the subject of diplomatic intercourse and privileges and of jurisdictional immunities of foreign States, their heads, their ships and their public property; it has an elaborate machinery for concluding treaties; manifold agreements regulate an intricate variety of interests. But in fundamental matters, traditional and to a large extent existing international law abdicates any regulative or remedial function. It leaves to the State a degree of freedom of action which reduces law to a very secondary factor in the life of States. It fully admits that subjects like economic policy and migration are entirely within the so-called sphere of exclusive jurisdiction of the State – matters which are among the most fruitful sources of friction. It leaves to States full freedom of action in framing laws concerning acquisition and

[1] Sir William Malkin's article entitled 'International Law in Practice', *L.Q.R.* 49 (1933), 487–510, provides an instructive survey of the daily work of the Foreign Office in connection with the application of international law.

[2] The italics are mine.

loss of nationality, with the resulting hardships and complications which follow upon double nationality and statelessness. It sets no limit to the discretion with which a State may treat its subjects regardless of the consequences of such action for other States. It concedes to States the right to refuse to submit to impartial adjudication disputes with other States – for there is, in principle, no obligatory jurisdiction of international tribunals. The result is that, in flat contradiction to the principle of equality and independence of States, each State has the right to constitute itself judge in disputes with its neighbours. Moreover, accepted international law declines to protect the very life and independence of States, for it permits war not only for the sake of enforcing rights, but also for the purpose of attacking and destroying existing rights – including the right to continued national existence. Even Members of the League of Nations did not fully abandon the right of war. The recognition of that right carried with it consequences repulsive both to common sense and to ordinary juridical thinking, like the rule that duress does not invalidate a treaty or that conquest confers territorial title.

It would therefore appear that it is not so much the lacking observance of existing rules which detracts from the reality of international law as the fact that – apart from the obligations of the General Treaty for the Renunciation of War and the Covenant of the League – there is little of substance to observe. Even if traditional international law were fully observed or, failing that, fully enforced by judicial and executive action, it would still partake of a substantial degree of unreality because of the narrow scope of matters subjected to its sway. This particular manifestation of the weakness of international law is not one which has conspicuously attracted the attention of its critics. And yet it is a defect of no less consequence for the legal nature of the rules of international law than the absence of enforcement, the absence of an international Legislature developing and declaring the law with an effect binding upon the majority and minority alike, and the absence of compulsory jurisdiction of international tribunals for settling disputes and clarifying any uncertainties in the existing law.

4. THE SHORTCOMINGS OF INTERNATIONAL LAW AND ITS PLACE IN JURISPRUDENCE

What is the total effect of these imperfections of international law? The answer to this question must to a large extent be found in the fact that no one of the typical constitutive requirements of law is so unchallenged and indispensable that its absence is in itself a sufficient cause for denying the quality of law to any rule of conduct. Thus it has been maintained, on high authority, that enforcement is not the essential *differentia specifica* of law. Sir Frederick Pollock refused to accept the proposition that law is law because it is enforced by the State; he insisted that law is enforced by the State because it is law.[1] There may be some hesitation in subscribing to that view without qualifications,[2] but it is not an opinion which can be brushed away as a mere quibble of an apologist. The view that the existence of a central authority with the power to issue binding commands is an essential element of law has been generally regarded as the main weakness of the analytical theory of law as based on the Austinian tradition. And there have been many who denied that the existence of tribunals endowed with compulsory and effective jurisdiction for settling disputes is as much of the essence of the law as has been frequently maintained.[3]

There is some substance in this refusal to reduce law to a single element. The fact is that the legal quality of a rule or of a body of rules is a matter of degree and that – like the sources of the law – it is the result of a complex variety of elements. However, while the inadequacy or even the absence of any of these constitutive elements of law does not in itself detract decisively from the legal character of rules of conduct, it is clear that the law increases in stature and effectiveness in proportion as these elements gain in intensity, and that the cumulative effect of their absence or of their insufficient development tends to render purely nominal the asserted legal quality of the rules in question. The same applies to the shortcomings

[1] *First Book of Jurisprudence* (5th ed. 1923), p. 29. See also Brierly, *The Law of Nations* (2nd ed. 1935), p. 60.

[2] It may well be true that a rule of law is not law for the mere reason that it is enforced. However, in the long run the absence of enforcement cannot remain without influence on the character of the rule.

[3] 'Whenever by a system of treaties the leading states of the world agree to submit certain classes of rights to compulsory arbitration and adjudication by a court whose judgments can be enforced by physical means, then, to that extent, the international rules regulating such classes of rights will be transmuted into positive law as to the states interested' (Hannis Taylor, *The Science of Jurisprudence* (1908), p. 610).

of international law. It is possible to explain the absence or insufficiency of any of the usual characteristics of law in what passes by the name of international law, but the general effect of the deficiencies in all these directions tends to bring international law to the vanishing point of jurisprudence – if it is maintained at the same time that these defects are of a permanent nature and indissolubly bound up with the very nature and structure of international relations.

These defects, even when viewed in their alarming comprehensiveness, are not destructive of the legal nature of international law so long as they are conceived as associated with a transient state of immaturity which humanity, prompted by the growing interdependence of the modern world, is destined to overcome by conscious effort. So long as this is borne in mind, it is better to admit the various defects of international law than to try to explain them away by unconvincing arguments such as, for instance, that which asserts the enforceability of international law by means of a war of reprisals,[1] or of the power of public opinion,[2] or, in general, by reference to the rudimentary systems of law obtaining within primitive communities. So long as this is borne in mind it is proper and convenient to describe rules of international law as rules of law rather than to choose another designation. The fact is that, in many essential respects, they approach the categories of law rather than those of any other system of norms of conduct. They are external in their nature; their ultimate binding force is generally regarded as grounded in a source superior to the will of States; even if not habitually enforced, they are deemed to be enforceable by external compulsion. Neither is it permissible to dismiss lightly the fact that they are considered to be and treated as law both by the executive and by the political

[1] As Allen says, to attempt to treat war and reprisals as an instrument of the legal system in a way comparable to self-help in primitive communities 'is to reduce legal doctrine to a mere figure of speech; and, even as a metaphor, it is far from exact': *Law in the Making* (3rd ed. 1939), p. 57.

[2] This kind of complacency is not confined to international lawyers. Thus we find Professor McIver saying that public opinion is the only support or sanction necessary for the effective operation of international law (*The Modern State* (1926), p. 289). With this may be compared the view expressed in 1919 by the late Mr Taft, President of the United States and Chief Justice of the Supreme Court, to the effect that if the moral sanction were to be the only sanction of the League of Nations 'it will be a failure and a laughing-stock' (as cited in Fleming, *The United States and the Leagues of Nations, 1920* (1932), p. 96). In the period after the First World War the idea of sanctions and of enforcement became associated in the minds of many with the desire of some States to perpetuate by force a questionable *status quo* and to refuse co-operation in the constructive efforts to improve international conditions. For this reason the idea of enforcement became suspect and tended to be disparaged by some international lawyers.

organs of States.[1] The analytical lawyer will, of course, argue that the definition of rules of conduct as law or otherwise is a matter properly determinable not by courts or Governments, but by the jurist. Even if this view be admitted, it is clear that the attitude of courts and Governments is a factor which the analytical jurist is entitled and bound to take into consideration in framing his definition. Finally, it is not without significance that so much of the substance of international law has been developed with the help of and is permeated with rules and notions of that typical and acknowledged law, namely, private law.

For these reasons it is probably more practicable and more accurate to describe traditional international law by that, rather than by any other name. Whatever that other name might be, what is now known as international law would still be the legitimate object of scientific study and question. The attempt to include it within the field of philosophical or social disciplines would be fraught with such difficulties as to bring home the comparative advantage of its traditional treatment as part of jurisprudence. But, as suggested above, the present terminology is profitable only so long as it is understood that the definition is one chosen without complacency and that the acknowledged shortcomings of international law are not a quality inherent in the very nature of the international legal system (as has, for instance, been suggested by the radical exponents of State sovereignty in Germany, from Triepel to National-Socialist writers, who consider international law to be a 'law of co-ordination' based on agreement as distinguished from command) but a transitory stage in the rational progression towards a full and effective system of law among nations.[2] So long as we bear these precautions in mind we shall be fully justified in assuming that in speaking of international law we are not lulling ourselves and others into an illusory state of security, but that, on the contrary, we are giving expression to a notion which, while already grounded in experience to a sub-

[1] There is an excess of simplification in the suggestion that they are regarded as law by municipal courts only because and in so far as they have been incorporated into domestic law and *pro tanto* endowed with a sanction. Their legal quality is pre-existent to and a condition of their recognition as part of the law of the land.

[2] In this respect the weakness of international law presents a problem similar to that of the philosophical problem of evil. The attempts to solve the difficulties confronting the notion of international law by dint of the adoption of an *a priori* comprehensive conception of law find a parallel in the frequent attempts, as in Leibnitz's *Theodicy* (1710), to solve the problem of evil by reference to the *a priori* assumption of the existence of God and the goodness of the Deity in relation to which evil is merely the product of the deficiencies of the human intellect. The answer is as unsatisfactory as the argument based on the incidental beneficence of evil or its logical necessity as the indispensable condition of good. The more satisfactory attempt at a solution is to acknowledge the practical duty to curb its malevolence by dint of unremitting effort.

stantial degree, is, at the same time, a reminder of the imperfection of the achievement and as such implies a perpetual call to human endeavour.

These considerations also explain why the question of the reality of international law *qua* law has been discussed here in some detail. This is so because it is closely connected with the more practical and urgent question of its reality as a body of rules actually governing the conduct of States. The requirements necessary for the inclusion of international law within the sphere of jurisprudence are essentially the same as those necessary for making it a potent force in maintaining peace and ordered progress in the relations of States. For this reason, the doctrinal discussion as to the nature of what is called the Law of Nations is substantially identical with the question of its reality and efficacy as a regulative factor in the life of nations. It is not a mere question of classification or terminology.

5. STATE SOVEREIGNTY AND THE REALITY OF INTERNATIONAL LAW

The preceding observations lead to one of the main and rather obvious conclusions of this paper. The deficient reality of international law is the result not so much of its deliberate breaches by States as of their refusal to submit, in the first instance, to the normal incidents of the rule of law as generally understood. That attitude is commonly described as the unwillingness to abandon part of the sovereignty of States in the international sphere. That description, though trite, and nearly tautologous, is accurate. International law is much more than the will of States; but it is primarily the product of the will of States. It is not *proprio vigore* a motivating power or a source of benefits. It is the refusal of States to submit to the restraints of the law, and not any weakness inherent in international law or in the very nature of international relations, which accounts for the artificiality, in substantial respects, of the Law of Nations conceived as a system of the effective rule of law. I say 'the Law of Nations conceived as a system of the effective rule of law' for this is its natural although not necessarily its traditional or technical connotation. A system of rules which, while limiting itself to the regulation of subjects of secondary importance and while leaving outside its orbit matters affecting the very life of the members of the community, pretends to be a body of law – such a system puts forward a claim which to the ordinary man is, not unnaturally, a source of confusion and an occasion for an exhibition of sarcasm.

However, this instinctive reaction of the average person bids us to go a stage further in the analysis. When we say that the deficient reality of the Law of Nations is due to the historic attitude of sovereign States, we must necessarily mean the attitude of the bulk of the citizens of those States. It is here that we must squarely face a phenomenon which is to any honest thinking man even less acceptable than the seeming complacency of the lawyer is to the man in the street. The average citizen is inclined to regard international law as being the product of agencies almost supernatural and external to his own will, intelligence and foresight. He tends to nurse a grievance if it fails to exhibit a power with which he has consistently refused to endow it. It is a frequent occurrence that the persons who are most keenly disappointed with the achievements of international law and who are most vocal in their denunciation of its shortcomings are those who shrink with horror from the suggestion that their own State should abandon part of its sovereignty and of its freedom of action. This disingenuousness is in some cases aggravated by the circumstance that the critics do not put forward their obstructive scepticism as an expression of their own personal conviction. They shift the responsibility upon the anonymous shoulders of the uninstructed mass of the people unable to learn from experience. This is an attitude which is even less helpful than that of the small minority who hold the view that the relations of States can only be governed by a precarious balance of physical forces as distinguished from law; that war is a necessary – and perhaps beneficent – natural phenomenon, impervious to human will and intelligence; and that individuals organized as States cannot, in their external relations, be governed by those standards of morality, foresight and social progress which make possible the rule of law within the State.

In times of crisis – and the Second World War is a time of crisis – it is incumbent upon the student of international affairs to overcome the disinclination to give currency to views whose edge seems to have been somewhat blunted by repetition. This being so, it may be stated – what has become almost a platitude – that the degree of the reality of international law is determined by the extent of the surrender, in appropriate spheres, of the sovereignty of States, and that sovereignty, as fully recognized by existing international law, is, and has in many respects proved to be, inconsistent with the idea of order of which States are the trustees. To say that it is only the abuse of sovereignty which is at the root of the evil is to understate the gravity of the problem. It was the anxious craving for order, peace and stability threatened by the horrible experience – which they witnessed – of civil struggle and religious dissension that underlay the extreme mechanistic formulation of the doctrines of sovereignty of Hobbes and Bodin. They would have recoiled with amazement and dismay at the sight of those very evils which they laboured to banish and which have now engulfed the peoples of the modern world as the result of the unbridled and uncompromising dogma of sovereignty transposed into the international arena.

There is, in these days, a particular reason for a clear understanding of this central issue of international law and relations. The prolonged upheaval which preceded the Second World War consisted not only in the violation of major political treaties imposed by force or voluntarily accepted. It found expression not only in successful acts of aggression against the very life of independent nations. It manifested itself in the disregard, on a large scale, of many of the accepted rules of international law and comity. This state of affairs was, of necessity, temporary, and those loud questioners who inquire whether there is any international law left may be correctly answered that the fact and the magnitude and the acknowledged meaning of this present struggle are a proper measure of the essential reality of the Law of Nations. At the same time, the successful assertions of force have undermined not only the authority of law, but also the effects of that criticism of sovereignty, both internal and external, which we have learned to regard as a permanent gain of the science of law and of politics in our generation. Some States, in their triumphant departure from established canons of conduct, have proved to be so powerful, and so much power is in turn required to compel them to revert to the channels of legality, that sovereignty – the embodiment of the organized might of the State – has once more come into its own, with a vengeance. This trend, although perhaps unavoidable, must be regarded as transient. Constructive thought in the field of international organization must continue to be based on the view that while the protection of true sovereignty, conceived as independence of the power of other States, is the main purpose of international law, its reality has been thwarted by certain manifestations of State sovereignty and that a surrender or limitation of some aspects of that sovereignty are still the essential condition of the effectiveness of the Law of Nations. The fulfilment of that condition depends not only on the acquiescence but on the active determination of the individual citizen.

6. ADAPTATION OF INTERNATIONAL LAW TO FACTS

Alongside the problem of sovereignty as a cause of the weakness of international law, both the lawyer and the student of international affairs in general have been confronted in the last decade with exhortations to adapt the law to what have often been described as facts, namely, to the successful assertions of force and to conditions created by government based on mere force. Tendencies of this kind, fostered by a superficially conceived realism, must be resisted. We ought to regard the experience of the decade preceding the Second World War as one of a period of retrogression from which certain cogent lessons may be derived. But we must refuse to treat it as a period heralding a new international and national revolution, to which international law, if it is to be real, ought to adjust itself. It is futile to try to adapt the Law of Nations to any wave of lawlessness which may happen to sweep over the world and temporarily engulf parts of it. This has been done occasionally by sycophantic national writers, as, for instance, when Russian international lawyers were laboriously forging a system of Soviet International Law as a law of a period of transition prior to the advent of the communist world revolution or when National-Socialist writers were defining international law as an inter-corporative system of co-ordination based on racial consanguinity and – up to 1939 – on equality and fundamental rights of States.

Neither ought we to exhibit undue haste in adapting international law to some of the manifestations of totalitarian and dictatorial régimes. It is too early to assume their permanency in their present form; and it is an excess of optimism to believe that in case of their survival international law will be able to develop at all. For this reason, we must, for instance, treat with caution the suggestion that the rules of international law relating to State responsibility and to the separation, in certain matters, of the duties of States from those of their citizens should adapt themselves to the fact of the regimentation of the individual in totalitarian States.[1] Similarly it would have been of advantage if lawyers and statesmen had not occasionally disparaged the principle and practice of non-recognition of situa-

[1] See, e.g., Friedmann in *B.Y.* 19 (1938), 142–7.

tions brought about by means contrary to fundamental international obligations on the ground that law must follow facts. Apart from the basic consideration that an illegality confers no right, it is proper for the law-abiding not to attribute an undue probability of permanence to facts grounded in illegality.

The reality of the Law of Nations will not be enhanced by making it follow facts of this nature. We must avoid the danger of reducing international law to a catalogue registering successive illegalities – just as, as historians, we must refuse to interpret the injunction of learning from history as meaning that it is our right and duty to copy history and that war is destined to be a permanent feature of the future for the reason that it has been so in the past. It is of the essence of the law that to some facts it denies any results at all – other than condemnation and repression. It is understandable if sympathetic outsiders who possess a nodding acquaintance with international law are anxious, in the spirit of realism, to incorporate into the Law of Nations any excrescence of force which succeeds in maintaining itself for a while. But this is not a kind of reality which is congenial to or consistent with the Law of Nations.

7. THE REALITY OF THE LAW OF WAR

Similar considerations apply to the impact of the new facts and changes upon the question of the reality of the branch of international law usually referred to as the law of war and neutrality. In so far as these new facts have expressed themselves in lawlessness pure and simple, they may and ought to be disregarded. Thus, for instance, to the extent to which there exists a rule of international law prescribing a declaration of war prior to the opening of hostilities, that rule has not been affected by the crude and uniform German practice to the contrary in the Second World War. In so far as these new facts have their origin in changed conditions of warfare, their bearing upon the development and the observance of the law deserves careful consideration. For it is in particular with regard to the law of war that the charge of a mischievous propensity to unreality has been levelled against the science of international law. The very idea of a legal regulation of a condition of mere force has appeared to many incongruous to the point of absurdity.[1] This view, which is entitled to respect, is controversial – at least so long as the law permitted or

[1] See, e.g., Professor Quincy Wright's essay on 'International Law and the World Order', in *Harris Foundation Lectures* (1940), pp. 127, 128.

even authorized resort to war. And it may be argued that even if war were to be unconditionally renounced and prohibited – which is not as yet the case – juridical logic would have to stop short of the refusal to provide a measure of legal regulation, for obvious considerations of humanity, of hostilities which have broken out in disregard of the fundamental prohibition of recourse to war. The same applies to hostilities and measures of force taking place in the course of collective enforcement of international law or in the course of civil wars.

The argument against the law of war as such can, of course, be based on grounds weightier than purely analytical considerations. The fact is that many rules of warfare partake of a high degree of artificiality so far as their content and their binding force are concerned. The general participation clause – which makes the applicability of a rule dependent on its being formally binding upon all belligerents – in the Hague Conventions and in a number of other treaties regulating the conduct of war have made illusory the binding force of most of those conventions. The use of reprisals, on whose broad shoulders most of the departures from accepted rules have been made to rest in the two World Wars, has had the same effect on both customary and conventional rules. The operation of the doctrine of the plea of superior orders as a valid excuse in the matter of war crimes must necessarily have a disintegrating effect on the restraints of the law of war. The same applies to the absence of any legal duty on the part of neutrals to protest against violations and insist on the observance of rules of war. Finally, although the overwhelming majority of legal opinion has rejected the view that military necessity overrides the law of war, the fact remains that the doctrine of self-preservation, fully recognized in time of peace, cannot be altogether eliminated in the relations of belligerents fighting for their lives.

To these limitations of the effectiveness of the rules of war there must be added the fact, which may prove decisive for the future of the law of war, that there has not yet taken place an agreed adaptation of the law to the advent of new weapons – like the air arm and the submarine – and to the claim of their effective use unhampered by traditional restrictions. Neither has there taken place an adaptation of the law to the undeniable, fundamentally new and most comprehensive extension of the scope of modern warfare and to the resulting obliteration in some respects of the distinction between combatants and non-combatants – a distinction which has been the basis of the modern law of war – and which, in turn, is jeopardized by the circumstance that the fully effective use of these new weapons is in itself incompatible with respect for the life and property of non-combatants. The question whether the law of war must adapt itself to the requirements of effectiveness of the new instrumentalities or whether these must be used within the orbit of and subject to the traditional and basic rules of war has not been solved either by agreement of States or by any consensus of opinion.

Even before these difficulties had been fully revealed, many had urged that, in the light of the history of warfare, it is futile and harmful to frame rules of war and, by their scientific exposition, to strengthen the illusion that they would be observed; that history had shown that rules of warfare are an uneven compromise between considerations of humanity and chivalry on the one hand and military necessity on the other; that, in general, such restrictions only have been adopted as did not or were not likely to interfere seriously with belligerent needs and operations; and that restraints have been abandoned as soon as it became clear that they interfered with military necessity. International lawyers have been conscious of these objections as well as of the possibility that by continuing to devote their energies to the exposition of the law of war they have been assisting indirectly in lending some support to war as an institution and in checking the development initiated by its formal renunciation in the Pact of Paris. At the same time, they could not disregard the fact that, even after the adoption of the Covenant and of the Pact of Paris, Governments continued to frame rules of war, as in the Gas Protocol of 1925, in the Conventions of 1929 relating to the treatment of prisoners of war and of sick and wounded members of armed forces, and in the instruments of 1930 and 1936 concerning the use of submarines against merchantmen. Neither could they forget that the welfare of the individual human being is the primary object of all law; that the aim of most rules of war is to diminish the sufferings and cruelties to which the individual is exposed as the result of war; that no historical analogies or arguments of logic absolve them of their part in contributing to that purpose; and that it is their duty to contribute, though without sanguine hopes and without much enthusiasm, to the achievement of that humanitarian object. On the other hand, it is possible that many lawyers will come to the conclusion that the harm resulting from the continued attention paid to rules of war is greater than its hypothetical advantages; that, although Governments may attach importance to continuing with the fiction of rules of war, this is not a decisive reason why lawyers should take the official attitude at its face value; and that no scientific inventiveness and foresight can effect the adaptation of the law of war to the two paramount factors of modern warfare, namely, the radical extension of its scope and the advent of new weapons, for the reason that such reconciliation is impracticable inasmuch as modern war has outgrown the possibility of legal regulation.

These problems confronting the question of the reality of the law of war have been sketched here rather summarily. But they suffice to show that, whatever the future may bring, the past preoccupation with and exposition of the law of war have not been the product of mere habit.

8. THE REALITY OF THE LAW OF NEUTRAL RIGHTS AND DUTIES

In so far as the relations between belligerents aud neutrals have been the counterpart of the mutual relations of belligerents – as, for instance, when they have been vitally influenced by the successive waves of reprisals sweeping over the established law – they have to that extent shared the artificiality of the rules of war. But the law of neutrality has been affected even more profoundly than the law of war by the extension of the scope and the resulting change of the character of modern war. This applies conspicuously to that part of the law of neutrality which is concerned with the neutral rights of commerce, namely, the law of prize in the matter of contraband and blockade. In this respect the traditional law of neutrality has been the result of a compromise between a variety of conflicting factors. These have been the relative strength of the belligerents and of the neutrals; the wise consideration given by the belligerent, in his own interest, to the neutral estimate of the justice and fairness of the belligerent measures; and, above all, the military requirements of the belligerents and their determination to prevent the enemy from receiving goods of importance for the conduct of the war. At the time when the scope of war was limited and when the range of articles and goods useful for war was correspondingly small, the concessions which the belligerents could afford in relation to neutral trade were relatively large. The position has changed in modern warfare, in which the entirety of national life is indissolubly connected with the immediate war effort and in which the increase of the numbers of combatants and the mechanization of war have added immeasurably to the range of articles and commodities which are of immediate military importance. The obliteration of the distinction between relative and absolute contraband and the sweeping comprehensiveness of the list of both kinds of contraband as adopted in the two World Wars give an adequate picture of the situation. To these and other changes in the law of contraband neutrals have never consented; on these changes belligerents have insisted throughout, independently of any operation of reprisals. Neither has there taken place any approximation to agreement on the question whether, in such matters as immunity of postal correspondence, search at sea and bringing of neutral vessels into port for search, the belligerent or the neutral has to bear the brunt of changes in conditions. There is no higher test of distributive justice by dint of which it is possible to reconcile these conflicting claims – unless we admit that the interest of the belligerent in emerging victorious from the life and death struggle is more entitled to respect than the interest of the neutrals in the maintenance or in the increase of their commercial intercourse with the outside world. But this is not an admission which can be confidently expected from the neutrals.

At present, the degree of unreality attaching to the law of neutrality in the matter of neutral rights is even higher than in the case of the law of war. It is probably true to say that there exists no such agreed law of neutrality on the matter as could properly be applied by an international tribunal. For this reason the decision taken by the British and French Governments in 1939 to except from the jurisdiction of the Permanent Court of International Justice matters arising out of the conduct of the war – the avowed reason for the decision being principally the unsolved controversies in the matter of neutral rights – was both proper and in the best interest of the Court itself.

Secondly, the reality of the traditional law of neutrality has now been most substantially affected in its other principal aspect, namely, in respect of the duties of neutral States. It has been so affected as the result of the change in the legal position of war brought about by the Covenant of the League and by the General Treaty for the Renunciation of War.

The principle of absolute impartiality – and impartiality being one of the main features of the neutral duty of abstention and non-participation – was the corner-stone of the law of neutrality in the nineteenth century and in the first two decades of the twentieth.

That principle was abandoned in the Covenant of the League as between the Covenant-breaking States and States applying sanctions in pursuance of their obligations under the Covenant. The Covenant thus marked the return to the seventeenth-century conception of qualified neutrality. The Pact of Paris, in displacing war from its position as a legally recognized instrument for enforcing and changing the law, finally removed the historical foundations of the doctrine of neutral duty as an attitude of impartiality. For this reason, the measures so far taken by the United States in pursuance of its policy of aiding the Allies by all means short of war – as well as any further measures implied in that policy and in the resolve to render it effective – while contrary to specific rules of neutrality as embodied in the Hague Conventions and the customary law of the nineteenth century cannot be deemed to be inconsistent with international law viewed from the larger perspective of its historical development.

It would thus appear that the reality of the traditional law of neutrality is being assailed on both flanks – in the matter both of neutral rights and of neutral duties. The imperative reasons of a humanitarian nature which, according to some, militate in favour of the continued existence of the law of war, do not seem to apply to the law of neutrality. It will not therefore be surprising if, with a cogency even greater than in the case of the law of war, the problem of the law of neutrality will become once more a subject of discussion from the point of view both of feasibility of legal regulation and of international morality.

9. THE TASK OF THE SCIENCE OF INTERNATIONAL LAW

The impact of recent developments, in the two principal directions[1] outlined above, on the law of neutrality shows that while the science

[1] In comparison with these major problems the questions raised by the increased measure of State control over private activities in totalitarian and communist countries in relation to the traditional separation between the duties of the neutral State and those of its subjects appear to be of minor importance. It is too early to say that the system of regimentation of the individual has reached an extent and a probable permanency which warrants a substantial modification of the existing rules. There are two further considerations which tend to reduce to its true proportions the somewhat exaggerated importance attached in this matter to recent developments in State-managed economy. The first is that, whatever may be the position in time of peace, State control of private activities becomes in time of war a conspicuous feature in both belligerent and neutral countries. Secondly, the established law, while prohibiting neutral States from selling to belligerents arms and munitions of war, contains no such prohibitions with regard to other articles, like raw materials, whose importance is increased in modern warfare. In

of international law must resist the temptation to follow facts in the sense of interpreting successive breaches of law as part of the international legal system, it must constantly take into account both the developments occurring in the various branches of international law and the social changes taking place in society. Secondly, the way in which the doctrine of neutrality, in so far as it remains a legal institution, has adapted itself to parallel changes in other fields of the law by drawing upon some of the fundamental principles of international law, shows that we ought to exercise caution in urging that traditional international law must be thrown overboard in an attempt 'to make a fresh start'.

In this connection it is pertinent to inquire into the part which the science of international law may legitimately play in strengthening the element of reality of international law. International lawyers have in this matter been exposed to criticism which is not necessarily altogether groundless for the mere reason that the various exhortations occasionally addressed to them have been mutually exclusive. While some have charged them with creating the illusion of a law when none existed, others have accused them of conservatism and lack of vision in the building of a new world of international order. There may be an element of accuracy in both charges, but in their underlying assumptions both seem to be too sweeping to be helpful.

In the first instance, it is clear that any startling developments in international law cannot be the work of international lawyers. They must be the result of the practice of States; they must be the outcome of a changed attitude of Governments prompted and supported in this matter by an enlightened public opinion. International lawyers can admittedly do much in addition to their primary function of expounding the practice of States and, if possible, reducing it to a coherent scientific system. They can help to reveal its inconsistencies; they can evaluate the practice of States by reference to generally recognized principles of law; they can help in restoring to its full dignity the identity of moral standards which ought to govern the conduct of individuals and States alike; they can further the progress of the law by interpreting existing rules in the light of the supervening changes both in international conditions and in international agreements; they can suggest rules for further improvements in the law; they can do their share in imparting and keeping alive the

comparison with this new factor, the general extension of the sphere of economic activities of States is of secondary importance. For an emphatic presentation of a different view see Friedmann, in *B.Y.* 19 (1938), 130–8, and in *Grotius Society*, 26 (1940), 218–21.

consciousness of the fact that progress in international law cannot be achieved without a gradual limitation of the sovereignty of States within the framework of a politically organized international society; and they can show initiative in discerning and drawing conclusions from the inroads already made by the practice of States upon the dogma of the absolute sovereignty of States as the exclusive source of international law. But, essentially, any 'fresh start' on major issues must come not from the science of international law but from international practice. We cannot hope to hasten that development by the use of incantations such as that the method of the science of international law must become sociological, or pragmatic, or 'engineering', or realist.

Secondly, for reasons both of the continuity and the fruitfulness of future effort, the desire for a 'fresh start' ought not to be allowed to obscure the fact that a departure of revolutionary significance for the entire system of international law has been made in the Covenant of the League and the General Treaty for the Renunciation of War. These fundamental instruments provide a broad and firm basis for an orderly development of international society towards the final goal of the Federation of the World. It is within the province of the science of international law to supply a progressive interpretation of these constitutional charters and of any supplementary instruments calculated to add to their effectiveness and their authority. Such a progressive interpretation is fully consistent with the main established canons of construction, namely, with the principles of effectiveness and interpretation by reference to general legal principles and the social ends of law.

It cannot be claimed that international lawyers have been uniformly inclined to adopt that progressive interpretation. From this point of view there seems to be no substance in the charge that they have tended to create an illusion of reality where none existed and that they have been prone to confuse what is with what in their view ought to be. In some vital respects the contrary seems to be true. Many international lawyers, far from attempting to impart an exaggerated measure of reality to artificial creations of their fancy, have occasionally been so 'realist' and 'positivist' as to fail to acknowledge and to bring into full prominence those elements of legality and submission to law which express agreement and the necessities of international intercourse have carried to fruition. The extreme positivist school of thought, which for a long time dominated the science of international law and which insisted that the expressly manifested will of States is the only source of international law, did not in fact take into account the entirety of international practice and of international law. In its anxiety not to give prominence to a source of law not expressly deducible from the will of States, it failed to recognize the creative part which private law played in the development of the Law of Nations from its very inception. In this as in numerous other matters, some international lawyers, disregarding the developments in actual conditions and in the law, tended to rationalize and to generalize the extreme assertions of national sovereignty. For the same reason, they failed to pay sufficient attention to those changes in the law which showed that States, while exclusively entrusted with law-creating functions in the international sphere, are not the exclusive subjects of international law. In disregard of much evidence to the contrary, many international lawyers have insisted that, by the very nature of international law, sovereign States are not amenable to repressive punishment and that the mere fact that individuals organize themselves as States is sufficient to relieve them, in their collective capacity, of the consequences of their criminal actions. By reference to such theories, attempts, not wholly unsuccessful, were made to question the significance and to reduce the effect of the innovation implicit in the provisions of the Covenant of the League of Nations relating to sanctions. At the same time a rigid conservatism was observed in interpreting the provisions of the Covenant relating to the requirement of unanimity. Even after the Permanent Court of International Justice had laid down in its Advisory Opinion concerning the *Mosul* controversy that the rule on unanimity must be interpreted subject, in appropriate cases, to the principle that no one can be judge in his own cause, jurists showed no disposition to apply that ruling to the not too remote case of the interpretation of Article 11 – one of the crucial provisions of the Covenant. In deference to the traditional doctrines of absoluteness of sovereignty, many international lawyers have adhered for a long time to the view that territorial sovereignty is indivisible – a view which the practice of States has repeatedly tended to disprove and which is inimical to territorial adjustments and neighbourly arrangements falling short of the drastic remedy of full cession of territorial sovereignty. In disregard of substantial, though not uniform, practice, the majority of international lawyers have taught that the recognition of States, of Governments and of belligerency – a function of fundamental importance in international society – is an act governed not by law but by shifting and arbitrary considerations of national policy. The majority of international lawyers have given currency to the doctrine, directly opposed to legal principle and self-contradictory in its conflicting formulations, that by the very nature of international law and relations there exist disputes – so-called non-justiciable or political disputes – which are inherently incapable of judicial settlement within any scheme of obligatory jurisdiction of international tribunals. Some international lawyers – though certainly not the majority of them – have gone to the length of refusing to admit the significance and the authority of the fundamental departure in international law implicit in the General Treaty for the Renunciation of War on the ground that its signatories attached importance to specifying expressly the reservation of self-defence – an exception which is in any case implicit in any international treaty or custom. Nor has there been any general disposition to draw from that Treaty the legitimate conclusion that one of its results has been to alter the existing law inasmuch as it disregarded the vitiating influence of duress upon the validity of treaties and inasmuch as it treated conquest as conferring a valid title.[1] The fact is that international lawyers, far from creating the illusion of a reality when none existed, have often lagged behind developments in their desire not to lose sight of what seemed to them the paramount reality, namely, the sovereignty of the national State. There ought to be no doubt that in this respect a change both of attitude and of emphasis will be necessary if the science of international law is to fulfil effectively its legitimate twin function of accurately expounding and creatively assisting in developing the Law of Nations.

10. THE PURPOSE OF THE LAW OF NATIONS

It has been suggested that we cannot hope to make a helpful contribution to the reality of the Law of Nations by exhorting its exponents alternately to modesty and to boldness. Neither do we facilitate their labours by expecting them to adjust international law to mani-

[1] There are borderline cases in which the jurist, while inclined to make use of an opportunity calling for a bold interpretation, must take into account the indications of a contrary intention on the part of the contracting Governments. This circumstance explains why some writers – including the author of this paper – were unwilling to admit that the immediate and automatic effect of the General Treaty for the Renunciation of War was to change the law of neutrality. But, quite apart from the right to resort to discriminatory action by way of reprisals, it is clearly within the legal power of the principal signatories of the Treaty, confronted with the fact of its continuous violation by one of its signatories, to effect at any time the change locally inherent in its provisions by resorting to discriminatory treatment against the law-breaker.

festations of lawlessness. Their legitimate province is and must remain the exposition and progressive interpretation of the existing law in terms of the abiding purpose of the Law of Nations. What is that purpose?

That purpose is, first, to protect and secure the independence of States by the prohibition of the use of force and by the collective enforcement of that prohibition. That purpose is, secondly, to render the elimination of force tolerable and durable by the provision of an absolute duty of judicial settlement of disputes and of submission to the decisions of a supra-national political authority decreeing changes in the existing law and existing rights. It is, thirdly, to give effect, through appropriate limitations and international supervision of the internal sovereignty of States, to the principle that the protection of human personality and of its fundamental rights is the ultimate purpose of all law, national and international. It is, fourthly, by fostering the sentiment of and obedience to law among nations, to develop and finally establish the consciousness of the essential identity of moral standards applicable to States and individuals alike. That purpose is, fifthly and lastly, the creation of conditions and institutions calculated to bring about the transition to the realizable and certainly not infinite ideal of the Federation of the World conceived as a commonwealth of autonomous States exercising full internal independence, rendered both just and secure by the power of the impersonal sovereignty of the *civitas maxima*.

This latter consummation is probably a matter of prolonged – though not infinite[1] – development. In the meantime we must bear in mind that the reality of the law is to a large extent dependent upon the existence of institutions within which and through which it operates. Of these institutions the State is, in the relations of the individual, the normal and typical manifestation. Even if law can exist without the State – an assumption which many will deny – such law must be haphazard, precarious and faulty. These are in fact the drawbacks of international law in the absence of an international commonwealth organized as a State. However, like the law itself, so also statehood is a matter of degree. International law will not achieve a full measure of reality until it is organically woven into the fabric of a supra-national entity. But in the meantime it may be able

[1] The notion of perpetual peace as an infinite ideal incapable of realization originates with Kant. His explanation of the infiniteness of this ideal is singularly unconvincing. However, in his 'Essay on Perpetual Peace', Kant insisted that the political principles directed towards the formation of associations of States for the purpose of approximating gradually to this aim are not impossible of realization.

to fulfil the primary purpose of statehood, namely, to render secure the life and independence of the members of the community by the prohibition and collective suppression of violence and war. The League of Nations, when suitably strengthened for the fulfilment of that fundamental purpose – without which the notion of a political organization of mankind is an abuse of language – may be regarded as an institution of this nature. Both it – the League – and any other possible association of States fulfilling that primary purpose, are a legitimate and indispensable object of inquiry by the student of international law. They are the soul of a properly conceived science of international law. International lawyers bent on leaving this issue rigidly alone run the risk of finding themselves in the position of that disciple of Pomponazzo, the philosopher of the Renaissance, who, in order to obviate complications with the church authorities, carefully avoided the subject of the immortality of the soul and began his lectures with the exposition of Aristotle's meteorological treatise. He was interrupted by the turbulent shouts of the audience: '*Quid de anima?*', 'What of the soul?'

The various purposes of the Law of Nations as outlined above ought, in order to be fully effective, to be achieved *pari passu.* Their simultaneous or parallel achievement must, accordingly, be the object of intelligent endeavour if international law is to become both real and rational. But it is a grave mistake to assume that the absence or the difficulties of accomplishing any single one of them are a good reason for abandoning others or for disparaging their importance. The fact that there is not as yet in existence an international Legislature for remedying the law is an inadequate argument for doubting the indispensability of obligatory judicial settlement or of the enforcement of the existing law. Parallelism in achieving progress is a valuable political principle of action. But care must be taken lest it become a source of inertia and obstruction.[1] We ought not to become oblivious to the general beneficence of ascertaining and enforcing the law by regular processes for the mere reason that some of it is unsatisfactory and that there is as yet no appropriate organ for changing it.

[1] This is what has taken place in connection with the problem raised by the absence of adequate machinery for changing international law. That problem has been the main argumentative starting-point for questioning the propriety of the obligatory jurisdiction of international tribunals and of enforcement of international law. At the same time, there has been a tendency on the part of those questioners to deny the possibility of setting up an effective organ in the form of an international Legislature for the purpose of remedying the law. The progress of international law is thus made dependent upon a condition whose realization is declared to be impossible.

II. THE VINDICATION OF THE LAW OF NATIONS IN THE SECOND WORLD WAR

The proper understanding of these purposes of the Law of Nations makes it possible to attempt an answer to the doubts and anxieties of those who take a sincere and sympathetic interest in the future and, in particular, in the present apparent impotence of international law. To these persons the following observations may suitably be addressed. The fact and the magnitude of the Second World War are in themselves a vindication, in a double sense, of the reality of the Law of Nations. This is a contest for definite spiritual values and, we may admit without embarrassment, for paramount material interests. Only the superficial brilliancy of the cynic can find fault or insincerity in our profession of attachment to an ideal for the mere reason that pursuit of it coincides with our interests. These spiritual and material values are menaced by the same threat and the same challenge which have been thrown out and which hover over the shaken structure of the rule of law within the as yet amorphous society of States. That structure was artificial and transparent in the international law of the nineteenth and twentieth centuries – in that law which proclaimed and left intact the unlimited right of war, which failed to impose any duty of obligatory judicial settlement, and which, generally, made unrestricted sovereignty the main factor in international relations. But the two decades which followed the First World War marked a radical change in various directions – a change none the less revolutionary because it was qualified and subsequently brutally halted. Wherein lay those changes?

They lay in the practical – though not formal – renunciation in the Covenant of the League of the unlimited right of war, in the adoption of the principle of the collective enforcement of peace by the Members of the League, and in the recognition of the right of intervention of the League in disputes between its Members; they lay in the wide though still qualified acceptance of the principle of obligatory arbitration and judicial settlement; they lay in the formal renunciation of the right of war in the Pact of Paris.[1]

Secondly, those changes expressed themselves, less conspicuously but significantly, in the provision of safeguards for the protection of human personality through the institutionalized protection of minorities, the régime of mandated territories, the attempts – at the

[1] For an impressive survey of the significance of these developments, see Dr McNair's inaugural lecture on *Collective Security* (1936).

Hague Codification Conference and in subsequent arrangements – to mitigate the consequences of statelessness, and, above all, in the establishment of the International Labour Organization. Circumstances were not propitious for perfecting these developments. The advent of dictatorships, for which the sanctity of human personality had no meaning, and the actual or supposed necessity for co-operating with them, put the clock back on this weighty issue. But these setbacks did not deprive the initial achievements of their significance as a step in the direction of the protection of human personality as the ultimate purpose of all law. For the historically minded, these changes signified the repayment of an old debt which the Law of Nations owed to the individual. For much of the sixteenth- and seventeenth-century law of nature had its origin in the desire to establish those principles of reason and justice which, it was thought, could assist the cause of individual liberty against the encroachments and tyranny of the newly risen territorial national State of the Reformation. And much indeed of the Law of Nations was due to the law of nature thus resuscitated.

Finally, those changes manifested themselves in the unprecedented development of international institutions of common concern and, in particular, of the Permanent Court of International Justice, which, although still shorn of the normal attributes of compulsory jurisdiction, fully revealed the potentialities, legal and political, of international judicial settlement wielded by an authoritative tribunal.

International law was becoming real – real when judged not by the controversial test of normal observance of narrowly conceived duties, but by the test of the subjection to law of issues that matter. For these reasons the Second World War will probably be viewed by the historian as having been in a double sense a struggle for the vindication of the reality of the Law of Nations. On its outcome depends, first, the survival of what is valuable and enduring in traditional international law, namely, the free existence of equal members of the community of nations and the exclusion of world domination by a single earthly power. On its outcome rests, secondly, the continuance of the progress, which had clearly begun, towards a more integrated system of international law and an effective legal organization of peace.

If we fix our gaze on the enduring purposes of the Law of Nations and if we bear in mind that they are identical with the issues which are now being decided on the field of battle, we shall neither get despondent in times of adversity nor succumb to the temptation of gauging the reality of international law by the ignoble test of temporary triumphs of force wielded by lawless States or to the craving to adapt international law to other manifestations of their inferior statehood. Above all, we shall then be better in the position to remember that the degree of the reality of the Law of Nations is in the last resort determined not by Governments, nor, even less so, by international lawyers, but by the will and the exertion of the citizen. Westlake's insistence that the rights and duties of States are the rights and duties of man expresses a profound truth in more senses than one. The cause with which the Law of Nations is totally identified is being defended, in this Second World War, by the common effort and suffering of the individual citizen to a higher degree than at any previous period in history. It is therefore legitimate to hope that the individual will succeed henceforth in giving to that experience – superadded to the lessons of the First World War and of the preceding centuries of international anarchy – an expression commensurate with the magnitude of the greatest political task which has confronted mankind since the inception of history; that by the action of his Governments, he will revive and strengthen the existing institutions of international order; and that, by dint of his own municipal law and of precise international obligations, he will safeguard these achievements from the vicissitudes inherent in the fallibility of Governments and in the imperfections of collective memory.

CHAPTER 3

ON REALISM, ESPECIALLY IN INTERNATIONAL RELATIONS

Editor's note This chapter consists of a paper given at a meeting of the Carlyle Club on 10 October 1953.

The Club was founded in 1909 upon the initiative of A. J. Carlyle and his brother E. J. Carlyle. It was originally called the Political Philosophy and Science Club but was re-named in 1943, in memory of A. J. Carlyle, who died in that year, having acted as the Club's Secretary for thirty-four years. The object of the Club was 'to promote the better organization of political studies, and especially the co-ordination of the various branches of philosophy, history and science which are related to these studies'. The Club's members have included some of the most distinguished names in the study of politics, history, sociology and law in England, including Lowes Dickinson, William Beveridge, A. D. Lindsay, Ernest Barker, Graham Wallis, Maynard Keynes, C. K. Webster, G. D. H. Cole, H. J. Laski, A. J. Toynbee, R. H. Tawney, T. H. Marshall, Arnold McNair and Morris Ginsberg. The Club meets three times a year over dinner, for a discussion preceded by a paper.

Lauterpacht became a member of the Club in 1952. His paper was delivered on 10 October 1953 at a meeting held at Gonville and Caius College, Cambridge. Fifteen members and one guest were present.

The very existence of this text is a reflection of the seriousness of purpose with which Lauterpacht approached every task he undertook. Here, albeit in a society where the delivery of a formal paper was customary, Lauterpacht carried his preparation to the point of producing a typescript virtually suitable for publication as it stood. Yet even though he no doubt had the text before him as he spoke, it was his practice to have studied it so carefully that when delivering it he gave scarcely any impression of reading.

What I propose to say by way of opening this discussion on 'Realism, Especially in International Relations' is perhaps not what is generally expected. The natural expectation is probably that I may, in the light of recent experience, add to the considerations pointing to the virtues of realism and to the dangers of Utopian idealism. It is not unnatural to expect that, in the field of international affairs, our respect for the soundness and wisdom of realism may receive support from one whose study brings him into closer touch with the subject. This, I fear, is not the object of this paper. Its purpose is to put some questions pointing to the dangers and exaggerations of what goes by the name of realism in the field of political action in general and of international affairs in particular. These questions may suggest the conclusion that appeal to so-called realism is an inducement to facile and complacent thinking; that, as a method of argument and discussion it may often be, in effect, open to the charge of being intellectually dishonest; that it is a convenient and much abused cloak for opportunism or worse; and that it has tended to treat with contempt long-range principle as a standard of human action and to deny the value of human will as an agency shaping the destiny of men. This is a drastic indictment. What follows is an attempt to examine what justification there may be for it.

Before I proceed, I ought to state what is perhaps obvious, namely, that the distinction between so-called realism and idealism in the field of action has no necessary relation – or perhaps any relation – to the more meaningful distinction between realism and idealism in philosophy. There may be some, at first sight startling, relation between the two. Thus some prominent idealists in philosophy – to mention such names as Hegel and Bosanquet – have been so-called realists in politics, especially in international politics. The explanation of that fact may be that their philosophical idealism has led them to attribute an absolute value to the State and its sovereignty and to a denial of any binding law or morality outside the confines of the State and to a consequent political realism in its current connotation. The modern idealistic revolt against reason in some totalitarian States was accompanied by a political realism of a particularly brutal and cynical brand.

I have suggested, in the first instance, the possibility that as a method of argument and discussion the appeal to realism may be objectionable from the point of view of integrity of method of discussion. For what is the method of the typical realist who confronts us in argument? He says: 'I am a realist; I am a sound person; I am a practical man; I look to realities; I see things as they are and not as I would like them to be.' To his opponents he says: 'You are a Utopian; you are a dreamer; you see people and events as what you think they ought to be and not as what they are.' That attitude of the realist is upon analysis an exclusive claim to wisdom. It is an assertion of victory even before the argument has started. It is an attempt to reduce the opponent, at the very outset, to a lower intellectual status and to gain the confidence of the others. For those others have a weakness for realism; they like to repose their trust in the sound man. If at the very outset we proclaim ourselves to be realists they will be inclined to listen to our arguments with confident understanding and to think of our opponent with sympathetic or impatient incredulity. For this reason a person who at the commencement of the discussion has successfully annexed for himself the attribute of realism starts with a clear, though unmerited, dialectical and psychological advantage.

However, fairness seems to suggest that if we are determined to do ourselves justice, we may be entitled to address the person who calls himself a realist and us, by implication or expressly, Utopians, in some such terms: 'My dear man, do not give yourself airs; we are all, *ex hypothesi*, realists in the sense that we wish to avoid a frustration of our effort; we are all anxious to find out what things actually are so that we can shape our conduct accordingly; we all wish our endeavours to be effective and not futile; we are all realists.' After all, realism in the realm of politics – and I may as well make the overdue attempt at a definition – is nothing else than the method, or temper, or attitude most calculated to realize our desires. Who but a crank or a fool does not wish to be a realist in that sense?

This adorning oneself with the epithet of realism is a game at which two can play. Let us re-enact, for instance, the exchanges which took place between the opponents and the adherents of the League of Nations when the time came to diagnose the causes of its failure. 'I was a realist' – said the opponent of the ideas embodied in the Covenant of the League – 'for I saw at the outset that it was Utopian to try to organize under the rule of law a multitude of States differing in outlook and interest and glorying in their sovereignty; to make them abide by their obligation to refrain from resorting to force; and, what is more, to sacrifice their own peace in order to enforce the law against the aggressor. I foresaw', he would say, 'that if the test came Mr Chamberlain would affirm that sanctions against Italy are midsummer madness and that Sir John Simon would proclaim that he would not wish to see a single British ship sunk in the defence of Abyssinian independence.' 'I was a realist' – the adherent of the League retorted – 'for I foresaw that it was Utopian to think of preserving peace and civilization among modern sovereign nations, armed and equipped with all the destructive instrumentalities of science, unless that sovereignty is effectively curbed by clear and unequivocal obligations not only to observe the peace but to enforce it, if necessary, and unless that obligation is accompanied by other improvements in the fabric of international organization which make peace not only durable but just, in particular by effective machinery for both the impartial ascertainment and the peaceful change of existing law.'

Or let us recall the discussions which preceded the adoption of the Charter of the United Nations – a document which, somewhat ominously, was repeatedly described by those responsible for it as being highly realistic. The salient feature of that document is that the Great Powers, on condition that they act in concord and achieve unanimity, have, in effect, the decisive power and the decisive responsibility for enforcing the peace – except when they themselves happen to be the law-breakers. It was possible both to approve of and to criticize the Charter on 'realistic' grounds. Its draftsmen and supporters said repeatedly: The Charter is a highly realistic instrument. It acknowledges that the equality of all Members is a useless notion for the purpose of maintaining the peace; that responsibility and rights must be commensurate with power; that the Great Powers have the power; that their unity and concord are the safest, and the only, guarantee of peace; that no legal machinery will be of the slightest use if they fall out amongst themselves; and that, therefore, the so-called veto, although open to abuse, is the only realistic solution of the problem of international organization. Mr Attlee and Mr Bevin, who uttered warnings against starry-eyed idealism, appealed to the imperative duty of a realistic approach to the subject. In his report to the President of the United States on the Charter of the United Nations in 1945, the then Secretary of State viewed the realism of the Charter as its principal characteristic. (It may be noted that in the speech to the General Assembly on 17 September 1953 the present Secretary of State attributed the cause of the failure of many of the hopes attached to the Charter to the fact that 'these hopes were not realistic'.) However, it was possible to say – and it was said – that the Charter thus conceived was highly unrealistic; that if the Great Powers are united and determined in their unity to keep and enforce the peace, no international organization is required for that purpose; that in the past the Great Powers and not the small States had proved a danger to peace; that the permanent unity of action of all the Great Powers is no more than an assumption of wishful thinking; that that unity is not always easy to maintain even in time of common effort in war; that after the First World War all Great Powers, members of the Great Alliance, went their different – and occasionally hostile – ways; and that therefore a realistic international organization must be built on the principle that it must be made to work notwithstanding – nay, for the very event of – the probably contingency of disagreement of the Great Powers and of the defection of some of them from the basic principles of the Charter.

Many other examples in the field of international affairs can be adduced as showing the frustrating ambivalence of the terms 'realism' and 'idealism' as currently used in public discussion. Thus it is possible to say that international progress can be achieved only by way of parallel and simultaneous advances on all vital lines of international organization; that disarmament, legal prohibition of war, the obligation to enforce the peace against an aggressor, the duty of obligatory judicial settlement, and – probably – legal and enforceable obligations to respect fundamental human rights must be attempted *pari passu*; that progress in any of these fields is illusory without a parallel advance in the others; and that such parallelism of endeavour is of the essence of realism. But it is possible to argue – and it has been argued with more success – that such building of the new world by way of comprehensive blueprints is utterly unrealistic; that progress must be achieved by stages; and that any other approach is no more than the product of Utopian dreaming.

A similar problem has arisen in the sphere of international treaties of a general character, so-called legislative treaties. There the choice often presents itself as to what is preferable – a treaty very widely signed but riddled with reservations which render the signature largely nominal, or a treaty signed by a limited number of States but involving substantial obligations for the contracting parties. Both alternatives – that of universality and of what has been termed the integrity of the treaty – have been advocated as realistic, especially that promising the maximum degree of universality as against the unrealistic, 'perfectionist' (for that is the usual gibe of the realistic school) who would rather have no treaty at all than a grandiloquent declaration of principle divorced from any enforceable legal obligation. It is realistic, it has been said, to have half-a-loaf rather than no bread, i.e., a treaty, however imperfect, signed by all or many States rather than a perfect treaty signed by none or only few. On the other hand, it has been represented as realistic to aim at a true treaty with but few signatories rather than at a transparently deceptive piece of verbiage of which it can be said, as it has in fact been said on occasions, that it is difficult to say less in more words.

Finally, in the same line of examples, there has been recently in the field of international relations a recrudescence of the kind of realism which, although most true to type, contains nothing the opposite of which could not, with equal justice, be described as realism. I am referring to the writings of Mr Kennan, the former United States Ambassador to Moscow and some other American authors.[1] They have, in their criticism of the policy of the United States in the last fifty years, invoked the virtues of realism in contrast to Utopianism, perfectionism, ideologism, legalism, sentimentalism and the like. They have deplored the tendency 'to achieve our foreign policy objectives by inducing other Governments to sign up professions of high moral and legal principle'. They have stressed the realistic necessity, 'instead of making ourselves slaves of the concepts of international law and morality', of confining these concepts 'to the unobtrusive, almost feminine function of the gentler civilizer of national interest in which they find their true realm'.[2] The primacy of national power and national interest, as against the appeal to ideologies and principles, have been invoked, once more, as preeminently expressive of realism. However, it is equally legitimate to argue that the opposite of such approach is truly realistic; that ideas and ideals are the truly abiding basis of power and national interest; that, as abundant experience shows, States which act upon and acquire a reputation for acting on principles of law and ethics, are in a better position to achieve long-range aims of national life than States pursuing so-called realistic policies contemptuous of these principles; that things which cannot be weighed in advance or weighed at all, may be decisively weighty in terms of true power; that man in the long run rejects a political philosophy which makes

[1] See, in particular, Kennan, *American Diplomacy 1900–1950* (1951). See also Morgenthau, *Politics among Nations* (1948); the same, *In Defense of National Interest* (1951); Herz, *Political Realism and Political Idealism* (1951). For a recent critical analysis of the views propounded in these works see Quincy Wright in *International Politics*, 5 (1952), 116–28 and McDougal in *A.J.* 46 (1952), 102–14. In England Professor E. H. Carr – in particular in his *The Twenty Years' Crisis, 1919–1939* (1939) – has been the main recent exponent of the realist view.

[2] Kennan, *American Diplomacy*, p. 54. Apparently in reply to Mr Kennan – and using the same language for opposite purposes – Professor Northrop, of Yale, wrote in 1952: 'The cultural values and moral principles of the world in all their living law diversity and also in their unity, rather than precedent, power politics, jockeying for momentary isolationist expediency, constitute the realistic basis for resolving the ideological conflicts and disturbances of our world by peaceful means rather than suicidal resort to war in an atomic age' (*The Taming of the Nations. A Study of the Cultural Bases of International Policy* (1952)). Professor Northrop, it may be added, who thus calls himself a realist, has drawn upon him the reproach of a reviewer to the effect that he has 'allowed a heavy idealism to cloud clear thinking' and that it would have been better if 'his feet were more firmly on the ground' (*International Affairs*, 29 (1953), 478).

the physical power of the State and not the dignity and rights of man the final value and that such policy is therefore utterly unrealistic; that, in the modern world, national power and interest conceived as the exclusive aim, 'realistically' pursued, must lead, if they become a general pattern of behaviour, to war and anarchy with all their implications destructive of most things which matter; and that from that point of view they must be described as wholly unrealistic.

I have been concerned so far with the terminological aspect of the question. I have tried to suggest that, except psychologically, we do not actually add weight to our argument or attitude by calling it realistic. We simply assume something which must be proven. Psychologically, of course, we gain an advantage if we succeed in making others believe that we are the realists. But this seems an intellectually questionable way of arguing. It is, to use a hackneyed phrase, a Machiavellian proceeding.

I am using that hackneyed phrase for the reason that it was Machiavelli who was among the first to attach importance to calling themselves realists. He says in a frequently quoted passage:

> It being my intention to write a thing which shall be useful to him who apprehends it, it appears to me more appropriate to follow up the real truth of a matter than the imagination of it . . . For many have pictured republics and principalities which in fact have never been seen and known. Because how one lives is so far distant from how one ought to live that he who neglects what is done for what ought to be done sooner effects his end than his preservation.

These realistic words found wide approval. He received a pat on the back from Bacon for 'saying openly and without hypocrisy what men are in the habit of doing, not what they ought to do'. Now this commendation by Bacon, although not so intended, brings to mind – and here I am turning from terminology to substance – one of the two characteristic features of realism as generally propounded. Lord Morley, in his essay on Machiavelli, which is always worth re-reading, says with regard to Machiavelli's claim to see the real thing: 'Machiavelli and his school saw only cunning, jealousy, perfidy, ingratitude, dupery; and yet on such a foundation as this they dreamed that they could build! What idealist or doctrinaire ever fell into a stranger error!' The gist of this remark is that the typical realist sees only the directly manifest aspect of things. It is perhaps here that he approaches, unconsciously, his namesake in philosophy. He sees what is obvious and what hits the eye. And it is the thing that hits the eye which, if generalized with facile ingenuity, appeals to many a mind as expressive of reality. Yet such a picture of the situation is no more than a half-truth. Let me, once more, give some examples in the sphere of international relations.

The basic notion of the idea of international progress, including that implicit in the elimination of war, is the conviction of the ultimate solidarity and harmony of interests of States. It is the conviction that though particular and important interests of nations, like those of individuals, often conflict, the conflict, however acute, is of secondary significance when compared with the transcending fact of the unity of the human race and of the growing and inescapable interdependence of States in the economic and other fields in an age in which science has done much to obliterate frontiers between sovereign States. But the realist sees only what hits the eye. He sees primarily conflicts of interests among States, in particular those arising out of rival claims to territories and raw materials. He is content to regard them as the fundamental phenomena of international relations. He is thus led to reduce most aspects of international politics to a conflict between the 'have' and 'have not' States. He regards this as *the* problem of modern international politics – a problem which, in his view, did not exist in the past when there was enough to go round and when, accordingly, the doctrine of a harmony of interests between nations appeared plausible. He does not explain why, if this was so, wars were rampant in the past. The realist is so impressed with the conspicuous phenomenon of conflicts of interest that there is no room in his philosophy for the reality of the ultimate identity of interest of States which consists in the preservation of peace both as an end in itself and as an indispensable condition of adjusting in accordance with justice the disparity between the 'haves' and 'have nots'. For him – and here reveals itself the realist's tendency to cynicism – the insistence on peace and law are primarily expressive of the desire of the satisfied States to be left alone in the enjoyment of what they have. His historical researches confirm him in the view that internationalism is mainly an ingenious device of those in power to perpetuate the existing *status quo*. He points out, for instance, that the Grand Design, the plans for organized peace in Europe put forward by two Frenchmen, Sully and Emeric Crucé, in the seventeenth century, at a time when French power was preponderant in Europe, were subtle schemes for perpetuating French power in Europe. He notes that internationalism gained a foothold in England in the nineteenth century at a time when the might of the British Empire was supreme and unchallenged.

Yet internationalism, based as it is on an enlightened view of national interest, has been propounded with vigour by thinkers of small nations. The internationalism and the pacific idea of the prophets, of Erasmus, of Grotius and of Fritjof Nansen were not a hypocritical glorification of the satisfied appetite of Great Powers.

A further example of the attraction which the obvious has for the realist is equally instructive. One of the bases of the international organization of peace is the fact – and the appreciation of the fact – that peace is indivisible. Which means that any aggressive war, or threat thereof, is a subject of direct concern to all; in this matter the world cannot be divided into watertight compartments. But the realist is inclined to ridicule the statement that peace is indivisible. For, he says, as a matter of actual fact, peace is divisible. Some States do stay at peace, and like to stay at peace, when other States are at war. Members of the League of Nations were at peace with Japan when she was engaged in making war on China. Soviet Russia was at peace with Germany when the latter was waging war on and invading the territories of the Members of the League, of which Russia formed a part. Some traditionally neutral States – neutralized and others – remain at peace, and have flourished on it, in the midst of general conflagrations. The obvious answer to that realistic assessment of events is that when we say that peace is indivisible we mean that in the long run it is indivisible; that in the long run the infection of lawless force cannot be isolated; that in the long run aggressive war tends to become universal and equally threatening to all; and that the tenuous and precarious peace of the few remaining neutrals merely confirms that major proposition.

Finally, as the third example in the sphere of international affairs of the realist tendency to see mainly the obvious and the conspicuous, there may be recalled the importance attached by the realist to the immorality of nations. He regards it as the typical and normal phenomenon in the relations of States. And as he sees mainly what is glaring and writ large, he tends to exaggerate the element of immorality in the conduct of States as compared with that of individuals. The realist's description of the hypocrisy and selfishness of nations almost seems to suggest that individuals in their private life and in their business relations are invariably selfless, upright, and without a trace of sanctimoniousness. Now the realist not only magnifies the extent of the immorality of States. He regards this double standard of morality – one for individuals, the other for States – as an enduring fact grounded inescapably in the very existence of

States as collective bodies and as sovereign States. For him the immorality of States is, in the first instance, only one aspect of the lower morality of groups as compared with that of individuals. It is a necessary and permanent quality. The moral restraints which determine the acts of the individual in his private life tend to be inoperative when he acts on behalf of his group or as a member of the group. There is an element of truth in that – though not as much truth as is often assumed. In any case this actual or supposed lower morality – this double standard of morality – of leaders of nations when acting on behalf of these nations is not an unalterable and immutable part of nature. It is subject to education, to moral enlightenment and, to some extent, to the abandonment, which has already largely taken place, of some notions of law and political science associated with the idea of the real personality of groups. But the realist does not see that. The immorality of the conduct of States – i.e., of those acting on their behalf – is to him a permanent factor inherent in their existence as collective units.

Moreover, to the realist who sees only the conspicuous fact of organized national society and the amorphous international community, that immorality is a necessary phenomenon for yet another reason. To quote Bosanquet:

> It [the State] has no determinate function in a larger community, but is itself the supreme community; the guardian of a whole moral world, but not a factor within an organized world. Moral relations presuppose an organized life; but such a life is only within the State, not in relations between States and other communities.[1]

Hobbes said the same thing, in almost identical words, two hundred years before. Realists have since copied one from the other, with some complacency, this characteristic exhibition of realistic thinking.

And this brings us to the second main characteristic of the realist. He has no faith in the capacity of human beings when acting collectively, especially in relation to other collectivities, to act intelligently and to learn from experience. He denies, in fact, the sovereignty of the human will, both in general and in the field of international affairs. In this sphere he questions the power of man to learn from experience and to advance to progress. Let me give two examples. The central issue in international organization is the problem of collective security which is, upon final analysis, the problem of the willingness of States to gain safety by undertaking mutually to defend the security of all others against aggression. But that problem cannot

[1] *The Philosophical Theory of the State* (4th ed. 1923), p. 302.

be solved unless States are willing to limit their freedom of action – their sovereignty – by undertaking not only to act when the security of others is at stake but also to abide by the collective judgment, reached by an appropriate majority of an impartial tribunal, as to whether a case has arisen for the fulfilment of that obligation. For unless some power resides in an outside body to determine whether the case for the fulfilment of an obligation has arisen, there is no effective obligation; if it depends on me to say whether I am bound to act, I am in fact not bound at all. Now the realist concurs in that analysis – it is difficult for him not to – but after having done so he will say wisely and sadly: 'Yes, but Governments will not have it; peoples will not have it; they will never agree to undertake to be bound to act in unforeseen contingencies at the behest of an external agency; they will not agree to surrender their sovereignty; we are up against a brick wall; we must be realistic. The Charter of the United Nations is to that extent a realistic document. Only the small States are bound by the obligations of collective security. The Great Powers are so bound only when each of them holds that an obligation has arisen.' To the suggestion that there is probably no alternative between the limitation of full sovereignty thus conceived and the continuation of international anarchy which threatens to destroy that very sovereignty, the realist replies that we are dogmatic and that we rely too much on principle (which, he urges, is in itself a sign of Utopian mentality). He will regale us with a story about that street hawker in Lisbon who, 250 years ago, was selling anti-earthquake pills and who, when it was suggested to him that this was not really a remedy, asked petulantly: Possibly, but have you anything else to put in its place? The realist does not admit that, though there is no remedy for earthquakes, there may be a remedy for the imperfections of human institutions. He has no faith in the part of the human will as an agency shaping the destiny of man. The realist recalls that when one of the founders of the League of Nations was asked whether its principles (which, in the realist view, did not take into account human nature) would work, he answered 'they must be made to work'. This to the realist appears ridiculous. He is pessimistic about the capacity of man to learn from experience, as indeed about the capacity of man to improve. For him, human nature does not change; and human nature is bad. Human nature is a natural phenomenon like an earthquake. Contempt for the 'little breed' of men is a dogma for the realist. It was so with Machiavelli and Hobbes. It is so with their modern successors.

With this, there are connected three other features of modern realism in particular in the field of international affairs. The first is mistrust of principle. Principle is suspect; it is an abstraction unrelated to realities. Instruments such as the Covenant of the League of Nations or the Charter of the United Nations, says the realist, are based on principles, on logic, on a scheme. As such they stand condemned. For the problems of international politics, it is said, cannot be solved in reliance on abstract formulae and legal rules. They must be solved - if they can be solved - by taking account of the complexities of each individual case. Yet, to deny the value of principle as a guide for human action is to deny the value of reason. No one, even a realist, can consistently act on a theory which denies the value of theory.

However, from the realist point of view, this successful attack on principle is essential, for only if we deny long-range principle can we act on the realistic view that what matters is the immediate advantage. In this sense opportunism is the hall-mark of political realism as generally understood. This explains, in the field of international relations, why realists have viewed with disapproval the idea of collective security. Collective security may require that we go to war in order to ensure peace. It may demand that we sacrifice the immediate advantages of peace today in order to make sure, so far as we can, of the more enduring peace under law. For, like other institutions of civilized life, collective security is in the nature of an insurance. The realist, when confronted with the choice, will prefer the immediate advantage of remaining at peace today rather than of securing it for the days to come. He prefers to act on the words of the prayer: 'Give us peace in our day, O Lord' – even if peace today means a precarious war tomorrow. For that reason between the two World Wars realists spoke disparagingly of the jargon of collective security. They suggested that the only means of strengthening the Covenant of the League of Nations was to take out of it the teeth of collective security.

Finally, the realist's attitude to collective security – which is the backbone of the international organization of peace and of international organization generally – helps to draw attention to yet another important and disquieting characteristic of political realism. Collective security, in so far as it means repression and punishment of aggression, implies a moral judgment. Of this the realist disapproves – and not only for the reason to which I have already referred, namely, that as accepted canons of morality do not operate in the relations of States, States cannot act immorally and that moral judgment on their actions is misplaced and irrelevant. There are other reasons. In the first instance, moral principle – being a principle – must be distrusted. There are, in the realist's view, no absolutely binding rules of conduct; nothing is wholly good or wholly bad; we must not assume the monopoly of righteousness; we must not judge others; there is no abstract international justice. The realist reminds us that not only Mr Churchill but also Hitler and Goebbels appealed to international justice, and that both the Kaiser and President Wilson invoked God and the righteousness of their cause. It follows that any such appeal, on either side, is no more than special pleading. We must not condemn aggression – the realists pleaded during the Italo-Abyssinian war and on similar occasions – for we have done the same or the similar thing in the past. Moreover, immoral or illegal aggression are terms dear to the hearts of the 'haves', of those in possession, of the satisfied States. They have no meaning in relation to States which ask for a change in the *status quo*. In recent years there has been added to that armoury of moral relativism the argument that the usurpation of the right of moral judgment upon States and the condemnation of the law-breaker leads to the ideas of punishment, of total victory and unconditional surrender and the consequent brutalization and prolongation of wars. There is a possible connection between that climate of opinion and the widespread attitude of indifference to or even condemnation of the punishment of soldiers and politicians who have committed crimes of a revolting character and an unprecedented scale against the civilian population. That attitude, for which there may be found a plausible political justification, constitutes a grave reflection on the state of public morality in the period following the Second World War. That realist approach of moral relativism may also explain the fact that in the controversy – for there is still a controversy – as to the right of moral judgment on the part of historians the scales have been turning, even in Cambridge, against Lord Acton.

These, then, are the features of the current realistic attitude in international affairs. In the first instance, the realist sees mainly the obvious and the conspicuous. It is for that reason that he magnifies the phenomena of conflict of interest and the immorality of States. Secondly, he is pessimistic about human nature and its capacity for improvement. He has no faith in the power of the human will to shape the fate of men. He is distrustful of principle. He is attracted by immediate advantage. He is a moral relativist. All these features of realism are, like its very name, superficially attractive. They appeal to men almost as much as their opposites; they are very plausible; and they are in practice easier to follow. They have been widely followed in the last quarter of the century. While the sombre events in the international sphere of that era may be explained by a variety of causes, it is my conviction that they have been powerfully influenced, for evil, by the temper of realism.

To return to the initial theme, I believe that when conceived as an argument in itself – and it is so often used either in good or in bad faith – the appeal to realism is intellectually faulty. It assumes at the very outset a quality of wisdom and soundness which it denies to the opponent. What, then, shall we do when confronted or in danger of being confronted with that kind of argument? Shall we steal the thunder from our opponent, get in first, and call *ourselves* realists and *him* a Utopian? I have occasionally, in this matter, advised undergraduates as follows:

If in the future, in argumentative zeal, you call yourselves realists, you should blush for very shame. For realism, properly conceived, is a quality which we must concede to our opponent in the same measure as we claim it for ourselves. Neither ought we to meet the egregious claim half-way by calling ourselves 'realistic idealists' or 'idealistic realists'. Let us distrust labels. If you ask me whether, apart from *calling* ourselves realists, it is not a good thing that we *should* be realists, my answer is that I am not certain what exactly a realist is. If it is the kind of realism which I have been describing, and which has been very real in recent years, my answer can be surmised from my questions. If it is the kind of realism which often goes by that name and which has been identified with the temporary successes of wilful men in history – the Borgias, the Frederick the Greats, the Napoleons, the Bismarcks, the Hitlers, the Mussolinis – the realism of lawlessness, opportunism, and denial of sanctity of man – then no answer is necessary. By all means let us see and learn to see things as they are – this is the main reason why you are in the University – but to know things does not mean to be content with them. Certainly, let us respect power, but let us not identify it with physical force, and let us not worship it unless as an instrument of right. Guns are propelled by ideas. Except in military language there are no self-propelling guns. By all means let us acknowledge the authority of facts. But we need not think of facts in terms of narrow realism. In the realm of human action ideas are facts. Revolt against injustice and prejudice is a fact. Projects of improvement are a fact. As such they must assuredly play a part – not as an infinite ideal, but in our time. Let us study them, all of them, whether they be projects of world federation, or of the constitution of the world, or of the revision of the Charter. Let us treat with serenity the gibe that we are engaged in producing perfectionist blueprints. If we must be realists, let us have a realism which does not merely register experience in a mood of pessimism or resignation, but which learns from experience and which is impatient of its defects as seen by reason. Nowhere are these defects more glaring and more destructive of the good life than in the external relations of States which are, mostly, civilized except in their mutual relations. If we are realists in that sense, perhaps we shall be forgiven if, in the heat of argument, we fall into the trap and resort to the little trick of calling ourselves so.

This is the advice which I have occasionally ventured to give to undergraduates. If pressed hard I might make so bold as to impart it to others. But I would not be inclined to exaggerate its importance. For it is possible that the matter is not one of substance, but of method of argument.

CHAPTER 4

PROFESSOR CARR ON INTERNATIONAL MORALITY

Editor's note This chapter contains an undated and apparently unpublished comment on Professor E. H. Carr's views on international morality. From the page references in the text it is possible to identify the passages under criticism as falling within chapter 9 of the first edition of Professor Carr's *The Twenty Years' Crisis, 1919–1939*, published in 1939. The references to Wellesley and Boston at p. 85 suggest that the piece may have been written while Lauterpacht was a visiting professor at Wellesley College, Massachusetts, in the autumn of 1941.

It is with some hesitation that I have included this uncharacteristic item – uncharacteristic because of its polemical tone and its relatively unrestrained style. Lauterpacht felt deeply about questions of international morality and appears to have reacted strongly to chapter 9 of Professor Carr's book. The strength of his reaction to the chapter was probably affected by conditions at the time when the piece was written. Perhaps more than most, Lauterpacht was influenced by the prevailing anxiety and tension of the period following the fall of France. Moreover, he must have been greatly worried about the fate of his parents and relations who lived in Poland.

Lauterpacht normally avoided the public pursuit of controversy, which doubtless explains why he put aside this piece without even correcting the typescript. It was, indeed, left in so rough a state that he never filled in the title of Professor Carr's work. Or perhaps he may have felt, writing as he appears to have done, within five years of the Hoare–Laval Treaty and at a time when Sir Samuel Hoare was still active in government, that it would have been inappropriate to publish this kind of comment on Sir Samuel's part in the conclusion of the Treaty. Such considerations no longer have the same force; and notwithstanding its obviously hurried composition the work seems worth publishing for the light it so strikingly sheds on Lauterpacht's own positive views.

As in previous chapters he [Professor Carr] gives himself an advantageous start by stating, without an effort at proof, that the monopoly of international studies by the Utopian schools in the post-war period has resulted in a concentration of interest on discussions of what international morality ought ideally to be; that there has been little discussion of the moral behaviour of States except to pass hasty and sweeping condemnation on it; and that there has been no discussion at all of assumptions held by the ordinary man about international morality. This claim to a monopoly of realism and novelty is not confined to this part of the book. It appears from Professor Carr's citations on p. 199 that at least two writers have expressed views on the assumptions of the ordinary man in the matter, but the bibliographical list could be enlarged very substantially indeed. The problem of international morality has, of course, been a persistent theme in political science before and after the [First] World War.

In fact, Professor Carr's chapter is to a large extent devoted to a discussion of what writers have actually said on the subject as, e.g., on p. 188, where he points out that writers on international morality are not clear whether what they wish to discuss is the morality of States or the morality of individuals.

Moreover, on the same page (187), he seems to admit that a discussion of the subject has been taking place, but that it has become merely a tool on the part of Utopian Anglo-Saxon writers, to assail those opposed to the maintenance of the *status quo*. Finally, in his introductory remarks Professor Carr once more follows his customary attitude of asserting an exclusive claim to scientific method by exhorting the student to maintain contact with his ambitions for the future and the realities of the present. He reminds the student of the anthropologist who, although disliking cannibalism, does not permit his feelings to obscure the objectivity of his exposition.

Professor Carr rightly assumes that the personification of the State is one of the central aspects of the problem of international morality. But it is not certain that he is right in assuming that the problem *began* with the personification of the State as distinguished from the personal ruler of the moment and that it was the personification of the State which made possible the creation of international law on the basis of natural law. Machiavelli's *Prince* is conceived in terms of the duties of the ruler, and yet it is the beginning of the modern discussion of the dualism of moral standards. And it is a fact that the systems of international law built by Grotius and other classical writers were largely – though not exclusively – expressed in terms of rights and duties of rulers of States. Neither can it be admitted that the principal drawback of the personification of States was that it emphasized not only duties but also rights and that the emphasis upon the latter became more and more conspicuous. The opposition against the abuses of personification of States (Professor Carr conveniently limits that opposition to modern Utopian writers – practically everyone who disagrees with Professor Carr is Utopian – among whom he includes Duguit) has come from the realization that it tends to conceal the fact that the agents of the personified States and the persons determining the policy of these agents and individuals are bound by ordinary standards of morality. Utopian writers have been opposing not the convenient device of the personification of the State, but the abuses of that personification, in particular the assumption that the personification of the State means that its actions are actions of an entity other than the individuals who compose or who govern it and that therefore the distinct personality of the State implies a distinct international morality.

The difficult question of State personality Professor Carr treats in a somewhat cavalier-like fashion. The controversy, he says, as to the attribution of personality to the State, is not only misleading, but meaningless. 'To deny personality to the State is just as absurd as to assert it. The personality of the State is not a fact whose truth or falsehood is a matter of argument' (p. 189). The personality of the State – as well as of other groups – is to him merely a convenient device for dealing with the complicated structure of modern society and for stressing the continuity of the group as distinguished from its members. This is probably an all too easy way of disposing of the difficulty. The distinct reality of the group has been asserted by representative exponents of philosophy and it has been no less emphatically asserted by philosophers and political writers. We have only to think of names like Gierke, Maitland, Dicey, Laski. Dicey's assertion of the real personality of the State and of other groups and his rejection of the view that such personification is merely a fiction of the law have become classical. To dismiss these views as absurd without specifying them and without further discussion will be regarded by many as an over-simplification of a difficult problem. The question is how, assuming the reality of the personality of the State, that reality can be maintained consistently with upholding a single standard of morality for States and individuals. A similar problem in the field of political theory reveals the true nature of the problem: both Hegel and Green asserted the reality of the State and of the general will. There may be more than a legal fiction in a corporation, in a club, in a partnership, in the institution of the family. But it does not follow from this that the actions of the members of these groups or of the agents appointed by them, are not actions of individuals; that the obligations of States are not the obligations of individuals acting on their behalf; and that the morality of States is different from the morality of individuals. But this is exactly what Professor Carr, without proving it, asserts. (And, curiously enough, he maintains that such distinct personality is in the nature of a fiction. For if it is a fiction, if, that is to say, it does not *actually* exist apart from the individuals composing it, then how can a different morality be attributed to it? How can any morality be attributed to it? Professor Carr attempts some kind of an answer to this question. He does not deny that the actions of States are in fact actions of individuals and that the moral behaviour and the (distinct) morality of States are in the nature of a hypothesis, of a fiction. But he maintains that that fiction is real inasmuch as it guides and influences individual behaviour to the extent of making those acting on behalf of the State believe that they are acting on behalf of a separate personality endowed with duties and rights of its own and that, therefore, in thus acting they are not bound by the same rules by which they are bound as individuals. The *non sequitur* is so blatant as to be confusing.)

Although Professor Carr does not adduce proof, he adduces illustrations in support of his view. He points out that when, in 1935 the Opposition (was it only the Opposition?) denounced the Hoare–Laval Plan as a 'terrible crime', it did not denounce Sir Samuel Hoare as a criminal or regard him as such; 'it only found him guilty of an error of judgment'. It is not clear what conclusions Professor Carr draws from this incident, as presented. Does he conclude that a statesman, writing on behalf of a nation, may commit acts which are contrary to international morality, but which do not reflect upon the private morality of the agent – a phenomenon pointing to the existence of different standards in private and public morality? Or does he mean (as has, indeed, occasionally been argued by so-called realists and by protagonists of the Machiavelli–Hegel school) that an individual may, while acting on behalf of the State, pursue a line of conduct which would be reprehensible if acted upon, in an ambiguous situation, for his private purposes, and that this is, in fact, the way in which the ordinary citizen approaches the matter? Professor Carr apparently has in mind this second alternative, for, although he refers to the allegation of a 'terrible crime' on the part of Sir Samuel, he himself does not think that the act was contrary to international morality; the whole argument is intended to show that as international morality is different from private morality the act in question, although reprehensible from the point of view of private morality, did not necessarily offend against international morality. But this, apparently, was not the view of those who accused the Foreign Secretary of a 'terrible crime'. They seem to have thought that the act was criminal and immoral. And as, in Professor Carr's view, they did not attribute any private criminality or immorality to Sir Samuel Hoare, they must have thought that his conduct *was* contrary to international morality. Professor Carr thus proves the very contrary of what he intended to prove.

But, in fact, it is not at all certain that the accusers of Sir Samuel did not charge him with an act of which he ought to have been personally ashamed. They certainly charged him with something more than with an error of judgment. They did not accuse him of personal dishonesty for personal profit. But that particular motive is not necessary in order to render an individual morally responsible. If, in order to advance the interest of my family and without any thought of any private profit, I resort to lying or dealing disloyally, I still act immorally. If, in order to advance the interest of my club or team, I cheat or bully in the course of a game, I still act immorally. The fact is that those who criticized the Foreign Secretary charged him with an act which involved him personally. The fact is that his critics charged him with conduct which they considered reprehensible from the point of view of both international and private morality. The entire Hoare–Laval episode is indicative of the shallow inaccuracy with which the 'realist' writers adduce the attitude of the ordinary man in support of their contention that the ordinary man – unlike Utopian writers and philosophers – fully realizes and approves of the dualism of moral standards among individuals and States. What warrant is there for that contention? None, it is submitted. The fact is that the ordinary man tends to be indignant at any attempt to introduce such dual standards – often in a manner which, according to some, betrays a lack of comprehension of the complexities of international situations. In the Italian–Abyssinian war the ordinary man violently and passionately disapproved of the deal; he did not, as Professor Carr and other realists wanted him to do, pass by on the other side with an air of resignation and appreciation of the difference in private and public morality. So violent was his indignation that it swept like a cleansing breeze through the entrenched citadel of a Government supported by a powerful and docile parliamentary majority. But Professor Carr refers to the Hoare–Laval incident as demonstrating popular acquiescence in a loose standard of international morality. The fact is that popular feeling spontaneously and almost invariably disapproves of any manifestations of or attempts at inferior international morality. When the Soviet Government in the summer of 1939, by its clandestine deal with Germany, made itself responsible for an outrageous and rather petty piece of double-crossing, there was no disposition among sections of public opinion to condone the action taken by reference to a specifically conceived international morality – although there were attempts to find extenuating circumstances for that action in what was described as the condescending, half-hearted and humiliating tardiness of French and British attempts at a *rapprochement* with Russia.

Moreover, the realist not only misrepresents or exaggerates the degree of popular acquiescence in international immorality, he tends to exaggerate the extent of the immoral conduct of States. There has been an almost fatalistic tendency to assume that modern States do habitually act in a manner offending against the generally accepted conceptions of morality, and that the only task left to the student is to explain the reasons of that fact and to assist in building a new system of international morality different from that known in the relations of private persons. But are we actually confronted, as a normal and persistent phenomenon, with State conduct offending against obvious principles of morality? Let us take as an example the foreign policy of the United States of America or of Great Britain in the last fifty years. It would constitute an interesting topic for an essay to survey that policy and to try to find in it acts which were clearly immoral. We are on dangerous ground now, but let us not shirk the issue.

Let us take the United States first. What are the examples of clearly immoral conduct which will make the ordinary citizen blush? This is not the time to go into the details of isolated examples, but I submit that inquiry would show that there are remarkably few such examples and that those few are controversial. I can think of one which the student might feel inclined to adduce. It is the incident of the premature recognition of the Republic of Panama. This sounds bad enough. It was not a rash act of an executive officer. It gave expression to a deliberate and considered act of policy which was defended at great length in the protracted correspondence between the United States and Colombia. It would clearly be misplaced to attempt to justify or to minimize the seriousness of this act of the United States. It was undoubtedly an example of a Great Power using in a ruthless fashion its physical strength to brush aside the legal right of a small state. The United States subsequently recognized that there was room for amends, for in a subsequent treaty, concluded many years after the event, compensation was granted to Colombia. However, after all this has been said, the fact remains that the immorality of the action taken by the United States – as distinguished from its undoubted illegality – is controversial. Westlake, a distinguished international lawyer, with an exacting standard of international morality, was not prepared to condemn the action of the United States. For him it was a case in which a State, in the absence of an international legislature, had been called upon to act as a legislator for the wider good of the international community. The issue was whether a beneficent and civilizing enterprise should be delayed or obstructed by a State which happened to be in possession of the territory in question.

I must leave it to others to inquire into the immorality of British foreign policy in the period discussed. But I submit confidently that a survey of the foreign policy of modern States will show that the immorality of international conduct is something in the nature of a myth. Anyone who has had occasion to study the records of the foreign offices or state departments must be impressed by their reasonableness and straightforwardness in the routine of international intercourse.

Those in whose minds international morality looms in an excessive proportion are much preoccupied with the fact that practically all States spend large sums of money for spying and, generally, for obtaining information by means which no self-respecting individual would employ for his private purposes. It is probably no excess of optimism to believe that the amount of money expended for these purposes as between Canada and the United States of America, the United States of America and Great Britain, or Norway and Sweden, or Holland and Belgium, is negligible – assuming that it is expended at all. Spying is an incident of latent warfare between States for whom war is in the range of practical politics.

Undoubtedly, war looms large in the foreign policy of States, but war is an imperfection of international law and of international organization, not of international morality. There may be some – although not much – substance in the suggestion that that state of the law is in itself due to a low level of international morality. However that may be, two facts must be borne in mind in this connection. The first is that in the last quarter of the century attempts have been made, of fundamental importance for the structure of international law, to limit and, in the Kellogg–Briand Pact, to abolish the institution of war as an instrument of national policy. The second is that, as a matter of historical fact, instances of a democratic State resorting to aggressive war as an instrument of national policy are in the nature of a rare exception.

This latter point – this reference to democratic States – brings us to one of the principal aspects of the problem of international morality, namely, its connection with the democratic way of life. Democracy – as events have shown – is not the best instrument for operating a long-range foreign policy. It does not exhibit a temerity of purpose and a degree of foresight necessary for the effective organization of an international system of peace and collective security. Unless aided by enlightened and determined leadership or by precise legal institutions and obligations supplying the deficiencies of collective memory, it fails to exhibit the necessary loyalty and fidelity to obligations undertaken on its behalf in the field of collective international endeavour. But while it is not an ideal instrument for positive and constructive action in the international field, it is at the same time a powerful brake upon positive immoral conduct. Democracy, after all, is government by the people and there are obvious limits to the separation of the State from those who compose it and act on its behalf. There are natural and inescapable limits, in a democracy, to the personification of the State and to the assertion of its absolute value as against the ephemeral and incidental existence of the individual. In the final analysis, the individual remains the ultimate unit of Government and of State action. This is the reason why the doctrine of duality of moral standards has never struck deep roots in democracies. Occasionally, very occasionally, it has been preached there by sycophantic writers and by those hankering after realism, but, essentially, it has originated from, and been practised under, the régimes of absolutism and dictatorship. The absolute ruler of Machiavelli, or Frederick the Great, or the State idolized by Nietzsche, or the modern brands of dictatorships will tell the same tale. Once the State becomes an absolute, mystical, irrational entity divorced from and infinitely superior to the transient beings who compose it, it acquires a claim to a different morality or, what is the same, to an absence of morality as understood by individuals. This is so because it is supposed to be both different from and superior to individuals. And this is so also for the third and in itself decisive reason that tyranny is essentially immoral *per se*, regardless of any immediate objects at which it aims; in the long run, it depraves those who wield it. It is not to be expected that an institution which *pro bono publico* violates the fundamental moral postulate – that of freedom – will exhibit a respect for moral standards above the dictates of convenience.

There thus emerge three facts from what has been said. (1) The immorality of the international conduct of States is a less frequent phenomenon than realist writers would make us believe. Upon analysis it proves to be a fiction asserted by political writers in support of questionable theories of the State. (2) The attitude of the ordinary man to manifestations of State immorality is more critical and condemnatory than is often represented. (3) There is a close connection between the form of government of States and the morality of their international conduct in the sense that the excessive personification and sanctification of the State inherent in dictatorships, inevitably leads them to the abandonment of the accepted canons of private morality.

(With regard to the latter point it is perhaps useful to stress in these days this particular advantage of democracy and this particular danger of dictatorships. Dazzled by the temporary triumphs of force, political writers have acquired the habit of questioning or ignoring some of the advantages usually associated with democracies. One of these is their inherent peacefulness and disinclination to resort to war. Kant insisted that one of the conditions of international progress in the direction of a Federation of the World was the spread of the republican form of government. The meaning of that view has not lost its vitality. It is not necessary to expatiate on the reasons for that view. One of them may be noted, however. Dictatorships are typically in need of and capable of the necessary ruthlessness for using a foreign war as a diversion from internal crisis and unrest.)

Is the attitude of most States in the matter of migration and of admission of aliens contrary to international morality?

In what has been said so far there has been no intention to suggest that the problem of international morality is non-existent or that it is right that it should be wholly disregarded. For in so far as the State is a group – and it is so to a substantial extent – it raises in the field of morality the same general problem of group morality. The problem lies not in the fact that group personality is entirely distinct from that of the component units – for that is controversial. The problem arises from the fact that the group, even if it is merely a legal fiction, is a convenient instrument of thinking. It lies in the fact that the existence of a group is a powerful inducement to laxity in conduct. The opportunity to shift the burden or moral doubt upon the impersonal shoulders of the amorphous association is a motivating force in the nature of a temptation which only a most scrupulous fortitude of mind and principle can hope to overcome with ease. There is nothing mystical about the group. But there is about it the constant threat of the suggestion that it represents an interest greater in the scale of values than the private interest of the acting individual. From this there is only one step to the view that the individual is entitled to gauge the action to be taken by a standard different from that which he would be bound to adopt if he acted on his own behalf. From this it is only another step toward the final view that the individual is not at liberty when acting as trustee for others to afford the luxury of private morality. This particular argument has been repeatedly put forward. A moment's consideration shows that the argument is grotesquely inadequate. It is difficult to understand why the interests of other persons on behalf of whom we are acting should be so different and so much higher in the scale of values than our own as to warrant the adoption of different moral standards. Undoubtedly, the fact that we are acting on behalf of others ought to imbue us with a measure of caution in the sense that we ought not to show a refinement of morality or generosity which we would not be inclined to show in dealing with our own business, but this is the only limitation.

But let us return to Professor Carr's illustration of the contention that the ordinary man distinguishes and approves of the distinction between private and public morality. He points out that while most Englishmen were 'ashamed' of the Munich settlement of 1938, they were not ashamed of Mr Chamberlain (who, in their belief, acted honestly, although mistakenly) or of themselves ('for they would have done anything in their power to prevent it'), but they were ashamed of the 'cowardly act' of Great Britain which subsequently granted a loan of £10,000,000 to Czechoslovakia – a species of 'conscience money' paid by a moral delinquent (see p. 192). This account of the situation is, of course, an inaccurate simplification of the situation. The majority of Englishmen were not ashamed either of themselves or of Mr Chamberlain or of Great Britain. They approved of what Mr Chamberlain did at Munich as a measure of unavoidable – although humiliating – political necessity imposed upon a nation which, as the result of the shortcomings of its leadership, had neglected the necessary precautions both in the field of armament and of collective security. That distressing and resentful approach was coupled with the determination to strengthen the defences of the country and to turn away from the path of appeasement. It was followed by an active measure of sympathy towards the nation directly afflicted as the result of the shortcomings of British policy. (It will be noted that there was, in connection with the Munich settlement, no question of a breach of clear legal obligation towards Czechoslovakia. It will also be noted that inasmuch as Professor Carr represents the loan as 'conscience money' by a shame-covered Britain, he admits the presence, with the ordinary man, of the consciousness of an international morality identical with that of morality in general.)

However, there was a minority of people in Great Britain who disapproved violently of the Munich settlement and who regarded it as dishonouring the country which bought its security or a short-lived respite at the expense of the vital interests of a small and trusting nation. That minority was far from regarding Mr Chamberlain's conduct as a mere intellectual error. It viewed it in the same light in which the majority viewed the conduct of Sir Samuel Hoare in the Hoare–Laval deal. There was no inclination to draw a hard-and-fast line between the moral qualities of Mr Chamberlain as a person and as a politician. But it would not be proper to expatiate on that.

Professor Carr does not deny that there exists an international morality. This, he says, is only the view of 'realists' – among whom he includes Hegel and Bosanquet, a disciple of Hegel and one of the leading exponents of idealistic philosophy in England, who was even more emphatic in denying international morality – another example of the arbitrariness of Professor Carr's use of the term 'realist'. But he denies that the same standards are applicable to the morality of States and of individuals. This, he says, is the view of 'Utopians' like Presidents Wilson or Roosevelt or Dr Benes. This assertion, it will be shown, amounts to a denial of international morality although it is plausibly wrapped up in the advocacy of a specifically conceived international morality.

For the sake of clarity, it ought to be stated at the outset that there is very little difference between denying that there exists an international morality and maintaining that there exists an international morality different from private morality. As a matter of experience, we know only of the fundamental canons of private morality. Occasionally, individuals acting on behalf of States have departed from that morality. By dint of felicitous turn of phrase, these deviations may be described as, or generalized into, an 'international morality', but the classification thus adopted ought not to obscure the true nature of the conduct in question. The conduct of the State – being the conduct of individuals – is like the conduct of any other group, either moral or immoral from the point of view of accepted standards of international conduct. Professor Carr's general thesis – although adroitly dissociated from that of the 'realist' – amounts in fact to a denial of international morality. This may best be seen from the kind of proof which Professor Carr adduces in support of the existence of international morality as he conceives it.

(1) The first is that statesmen have, in their professions, always acknowledged and appealed to some kind of international obligation (it is clear from the examples given by Professor Carr that he does not distinguish between the professions of legal and moral obligation). He quotes extensively Herr Hitler, Dr Goebbels and Signor Mussolini as appealing eloquently to international justice.

(2) The obligation not to inflict unnecessary death or suffering. This rule, of course, has nothing to do with international morality. It is a principle of the law of war which has developed largely from considerations of chivalry and which has been enshrined in Hague Convention No. 4 on the Rules and Customs of War on Land. (The principle refers only to unnecessary suffering – not to death or suffering.)

(3) Constant references in diplomatic practice to international comity. It is well known that in international practice and in the language of courts international comity means 'international law'.

(4) The automatic obligation of States newly admitted to the international community to be bound by international *law*(!).

(5) The professed obligation of States to be bound by treaties. This again is an obligation of international law.

After this half-hearted – and therefore unconvincing – proof of the existence of some international morality, Professor Carr proceeds to show 'why states are not ordinarily expected to observe the same standards of morality as individuals'. The view that States are not ordinarily expected to act in this way is, as has been pointed out before, highly controversial. But it is of interest to see what reasons Professor Carr adduces in support of that assumption.

The first reason is the 'difficulty of ascribing to the State or to any other group of persons, love, hate, jealousy and other intimate emotions which play a large part in individual morality'. It seems plainly incongruous to say, as an eighteenth-century writer said, that 'a nation must love other nations as itself'. It may be a matter of controversy to what extent these sentiments are the basis of morality, but even Professor Carr does not deny that these sentiments cannot exist altogether in a group or in the State. He gives examples showing that a corporation, acting through its agents, can be generous and charitable. It would be surprising if it were otherwise. It is not easy to see why individuals acting for some common purpose should, while so acting, be incapable of being swayed by the same or similar emotions which determine individual conduct. Individuals acting as a State can love and hate or be generous or jealous. It would be an interesting and not altogether unprofitable subject to survey instances of State generosity – a task which, rather surprisingly, has not so far been undertaken. And it is almost a platitude to suggest that the action of States has often been determined by the prejudices of hatred or jealousy or compassion. The attitude of Great Britain – that is to say, of the British Government and people – to German re-armament since the Treaty of Versailles was a curious mixture of generosity expressed in the (mistaken) belief that it is 'impossible' – surely, not physically impossible – to keep a great nation permanently disarmed, and of jealousy about French military supremacy.

But while Professor Carr himself acknowledges that the 'initial difficulty' is not a substantial factor in the situation, he imperceptibly shifts the ground of the discussion by pointing out that the 'State' is incapable of showing and is not entitled to show those sentiments of altruism and self-sacrifice which underlie the moral conduct of individuals. This argument, although it succeeds in befogging the issue, is highly irrelevant. Self-sacrifice and altruism in the nature of self-sacrifice are not the basis of private morality. Morality does not enjoin us to sacrifice our life and interests for the good of others. An exalted religious precept may have given expression to such duty, but even religion enjoins us to love our neighbour *as* we love ourselves – it does not enjoin us to love our neighbour more than we love ourselves. Even Professor Carr agrees that this duty 'might be limited by duty to family or dependents'.

The second reason for the different international morality of the State is that the individual 'expects from the group person certain kinds of behaviour which he would definitely regard as immoral in the individual'. (The reader will note the admission that the 'different international morality' is tantamount to conduct which is immoral in the individual.) And that the group is definitely associated with pugnacity and self-assertion, which become positive virtues of the group person. In support of this view Professor Carr adopts wholesale a series of assertions propounded by Dr Niebuhr and calculated to explain the alleged phenomenon of the moral man in the immoral society. It is instructive to quote the entire passage (from pp. 202–3) for it is difficult to deal by way of general refutation with a series of loose *non sequiturs*.

It is, however, not merely true that the ordinary man does not demand from the group person certain kinds of moral behaviour which are demanded from the individual; he expects from the group person certain kinds of behaviour which he would definitely regard as immoral in the individual. The group is not only exempt from some of the moral obligations of the individual, but is definitely associated with pugnacity and self-assertion, which become positive virtues of the group person. The individual seeks strength through combination with others in the group; and his 'devotion to his community always means the expression of a transferred egoism as well as of altruism' (*Moral Man and Immoral Society*, p. 40). If he is strong, he converts the group to the pursuit of his own ends. If he is weak, he finds compensation for his own lack of power to assert himself in the vicarious self-assertion of the group. If we cannot win ourselves, we want our side to win. Loyalty to the group comes to be regarded as a cardinal virtue of the individual, and may require him to condone behaviour by the group person which he would condemn in himself. It becomes a moral duty to promote the welfare, and further the interests, of the group as a whole; and this duty tends to eclipse duty to a wider community. Acts which would be immoral in the individual may become virtue when performed on behalf of the group person. 'If we were to do for ourselves what we are doing for Italy,' said Cavour to D'Azeglio, 'we should be great rogues' (quoted in Woodward, *Three Studies in European Conservatism*, p. 297). The same could truthfully have been said by many directors of public companies and promoters of good causes. 'There is an increasing tendency among modern men', writes Dr. Niebuhr, 'to imagine themselves ethical because they have delegated their vices to larger and larger groups' (*Atlantic Monthly* (1927), p. 639). In the same way we delegate our animosities. It is easier for 'England' to hate 'Germany' than for individual Englishmen to hate individual Germans. It is easier to be anti-Semitic than to hate individual Jews. We condemn such emotions in ourselves as individuals, but indulge them without scruple in our capacity as members of a group.

Is it really the product of daily experience that the group is definitely associated with pugnacity and self-sacrifice and that for that reason the individual expects from a group a kind of behaviour which is definitely regarded as immoral in the individual? Does this statement reflect the true position with regard to that manifold variety of associations into which individuals group themselves for diverse purposes? What part does pugnacity and self-assertion, with the resulting inferiority in moral standards, play in the life and the purpose of a College or of associations for the promotion of cultural or humanitarian purposes? What part do they play in groups organized for the protection of economic interests, like associations of employers and workmen? Undoubtedly, such groups exist for the protection of economic interests vital to their members. Undoubtedly, such groups are often engaged in conflicts for the protection of these interests. But is their pugnacity and self-assertion greater than those of individuals? Their seemingly militant nature may, on occasions, be accentuated by the fact that they are devoted to the pursuit of a single interest, whereas in the individual the rough edges of his various purposes are smoothed out in the total blend of his personality. But this does not mean that pugnacity and self-assertion, as distinguished from the true object of the group, constitute its main purpose or its main characteristic feature. Psychologists tell us – and rightly so – that pugnacity and aggressiveness constitute a primary factor in the emotional make-up of the individual, but is there any compelling evidence which leads us to accept the view that membership of the group necessarily accentuates that aggressiveness? Does not experience show that such aggressiveness, when contained in the impersonal channels of group action, freed of the elementary and immediate complex of individual passions, may loose much of its roughness? It is true that some individuals develop the habit of easily pacifying their conscience by screening themselves behind the impassioned entity of the association in order to cover ruthless or immoral conduct, but is this typical of group activity or of the individual approach? A moral person does not use the screen of the association as a justification of immoral conduct. An immoral person may do it and often does it, but there is no reason to regard him as the typical phenomenon or – still worse – to picture it as the normal incident of the existence of groups. A rash investigator, given to generalization, will maintain that this lowering of private morality is a typical and necessary consequence of group activity. A careful researcher will find that this is not the case. The converse is often true. Many persons, far from wishing their side to win at any cost, will exact from themselves in their collective behaviour a specially high degree of exacting care in the matter of correctness of action in order to leave the name of their group untarnished. Professor Carr quotes, once more with approval, a passage from Dr Niebuhr's book: 'There is an increasing tendency among modern men to imagine themselves ethical because they have delegated their vices to larger and larger groups.' This statement is accurate inasmuch as it reveals one of the dangers of the operation of corporate personality – a danger against which a properly conceived science of ethics and politics ought to put the individual on his guard. It is inaccurate if interpreted as a normal and inseparable condition of group life. But that is exactly what Professor Carr does. (It is in this way that, in his view, we delegate our animosities. 'It is easier for "England" to hate "Germany" than for individual Englishmen to hate individual Germans' (see p. 203). And yet on p. 200 he describes as one of the principal reasons of different international morality the fact that it is difficult to attribute hate and other emotions to a State.)

These immoral tendencies of groups are, in Professor Carr's view, immeasurably accentuated in the case of the State (although he insists elsewhere (p. 202) that the loyalty to the group tends to eclipse the moral duty to the international community – this would mean that the loyalty to the group within the State is seriously affected by the loyalty to groups outside the State). The reason for this is that the State embraces a much larger field of activities, that it demands much greater sacrifices from the individual than any other group, and that it therefore more easily comes to be regarded as a moral end in itself. 'The good of the state comes more easily to be regarded as a moral end in itself.' If we are asked to die for our country, we must at least be allowed to believe that our country's good is the most important thing in the world. This reasoning is a plausible *non sequitur*. The fact that persons are willing to die for their State does not mean that they regard it as the most important thing. A person may be willing to die for his family, or for freedom, or for justice, or because honour so demands. All these things are important; none is the most important. Moreover, the State is not in itself a self-motivating power. It derives its strength from the meaning of things for which it stands, for such very things as freedom, justice, and honour. It is only for the militant jingoist or the adherent of the Hegelian theory of the State that the State is automatically identified with morality. When a State goes to war, it invokes justice and morality in order to enlist not only the support of foreign public opinion, but also that of its own. States do not go to war professing that they are above moral obligations.

Contrary to Professor Carr's view, the frequently asserted right of self-preservation of the State need not override its moral obligations. Undoubtedly, the appeal to the right of self-preservation has often been abused, but there are clearly cases in which an appeal to the right of self-preservation, although violative of the legal rights of another State, is not inconsistent either with legal or moral obligations. International law fully recognizes the right of a State to override, in certain contingencies, the legal rights of other States. If the seizure of the Danish fleet in 1807 had been brought about as the result of a justifiable belief that the very existence of Great Britain was at stake, the action would not have been inconsistent either with international law or with international morality. The only question which has divided writers on this point was whether the emergency was in fact such as to justify the action taken. Undoubtedly, a State's right to existence must not be asserted in such a way as to deny the same right to the other State, but law and morals admit that a particular interest of a State may legitimately be made to yield to the good of the international community.

In general, Professor Carr finds it difficult to distinguish between international law and international morality, and this difficulty leads him to somewhat naïve explanations of asserted inferior international morality. One of these explanations is that there is no authority above the State's to impose a minimum of moral standards in the same way in which a State imposes moral conduct upon groups within its borders. We should have thought that so far as morality is concerned, the absence of a superior authority is irrelevant. It is of the essence of morality, as distinguished from law, that its observance is dictated by motives other than the application of external sanctions by a superior authority. As a corollary of this absence of an external agency imposing sanctions, Professor Carr cites the right of self-help in remedying just grievances. This, again, is merely the result of a legal imperfection of international organization; to some extent self-help is admitted in municipal law. In any case, the relevance of admissibility of self-help is not apparent in relation to international morality.

Another corollary, in Professor Carr's view, of the absence of a compelling supra-national agency, is that, as moral standards are determined by common practice and the common practice of States is frequently immoral, 'a higher standard of morality is not expected from States'. And he quotes Spinoza as saying that States could not be blamed for breaking faith, for every one knows that other States would likewise break faith if it suited their interests. This argument is based on two inaccurate assumptions. One is that in fact immoral conduct is rampant among and typical of States. This view has already been refuted. The second is that our moral standards are influenced by the probability of their being observed by others. If treaty breaking, diplomacy by lying, blackmail or assassination were a normal feature of the international conduct of States, we would still regard these manifestations as an offensive and intolerable challenge to morality and we would still continue to condemn them. The fact is that States cannot create a morality *sui generis* so long as it is remembered that the actions of States are the actions of individuals.

It is generally accepted that the existence of a community is the natural pre-requisite of morality, and those who have been elaborating the theme of the shortcomings of international morality have made much of the alleged absence of a true international community. Professor Carr does not, it is true, go to the length of denying the existence of an international community although he implies that such a community exists only because people have been led to think that it exists. 'There is', he says, 'a world community because as Señor de Madariaga puts it, we have smuggled that truth into our store of spiritual thinking without preliminary discussion.' (*The World's Design*, p. 3.) (In fact, Señor de Madariaga's book is one of the most cogent descriptions of the actual purity and solidarity of the modern world.)

The degree of the existence of an international community is discussed elsewhere. But it is of interest to examine the two factors which Professor Carr regards as indicative of the absence of a true international community.

The first of these is, in his view, that 'the principle of equality between members of the community is not applied, and is indeed not easily applicable, in the world community'. What does this mean?

There is no equality in the international community because, in Professor Carr's view, individuals in one country do not have the same feeling of understanding of and sympathy and solidarity with individuals in another country as is the case within the State: an Englishman or an American does not show that same or comparable degree of sympathy with the sufferings of a person in China, or in any other remote part of the world, as he shows for a citizen of his country. This amounts to discrimination, and discrimination is a denial of equality. The argument, which is highly irrelevant to the question of equality, is both specious and inaccurate. Professor Carr quotes in support of his view the saying of an American correspondent to the effect that an accident is worth reporting if it involves the death of one American, five Englishmen or ten Europeans. The irrelevancy of this argument is too patent to require detailed examination. A local newspaper in Wellesley will give a detailed account of a fatal accident in Wellesley because this, not unnaturally, enlists the particular interest of people in Wellesley; the account will be less detailed if the accident happens in Boston; it will be even more general and summary if it happens in New York; it will totally escape attention if it has taken place in Georgia or Alaska. The reason is not that there is absence of equality destructive of a feeling of community, but that the capacity for interest and sympathy is naturally determined by the geographical factor. An earthquake in our own town is naturally of greater interest than in a distant province of our own State. But this does not mean a denial of sympathy or of community or of equality. People are naturally concerned with what is nearer to them, but this does not mean that they deny in others the fact or capacity for suffering. Distance blunts the edge of imagination, but this is not a denial of equality! Persons in the United Kingdom or in the United States may tend to be less sensitive to the effects of the bombing of the civilian population in China or Spain than they would be if such matters happened in their own country for various reasons – including a narrowly conceived realism – but the absence of equality is certainly not one of them. Professor Carr represents as the typical critical reaction of the ordinary Englishman a passage in Mr Chamberlain's broadcast during the Czechoslovak crisis on 22 September 1938. Chamberlain said: 'How horrible, fantastic, incredible it is that we should be digging trenches and trying on gas masks here because of a quarrel in a faraway country between people of whom we know nothing!' It may be doubted whether this statement represented the feelings of even the typical unenlightened Englishmen. It is more probable that the vast majority who condoned the Munich settlement nevertheless regarded the words of the Prime Minister as the words of a singularly uninformed and narrow-minded man – words which they possibly condemned. They approved of the settlement because of what they regarded as a humiliating practical necessity brought about by shortsighted leadership. It had nothing to do with the alleged fact that 'our normal attitude to foreigners is a complete negation of that absence of discrimination on irrelevant grounds which we have recognized as the principle of equality' (p. 209).

Even less accurate is Professor Carr's assertion of the inequality between States themselves. 'The existing inequalities among a handful of known States subject to no external control are infinitely more glaring, more permanent and more difficult to forget than the inequalities between the anonymous mass of citizens subject, at any rate in name, to the same law.' It might be said that the inequality between a Rockefeller and an unemployed and unemployable pauper, between a cripple and an athlete, between a genius and an imbecile, is as great as between Russia and Norway or Siberia and the United States of America. But the point is both obvious and irrelevant. The fact – which is known to most students of international law and relations – is that the unavoidable inequalities in size, population and wealth are countered by the full recognition of the equality of all States before international law. All States – small or great – enjoy equal protection before the law of such rights as they possess. Moreover, international law grants to all States equality of representation and voting – a measure of equality which many have considered to be artificial, unnecessary, unethical and, because of the necessary correlation of right and power, obstructive of international progress. According to Professor Carr, the equality in the exercise of the existing – though unequal – rights is meaningless because it is always at the mercy of the more powerful State. He says:

> The trouble is not that Guatemala's rights and privileges are only proportionately, not absolutely, equal to those of the United States, but that such rights and privileges as Guatemala has are enjoyed only by the good-will of the United States. The constant intrusion, or potential intrusion, of power renders almost meaningless any conception of equality between the members of the international community (p. 210).

The argument is characteristic. It ignores the fact that normally the equality – conceived both as equality before the law and equality of representation – is an outstanding phenomenon in international life. It is a reality. In some respects it is an obstructive reality in the sense that equality becomes inconsistent with justice and international progress. Coupled with the doctrines of sovereignty and unanimity, it has been a powerful obstacle in the way of international legislation. But because that reality is in danger – which experience has shown to be exceptional – of being set aside by the Great Powers, Professor Carr feels justified in denying its existence and in using the absence of equality thus proved as a reason for denying the existence of an international community as a basis of international morality.

Another example of the reasoning adopted is the argument pointing to the absence of equality on the ground that demands for it loom so large in diplomatic phraseology and correspondence. Professor Carr lists as examples such conceptions as 'most-favoured-nation treatment', the 'Open Door', 'freedom of the seas'. It is, of course, clear that all these conceptions have nothing to do with the existing inequalities between great and small powers. The principle of the 'Open Door', for instance, has its origin in the desire of the Western Powers to secure equal advantages and opportunities in and at the expense of China. When Denmark agrees in a commercial treaty to grant most-favoured-nation treatment to Great Britain, what issue of equality, in the sense contended for, is raised therein? The free and equal use of the sea is a postulate and a rule devised in the interest of all States, great and small; it has become a rule of law and of practice; it is a denial of any inequality of right. It is a feature of Professor Carr's reasoning that, in support of his thesis, he relies not only on alleged existing inequalities, but also on achieved equalities. Undoubtedly, demands for equality – like demands for just and fair treatment – loom large in international intercourse. They do so within the State, where equality is an abiding theme of political discussion and theoretical argument. But there is no warrant for using all this as an argument showing the absence of equality in the international sphere and, with it, of a true international community.

The second principal factor which, in Professor Carr's view, accounts for the absence of an international community is that 'we find an almost . . . universal reluctance to admit that, in this international community, the good of the part (i.e. our own country) can be less important than the good of the whole' (p. 211). And he asks: 'If we refuse altogether to recognize the overriding claim of the whole, can any world community or any kind of international morality be said to exist at all?'

The outlook both for the international community and for international morality is black if we accept Professor Carr's premises and facts. We are under no compelling necessity to do either. It is true that the existence of a community depends to a large extent upon the recognition of the superiority of the general interest over the particular interest of the individual, but this does not imply any admission of the absoluteness of the claim of the State or of self-sacrifice as the basis of the relationship between the State and the individual or of the elimination of the ultimate interest of the individual as the basis of his services and sacrifices for the State. When we proclaim our readiness to sacrifice our life for the State, say, in order to defeat Nazi Germany, we do so not because of any abstract duty of sacrifice for the State, but because we think, and we are not ashamed of proclaiming it, that our individual freedom is at stake, because we see values imperilled to which we attach an importance greater than life itself. When the Chancellor of the Exchequer justifies the increase in the income tax by telling us that the measure will, ultimately, make us better off, we are not, unlike Professor Carr, to treat that as humbug. In so far as we pay for reasons other than the whip of the collector and of the bailiff, we pay increased income tax for reasons of enlightened self-interest. The same applies to the relation of the State to the international community. Its basis is not self-sacrifice nor blind acceptance of the overriding superiority of the general interest of the international society, but enlightened self-interest which admits the advisability, in given circumstances, of the sacrifice of an immediate sectional interest for the sake of the general interest.

While it is thus impossible to accept Professor Carr's theory in the matter, it is equally impossible to accept his account of the general attitude to the international good. In his view, that general attitude is to identify, in various forms, the general international good with the national good. Thus, he says, Herr Hitler identifies the general good with the good of the fittest (p. 211) – which probably means an adequately armed German State. The neo-liberal doctrine of Woodrow Wilson, Lord Cecil and Professor Toynbee, he says, does in effect the same. They identify the good of the whole with the security of those in possession. And Professor Carr refers to President Wilson as saying that American principles are the principles of humanity, and Professor Toynbee as saying that the British Empire is 'the supreme interest of the whole world', and, on another page, Lord Cecil as speaking of 'our duty to our country, to our Empire and to humanity at large'. This, Professor Carr says, is in effect identical with Herr Hitler proclaiming that his countrymen are 'the bearers of a higher ethic'; it is a denial of the 'overriding claims of the whole', it is the assertion of the national interest as the supreme value. This kind of argument and of interpretation is, unfortunately, typical of Professor Carr's book. It could be left safely aside, but for the fact that it has a bearing on the general aspects of the subject. The philosophy which underlies these and similar pronouncements of advocates of international progress and co-operation is that enlightened self-interest, apart from other considerations, is a powerful reason for promoting international co-operation, for undertaking and honouring commitments for the preservation and enforcement of the rule of law in international society, for limiting sovereignty in the interests of a just and equitable development of the relations between States and for sacrificing immediate and partial interests of any single country for the sake of its larger and ultimate interest in the peaceful functioning of the whole. Such pronouncements are obviously intended to convey that the sacrifices which nations are asked – and compelled – to make by abandoning certain sovereign rights and a certain freedom of action are dictated by the highest considerations of their ultimate interests. It is only a dialectical desire for over-simplification that makes Professor Carr adduce the pronouncements of Herr Hitler and those of President Wilson, Lord Cecil and Professor Toynbee as evidence of the same phenomenon. They are diametrically different in a vital and essential respect. One is an affirmation of triumphant natural force as the regulative and dominant factor in international affairs. The other is based on the view that the supreme national interest is identified with the rule of law among States, with a submission to the impersonal sovereignty of the law, with the willingness to forego progressively rights of sovereignty for the sake of the greater whole ultimately beneficial to the component parts. If Professor Carr's vision is spoiled by the original belief that that willingness to submit to law and to co-operate for its maintenance is prompted by the fact that the existing law is all in favour of those who urge submission to it, then that cynicism is unjustified for a variety of reasons. In the first instance, by the very willingness to undertake commitments for observing and enforcing the law, the States in question give up some of their substantial rights. Secondly, in thus agreeing to a scheme of international organization, they may undertake progressively to accept machinery for further changing their existing rights. But these are minor considerations in comparison with the principal aspect of the question, that, except in an ideal and truly Utopian society, there is a constant disparity between the 'haves' and the 'have nots'. Society and law perform two seemingly contradictory functions. They protect the 'haves' and thus in a sense perpetuate the disparity. (It will be noted, at the same time, that they also protect the rights of the 'have nots' – for even the 'have nots' have rights, often very substantial ones, which are in need of protection.) But society and law perform also another function, and that is the creation of conditions and institutions for changing by proper political processes the existing law in accordance with equity and distributive justice. It is possible, as Professor Carr does, to picture those who identify national interest with the organized and effective rule of law among States as hypocrites who see in international order the best means of preserving what they have acquired. But it is also possible to see in their advocacy of an effective rule of law among nations a summons to the creation of international conditions and institutions in which the balance between the rich and the poor is adjusted not by the rough and haphazard instrumentality of force, or by spasmodic eruptions of self-sacrifice, but by the orderly processes of a politically organized community. It is only within an organized world, free of the precariousness and anarchy of force, that altruism and self-sacrifice can be nationally effective.

Whenever in the last 200 years appeals have been made to the human spirit pointing to the necessity of an effective organization of peace, they have been unavoidably made by reference to the imperative interest of nations. The persuasive argument has been that the general good, for the sake of which sacrifices of sovereignty have been urged, is not something separate from and foreign to national interest, but identical with it or, conversely, that intelligently conceived national interest is identical with the general international good. This – unless one appeals to self-sacrifice as the mainspring of international conduct and morality – is a sound and proper reasoning. But Professor Carr chooses to interpret it as pointing to a selfish assertion of the overriding supremacy of national interest comparable in substance with the pronouncements of Hitler and Mussolini. Self-interest, enlightened self-interest, has traditionally formed the basis of ethics.

Undoubtedly the very action of enlightened self-interest implies the necessity of secondary sacrifices for the sake of the ultimate good, but the supreme problem is to make such sacrifices effective and rational within the scheme of an organized life. This Professor Carr rejects, and the reader to his astonishment (and to his utter confusion) is presented with the demand for sacrifice on the part of States as the principal basis of international ethics and of an international community and with the mocking description of those holding to the identity of national and international interests as indistinguishable from those asserting the overriding supremacy of national interest. The result is astonishing and confusing in its suddenness because one of the principal features of Professor Carr's scepticism about international morality is that nations, unlike individuals, cannot easily manifest and are not expected to manifest feelings of sacrifice and generosity. The result is sudden and astonishing because, after having reduced the possibilities of international morality to next to nothing, Professor Carr finishes by basing it on the rigid and exacting test of sacrificial obligation as distinguished from interest.

The result is astonishing but only so long as we are not conscious of the underlying purpose of the book. That purpose is to supply a justification for the policy of negation towards effective international organization which characterized the conduct of the principal Governments in power in Europe since 1920. The best way of proving this is to show that the ideal of international organization, conceived often as the effective rule of a supra-national authority or, in the absence of such authority, as the collective enforcement of peace, is unsound and Utopian. The principal theme in that negative proof is that there is in fact no common interest in the preservation of peace because, owing to the disparity between the 'haves' and 'have nots', peace, conceived as an effective rule of law, works only in the interest of those in possession. The primary factor in international relations is not harmony but conflict of interests. Those who advocate the political integration of the international society are merely the deliberate or unconscious advocates of the preservation of the *status quo*. Conflicts of interests – impervious to any regulative scheme of legal organization – are the basic elements. A harmony of interests expressed in the postulate of an international community, securing under the reign of law the full development of its members and the progressive levelling of removable injustices, is a dream of Utopians as distinguished from realists. (Nine-tenths of the book are devoted to attacking the Utopian position, although Professor Carr, in order to render the assault more effective, affects an intermediate position between realists, whom he occasionally attacks *pour mieux sauter*, and Utopians.) These conflicts, in his view, are a perennial feature of international life. He gives reasons why they cannot be solved or kept within bounds by any scheme of international law or organization. For in the absence of an international legislature, international law is static because it has no machinery for effecting changes in the *status quo* so as to bring about a just solution of conflicts. The problem of peaceful change is thus the central problem of international society. But unlike within the State it is not a problem capable of solution by way of the establishment of a supra-national authority decreeing changes in the existing law. Change must remain a function of power. But, and this is the comfort which Professor Carr offers, it need not remain exclusively a function of power. States may show that enlightened spirit of sacrifice, generosity and morality (which we are told elsewhere they ought not, and cannot be easily expected, to show) which may render the use of power on the other side unnecessary. But power – not the organized and important power of the community, rather the power of each interested party – is, and must remain the *ultima ratio* of the central problem of international relations.

II

HISTORY OF INTERNATIONAL LAW

CHAPTER 5

INTERNATIONAL LAW AND COLONIAL QUESTIONS, 1870–1914

Editor's note This chapter appeared as chapter XVIII of volume III of the *Cambridge History of the British Empire* (1959). It bore an indication that it was written jointly by Lauterpacht and R. Y. Jennings, who was at that time a lecturer in the Faculty of Law. In 1954 he succeeded Lauterpacht as Whewell Professor of International Law upon Lauterpacht's election as a judge of the International Court of Justice.

Professor Jennings has, therefore, been in a position to provide a helpful indication of the circumstances in which the chapter came to be prepared and of the method of work adopted. He has written:

> 'There is no question that your father made a substantial contribution to the article. The method of work was this. Your father sent me a ms. which was in effect the plan of the whole article, with some parts completely written and others left blank. I filled in the blanks. The result is that some paragraphs are almost entirely your father and some almost entirely me. Speaking from memory I would say the distribution must have been very nearly 50:50 . . .
>
> 'If you want to include it of course you may. As far as I am concerned the value of this article to me is not my part in it but the fact that your father asked me to collaborate with him.
>
> 'At the same time, I do not feel it is one of the better products of either of us. For one thing it was done in a very great hurry. We had to finish inside a few weeks (it then lay at the press for 2 years or more, so the next time we saw it neither of us could bear to look at it). Moreover your father was just a little impatient I think of the thing and rather wanted to get it off his hands; and I do not think that the assessment of historical materials was ever a study that quite kindled the full spark in him . . .'

Professor Jennings subsequently added:

> 'The important point is that the conception and framework of the whole of the article was your father's. He brought me in when he already had the basic scheme worked out. My part, therefore, was essentially that of an assistant.'

In the history of international law the period 1870–1914 is in some ways more significant than any other period of comparable length. During this period international society seemed to have a pronounced degree not only of well-being but also of stability. Yet, in essence, the mutual relations of civilized States continued to be those of primitive communities. Although nearly two generations had elapsed without a major war in Europe, a profound observer was able to write in 1908: 'the spectre of war has become terrible';[1] that the 'irresponsibility of international action' had become the transcending phenomenon of the time;[2] and that 'to bring that action under some responsibility is the object of a great cry which goes up from modern Europe, a cry based on no new spiritual vision, but wrung from suffering and fear'.[3] In some ways the period from 1870 to 1914 produced a conscious effort on the part of the leading States to live up to that responsibility. But the attempt was rudimentary. It was directed towards mitigating the evils of war, not towards eliminating it or providing effective procedures for its avoidance.

Yet even in that field important, though hesitating, developments took place. International arbitration emerged from the realm of mere theory. Some significant arbitrations were conducted; steps were taken in the direction of setting up permanent agencies for that purpose; the first treaties of obligatory arbitration were concluded. In this and other spheres Great Britain, partly in collaboration with the United States, assumed a position of leadership. The adherent of the economic interpretation of history may urge that, as the British Empire at that juncture reached the zenith of its territorial expansion and of corresponding political and strategic power, its interests became identified with the requirements of international stability and order, of which an effective international law was an essential condition. Be that as it may, the fact remains that in this period some of the salient features of British foreign policy constituted a distinctive contribution to a progressive development of international law. That contribution included those parts of international law which are concerned with the protection of the dignity and the freedom of human personality, such as the prohibition of the slave trade (a constant theme of British international action in the nineteenth century), the limitation of slavery and forced labour, and the protection of minorities. With regard to the law based on the principle of asylum and non-extradition of political offenders, Great Britain continued the liberal policy of the preceding period. In the same category must be included British policy concerning recognition of Governments: a practice which, by insisting on the subsequent

[1] Westlake, *Papers*, p. 532.
[2] *Ibid.*
[3] *Ibid.*

legitimation of revolutionary changes through constitutionally expressed popular approval, tended to encourage political freedom and the ideals of democracy. In the matter of acquisition of territory the British contribution was of distinct usefulness in mitigating the rigours of annexation and in devising territorial adjustments such as *condominia* and leases which, in falling short of the drastic expedient of outright cession, assisted in solving the recurrent problems of the most potent source of international friction. Great Britain was actively associated in surmounting, through the decisions of the Berlin Conference of 1884–5, some of the difficulties resulting from the unregulated scramble for colonial acquisitions in Africa. She took a prominent and, in some cases, a leading part in the formulation of rules of war on land and at sea. The nature and extent of her contributions in these various fields will be surveyed in this chapter. It may be added that in the internal sphere English courts continued, with one exception, the tradition of the most enduring contribution of the common law to the law of nations – the tradition of the incorporation of international law as part of the law of England. In the case of the *Franconia*,[1] some of the Judges of the Court of Crown Cases Reserved held that even if, according to international law, English courts were entitled to exercise jurisdiction over an alien in respect of an offence committed in British territorial waters, they could not, according to English law, exercise such jurisdiction unless there were a clear rule of English law, statutory or other, conferring that power upon them. This aspect of the decision gave rise to some trenchant criticism. Sir Henry Maine came near to suggesting that by that decision Great Britain placed herself outside the orbit of civilized countries.[2] A subsequent Act of Parliament – the Territorial Waters Jurisdiction Act, 1878 – laid down that British courts had – and always had had – jurisdiction over territorial waters. Apart from the *Franconia* case, there was no interruption of the 'even and accustomed' flow of 'the majestic stream of common law, united with international law'.[3]

I

The period under review opened with two events of significant, though of unequal, importance for international law. The first was the Protocol of 17 January 1871, between Austria, Great Britain,

[1] *Reg.* v. *Keyn* (1876), 2 Ex. Div. 63. [2] Maine, p. 38.
[3] Judge Moore in the case of *The Lotus* (*P.C.I.J.* Series A, no. 10, p. 75).

France, Germany, Italy, Russia and Turkey – all signatories of the Treaty of Paris of 1856 – affirming the binding force of treaties. The second was the Treaty of Washington of 8 May 1871, between Great Britain and the United States, referring to arbitration what has since become known as the *Alabama* controversy. The Protocol of January 1871 was adopted at a Conference convened in London on the initiative of Great Britain, who was the first to protest against the unilateral Russian denunciation of the provisions of the Treaty of Paris relating to the Black Sea. On 31 October 1870 Prince Gortchakof, relying on the preoccupation of the signatories of the Treaty of Paris with the events of the Franco-Prussian war,[1] informed the signatory Powers that Russia no longer considered herself bound by the obligations of the Treaty of Paris in so far as they limited her sovereign rights in the Black Sea. Great Britain protested. In his dispatch of 10 November 1870, to Sir A. Buchanan, the British Ambassador at Moscow, Earl Granville instructed the Ambassador to voice the strongest objection on the part of Great Britain to the Russian method inasmuch as it amounted not to a request by a signatory State for the reconsideration of the Treaty but to an announcement that 'it has emancipated itself, or holds itself emancipated, from any stipulations of the Treaty which it thinks fit to disapprove'. It was quite evident, the Foreign Minister said, that 'the effect of such doctrine, and of any proceeding which, with or without avowal, is founded upon it, is to bring the entire authority and efficacy of Treaties under the discretionary control of each one of the Powers who may have signed them; the result of which would be the entire destruction of Treaties in their essence'.[2]

The London Conference did not undo the results of the Russian denunciation. It abrogated previous treaties in so far as they referred to the neutralization of the Black Sea and the limitations imposed upon men-of-war in it. But the acceptance of the Protocol affirming the binding force of treaties disapproved by obvious implication of the Russian action and saved as much from the wreckage as circumstances permitted. The Declaration was in the following terms: 'C'est un principe essentiel du droit des gens qu'aucune Puissance ne peut se délier des engagements d'un traité, ni en modifier les

[1] See Headlam-Morley, *Studies in Diplomatic History* (1930), pp. 232, 233, for a graphic description of the situation.

[2] *Parl. Pap.*, 1871, LXXII, p. 15 [245, p. 7]. See also, for Prince Gortchakof's explanation given to Sir A. Buchanan, *ibid.* p. 24 [p. 16]. And see, for the statements by other Powers, *Fontes Juris Gentium, Digest of the Diplomatic Correspondence of the European States, 1856–1871*, ed. by Markarov and Schmitz, I (1932), 758–68.

stipulations, qu'à la suite de l'assentiment des parties contractantes, au moyen d'une entente amicale.'[1] The Declaration is occasionally referred to as a typical example of the euphemistic insincerity and ineffectiveness of diplomatic language; this is to underestimate its importance. In comparison with what was to follow, this was a law-abiding age. In fact, apart from the annexation by Austria-Hungary, in 1908, of Bosnia and Hercegovina in violation of the Treaty of Berlin, there is no instance in this period of a major violation of a treaty by a Great Power – though it is difficult to assess to what extent, if any, this was the result of the solemn affirmation, in the Declaration of 1871, of the sanctity of international compacts.

The second event – one of considerably greater importance for international law – was the conclusion of the Treaty of Washington providing for arbitration of the claims of the United States in the matter of the *Alabama* and other vessels. That Treaty (of which it is convenient to give an account in another part of this chapter)[2] is also a milestone in the history of Anglo-American relations. The same double significance is true, within a more limited compass, of the British Naturalization Act of 1870 in so far as it bears upon the right of expatriation. This Act abandoned the traditional doctrine of the common law according to which the subject cannot at will renounce his allegiance. As a corollary of that doctrine Great Britain, prior to the Act of 1870, continued to claim the allegiance of British subjects naturalized in a foreign country, and the impressment into the British Navy of British subjects naturalized in the United States was one of the contributory causes of the Anglo-American War of 1812. After the American Civil War the growth of the Fenian movement brought the controversy to a head once more. When naturalized American citizens of British origin were arrested in Ireland while engaged there in revolutionary activities, Great Britain, who regarded them as British subjects, denied the right of the United States to afford them diplomatic protection. On 27 July 1868 the Congress of the United States declared 'the right of expatriation' to be an 'inherent right of all people' and instructed the Government to adopt, when necessary, any requisite measures, short of war, for the protection abroad of naturalized American citizens. In the same year a Royal Commission was appointed to inquire, in this connection, into 'the legal position of natural-born subjects, who may depart from and reside beyond the realm in Foreign Countries' and 'the legal position

[1] See Martens, *N.R.G.*, 18, 278.
[2] See below, p. 121.

of persons, being aliens, entering into or resident within the realm and becoming naturalized as subjects of the Crown'.[1] The main point covered by these studiously general terms of reference was the question of the right of expatriation. The Commission came to the conclusion that the common law doctrine of the 'indelibility' of allegiance was 'neither reasonable nor convenient' and that it conflicted with the 'freedom of action which is now recognized as the most conducive to the general good as well as to the individual happiness and prosperity'. The Commission recommended the abandonment of the common law doctrine on the subject. A Convention, on the lines of the recommendation of the Commission, was concluded in 1870 between the United States and Great Britain.[2] One of the objects of the Naturalization Act was to give effect to that recommendation. The result was not only the removal of an irritating source of friction between the two countries: it also signified the acceptance, as part of international law, of a view more congenial to the humanitarian and liberal tradition of British foreign policy in matters involving the dignity and freedom of the individual. Both are incompatible with a legal doctrine which transforms the State into a prison and allegiance into an unwilling relationship of bondage.

The humanitarian tradition of the past was continued with vigour in the granting of asylum to political refugees and others. A constitutional lawyer, writing in 1890,[3] summarized the legal position on the subject in the sense that the Executive had no constitutional power to refuse admission to any person. Although, in 1905, such power was granted on the ground of 'undesirability', political and religious refugees were expressly exempted.[4] In 1871 asylum was granted to the French Communards; in 1885 to the Comte de Paris, the claimant to the French throne; in 1889 to General Boulanger, accused in France of high treason. Belgium had previously declined to admit the Communards, and had expelled General Boulanger. In 1906 the Home Secretary made an order laying down that, in cases where it was uncertain whether persons claiming admission were political refugees, such persons should be given the benefit of the doubt if they came from politically-disturbed countries.[5] More-

[1] For an account of the work of the Commission see Jones, *British Nationality Law and Practice* (1947), pp. 76–88.

[2] See *Parl. Pap.*, 1870, LXIX, p. 471 [C. 192], and *ibid.* 1871, LXX, p. 59 [C. 345], for the supplementary Convention of 23 February 1871. See also, for previous correspondence with the United States on the subject, *Parl. Pap.*, 1868–9, LXIII, p. 735 [4144].

[3] Craies in *L.Q.R.* 6 (1890), 39.

[4] 145 *H. C. Deb.* 4s., col. 743.

[5] 5 Edw. VII, c. 13, 1 (3).

over, no onerous restrictions were placed upon the political activities of the refugees thus admitted. In *Rex* v. *Antonelli and Barberi*,[1] the Court declined to hold that publications directed against foreign Governments constituted criminal libel. Phillimore, J., delivering judgment in this case, said: 'Seditious libels are such as tend to disturb the government of this country, and in my opinion a document published here, which was calculated to disturb the Government of some foreign country, is not a seditious libel, nor punishable as libel at all... To hold otherwise... would make our great statesmen guilty of seditious libel, and those persons also who espoused the cause of Italian liberty.' Although the Aliens Restriction Act of 1914[2] expressly conferred upon the Home Secretary the discretionary power to refuse admission or to authorize expulsion, such power was limited to the time of war; it was only in 1919 that it was extended to peace time.[3]

2

It was during the period under review that international law clearly emerged from the stage of being merely a law between States, and began to be concerned also with the individual. This important development began in the movements to protect three main classes of persons: the native races of colonial territories, minority peoples in the new national States of the old world, and finally the labouring classes in the countries of western Europe and the United States.

Efforts to ameliorate the lot of native peoples and in particular to eradicate slavery and the traffic in slaves continued throughout the latter part of the nineteenth century.[4] Some progress had already been made towards giving practical effect to the sentiment expressed at Vienna in 1815 that the slave trade was 'repugnant to the principles of humanity and to the universal laws of morality'.[5] It was clearly impracticable, however, to control the slave trade unless warships were given rights of visit and search over vessels suspected of carrying slaves; and such a right they did not possess under customary international law.[6] Accordingly the right could only be secured by treaty. Great Britain had succeeded in negotiating a

[1] (1905) 70 J.P.4. [2] 4 and 5 Geo. V, c. 12.

[3] 9 and 10 Geo. V, c. 92.

[4] See Coupland, *The British Anti-Slavery Movement* (2nd ed. 1939).

[5] Annex XV of the Vienna Final Act.

[6] See the judgment of Lord Stowell in the case of *Le Louis* (1817), 2 Dods. 210; and the American decision in *The Antelope* (1825), 10 Wheaton, 66.

number of such treaties with several of the principal European Powers,[1] but bilateral treaties were of little avail so long as flags remained under which the slave-traders could enjoy immunity from visit and search. Efforts to conclude more general treaties had been only partially successful owing to the distrust in some quarters of a measure which might have the incidental result of increasing the powers of the British Navy. A different but closely related problem was how far a warship might lawfully grant asylum to a fugitive slave. In July 1875 the British Admiralty issued a circular instruction to officers of the Royal Navy allowing that a captain might receive fugitive slaves on board his warship, but adding the proviso that, if the ship entered a port of the country from which a slave had escaped, he must be handed over on a properly authorized demand from the local authorities. This circular, which appeared to be a reversal of former British policy, aroused a storm of protest in the country and in Parliament. On 4 November 1875 'Historicus'[2] wrote a letter to *The Times* newspaper in which he argued that foreign jurisdiction could not run on board a British warship even in foreign waters, that the captain could do no other than administer English law on board the vessel, that as English law did not recognize slavery the slave once on board was a free man, and that therefore he could not thereafter lawfully be handed over as a slave.[3] In the following year a strong Royal Commission made an exhaustive inquiry into the law involved. Its report[4] showed that there was room for differences of opinion, and that, while certain principles were undoubtedly accepted, the limits of their application could not always be precisely stated. A revised Admiralty circular of 1876 attempted a compromise between the requirements of law and humanity, and went some way towards meeting the demands of a liberal public opinion.

It was clear, however, that the trade could not be satisfactorily dealt with except by means of a multilateral convention, and the British Government continued to work towards this end. The question was raised and discussed at the Berlin Conference of 1885; but the only result was a vague clause in the Final Act condemning slave trading in general terms and an undertaking by the signatory Powers to use 'the means at their disposal' for putting an end to it. Effective

[1] See *Cambridge History of the British Empire*, II, 854.

[2] Sir William Vernon Harcourt, afterwards first Whewell Professor of International Law in the University of Cambridge. See Gardiner, *Life of Harcourt* (1923), I, 296 *et seq.*

[3] *Somersett* v. *Steward* (1772), Lofft. 1.

[4] *Report of the Royal Commission on Fugitive Slaves: Parl. Pap.*, 1876, XXVIII, p. 285 [C. 1516–1].

action was at last taken, however, at the Brussels Conference convened in 1890 by the King of the Belgians at the suggestion of the British Government. The Brussels Act[1] provided systematic measures for the suppression of slave trading in the Indian Ocean, the Red Sea and the Persian Gulf, including a limited reciprocal right of visit and search in certain zones, the reception of fugitive slaves aboard government vessels, and the establishment of an International Maritime Office at Zanzibar.[2]

The fight against slavery, however, was only part of the movement to secure the welfare of native peoples. This period of active colonial expansion also raised anew the old question of the duties of colonial Powers towards the native peoples of occupied territories. The basic rule of international law was that a State might do as it pleased in its own territory, subject of course to the somewhat vague requirements of natural law – requirements which had from time to time received authoritative expression,[3] but were necessarily lacking in precision and sanction. The latter part of the nineteenth century, however, saw the beginnings of more effective protection of native peoples by means of treaty obligations. The primary objective of the Berlin West African Conference of 1884–5 was to ensure that all the interested Powers should have a say in the development of the Congo Basin;[4] but several delegates took the occasion to speak of the need for positive measures for the welfare of the natives, and the Berlin Act provided not only for the freedom of navigation and commerce for all nations in the regions of the Congo and Niger Basins, but also, by Article 6, the Powers exercising rights in the Congo Basin undertook to suppress slavery and the slave trade and to care for the improvements of the moral and material conditions of the natives and to guarantee 'freedom of conscience and religious toleration'. The Brussels Act of 1890 too, though mainly concerned, as we have seen, with the suppression of the slave trade, contained promises of positive measures for the improvement of the natives' lot.

The question of the legal nature of these treaty obligations was

[1] Ratified by Great Britain, Germany, Austria-Hungary, Belgium, Denmark, Spain, the Independent State of the Congo, the United States of America, France, Italy, Holland, Persia, Portugal, Russia, Sweden–Norway, Turkey, and Zanzibar. France ratified but with reservations to the articles dealing with reciprocal rights of visit and search and detention of suspected vessels.

[2] For an important controversy between Great Britain and France over rights of visit and search see the award of the Permanent Court of Arbitration in the case of *The Muscat Dhows* (1905): Scott, *Hague Reports*, I, 1–95. See also Westlake in *L.Q.R.* 23 (1907), 83–7, and in *Papers*, pp. 523–30.

[3] See, e.g., the precedents collected in Lindley, ch. XXXVI.

[4] See *Cambridge History of British Foreign Policy*, III, 308 *et seq.*

subsequently raised in an acrimonious dispute between Great Britain and the Independent State of the Congo.[1] The Free State of the Congo was under the personal dominion of Leopold II, and united with Belgium only by a personal union. It became apparent from the reports of British missionaries and traders that a monopolistic system of exploitation had been set up by which, with almost insignificant exceptions, the entire natural wealth of the land was claimed as the private property of the State or its concessionaires, this being accompanied, moreover, by taxation in the form of compulsory labour, in practice hardly distinguishable from slavery. Against this state of affairs the British Government, acting for the most part alone, carried on a protracted but ultimately successful campaign, the British Government itself being driven by an informed and insistent public opinion instructed by influential organizations such as the 'Aborigines Protection Society'. A most effective diplomatic weapon was found in the legal argument that this policy of the Congo Government was a clear breach of the provisions of the Berlin Act, both those which safeguarded the rights of the natives and those which required freedom of commerce. The legal argument of the right of intervention arising from the treaty obligation of the Congo Government was from the outset made the gravamen of the campaign; as appears from the wording of Mr Herbert Samuel's (as he then was) motion in the House of Commons on 20 May 1903, which was accepted by the Prime Minister and carried without a division:

> That the Government of the Congo Free State having at its inception guaranteed to the Powers that its native subjects should be governed with humanity, and that no trading monopoly or privilege should be permitted within its dominions; this House requests the Government to confer with the other Powers, signatories of the Berlin Act, by virtue of which the Congo Free State exists, in order that measures may be adopted to abate the evils.

Lord Lansdowne, indeed, suggested that the question whether the acts complained of were permissible under the Berlin Act might be referred to the newly-created court at The Hague; but this suggestion met with no response from the Government of the Congo or, for that matter, from the other parties to the Berlin Act. The sheer weight of the evidence eventually compelled the Congo Government to submit to a Commission of Inquiry which reported in 1905, and in the following year Leopold signed decrees which purported to give effect

[1] See *ibid.* III, 366–73, 424–9.

to the Commission's recommendations. The decrees were accompanied, however, by a provocative declaration denying the legal right of any other Government to interfere in the government of the Congo, which Leopold apparently regarded as a matter purely personal to himself. Moreover, it immediately became apparent that the scandalous situation in the Congo was still continuing, and it seemed unlikely to be effectively remedied until the Congo State was rescued from the personal rule of the King and annexed to the Belgian State. The British Government was now no longer acting alone; the United States Minister in Brussels supported his British colleague, and in November 1908, as a result of joint pressure, the Congo was annexed to Belgium. At once, therefore, the British Government was possessed of yet another legal weapon in the form of recognition; though France and Germany immediately recognized the annexation, Great Britain refused recognition in the absence of actual guarantees of reformed government. In fact, recognition of the annexation was not given until 1913, when the British Government was finally satisfied that the abuses had ended. This humane campaign of the British Government, acting for the most part in isolation, marks therefore an important step in the gradual transition of the natives' rights, and indeed ultimately of human rights in general, from the sphere of the sovereign discretion of each separate government to the higher plane of general international law.

In many ways the most significant of the trends towards the international protection of the individual was the movement for the protection of labour. The suppression of slavery had necessarily raised the problem of the protection of labour in general; for the line between slavery and the compulsory recruitment of underpaid labour was difficult both to draw and to maintain. A beginning had already been made with bilateral conventions protecting particular classes of native labour in the colonies; e.g., the 1860 Convention between Great Britain and France regulating recruitment of natives of Bengal to work in French colonies, and a Convention of the same year between Great Britain and China concerning Chinese labour in British colonies. The latter part of the nineteenth century, however, saw the beginnings of international action to protect labour in the principal European countries themselves; a movement which, though initially concerned with domestic labour, was to lead to general standards by which conditions in colonial as well as in metropolitan territories would be judged. The idea was not new; indeed, a British cotton manufacturer, Robert Owen, had presented a memorandum on the subject to the delegates at Aix-la-Chapelle in 1818. It was not, however, until after the turn of the century that the spread of industrialization and increased competition, together with popular agitation for betterment of the lot of the workers, gradually created a realization that the problem was international and not merely domestic. In England, far and away the most industrialized country, the battle for domestic labour legislation had already been fought and won under the influence of men like Robert Owen and Richard Oastler;[1] but the British Government, like almost all others at this time, was at first suspicious of what it tended to regard as foreign interference in a domestic matter. It was the Swiss Government that supplied an initiative which resulted in the Berlin Conference of 1890. However, the Conference did not attempt to do more than offer recommendations in general terms. In particular, the British delegation made it quite clear that they must oppose regulation by international convention, which 'could not take the place of legislation peculiar to each country'. For a time, the leadership of the movement then passed to private enterprise in the shape of the International Association for Labour Legislation, founded by a group of scholars at Paris in 1900. This unofficial but influential association carried out necessary preparatory studies of particular problems, and in 1905 the way was open for the Swiss Government to call a further technical conference at Berne to consider two questions: the employment of women at night, and the use of white phosphorus in the manufacture of matches. This purely technical conference of 1905 was successful, and was followed by a diplomatic conference in 1906, which actually drafted the appropriate conventions for ratification by States. Between the first and second Berne conferences the British Government informed the Swiss Government of its willingness to enter into a convention, subject to adherence by all countries 'whose competition in the industries affected was likely to be serious'. It also took the opportunity to point out the importance of adequate means of enforcement, and suggested that execution of the conventions should be supervised by an international commission, any differences arising between the parties being settled by arbitration. In addition, the memorandum pointed to the need for providing proper procedures for settling such matters as the agenda of future conferences, procedures and so forth. These British proposals were pressed very hard at the 1906 conference by the first British delegate,

[1] See Clapham, *An Economic History of Modern Britain: the Early Railway Age*, ch. xiv.

Mr Herbert Samuel. Opposition by the Central Powers and Belgium prevented for the moment the general acceptance of the British proposals, even in a modified form, but their importance for the subsequent development of the international regulation of labour should be emphasized. Moreover, the acceptance in 1906 of the general principle of regulation by multilateral convention was a great step forward. Although the British Government had at first been shy of international regulation in what appeared to be a domestic matter, it was clear by the end of our period that Great Britain was henceforth to take a leading part in the working out of an adequate organization and techniques, and also to make a substantial contribution to the movement, which reached a new and decisive stage in 1919 in the establishment of the International Labour Organization.

3

What has been described as the liberal tradition of British foreign policy in this period manifested itself also in the consistent British practice in the matter of recognition of Governments. The principle of legitimacy was definitely abandoned. On the other hand, there was no inclination to adopt the easy and automatic test of recognizing any *de facto* authority for the mere reason that it is in power and enjoys the obedience, however unwilling and resentful, of the bulk of the population. What was required – and always insisted upon – was that the Government *de facto* either should be freely-chosen or, after having come to power by revolutionary means, should be confirmed by a free expression of popular approval. That principle had already been formulated, with some clarity, in 1852 after the *coup d'état* of Louis Napoleon. On that occasion Lord Malmesbury stated in the House of Lords on 6 December 1852: 'It has been our usual policy . . . to acknowledge the constitutional doctrine that the people of every country have the right to choose their own sovereign without any foreign interference, and that a sovereign having been freely chosen by them, that sovereign, or ruler, or whatever he may be called, being *de facto* the ruler of that country, should be recognized by the sovereign of this.'[1] In the period under review the principle of popular consent as a requirement of recognition received the imprimatur of a consistent and reasoned practice. When M. Thiers visited England in September 1870 and urged the recognition of the Government of the new French Republic he was informed by

[1] 123 *H.L. Deb.* 3s., col. 971.

Lord Granville that it would be 'contrary to precedent to do so at present' and that the new Government had no legal sanction so long as it had not been confirmed by a freely elected constitutional Assembly.[1] In a dispatch of 1 October 1870 to the British Ambassador in Paris Earl Granville said that he had 'pointed out to him (M. Thiers) that the Government, though administering *de facto* the affairs of France, itself recognized that the voice of France speaking in a Constituent Assembly could alone determine the form and the character of the Government to whom the destinies of France should be finally committed'.[2] In a further communication the Foreign Secretary insisted that

> the first element of recognition was still wanting and that, as the Government of National Defence itself admitted that it does not possess that stability which a formal vote of the Constituent Assembly alone could bestow upon it, it would be premature for Her Majesty's Government to recognize, as the national Government of France, a Government which is only administering the affairs of the country pending its decision as to the form of government under which it may ultimately elect to live.[3]

It was not until February 1871 that these conditions of recognition were deemed to have been fulfilled.

An identical practice was followed in connection with the recognition of the successive revolutionary Governments in Spain in 1869 and 1874.[4] Again, after the establishment of the revolutionary Government in Portugal in 1910, the British representative in Lisbon was instructed to inform the local authorities that 'as soon as Portugal shall, by a formal vote of a constituent assembly, or in some other unambiguous manner, have determined the form and character of the future Government of the country, His Majesty's Government will be prepared to advise the King to recognize it, and will be happy to enter into official relations with it when established in accordance with popular vote'.[5]

The insistence on popular approval of the revolutionary régime as a condition of recognition continued to be a prominent feature of

[1] *Br. and For. St. Papers*, 61, 751.

[2] *Parl. Pap.*, 1871, LXXI, p. 125 [C.244, p. 111]; *Br. and For. St. Papers*, 64, 802.

[3] *Parl. Pap.*, 1871, LXXI, p. 273 [C.266, p. 259]; *Br. and For. St. Papers*, 61, 995.

[4] 222 *H.L. Deb.* 3s., col. 1382. See also Smith, I, 198–205.

[5] As quoted in Lauterpacht, *Recognition in International Law* (1947), p. 122. When, during and after the Second World War, the right of man to government by consent became inevitably part of those human rights and fundamental freedoms the enthronement of which had been declared to be one of the major purposes of the war, the practice of recognition showed a pronounced tendency to revert to standards more closely in keeping with British notions of the rule of law and of the rights of man.

the British practice until the period following the end of the First World War. In that period the establishment of dictatorships in a number of States led Great Britain – and other countries – to base their policy of recognition on the purely factual test of control.

4

The colonial expansion of the Great Powers in Africa and the Far East had important results in the clarification and elaboration of the law concerning the acquisition and government of territory. Two main tendencies can be distinguished: first, an increasing strictness in the conditions required for the acquisition of full territorial sovereignty by the traditional mode of occupation; and secondly, elaboration of the law by new concepts sanctioning the acquisition of an authority or interest falling short of territorial sovereignty.

'International law,' said the arbitrator in a modern case, 'the structure of which is not based on any super-State organization, cannot be presumed to reduce a right such as territorial sovereignty, with which almost all international relations are bound up, to the category of an abstract right, without concrete manifestations.'[1] Ever since the eighteenth century there had been an increasing tendency to insist on the actual display of authority over territory as a condition of the acquisition of the corresponding right of sovereignty over it. In the latter part of the nineteenth century Great Britain's influence was strongly asserted in this direction both at international conferences and in her attitude towards territorial claims as, for example, in her argument in the *Delagoa Bay Arbitration* of 1875;[2] in 1876 by protests over Spanish activities short of actual settlement in the Sulu Archipelago; in 1885 by the recognition of Spanish sovereignty over those parts of the Sulu Archipelago which had been effectively occupied; and in 1877 in an intimation to Portugal that effective occupation and the exercise *de facto* of jurisdictional powers were essential conditions for the acquisition of territories in Central Africa and that the British Government could not recognize Portuguese sovereignty over territories 'not occupied by her in sufficient strength to enable her to maintain order, protect foreigners, and control the natives'.[3] Nor was she alone in this attitude, for it was generally realized, at any rate amongst the more important Powers,

[1] Judge Huber in *The Island of Palmas Arbitration* (1928), *Annual Digest*, 4 (1927–8), p. 103.

[2] See Hall, para. 33.

[3] All these precedents are discussed in Lindley, ch. xix.

that a mere paper claim could not be regarded as creating dominion without the risk of divorcing sovereignty from responsibility.

This general opinion of statesmen and jurists was formally stated in the Final Act of the Berlin Africa Conference of 1885.[1] Article 34 provided that future takings of possession of any territory on the coasts of the African Continent, or the establishment of protectorates there, should be accompanied by a notification addressed to every other signatory Power, to enable them, if need be, to make good any claims of their own. Article 35, which referred only to annexations and not to protectorates, recognized the obligation of the parties to ensure 'in the regions occupied by them on the coasts of the African Continent' the establishment of authority 'sufficient to protect existing rights and, as the case may be, freedom of trade and of transit under the conditions agreed upon'. The usefulness of the notification required by Article 34 is manifest, but in contrast with Article 35 there is no doubt that Article 34 went further than existing customary law required; nor has notification even since the Act become a requirement of general law. The position was accurately stated by the British representative that notification was 'rather an act of courtesy than a rule of law'.

On the other hand, Article 35, in requiring a claim to sovereignty to be supported by the exercise of *de facto* authority, probably went no further than existing law required. For this reason the British representative at the Conference had at one point suggested that the Article might be expressed to cover the whole of Africa and not merely the coasts. Although his suggestion was not accepted, it was clear at the Conference and afterwards that in the British view the Declaration had done no more than emphasize in particular respects already established rules of international law. Thus when, in 1887, Portugal laid claim to a region in Central Africa lying between her existing possessions of Angola and Mozambique, and argued that effective occupation was not a requirement in central as opposed to coastal Africa, Lord Salisbury asserted that the Berlin Act 'did not in any way affect the well-established principles of international law in regard to the occupation of lands in the interior', and that 'no paper annexation of territory can pretend to any validity as a bar to the enterprise of other nations'.[2]

In the original draft of Article 35, the requirement of effective

[1] The Final Act was signed by Austria–Hungary, Belgium, Denmark, France, Germany, Great Britain, Italy, the Netherlands, Norway, Portugal, Russia, Spain, Sweden, Turkey and the United States.

[2] *Parl. Pap.*, 55, 1884–5, LV, p. 10 [C.4361].

authority was declared to apply to the establishment of protectorates as well as to the acquiring of sovereignty by occupation. The reference to protectorates, however, was struck out on the insistence of the British Government.[1] This was logical enough if 'protectorate' were used in the proper sense of a treaty relationship between two States. In the uncivilized regions of Africa, however, there was no 'State' with which such a treaty relationship could exist, and the so-called 'colonial protectorates' with which the Conference was in fact concerned were no more than steps towards the acquisition of sovereignty over the territories in question. The term 'colonial protectorate' had, as Westlake said,

> 'the double advantage of giving a flavour of international law to a position intended to exclude other States before such exclusion could be placed on the ground of duly acquired sovereignty, and at the same time of allowing that position to be abandoned with less discredit than attaches to the abandonment of sovereignty.'[2]

The pretence that such colonial protectorates were analogous to orthodox protectorates, where the protecting Power derives its authority by cession from the protected State, was to say the least disingenuous; for while it must be conceded that the colonial protectorate differed from annexation, this distinction, as Westlake pointed out,

> even while it lasts, is attenuated by the circumstance that a colonial protectorate is intended by the State assuming it to exclude the action of other powers as completely as it would be excluded by annexation, since otherwise the protectorate would not have the desired effect of earmarking the country for the future enjoyment of the assuming State.[3]

It is significant that the British Government, in spite of the attitude adopted at the Conference, seems shortly afterwards to have been prepared to read into the Final Act an implied provision not unlike the express provision that it had so strenuously opposed. Thus in the African Order in Council, 1892,[4] it was recited that

> by the General Act of the Conference of Berlin signed in 1885, the several Powers who were parties thereto declared, with respect to occupations in Africa by any of the Signatory Powers, that the establishment of authority in protected territories was an obligation resting upon the respective Protecting Powers.

[1] For the political background of the British attitude see Crowe, *The Berlin West African Conference, 1884–1885* (1942), pp. 179 *et seq.*

[2] Westlake, *International Law* (1st ed. 1904), I, 120.

[3] *Ibid.* p. 123.

[4] *Br. and For. St. Papers*, 84, 290.

The increasing strictness in the conditions for acquiring full sovereignty encouraged the Powers to experiment with new legal devices, usually based on analogies of municipal law, by which they could support claims to the acquisition of an authority which, while falling short of full sovereignty, might nevertheless be sufficient for their immediate aims. There was an obvious advantage in giving these lesser claims the appearance of perfect legal rights rather than the appearance of inchoate attempts at annexation. One important method frequently employed, both in Africa and in the Far East, was the 'lease'[1] of territory. There is, of course, no reason why one State should not lease to another the beneficial enjoyment of land for a period of years, following strictly the analogous institution of municipal law.[2] The so-called 'political leases', however, are quite different, in that what is leased includes not only territory but also political authority within the leased territory. In this way Great Britain, as well as Italy and Germany, acquired grants of territory from the Sultan of Zanzibar;[3] the leases were in the first instance for fifty years, but the British interest was in 1891 converted into one in perpetuity in consideration of an annual payment of rent to the Sultan, and was transferred to the Crown in 1895. Several Powers acquired important territorial interests in China by lease. In 1898 Great Britain was granted a lease of Wei-hai-wei 'for so long a period as Port Arthur shall remain in the occupation of Russia', and there was no stipulation for compensation to China.[4] Other leases of Chinese territory, e.g., Port Arthur to Russia, Kaulmang to Great Britain, Kiauchau to Germany, Kwangchauwan to France, were made for a period of years.[5]

Such 'leases' come near to being cessions; and clearly they were often intended to be virtual cessions disguised so as to appear less offensive to the susceptibilities of the lessor State. At the same time they were not cessions in law, for the use of the lease analogy must be given some legal meaning, which could only be that the arrangement

1 See Westlake, *International Law* (1st ed.), pp. 133–4; Lindley, ch. xxv.

2 For examples see Lauterpacht, *Analogies*, p. 183.

3 Grants were made by the Sultan to the British East Africa Company in May 1887, October 1888 and March 1890.

4 Wei-hai-wei returned to China under the Washington Agreements of 1922.

5 A curious example of the use of the term 'lease' is in the Anglo-Congolese Agreement of 1894. Great Britain and the Congo State granted leases of African territory to each other for 'so long as the Congo territories as an independent State or as a Belgian colony remain under the sovereignty of His (Belgian) Majesty and His Majesty's successors'. In this Agreement, it is to be noted, Great Britain was purporting to grant a lease of territory she had never in fact occupied, nor was there in this Agreement any stipulation for a rent. The arrangement was rescinded by the Treaty of London, 1906.

must be interpreted as leaving at any rate the ultimate or residuary sovereignty vested in the lessor. Thus, at the Washington Conference in 1921 the Chinese delegate was able to say concerning the Chinese leases:

While the measure and extent of control by the lessee Powers over these leased territories varied in different cases, the leases themselves were all limited to a fixed period of years. Expressly or impliedly they were not transferable to a third power without the consent of China. Though the exercise of administrative rights over the territories leased was relinquished by China to the lessee Power during the period of the lease, the sovereignty of China over them had been reserved in all cases. The leases were all creatures of compact, different from cessions both in fact and in law.[1]

Another private-law analogy pressed into service at this time was '*condominium*', by which two Powers might conjointly enjoy the sovereignty over a territory. The most notable example was the Agreement of 19 January 1899, between Great Britain and the Khedive of Egypt, whereby the Sudan became subject to a *condominium* of Great Britain and Egypt, expressed as a regularizing of the situation created by the fact that the reconquest of the Sudan had been a joint enterprise of the two Powers. In practice, of course, Great Britain was, to say the least, the major partner in the exercise of the joint sovereignty, more especially as Egypt was at the time subject in fact to her authority. In 1882 Egypt had been occupied by the British. At this stage the occupation was intended to be of a temporary character, with the sole purpose of restoring order and financial stability in the country; but it tended to become permanent by reason of its very success, and the position of the British in Egypt was recognized by France in the Agreement of 1904 and later by other Powers; although it was not until 1914, after the outbreak of war with Turkey, that Egypt was formally declared a British Protectorate. Nevertheless, despite the inequality of the partnership in the government of the Sudan, the term '*condominium*' can only be interpreted as having legal results in conformity with the analogous institution of private law and is by no means to be regarded as a mere formula covering a unilateral assumption of power; and the significance of the term has of course become more apparent as Egypt has progressed towards independence.[2]

[1] Cited by Lauterpacht, *Analogies*, p. 186, where also there is a full discussion of this question on pp. 181–90.

[2] The Treaty of Alliance of 1936 between Great Britain and Egypt reserves the question of the Sudan, and according to the Annex to Article 11, the participation of the Sudan in international conventions is effected by joint action of Great Britain and Egypt.

Another method of acquiring authority, without prejudice, as it were, to the ultimate disposal of sovereignty, was to enter into a treaty granting the right to occupy and administer the territory. By an Anglo-Turkish Convention of 1878, expressed to have 'the object of securing for the future the territories in Asia of His Imperial Majesty the Sultan', the Sultan agreed 'to assign the Island of Cyprus to be occupied and administered by England'.[1] It was further provided in an Annex that England would pay the Porte 'whatever is the present excess of revenue over expenditure in the Island', and also that 'if Russia restores to Turkey Kars and the other conquests made by her in Armenia during the last war, the Island of Cyprus will be evacuated by England'. It was made clear that the authority transferred in this arrangement included full legislative power, and indeed third States recognized this to the extent of foregoing their capitulatory rights in the Island. The natives of the Island were not, however, regarded as British protected persons and there remained in the Sultan a part of the external sovereignty which was, as Westlake said,[2] not quite a *nudum jus*, but was insignificant. On the outbreak of war with Turkey in 1914, the island was formally annexed by Great Britain. A somewhat similar arrangement in the Treaty of Berlin, 1878, and in a convention of the following year, gave rights of occupation and administration in the Turkish provinces of Bosnia and Hercegovina to Austria–Hungary.[3]

It will be apparent that all these new institutions of public law were from one point of view mere devices of diplomacy; they offered a means of acquiring sufficient power where downright annexation was thought to be politically inexpedient, and quite often they were employed as preparations for annexation. Nevertheless, it is important to remember that in law they were not equivalent to annexation. When a legal term of art is used which clearly means in law the transfer of something less than sovereignty, it cannot be argued by any proper canon of interpretation that sovereignty is transferred. A lease necessarily implied the existence of some reversionary interest in the lessor; a grant of the right to occupy and administer carried the implication that some remnant of sovereignty remained in the former sovereign; and even a colonial protectorate was at least an admission that full sovereignty had not yet been formally

[1] For the political background of the Cyprus Convention, see Headlam-Morley, *Studies in Diplomatic History* (1930), ch. vii.

[2] Westlake, *International Law* (1st ed.), p. 138.

[3] This is discussed in detail in *ibid.* pp. 135–7.

acquired.[1] In short, the significance of these institutions lay in the fact that each of them carried with it a specific legal connotation which excluded the possibility of their being interpreted as mere euphemisms for annexation. In the development of international law, these admittedly subtle legal distinctions are important in that they mark the beginning of that shyness of annexation which, coupled with the marked development in international responsibilities towards native peoples, culminated in 1919 in the Mandates system of the League of Nations and, later, the Trusteeship system of the United Nations.

In connection with acquisition of territorial sovereignty reference may be made to developments in the law of State succession following upon territorial changes. When a State ceases to exist by absorption into another State, whether by cession or conquest, the difficult question arises how far the absorbing State succeeds to the obligations as well as to the rights and territory of the former State. When, in 1886, Great Britain annexed Upper Burma, she recognized the existing financial obligations while refusing to admit any legal obligation to do so. Much the same attitude was adopted when in 1900 Great Britain annexed the two Boer Republics.[2] A Commission was appointed under the chairmanship of the Hon. A. Lyttelton to examine the maintenance of concessions granted by the former Transvaal Republic. Their report maintained that 'it is clear that a State which has annexed another is not legally bound by any contracts made by the State which has ceased to exist, and that no court of law has jurisdiction to enforce such contracts if the annexing State refuse to recognize them.'[3] It seems, however, as Westlake suggested,[4] that the Commissioners were using the term 'legal' in a very narrow sense to mean only such rights as were enforceable in the municipal courts.[5] The absence of a remedy in a municipal court does not dispose of the question of succession in international law, and indeed the Commissioners go on to admit that 'the modern usage of nations has tended in the direction of the acknowledgement of such contracts'. After this somewhat unpromis-

[1] See *R.* v. *Crewe* [1910] 2 K.B. 576, where Vaughan-Williams, L. J. said that Bechuanaland was 'under His Majesty's dominion in the sense of power and authority, but is not under his dominion in the sense of territorial dominion'.

[2] The Orange Free State was annexed by proclamation on 24 May 1900, and the South African Republic by proclamation on 1 September 1900. The proclamations were premature, for the surrender of the Dutch forces was not received until 31 May 1902.

[3] *Parl. Pap.*, 1901, xxxv, p. 7 [Cd. 623, p. 7].

[4] *International Law* (1st ed.), p. 82. See also Westlake in *L.Q.R.* 17 (1901), 392, and 21 (1905), 335.

[5] Following *Cook* v. *Sprigg* [1899] A.C. 576.

ing introduction, however, they examined the several concessions on their merits, recommending the recognition of some and rejection of others, though all the while regarding this process as a matter of ethics rather than of law. Yet, although the Commissioners were unduly influenced by 'the baneful effects of Austin's definition of law',[1] their report was valuable in making practical distinctions between different classes of cases, and provided material for the later elaboration of what are now generally acknowledged to be rules of law. Even then it was significant that the British Government paid compensation in most cases involving foreign creditors whose claims were supported by their Governments.[2]

However, in *West Rand Central Gold Mining Company* v. *The King*,[3] the High Court rejected a claim by the underwriters to recover from the British Government the value of gold commandeered by President Kruger on the eve of the South African War, and committed themselves to the view that there was no principle of international law by which, after annexation of conquered territory, the conquering State becomes liable, in the absence of express stipulation to the contrary, to discharge the financial liabilities incurred by the conquered State before the outbreak of the war. In this case, however, the plaintiff was in fact a British company, and the decision could not therefore give rise to an international claim. It is doubtful whether this dictum would even at that time have been accepted by an international court. On the other hand, it is generally agreed that there is no State succession to obligations arising from tort, and an Anglo-American Claims Commission held that the British Government was not liable in international law for a denial of justice suffered by an American citizen in the courts of the former South African Republic.[4]

Before leaving the question of territory, mention must also be made of the Suez and Panama Canals. These canals were of such strategic and commercial importance that they could hardly be left as internal waters of the States through which they passed. Particular legal régimes were therefore devised to govern their use.[5] The Suez Canal was opened in 1869 and, although proposals for the 'neutralization'

[1] Westlake, *International Law* (1st ed.).

[2] See Feilchenfeld, *Public Debts and State Succession* (1931), pp. 380 *et seq.*

[3] [1905], 2 K.B. 391.

[4] 'The Claim of Robert E. Brown', in *A.J.* 19 (1925), 193–206.

[5] See Westlake, *International Law* (1st ed.) p. 321, and the entire chapter xv, which has a valuable account of the legal history of the Suez Canal.

of the canal had been made even before work on it was begun, it was not until some years afterwards that the legal problem was solved. In 1875 Great Britain had acquired a controlling interest in the Canal shares and two years later made it plain to a general meeting of shareholders that 'an attempt to blockade or otherwise interfere with the Canal or its approaches would be regarded by His Majesty's Government as a menace to India and a grave injury to the commerce of the world'. There was, moreover, general acceptance among the Powers of the principle that the Canal ought to be removed from the theatre of war. Great Britain was at first chary of this principle being put in the form of a general treaty; and indeed the first warlike operation in the canal zone was Sir Garnet Wolseley's landing at Ismailia in 1882 and his successful expedition against an insurgent Egyptian Government, leading to the British occupation of Egypt. As this operation was undertaken in order to protect the Canal, the other Powers did not complain. However, with Egypt now occupied by a strong Power it had clearly become appropriate that the general understanding about the Canal should be given legal form in the shape of a general treaty, and Lord Granville proposed this in a circular of 1883.[1] A conference met at Paris in 1885 and the Suez Canal Convention was signed in 1888, by which the Canal was to be 'open, in war as well as in peace, to ships of war and merchant ships of all flags; and is never to be blockaded'. Owing to the transitory state of affairs in Egypt the British Government only became a party to the treaty subject to a substantial reservation which, however, was removed after the Anglo-French understanding of 1904.

An even more important role was played by Great Britain in the creation of the legal régime of the Panama Canal, which indeed still depends principally upon the terms of a bilateral Treaty between Great Britain and the United States. As early as 1850, when the idea of an inter-ocean canal was first mooted, the Clayton–Bulwer Treaty between the two Powers had provided for the free navigation and 'neutralization' of the proposed canal in terms that prevented either Power from independently making or owning the canal. After the failure in 1888 of the de Lesseps scheme, the United States Government again became interested in the project, but found the 1850 Treaty a serious embarrassment, more especially as the

[1] The opinion of writers on international law had already hardened in favour of a special legal régime for the Canal. In 1875 Sir Travers Twiss had advocated the 'neutralization' of the Canal in an article in *R.I.* 7 (1875), 682, and the Institute of International Law had voted in favour of a general treaty in 1879, see *Annuaire*, 3 and 4 (i), 349.

strategic importance of such a canal was very evident and American opinion had begun to harden in favour of an all-American canal. Lord Salisbury, however, readily agreed to a modification of Great Britain's right under the 1850 Treaty, and to the surrender of her right to participate in the construction of a canal. By the Hay–Pauncefote Treaty of 18 November 1901, all obstacles to the construction of a canal by the United States and to the exclusive regulation and management of the proposed canal by her were removed. Provision was again made, however, for the so-called 'neutralization' of the canal in terms substantially following those of the Suez Canal Convention: it was to be open to the vessels of commerce and of war of all nations on terms of entire equality: it was never to be blockaded, and no act of war or hostility was to be committed within it.

The Hay–Varilla Treaty of 1903 between the United States and the newly created Republic of Panama gave the United States a lease in perpetuity of the required territorial rights, and the Panama Canal was opened on 14 August 1914. In the meantime, however, a dispute had arisen between Great Britain and the United States over the interpretation of the Hay–Pauncefote Treaty. By Article 3 of that Treaty, the Canal was to be free and open to the vessels of commerce and of war of 'all nations', and on 'terms of entire equality': but in 1912 Congress passed a bill, section 5 of which authorized the President to prescribe the tolls to be charged, but provided that no tolls should be charged upon vessels engaged in the coastwise trade of the United States. The British Government had already protested against this provision as being contrary to the Hay–Pauncefote Treaty, arguing that 'all nations' must include the United States. The United States replied that their coastwise trade was in any case limited to United States vessels by municipal law and that the 1912 Act, therefore, was not introducing any new discrimination. Although, however, the United States' arguments showed that the proposed exemption of her coastwise shipping from tolls was not unreasonable, they did not touch the charge that the exemption was in plain contravention of her treaty obligations, and on this point the British Government quietly but firmly insisted, while offering nevertheless to have the legal question submitted to the Hague Court. This the United States Government refused to do. The controversy was not settled until Taft went out of office and Wilson came in, Wilson's advisers had no doubt that the British objection was well founded and Wilson settled the matter in a statesmanlike way by waiving the American claims.

5

Probably the most important British contribution to international law in the period under review was in the field of international arbitration. It falls under three heads: the first, and most important, is the actual submission to arbitral settlement of territorial and other disputes; the second is the contribution made by Great Britain to the development of international organs of arbitral settlement; the third lies in the British participation in the movement to bring about a wider measure of obligatory settlement of disputes.

Settlement of disputes by arbitration

In the first – and most significant – of these three spheres the British contribution was effected in close co-operation and partnership with the United States. The history of international arbitration in the nineteenth century – and in particular in the last quarter of the nineteenth century – is to a large extent the history of the arbitral settlement of disputes between Great Britain and the United States. In a very real sense the Jay Treaty of 1794 between these two States had marked the beginning of modern arbitration. That Treaty submitted to arbitral settlement, through mixed commissions adjudicating on the basis of law, not only troublesome boundary disputes affecting vast stretches of territory: the commissions were also given jurisdiction to decide upon claims arising out of alleged violations of neutral rights as the result of the conduct of maritime war by Great Britain, and of breaches of obligations of neutrality by the United States in the course of the war with France. These were questions which, to use the modern terminology, affected the 'vital interests' and 'honour' of the parties. However, notwithstanding delays, disagreements and occasional bitterness of argument, the commissions proved equal to their task. They paved the way for a series of similar commissions under the Treaties of 1814 (the Treaty of Ghent), of 1822, of 1842 and of 1854, and of 1863.[1] The cumulative result of their experience was the imposing series of five great arbitrations between the United States and Great Britain in the last thirty years of the nineteenth century and the first decade of the twentieth: The *Alabama Arbitration* of 1871 and 1872; the *Behring Sea Arbitration* of 1893; the *British Guiana Arbitration* of 1897 (for although

[1] The work of these commissions is surveyed in Moore, *International Arbitrations*; Moore, *International Adjudications, Ancient and Modern* (6 vols. 1929–33); Lapradelle-Politis, I (1905), covering the period 1798–1858, and II (1924), covering the period 1858–72.

the parties to these proceedings were Great Britain and Venezuela, this was, in many ways, a British–American arbitration); the *Alaskan Boundary Arbitration* of 1903 (although the parties were the United States and Canada, this was essentially a British–American arbitration); and the *North Atlantic Fisheries Arbitration* of 1910. These arbitrations were the first to reveal on a large scale the potentialities of international judicial settlement. They were preceded by an exchange of written pleadings – cases, counter cases, replies, arguments and counter-arguments, rejoinders and sur-rejoinders – occupying bulky volumes. They were argued with zest and acumen in oral proceedings lasting weeks, if not months. They would not have been possible had they not been conducted between two nations bound by the tradition of the common law, speaking the same language and animated by the same respect for the peaceful solution of international disputes.

The *Alabama Arbitration* was the greatest and, in many ways, the most significant of those arbitrations. Its origins and circumstances are recounted elsewhere in these volumes, and the observations which follow are – as with the four other arbitrations mentioned above – limited to a survey of their contribution to the general development of international law and of the judicial settlement of international disputes. The *Alabama Arbitration* was the first example of the arbitral settlement of an international issue which one of the parties regarded as affecting its national honour and which it had for that reason originally declined to submit to arbitration. While, for the United States, reparation for the wrong inflicted upon them as the result of alleged violations of neutrality on the part of Great Britain became a question of national dignity, Great Britain, on the other hand, deemed it inconsistent with her honour to submit to a foreign judgment on the questions whether her Government observed duties of neutrality in good faith and whether the Law Officers properly interpreted the neutrality laws.[1] Earl Russell was emphatic on that point when in 1865 the United States asked for an impartial determination of the controversy: 'It appears to Her Majesty's Government that neither of these questions could be put to a foreign Government with any regard to the dignity and character of the British Crown and the British nation. . . Her Majesty's Government are the

[1] *Parl. Pap.*, 1864, LXII, pp. 1 *et seq.* and 109 *et seq.* [3241]; and *ibid.* 1868–9, LXIII, pp. 735 *et seq.* [4144]. See also on this, and other, aspects of the controversy Lapradelle-Politis, II, 902–83; Bernard, *A Historical Account of the Neutrality of Great Britain during the American Civil War* (1870), pp. 385 *et seq.*; Cushing, *The Treaty of Washington* (1879); Nevins, *Hamilton Fish* (1936), pp. 296–301, 423–48, 481–90.

sole guardians of their own honour.'[1] Neither was the national dignity of the United States fully appeased by the Convention of 1869 which provided for the settlement of the American claims. The Senate refused to ratify the Convention for the reason that its conclusion was not accompanied by a suitable expression of regret for the events which led to the American claims. That satisfaction was given in a declaration made by the British negotiators of the Treaty of 8 May 1871 which submitted the *Alabama* claims to an international tribunal. In that declaration the British representatives expressed 'in a friendly spirit the regret felt by Her Majesty's Government for the escape, under whatever circumstances, of the *Alabama* and other vessels from British ports, and for the depredations committed by those vessels'. The American Commissioners, it was stated, 'accepted this expression of regret as very satisfactory to them and as a token of kindness, and said that they felt sure that it would be so received by their Government'.[2] The principal provision of Article 6, which defined in advance much of the law to be applied by the arbitrators, was as follows:

> A neutral Government is bound:
> First, to use due diligence to prevent the fitting out, arming, or equipping, within its jurisdiction, of any vessel which it has reasonable ground to believe is intended to cruise or to carry on war against a Power with which it is at peace; and also to use like diligence to prevent the departure from its jurisdiction of any vessel intended to cruise or carry on war as above, such vessel having been specially adapted, in whole or in part, within such jurisdiction, to warlike use.

Great Britain, while agreeing that the Tribunal should decide according to the rules laid down in that Article, declined, in an express statement made in that Article, to agree that it was part of international law at the time when the claims arose. The two parties agreed nevertheless, in the same Article, 'to observe these rules as between themselves in the future, and to bring them to the knowledge of other maritime Powers, and to invite them to accede to them'.[3]

The fact of this submission of a grave issue to arbitration, and the circumstances surrounding it, were even more important for the future of international arbitration than the legal questions involved

[1] Moore, *International Arbitrations*, p. 496.

[2] Moore, *International Arbitrations*, p. 544. See also *Parl. Pap.*, 1871, LXX, p. 25 [C. 346], and *ibid.* p. 45 [C.386], for the text of the Treaty of 8 May 1871.

[3] See *Correspondence with the Government of the United States respecting the communication to other Governments of the Rules of the Treaty of Washington: Parl. Pap.*, 1874, LXXV, p. 1 [C. 1012].

in the arbitration and decided by the Tribunal which met in Geneva on 15 December 1871 and which, after various adjournments, gave its award on 14 October 1872.[1] Nevertheless, the legal matters decided by the Tribunal were in themselves important. In its answer to the question of what constitutes the 'due diligence' required from a neutral in the discharge of the obligation defined in Article 6 of the Arbitration Treaty the Tribunal held that: 'The due diligence . . . ought to be exercised by neutral Governments in exact proportion to the risk to which either of the belligerents may be exposed from a failure to fulfil the obligations of neutrality on their part.'[2] The findings of the Tribunal on the matter, although subjected to much criticism, did not differ materially from the formulation subsequently adopted in Article 25 of Hague Convention No. XIII of 1907 defining neutral duties in maritime warfare. In any case the voluminous discussions before the Tribunal made a substantial contribution to the elucidation of that intricate branch of international law.[3]

In one respect the contribution of the Tribunal to international law was purely negative, namely, on the right of States to indirect damages for injuries sustained by them. The Tribunal, in an interlocutory decision announced on 19 June 1872, held that its members had arrived 'individually and collectively' at the view that indirect losses 'do not constitute, upon the principles of international law applicable to such cases, good foundation for award of compensation or computation of damages between nations'.[4] The rule thus enunciated is contrary to general principles of law and has been consistently disregarded by international practice. The explanation lies in the character of the claims advanced by the United States. These included damages for losses suffered by the transfer of the American commercial fleet to the British flag (a device adopted in order to protect American vessels from depredation by insurgent ships equipped in British ports), the enhanced payments of insurance, the prolongation of the war and the suppression of the rebellion; and moreover these claims were advanced subsequent to the signature of the arbitration agreement. They became the subject-matter of an

[1] See *Papers relating to the Proceedings of the Tribunal of Arbitration at Geneva*, Part I. *Protocols, Correspondence, etc.: Parl. Pap.*, 1873, LXXIV, p. 9 [C. 688].

[2] *Award of the Tribunal, and the Reasons of Sir Alexander Cockburn for dissenting from the Award: Parl. Pap.* 1873, LXXIV, p. 419 [C. 689].

[3] See *Cases, Counter Cases and Arguments presented by Great Britain: Parl. Pap.*, 1872, LXIX, [C. 469], [C. 476], [C. 505], [C. 506], [C. 506–VII], [C. 531], [C. 545], [C. 548], [C. 566], [C. 570], [C. 571].

[4] For this aspect of the award see Lauterpacht, *Analogies*, pp. 219–21.

emphatic repudiation in the Queen's Speech and of an indignant and heated debate in Parliament. If not disposed of by the Tribunal, they would have rendered the continuation of its work, with the participation of the British arbitrator, impossible.[1] In disposing of them in a summary way, the Tribunal performed what was in fact a political function. But this very fact showed, indirectly, the significance of the *Alabama Arbitration*. It is probably not an exaggeration to say that, if the Jay Treaty marks the beginning of modern arbitration, the proceedings and the award in the case of the *Alabama* revealed the full political potentialities of judicial settlement among States and the inaccuracy of the widely adopted view that international arbitration is necessarily confined to minor issues and that it must stop short of questions that matter. It is in that vital respect that the influence of the British–American contribution to the cause of international arbitration has been beneficent and lasting.

The same considerations apply to the *British Guiana Arbitration* of 1897 between Great Britain and Venezuela. In law the United States was not a party to the dispute, but it was so in fact. It insisted on the arbitration and brought it about by intervention based on the unilateral assertion of the Monroe Doctrine and by what some considered to be a threat of war. The President proposed to the Senate the appointment of an American Commission charged with the task of investigating the dispute between Great Britain and Venezuela and of submitting a report to be acted upon by the United States. Citizens of the United States played a prominent part in the composition of the Arbitration Tribunal and in the oral proceedings before it. It was this complexion of the arbitration which, once more, imparted to it the character of a controversy affecting the honour of the parties. John Westlake, who did not easily yield to excesses of national pride, wrote in *The Times* newspaper on 6 June 1896 that the message of the President of the United States, in which the intervention by the United States was asserted in a manner both drastic and peremptory, 'had first to be met in this country by an assertion of our own dignity and independence'.[2] But after having said that, Westlake made practical suggestions which were, in effect, accepted by Great Britain and the United States and which formed the substance of the crucial provision of Article 4 of the Arbitration Treaty of Washington of February 1897. That Article provided: 'Adverse

[1] *Correspondence respecting Claims for Indirect Losses put forward in the Case presented by the United States Government: Parl. Pap.*, 1872, LXIX, pp. 653 *et seq.* [C. 545].

[2] The letter is also printed in Westlake, *Papers*, pp. 414–16.

holding or prescription during a period of fifty years shall make a good title. The arbitrators may deem exclusive political control of a district, as well as actual settlement thereof, sufficient to constitute adverse holding or to make title by prescription.' The effect of that provision was to circumscribe at the outset the powers of the Tribunal and to remove the possibility of long peaceful possession being challenged before the Tribunal. This precaution did not prevent lengthy and able argument by British and American lawyers before the Tribunal on the meaning of prescription in private and in international law. In this matter, as well as on the general question of occupation and discovery as original title to territorial sovereignty, the proceedings of the Tribunal contributed to a clarification of a difficult branch of international law. Thus there was no hesitation in resorting to the technicalities of the common law doctrine of estoppel with regard to a substantial aspect of the case before the Tribunal.[1]

The antecedents of the *Alaskan Boundary Arbitration* were less dramatic than those of the *British Guiana* case, but the arbitration did not materialize without much initial difficulty. There was a tendency in the United States to regard the Canadian claim as frivolous. Thus, T. W. Balch, who had the cause of international arbitration much at heart, wrote:

> There is no more reason for the United States to allow their right to the possession of this unbroken Alaskan lisière to be referred to the decision of foreign judges, than would be the case if the British Empire advanced a claim to sovereignty over the coast of the Carolinas or the port of New York and proposed that this demand should be referred to the judgment of subjects of third Powers.[2]

The submission of the dispute to arbitration was not secured, therefore, without resort to a precautionary device which caused the Tribunal to resemble, in some respects, a body of political negotiators rather than a court adjudicating upon the basis of law. The United

[1] See *British Guiana Boundary Arbitration with the United States of Venezuela: Case, Counter Case and Argument, with Appendices and Maps* (9 vols., printed at the Foreign Office, London, 1898); *Venezuela-British Guiana Boundary Arbitration: the Case of the United States of Venezuela* (3 vols.), *the Counter Case* (3 vols.) *and Argument* (2 vols.), printed in New York, 1898; *British Guiana-Venezuela Boundary Arbitration* (*Oral Argument*, 11 vols., Paris, 1899). See also Cleveland, *The Venezuelan Guiana Boundary Controversy*, 1913; and Moore, *International Arbitrations*, VI, 966; see also *Parl. Pap.*, 1896, XCVII, pp. 1–988 [C. 7972], [C. 8012], [C. 8016], [C. 8194], [C. 8195] for the correspondence preceding the arbitration; and *Parl. Pap.*, 1899, CXI, pp. 217 *et seq.* [C. 9336], [C. 9337], [C. 9338], [C. 9499], [C. 9500], [C. 9501] for the British and Venezuelan written pleadings and for the Venezuelan *Argument*; and *Parl. Pap.*, 1899, CXII [C. 9533], for the Award of the Tribunal.

[2] See *The Alaskan Frontier* (1903), p. 178; see also, *Correspondence respecting the Alaska Boundary: Parl. Pap.*, 1904, CXI, p. 5 [C. 1877].

States originally rejected the proposal to arbitrate the dispute. It was agreed eventually to submit the matter for a decision of 'six impartial jurists of repute', three to be appointed by each party. The impartial jurists chosen by the United States were said by the President of the United States to be 'men who had already committed themselves on the general proposition'.[1] A decision by a tribunal thus constituted was made possible by Lord Alverstone voting in favour of the American contention. However, the written and oral proceedings before the arbitrators were strictly in the nature of legal proceedings concerned largely with the interpretation of the Treaty of 1825 between Great Britain and Russia (to whose rights the United States succeeded as the result of the purchase of Alaska in 1867). The proceedings abounded in much learned argument not only on the interpretation of treaties but also on the place, in international law, of prescription and estoppel and the authority of Roman law and common law rules of evidence.[2]

The *Behring Sea Arbitration*, decided in 1893 by an imposing tribunal sitting in Paris, was concerned with a jurisdictional issue closely related to the freedom of the high seas; an issue upon which maritime States feel strongly.[3] The main question put to the Tribunal was: 'Has the United States any right, and, if so, what right, of protection of property in the fur seals frequenting the islands of the United States in Behring Sea where such seals are found outside the ordinary three-mile limit?' The United States based its claim to exercise jurisdiction over foreign vessels engaged in fur seal fishing in the Behring Sea on purely legal, though unorthodox, grounds. The seals, having been born and reared on islands belonging to the United States and having retained throughout the *animus revertendi* to these islands, were the property of the United States; the continued existence of the species depended upon the care and protection by the United States. This part of the argument was conducted with much reliance on the rules of Roman law and common law on the subject of animals *ferae naturae*. The United States also appealed, not unnaturally in the circumstances, to the law of nature. The Tribunal, however, considered the principle of the freedom of the seas to be paramount and gave its award accordingly. At the same

[1] See *Selections from the Correspondence of Theodore Roosevelt and Henry Cabot Lodge*, II, 67.

[2] The printed *Cases, Counter Cases, and Arguments* of both parties, as well as the oral proceedings are printed in *Proceedings of the Alaska Boundary Tribunal, U.S.A.* 58*th Cong. 2nd Sess. Sen. Doc.* no. 162 (7 vols. 1904).

[3] For the prolonged and occasionally bitter correspondence preceding the arbitration see *Br. and For. St. Papers*, 82, 202–91, and *ibid.* 83, 306–55.

time – and here lies the principal significance of the *Behring Sea Arbitration* – the Tribunal availed itself of what constituted an entirely novel feature of arbitral procedure, namely, of the power conferred upon it to propose recommendations. Article 7 of the Arbitration Agreement of 29 February 1892 laid down that, should the answer of the Tribunal leave the subject in such a position that the concurrence of Great Britain was legally necessary for the establishment of regulations for the proper protection and preservation of the fur seals, the arbitrators shall, in addition to the award, determine which concurrent regulations are necessary outside the jurisdictional limits prescribed by international law.[1] The Tribunal availed itself of that authorization and framed detailed regulations which were subsequently accepted by the parties.[2] Thus the ingenuity and the good will of the statesmen of the two countries enriched international practice by a useful expedient amounting to a conferment of legislative authority upon an international tribunal in cases when the situation demands the adjustment of the law to the exigencies of the situation. An expedient of this nature is of special usefulness in the international sphere where there is no legislature having the power to adapt the law to the changing conditions of society.[3]

That innovation was repeated, in a somewhat different form, in the Arbitration Agreement of 27 January 1909 between Great Britain and the United States which provided for the settlement of the serious dispute which arose between the two States concerning the North Atlantic Fisheries. The Agreement provided that, after making the award, the Tribunal should recommend, for consideration by the parties and in accordance with the principles of the award, rules and procedures for the settlement of future disputes concerning the exercise of the rights of fishery. The award of the Tribunal was in favour of Great Britain. It declined to accept the contention of the United States that the Treaty of 1818, which created certain fishery rights in favour of the United States, was in the nature of an international servitude necessitating prior consent of the United States to any legislative regulation of the subject by Great Britain and Canada.

[1] *Parl. Pap.*, 1892, xcvi [C. 6639].

[2] The regulations of the Tribunal which prescribed the periods and methods of seal-fishing were fully incorporated in the Schedule to the Behring Sea Award Act, 1894 (57 Vic., c. 2; Hertslet's *Commercial Treaties*, 19, p. 925).

[3] See *Parl. Pap.*, 1893–4, cx [C. 6918], [C. 6919], [C. 6920], [C. 6921] for the British *Case, Counter Case and Argument* and for the *Case, Counter Case and Argument* of the United States. See *ibid.* cxi [C. 6949], [C. 6950], [C. 6951], [C. 7161], pp. 955 *et seq.* for the Papers relating to the Proceedings of the Tribunal, and [C. 7107], p. 1065 for the award.

But the recommendations proposed by the Tribunal and accepted by the parties[1] came very near to making such consent necessary. In addition, the award and the proceedings, which were conducted under the aegis of the Permanent Court of Arbitration in the great forensic tradition of the previous Anglo-American arbitrations, threw much light on such questions as the doctrine of international servitudes and the extent and measurement of bays. The importance of that particular arbitration in the relations of the two States may well be gauged from the following passage, which, because of its general significance, may be quoted here in full, from the opening remarks in the oral argument by Senator Root before the Tribunal:

> It is not alone a controversy that, through lapse of time, has acquired historic interest, that, through the participation of many of the ablest and most honoured statesmen of two great nations through nearly a century, has acquired that sanctity which the sentiment of a nation gives to the assertion of its rights, but it is a controversy which involves substantial and, in some respects, vital interests to portions of the people of each nation...
>
> When two great nations, bound to protect the interests of their citizens, however humble, find themselves differing in their views of rights which are substantial, find themselves differing so radically that each conceives itself to have a right which it cannot abandon without humiliation, and cannot maintain without force, a situation arises of the gravest importance and the first dignity.[2]

Reference may also be made in this connection to the Convention of 1910 between the two countries in which they set up the British-American Claims Tribunal for the settlement of a variety of claims arising from events prior to the annexation of the South African Republics.[3] The Tribunal gave awards in a large number of cases and had not concluded its work by the time the First World War broke out.

While arbitrations with the United States constituted the bulk of active British participation in the arbitral settlement of disputes, a number of interesting arbitrations also took place in that period between Great Britain and other States. These included the *Savarkar Arbitration* with France, decided on 24 February 1911 by a Tribunal of the Permanent Court of Arbitration, an interesting case in which France claimed, unsuccessfully, that Great Britain was bound to

[1] See Agreement of 20 July 1912 between the United States and Great Britain (Hertslet's *Commercial Treaties*, 27, p. 1095).

[2] *Argument of the Honorable Elihu Root on behalf of the United States*, ed. by Scott (1912), pp. 1, 2.

[3] *Parl. Pap.*, 1912–13, CXXII, p. 627 [Cd. 6201].

surrender to France an Indian political prisoner who, while being conveyed in a British ship to India, escaped from that ship in Marseilles and whom the French police, apparently in ignorance of the law of extradition, handed over to the authorities of the British ship;[1] the *Delagoa Railway Arbitration* decided in 1900, between Great Britain and the United States on the one hand and Portugal on the other;[2] the arbitration with Brazil in 1904 concerning *British Guiana*;[3] and the arbitration with Germany in 1911 concerning the *Walfisch Bay Territory*.[4] The well-known Dogger Bank incident with Russia which, according to some, brought the two countries to the brink of war[5] was settled as the result of the findings of a Commission of Inquiry set up in accordance with the provisions of the Hague Convention for the Pacific Settlement of International Disputes.

Contribution of Great Britain towards the development of international organs of arbitral settlement

The experience of a century of arbitration by sporadic tribunals made feasible the consideration, at the end of the century, of permanent organs of international arbitration. To that development Great Britain, once more in partnership with the United States, made a major contribution. As early as 1825 James Mill, in one of his essays published in a supplement to the *Encyclopaedia Britannica* and entitled 'The Law of Nations', had discussed such subjects as 'The Constitution of an International Code and an International Tribunal; How an International Tribunal should be constructed; Form of Procedure before an International Tribunal'. John Stuart Mill's *Essay on Representative Government* included a section on a Federal Supreme Court. However, it was at the first Hague Conference of 1899 that an opportunity was given to Great Britain to make a distinct contribution in this field.

In the matter of arbitration the first Hague Conference was confronted with two distinct problems. The first was the formulation and acceptance of obligations of compulsory arbitration, and in that sphere the achievements of the Conference were purely nominal.[6] The second was the creation of a permanent international arbitral

[1] See Treaty Series, No. 25 (1910) [Cd. 5394] for the Arbitration Agreement.

[2] *Sentence Finale du Tribunal Arbitral du Délagoa* (1900).

[3] For the arbitration agreement see *Parl. Pap.*, 1902, CXXX, p. 53 [Cd. 916]; and *ibid.* 1904, CX, p. 1 [Cd. 2166], for the award of the King of Italy.

[4] See *ibid.* 1911, LII, p. 745 [Cd. 5857], for the award of the arbitrator.

[5] See, for the correspondence on the subject, *ibid.* 1905, CIII, p. 369 [Cd. 2350] and *ibid.* p. 437 [Cd. 2382].

[6] See below, p. 129.

tribunal. Proposals submitted to that end were opposed by some States not only because the very notion of a judge over sovereign States seemed to be incompatible with the sovereignty of States; they were also opposed on the ground that the mere existence of an international tribunal, even if not endowed with obligatory jurisdiction, might be dangerous as implying an indirect pressure to submit disputes to it. It was for this reason that the Russian proposals on the subject rejected in effect the idea of an international tribunal.[1] According to these proposals the Conference was to designate five Powers which, when so requested by the parties to a dispute, should each name a judge either from among its own nationals or others. The proposal of the United States was to establish an international tribunal composed of members appointed by the highest court of justice of each State; a supplementary convention between the parties was to determine whether in any particular case all the members of the tribunal or several of them were to sit. The British project, which was a compromise between the Russian and the American plans, was accepted as the basis of the work of the Conference and eventually adopted, in substance, by the Conference. According to that plan each of the signatory Powers was to designate an equal number of arbitrators to be entered upon a general list as members of the court. From this list parties to a dispute could select members to form a tribunal in any particular case. This was the Permanent Court of Arbitration as established by the first Hague Conference[2] in the Convention for the Pacific Settlement of International Disputes. It was neither a court nor permanent. It was a panel of arbitrators. However, with the help of a permanent bureau and a code of procedure framed by the Conference and embodied in the Convention, it provided the necessary facilities for the arbitration of a number of important disputes.[3] After the First World War it was overshadowed – and, in effect, replaced – by the Permanent Court of International Justice set up by the League of Nations.

Contributions of Great Britain to compulsory arbitration

While the proposals of the United States for an international arbitral tribunal were more ambitious than those put forward by Great Britain, the latter took the leading part in the movement for

[1] For the text of the Russian, American and British proposals see Carnegie Endowment for International Peace, *Reports to the Hague Conference of 1899 and 1907*, ed. Scott (1917), pp. 101, 110, and 108 respectively. [2] *Parl. Pap.*, 1902, cxxx, p. 517 [Cd. 798].

[3] For a collection of the awards rendered by the various Arbitrators of the Permanent Court of Arbitration see Scott, *Hague Reports* (1916); 2nd ser. (1932).

obligatory arbitration. No substantial progress was made in this respect, however, by either of the Hague Peace Conferences. Article 16 of Convention no. I of 1899 for the Pacific Settlement of International Disputes amounted, when stripped of the niceties of diplomatic language, to a rejection of obligatory arbitration. It provided that 'in questions of a legal nature, and especially in the interpretation or application of international conventions, arbitration is recognized by the signatory Powers as the most effective, and at the same time, the most equitable, means of settling disputes which diplomacy has failed to settle'. The second Hague Conference emphasized in effect the purely nominal character of this provision (which became Article 39) by adding to it the following sentence: 'Consequently, it would be desirable that, in disputes about the above mentioned questions, the contracting Powers, if the case arise, have recourse to arbitration, in so far as circumstances permit.' The efforts to accept the principle of obligatory arbitration with regard to specified categories of disputes failed owing to determined opposition in which Germany took the most vocal, though not the exclusive, part. Great Britain's affirmative attitude to the proposals found eloquent expression in Sir Edward Fry's reply to Baron Marschall von Bieberstein's outspoken repudiation of any system of obligatory arbitration worthy of that name.[1] In view of this the efforts of successive British Governments were directed towards securing compulsory arbitration by way of bilateral treaties. In 1903 Great Britain concluded with France what was the first treaty of obligatory arbitration. The crucial Article 1 of the Treaty provided as follows:

> Differences which may arise of a legal nature, or relating to the interpretation of treaties existing between the two contracting parties, and which it may not have been possible to settle by diplomacy, shall be referred to a Permanent Court of Arbitration established at The Hague by the Convention of 29 July 1899, provided, nevertheless, that they do not affect the vital interests, the independence, or the honour of the two contracting States, and do not concern the interests of third Parties.[2]

Before the outbreak of the First World War Great Britain had concluded sixteen treaties of that type. At the same time British efforts were directed towards securing obligatory arbitration with the United States. These efforts were not successful. While the United States, together with Great Britain, could justly claim to have partici-

[1] See *Parl. Pap.*, 1908, cxxiv, p. 402 [Cd. 4081, p. 368]. See also Higgins, *The Hague Peace Conference* (1909), pp. 82–4, and Hull, in *A.J.* 2 (1908), 740.

[2] Hertslet's *Commercial Treaties*, 23, 492; *Parl. Pap.*, 1904, cx, p. 351 [Cd. 1837].

pated in a greater number of international arbitrations than any other country, it exhibited, through its Senate, a conspicuous reluctance to enter into commitments of obligatory arbitration for the future. American Governments and statesmen viewed with favour – and with fervour – the conclusion of such treaties. But these, once signed by the Executive, were subsequently amended by the Senate in such a way as to deprive them of their obligatory character. Following upon the Arbitration Treaty with France, the United States signed identical agreements with Great Britain and other countries. In February 1904 the Senate amended these agreements by substituting in each case the word 'treaty' for 'agreement', in such a way that in each dispute as it arose, the advice and consent of two-thirds of the Senate would have been required for its submission to arbitration. As this would have divested the treaties of their obligatory character, the Executive did not proceed with the matter.[1] Previously the Olney–Pauncefote Treaty, signed on 11 January 1897 and warmly recommended to the Senate in a special message by President Cleveland, had failed to secure the concurrence of the Senate.[2] This was also the fate of the Treaty concluded between the two States on 4 August 1908.[3] The last of these attempts – the Knox Arbitration Treaties – was made in 1911.[4] But these efforts, while not successful in relation to the United States, were not without indirect influence upon the movement for obligatory arbitration in general.[5]

6

Parallel with the developments in the sphere of international arbitration, various efforts were made to codify the laws of war. Before 1870 these efforts were limited to the humanitarian aspects of the regulation of warfare. The Geneva Red Cross Conventions of 1864 and 1868, and the Declaration of St Petersburg of 1868, have been mentioned elsewhere in these volumes.[6] After 1870, however, efforts began to be directed towards the improvement and codification of the laws governing the conduct of war. In 1874 the Czar Alexander II of Russia convened a conference at Brussels to consider a 'project

[1] *Parl. Pap.*, 1904, CX, pp. 103, 104 [Cd. 1837].

[2] For details see Moore, VII, 74–88.

[3] Hertslet's *Commercial Treaties*, 25, 203.

[4] See Taft, *The Presidency* (1916), pp. 102–4.

[5] An arbitration treaty of more limited compass, safeguarding the powers of the Senate, was concluded and duly ratified in 1908: *Parl. Pap.*, 1908, CXXV, p. 907 [Cd. 4179]; see *Parl. Pap.*, 1914, CI, p. 759 [Cd. 7357], for a renewal of that Treaty.

[6] *Cambridge History of the British Empire*, II, 881.

for an international code, with the object of determining the laws and usages of warfare'. The British Government seems to have viewed the conference with some suspicion, as it was feared that the question of maritime capture might be reopened. The Foreign Secretary accordingly required and got an assurance from the other Governments that there was no intention of discussing the right to capture private property at sea, before consenting to send a British delegate. Even so the British Government made it clear that the British delegate would not have plenipotentiary powers and that his function would be merely to observe and report the proceedings, Her Majesty's Government retaining entire liberty of action, and that the British delegate would not be free to discuss 'general principles of international law not already universally recognized and accepted'. Perhaps, as Maine said,[1] the Conference was held too soon after the Franco-Prussian War, and the suspicion with which the British Government viewed the proceedings at Brussels is no doubt readily understandable when viewed against the contemporary political background. The nature of that suspicion is very clearly revealed by a passage in a dispatch of Lord Derby to the British Ambassador at St Petersburg, in which he announces his refusal to enter into any arrangement which would facilitate aggressive wars and 'paralyse the patriotic resistance of an invaded people'.[2] However, in spite of the unfavourable atmosphere, the delegates did manage to draw up a Declaration of fifty-six articles covering some of the more important questions of the laws and customs of war on land.[3] The Declaration, however, could only be signed by the delegates as a record of the proceedings of the Conference, even though in the form of a draft convention, and without pledging their Governments. It was never ratified. The so-called Brussels Rules, however, were later to provide a useful basis of discussion at the 1899 conference at The Hague.

When Czar Nicholas II called the first Hague Conference of 1899 to discuss 'the maintenance of universal peace and a possible reduction of the excessive armaments', Her Majesty's Government this time at once accepted the invitation, pledged co-operation, and sent a strong delegation to The Hague under Sir Julian Pauncefote. The disarmament proposals failed, in large measure owing to the technical difficulty of the subject, and on this matter the Conference

[1] *Whewell Lectures on International Law*, 1877 (1915), p. 128.

[2] Cited in Woolsey, *Introduction to the Study of International Law* (6th ed. 1888), p. 237.

[3] There is a useful summary of the proceedings of the Conference in the Report of the British Delegate, Sir A. Horsford, to Lord Derby, which is reprinted as Appendix II to Lorimer's *Institutes of the Law of Nations* (1884), II, 337–402.

had to be content with a resolution that the restriction of military budgets was extremely desirable. The Conference settled down, therefore, to efforts first to provide means for the pacific settlement of disputes, as described above, and secondly to codify the laws and customs of war. Differences of opinion amongst military and naval experts made it impossible to do more than attempt a partial codification of existing rules. The United States delegation, following traditional American policy, tried to press for the immunity of private property from capture at sea; but the British delegates, following their explicit instructions, refused to enter upon a discussion of the subject.[1] There was a sufficient area of agreement, however, to enable the drawing up of a Convention on the adaptation of the principles of the Geneva Convention to maritime war (based in part on the Additional Articles of 1868). It was reasonable to expect that some headway could be made also with the work on the laws and customs of war on land, for the subject had already been studied *in extenso*: Francis Lieber's Code of the rules of land warfare had been prepared for the United States Government as early as 1863, and the American example had been followed in several European countries; there were the Brussels Rules of 1874; and the Institute of International Law meeting in Oxford in 1880 had prepared the so-called 'Oxford Manual'. In 1883 the British War Office had allowed Lord Thring to add a chapter on the customs of war to the *Manual of Military Law* (though it was labelled as having 'no official authority', and it was not until 1904 that T. E. Holland was permitted to write an official manual). This expectation was fulfilled and a Convention was signed containing the agreed rules of warfare in an Annex (the so-called Hague Regulations), the parties undertaking to issue instructions to their land forces in conformity with these regulations. The Convention was not reached, however, without difficulty. In particular there was an important difference of opinion over the vital question of the qualifications of belligerent forces and the position of the levy *en masse*. This difficulty had already appeared at Brussels in 1874. Germany and the other Continental Powers naturally wished to restrict the privileges of the Convention – such as the status of prisoners of war – as nearly as possible to professional armies. This had some historical justification, for the effective application of rules governing the conduct of war had first become a practicable proposition with the advent of disciplined professional

[1] See letter from Sir Julian Pauncefote to the Marquess of Salisbury of 28 June 1899: *Parl. Pap.*, 1899, cx, p. 206 [C. 9534, p. 108].

armies. Smaller Powers, however, which had perforce to depend for their defence upon the improvised organization of local militia, naturally tended to regard the proposed rules as a threat to their security and as putting a premium upon prepared aggression; there were also lively memories of the severe treatment of '*franc-tireurs*' by the Germans in 1870. In this the smaller Powers were strongly supported by the British military delegate, who proposed an additional article that 'nothing in this chapter be considered as tending to diminish or suppress the right which belongs to the population of an invaded country to patriotically oppose the most energetic resistance to their invaders, by every legitimate means'.[1] In the result a compromise was reached partly by modification of the offending articles and partly by a formula in the preamble stating that it had not been possible to agree on provisions embracing all circumstances that might occur in practice.[2] It was not, however, until after the Russian delegate, M. de Martens, had pleaded with the Conference and had pointed out the possible disastrous effect of yet another failure to agree following the failure at Brussels in 1874, that the Convention was signed; yet it was apparent that the agreed Regulations, useful as they were, in some measure obscured or avoided fundamental disagreements.

Although the initiative in calling together the second Hague Conference of 1907 came originally from the United States, it was actually summoned by Czar Nicholas II at his own desire. It was proposed by Russia that the Conference should seek to secure improvements in the working of the Hague Court and to draw up conventions on the rules of land and sea warfare and the rights and duties of neutrals at sea, 'leaving untouched, however, those questions which might affect the limitation of military or naval forces'.[3] The British Foreign Secretary replied that the British Government wished to see disarmament included in the agenda of the Conference.[4] Despite German opposition the question of disarmament was in fact raised by Sir Edward Fry at the Conference, with the support of the United States, France and Spain; the matter, however, was disposed of by a reaffirmation of the 1899 resolution, and thereafter the Con-

[1] For the report of the British military delegate, Sir John Ardagh, on this part of the discussion, see *Parl. Pap.*, 1899, cx, pp. 257–61 [C. 9534, pp. 160–3].

[2] Westlake's comment is pertinent: '... since it applies only to cases not included in the Regulations, it does not profess to relax those Regulations as operative in the cases which they include; and [one] may wonder how it produced the assuaging effect which it is recorded to have produced' (*International Law*, II (1907), p. 62).

[3] Count Benckendorff to Sir Edward Grey, 3 April 1906, see *Parl. Pap.*, 1908, CXXIV [Cd. 3857, p. 2].

[4] *Ibid.*

ference concentrated on the pacific settlement of disputes and the rules of warfare and neutrality.

After four months' work the participating States were able, in the Final Act of the Conference, to record the conclusion of thirteen Conventions.[1] Three of these were revisions of the corresponding Conventions of 1899. The others covered between them a much wider field than it had been found practicable to attempt at the earlier Conference. It is not possible within the limits of this chapter to discuss the work in any detail, and it must suffice briefly to indicate the British participation in those parts of the discussion in which she was chiefly concerned; mainly, of course, questions of maritime law. Discussions on neutrality laid bare the old disagreements about the test of enemy character. The Anglo-American 'domicile' school opposed the Continental 'nationality' school, and this particular point had to be avoided in the Conventions. Serious disagreement was revealed over the position of enemy merchantmen found in port at the outbreak of war. The majority wished them to be allowed time to depart, but the British insisted on the rules laid down in their prize courts[2] that such vessels were liable to seizure and condemnation; in the end the Convention avoided the difficulty by the use of the formula 'it is desirable' that such vessels should be allowed time to depart. The British attitude was much condemned at the time, but experience since then has shown that it was clearly right. On the other hand, the British delegation was bitterly opposed to the legalizing of the use of submarine contact mines in the maintenance of blockades. 'We declare without hesitation,' said Satow, 'that the right of the neutral to security of navigation on the high seas ought to come before the transitory right of the belligerent to employ those seas as the scene of the operation of war.' The use of mines, however, was defended by Germany on the ground of military necessity, and the Conference was able to agree only upon unsatisfactory provisions forbidding certain types of mines, in view of which Great Britain

[1] Conventions are: I. The pacific settlement of international disputes; II. The limitation of the employment of force for the recovery of contract debts; III. The opening of hostilities; IV. The laws and customs of war on land; V. The rights and duties of neutral powers and persons in case of war on land; VI. The status of enemy merchant-ships at the outbreak of hostilities; VII. The conversion of merchant-ships into warships; VIII. The laying of automatic submarine contact mines; IX. Bombardment by naval forces in time of war; X. The adaptation to maritime war of the principles of the Geneva Convention; XI. Certain restrictions with regard to the exercise of the right of capture in naval war; XII. The creation of an International Prize Court; XIII. The rights and duties of neutral Powers in naval war.

[2] E.g. by Lord Mansfield in *Lindo* v. *Rodney* (1781), 2 Doug. 612, and by Lord Stowell in the *Boedes Lust* (1803), 5 C. Rob. 245.

felt it necessary to enter the caveat that 'it is not permissible to presume the legitimacy of an action, for the mere reason that this Convention has not prohibited it'. The question of the conversion at sea of merchantmen into warships had been brought to a head by the incident in 1904, during the Russo-Japanese War, when the Russian vessels *Petersburg* and *Smolensk* sailed through the Bosphorus and Dardanelles and the Suez Canal under a commercial flag, then hoisted a naval flag at sea and stopped and captured neutral merchantmen. A British proposal to forbid such conversion at sea was whittled down to an innocuous provision to prevent the evasion of the 1856 rule abolishing privateering. It was found possible to agree upon a Convention limiting the bombardment of coastal towns and villages in time of war, a practice which had already been condemned as contrary to the modern rules of international law by Professor Holland in letters to *The Times* newspaper.

More important general issues arose concerning the whole question of maritime capture and commercial blockade. As always, the United States proposed the adoption of the principle of the immunity of private property from capture at sea, except when contraband or bound for a blockaded port; a proposal which, as an American observer has said, had 'long been a favourite doctrine, though never the practice of the United States',[1] but one to which Great Britain as the leading maritime Power was traditionally opposed.[2] The British argued the case for commercial blockade as a weapon at once powerful and less cruel than military operations on land. Nevertheless the British attitude was conciliatory, and it was indicated that His Majesty's Government would be prepared to consider sacrificing even this vital weapon if it could prove a means of bringing about a measure of general disarmament; for one of the grounds on which Germany was demanding a large navy was that it was required to defend merchant shipping in time of war. Although the Americans were able to organize an impressive majority for a test vote on a side issue, the opposition was too important, and the matter was shelved by the adoption of a non-committal *vœu*.

It was Great Britain herself, however, who startled the Conference by a revolutionary proposal for the abolition of contraband. The proposal was in the following terms: 'In order to lessen the difficulties suffered by neutrals in case of war, the Government of His Britannic

[1] See Scott, *The Hague Peace Conference, 1899 and 1907*, I, 699.

[2] Others were France, Russia, Japan, Spain, Portugal, Mexico, Argentina and Colombia.

Majesty is ready to abandon the principle of contraband in case of war between Powers signatory of a convention to this end. The right of visit shall only be exercised to establish the neutral character of the merchant vessel.' At first sight it seems barely credible that within seven years of a war, in which the British were to be compelled rapidly to extend the contraband lists until they covered almost every conceivable commodity, the British Government could have proposed the total abolition of this vital technique of naval warfare. The British argument makes curious reading today: it seeks to show that, by reason of scientific advances in the warlike use of materials, the difficulty of searching modern merchant vessels on the high seas and the complicated voyages with calls at many neutral ports possible for steam vessels, the law of contraband was in danger of becoming so extended that 'the prohibition to be useful must be stretched to the point of rendering the Declaration of Paris a dead-letter'. These, of course, are precisely the reasons which shortly afterwards did indeed cause the growth of contraband out of all proportion in the two World Wars. To that extent the British case was founded on a correct appreciation of the situation. It was true that the law of contraband must in the near future be either enormously extended or entirely abolished; what is astonishing is that it could have been supposed that Great Britain could afford to press for the latter alternative on the ground that the first would 'inflict upon neutral commerce a trouble disproportionate to the legitimate interest of the belligerent'.[1]

The fact of the matter was that Great Britain had ceased for the moment to be a Power which approached these questions exclusively from the standpoint of a potential belligerent. Already in 1887 Sir Henry Maine pointed to the tendency to establish new classes of contraband as constituting a source of 'unexampled danger' to Great Britain. He predicted that in any future war of larger dimensions coal and provisions would be included as contraband at the very outbreak of the hostilities, and he went so far as to counsel early adherence by this country to the principle of immunity of private property at sea advocated by the United States.[2] Professor Westlake also, giving evidence in 1905 before the Royal Commission on the supply of food and raw materials in times of war, considered the immunity of private property at sea to be a practical proposal.

[1] It is instructive to compare this argument with the decisions in the leading cases of the First World War, *The Stigstad* [1919] A.C. 279 (*Annual Digest*, 1 (1919–22), 429); and *The Leonora* [1919] A.C. 974 (*Annual Digest*, 1 (1919–22), 429).

[2] Maine, p. 121.

He was generally of the opinion that the attitude of Great Britain, as a country vitally dependent on supplies from overseas, should be directed rather towards what he described as neutral rights than belligerent rights.[1] He clearly envisaged the practicability – and desirability – of abolishing contraband: a view from which his Oxford colleague, Professor T. E. Holland, dissented.[2]

The deliberations of the Royal Commission, moreover, were clearly influenced by the revealing experience of the Russo-Japanese War, on the outbreak of which Russia had declared both coal and provisions to be absolute contraband. Great Britain protested vigorously. In a statement made to a deputation representative of British shipping interests Mr Balfour, the Prime Minister, laid it down as being 'in absolute conformity with the Law of Nations' that, while coal carried to a belligerent for the purpose of aiding him in his warlike operations was undoubtedly contraband and while the same applied to foodstuffs carried to a beleaguered fortress or to an army in the field, coal, foodstuffs and cotton could not lawfully be declared to constitute absolute contraband (i.e., contraband irrespective of their destination). Russia partially complied with the British protest by agreeing to treat foodstuffs as conditional contraband. Even so, it appeared that the concession was rendered largely illusory by the insistence of Russian prize courts on the owners proving that the captured cargo might not come into the hands of the enemy forces: an almost impossible task.[3]

It is not after all surprising, therefore, that the proposal to abolish contraband altogether should have gathered sufficient momentum to be put forward officially by Great Britain at the second Hague Conference. Twenty-five States rallied in favour of the British proposal; only five opposed. Yet some of the support was clearly half-hearted. For when Great Britain proposed that the States in favour of abolition of contraband should conclude as between themselves a Convention to that effect, no favourable response was forthcoming. For the rest the Conference found itself fatally attracted towards the traditional but hitherto insoluble problem of drawing up agreed lists of contraband, so that, in the end, nothing came of this extraordinary proposal.

In many ways the most ambitious of the proposals actually adopted by the Conference was that for the setting up of an international

[1] *Report of the Commission: Parl. Pap.*, 1905, XXXIX, p. 241 [Cd. 2643], [Cd. 2644], and XL [Cd. 2645].

[2] *Ibid.* p. 236.

[3] Smith and Sibley, *International Law as Interpreted during the Russo-Japanese War* (1907), p. 216.

court of prize. This was not on the original agenda, but both the British and the German delegations came to the Conference armed with draft schemes. The German scheme was for a tribunal of five members (two admirals and three members of the Permanent Court of Arbitration) which would be set up *ad hoc* at the outbreak of hostilities, to hear appeals, which might be brought even by individual litigants, from national prize courts. The British scheme was for a permanent tribunal of judges nominated by signatories whose mercantile tonnage exceeded 800,000 tons; this was to be a court of appeal from national tribunals, but competent only in matters affecting a neutral, and on the motion of the neutral State concerned. Convention no. XII was reached largely by way of compromise. There was to be a permanent court at The Hague, with competence to hear appeals by neutral States or individuals and in certain cases by belligerents, and consisting of fifteen judges, eight permanently representing the Great Powers of Europe, the rest representing minor States on a rota system. The proposed constitution of the court aroused bitter opposition from many of the smaller States led by Brazil, in spite of the argument of Sir Eyre Crowe, the British representative, that the scheme based on a combination of political power and mercantile tonnage meant that the privileged States were those who were making the most real sacrifice in assenting to the setting up of a court, and that the smaller Powers had much to gain and little to lose by the success of the scheme.

However, the principal difficulty was to decide what law the proposed court should apply; for clearly the projected court might have to decide precisely those questions of maritime rights on which the Conference had been able to register only a fundamental cleavage of opinion. Article 7 of the Convention provided that the Court should give its decisions, in the first instance, on the basis of treaties applicable between the States concerned. In the absence of such treaties the Court was to apply generally recognized rules of international law. Where that source failed, judgement was to be given 'in accordance with the general principles of justice and equity'. This elastic formulation of the sources of law to be applied by an international court would have been bound to cause misgivings even if its jurisdiction were confined to administering the law of peace. The clause conferring upon the Tribunal the power to decide in accordance with 'justice and equity' was to be found occasionally in treaties creating *ad hoc* arbitration tribunals. It found no place in such general instruments of compulsory arbitral settlement as existed at the time. (In the Statute of the Permanent Court of International Justice set up in 1920 the Court was given the power to decide *ex aequo et bono* only if the parties expressly agreed thereto.) Here it was proposed to confer wide powers of judicial discretion, under the name of 'justice and equity', in the most controversial and elastic branch of international law. It was therefore clear from the outset that, unless this part of the law of sea warfare could be codified with some approximation to precision, the prospects of the Convention being ratified by a considerable number of States were indeed tenuous. It was agreed therefore that ratification of Convention no. XII should be delayed until a further conference had agreed upon a codification of prize law.

The necessary initiative came from Great Britain. On 27 February 1908, the British Government proposed that a Conference should be held

'with the object of arriving at an agreement as to what are the generally recognized principles of international law within the meaning of paragraph 2 of Article 7 of the Convention, as to those matters wherein the practice of nations has varied, and of then formulating the rules which, in the absence of special treaty provisions applicable to a particular case, the Court should observe in dealing with appeals brought before it for decision'.[1]

The British Government referred to the impression created at the second Hague Conference 'that the establishment of an international Prize Court would not meet with general acceptance so long as vagueness and uncertainty exists as to the principles which the court, in dealings with appeals brought before it, would apply to questions of far-reaching importance affecting naval policy and practice'. The invitation to attend the Conference, to be held in London, was extended to a limited number of States only, namely, Austria–Hungary, France, Germany, Italy, Japan, Russia, Spain, Holland and the United States of America. The work of the Conference, which sat between 4 December 1908 and 26 February 1909, resulted in a *Déclaration relative au droit de guerre maritime*, commonly referred to as the Declaration of London.

There were three main topics on which a reconciliation of the divergent views proved to be unattainable: the essentially British doctrine of the Rule of War of 1756[2] according to which a vessel loses her neutral character if she engages in trade which the opposing

[1] *Parl. Pap.*, 1909, LIV [Cd. 4554]; see also Gooch and Temperley (eds.), *British Documents*, VIII, 306 *et seq.*
[2] *Cambridge History of the British Empire*, I, 551.

belligerent, before the war, reserved for his own trade; the question whether the test of the enemy character of cargoes should be the domicile or the nationality of the owner; and the conversion of merchantmen into men-of-war on the high seas. Outside these topics, however, the Declaration provided a comprehensive scheme of laws for six major questions of the law of prize: wartime blockades, contraband, unneutral service, destruction of enemy prizes, transfers to a neutral flag, and the right of convoy. Of these, the vital questions were of course blockade and contraband. The chapter on blockade represented almost entirely the British view. It is true that Great Britain abandoned her claim to capture blockade runners at any distance from the blockaded coast. On the other hand, the former Continental view, which the Armed Neutralities of 1780 and 1800 had attempted to enforce, that a lawful blockade could only be maintained by stationary vessels, was rejected; and so also was the requirement of a special notification to the captured vessel of the existence of the blockade. The problem of contraband was more obdurate. The difficult question of the limits of the doctrine of continuous voyage was apparently solved by permitting its application to absolute contraband and rejecting it for conditional contraband; however, this and indeed almost every other matter concerning contraband depended in the long run on the solution of the persistent problem concerning the lists of contraband. The Declaration boldly attempted a solution by agreed lists. That provision, the crux of the Declaration, requires some explanation.

The Declaration adopted an elaborate distinction between goods placed on the 'free list', which could not in any circumstances be declared to constitute contraband; secondly, absolute contraband, namely goods which were always contraband provided they had enemy destination; and – most important of all – goods within the category of 'conditional contraband'. These last included the vital category of foodstuffs. With regard to conditional contraband, Article 33 of the Declaration seemed to adopt the traditional British principle as enunciated by the Prime Minister during the Russo-Japanese War. It laid down that conditional contraband is liable to seizure and condemnation only if it is actually destined for the armed forces or the government departments of the enemy State. But Article 34 added certain presumptions of enemy destination which critics in Great Britain considered to be of devastating comprehensiveness: for example, the destination required in Article 33 to be presumed to exist where goods were consigned to a merchant in the enemy's country who, 'as a matter of common knowledge', supplies the enemy with goods of that kind. The Article thus formulated lent itself to the construction that it covered the furnishing of provisions to the enemy population in general. The official Report, which accompanied the Declaration and which the Conference treated as authoritative, attempted to allay that apprehension by explaining that the intention of Article 34 in this connection was to cover the case of a merchant notoriously furnishing provisions to the enemy Government. The second presumption, equally disquieting, established by that Article was that goods were to be treated as contraband if they were consigned to a place serving 'as a base for the armed forces of the enemy'. The critics of the Declaration pointed out that this might include any port in the United Kingdom. The General Report explained that the intention was to refer to a base either of operations or of victualling (*revitaillement*) – a form of words which indicated a necessary connection between a commercial port and the military or naval operations.

Thus one of the most vital aspects of the code of maritime law was made to hang on the slender thread of the controversy as to the authority of the General Report of the Conference. The Report was drafted by M. Renault, a jurist of acknowledged distinction. It received the endorsement of the Conference as a whole. But it was not ostensibly an integral part of the Declaration. It was extremely unlikely that any international tribunal acting in good faith would have disregarded it as a legitimate instrument of interpretation. But the fact remained that a vital aspect of the Declaration – there were others[1] – now hinged on the uncertain results of discussion, familiar to lawyers but disconcerting to the layman, on the place of the so-called *travaux préparatoires* in the interpretation of treaties.[2] It is perhaps not surprising that Professor Westlake, the most distinguished British international lawyer of the time, who was otherwise an emphatic advocate of the Declaration, eventually suggested that, unless the Powers represented at the London Conference met again and formally declared the General Report to be an official and authoritative commentary binding upon the judicial, military and administrative authorities of the Contracting Parties, it would be preferable not to ratify the Declaration of London.[3] There was the further relevant fact that, in addition to the questions which the

[1] See McNair, *The Law of Treaties* (1938), p. 264.
[2] See *ibid.* ch. XXV.
[3] Letter to *The Times* newspaper, ' March 1911; also printed in *Papers*, p. 670.

Declaration clearly left unsolved, the solution of some others was so elastic and nominal as to leave a wide field to the exercise of judicial discretion by the application of not only generally recognized principles of international law but also those of justice and equity. These considerations determined the fate of the Declaration when the question of its ratification came before the House of Lords. Before the House of Commons the Government expressed itself strongly in favour of ratification. Mr McKenna, the First Lord of the Admiralty, said:

> In this matter of international law, under the practice of the Admiralty, the expert adviser is the Director of Naval Intelligence who is always an admiral of distinction and whose office is one of the most important of the Admiralty outside the Board. I know for certain the opinion of four Directors of Naval Intelligence upon this point, and I believe I know the opinion of a fifth, and they are unanimously in favour of the Declaration of London.[1]

The House, with diminishing majorities, approved the Bill before it. The House of Lords rejected it.

Thus came to an unsuccessful conclusion the most ambitious attempt ever undertaken to codify a substantial branch of international law. In this effort Great Britain took a leading part. Even after the rejection of the Declaration by the House of Lords the British Government did not altogether jettison its principles. When the First World War broke out in 1914, the Government, through an Order in Council, declared their intention to act on its principles. The courts, with some hesitation, applied it for a while. But the realities of total war soon cut short the span of its precarious life. On 7 July 1916 the Declaration was formally abandoned. However, this fact in no way detracts from the historic significance of the Declaration. Much of that significance is of a negative character. While the effort to put the Declaration on the international statute book revealed the laudable determination to introduce an element of order and legality into the relations both between the belligerents themselves and between belligerents and neutrals, it is probable that, even more than in the case of war on land, the very basis of the codifying and legislative effort of the Declaration of London was artificial and unreal. That basis was the assumption that the conduct of modern war can be effectively regulated by reference to a workable distinction between the belligerent State and its nationals,

[1] House of Commons, 28 June 1911: 27 *H.C. Deb.* 5s., col. 546.

between the military effort of the State engaged in a struggle for survival and the normal pursuit of its economic life. To demonstrate the falseness of that assumption it is sufficient to compare the lists of articles of contraband as formulated by the Declaration of London and those which finally emerged at the end of the First World War. Indeed, in contrast with the changes, during this period, in the law of peace – where the foundations were laid of new developments in international law which were to become of increasing importance – the efforts made in the field of the laws and customs of war were in large measure an attempt to codify rules which had already served their purpose and which were shown to be outmoded as soon as they were put to the test of a total war.

[Bibliography omitted.]

CHAPTER 6

INTERNATIONAL LAW AFTER THE COVENANT

Editor's note This chapter was published in *Problems of Peace*, 10th series (1936), pp. 37–56. The series was based upon lectures given at the Geneva Institute of International Relations and constituted an important element in the output of books on peace which was so prominent a feature of the literature of international relations in the 1930s.

I. THE DEVELOPMENT OF INTERNATIONAL LAW

What is the sum total of the contribution of the post-war period to the idea of world order? This is the question with which we are concerned in this course of lectures. And as world order is, on analysis, identical with the organized supremacy of law over force in international relations, our task will to a large extent amount to an inquiry as to the development of international law in the post-war period. Now the answer to the question thus interpreted must, it is submitted, be that international law, conceived as the expression of world order, has suffered a severe set-back in the period from 1920 to 1934. This estimate is subject to some qualifications, but the historian of the future will probably be right in saying that, not very long after the setting up of the Covenant, humanity recoiled – as if in astonishment at the implications of the change and in fatigue wrought by the material and mental devastation of the war – before the magnitude of the new departure, and was reverting to the essential characteristics of a system whose re-appearance many regarded in 1919 as inconceivable. The answer, in a word, will probably be that in the field of international law taken as a whole there was, in that period, no progress but retrogression.

This negative result, it must be pointed out at the outset, is only a relative one. The history of these fifteen years is a history of relapse only when compared with the promise held out by the Covenant. But it might well be regarded as a history of rapid progress when contrasted with the state of international law in 1914. This divergence of assessment is due to the Covenant of the League. If we discard the accurate although somewhat trite statement that the

Covenant of the League is not a super-State, and if we set aside for a moment the imperfections which, if removed, would transform it into one, then the Covenant as laid down in 1919 stands out for radical changes, express and implied, in the structure of international law. In comparison with these changes, the normal development of international law must appear to be trifling. If the Covenant and the question of its fulfilment are forgotten, then it is clear that this has been a period of unprecedented progress in the creation and clarification of international law. Some instances may be mentioned. There has never before been such intensive judicial and arbitral activity in the international sphere. The record of any of the years between 1919 and 1932 more than exceeds in this respect that of any of the years before the World War. The Permanent Court of International Justice has not, except in one or two isolated cases, been called upon to decide disputes of conspicuous political importance. But it has served the cause of international law by applying, illustrating, and developing rules and principles of international custom and treaties. There is hardly an important branch of the international law of peace which has not been enriched by a pronouncement of the Permanent Court. The very Statute of the Court signified an important advance by the manner in which it formulated the sources of international law. By authorizing the Court to apply general principles of law as recognized by civilized States, it enlarged the basis of judicial decision and put an end to the predominance of a barren doctrine of positivism which, by relying on the consent of States as the only source of law, lent its support to an extreme conception of State sovereignty. Moreover, the Permanent Court of International Justice has not been the only tribunal in existence. A number of Mixed Arbitral Tribunals and Mixed Claims Commissions were created to deal with private claims against the former Central Powers and other States, as well as with other matters. And an unusual accumulation of arbitral bodies not connected with the peace settlements have done much to add to the growing body of international jurisprudence.

The well-established rule that no State is bound to submit its disputes with other States to impartial adjudication, unless by virtue of an obligation undertaken in advance, continued in all its abstract rigidity, and the Permanent Court of International Justice has repeatedly re-affirmed this principle. But, subject to this rule, and apart from more or less comprehensive reservations, the scope of treaties of obligatory arbitration and judicial settlement has grown almost out of recognition when compared with similar treaties obtaining before the World War. The Optional Clause, by which most States are bound, may have flaws – some real, and some imaginary. In fact, it is so comprehensive as to cover practically every conceivable dispute.

There have taken place improvements in the technique of the treaty-making process, and promising attempts have been made to obviate to some extent the terrors of delay inherent in the requirement of ratification of multilateral treaties. The number, character, and variety of these general treaties – conveniently, but somewhat inaccurately, referred to as international legislation – constitute another striking contribution to international law. Even the abortive effort to codify parts of international law has not been altogether without some advantages.

A further notable achievement has been the increased interest which international law, as laid down in treaties and institutions created by them, has shown in the betterment of the lot of the individual in cases in which it appeared that international action or supervision is necessary to that end. The Peace Treaties, in establishing the International Labour Organization, expressly recognized the direct connection between international peace and the securing of a minimum standard of treatment for wage-earners. It is no exaggeration to say that the activity displayed by the International Labour Organization and the conventions concluded under its aegis have surpassed all expectations. The principle of the protection of the religious and cultural interests of the individual, as adopted in the various Minorities Treaties and Declarations, has been applied by the organs of the League in a way which, although it has invited criticism in some quarters, has certainly not been disloyal to the intentions of the framers of these Treaties. The interpretation of these treaties by the Permanent Court of International Justice, in particular of the term 'equality before the law', is of lasting value. In the field of the purely humanitarian protection of the individual, the Opium Conventions, with their elaborate system of supervision and experiment, constitute a most instructive example of the new developments. So does the protection of stateless persons and refugees by conventions and arrangements concluded under the auspices of the League. Even the framing of an international code designed to lay down a minimum standard for the treatment of prisoners has occupied the attention of the Council of the League. On the other hand, note must be made of the fact that the protection by international law of the fundamental human and political rights of the individual from assault on the part of the omnipotent State has receded into the background in comparison with the ideals and aspirations prevailing before the World War. It would appear that the conception of 'intervention for the sake of humanity' is less acceptable to civilized Governments than it was thirty or forty years ago.

In the domain of the law of war, the innovations have been less marked. No serious attempt has been made to solve the problems raised by the unprecedented extension of the scope of modern warfare and the resulting inducements to an obliteration of the distinction between combatants and non-combatants – a distinction which has been the basis of the laws of war and of civilized warfare generally. Much of the violation of the laws of war during the World War was due to the fact that the Hague Conferences, working as they did in an atmosphere of unreality, ignored these developments. It is probably true to say that there exists today no generally recognized law of prize in regard to some of its most important aspects. Neither has there been a determined effort to cope with the situation arising out of the changes in the instrumentalities of war, in particular in the matter of air warfare. But, on the other hand, there have been some noteworthy improvements. The Convention of 1929 on the Treatment of Prisoners of War constitutes a distinct progress in the humanitarian sphere; so does the Convention of the same year on the treatment of sick and wounded in armies in the field. These conventions are also conspicuous for some of their general provisions like the prohibition of reprisals against prisoners of war, and the abolition of the so-called general participation clause which reduced most of the Hague Conventions to a state of utter precariousness if not worthlessness. As to the new instrumentalities of war, the London Naval Conference of 1930 re-affirmed the customary rule of international law on the protection of non-combatants in submarine warfare, and the Geneva Gas Protocol of 1925, in re-enacting the provisions of some former treaties, applied to this new weapon the customary prohibition of international law relating to the use of poison. But such is the degree of unreality or caution in these conventions that the Geneva Convention of 1929 relating to prisoners of war included gas masks among the private belongings which prisoners must be allowed to retain. What is the purpose of mentioning gas masks, some of the delegates to the Conference asked, if the use of gas is prohibited? The answer was, of course, that gas masks may be worn as a precaution against breaches of the Protocol.

The same kind of reply is at times given to the question as to the necessity of rules of war in view of the General Treaty for the Renunciation of War, or the so-called Kellogg–Briand Pact of August 1928. More persuasive answers could be given. For reasons which need not be elaborated here, that Treaty has not rendered unnecessary the formulation and study of rules of warfare. Nevertheless, there ought to be no doubt that it constitutes the most important achievement in this history of international law since the Covenant. Its significance has been obscured on the one hand by sceptics or cynics who see in it a legally worthless declaration which does not deceive any one and which is not even intended to deceive. On the other hand, its authority has been undermined by zealous commentators who read into it obligations of sanctions and changes of neutrality which its signatories might have adopted had they intended the Treaty to be truly effective, but which they did not in fact adopt. The Treaty has done more than any other agreement among States, perhaps even more than the Covenant itself, to make it possible to contemplate the relations between States as governed by legal rules; it has contributed perhaps more than any other legal provision or principle towards rendering possible an affirmative reply to the question whether international law is law. Before the Kellogg–Briand Pact, war was not only a legal means of self-help and redress; it was – incomprehensible as this may be for ordinary juridical thinking – a legally recognized instrument for challenging and defying existing law. International law recognized a violation of the most fundamental rights of States so long as this was done under the cover of a formal declaration of war. This is no longer the case. Resort to war has been legally reduced to a position even more limited than it occupied in the view of the scholastic writers and some of the founders of international law. Except in cases of self-defence, it is not even a legal remedy. The Treaty is said to have been circumscribed by reservations, express and implied, formal and informal, but these do not essentially detract from the overwhelming legal reality of the Treaty.

This strong emphasis on the legal merits of the Treaty is likely to provoke opposition. Is it not true, it may be said, that even if the Treaty has effected a radical change in the system and the textbooks of international law, its political reality is negligible? This is to a large extent, although not entirely, true. It would not be a complete answer to urge that after all law unavoidably forms part of political reality. And it would be mere flippancy to insist that this is a lecture on international law and not international politics.

The fact is that there *is* a discrepancy between the legal content and the political significance of the Treaty. This is an anomaly which requires explanation. The explanation is that, by a natural process of contamination, the General Treaty for the Renunciation of War has shared the lot of international law as a whole, and in particular of one of its major and more fundamental instruments, namely, the Covenant of the League. It has become infected by the fate which has befallen the Covenant politically and probably also legally.

2. THE COVENANT

What was the legal promise of the Covenant? And in what has its non-fulfilment consisted so as to affect other instruments by a process of contagion and to make appear insignificant the undoubted developments in international law in many a sphere? We have reached a moment in history when it is perhaps not altogether without advantage to look back and to recapitulate the changes of a general character introduced by the Covenant.

(1) The first change is the limitation of the right of war. The Covenant did not, it is true, deprive the Members of the League of the right of war to the same extent as the Kellogg–Briand Pact. But indirectly it undermined, in law, the institution of war as the result of the obligation of Article 10 to respect and to preserve as against external aggression the existing political independence and territorial integrity of all the Members of the League. That Article attacked the very object of war. If loyally observed in letter and spirit, it would in itself have signified the end of war as a normal means for achieving political aims. It was no mere phrase when that Article was described as the backbone of the Covenant. It embodies the idea that political independence and territorial integrity are for States what life is for individuals, and that it is the first and vital condition of political society to guarantee, so far as the power of the law permits, that most elementary of all possessions. No such obligation of respect and guarantee existed before the Covenant. On the contrary, it was part of the established law that while in time of peace States owed one another a meticulously circumscribed duty of non-interference and ceremonious respect for the minutest aspects of their independence, they were freed of that duty by the simple device of a declaration of war.

(2) No less radical was the innovation introduced by Article 16. It had previously been a canon of international law that sovereign States could not be coerced or punished by collective action. The very notion of sovereignty, as then interpreted, excluded the idea of punishment. Individuals organized as States acquired an immunity which they did not otherwise possess, and which was in itself destructive of the idea of an organization of States under the reign of law. The idea of compulsion, which is of the essence of law, was known only in the form of self-help. The Covenant definitely abandoned that principle.

(3) Thirdly, in connection with sanctions, the Covenant effected a substantial change in the conception and law of neutrality as between Members of the League. It has, by implication, reintroduced the classical conception of qualified neutrality. If a State resorts to war against a Member of the League in violation of the Covenant, other Members of the League may declare war upon it. But if they do not elect to adopt that extreme measure and retain thus the formal status of neutrality, it is not a kind of neutrality accepted by international law in the nineteenth and twentieth centuries. It is a neutrality qualified by the right and duty of the neutral members of the League to discriminate, by means of applying sanctions, against the guilty belligerent who, by signing the Covenant, has accepted in advance the obligation to submit to such discrimination. A change was thus effected which subjected resort to war to the legal judgment of the non-participants and constituted them to a large extent the organs of the law.

To describe these innovations in detail is to expose oneself to the reproach of being too rigidly academic. For, it may be asked, is it not true that the years following upon the adoption of the Covenant have witnessed a frustration of the purpose of these changes and a denial of their obligatory force? This, as we shall see, is not entirely true. But neither is it entirely false. And the element of accuracy which it contains is so conspicuous and has loomed so large in actual practice and in general consciousness that it is not the legal promise of the Covenant but the absence of achievement which has given the decisive impress to post-war international law.

This being so, what is the nature and the explanation of that phenomenon of non-fulfilment? The explanation, it is believed, lies largely in the fact that the radical innovations introduced in the Covenant were deliberately combined with the maintenance of some traditional features of established international law and of

State sovereignty. Some examples will illustrate this proposition: Members of the League accepted the obligations of mutual guarantee and of direct suppression of unlawful recourse to war. These obligations are necessarily of a collective nature; they retain a sense and purpose only when thought of not as an isolated measure of any single Member of the League but as collective action of all its Members. However, the Covenant stopped short of treating them as such, it stopped short of providing a basis, expressed in binding and effective obligations, for the collective effort. The non-participating Members of the League have retained the right to judge for themselves whether unlawful resort to war has taken place and whether the duty of enforcing the Covenant has arisen. No such right of effective decision or even opinion binding upon a dissentient minority has been given to the Council or Assembly. The very term 'resort to war' on which the individual obligation to apply sanctions depends, is surrounded by an ambiguity which, in the opinion of many, tends to defeat one of the principal objects of the League. Thus it was possible for Members of the League to refrain from regarding the invasion of Manchuria by Japan as 'resort to war' and yet to remain legally within the four corners of the Covenant. It will thus be seen that not only have Members of the League remained judges of their obligations, but that the Covenant is so framed as to add substantially to the scope of their discretion. The result is that while the *principle* of enforcement of the law is recognized, the legal effectiveness of that principle may be frequently rendered illusory for the reason that its application is doubtful or discretionary or rendered theoretical because of the absence of legal machinery for making it effective. The same applies to the question of neutrality. The general law of neutrality has undergone a significant change, but the possibility of that change being given effect has been limited because of the legal admissibility of war in many cases and because of the very large margin of legal discretion left to the Members of the League in deciding whether occasion has arisen for giving effect to that change. Neither has the requirement of unanimity added to the reality of the provisions of the Covenant in this field.

But there is no room for multiplying examples. Suffice it to say that the adherence to some of the traditional tenets of international law has created a gap between the actual legal structure of the League and its professed function as the organization of peace and order. Very likely the framers of the Covenant wished to leave it to the future to fill the gaps. But the future, as the result of political conditions largely unforeseen by the authors of the Covenant, instead of filling the gaps, allowed them to broaden and to sap the very bases of the new international order said to have been established by the Covenant. Owing to the juxtaposition of the two incongruous elements – the new and the old – the Covenant, conceived as a legal document, is not so much an instrument imposing legally effective obligations in the field of collective enforcement of the law as a legal authorization to act in that capacity. This in itself was a tremendous achievement. No such authorization existed before. In cases in which the individual interests of individual Members of the League should happen to coincide with the purpose of the Covenant, this authorization may prove of tremendous value. The Covenant, even if it has not created an effective legal obligation to act for the common good, has created a right so to act. But a right if permitted to rest unexercised in matters in which the moral sense of mankind requires it to be used is a source of disintegration and demoralization. Moreover, the value of the relevant provisions has been impaired in a number of cases not only by the failure to put to use the authorization contained therein but also by Governmental interpretations and by the few isolated cases of actual disregard of unequivocal obligations of the Covenant. It may be difficult to deny that Members of the League have failed in their legal duty under Article 10 to preserve the territorial integrity of China or to apply Article 16 against Paraguay after she was found to be resorting to war contrary to the provisions of the Covenant.

The extent of this process of attrition can best be gauged by the character of the answer that must be given to questions like these: How much of Article 10 is still law? How much of Article 16 is still binding? It is a fact that these questions are being increasingly and legitimately asked – and yet these are questions pertaining to the most fundamental and most solemn treaty ever concluded. An impressive legal argument could be put forward in favour of the contention that nothing or little has happened to take away effectively from the legal force of these obligations. There has been no formal amendment of the Covenant of any consequence. As to the frequently cited cases of the non-observance of the Covenant, the Members of the League were, it may be argued, entitled to refrain from regarding as 'resort to war' not only the action of Italy in Corfu but also the Japanese action in Manchuria. In law, therefore, save for the Paraguayan incident, Article 16 stands today as it did when it was framed in 1919. In spirit nothing has happened to detract from the formidable obligation of Article 10. If in one isolated case that Article remained a dead letter, such an event is of no more importance than the breach of a law within the State. There is no process of obsolescence of international law as the result of non-observance – especially when such non-observance is confined to single cases.

All this is true. But the legally relevant fact remains that the new international law as laid down in the Covenant has, in its essential aspects, remained in the rudimentary state in which it was in 1919. I say 'in its essential aspects' because there have been developments in many other spheres. But in what must be regarded as its vital aspect, the discretion left by the Covenant has been exercised only in one direction, to wit, in such a way as to bring into relief the traditional freedom of action enjoyed by sovereign States and as to obscure the fundamental changes which were generally associated with the Covenant at the time of its inception. The potential advance has not been implemented. For this reason it may be true to say, somewhat paradoxically, that although on the whole the law as laid down in the Covenant has not been formally altered or abrogated, the new international law which it embodies has suffered a relapse. There is little comfort in the suggestion that by a healthy process of trial and error the more audacious parts of the Covenant have by common consent been allowed to disappear. For there is an obvious element of danger in the suggestion that as constitutions within the State grow and develop through practice and experience, so also parts of international law may become obsolete by the same process. Such obsolescence cannot be lightly attributed to laws which were regarded as being of the essence of the system and as embodying the highest hopes of many nations.

The legal purist or 'positivist' will argue that this relapse has been mainly political and psychological. He may be right. But in these matters the borderline between fact and law is not very rigid. In an unorganized society facts translate themselves into law more quickly and more imperceptibly than in an organized community. It is exactly the positivist view which sees in manifestations of fact in the international sphere a potent source of international law. So potent, indeed, has been the influence of political facts and conditions that even those parts of the Covenant which signify clear and unequivocal obligations are being increasingly regarded as political declarations of principle rather than as clear legal duties capable of ascertainment and interpretation like any other treaty. Would it be difficult to find statesmen, professed adherents of the League, who would yet be quite prepared to proclaim that Article 10 or 16 must not really be taken literally like a private contract or even an ordinary international convention?

The consequences of this situation have been truly far-reaching for international law as a whole. *Corruptio optimi pessima.* Never before, perhaps, has this saying been verified on a more gigantic scale. Any decrease in the authority of the Covenant – the most fundamental of all expressly accepted international obligations – must unavoidably be followed by a decrease of the authority of international law in general. There has, in the period under review, been a disquieting wave of disregard of the binding force of treaties. The authority of the law as a factor determining the action of States has weakened. It would seem that the equilibrium of physical forces, and not legal restraint, is becoming the decisive element in the conduct of States. It is not very difficult to find the explanation. If treaties – especially treaties to which the highest hopes of mankind were attached – are broken or interpreted out of existence or simply not acted upon, subsequent treaties lose the vital force of their being. If Article 10 of the Covenant – and the Covenant generally – had remained in the consciousness of nations and Governments what it was intended to be in 1919, there would have been no necessity for most of the subsequent pacts of guarantee, of non-aggression, and so on. What superior virtue, except political expediency, is there in a new treaty after its predecessor *in pari materio* has not been treated with the respect due to a solemn obligation? What authority, moral or juridical, is there in a pact not to go to war for a period of ten years if the contracting parties are already bound not to go to war for ever? What reassuring force is there in a regional pact if the general pact laying down the same obligation has been treated like a scrap of paper? Any attempt to restore the diminished authority of international law will have to start from a re-affirmation of the binding force of the vital parts of the Covenant.

3. THE FUNCTION OF INTERNATIONAL LAW

In the meantime, it may be fittingly asked, what is the function, in the situation with which we are confronted, of the science of international law? Its power is limited both in practice and as a matter of scientific propriety, but within its limitations it may exercise an influence of significance. In the first place, in so far as it is confined to an exposition of existing law, it is certainly within its province to present in all its implications and in all its dignity the law which was created in 1919, and which has not been formally abrogated. The fundamental changes effected by the Covenant are still part of the law. Legal rules and institutions, including those laid down by treaties, have been frequently exposed to criticism on the ground that they tend to stabilize conditions and that, being incapable of taking into account social changes, they create a gap between law and justice. This is so. But, on the other hand, law is the depository of mature social experience and responsible social compromise. It gives flesh and bones to that experience and renders it immune from the effect of transient moods and influences. International lawyers ought therefore to be in a position to take a long view. They must avoid any undue generalizations from the present condition of political regression as compared with the law as shaped in 1919 and with the ideas that moved nations and statesmen in shaping that law. The new international law then enacted must be interpreted by reference to those ideals and intentions, and not in a spirit of impatience, disappointment, or opportunism. There are certain fundamental ideas of international organization and international morality underlying the Covenant which ought to be treated with absolute respect and which must be approached with humility. This does not mean that the Covenant is above criticism. This paper is in many respects critical of the Covenant. It means that the greatest restraint ought to be exercised when, under the influence of temporary difficulties, we feel tempted to cast doubt upon those very features of the Covenant which, as a matter of historical fact, were at the time of its creation regarded as embodying new and decisive elements of international progress and order. To mention only one example:

Any one who has studied the history of the establishment of the League, as revealed in the projects for its creation and in the various drafts preliminary to its acceptance, cannot fail to perceive that the idea of the collective enforcement of the obligations of pacific settlement was one of the principal ideas of the Covenant. No doubt, the preservation of peace by way of mediation, conciliation, conference, and discussion was regarded as of paramount importance, and was justly placed in the forefront of the activities for the promotion of peace. The application and operation of Article 11 have fully shown the great possibilities of the principle embodied therein. But the idea of sanctions and enforcement, coupled with the mutual guarantee, as an *ultimum refugium pacis mundi* is one without which the Covenant would in 1919 have been regarded as deprived of its essential content. President Wilson could perhaps have secured the acceptance of the Covenant by the Senate of the United States at the price of the elimination of these fundamental ideas. But he and others would have rejected with surprise and scorn the suggestion that the League was merely an elaborate conference of States endowed with permanent organs. The framers of the Covenant deliberately stopped short of providing the League as such with the instruments of force to be wielded by the organs of the League, just as they stopped short of organizing the collective action of its Members, but this is another matter. When, therefore, it is said that the idea of force is foreign to the Covenant, that its sole and exclusive instrument and object is persuasion, and that any infusion of the idea of enforcement is yet another manifestation of the Continental as distinguished from the British or Anglo-American mentality – then such submissions must be regarded as a misinterpretation of the Covenant and as amounting in part to an attempt to elevate to the authority of a principle the psychological atmosphere of a temporary political relapse.

Secondly, international lawyers may be able to play a useful part in reducing to its true proportions the complacent and by now trite phrase that the League of Nations is not a super-State. That phrase is, of course, essentially true. It is true in the sense that Members of the League have not irrevocably surrendered their freedom of action in matters in which they are bound by the Covenant; they may release themselves from these obligations by withdrawing from the League. And it is accurate in the meaning that, while Members of the League, they are not bound to acquiesce in any addition to or extension of their obligations under the Covenant; they may, if they disagree with the majority on such issues, withdraw from the League. However, while it is of importance to bear in mind that the Covenant does not establish a super-State in the connotation suggested above, it is no less important not to make this fact a starting-point for a misrepresentation of the purpose and of the legal nature of the League. Thus it is very widely assumed that the absence of a super-State in the legal organization of the League means that it is a system of co-operation and nothing else. This is an entirely false conception of the nature of the League. The Covenant is much more than that. It is a system of binding obligations in matters which sovereign States have traditionally considered to be at the very root of their existence as sovereign units, namely, in the matter of the right of war.

Moreover, it is, in law, a system for the enforcement of those obligations. But in the first fifteen years of the history of the League the truism that the League is not a super-State has in practice frequently been invoked with the intention – and has often had the effect – of totally obscuring these two outstanding features of the Covenant. It is within the province of legal science to remove that misapprehension. After this has been successfully accomplished it will be time to approach the more difficult but hardly less urgent task of doing away with the prejudice and complacency which now stand in the way of a scientific consideration of the question of the relation of international law to the conception of the Federation of the World – commonly referred to as the super-State. But this is a matter which falls outside the province of this paper.

If the science of international law and public opinion generally are determined to take a long view, in the sense here suggested, in the matter of the interpretation of the Covenant, then the history of the last fifteen years need not necessarily be written off as a clear loss. In that case the very disappointments of that period constitute an indirect contribution to further development. They are a lesson and an experience. But they are much more than that. Within the frame of the still dominant old order and of old conceptions, there have taken place legal changes, detailed and numerous, far-reaching in their cumulative effect and of immense practical value when time has released their potentialities. A properly conceived science of international law can help to disclose their true significance and thus assist in maintaining faith in progress.

Postscript. This lecture was delivered before the outbreak of the war between Italy and Abyssinia. The future will show whether that event and the attitude adopted towards it by the Members of the League will have to be regarded as a continuation of the period reviewed in this lecture or as the beginning of a new phase in the history of the League and of international law in general.

CHAPTER 7

INTERNATIONAL LAW AFTER THE SECOND WORLD WAR

Editor's note This is one of two lectures which Lauterpacht delivered at the Hebrew University of Jerusalem on 7 May 1950 as part of the celebrations marking the twenty-fifth anniversary of the foundation of the University. He recalled that he had been present at the opening ceremony in 1925. At that time he was the president of the World Federation of Jewish Students. His own connection with the University has been commemorated by the establishment there in 1968, as a result of gifts made by numerous friends and former students all over the world, of the Hersch Lauterpacht Chair in International Law.

I hope to have your indulgence if I begin this lecture on 'international law after the Second World War' on a personal note and with an expression of deep appreciation of the honour of being invited to participate in the semi-jubilee celebrations of the Hebrew University of Jerusalem. I was present twenty-five years ago at the opening ceremony. This week I can pay my tribute to an inspiring achievement of a quarter of a century, make my small contribution to this auspicious occasion and join with you in the expression of high hopes for the future of the University. I am also here, as the representative of the University of Cambridge, to convey the greetings and good wishes of the Vice-Chancellor and the Council of the Senate of my own University. This Hebrew University is bound to become one of the most respected seats of learning in the world in every branch of humanities and scientific endeavour. No subject in its precincts can, by itself, claim pre-eminence over the other. But for me – and I am sure for others – there is a profound significance in the fact that international law, under the distinguished leadership of the present Dean of the Faculty of Laws, has been assigned a distinct and important place in this University. What can be more proper than that the discipline of the rule of law among nations should be taught in the City of the Prophets who first proclaimed, in resounding language which will stir mankind even after the Federation of the World has become reality, the ideals of international peace and brotherhood among the nations of the earth?

After the First World War it became customary to quote with approval and some satisfaction a remarkable passage in the preface to the third edition of Hall's *Treatise on International Law*. In that passage, written in 1889, one of the leading British international lawyers prophesied that 'conduct in the next great war will certainly be hard' and that 'it is very doubtful whether it will be scrupulous, whether on the part of the belligerents or neutrals'. But, he added, 'there can be very little doubt that if the next war is unscrupulously waged, it also will be followed by a reaction towards increased stringency of the law'. After the First World War it was widely held that that prophecy was being fulfilled. These, in fact, were the words which I used in the first sentence of my first article which I published in the year in which this University was founded.

The position seems different after the Second World War. There is a widespread feeling that, after the war proclaimed to have been fought for the vindication of the Law of Nations, there has been no progress in securing the rule of law among states and that no tangible evidence of any appreciable advance in the near future can be expected. The historian of the future will note, probably with good reason, that in the period immediately following upon the Second World War there was a growing conviction of the reality of power in international relations and a diminishing faith in the reality of law. How will he attempt to explain that phenomenon?

He will point, in the first instance, to the fact that the Second World War was a period of such complete negation of the accepted rules and fundamental principles of war that Hall's gloomy reference to hard and unscrupulous conduct appeared to be an incongruous underestimate. In the field of prize law – a large section of the traditional law of war – the Second World War showed clearly the obsolescence of the time-honoured rules of blockade and contraband. Another substantial portion of the law of war, namely, the law of neutrality was relegated into insignificance, not only because there were only few neutrals left, but also because practically all who were left lived under the shadow of the lawless forces of the Axis belligerents and were compelled to shape their conduct accordingly. The fundamental basis of the law of war, namely, the distinction between combatants and non-combatants and the rule that civilians must not be made the object of indiscriminate military attack, became a mere figure of speech in a war in which strategic bombing, culminating in the use of the atomic bomb, proved to be one of the decisive factors of the conduct of the war. The rules relating to the respect of the life of civilians on the high seas were swept away – and it is significant that the International Military Tribunal at Nuremberg declined, for reasons which hardly command general assent, to find the two German admirals concerned guilty of the charge of sinking merchant vessels without warning. Above all, the law of belligerent occupation was trampled upon contemptuously and brutally in a way which numbs the imagination and which will forever constitute an indictment not only of the régime of National-Socialist Germany, but of modern civilization. The murder of six million Jewish inhabitants of the occupied territories was in its essence, in its conception, and in the cruelty and magnitude of its execution, a crime against humanity. In law it was a war crime pure and simple. It was the most terrible breach of the law of belligerent occupation. So, in a different sphere and degree, was the policy of deportation to slave labour. When in 1916 Germany deported a limited number of inhabitants of occupied Belgium for compulsory labour in Germany, the protest of the civilized world was so emphatic and, at that time, still so effective that Germany desisted from her practice. During the Second World War eight million inhabitants of occupied territory were deported by Germany to slave labour in conditions of revolting contempt for human dignity and the laws of warfare. The only part of the laws of war which secured some observance were the humanitarian provisions of the law relating to prisoners of war. But even these were observed only between Germany and the Western Powers. It is not an exaggeration to say that, by and large, in the Second World War the traditional laws of war prevailed only to the extent to which fear of reprisals prompted their observance.

I have dwelt at some length on that fact – not of obsolescence – but of wholesale violations of the law of war in the Second World War because it explains much of the state of international law after it. That unprecedented denial of all legal restraints had a triple effect – all of which have been inimical to the maintenance and the authority of international law after the termination of the war. In the first instance, already during the war the lawlessness of Nazi Germany necessarily brought about, as the result of reprisals and otherwise, the general lowering of the standards of legality and humanity in warfare. Thus while the large-scale bombing of centres of civilian population, initiated by Germany, and followed by the Allies, brought into prominence the problem of the adaptation of international law to the conditions of total modern warfare where the entire population forms part of the supreme effort of the State, it raised the even more fundamental question of the distinction between combatants and non-combatants. It culminated in the use of the atomic bomb. This is not the proper occasion for examining or passing judgment upon the legality of the use of that weapon, but it is clear that it raises a central issue of international law and that it is but an example of the consequences of the lawlessness which Germany let loose upon the world. I shall consider it my duty to say something about this weighty issue before I conclude this lecture.

The second result of the era of illegality both before and during the Second World War has been that it made difficult a speedy transition to the full application of established rules of law. Thus when the Allied Powers occupied Italian territory they were not in the position to apply the customary and conventional rule of belligerent occupation according to which the laws of the occupied territory must, in general, remain in force. For many of these laws enacted by a ruthless dictatorship were utterly contrary to the accepted rules of law. In fact some of the major purposes of the war waged by the Allies was to eradicate such laws contemptuous of human rights and dignity. The same considerations would have applied to Germany if the occupation of that country had been in the nature of belligerent occupation and not of full – though temporary – sovereignty acquired by virtue of the unconditional surrender of Germany.

Finally, and this is perhaps the most weighty factor in the situation, there is no doubt that seldom in the history of the world has power been the object of greater veneration as in the years immediately following upon the Second World War. It may be said, with some justice, that this is so because the law is weak and unable to afford protection. But it is also true that law has been relegated to second place because of the hold which adulation of power has acquired over the minds of men. What is the explanation of that reverence for and attraction of force? Part of the explanation lies in the fact that so much power was required for asserting the triumph of justice and of the dignity of man that power has begun to be viewed not as an instrument to a greater end, but as an end in itself.

With that feature of the post-war period has been connected the cognate tendency to a realism which confuses immediate success with the ultimate aim and which does not therefore seriously attempt to grapple with what it considers to be the irreducible fact in international life, namely, the power of Great Powers. That realism has found expression in the main aspects of the new political organization of mankind as embodied in the Charter of the United Nations. It was responsible for that aspect of the Charter of the United Nations which is based on the assumption of permanent unanimity among the permanent Members of the Security Council – an assumption not justified either by experience or by a wise anticipation of probabilities or by an accurate assessment of the main political purpose of a general organization of States. That purpose is to provide machinery and to devise means for safeguarding the peace of the world and securing international co-operation for the very contingency that no absolute unanimity can be obtained between the Great Powers. But it was on the assumption of unanimity that the authors of the Charter based the working of the most important organ of the United Nations. The resulting weakness of the international organization signifies a consequent weakening of international law. It may – as it has done in fact – develop in important details showing the essential interdependence of the international community and the even vaster possibilities of its further expansion. But these developments, important as they are, are precarious and unreal, so long as the society of States is so constituted that it is legally unable to act effectively in a world divided by warring ideologies represented by the leading Powers.

I have been surveying so far the causes of the recession in international law in the period after the Second World War. They are, first, the lawless conduct of the Second World War, on the part of Germany and her allies, and the resulting general abolition of the restraints of rules of warfare. Secondly, there have been the problems accompanying the transition from that phase of challenge to the law to a phase of legality. Thirdly, the very part which power played in conquering lawlessness has tended to enthrone power as an end in itself. Fourthly, that veneration of power has found expression in a form of shortcut which, by reducing the basic problem of the United Nations to the rigid requirement of the unanimity of the Great Powers, has tended, to a large extent, to make unreal both the political organization of mankind and the normal functioning of international law upon which it depends.

However, it would be wrong – and particularly wrong on this occasion – if I were to give a one-sided and therefore unduly pessimistic picture of international law after the Second World War. For, in a distinct sense, the retrogression that has taken place is only relative. It is a retrogression when measured by reference to the high hopes which had been raised during the War and to the needs of rational international order. Thus in relation to the Covenant of the League of Nations the requirement of unanimity of the Great Powers – the Permanent Members of the Council – is not a retrogressive step. It is an advance. For the Covenant contemplated the unanimity of all its members, whether permanent or not, as a condition of the validity of its decisions. The Charter requires only the unanimity of the Permanent Members of the Council. Much has been heard of the right of veto of the Great Powers in the Security Council. But under the Covenant *any* member of the Council had the right to a veto. There is thus no doubt that in that respect the Charter constitutes an advance. It is an advance, it may be objected, at the expense of the equality of States. For it implies in effect that the vote of Permanent Members of the Council counts for more than the vote of other members. That is so. But, then, the abandonment of the mechanical principle of equality of representation and responsibility is in itself one of the conditions of international legal and political progress.

The second important improvement which the Charter makes upon the Covenant is that the former – although it does not expressly recognize the formal international personality of the United Nations in the international sphere – in fact treats the United Nations as an entity separate from that of its Members. While the Covenant referred to the Members of the League, the Charter speaks of the United Nations as such. The International Court of Justice – which unlike its predecessor is declared to be the judicial organ of the international community – has gone beyond that. It has laid down, in an Advisory Opinion, that the United Nations, although not a State, is an international person and a subject of international law. The importance of that Opinion is enhanced by the fact that it has been the only pronouncement so far unanimously given by the International Court of Justice. It is, it may be added, of profound significance for the further reason that expressly and by implication it denies that States are the only subject of international law – a decision which in 1925 would have been regarded as revolutionary.

Thirdly, the Charter marks a far-reaching advance in as much as it lays down, more definitely than did the Covenant, the principle of prohibition of resort to force. The Covenant limited – it did not prohibit – recourse to war. It was silent on recourse to force falling short of war. By implication it permitted it so long as it did not approximate to actual hostilities on a large scale. The Charter is, on this matter, clear beyond doubt. It prohibits recourse to force or threats of force for the settlement of disputes.

Finally, the Charter, more explicitly than the Covenant, provides for the enforcement of the obligation not to have recourse to force. Under the Covenant every Member of the League had the right to determine whether a violation of the Covenant in the matter of pacific settlement had taken place. Moreover, there was no obligation to accept any decision of the Council on the question how to give effect to the duty to enforce the Covenant. The Charter signifies an advance in both these respects. Admittedly, it is an advance whose application in practice is conditioned by the unanimity of the Permanent Members of the Council and which is not operative against any of them. But progress it is. For enforceability and enforcement are of the essence of the law. To the extent to which they are lacking, the legal nature of rules of conduct is weakened.

The progressive features of the Charter are a landmark of paramount importance for international law. They may remain in the background in a period of turmoil and uncertainty, but they constitute a solid accession to the strength of international law. They are more significant than the defects of the Charter (as compared with the Covenant), such as the absence of express provisions for peaceful change of treaties and customary international law, which constitute a source of danger to international peace, or some retrogressive details in the system of trusteeship.

Another development of lasting value for international law has been the effective recognition of enforcement of its obligations not only as against States but also against individuals whether acting for private gain and lust or when acting as agents of the State. Another Charter – that of the International Military Tribunal of Nuremberg – has in this respect immeasurably increased the authority of international law. Before very long the argument as to whether aggressive war was in 1939 criminal or merely illegal will become a matter of the past. The stature of the Nuremberg Charter and Judgment will grow with the passage of years as a vital event in the maintenance of the authority of the very preservation of international law. There was only one accused at Nuremberg who was sentenced, not to death, for the crime against the peace alone. Only two were sentenced, and only one executed, for crimes against humanity alone – although even in their case the Tribunal, for reasons which are controversial, limited the responsibility of the accused to crimes against humanity committed in connection with the war and thus assimilated them to war crimes proper. History and the conscience of the world will judge whether in the case of these two accused the penalty was too severe. All other accused were sentenced, in addition to other crimes, for crimes against the law of war – for crimes with regard to which international law has always recognized the full jurisdiction of the belligerent and, indeed, as in the case of piracy, of all nations. The innovation – such as it was – was one of fact, not of principle. It was for the first time that leaders of the civil government and of the armed forces, as distinguished from humble soldiers, were arraigned for war crimes. Apart from that there was essentially no innovation in bringing to justice the authors of these crimes. If the Allied statesmen had been intent upon simplifying their task, they would have achieved all – or practically all – that was achieved in this and similar trials by limiting the indictment to war crimes proper. They took the more difficult and the wiser course. They resolved that the enforcement of international law must cover not only war crimes but also the crime of war – which is the cause and the parent of war crimes. They thus took a decisive step towards the enforcement of international law in its most vital aspect. They made it possible for the Tribunal to reject emphatically the view that international law is concerned only with actions of sovereign States and that it provides for no punishment for individuals. 'Crimes against international law', said the Tribunal, 'are committed by men, not by abstract entities, and only by punishing individuals who commit such crimes can the provisions of international law be enforced.'

The third principal contribution to international law in this period is the joint product of the two Charters – that of San Francisco and that of Nuremberg. The latter enacted that offences against humanity constitute an international crime and are subject to the jurisdiction of an international tribunal. It thus laid down that there are fundamental human rights superior to the law of the State and that their violation is a crime even if committed in obedience to the law of the land. The Charter of the United Nations expressed in a more direct manner the principle that the individual is possessed of inalienable rights independent of the law of the sovereign State. It recognized these rights and pledged the Members of the United Nations to their promotion and encouragement by just and collective action. As a matter of interpretation or good faith and common honesty that pledge includes the obligation to respect human rights and fundamental freedoms. It is probable that as the result of these provisions of the Charter the observance of human rights has ceased to be a matter which is essentially within the domestic jurisdiction of

States. But even if – as some maintain – it has not, the United Nations is under a duty and possesses the right to ensure the fulfilment of that obligation by all means short of forcible intervention. Moreover, such forcible intervention is permissible and obligatory whenever the violation of human rights is on such a scale and of such a degree as to imply a threat to international peace. Thus the Charter of the United Nations in recognizing the individual as a subject of rights independent of the law of the State has opened a new chapter in human government and has endowed international law with a new function of transcending significance. In the initial stage of its activity the United Nations was not in the position to give full scope to that radical innovation implied in the Charter. Some believe, indeed, that the organs of the United Nations, in particular the Commission of Human Rights, have taken a limited view, not warranted by the terms of the Charter, of its rights and obligations in that sphere. In this as in other respects the effectiveness of the United Nations is the function of its political authority and of the political conditions of the world in the realm of international relations. On the other hand, it is probably true to say that the authority of the United Nations and international peace must depend to a large extent upon the way in which the vital purpose of the Charter in the matter of human rights will be brought to fruition.

These, then, are the three principal contributions of the post-war period to the development of international law: they lie mainly in the undoubted improvement of the structure of international organization; in the growing acceptance of the principle of enforcement of international law not only in relation to States, but also against individuals acting on their behalf; and in the recognition of the inalienable rights of the individual conceived as the ultimate unit of all law. The reality of that progress has been obscured by the more tangible and menacing reality of the division of the world into two opposing groups of States – a cleavage which seems to engulf hope and to rule out further improvement. The outlook is dark unless that ideological cleavage – otherwise legitimate and, subject to the respect of the sanctity of human personality, in some respects beneficent – is contained within the secure channels of the law. What can international law offer as its own contribution to that end? Its help must be limited for the reason that law is primarily the function and the result of the will of States. International law is not the product of writings of publicists. It exists effectively to the extent to which sovereign States submit to its rule. It cannot feasibly be urged, at the present juncture of history, that they should do so irrevocably in matters which directly and immediately affect their safety and independence. But there are matters with regard to which States are in the position – and may be reasonably urged – to make their contribution towards fostering the rule of law without sacrificing their vital interest at a time when they deem themselves in peril. What are these questions? I can mention only four of them.

In the first instance they may agree, in a manner more pronounced than they have done hitherto, to implement the purpose of the Charter in the matter of human rights and fundamental freedoms. In the first phase of its existence the Commission on Human Rights, composed as it is of representatives of States, adopted a restrictive interpretation of its powers with regard to violations of human rights. Little progress has been achieved in the matter of a true and effective International Bill of the Rights of Man. The General Assembly of the United Nations adopted in 1948 the Universal Declaration of Human Rights – an instrument which has no legal validity and which lends itself to the criticism that it has been accepted by all – or practically all – for the reason that it is not binding upon any. And yet the provision of effective international obligations and guarantees for ensuring respect for fundamental human rights and freedoms is not only an essential condition of political progress and an imperative call of duty. It is in the long run an essential condition of peace. It cannot be achieved without a substantial sacrifice of sovereignty. But it is a sacrifice which does not imperil the existence of States as independent units. It dignifies and glorifies their sovereignty and raises it high above the level of a mere instrument of power.

Secondly, States can lend greater support than they have done in the period following immediately upon the Second World War to the principle of obligatory arbitration and judicial settlement. International law is still under the sway of the rule that no State is bound to submit its disputes with other States to the arbitrament of law. Many States, it is true, have subscribed to the obligations of the Optional Clause of Article 36 of the Statute of the International Court of Justice in which they agree to the compulsory jurisdiction of the Court in all or some classes of so-called legal disputes. But that obligation has been undertaken in many cases subject to far-reaching reservations which seriously impair the value of the principal undertaking. Here again enlightened States can, without imperilling their vital interests, afford to agree to a limitation of their sovereign right to be judges in their own cause and contribute to enhancing the authority of the rule of law among nations.

Thirdly, the authority of international law and urgent considerations of international morality require that Members of the United Nations should formally and solemnly declare themselves as bound by the principles of the Charter of the International Military Tribunal which they set up in 1945. They have not done it so far. In the Resolution of the General Assembly of December 1946 they 'affirmed' the so-called Nuremberg principles. The question of the nature and of the binding force of that Resolution are necessarily controversial. In a Resolution adopted in 1947 the General Assembly directed the International Law Commission to 'prepare a draft code of offences against the peace and security of mankind, indicating clearly the place to be accorded to the principles . . . of international law recognized in the Charter of Nuremberg Tribunal and in the judgment of the Tribunal'. Undoubtedly, a Code of that nature will enhance the standing and the usefulness of these principles. But they, and the Judgment which is based on them, will continue to be a source of controversy and of misinformed and malevolent reproaches of retroactive legislation, unless the principal Powers who framed them – as well as other States – expressly accept them as law which has always been and which will be in the future binding upon them. The explicit enactment of crimes against humanity, of the criminality of aggressive war, and of the principle of criminal responsibility both of States and of individuals acting on their behalf, are of the greatest value for international law and international peace. There should be no reproach that their enactment was merely the product of the vindictiveness of the victor wreaking his vengeance upon the defeated.

Finally, and I would be failing in my duty on this important occasion if I avoided the subject, there is the problem of atomic warfare, which has cast a deep shadow over international peace and, indeed, over the chances of survival of civilization. It is a subject in which I must weigh my words carefully and avoid unprofitable controversy as to the past. Lawyers will debate for a long time the legality of the use of the atomic weapon at the end of the Second World War. They will discuss it in the light of the fundamental distinction, without which the laws of war become a mockery, between combatants and the civilian population; of considerations of humanity; of the Declaration of St Petersburg of 1868, in which the Signatory Powers gave their assent to the proposition that 'the employment of arms which uselessly aggravate the sufferings of disabled men or render their death inevitable' is 'contrary to the laws of humanity'; of the Geneva Gas Protocol which prohibits the use not only of asphyxiatory, poisonous and other gases, but also of 'all analogous liquids, materials, or devices'; of the difficulty of distinguishing, except as a matter of degree, between mass strategic bombing of centres of civilian population and the use of the atomic weapon; and, finally, whether its use may be justified against an enemy, or his allies, who have outraged the laws of war and humanity alike. I do not propose to enter into that controversy. But I submit that it is consistent with – and in fact required by – the fundamental laws of war and humanity that the use of the atomic weapon should be prohibited in the future and, except in self-defence following upon the actual recourse to it by the other belligerent, rendered criminal. The express and solemn adoption of that obligation and prohibition is independent of the solution of the problem of international supervision of the production and use of atomic energy and of cognate problems. We must all hope that, for the sake of the dignity of man and of his survival as a civilized being, these weighty issues will be solved. Pending their solution States cannot be expected to relinquish the right and the duty of making preparations which they deem vital for their safety. But it must become a solemnly proclaimed and accepted rule of international law that the use of that weapon, except in self-defence, is prohibited and criminal. We must cherish no illusion as to the efficacy of such prohibition. But we must not succumb to facile pessimism and consider it as a snare and a delusion. Law in so far as it embodies compelling dictates of humanity and decency is of some potency, both persuasive and deterrent, in governing the conduct of men and in forming their habits. In any case, we must do our duty, in so far as it lies in us. We must not act – or fail to act – as if the future of the human race were a product of blind fate impervious to the will, intelligence, and moral responsibility.

I trust I may be forgiven for marring a festive occasion with the consideration of a subject the very nature of which must cast a gloom. For I have touched also on brighter and more hopeful aspects. But I have thought it fit that this call should come, at this time, from Jerusalem. There is a future of promise and deep meaning for the science of international law – and for other sciences – in the City in which Isaiah proclaimed the message of eternal peace and of transformation of weapons of death into implements of creative effort by all men of good will.

III

SOURCES OF INTERNATIONAL LAW

CHAPTER 8

PRIVATE LAW SOURCES AND ANALOGIES OF INTERNATIONAL LAW

Editor's note Lauterpacht was always opposed to writing about 'topical' subjects of international law. His real interest lay in fundamental and abiding issues. This explains why his early works, namely, *Private Law Sources and Analogies of International Law* and *The Function of Law in the International Community* still remain of value and are quoted more than forty years after they were originally published. But as the years went by, Lauterpacht began to feel that new editions of his earlier works were called for. In one case, a second edition appeared very soon after the first. Thus *An International Bill of Rights*, published in 1945, was rewritten and expanded to appear in 1948 as *International Law and Human Rights*. In 1958, after he had become a judge of the International Court he published *The Development of International Law by the International Court*, which was a fundamentally rewritten and generously expanded revision of his earlier work published in 1935.

During the last decade of his life he succeeded in finding time to begin the preparation of new editions of *Analogies* and of the *Function of Law*. He made little progress with the latter, but amongst his papers there was found a typescript of seventy-nine pages containing a revision of chapter 1 of *Analogies*. It has seemed right to print this here, for some sections are significantly expanded.

THE SCIENCE OF INTERNATIONAL LAW AND THE PROBLEM OF PRIVATE LAW ANALOGIES

§1. *The points of contact between international and private law*

The points of contact between international public law and private law can conveniently be grouped in two classes. The first relates to rights and obligations of States as political entities endowed with attributes of government. It comprises cases in which legal relations normally forming the subject-matter of international public law are being shaped in accordance with or by analogy to a conception of private law. When, for example, the question of sovereignty over a portion of territory is decided by application of the rules of prescription; when restrictions of territorial sovereignty are construed by analogy of easements or servitudes in private law; when recourse is had to private law rules of inheritance and succession for the purpose of determining certain rights and duties of States arising out of changes of sovereignty; when the conditions and standards of responsibility of States for international wrongs are established according to principles of private law; when the rules and principles of the law of contract are resorted to for the purpose of construing and applying a treaty regulating the normal political relations of States; or when the principles of the law of nuisance are applied for determining the obligations of territorial sovereignty in relation to the territory of neighbouring States; when before an international tribunal the conduct of a State is judged in accordance with a private law rule of evidence; when the rules of procedure as developed in the sphere of arbitration between private persons are used as a basis of the procedure of international courts and tribunals; when the question of payment of moratory interest for delay in the settlement of a war indemnity is decided by application of rules of private law – in all these cases the legal relations to which analogy is applied are directly related to the political and public functions of the State conceived as an entity endowed with and wielding *imperium*. It is only and exclusively with this aspect of the problem that this book is concerned.

To the second category belong cases in which States enter into relations which, but for the fact that the parties to it are States, would constitute relations of private law *prima facie* calling for the application of private law rules and principles. This arises, for instance, when States conclude a treaty providing for a loan or the opening of a credit, or a guarantee of a loan for purchase of goods, or a lease of real property, or when they enter into an arrangement for the purpose of constructing and maintaining a bridge or installations on a river dividing their territories. Some examples, selected from treaties concluded in the period following upon the Second World War, will illustrate this aspect of international conventional law.

An Agreement of 23 March 1948 between the United States of America and the United Nations provided for a loan to the latter, without interest, of a sum not exceeding $65,000,000 for the construction and furnishing of the permanent headquarters of the United Nations. The Agreement laid down in detail the dates and amounts of instalments to be paid in the currency of the United States, 'which is legal tender for public debts on the date such payments are made'. It provided that while any indebtedness under the Agreement is outstanding and unpaid, the United Nations shall not 'create any mortgage, lien or encumbrance on or against any of its real property in the headquarters district'.[1]

An Agreement of 28 June 1950 between the Governments of the United Kingdom, Australia, India, Pakistan and Ceylon on the one hand and the Government of Burma on the other hand, provided for a loan, and the modalities of its payment, to be made to the latter by the five Commonwealth Governments.[2] While in this and similar cases the lending of money or the opening of a credit[3] have been the exclusive objects of the transaction, in others they have been attached to a particular object, such as the purchase of goods in the country providing the loan or the credit. Thus the Financial Agreement of 5 February 1946 between Canada and the Netherlands provided for a loan to the latter of an amount not exceeding $125,000,000 to enable her to pay the cost of Canadian produced goods. The Agreement, which fixed the payment of interest at the rate of 3 per cent per annum, provided for the issue by the Netherlands of various categories of bonds representing its consolidated debt 'which bonds shall constitute valid, binding, absolute and unconditional obligations of Government of the Netherlands'. It was also agreed that payments by the Netherlands should be in Canadian dollars or fine gold at the option of the Government of the Netherlands.[4]

A considerable number of treaties have been concluded for the sale and purchase of goods – a phenomenon not unnatural in a period characterized by the growing direct management – as distinguished from regulation – by the State of the economic life of the nation.[5]

[1] *U.N.T.S.* 19, 44.

[2] *U.N.T.S.* 87, 154.

[3] Agreement of 1 July 1946 between Yugoslavia and Albania concerning a credit to be extended to the latter: *U.N.T.S.* 111, 83.

[4] *U.N.T.S.* 43, 4. Similar Financial Agreements were concluded with China, France, Norway and Czechoslovakia (pp. 23, 43, 67, 81). See also Exchange of Notes between the United Kingdom and Yugoslavia of 28 December 1950 granting a credit of £3,000,000 to Yugoslavia for the purchase of consumer goods, foodstuffs, etc.: *U.N.T.S.* 88, 330; and Agreement of 18 March 1947 between Sweden and Poland concerning the participation of Sweden in the reconstruction of Polish economy in exchange for the provision of Polish coal and coke: *U.N.T.S.* 12, 315.

[5] See Economic Agreement of 17 September 1946 between the United Kingdom and Argentina in which, apart from the regulation of questions relating to railways and payments, the United Kingdom agrees to purchase the exportable surplus of meat at prices laid down in the Agreement: *U.N.T.S.* 88, 40.

In the Agreement of 4 March 1948 the Government of the United Kingdom agreed to sell and that of Denmark to purchase certain aircraft and equipment: *U.N.T.S.* 77, 58.

See an Exchange of Notes between the United States of America and the Dominican Republic of 10 June 1943 relating to the purchase by the former of the exportable surplus

In some cases it has been found necessary to regulate by contractual agreement the conditions of what has been no more than an outright gift.[1] In a different sphere contractual arrangements relying upon the use of private law notions have been concluded for regulating what is in essence a gift made in the interest of neighbourly relations and equitable economic conditions. Thus the Agreement of 6 April 1951 between Belgium and the United Kingdom[2] provided for the grant of a lease to the former of a site in the Port of Dar-es-Salaam to facilitate Belgian traffic through the territories of East Africa through the construction of a deep-water berth in that port. The rental was fixed at 1 franc per annum.[3] The same applies, essentially, to cases in which the consideration obtained has been not in the exclusive interest of the donating State but in the general interest such as freedom of international traffic.[4] To the same cate-

of certain Dominican food products in a purely commercial contract with detailed specifications of the quantity and quality of the goods purchased: *U.N.T.S.* 21, 278. See also *ibid.* 7, 132, for an Exchange of Notes on 19 September 1946 between the United States of America and Argentina where the latter 'pledges itself to sell' to the United States certain oil products at a specified price: and see Exchange of Notes of 17 May 1946 between the United States of America and Portugal relating to supply to the former of Portuguese colonial sisal: *U.N.T.S.* 126, 4.

In 1946 the United States concluded a series of agreements for purchasing natural rubber: see Agreement of 28 January 1946 with France (*U.N.T.S.* 3, 239); with the Netherlands (*ibid.* 247); with the United Kingdom (*ibid.* 293). See the Agreement between the United States and the Philippines of 11 September 1946 for the sale of certain surplus war property with Articles on Property Sold and Granted, Transfer of Possession, Distribution, Warranties, and Consideration in *U.N.T.S.* 43, 232.

A detailed Agreement—occupying an entire volume (114) of the *U.N.T.S.*—of 24 July 1947 between Yugoslavia and Hungary provided for the purchase in Hungary over a period of five years of complete plants, mechanical equipment, machines and materials to be paid from the proceeds of specified exports from Yugoslavia. See, further, Convention of 23 December 1946 between Yugoslavia and Roumania concerning the loan of grain: *U.N.T.S.* 116, 33; the Agreements between Yugoslavia and Russia of 30 November 1945 concerning deliveries of petroleum products: *U.N.T.S.* 116, 153; of 26 April 1946 concerning delivery of grain (*ibid.* 163); concerning the creation of the Yugoslav–Soviet Danube Steamship Joint Stock Company (*ibid.* 171); concerning the sale to Yugoslavia of railway rolling stock (*ibid.* 296).

[1] See, e.g., Exchange of Notes between Australia and Hungary of 28 June 1948 concerning a gift of wool to Hungary: *U.N.T.S.* 22, 3. It provides, *inter alia*, that the object of the gift shall be distributed without discrimination of race, language, sex, or religious or political grounds, and that it shall not be used for the armed forces or other military or similar purposes: *U.N.T.S.* 22, 3. And see *ibid.* pp. 11, 17 and 25 for similar agreements with Italy and with Yugoslavia.

[2] An Agreement confirming the previous Convention of 15 March 1921: *L.N.T.S.* 5, 319.

[3] *U.N.T.S.* 110, 4.

[4] See, for instance, Article 3 of the Agreement of 31 December 1943 between the United States of America and Liberia: 'The Government of the Republic of Liberia agrees to the establishment of the port as a free port, or foreign trade zone, to be operated for the mutual benefit of the United States of America and the Republic of Liberia and all nations with which the Government of the United States of America and the Republic of Liberia maintain friendly relations' (*U.N.T.S.* 106, 202). See also Exchange of

gory, though in a different sphere, belong arrangements such as the Agreement of 11 June 1946 between the United Nations and the Swiss Confederation on the Ariana site, which provides that the land on which the United Nations buildings are situated shall be subject to a transferable and exclusive right of user – 'un droit réel de superficie cessible et exclusif' – to continue so long as the buildings themselves; that the same shall apply to certain roads leading to or connecting the buildings; and that the United Nations 'shall enjoy a servitude personnelle of non-transferable and exclusive user' over certain other plots of land.[1] Finally, reference may be made to contractual agreements between Governments for the joint construction and operation of works and installations of common interest. Thus in the Treaty of 14 November 1944 between the United States of America and Mexico the two Governments agreed to construct jointly various works in the main channel of the Rio Grande, the cost of the construction to be divided between them in proportion to the benefits which the respective countries receive therefrom, as determined by the Commission set up by the Treaty and approved by the two Governments.[2]

Notes of 18 May 1948 between the United States of America and Guatemala: 'the latter will not impose any restriction on the use of the Inter-American Highway, nor levy directly or indirectly any tax or charge for such use . . . that do not apply with equal force to the like use of the highway by traffic or vehicles of Guatemala' (*U.N.T.S.* 67, 162). Agreement of 14 February 1947 between the United States of America and Philippines, regarding a road, street, and bridge programme (*U.N.T.S.* 16, 5) Article VII provided as follows: 'The Republic of the Philippines agrees to provide all lands, easements, and rights of way necessary for the execution of the projects under the programs to which this Agreement relates.'

[1] *U.N.T.S.* 1, 154. See also the Agreement of 1 March 1948 between the United States and Canada relating to the future operation and maintenance of the war-built land line communications system between Edmonton, Alberta and Fairbanks, Alaska. The Agreement refers repeatedly to the 'lease' of the facilities in question. There was a rental stipulated of $271,000: *U.N.T.S.* 81, 286.

[2] Article 5, *U.N.T.S.* 3, 32. For the Exchange of Notes of 20 July 1925 between Colombia and Venezuela concerning the construction of an international bridge on the river Tachira, see *L.N.T.S.* 39, 15–24.

The above classification is necessarily of an elastic nature. The public and private law elements are frequently united in one transaction as may be seen, for instance, from the Treaty of 1865 between Chile and Peru, in which a political alliance and the unification of naval forces for the purpose of conducting the war against Spain were combined with what may be called an agreement for a limited partnership with regard to the expenses connected with the common operations (see Moore, II, 2085–105). An Agreement of 21 January 1948 between Yugoslavia and Poland provided that the Government of the latter should authorize and instruct the Polish State enterprise—the Bureau of Industrial Planning and Construction—to construct and equip fully a powder factory in Yugoslav territory. While it was provided that the factory should be constructed in virtue of a contract between the respective Polish and Yugoslav institutions, it was agreed that Yugoslavia guaranteed to pay to Poland the sums due to it for the goods produced by the factory (*U.N.T.S.* 115, 160).

The examples here adduced suggest that it may not be altogether accurate to assert that in such cases States act in a purely business or private capacity without reference to the exercise of *imperium*. For the distinction, as revealed – for instance – in connection with the problem of jurisdictional immunities of States, between the private law and public law activities of a State, may be of less substance than appears at first sight. Thus, with regard to a contract for the purchase of shoes for the army, while some courts have held the transaction to be of a purely private law nature disentitling the State concerned from relying on jurisdictional immunity, other courts have considered the same transaction to have been entered for the purposes of pursuing the highest interests of the State and thus coming within the orbit of the traditional rule of immunity.[1] Even when constructing a contract as a *fiscus*, the State still acts in its sovereign capacity in pursuance of public welfare; it cannot act otherwise. For this reason, although treaties such as those enumerated above seem, *prima facie*, to use the terminology of private law, it is doubtful whether, unless expressly provided to the contrary, the private law in question is one of a particular municipal system. There is room for the view that any transaction between sovereign States constitutes, by that very fact and notwithstanding its typical private law content, a transaction of public international law. It may be the business of the latter to formulate and develop those international[2] rules of private law which may have to be applied when both contracting parties are States. The thus evolved law of State contracts of a private law nature must necessarily be determined by, or be identical with, the general principles of law applicable in the matter (in the formation of which comparative law must form a legitimate and important part) or the general principles of the law of contract as adapted to the requirements of international rela-

[1] For references to the cases and other examples see Lauterpacht, in *B.Y.* 38 (1955), 223.

[2] See Fischer Williams, *Chapters*, p. 259 and other authors referred to by Mann, in *B.Y.* 21 (1944), 24, n. 1. And see, generally, the latter article by Mann, *ibid.* pp. 10–33 for an illuminating discussion of 'the law governing State contracts'. He says: '... if one party to a contract is an international person, particularly a State, there exists *ipso facto* a sufficient connection with supernational rules which ... may enable and justify the parties to de-localize their contract and to submit it to what may be called public international law, i.e. to internationalize it' (at p. 19). As appears from the sentence which follows, the learned author, in referring to public international law, has in mind the 'general principles of law' referred to in Article 38 of the Statute of the Permanent Court of International Justice, as largely identical with 'private law to be ascertained on a broad comparative basis'.

tions and the specific practice of States.[1] This is so although it is only seldom that an international agreement which resorts to typical private law terminology lays down expressly that it shall be interpreted in accordance with 'general principles of law' – a provision to be found in Article 12 of the Agreement, referred to above, of 1946 between the United Nations and the Swiss Confederation concerning the Ariana site for the United Nations.

Probably there is no question of applying by analogy the rules of private law to relations of States which are outside the typical domain of public international law. The same applies to the group of cases in which parties to a treaty avail themselves of a conception of private law in order to determine private rights, and the question subsequently arises as to the meaning of the particular term thus used.[2] However this may be, this second category of relations, as instanced

[1] The same, it may be added, applies probably to what may be described as 'internationalized' contracts—i.e. contracts between States and foreign nationals (whether individuals or companies) which either expressly or by implication rule out the application of the municipal law of either party. Thus the 'Convention' concluded on 29 April 1933 between the Government of Persia and the Anglo-Persian Oil Company provided, in Article 22, that the award of the arbitration tribunal for the settlement of disputes between the parties 'shall be based on juridical principles contained in Article 38 of the Statute of the Permanent Court of International Justice' and that the procedure of the arbitration shall be that followed by the Court (for the text of the Convention see *Anglo-Iranian Oil Co.* case, *I.C.J. Pleadings*, p. 258). In the *Lena Goldfields Arbitration* of 2 September 1930 the Tribunal seems to have accepted the contention of the plaintiff company to the effect that 'the proper law of the contract' was not the law of Russia but general principles of law such as those recognized in Article 38 of the Statute of the Permanent Court of International Justice: *Annual Digest*, 5 (1929–30), p. 3. In the case of *Petroleum Development Ltd.* v. *Sheikh of Abu Dhabi* the arbitrator (Lord Asquith) was called upon to apply Article 17 of the Agreement between the parties which provided that 'the Ruler and the Company both declare that they base their work in this Agreement on good will and sincerity of belief and on the interpretation of this Agreement in a fashion consistent with reason'. He held that that Article 'repels the notion that the municipal law of any country, as such, could be appropriate'. He said: 'the terms of that clause invite, indeed prescribe, the application of principles rooted in the good sense and common practice of the generality of civilized nations—a sort of "modern law of nature"'. However, he held that although English municipal law was inapplicable as such 'some of its rules are . . . so firmly grounded in reason, as to form part of this broad body of jurisprudence—this "modern law of nature"'. Thus, while denying the applicability of the English rules of evidence declaring largely inadmissible the correspondence relating to the negotiations preceding the agreement, he held applicable the rule which attaches decisive importance to the actual language used in the final agreement. While admitting the possible exaggerations of the rule *expressio unius est exclusio alterius*, he thought that when 'confined within its proper borders' it was 'mere common sense'. He had grave doubts as to the application of the rule *contra proferentem* or the rule that grants by a sovereign are to be construed against the grantee: 'The latter is an English rule which owes its origin to incidents of our own feudal polity and royal prerogative which are now ancient history' (*I.L.R.* 18 (1951), 144 *et seq.*).

[2] See, for instance, the Treaty of Commerce and Navigation, of April 1896, between Japan and Germany: Martens, N.R.G., 2nd series, 23, 269, and Lauterpacht, *Analogies* §124. For a scholarly exposition of the relevant principles, see Ruegger in *Z.I.* 27 (1919–20), 426–502.

by the treaties here enumerated, does not fall within the orbit of this book which is concerned with the relation of private law to public international law in its traditional aspect as the law governing the relations of States as wielding *imperium* in its traditional connotation.

§2. *Private law in international public law proper*

Prior to the impetus given to the subject by the inquiry into the meaning and the application of the 'general principles of law' as formulated in Article 38 of the Statute of the Permanent Court of International Justice, little systematic attention was paid to the problem of private law sources and analogies in international public law. We say 'systematic attention' for, given the actual area of contact between the two branches of law, it has been difficult for writers not to define occasionally their views on the admissibility of some particular concept of private law. The problem includes not only the vast subject of treaties and their analogy to contracts of private law with regard to rules governing their formation, validity, and termination (the juridical nature of treaties, the inconsistency of treaties with those already binding upon the parties, the influence of fraud, error and duress, the relevance of constitutional limitations upon the treaty making power, the *pacta in favorem tertii*, the *clausula rebus sic stantibus*, rules of interpretation), and the part of international law relating to acquisition and loss of territory. It affects almost every branch of the international law of peace. The international law of tort and the problems of State responsibility, including that of abuse of rights and of nuisance; the measure of damages; the question of interest, moratory and compensatory; the doctrine of State succession; extinctive prescription; real rights in relation to State territory such as international servitudes and leases; international mandates under Article 22 of the Covenant of the League of Nations and trust territories under the Charter of the United Nations; private law rules of evidence and procedure, especially those of estoppel and *res iudicata*; the analogy of States and individuals as it has affected the doctrine of fundamental rights of States – they all come within its scope. To those instances cases may fairly be added in which doctrines originally created in close contact with Roman and private law developed subsequently without leaving visible traces of their private law origin. The historic influence of the institution of property on the formation of the theory of sovereignty, and the influence of the Roman law rules of possession and property on the conception of the freedom of the sea and on that of territorial waters, may be mentioned in this connection. How far has international law drawn, in these and similar cases, from the rich source of private law? Is this application of analogy a matter of form and metaphor, or of legal substance? If it is the latter, who is responsible for it? Is it the practice of States and the very nature of international relations, or a regrettable absence of originality on the part of writers who, unable to grasp the special and quite peculiar character of international relations, proceed to mould them after the private law pattern? Does the recourse to private law strengthen the independent and scientific character of international law *qua* law, or does it result in transforming it into mere speculation or philosophy of law? And, finally, has the application of private law been conducive to the realization of ideals of justice in the domain of international law in the sense of bringing about a closer approximation of its rules and principles to the sentiment and canons of morality?

§3. *The science of international law and the application of private law*

The fact that the treatment of these questions has been, on the whole, casual and sporadic can be attributed largely to the circumstance that the problem has become intimately connected with the controversy between the positivist and the natural law tendencies and with the ascendancy of the positivist school. The reign of the latter at the end of the nineteenth century and the two decades which followed it was undisputed. The reaction against the purely positivist way of thinking is, in international law, only of recent date.

Now, the chief postulate of the positivist school can be expressed in one word: self-sufficiency. It rejects the taking over of rules and precepts from sources other than international custom or treaties. This is so for the simple reason that if the will of States is the only source of international law – and this is the essence of the positivist doctrine – then there is no room for sources of law extraneous to that will; it does not matter that reliance upon them is introduced through the back door of analogy. Such borrowing, it is alleged, of rules and principles from an outside system of law destroys the independence of international law and hampers its free development. That this independence has in fact been threatened by the gigantic edifice of human thought and experience embodied in private law, is obvious. Here – apart from justifiable manifestations of impatience at far-fetched recourse to analogy – lies the explanation of the attitude adopted by those writers who reject the idea of any meaningful connection between the two branches of law. The same forces which were fighting the influence of the law of nature advocated with vigour the purification of international law from its private law ingredients. The positivist disapproval of recourse to private law found, on the other hand, an ally in the current doctrine of the sovereignty of the State, conceived as the bearer of the highest and vital interests of the nation, which encouraged a conception of international law as regulating interests of a higher value and adjusting public rights of an 'eternal and inalienable'[1] character; it seemed quite natural that such rights and interests should not be amenable to ordinary standards of private law deemed to be concerned mainly with the regulation of economic interests.

Moreover, in relation to the question of sources of law, positivism and State sovereignty in the international sphere are – upon analysis – synonymous. They both view the will of the State as the exclusive source of obligation and as the final judge of its actions. It is largely for this reason that a subsequent chapter of this book is devoted to an examination of the present position in international law of the doctrines both of positivism and sovereignty. This task will be attempted although it may be said that as a matter of positive law the substantive problem with which this book is concerned has been put beyond the realm of controversy as the result not only of actual previous practice of Governments and international tribunals but also of the specific provision of Article 38 of the Statute of the International Court of Justice which, in elevating 'general principles of law recognized by civilized States' – principles which are substantially identical with general principles of law – to the authority of a formal source of law, may be said to have put the impress of finality upon a process hitherto controversial. For the previous practice lends itself to divergent interpretations. It may be represented as an expression of the immaturity of a transient phase in the history of international law. The voice of Article 38, it may be said, is no more than the voice of a treaty which is general, but not universal, in character and which is subject to the vicissitudes to which all treaties are liable. Above all, however great and widely acknowledged the authority of that treaty may be, the manner of its interpretation and application may be to a large extent dependent upon the power of conceptions, such as positivism and sovereignty, whose influence and vitality are by no means spent.

[1] See Oppenheim, quoted below, §11.

The same applies to cognate doctrines which, historically and as a matter of legal analysis, have developed alongside the conceptions of positivism and sovereignty and as such influence powerfully the development of international law. It is for this reason that it will be necessary to digress here and give an account of the present position with respect to the general relation of international and municipal law – for private law is a no mean part of municipal law – and with respect to the subjects of international law. For if it is a fact that international and municipal law are fundamentally disparate in respect of their subject matter and that, as a matter of actual practice, there is no mutual recognition of each other, then that circumstance must decisively affect recourse to analogy as a significant source of action and decision. That circumstance would not, however, exclude altogether the use of analogy, for nothing can exclude its inherent persuasive force.

Secondly, there is no room for analogy if the subjects of the two systems of law are wholly different – namely, if the subjects of international law are the personified entities of States only and exclusively. The position is wholly different if the traditional doctrine, as it dominated international law for generations prior to the First World War, is regarded as having been modified in two ways: (1) by the realization that international practice has recognized persons and entities other than States as subjects of international duties and as direct beneficiaries of international rights; (2) by the realization that even when the personified entity of the State is regarded as a subject of international rights and duties the latter are – in fact and, ultimately, in law – the rights and duties of individual human beings.

These are the reasons why it will be necessary to survey and discuss these general problems of international law in the context of the present monograph.

The neglect of the general problem and of the specific applications of sources and analogies of private law, the explanation of which has been attempted in the preceding sections, has been remedied to a large extent, subsequent to the establishment of the Permanent Court of International Justice, by the increasing attention given to the place of 'general principles of law'. However, even prior to that development there were two groups of writers who faced the problem in a more general and comprehensive manner. The question was examined in some detail by several representative writers of the positivist school of international law on the continent of Europe. It was answered, from a different angle, by English writers of the authority of Manning, Maine, Phillimore, and Westlake, who discussed with some thoroughness the relation between Roman law and the Law of Nations.

§4. *The founders of international law and the problem of analogies*

The customary repudiation of private law as a source of international law seems, at first sight, to have received some support both from Grotius and from his forerunners and successors. This fact shows that the controversy is not of recent date, and that the writers of the classical period, who notoriously were relying to a large extent upon Roman and other private law, were not doing so merely owing to their inability to perceive the differences between private law and international law. The problem in its entirety was not examined by the general body of the writers of that period. The great majority do not mention it at all. The isolated utterances, often contradictory of others, have been, rather inconsistently, quoted by modern positivists both as showing that the danger of indiscriminate recourse to analogy was already fully appreciated by the founders of international law and as an instance of the hampering effects of indiscriminate recourse to analogy on the part of classical writers. Both the first and the second inferences are too general not to be misleading. For the problem which confronted those writers was not, on the whole, identical with that which modern international law has to solve, namely, how far analogy is admissible between the rules of two apparently different systems of law (for so they are described) with different subjects and objects. The question before them was how far the law of one ancient Empire may, by reason of its comprehensiveness and its universally recognized conformity with right and justice, be resorted to as a source of international law.

Thus conceived, the question did not present to them a problem at all. For reasons to be stated presently, Roman law, which for most practical purposes was Roman private law, was almost the preordained element in the formation of international law. This was so at the time both prior to the dissolution of the temporal and spiritual unifying bond of the Holy Roman Empire and in the following period in which that unity disappeared and which gave birth to modern international law. It seems strange, at first sight, that Roman law fulfilled that function in periods characterized by different and opposing principles of political organization and obligation. In the Middle Ages Roman law was, to a large extent, coterminous with law. Roman law was the law of the Roman people. 'In a sense', we find Bartolus saying, 'all peoples, who owe obedience to our mother, the Church, belong to the Roman people, including those who by privilege or prescription or some other legal title are no longer within the world embracing dominion of the Roman Emperor'.[1] Moreover, the *jus gentium*, the precursor of the law of nature which was destined to play its great part in the birth and growth of international law – was considered as sanctioned by and as part of Roman law. Also, insofar as Roman law was the law of the *princeps*, it became the law invoked by the territorial rulers, who claimed not to recognize a superior, not only against the vanishing power of the Roman Emperor but also – and above all – against the pretensions of the Papacy to the temporal rule over the world. In fact it was through Roman law that the antique theory of the omnipotent State asserted itself in the late Middle Ages and undermined their unified political structure. For the Roman *princeps*, as represented by the head of the Roman Empire (who was *legibus solutis*), there was substituted the *princeps*, the kings and rulers of the smaller territorial units. The Papacy in the course of its struggle against the kings and princes – it was apparently Innocent the Third who first employed the formula *superiorem non recognoscentes*[2] – aided in that transformation which eventually turned its edge against the Papacy itself. The support which Roman law lent to the claims and doctrines of the rising power of the territorial rulers explains partly – the more substantial explanation lies, as will be seen, in the acceptance of its authority as the repository both of *jus gentium* and *jus naturae*[3] – the use of civilians in international intercourse in the Middle Ages and in the following period. Savigny tells us that between 1273 and 1281 Franciscus Accursius, the great glossator, appears repeatedly as the envoy of Edward I and that most of the famous civilians of the thirteenth and fourteenth centuries, such as Odofredus, Alberic of Rosciat and Bartolus, were employed on diplomatic missions. In Rymer's *Foedera* there is an abundance of information to the same

[1] Woolf, *Bartolus of Sassoferrato* (1913), p. 25.

[2] See Ch. de Visscher, *Théories et realités en droit international public* (1953), p. 21, n. 1.

[3] See Frey, *Das öffentlich-rechtliche Schiedsgericht in Ober-Italien im XII. und XIII. Jahrhundert* (1928), pp. 155 *et seq.*, who points out that when in arbitration agreements in the thirteenth century the parties referred to 'law' as a source of decision, what they had in mind was Roman law. And see Von der Heydte, *Die Geburtsstunde des souveränen Staates* (1952), p. 157.

effect. Beginning with the sixteenth century the use of civilians, largely as represented by the Doctors Commons, becomes a regular occurrence in English diplomatic and international intercourse – an absorbing chapter of legal history to which Nys first drew attention in a valuable essay and which has been recently treated by Lord McNair in revealing and absorbing detail.[1]

However, there were deeper and more pertinent explanations of the part which Roman law played in the formative period of international law. It was not only the fact that for many purposes Roman law was identified with law in general. What was more important was, first, that its individualistic character was particularly suited for regulating the relations of territorial and sovereign units which now had definitely taken the place of the system of political unity of the Western world. Moreover, it was Roman law that for most practical purposes formed the articulate content of natural law, equally individualistic, which – prompted by the ideas of reformation and rising capitalism – became the main ingredient, embodying the aspirations of justice and right reason, of the law which had to be created, the Law of Nations. Max Huber, a great lawyer and humanist writing in 1910, summarized that development in a pregnant sentence: 'The individualistic character of natural law, which made international law appear essentially as a kind of absolute private law at large, while consonant with the principles of the sovereignty of the modern State, at the same time confronted the State with ethical duties and postulated the ethics of international intercourse.'[2]

As that part of Roman law which was most developed and which was, accordingly, most used for the purpose of extracting analogies was private law proper, an examination of the part played by Roman law in the writings of some representative writers of that period is directly germane to the subject under discussion.

§5. *Gentilis*

Thus we find Gentilis urging gravely that civil law must not be cited rashly, and that 'what applies to a State must not be extended beyond the State absurdly'.[3] This attitude he explained by pointing

[1] 'The Debt of International Law in Britain to the Civil Law and the Civilians', in *Grotius Society*, 39 (1953), 183–204.

[2] 'Beiträge zur Kenntnis der soziologischen Grundlagen des Völkerrechts und der Staatengesellschaft', in *Jahrbuch des öffentlichen Rechts*, 4 (1910), 56 (reprinted in his collected writings under the title *Gesellschaft und Humanität* (1948), p. 85).

[3] *Hispanicae advocationis libri duo* (1613), in Scott's 'Classics of International Law', with English transl. by F. F. Abbott (1921), p. 110.

out that while the ancient world constituted a single State the world is now divided into 'separate jurisdictions or principalities'. Probably it was under the influence of these and similar passages that writers express the opinion that Gentilis 'broke away from his predecessors . . . in giving up largely the attempt to cast the Law of Nations in the mould of Roman civil law',[1] or that even when resorting to Roman law he did not refer to it as implying an authoritative solution, but rather as illustrative of certain universal principles.[2]

However, it is not certain that statements such as these convey a correct appreciation of Gentilis's method. Probably the opposite is the case. We can imagine that Gentilis himself, to whom the application of Roman law was not a matter of mere imitation, but a question of principle, would have protested against such an imputation. He had no desire to be classed among the positivists of the day who were issuing warnings against the application of Roman law.[3] He reminded these positivists that 'sana ratio exemplis anteponitur',[4] and that 'nuda historiarum recitatio' is fruitless. 'Facta nos non quaerimus', he says, 'aut ex factis ius constituimus, sed ex iure examinamus facta.'[5] Reliance on Roman law is accordingly a characteristic feature of his writings. Apart from numerous references to it on particular questions,[6] he frequently voices his opinion in a more general form. 'All Sovereign Princes', he says, 'are obliged to be governed by the Civil Law in the disputes between them';[7] 'Every one submits to the Civil Law as to a sort of Law of Nations.'[8] He expresses the same view when giving an account of the instructive incident to which civilians and lawyers of his time devoted much discussion. Philip II, when confronted with the question of succession to the throne of Portugal, rejected the learned opinion of the civilians from the Academy of Coimbra, who, basing themselves on Roman law, decided in favour of the Duke of Bragance. But the Emperor

[1] Abbott, in *Hispanicae advocationis libri duo*, Introduction, p. 19a.

[2] Phillipson, in the *J.C.L.* new series, 12 (1912), 58. See also Nézard, in *Les fondateurs du droit international* (1904), p. 83.

[3] See, for instance, Bodin (to whom he refers), *De la République* (1577), book v, ch. vi.

[4] *De Jure Belli* (1598), book II, ch. xviii.

[5] *Ibid.* book I, ch. xx.

[6] See, for instance, his treatment of military pacts from the point of view whether they are *bonae fidei* or *stricti iuris* (book I, ch. XXII), or of the question of exterritoriality of ambassadors (*De Legationibus* (1585), book II, chs. XVI, XVII, edited in Scott's 'Classics of International Law', with English transl. by Laing, 1924).

[7] *De Jure Belli*, book I, ch. v. See especially the much-quoted passage, *ibid.* ch. III: 'ius etiam, illis perscriptum libris Iustiniani, non civitatis est tantum, sed et gentium, et naturae et aptatum sic est ad naturam universum, ut imperio extincto, et ipsum ius diu sepultum surrexerit tamen, et in omnes se effuderit gentes humanas.'

[8] *Advocatio Hispanica*, book I, ch. xxi.

would not rely even upon the opinion of his own jurists, who urged that disputes between princes should be decided by application of the Law of Nations, and not of the fictions of the law of Justinian. He preferred his own view, namely, that 'Empires are not given or taken away in accordance with the opinions of jurisconsults, but it is necessary to acquire and retain them by recourse to arms.' He acted upon this view with complete success. Gentilis, however, when discussing the question, had no hesitation in affirming that the law of Justinian is not a particular law, but the Law of Nations.[1] In fact, it is as a staunch civilian in matters of international law that he is regarded by writers, frequently not without reproach. From Selden, who emphatically rejected his opinion on the universally binding force of Roman law,[2] and De Ferrière, the historian of Roman law, whose enthusiasm for the subject did not prevent him from pointing, not without some surprise, to the fact that Gentilis had gone so far as to identify Roman law and the Law of Nations,[3] through Ward, who thought that 'Gentilis cramps himself by supposing the Roman law to be the Law of Nations',[4] to modern authors, there is almost complete agreement on this point.[5] Some have attempted to absolve him from a portion of the guilt by referring to passages, mentioned above, in which he exhibits a certain reluctance to adopt a rule of civil law. These passages, however, relate, as may be seen on closer investigation, to such rules of Roman law, mainly public law, as are peculiar to the Roman State and to its time, and which, to use Sir Robert Wiseman's expression, 'look homewards'.[6]

§6. *Grotius*

Grotius himself has become, with regard to the question under discussion, a source of misunderstandings. There is scarcely a chapter in the three books of the *De Jure Belli ac Pacis* in which he does not reject a rule, because, as he says, it belongs to the civil law only and

[1] *De Juri Belli*, book I, ch. iii. For an account of this case, see Sir Arthur Duck, *De Usu et Authoritate Juris Civilis Romanorum in Dominiis Principum Christianorum* (1653), II, ch. vii, §§15, 16.

[2] *Mare Clausum sive de Dominio Maris Libri duo* (1635), book I, ch. xxiv (Needham's transl. 1652, pp. 152–6).

[3] *Histoire du Droit Romain* (1718) (English transl. 1724, p. 136).

[4] *An Enquiry into the Foundation and History of the Law of Nations* (1795), II, 613. See also Reddie, *Inquiries into International Law* (2nd ed. 1851), p. 26.

[5] See, for instance, Kaltenborn, *Die Vorläufer des Hugo Grotius* (1848), p. 231; Holland, *Studies*, p. 22; Vinogradoff, Historical Types of International Law', *Bibliotheca Visseriana*, I (1923), 56; and also Phillipson, in *J.C.L.* new series, 12 (1912).

[6] *The Excellency of the Civil Law* (1656), p. 62.

not to the Law of Nations.[1] Text-books quote eagerly his refusal to acknowledge that 'the contracts of kings and peoples are to be interpreted according to Roman law; except when Roman law has been accepted as belonging to the Law of Nations; which is not lightly to be presumed'.[2] His view on prescription is cited as another example. But there is, on the other hand, no doubt that this work 'bristles with analogies',[3] and Gessner's statement to the effect that Grotius's chapters on treaties read like a Roman private law treatise mixed with natural law ideas[4] is quoted with approval by many authors.

This contradictory attitude, however, is startling only when we forget that some of the difficulties in the writings of Grotius which puzzle the student or the commentator are due to the fact that unfailing exactitude of terminology cannot be regarded as one of the accomplishments of that great lawyer. What confusion has, for instance, been caused as a result of his having chosen to attribute so many different meanings to his conception of *ius gentium*! Similarly, what he understood by civil law is not private law in general or Roman law, but rather positive municipal law, both private and public, in contradistinction to the law prevailing between nations. We see this at the very beginning of his work when he speaks of 'civil law both that of Rome and that of each nation in particular';[5] or of ambassadors who are not bound 'by the civil law of the people among whom they live';[6] or of the 'representatives of provinces, towns and others who are not governed by the Law of Nations but by civil law';[7] or of crimes which, by 'civil law', may justly be punished by death.[8] It is obvious, therefore, that the numerous statements in which he repudiates the use of civil law cannot have the meaning attributed to them now, namely, that of rejection of private law as such. He used the term 'civil law' as connoting rules of

[1] See, for instance, book II, ch. iv, §§10, 12, 13; ch. v, §§7, 10, 15, 29; ch. vi, §§1, 2; ch. vii, §§1, 12.

[2] Book II, ch. xvi, §31.

[3] Dickinson, *The Equality of States in International Law* (1920), p. 50.

[4] Holtzendorff, III, 11. Cf. also Walker, *History*, p. 334.

[5] *Proleg.* 1.—'Jus civile', says Cocceius commenting upon this passage, 'i.e. jus statutarium cujusque populi'. He says again, when commenting upon book II, ch. xvi, §31: '. . . sane si plures gentes idem forte ius suis subditis statuunt, id non est jus gentium, sed jus civile, quod non inter civitates obtinet, sed in singulis saltem civitatibus'. The following passage from book IX, *Dig.*, *de iustit. et iure*, I. i. (taken from Gaius) will illustrate this conception of *ius civile*: 'Nam quod quisque populus ipse sibi constituit, id ipsius proprium civitatis, vocaturque civile.' It is also in this meaning that the term is used by Gentilis; see, e.g., *De Legationibus*, book II, ch. xvii. Cf. here also Fiore, *Code*, p. 83.

[6] Book II, ch. xviii, §4 (Whewell's transl.).

[7] Book II, ch. xviii, §2.

[8] Book II, ch. i, § 14. Cf. also book II, ch. xi, §5, where he deals with the requirements of the validity of promises.

municipal law aiming at the 'tranquillity of *one* community'. And for this civil law he could have no use in a Law of Nations by which he understood rules applicable to the intercourse *between* States and sovereigns.[1]

Secondly, although he did not identify the law of nature with the Law of Nations, he regarded the first as the obvious source from which we may fill the gaps of the 'instituted' Law of Nations. These gaps were wider than the area of rules actually adopted. In this light – in the light of the Grotian acceptance of the law of nature as an independent source of international law – the view of those writers who imputed to Grotius the identification noted above is, after all, not so misleading. For what were the sources or the evidence of this natural law? They, in turn, were in most cases identical with those rules of private and especially of Roman law which appeared to him as of sufficient generality and as suitable for the purposes of international law. 'Rationes saepe optimas suppeditant ad demonstrandum id, quod iuris est naturae; et eidem iuri neque minus gentium iuri testimonium saepe praebent'.[2] He did not accept private law (or Roman law) as having *per se* obligatory force in international law, but he was taking over, under a different name, its rules and principles whenever he deemed it to be evidence of the law of nature applicable to a given case. What the right hand of the builder of a more positivist system – of the *ius gentium voluntarium* – formally rejected (if rejection it was in view of his conception of civil law), the left hand of the great expounder of natural law, of justice, and convenience was adopting with far-reaching thoroughness.[3] This is hardly surprising if we bear in mind the fact that the

[1] This conception of civil law as understood by Grotius is discussed with much lucidity by Textor in his *Synopsis Juris Gentium*, 1680 (edited in Scott's 'Classics of International Law', with English transl. by Bate, 1916). He points out that the Law of Nations embraces law common to all or many nations, both public and private (see ch. viii, 41; ch. ii, 14, 15), and that it is not exclusively public law, although it is akin to public law and politics, 'some of its special topics being matters of the prerogative, like war, peace, treaties, etc.' (ch. i, 12).

[2] *Proleg.* 53.

[3] That it was his constant recourse to Roman law, and not his rejection of it, which was of decisive influence may be seen from the testimony of that great enthusiast of Roman law, Sir Robert Wiseman (*The Excellency of Civil Law*, p. 61). About a hundred years later, J. J. Moser, the positivist, observes dryly that the constant invoking of Grotius for the purpose of proving the admissibility of recourse to Roman law is quite irrelevant, because Grotius's book is a private work which cannot dictate laws to free nations (*Teutsches Staatsrecht* (1738), part II, book I, p. 214). That, on the other hand, some expressions of Grotius were taken in their literal sense may be seen, for instance, from the vigorous attack delivered upon Roman law by Johann Gottfried Heineccius, the influential expounder of the law of nature in its application to states and the commentator of Grotius. He opens his *Elementa Juris Naturae et Gentium* (1737) with a preface solely devoted to the refutation of Roman law as a source of authority in international law: 'Ea tamen

recognition of the essential identity of States and individuals is one of the main features of Grotius's teaching.[1] However, in general – in this as, indeed, in many other matters – it is not possible, without being inaccurate, to say what was Grotius's considered view and practice. They varied – to the point of inconsistency.[2] Their importance lies in their testimony to the ever-present vitality of the problem and in the actual influence which they exercised.

§7. *Bynkershoek*

Bynkershoek too, the positivist, is praised by some writers as a writer who recognized in time the dangers or recourse to Roman law.[3] There is, no doubt, some evidence in his writings to support such an assertion. Thus he states, in one place, that the Roman law 'will not decide questions which belong to the Law of Nations'.[4] In another, he quotes approvingly Wicquefort to the effect that rules of public law cannot be derived from civil or canon law, because the two systems deal with different objects, and different principles must therefore apply to them.[5] But the same Bynkershoek is, on the other hand, extolled as a great admirer of Roman law, and as one whose recourse to it was by no means infrequent.[6] He does not fail to supply an explanation of this apparent inconsistency. He says: 'Non quod in iis quae sola ratio commendat a iure Romano ad ius gentium non tuta sit collectio.' For him 'the reason of the thing' thus becomes the form in which the reception of Roman law takes place. 'Quamvis non de Populi Romani sed de Gentium jurisprudentia agamus', he says in another work, 'non abs re tamen erit de Jure Romano quaedam praemonuisse, cum qui id audit, vocem fere omnium Gentium videatur audire.'[7]

[jurisprudentia Romana] nihil auctoritatis habitura sit in definiendis integrarum gentium litibus et controversiis, quippe, quae inter se non alio iure, quam quod ipsa natura inter homines peraeque constituit, reguntur; iure inquam, illo universali quod in foederibus, pactionibus, conditionibus populorum . . . versatur.' (The English translation of the work appeared in 1789, without the preface.)

[1] See Lauterpacht, in *B.Y.* 23 (1946), 26–30.

[2] See as to this aspect of *De Jure Belli ac Pacis*, Lauterpacht, in *B.Y.* 23 (1946), 4–9.

[3] Phillipson, in *J.C.L.* new series, 9 (1908) 33; Delpech in *Les Fondateurs du Droit International* (1904), pp. 390, 391.

[4] *De Dominio Maris* (1702), ch. ix (p. 95 of Magoffin's transl. in Scott's 'Classics of International Law', 1923).

[5] *De Foro Legatorum* (1721), ch. vii; see also *ibid.* ch. ii and viii *in fine*.

[6] See Phillimore, I, 31.

[7] *De Foro Legatorum*, ch. vi.

§8. *Moser*

J. J. Moser is perhaps the only leading positivist of that period who is consistent in his rejection of Roman law. He regards it as a ridiculous *petitio principii* that disputes between free nations should be decided in accordance with the law of Justinian. He adduces, not without sarcasm, the example of a civilian who advised the King of France to bring an action based on the *Lex Aquilia* against a German prince who invaded his territory. To those who point to the lead given by Grotius in this regard, he gives the curt reply that Grotius's book is a private work with no binding authority attached to it.[1] The reason which explains the consistency of his attitude – whereas the writers mentioned above were not – is easily explained by the fact that the numerous and bulky volumes written by this learned chronicler in no way go beyond a systematic collection of provisions of treaties. It may be said, without disrespect to Moser's prodigious industry, that he obviously neither claims nor attempts a jurisprudential discussion of the principles of international law.[2]

§9. *Neyron*

Finally, Neyron, a writer less known but typical of the authors of monographs written in the seventeenth and eighteenth centuries, may be mentioned as an example of the characteristic attitude of alternately rejecting and adopting Roman law.[3] He complains, on one hand, of the great insecurity and confusion occasioned by exaggerated recourse to civil law, especially with regard to treaties. He shows how frequently Roman law had been used as an instrument in the hands of skilled civilians in order to defeat or to explain away provisions of a binding treaty. At one moment, he says, they discovered a flaw in the form of the treaty; at another, they put forward the plea of lesion, or of restitution on account of minor age, or of duress or fraud, and so on.[4] This went so far that in many treaties a mutual renunciation clause had to be inserted to the effect that both parties renounced the benefits of civil law. Nevertheless, although he is fully alive to the dangers, practical and theoretical of

[1] See above, p. 190, n. 3.

[2] His opinion, mentioned in the text, on the authority of Roman law is expressed in an obscure passage of *Teutsches Staatsrecht*, part II, book I, p. 214. For a melancholy, but true and accurate, account of the results of the uncompromisingly positivist method adopted by Moser, see Verdross, in *Z.ö.R.* 3 (1923), 16–102.

[3] He is the author of an excellent monograph entitled *Essai historique et politique sur les Garanties* (1777).

[4] *Ibid.* p. 70.

recourse to analogy – he speaks of the 'difference of relations between individuals subject to authority and equal nations' – he devotes a whole chapter to the 'Advantages brought by Roman Law to Public Treaties', and impresses upon the reader the fact that 'many principles of Roman law, salutary in themselves and independent of Roman constitutions, have been adopted by the European Powers and retained by reason of their intrinsic value until today'.[1]

§10. *Modern international law. The positivist school in Germany*

In turning to more modern international law, we are confronted once more with the same picture of alternate rejection and adoption of the recourse to private law, its repudiation in form going hand in hand with its adoption in substance, although under the more acceptable designation of 'concepts of universal jurisprudence' or 'general principles of law'. In fact, a great deal of the discussion on the subject has since followed a not unfamiliar pattern of doctrinal dialectics. Recession from an increasingly untenable position begins with a renewal of the attack; the withdrawal, dignified and orderly, takes place under the cover of a terminological device. On the face of it, there was in the second part of the nineteenth century no change from the position previously adopted except that the object of the attack changed in so far as Roman law was replaced largely by private law in general. This may be seen especially in the German positivist jurisprudence. Although Heffter, who adopted the private law division into persons, things, and obligations, and who omitted no opportunity of moulding international law relationships into institutions of private law, was the most influential German international lawyer of his time, there was the increasing tendency to eliminate altogether private law as a source of international law. The movement begins with warnings against exaggerated use of analogy; it does not yet exclude it as a matter of principle. Moreover, some writers expressly urge the admissibility, within limits, of recourse to analogy. Meier admits, in his *Abschluss der Staatsverträge*, that rules of international law are often only deductions from private law, and he adds: 'Arguments drawn from private law are *per se* permitted, although they ought to be used with caution.'[2] Bergbohm still adheres to the same opinion, although, as an avowed positivist, he allows only for a partial identification of international treaties – not, however, of law-making treaties – with private law contracts.[3]

[1] *Ibid.* p. 76. [2] (1874), p. 38.
[3] *Staatsverträge und Gesetze als Quellen des Völkerrechts* (1877), p. 79.

But the rejection of private law on the ground of wider juridical principle was receiving the support of writers of the authority of Holtzendorff and Bulmerincq. The first rejects not only Roman law, 'the analogies to which are more misleading than enlightening',[1] but also the recourse to private law in general. He says: 'It can hardly be maintained that international law may, in deciding disputes between States (which are independent), follow the analogy of private relations between individuals (who are permanently subject to authoritative legislation).'[2] Bulmerincq, who follows the same line of argument, is even more emphatic. He asserts that frequent recourse to analogy has impeded the growth of international law, and that it should never have been undertaken.[3] However, although we see here already the beginnings of a more systematic treatment of the problem, there is hardly an attempt to explain what appears to be its crux: how, after all, do conceptions of private law enter into the corpus of international public law and remain embedded there while even the most sweeping positivism is unable to eliminate them?

§11. *Jellinek, H.B. Oppenheim, Nippold, Triepel. 'Conceptions of universal jurisprudence'*

Here, as in many other directions, the important step has been taken by Jellinek. This great lawyer made only casual excursions into the domain of international law, but where he did so his influence was by no means negligible. He rejects, in principle, any analogy whatever. There is, to his mind, no justification for applying conceptions of a self-contained system of law as a *ius cogens* in a quite different sphere of law.[4] Analogy, he says, can only be permitted when it is expressly recognized as a source of law by a given system of law. But how are we to explain the actual similarity of rules which exists, for instance, between the law of private contracts and of international treaties? The explanation, he points out, consists in the fact that both private and international law contracts are 'universal conceptions of law', conceptions of general jurisprudence to which by the very nature of things similar rules must apply. Accordingly, these rules are not taken from private law, 'although private law has raised the universal element of contract into scientific legal consciousness'.[5]

[1] Holtzendorff, I, 72.
[2] *Ibid.* p. 126.
[3] *Praxis, Theorie und Codification des Völkerrechts* (1874), p. 130.
[4] *Die rechtliche Natur der Staatenverträge* (1880), p. 51.
[5] *Ibid.* p. 51.

This view was not altogether original. It had been expressed as far back as 1845 by H. B. Oppenheim, who in his *System des Völkerrechts* voiced the opinion that analogy to private law is to be rejected, or, when used, to be applied *cum grano salis*.[1] To approach problems of public international law from the angle of private law is, to his mind, as disruptive in the field of international law as the idea of State contract was in the sphere of political theory.[2] But, he adds, this does not apply to the relation between international law and the philosophy and logic of law. Thus the notion of property cannot be altered, no matter who is the subject of that right; neither can the nature of contract be different in international law, for instance, with regard to the rule that only a free declaration of will constitutes a binding obligation. This is also true of the rule *pacta tertiis nec nocent nec prosunt* or *nemo plus iuris in alterum transferre potest quam ipse habet*. However, it needed Jellinek's authority to establish this theory of the legal universality of some notions common to different branches of law.

Nippold, in a comprehensive examination of treaties, follows closely this line of argument, and, adopting Jellinek's view on the question, concludes the chapter on the relation between international and private law with the following strong appeal: 'It is an obvious task of the theory of international law to cease looking towards other branches of law, to constitutional or private law, for this is as unjustifiable as the artificial filling of the unfortunately small building of international law with natural law ideas or political maxims.'[3] As a precaution and a remedy against mechanical borrowing from private law, he advises the creation and adequate development of a general science of law which should include conceptions common to all branches of jurisprudence. From this source international law could draw the necessary reinforcements without having recourse to private law. Thus, with special reference to treaties, he says: 'The notion of contract is part . . . of general conceptions of law. Consequently, rules which follow from those notions apply equally to treaties in international law. For the latter is governed by general principles of law in the same way as private law.'[4] In the light of this statement, which is unobjectionable, the thrust against private law assumes the complexion of dialectics.

Triepel, one of the most influential German authors prior to the

[1] (2nd ed. 1866), p. 8.
[2] *Ibid.* p. 80.
[3] *Der völkerrechtliche Vertrag, seine Stellung im Rechtssystem und seine Bedeutung für das internationale Recht* (1894), p. 91.
[4] *Ibid.* p. 88.

First World War, was typical both in his emphatic rejection of private law and in the recognition, in substance, of its effective part as a source of international law. His attitude, actuated by the desire to establish the formal dualism of international and municipal law, may be briefly stated. He does not deny that international law has, in the past, taken over large parts of private and especially of Roman law; in common with other writers he explains this as being due to the domination of the natural law tendency in the formative period of international law, and to the fact that the Roman law, the *ratio scripta*, was regarded as approximating very closely to the law of nature. But he denies that international law of today has accepted those principles. This, he urged, was undoubtedly the case in the international practice at the time of the predominance of the patrimonial conception; however that method is not only, as Bluntschli says, unworthy of our time, but it is simply a matter of the past.[1] There remain only the cases in which States stand in economic relations to one another, as, for instance, when they lend money to one another, when they take over a collective guarantee for a loan, when they enter into actual economic partnership, and so on.[2] What rules are to be applied here if treaties are silent and if there is no custom forthcoming to fill the gap? Triepel denies that there is, even here, any need to apply a particular rule of private law, or that Roman law forms an exception to the general rule.[3] He then proceeds, in the approved manner, to modify substantially the negative attitude thus adopted. He points out that the damage resulting from that attitude is negligible, considering that there remains that eternal source of all law which we call morality or the reason of the thing, and on which we may fall back whenever necessary. Thus when, e.g., private law rules of contract and international law rules regarding treaties happen to be identical, they are not so as a result of analogy or deliberate adoption, but in consequence of the very nature of things. Jellinek, nearly two decades before, used almost identical language: 'The relations of States give rise necessarily and by the very nature of things to principles identical with those which derive from private law.'[4]

[1] *Völkerrecht und Landesrecht* (1899) (transl. into French in 1920); see especially the chapter dealing with private law, pp. 211–25.

[2] For instances, see *ibid.* pp. 222–3.

[3] See, however, Triepel, in *Hague Recueil*, I (1923), 101, where he admits that to certain treaties with private law contents rules of private law of one of the contracting parties may be applied.

[4] *Die rechtliche Natur der Staatsverträge* (1880), p. 51.

Most German writers, fortified by the authority of Triepel, combined iconoclasm with expectancy stemming from the realization of the potentialities of 'general principles of jurisprudence'. 'International law', says Liszt, 'is an independent branch of law . . .; that does not mean that the rich spiritual output of private law cannot be used for the purposes of international law. What really takes place is a developing of general notions and principles common to all law (general jurisprudence).'[1] However, many writers continued to support their views on controversial subjects by referring to the devastating influence of private law. With them it was a commonplace to speak with regret of the damage done to international law by obsolete private law analogies.[2] Authors often hoped to obtain a tactical advantage by suggesting that their opponents' standpoint was nothing more than an obsolete private law analogy.[3] The warning 'beware of private law' became a catchword uncritically accepted, eagerly copied, and widely disseminated. Its prestige continued undimmed by the fact that the banished phantom reappeared with some regularity under the garb of 'general jurisprudence' or some such concept.

§12. *English authors on the application of Roman law: Zouche, Sir Robert Wiseman*

Although the apparently – we need not put it higher than that – negative attitude of German positivist writers gained much promin-

[1] Liszt, p. 79; cf. also Ullmann, *Völkerrecht* (1908), p. 248. It is of interest to note the similar opposition in Germany to the application of conceptions of private law in the field of administrative public law, as well as the reluctant acquiescence in the use of some of them as universal conceptions of law. See, for instance, Jellinek, *System der subjektiven öffentlichen Rechte* (1892), p. 62 (as such conceptions he regards those of negligence, error, condition, set-off, prescription), Tezner, in *Archiv für öffentliches Recht*, 9 (1894), 563, and recently Meier-Branecke, *ibid.* new series, 11 (1926) (ii), 230–85.

[2] See, for instance, Strupp, *Das völkerrechtliche Delikt* (1920), p. 57, n. 1; the same in Schücking, *Das Werk von Haag* (1914), II, 128. See also Ruegger in *Z.I.* 28 (1919–20), 427; Schönborn, *Staatensukzessionen* (1913), *passim*; Hofer, *Der Schadenersatz im Landkriegsrecht* (1913), who devotes a whole chapter to the question of the influence of private law (pp. 16–22); the author, however, follows the well-trodden path adopted by the writers mentioned in the text.

[3] This method of approach is not limited to the orthodox school of positivist writers. Even recent writers of unimpeached independence of thought, who discuss questions of international law on the basis of 'the pure discipline of law' (*reine Rechtslehre*), exhibit here a deplorable lack of original judgment. See, e.g., Henrich, *Theorie des Staatsgebietes* (1922), *passim*, and Kunz in Strupp, *Wört*, I, 627 and II, 340. Spiropulos in *Z.I.* 35 (1925–6), 129, repeats H. B. Oppenheim's phrase (*System des Völkerrechts*, p. 7) on the 'eternal and inalienable rights' protected by international law; he is, however, a staunch believer in 'general principles of law'. And see his *Théorie générale dudroit international public* (1830), for a balanced account (pp. 97 *et seq.* and especially p. 101, n. 3). See, on the other hand, Fleischmann's note 2, at p. 79 of his edition of Liszt, as an indication of a more critical attitude.

ence in international jurisprudence both in and outside Germany, it would nevertheless be a mistake to assume that it alone held the field. In fact, it seems that British and American international jurists adopted an attitude which, it is believed, is more in keeping with the history and the organic growth of international law. It is true that English writers in the nineteenth century confined themselves to one part of the investigation only, namely, to that of the authority of Roman law as a source of international law. Within these limits, however, their answer to the question is, with scanty exceptions, in the affirmative. They adopt Roman private law not only as a source of international law in the historical sense, i.e., as evidence of the part played by Roman law in the formation of the Law of Nations, but also as a living source from which its numerous gaps may be filled. Unlike the continental writers, they never discarded the idea that Roman law is the source most likely to contain the 'reason of the thing' on many a question of international law. Indeed, it may be said that the great respect for Roman law and the acknowledgment of its importance as a subsidiary source of international law have become one of the characteristic features of British international jurisprudence. We have seen how strongly Gentilis, Grotius's most scientific predecessor and Professor of Civil Law at Oxford adhered to this view. Such was also the attitude of one of his successors at Oxford, the distinguished civilian and 'second founder of international law', the positivist Richard Zouche. His classification of both the law of peace and that of war into *status*, *dominium*, *debitum*, and *delictum* is based on Roman law, and he refers to the laws of Rome on many controversial subjects.[1] Dr Arthur Duck, the learned civilian and Zouche's colleague at Oxford, was at the same time extolling the virtues of Roman law as a source of the Law of Nations.[2] Three years later appeared that enthusiastic essay of Sir Robert Wiseman, an eminent practitioner in the Court of Admiralty, entitled: *The Law of Laws: or, the Excellency of the Civil Law, above all other Human Laws whatsoever. Shewing of how great use and necessity the Civil Law is to the Nation.*[3] The author took it for granted that the authority of Roman law extends to the Law of Nations, 'under the regulations of which come Embassies, courteous entertainment of

[1] *Juris et Judicii fecialis*, etc. (1650). See Holland's Introduction to the Classics edition (1911), p. xiv; Phillipson, in *J.C.L.* new series, 9 (1908), 285–6; Scelle in *Les Fondateurs du Droit International*, pp. 276–77.

[2] *De Usu et Authoritate Juris Civilis Romanorum in Dominiis Principum Christianorum* (1653), especially book I, ch. ii ('De Justitia et Encomiis Legum Romanorum').

[3] First ed. 1656.

foreigners and strangers, Laws of Arms, freedom of Traffique, right of Contracts, free passage through each other's Borders, Reprizalls, the preserving and redemption of captives, Leagues, Truces, Articles and such like'.[1] He admitted that not the whole Roman law may be resorted to, especially that 'circumstantial and positive part which was a Law to the Romans . . . being made for that people, climate and government only'.[2] 'But', he says, 'there is in it too a Law whereunto by the light of Reason men find themselves bound in that they are Men . . . a Law that may be applied to the communion and fellowship of all Mankind, or divers Nations . . .'[3] With regard to that law he entertained no doubt that it has been accepted by the general consent of nations as binding in disputes between them.[4] Lord Stowell was only giving expression to a widely held opinion[5] when, in the case of *The Maria*, he professed to act on the view that the Law of Nations is to a large extent based upon civil law.[6]

§13. *Nineteenth-century writers: Manning, Maine, Phillimore, Westlake*

The attitude of the nineteenth-century English writers does not differ appreciably from that adopted by the above-mentioned representatives of the Oxford School. The traditions of Doctors' Commons had not become extinct. From Manning, Maine and Phillimore to Westlake, they are almost unanimous in their opinion regarding the capacity of Roman law to serve as a source of international rule at hand. Roman law is, indeed, regarded as that general or universal science of law the development of which continental writers considered to be an urgent task of jurisprudence. William Oke Manning, one of the early writers of the nineteenth century, does not hesitate to explain the fact 'of the systematic writers on the Law of Nations having all been foreigners' by the absence in England

[1] *Ibid.* p. 60.

[2] *Ibid.* p. 63.

[3] *Ibid.*

[4] *Ibid.* pp. 65, 146, 156.

[5] Cf. here the passage in Edmund Burke's *Letters on the Proposals for Peace with the Regicide Directory of France*, 1797 (*The Works and Correspondence of Edmund Burke* (1852 ed.), v, 307), where the author, while pointing out that 'It has ever been the method of public jurists to draw a great part of the analogies, on which they form the Laws of Nations, from the principles of law which prevail in civil community', proceeds himself to construe the relations arising out of the dangers emanating from revolutionary France on the basis of the Roman law of neighbourhood pertaining to the *operis novi nunciatio*.

[6] 1 C. Rob. 363. And see *The Anna*, 5 C. Rob. 373, for the application, in relation to a group of small mud islands of the mouth of the Mississippi River, of the maxim of Roman law *quod vis fluminis de tuo praedio detraxenit, et vicino praedio attulerit, palam tuum remanet.* See Lord McNair in *Grotius Society*, 39 (1953), pp. 196–8, for an estimate, from this point of view, of Lord Stowell, whom he describes 'as the greatest of all our civilians'.

of a well-ordered study of Roman law.[1] Sir Henry Maine is even more emphatic. He describes it as an absurdity that England should appear on the stage of international affairs unequipped with the knowledge of Roman law.[2] Sir Robert Phillimore, speaking of the 'reason of the thing' as a source of international law, pays a weighty tribute to Roman law: '. . . To all nations, whatsoever and wheresoever, this Law presents the unbiassed judgment of the calmest reason, tempered by equity, and rendered perfect, humanly speaking, by the most careful and patient industry that has ever been practically applied to the affairs of civilized man.'[3] He goes so far as to assert the admissibility of recourse to Roman law in the case of interpretation of treaties between European and Asiatic nations.[4]

Westlake enumerates as sources of international law: custom, reason and Roman law. He says: 'The rules which flowed into international law from this source are now incorporated with the customary Law of Nations, and such is the respect still generally entertained for Roman law, which has been called written reason, that this part of the customary law is never contradicted even by the seekers after international right.'[5] These authors may fairly be regarded as representative of the general attitude of English writers on this question. The inquiry, interesting from many points of view, as to why the writers of a nation whose law preserved, with very slight exceptions, its complete independence of Roman law,[6]

[1] *Commentaries on the Law of Nations* (1839), p. vi. It is interesting to note how closely the idea of a universal jurisprudence is connected by Amos, Manning's editor in 1875, with the affirmative view on Roman law: 'It may be expected that one of the indirect consequences of the revived study of Roman law in England and of the growing desire to have the Law of Nations republished in a systematic form, will be the introduction of a common language of universal application in the wording of treaties' (at p. 129).

[2] He writes in 1856 in the *Cambridge Essays*: 'Englishmen . . . will always be more signally at fault than the rest of the world in attempting to gain a clear view on the Law of Nations. There cannot be a doubt that our success in negotiations is sometimes perceptibly affected by our neglect of Roman law.' See also Maine, pp. 20, 21, 26–9.

[3] Phillimore, I, 34. Similarly, Creasy, *First Platform of International Law* (1876), pp. 83–5, 205; and Wildman, *Institutes of International Law* (1849), pp. 22–4.

[4] Phillimore, I, p. 36.

[5] Westlake, I, p. 15.

[6] For whatever may have been the influence of Roman law on Bracton, or on the teaching of law at the universities (the Oxford School of Civil Law), or on the form of legal theory and of the science of law, or in the ecclesiastical courts, or in the Court of Admiralty and on the Law Merchant, and whatever may have been the reasons which were inducing, from time to time, different writers to urge the importance of teaching Roman law in English universities, the overwhelming weight of authority seems to be to the effect that its actual influence on English law as such is exceedingly small. See Pollock and Maitland, *The History of English Law* (1898), II, 131–5, 193–7, 333–7; Pollock, *A First Book of Jurisprudence* (3rd ed. 1911), p. 343; Scrutton, *The Influence of Roman Law on the Law of England* (1885).

remained staunch advocates of its applicability to international law, cannot be enlarged upon in this monograph.[1]

§14. *Lorimer*

It is James Lorimer, the eminent Scottish international lawyer, who seems to have made by far the most independent contribution to the question. In an article entitled 'Prolegomena to a Reasoned System of International Law',[2] he discusses the question whether international law may legitimately look for guidance to that department of jurisprudence in which positive law has long been a reality, namely, in municipal law. He concedes that the analogy between the units of private and international law is an imperfect one and that it breaks down in many directions. But although he admits that caution

[1] The reason for this affirmative attitude to Roman law so far as international law is concerned lies, if a short explanation may be ventured with diffidence, in the fact that English writers on international law, although following closely the practice of States, had never lost sight of what may be called the natural law foundation of international law. Sir Frederick Pollock suggests that to ignore this would mean ignoring the pronouncements of the most authoritative English judges and writers (see *Essays in the Law* (1922), n. 67.) This was notwithstanding the fact that the expression 'natural law' was not popular with English lawyers and that they preferred to use the term 'reason' (see the significant passage in *Doctor and Student*, Dial. 1, c. 5, in Pollock, *The Expansion of the Common Law* (1904), p. 109; and, by the same author, *Essays in the Law* (1922), p. 69, and *The League of Nations* (2nd ed. 1922), p. 28). Bryce expresses the same view in an article on the Law of Nature (*Studies in History and Jurisprudence*, II (1901), 164). He points to the Indian Code of Civil Procedure of 1882, which lays down that a foreign judgment is not operative as a bar if it is '... contrary to natural justice', and to the Courts in the British Indies, which are directed to apply 'the principles of justice, equity, and good conscience'. But whatever may have been the fate of the 'law of nature' in English law proper, it has never been totally discarded from the British conception of international law. With it, Roman law was being retained as embodying those legal rules which in the formative period of international law were deemed to give expression to the precepts of the law of nature. The fact is also not unimportant that the Court of Admiralty, which came into actual contact with many a question of international law, was engaged in administering the law maritime, a system founded, *inter alia*, upon Roman law, whose authority it successfully defended for a long time from the encroachments of the Courts of Common Law. It is also of interest to note that nearly all those writers who stressed the importance of Roman law for the Law of Nations were either practitioners or judges of the Court of Admiralty. On the whole, it seems natural that the cult and study of Roman law, diverted by historical circumstances from influencing English municipal law, should have asserted themselves in the field of international law (see Scrutton, *The Influence of Roman Law*, pp. 170–6; Senior, *Doctors' Commons and the Old Court of Admiralty* (1922); Holdsworth, *Sources and Literature of English Law* (1925), pp. 234–5; and also Nys, *Le droit Romain, le droit des gens et le collège des docteurs en droit civil* (1910), especially pp. 72–102). Lord McNair in his paper on 'The Debt of International Law in Britain to the Civil Law and the Civilians', in *Grotius Society*, 39 (1953), 183, goes further than the submissions of this note and suggests that the 'reception' of international law in England in the sixteenth and seventeenth centuries was due to two factors: its identification with the civil law and the labours of the civilian lawyers in England.

[2] *Studies, National and International* (1890), pp. 148–63.

is necessary, he urges that it must not become the guiding consideration. For, he says,

all analogies are imperfect in this respect, and yet the whole of our reasoning from experience . . . is reasoning from extremely imperfect analogies between past and present occurrences. The question is not, Are the conditions of the two problems the same? – for that may always be answered in the negative – but, Do they resemble each other closely enough for the old solution to be so modified as to apply to the new problem, or to suggest an analogous solution which may be applied to it?

He points out the exaggerations of which the founders of international law have become guilty while giving an affirmative reply to the question, and how frequently they rendered international law 'hidebound' by maxims and subtleties of Roman jurisprudence. This, however, does not affect his final judgment:

But the notion that, as in dealing with international relations they were still dealing with human rights and duties, the definitions which they had received in one class of relations might throw light on those which must be given to them in another class of relations, though differing considerably, was, I believe, a true notion. It is a notion, consequently, on which I have not hesitated to fall back.[1]

§15. *The American writers*

The American writers do not appear to have devoted special attention to the subject in question; they share, on the whole, the view of British authors. 'The introduction and study of the civil law', says Chancellor Kent in his *Commentaries on International Law*, 'must have also contributed largely to more correct and liberal views of the rights and duties of nations.'[2] Taylor considered it impossible to comprehend international law without some understanding of Roman jurisprudence, which he regards as constituting the philosophical basis of the Law of Nations.[3] Halleck, who, like Manning, connects the problem of Roman law with the demand for a universal jurisprudence, says:

It will generally be found that the deficiencies of precedent, usage, and express international authority may be supplied from the rich treasury o the Roman Civil Law. Indeed, the greater number of controversies between States would find a just solution in this comprehensive system of

[1] *Ibid.* p. 159. For an assessment of the wider significance of Lorimer's teaching, see Jenks, in *Grotius Society* 26 (1940), 35–65 and Campbell, *ibid.* 39 (1953), 211–29.

[2] (2nd ed. by Abdy, 1878), p. 26.

[3] *A Treatise on International Public Law* (1901), pp. 20–1.

practical equity, which furnishes principles of universal jurisprudence, applicable alike to individuals and to States.[1]

§16. *The French and Italian school: Rivier*

The French writers, such as Bonfils,[2] Despagnet,[3] and others, discuss at length the sources of international law and its relation to international private law, to constitutional law, to morality, to international courtesy, to politics and diplomacy, but no mention is made of private law proper. The same may be said of Italian writers in the nineteenth century. Subsequently, Italian positivists followed the German lead by either repudiating altogether the application of private law or by favouring the so-called conceptions of general jurisprudence. Thus Anzilotti, the leading Italian positivist, more than once gave expression to his disapproval of any recourse whatsoever to rules of private law. Similar was the attitude of Cavaglieri.[4]

That, on the other hand, the influence of the English approach was not confined to English-speaking countries may be seen in the treaties of Rivier, the Swiss–Belgian writer, who dealt with the matter in a comprehensive manner.[5] He approved of the application not only of Roman law but also of private law rules in general, although he advised a certain amount of caution.[6] When discussing the meaning of the phrase 'general principles of jurisprudence' used in arbitration treaties, he was clearly of the view that in the absence of the declared will of the parties the rules of Roman law, being common to various peoples of the international community, must be applied.[7]

§17. *Examination of the problem. The 'general jurisprudence' of the positivist school as connoting general principles of private law*

The insistence, so persistently voiced by the positivist school, on the complete independence of international law from private law could be regarded as well founded only if it could be shown: (I) that writers advocating a refutation of private law are able to maintain it in their own writings without introducing the rejected private

[1] *International Law* (4th ed. by Barker, 1908), p. 61; see also Davis, *The Elements of International Law* (3rd ed. 1908), p. 22. See, however, Hudson, quoted below, p. 35.

[2] Fauchille, I, part I, nos. 63 (4)–70.

[3] *Cours de droit international public* (4th ed. by Boeck, 1910), p. 55.

[4] Cavaglieri, pp. 100–1; and in *Rivista*, 16 (1924), 29.

[5] Rivier, I, 34; II, 123.

[6] 'Il faut procéder avec prudence et *mutandis mutatis*, en tenant compte toujours du motif de la règle et des conditions qu'elle suppose, ainsi que des obstacles que peuvent mettre à son application d'autres principes admis en droits des gens.'

[7] Rivier, II, 175. See, however, Nys, I, 206; and Calvo, I, 165.

law in a disguised form or under a different name; (2) that such refutation was in accordance with the practice of States; (3) that the judicial and arbitral settlement of international disputes is practicable and in fact takes place without recourse to private law rules and analogies. For, should an examination of the relevant literature show that this iconoclasm is only a matter of form and not of substance, and that it is opposed to the practice of States and international tribunals, then, obviously, that attitude is as inconsistent with the very principles of the positivist teaching as it is inaccurate in fact. This section is devoted to a preliminary examination of the first of the three questions; it will also indicate the manner in which the following chapters will deal with the two other aspects of the problem.[1]

[1] No attempt can be made here at a historical account of the recourse had to Roman law in the formative period of international law. This task, although it cannot be pursued here, is an urgent one. For the usual sweeping statement to the effect that early writers profusely and indiscriminately resorted to private law, is of little use. The literature on the subject is certainly exhaustive so far as the seventeenth and eighteenth centuries are concerned, especially in Germany. The problem is there, as a rule, treated in connection with the application of Roman law to public and constitutional law and to the mutual relations of the numerous independent German States, but the monographs in question throw, at the same time, ample light on the problem of the authority of Roman law in connection with international public law. Triepel mentions, for instance, the dissertation of Blütemeister, *De usu juris Romani aliorumque privatorum jurium in decidendis controversiis liberarum gentium* (1692). Of a similar character are: Engelbrecht, *De usu Juris Romani in Jure publico Romano-Germanico, huiusque variis Controversiis decidendis* (1692); M. H. Gribner, *De Proejudicio Principum Imperii ex abusu Juris Justiniani* (1717); U. Obrecht, *De Usu Juris Civilis in decidendis controversiis publicis* (about 1720).

However, even more instructive are the numerous writings on individual subjects of international law whose number in the seventeenth and eighteenth centuries seems to be much larger than in the two following centuries. Ompteda, for instance, gives in his *Literatur des gesammten sowohl natürlichen als positiven Völkerrechts* (1785, II, 512–14) a list of seventeen monographs on prescription written between 1710 and 1775, nearly all of them professing to deal with the question whether the private and Roman law rules relating to prescription had application as between States. Nearly as great is the number of authors writing on treaties of guarantee. Treaties of guarantee are of particular interest in this connection as showing how vast are the opportunities which that literature offers to the historian of international law, notably in connection with the subject of this book. How far, for instance, are the *warranti* or *reponsales* the result of a conscious application of the notion of *fideiussores* of Roman law and of the principles of suretyship as developed in pirvate law? The answer so far given by modern writers is conflicting and unsatisfactory. Some elaborate the distinction between guarantee in private and international law, pointing especially to the fact that while the former is of an accessory character, the second is not (see, e.g., Geffcken in Holtzendorff, III, 90, or Quabbe, *Die völkerrechtliche Garantie* (1911), pp. 69–91, who stresses the Gallo-Germanistic character of treaties of guarantee). Others insist on the fundamental identity of the two. Cf., e.g., Idman (*Le Traité de Garantie* (1913), pp. 84–7), who, however, denies the Roman law origin of treaties of guarantee. But it is of interest to note how Neyron (*op. cit.* p. 80), who cannot be charged with blind allegiance to Roman law, regards the notion of guarantee as an instance of the beneficent influence of Roman law; this is so although he stresses his consciousness of the differences in the application of the idea of suretyship in the two spheres of law. It is in a thorough investigation of the vast literature of that period, and not in the somewhat

As has been shown there is no good reason for generalizing the occasional rejection of Roman or private law by some of the writers of the classical period. The generally accepted view that they relied largely on that source remains unshaken – although it has often erred on the side of imputing to them an uncritical and rather naïve imitation of private law. For the resort to analogy was, with the majority of them, a method adopted deliberately and not without weighing the opposing considerations. In cases in which their repudiation of the rules of Roman and private law as such was genuine and consistent – and it was so only to a small extent – it was often counterbalanced by the fact that they were appealing, freely and without reserve, to Roman law as embodying the principles of the law of nature and right reason.

More difficult was the position of those modern positivist writers who found themselves rejecting not only private law but also the law of nature. Being unable to afford the consistency of totally ignoring both private and natural law, they put in their place 'the reason of the thing', 'the demands of logic', and 'the principles of general jurisprudence'. It is significant that many of those writers who were anxious to eliminate the application of private law regarded as essential for the development of international law the creation of a science embracing the general concepts of law common to all systems, international and municipal, private and public – this science to be called general jurisprudence. We have seen that it is, *inter alia*, from this source that they explain the identity of the rules governing international treaties and private law contracts. They foresaw the danger of this general jurisprudence becoming a purely abstract philosophy of law – the very natural law from which they wished to purify the science of international law. General jurisprudence must therefore, according to them, be empirical, i.e., drawn by means of generalizing induction from the existing systems of law.

However, it was here that they were confronted with a real – and, to them, insoluble – difficulty. A system of general jurisprudence meant as a generalization from existing systems of law, national and international, can possess a substantive meaning only when there are in existence developed systems of law, private and international, which form the constituent elements of the higher synthesis. Now, it was clear that in cases in which writers resorted to so-called general

uncritically accepted catchword on the now obsolete influence of the patrimonial theories of the State, that there will be found the explanation of the frequent use of Roman law in the literature and the practice of international law of that period.

jurisprudence, international law as such did not contribute towards this synthesis; it simply drew from that source when it found that its own rules, which it was called upon to develop in a comparatively short time and in conditions in which the border-line between law and mere force is often indistinguishable, afforded no answer. When, for instance, Liszt says that the *sedes materiae* of condition (treaties under a condition) is general jurisprudence, he needs must mean general jurisprudence of private law.[1] When, in international disputes, rules of general jurisprudence are referred to, what is meant is that not a rule of one particular system of private law is to be applied, but only such a rule – usually a private law rule – as has gained recognition by the general body of civilized nations. This is so for the simple reason that international law has not, in the particular sphere, developed any rules of its own. In fact, there would be no need to have recourse to general jurisprudence, if there were an international law rule ready at hand. Natural law performed, in the classical period, the function of a bridge between international and private law; it was the cover from under which international law drew from the rich source of private, notably Roman, law. In the days of the predominance of positivist tendencies it was 'general jurisprudence' which was called in to fulfil this function.

General jurisprudence is a useful and necessary notion for the purposes both of international practice and of the judicial settlement of international disputes so long as it remains clear that what we understand by that notion are rules which international law does not yet possess, but which have been evolved in the various systems of national law. Naturally enough, it is of rules of private law that we think primarily in this connection and not of general principles of criminal, constitutional or administrative law. For these are branches of public law concerned with the government of the State and the duties, enforced by criminal sanction, of the individual to the community. They have, as yet, a distinctly limited place in the relations of States whose undeniable subordination to international law – no international law is conceivable under any other hypothesis – does not alter the fact that it is primarily of a consensual, contractual character. From that point of view there is more than a manner of speech in the phrase that international law is private law writ

[1] See Rapisardi-Mirabelli, *I limiti d'obbligatorietà delle norme giuridiche internazionali* (1922), pp. 86–90, and Liszt, p. 245. See also Werveke, in *R.I.*, 3rd series, 1 (1920), 238–51, on acquisition of sovereignty under a resolutive condition in connection with Article 34 of the Treaty of Versailles, and, with regard to the Tacna-Arica dispute, see Lauterpacht, *Analogies*, pp. 291–2.

large. For the same reason, although rules of evidence and procedure are of importance also in criminal law and elsewhere, it is those rules of evidence and procedure which have developed in private law which are – and have proved to be – relevant to the purposes of international law. Moreover, unless the close connection between private law and general principles of law is sufficiently realized, the very notion of general principles of law – which is intrinsically elastic – assumes a complexion of uncertainty which tends to deprive it of much of its value. This explains why positivist writers, confronted with the application of general principles of law, almost universally held as such, to the relations of States, have often expressed doubts as to its quality as a general principle of law. Is, for instance, the notion of succession a general conception of all jurisprudence, as is maintained by some writers?[1] What may safely be said is that it is a general notion of municipal, notably of private, law. But its application, in the ordinary meaning attached to it, has been denied, in international law, by some positivist writers, The principle *res transit cum suo onere* is regarded by the great majority of writers[2] as an obviously general principle, but even this has been questioned by some positivists. It has almost become a truism that treaties being contracts – a universal legal conception – they are governed by principles of general jurisprudence; but the identification for this purpose, of treaties and contracts has been criticized.[3] Although, in deference to an obvious requirement of general jurisprudence, the vitiating effect of mistake and fraud is widely admitted, there are writers who deny that these rules of private law are applicable to international treaties. The recognition, by a tribunal of the Permanent Court of Arbitration, of the payment of interest as a general mode of fulfilment of pecuniary obligations has been subjected to severe criticism by several positivist writers, although others allege that modes of payment and fulfilling of obligations are general juridical categories not confined to private law.[4] Prescription, which is generally regarded as a principle common to all branches of law, is denounced by others as a purely private law notion. It would seem that it is a general principle of law that the

[1] See Cavaglieri, *Rivista*, 16 (1924), 29; he calls it 'un concetto generale, pertinente ad un' unica categoria, che si presenta nei vary rami del diritto, assumendo per ognuno di essi atteggiamenti specifici'; see also Guggenheim, p. 43, and Schönborn, *Staatensukzessionen* (1913), p. 3.

[2] Cf. Oppenheim, I, 147.

[3] Cf. Niemeyer, *Völkerrecht*, p. 126; Mayer in *Archiv für öffentliches Recht*, 38 (1918) (i), 8, 9; and Hudson in the *Cornell Law Quarterly*, 10 (1925), 433.

[4] So Jellinek, *System der subjektiven öffentlichen Rechte* (1892), p. 161; see, however, Kohler in *Z.V.* 12 (1912), 90, 91.

claimant party should bear the burden of proof, but this rule is, according to a widespread opinion, subject in international law to the qualification that the burden of proof rests upon the party alleging some measure of restriction of the sovereignty of another State. The principle that in awarding damages the *restitutio in integrum* should be aimed at is regarded by many as a rule of universal jurisprudence, but its application in international law has met with opponents.

These instances show with some clarity that there is, as a rule, nothing cogent and well defined in 'universal conceptions of law' – unless, indeed, we agree to regard them for most practical purposes as identical with generally recognized principles of private law. That identity positivists have refused to admit.

§ 18. *The practice of States*

While on a subject touching the foundations of international law it is legitimate and desirable to examine both the relevant literature and the doctrine, it is the practice of States that is best suited to throw light on the question under discussion. To the examination of this aspect of the problem, there will be devoted Chapters III, IV, and V of this book. An attempt will be made (a) to show how, historically, the development of international law has been facilitated, and its moral content strengthened, by its close connection with private law; (b) to inquire to what extent present-day international law draws from this source. In particular, the view will be examined which explains the influence of private law by reference to the patrimonial character of States in the formative period of international law. We shall have to inquire whether the causes are not deeper, and whether they do not obtain with undiminished force now when the patrimonial conception of the State is no more than a relic of the past.

The following appears to be the most suitable arrangement in this connection:

(1) There will be discussed, first, instances of private law analogy apart from treaties such as the influence of private law on the conception of State territory and on the theory and practice of acquisition of territorial sovereignty, on the modifications and division of territorial sovereignty through servitudes, leases, *condominia*, mandates, trusts and the like, on the development of the conceptions of the freedom of the sea, of the maritime belt and of the sovereignty of the air, of State succession, and of State responsibility and its conse-

quences, in particular with regard to the measure of damages for international delinquencies.

(2) The second class embraces instances of recourse to private law in connection with treaties, their conclusion and the conditions of their validity, their effect upon the contracting and third parties, their termination and interpretation.

(3) Thirdly, cases will be considered relating to the part of private law rules of evidence and procedure.

§ 19. *International arbitration and the problem of private law*

International arbitral and judicial settlement provides what is perhaps the most significant contribution to the subject. It does this not only by virtue of the intrinsic merit of judicial and arbitral decisions as a source of international law, but also because it furnishes the opportunity for expounding and testing the considerations of principle which have influenced the development of international law by reference to its private law sources and analogies. International arbitral awards and decisions not only have made use of private law, they have often asserted their right and duty to do so and have given reasons for it. Neither are the pleadings of the parties without instruction. The most convincing proof, however, of the growing importance of the problem and of the need for its systematic treatment is offered by a long series of cases of international arbitration. In the same measure as municipal courts pass judgment not only upon the claims of the parties but also, incidentally, upon the soundness of legal theories, so there is no better opportunity for testing the value of certain doctrines. The opinion may be ventured that, in the history of judicial and arbitral settlement of international disputes, there are not many cases of importance in which the tribunal was not called upon to deal in one form or another with the question of application of a rule or principle of private law as such or, in its more recent formulation, as embodied in a 'general principle of law'.

The long array of these cases begins with the British-American mixed commissions constituted under the Jay Treaty of 1794. Some of the main issues which confronted them, namely, the measure of damages and the right of an arbitral tribunal to determine its jurisdiction, receive here solutions, by reference to general legal principles, which required a century in order to become recognized as established rules of international law. Numerous minor arbitrations in the nineteenth century were dependent for their solution upon application of private law. Thus the cases, *Croft*,[1] *Williams*,[2] and *Fabiani*,[3] may be mentioned as being concerned, *inter alia*, with questions of damages, prescription, admission and waiver. It is, however, in the important and well-known arbitrations that evidence in support of the general proposition put forward in these pages will be sought. The Geneva Tribunal in the *Alabama Arbitration*[4] of 1871 had to deal not only with the meaning and scope of 'due diligence' as applied to States, and with the different forms of *culpa* known in Roman law; questions of the measure of damages and of the admissibility of interest proved also of no small importance for the decision of the main issues of the dispute. In the *Behring Sea Arbitration*[5] of 1893 between the United States and Great Britain, the question of the application in international law of conceptions of possession and property, as applied to a right claimed under international law, was widely discussed and answered in the judgment; whilst the problem of the development of international law in its relation to private and natural law occupied counsel for both parties to a considerable extent, as also did the question of damages and of prescription.

In 1899, in the *British Guiana Boundary Arbitration* between Great Britain and Venezuela, the doctrines of prescription, of estoppel, and of title by occupation played a conspicuous part in the written and oral argument.[6] In the *Pious Fund*[7] case of 1902 between the United States and Mexico, the questions of prescription, of estoppel, and of the extent of the application of the principle of *res iudicata* in international law were among the main points which the Court had to decide. The *Delagoa Bay Railway Arbitration*[8] between Great Britain, the United States, and Portugal of 1900 furnished a striking example of a purely private law solution of the question of the measure of damages, as also did, in 1902, the arbitration between Russia and the United States in the *Whaling and Sealing Claims*.[9] In a series of decisions of the commissions adjudicating, in 1903, claims against Venezuela, the questions of prescription, of interest, and the measure of damages were discussed before the individual commissions.[10] In the *Venezuelan Preferential Claim* case[11] of 1904 the questions of application of private law rules of bankruptcy, of hypothecation, of *negotiorum gestio*, and of estoppel were in the foreground of the proceedings. The general problem of the applicability of Roman law in

[1] See Lauterpacht, *Analogies*, p. 267.
[2] *Ibid.* p. 273.
[3] *Ibid.* p. 271.
[4] *Ibid.* p. 216.
[5] *Ibid.* p. 223.
[6] *Ibid.* p. 227.
[7] *Ibid.* p. 244.
[8] *Ibid.* p. 271.
[9] *Ibid.*
[10] *Ibid.* p. 272.
[11] *Ibid.* p. 250.

international law was here discussed at length in the cases and arguments of several States. In the arbitration decided in 1905 between Japan on one side, and Great Britain, France, and Germany on the other – the *Japanese House Tax* case – the tribunal was again called upon to decide on a question belonging to the domain of private law – the question of leases in perpetuity granted to private persons.[1] In the *Alaska Boundary* dispute of 1903[2] between the United States and Great Britain the problems of prescription, of private law rules of evidence, and of the authority of Roman law were argued at length. In the *Orinoco Steamship Company Arbitration*[3] of 1910 between the United States and Venezuela, private law rules regarding the nullity of judgment and essential error were the real point at issue. The *Grisbadarna* case[4] between Norway and Sweden, decided in 1909, afforded again an opportunity of discussing and applying the problems of prescription and of Roman law rules of possession.

The important *North Atlantic Fisheries Arbitration*[5] between Great Britain and the United States, in which the question of international servitudes was the central issue, showed again, both in the arguments of the parties and in the judgment of the tribunal, that the question of private law in relation to international public law must be dealt with in a systematic manner. The *Russian Indemnity* case between Russia and Turkey,[6] decided in 1912, is a classical instance of application not only in the pleadings of the parties, but also by the tribunal, of private law rules, especially those governing the question of moratory interest; the case itself was decided by the application of a private law rule amounting virtually to estoppel. The arbitrations between Great Britain and Brazil in 1904 concerning the frontiers of British Guiana,[7] between the United States and Mexico in 1911 (the *Chamizal Arbitration*),[8] and, in the same year, between Great Britain and Germany, the *Walfisch Bay Arbitration*,[9] offer important contributions to the question of prescription.

Two noteworthy awards of the Central American Court of Justice threw interesting light on the application of private law: one (between Honduras, Salvador, and Guatemala, decided in 1908)[10] dealt fully with the notions of *dolus* and *culpa* in relation to the degree of diligence to be exhibited by the neutral; in the other (between Salvador, Costa Rica, and Nicaragua, decided in 1917)[11] the Court

[1] *Ibid.* p. 262.
[2] *Ibid.* p. 233.
[3] *Ibid.* p. 265.
[4] *Ibid.* p. 264.
[5] *Ibid.* p. 237.
[6] *Ibid.* p. 255.
[7] *Ibid.* p. 227.
[8] *Ibid.* p. 276.
[9] *Ibid.* p. 277.
[10] *Ibid.* p. 287.
[11] *Ibid.* p. 288.

discussed thoroughly the questions of leases and co-ownership in application to State territory. A number of instructive cases decided before and after the First World War by the British-American Claims Arbitral Tribunal constituted under the Convention of 1910 are of special interest in this connection. They covered, *inter alia*, the question of the measure of damages, especially with damages for prospective profits, and with various aspects of admission and estoppel.[1]

It is convenient to postpone at this stage the further enumeration of instances of recourse to private law. The enumeration will be continued in a different context when an account will be given, in another part of this book, of the practical application by international tribunals – whether the International Court or other international tribunals administering international law – of the 'general principles of law recognized by civilized States'. Through that formula, adopted in Article 38 of the Statute of the Permanent Court of International Justice after the First World War, the previous practice of international tribunals assumed a complexion of codification and acknowledged respectability. It will be shown that in substance the application of these principles has amounted to an application of generally recognized principles of private law. That practice, now removed from the orbit of controversy, has emphasized the significance and the urgency of a systematic study, with the assistance of comparative law and otherwise, of the 'general principles of law' thus formally declared – for it is essentially no more than a declaration – to be a source of law. Upon the proper fulfilment of that task, henceforth unhampered by exaggerations of positivism, depends whether the practice of States and the settlement of disputes between them on the basis of law will benefit to the fullest possible extent from the potentialities of the authoritative formulation, accomplished in the Statute of the Court, of the sources of the Law of Nations.

It is proposed, in the chapter which follows, to consider in what manner the gradual erosions of the doctrines of positivism, of sovereignty, and of the exclusiveness of States as subjects of international law have assisted in the formal acceptance of general principles of law as a source of international law. These doctrines had not prevented the actual acceptance – mainly in the form of recourse to the sources and analogies of private law – of the general principles of law as a vehicle of development of international law and as a standard of action both of governments and international tribunals.

[1] *Ibid.* p. 280.

CHAPTER 9

SOME OBSERVATIONS ON THE PROHIBITION OF '*NON LIQUET*' AND THE COMPLETENESS OF THE LAW

Editor's note This chapter appeared as a contribution in *Symbolae Verzijl*, a volume of essays presented to Professor J. H. W. Verzijl on the occasion of his seventieth birthday. (It was published by Martinus Nijhoff, The Hague, 1958.) A detailed critique of Lauterpacht's position was subsequently published by Professor Julius Stone, entitled '*Non-Liquet* and the Function of Law in the International Community', in the *British Year Book of International Law*, 35 (1959), 124.

I

The Draft Convention on Arbitral Procedure which the International Law Commission submitted in 1953 to the General Assembly provided, in the second paragraph of Article 12, that 'the tribunal may not bring in a finding of *non liquet* on the ground of the silence or obscurity of international law or the *compromis*'. In the discussion which preceded the adoption of that provision the opinion was expressed that the prohibition of *non liquet* on the grounds stated was so firmly established both in universally accepted legal principle and in the practice of international tribunals that an express affirmation of it was unnecessary and, by exposing an acknowledged principle of customary law to the vicissitudes of codification, fraught with danger. The opposing view, which prevailed, was that a self-evident principle which is valid without saying so gains in effectiveness by being formally incorporated as part of codified law. There is force in both these views – neither of which questions the established authority of the principle as formulated in the draft of the International Law Commission. It is of interest to note that in the same year the Administrative Tribunal of the International Labour Organization found it necessary to affirm expressly the non-admissibility of *non liquet*. It said, using language strikingly reminiscent of that in the draft of the International Law Commission: 'One of the fundamental tenets of all legal systems is that no court may refrain from giving judgment on the ground that the law is silent or obscure.'[1]

However, although that principle, expressive of the completeness of the international legal order, is firmly based on practically universal arbitral and judicial practice, it has not always been received by writers without hesitation or questioning. Some have asserted the justification of *non liquet* as a safeguard against tribunals, faced with the absence of necessary evidence or of an applicable rule of law, deciding according to their personal whim or arbitrary discretion and thus discrediting the idea of settlement of disputes on the basis of law[2] – an apprehension largely due to that somewhat misunderstood award in 1831 of the King of the Netherlands in a boundary dispute between Great Britain and the United States of America.[3] Others have referred with some impatience, as savouring of a dogmatic formalism, to the insistence on the completeness of international law. Thus we find Judge Charles de Visscher, in the course of a discussion of the problem of justiciability of disputes, pointing to the 'sterile controverse d'école que suscite la thèse dite de la plénitude du droit international'. He adds: 'Ni les idées de justice, ni les exigences des rapports internationaux ne s'accommodent de cette représentation toute formelle et statique qui se satisfait en décrivant le droit comme "complet", tout en reconnaissant qu'il est gravement "imparfait".'[4] Others still, in addition to denying to it the character of a rule of universal validity, have questioned its claim to be a positive factor in the administration of international justice and the preservation of peace. They have suggested that the very contrary may be the case. This is the position, for instance, recently expounded by Professor Stone in his examination of the problem of *non liquet*.[5]

[1] *Desgranges* v. *International Labour Organisation*, International Labour Office, *Official Bulletin*, 36 (1953), 212–15; *I.L.R.* 20 (1953), 523, at p. 530. The passage in question occurs in the part of the Judgment relating to the competence of the Tribunal—a fact which probably gives to the passage the complexion of an *obiter dictum*. For the competence of the Tribunal seems to have been firmly established by the comprehensive terms of its Statute, which confers upon it jurisdiction in respect of 'non-observances . . . of the terms of appointment of officials . . . and of such provisions of the Staff Regulations as are applicable to the case'.

[2] See, for instance, Lapradelle-Politis, I, 100, and Asser, *ibid.* pp. 398, 399; Politis, *La justice internationale* (1924), p. 84; Carlston, *The Process of International Arbitration* (1946), p. 158.

[3] For an analysis of which, from this point of view, see Lauterpacht, *The Function of Law*, pp. 127–30. And see below, p. 219.

[4] *Théories et réalités en droit international public* (1953), p. 397, n. 2.

[5] *Legal Controls of International Conflict* (1954), pp. 153–64. See, on the other hand, for an exposition of the completeness of international law, Guggenheim, *Traité*, I, 139 *et seq.*;

He points out that, in the absence of an international legislature, decisions rendered in reliance on the theory of the completeness of the international legal order may fail to satisfy 'the inherent appeal to men's ethical and rational judgment'[1] and, as such, fail in their purpose as an instrument of international peace.

These considerations are entitled to respect. They bring to mind the frequent attempts to link the problem of justiciability of disputes with that of so-called peaceful change. For the occasional desire to leave open the avenue of a *non liquet* has not been confined to cases in which there is no clear rule of international law in existence – a lacuna properly so-called. It has been influenced by the possibility of situations in which the existing law, although clear, conduces to results which are contrary to requirements of peace and the sense of moral propriety – a situation which is occasionally described as a lacuna in the political sense, a gap improperly so-called. The question, with which the present essay is mainly concerned, is whether the practical preoccupations which have inspired that defence of *non liquet* can best be met by denying what, upon renewed examination, must be regarded as a fully established principle both of jurisprudence and of arbitral and judicial practice. The alternative course is to accommodate ourselves to what must be regarded as a fact and to enquire whether, within the sphere of administration of justice unreservedly based both on the application of existing law and on the prohibition of *non liquet*, there is room for judicial or arbitral methods calculated, in proper cases, to alleviate the consequences of the strict and full application of the law. It will be here suggested that some such methods cannot be ruled out as being illegitimate and that they deserve consideration.

2

With negligible exceptions,[2] international practice shows no instances of a *non liquet*. For that reason the subject seems to partake, to some extent, of a measure of unreality. In view of this it may be useful to attempt a clarification of the term in question. To

Sereni, *Diritto internazionale*, I (1956), 98 *et seq.* See also Witenberg, *L'organisation judiciaire. La procédure et la sentence internationales* (1937), pp. 312–15, and Gihl, *International Legislation* (1937), pp. 82–5. And see for an earlier expression of opinion to the same effect, Fischer Williams, *Chapters*, pp. 50 *et seq.*, and, even more emphatically, Brierly as cited below, p. 227.

[1] *Legal Controls*, p. 164.

[2] Such as the controversial instance of the award of the King of the Netherlands: see below, p. 219.

put it negatively, the prohibition of *non liquet* does not mean that a court must not decline to give a decision on any ground. It only means that a court, otherwise endowed with jurisdiction, must not refuse to give a decision on the ground that the law is non-existent, or controversial, or uncertain and lacking in clarity. A court may decline to entertain a claim on account of absence of jurisdiction – a reason of common occurrence in the international sphere where the jurisdiction of courts is in principle voluntary – but that contingency is not germane to the question of *non liquet*. The same applies to the refusal of a court to adjudicate upon a claim for the reason that the case is subject to the jurisdiction of a different court or that the plaintiff has no *locus standi* on account of age, status, or some other reason. It is only when the refusal to give a decision, after the court has assumed jurisdiction, is based on the absence or insufficiency of the applicable substantive law that the question of a *non liquet* may properly be deemed to arise.[1]

Secondly, the principle affirming the completeness of the international legal order (for this is the positive formulation of the prohibition of *non liquet*) does not mean that law and legal tribunals are the appropriate instruments for settling, to the satisfaction of the parties and in accordance with sentiments of morality, every dispute or conflict between States. It means merely that, in regard to contentious proceedings,[2] a legal tribunal is – and must always be – in the position to determine whether a claim is justified in law and whether judgment must therefore be given for the plaintiff or the defendant. Much unnecessary – and occasionally impatient – effort has been expended in the past on elaborating the proposition that the view emphasizing the completeness of international law is an embarrassing example of academic pedantry; that law and courts are not a panacea; and that, like most industrial and many other

[1] This is so although, as a matter of speculation (for there are no actual instances to exemplify that contingency), an international tribunal might 'decline jurisdiction' for the reason that it has been endowed with it only in respect of 'legal' disputes; that a legal dispute is one for the solution of which there exists a rule of law or a sufficient rule of law; and that, as in the case before it there does not exist such a rule of law, it has no jurisdiction. It is sufficient to state here that, as shown in this essay, the possibility of any such contingency is negatived both by singularly uniform practice and by decisive considerations of legal principle.

[2] In advisory proceedings the problem assumes a different complexion. As this essay is not concerned primarily with the jurisdiction of the International Court of Justice, it is not necessary to discuss this aspect of the question except to the extent of suggesting that the prohibition of *non liquet* applies there to the full extent in the sense that, as a rule, every question forming the subject-matter of a request for an Opinion may be couched in the form of a claim, for instance, in proceedings for a declaratory judgement.

disputes between groups within the State, some controversies between States – the so-called conflicts of interests – cannot be settled through law and judicial processes. Of course they cannot. But the argument is hardly relevant to the issue. Few, if any, suggest that all disputes between States should be settled by courts. It is tempting to judge the notion of completeness of the law by its capacity to remove political 'tensions' between States.[1] The latter test has all the attractions of the recurrent tendencies to what has been described as realism. However, it is not the function of courts to eliminate any particular cause of friction between the parties to a dispute – except in so far as tension can be removed, or reduced, by the realization that legal justice has been done and that a decision has been reached by a method more objective than the *ipse dixit* of an interested party. The question whether the existing law is satisfactory from the point of view of taking into account political or economic interests in accordance with justice and reason has nothing to do with its completeness. When it is said that the law is complete, the intention is not to assert that the law is excellent and above criticism. Neither need it be interpreted as a naïve and uncritical argument, savouring of dogmatic formalism, in support of the principle of obligatory judicial settlement of disputes. There may be better ways of settling a particular dispute than a decision according to existing law – though it is not easy to think of a better method for the purpose of obligatory settlement of future disputes. What the principle of the completeness of the law means is: (a) that once the parties have agreed to entrust a tribunal with jurisdiction they cannot avoid their obligation by contending that the dispute is not a legal dispute in the sense that there are no legal rules by reference to which it can be solved; and (b) that the tribunal cannot decline to give a decision on the ground of the absence of an applicable rule of law.

In the sense here described the principle of the completeness of international law – the prohibition of *non liquet* – constitutes one of the most indisputably established rules of positive international law as evidenced by an uninterrupted continuity of international arbitral and judicial practice. With isolated exceptions, neither the parties to the proceedings, nor international tribunals, have asserted the absence of a rule or principle of law essential to the decision. Even in those exceptional cases they have not considered the

[1] See Charles de Visscher in *Hague Recueil*, 86 (1954) (ii), 324.

absence of a rule, or of a clear rule, to provide a ground for a refusal to give a decision at all. In the case of the *Eastern Extension, Australasia and China Telegraph Co.*, decided in 1923 by the British-American Claims Commission,[1] it was urged by Great Britain that there was a gap in international law in the matter of compensation payable by a belligerent for cutting neutral cables. Perhaps naturally, Great Britain, being the plaintiff State, did not assert that if in fact international law contained no rule on the subject the duty of the Tribunal was to pronounce a *non liquet*. She merely urged that it was within the powers of the Tribunal, if it were not its duty, to lay down a new rule. But it is of interest to note that neither the Tribunal nor the defendant Government suggested that, if there were a gap, a *non liquet* would have been the necessary result.[2] In the event the Tribunal found that there existed principles of international law, as distinguished from a specific rule, enabling it to render an award. In the case of the *Mavrommatis Palestine Concessions*[3] the Permanent Court of International Justice, faced – for the first time in its activity – with a preliminary objection, stated that 'neither the Statute nor the Rules of the Court contain any rule regarding the procedure to be followed in the event of an objection taken *in limine litis* to the Court's jurisdiction'. The conclusion which the Court drew from the position thus ascertained was that 'the Court therefore is at liberty to adopt the principle which it considers best calculated to ensure the administration of justice, most suited to the procedure before an international tribunal and most in accordance with the fundamental principles of international law.' The Court, because of its reliance on the ordinary and natural meaning of terms, has only exceptionally admitted that a provision of a treaty is not clear. When it has

[1] *U.N.R.I.A.A.*, VI, 112.

[2] In a number of arbitration treaties the parties seem to have envisaged the possibility of gaps in the law—though not of a *non liquet*. Thus in the arbitration treaty between Germany and Switzerland of 3 December 1921 it was provided that if the tribunal finds that the three principal sources of law as enumerated in Article 38 of the Statute of the Court still leave a gap in the law then it 'shall decide in accordance with legal principles which, in its view, ought to prevail in international law' and that for that purpose 'it shall follow solutions sanctioned by doctrine and jurisprudence'. A number of similar treaties were concluded by Germany with other States—the last with Luxembourg in 1929: see *United Nations. Systematic Survey of Treaties for the Pacific Settlement of International Disputes, 1928–1948* (1949), p. 119. And see *ibid.* pp. 119, 120, for an enumeration of treaties which, following the pattern of the General Act for the Pacific Settlement of International Disputes, provide—in the Chapter on Arbitration—for settlement *ex aequo et bono* in case of the absence of a rule applicable to the dispute.

[3] *P.C.I.J.* Series A, no. 2, p. 16.

done so – as in the case of the *Lighthouses between France and Greece*[1] – the conclusion was not to assert a gap in the law, but to have recourse to extraneous sources of evidence. Similarly, it is only by way of rare exception that the Court has admitted that a situation with which it was confronted had not been envisaged by the authors of the Treaty. It did so in the Advisory Opinion concerning the *Employment of Women during the Night*.[2] This did not prevent it from answering the question put to it.

There seems to be but one controversial instance – the award given in 1831 by the King of the Netherlands acting as arbitrator between Great Britain and the United States in the matter of the *North Eastern Boundary* – in which the arbitrator, after finding that the available evidence did not enable him to lay down the boundary in accordance with law, proceeded to determine the boundary in a way which seemed to him most appropriate; he did not pronounce a *non liquet*.[3] It has been occasionally suggested that there has been an implied *non liquet* in cases in which arbitrators instructed to adjudicate according to rules of law have described their decisions as being *ex aequo et bono* – a not infrequent occurrence in the matter of award of damages. Actually in these cases the expression *ex aequo et bono* was resorted to not in the sense in which it is used in Article 38 of the Statute of the International Court of Justice. It was used as indicating a fair – equitable – assessment of compensation in situations in which the law cannot, in the nature of things, provide in advance a rigid mathematical assessment of the amount involved.[4]

Parties to proceedings before tribunals, international and others, are not averse to submitting arguments of a varying degree of

[1] *P.C.I.J.* Series A/B, no. 62, pp. 14, 20.

[2] *P.C.I.J.* Series A/B, no. 50, p. 377.

[3] For a discussion of this case see Lauterpacht, *The Function of Law*, pp. 127–30. See also Balasko, *Causes de nullité de la sentence arbitrale en droit international* (1938), p. 300; Carlston, *The Process of International Arbitration* (1946), pp. 88–90.

[4] See, for a confirmation of that view, the Advisory Opinion of the International Court of Justice in the *Unesco Officials Appeal* case (*I.C.J. Reports* (1956), p. 100; *I.L.R.* 23 (1956), p. 517). And see, to the same effect, the award of 10 June 1921 by Count Carton de Wiart in the *Campbell* case, between the United Kingdom and Portugal (*U.N.R.I.A.A.*, II, 1145). See also *ibid.* p. 1035, for the award of 30 June 1930, in the matter of *Certain Claims by Portugal against Germany*. The position in this respect is the same as with regard to resort to 'equity' in international arbitration. 'Equity' is there uniformly treated as legal equity and, as such, as part of international law. See Judge Hudson's Concurring Opinion in the case of the *Diversion of the Waters of the Meuse* before the Permanent Court of International Justice (*P.C.I.J.* Series A/B, no. 70, p. 76) and the authorities there quoted. See also Jenks, in *L.Q.R.* 53 (1937), 519 *et seq.* See, in particular, for a detailed exposition of the subject in this sense the *Cayuga Indians Claims* case before the British-American Claims Arbitral Tribunal (*U.N.R.I.A.A.*, VI, 173). And see Carlston, *Process of International Arbitration*, pp. 155 *et seq.* and Lauterpacht, *Analogies*, pp. 63–7.

persuasiveness – apparently disregarding the possibility that a bad argument may, through a process of infection, vitiate the sound aspect of their cause by rendering the judge or arbitrator sceptical as to the soundness of the presentation of their case. But it is significant that they seldom, if ever, assert the absence of an applicable rule of law[1] – not only as a reason for asking for a *non liquet* but also as a means of invoking the residuary rule of presumptive freedom of action following upon the absence of a limiting rule of law. In the course of the proceedings in the *Anglo-Norwegian Fisheries* case before the International Court of Justice, Norway repeatedly deprecated any intention of relying for that purpose on the argument that, in view of the apparent discrepancy of practice in the matter of drawing the base line of territorial waters and bays, there existed a gap in the law.[2] It may be suggested that, in thus refraining from invoking a *non liquet*, Governments, far from giving expression to any view as to its admissibility, did no more than abstain from relying on a doctrine which has received no support from international tribunals and reliance on which they have considered unnecessary in view of the availability of more convincing arguments.[3] Any such suggestion asserts a distinction without a difference.

The fact that the practice of international tribunals has rejected so consistently the notion of *non liquet*[4] is particularly significant seeing that the inducement to invoke and rely on it is more constant, and more pressing, in international than in municipal proceedings. For in the international sphere the 'gaps' – in some of their current, though not legal, connotations – are more ostensible and more frequent. In a sense, they are the rule rather than the exception. Even when the law is clear and generally accepted it

[1] For an exceptional occurrence see above, p. 218, the *Eastern Extension etc.* case.

[2] *I.C.J. Pleadings*, I, 371. And see Bourquin, in *Nordisk T.A.* 22 (1952), 107.

[3] See Stone, *Legal Controls*, p. 163.

[4] This disinclination, on the part of arbitrators, to incur the risk, however remote, of having to decline to pronounce a decision is shown by the following incident: When in 1889 the Emperor of Russia was invited to act as arbitrator in the dispute between France and the Netherlands in the matter of the Guiana boundary, he originally refused to do so on the ground that the Arbitration Agreement of 1888 bound him rigidly to either of the two lines proposed by the parties. He eventually accepted subject to the condition that he was authorized to choose an intermediate line. See Lapradelle-Politis, II, 399. In the award concerning the border between Guatemala and Honduras the Tribunal (presided over by Chief Justice Charles Evans Hughes) put it on record that, in the light of the declared purpose of the Treaty providing for arbitration to the effect that the Tribunal shall decide the boundary controversy finally, 'the Tribunal is not at liberty to conclude that the lack of adequate evidence to establish the line of *uti possidetis* of 1821, throughout the entire territory in dispute, relieves the Tribunal of the duty to determine the definitive boundary to its full extent' (Award of 23 January 1933: *U.N.R.I.A.A.*, II, p. 1352).

occasionally exhibits what some consider to be a lacuna – in the political and moral sense – inasmuch as it represents a rule which, as in the case of the disregard of the vitiating effect of duress, may be deemed to be morally questionable, or which has become politically reprehensible and obsolete on account of changed conditions,[1] or which leaves outside its orbit a situation clearly and urgently calling for regulation. Moreover, in so far as universal or quasi-universal agreement is a hall-mark of a rule of positive international law, the gaps – in the accepted sense of the absence of a legal rule – constitute a typical occurrence. For there is often no such agreement in international law. But international tribunals have not shown a disposition to act upon the view that there is in such cases a gap calling for the pronouncement of a *non liquet.* In the Advisory Opinion concerning *Reservations to the Convention on Genocide* the International Court of Justice was confronted with some divergence of practice – though, as in the *Anglo-Norwegian Fisheries* case, that divergence permitted a differentiation between the predominant and the minority practice. In neither case did the Court adopt the view that the apparently predominant practice represented the binding rule. But in neither case was the question raised of the inability of the Court to make a pronouncement on the ground that there was no rule or principle in existence upon which it could act. A substantial part of international arbitration and judicial settlement can be analysed in terms of some such situations. It may be a refinement to inquire whether that constant practice of international tribunals – in face of possible cogent inducement to the contrary – is a source of the rule of international law on the subject or an expression of it. It is probably both.

That uniform practice was firmly established even before the adoption of the Statute of the Permanent Court of International Justice which, in Article 38, elevated 'general principles of law recognized by civilized nations' to the authority of one of the three principal and formal sources of international law – an apparent innovation which in itself may not have been more than a declaration and confirmation of previous practice. However that may be, that apparent innovation added to the reality of the prohibition of *non liquet.* It did so in two ways. In the first instance, by making available without limitation the resources of substantive law embodied in the legal experience of civilized mankind – the analogy

[1] German writers refer to such gaps as unreal, legal-political (*rechts-politische*), gaps.

of all the branches of municipal law and, in particular, of private law – it made certain that there would always be at hand, if necessary, a legal rule or principle for the legal solution of any controversy involving sovereign States. Secondly, inasmuch as the principle of the completeness of the legal order is in itself a general principle of law, it became on that account part of the law henceforth to be applied by the Court.[1] As Sir Frederick Pollock said in relation to English law, it – namely, the rule that judges are bound to find a decision for every case, however novel and even if not covered by any existing rule of law – is 'the first and greatest rule of our customary law'.[2] Whether by way of positive or negative express provisions of codes or otherwise, it is a uniform feature of the administration of justice in all systems of law. It is perhaps the most general of the general principles of law. Professor Brierly, writing in 1930, put the position with all requisite clarity and emphasis:

Surely when we speak of 'gaps' in the law, international or municipal, we are using a tendencious metaphor appropriate to critics, but not one of the jurist's terms of art. We are thinking of contingencies in which we know that the only answer a court can give to the complainant state or individual is that his grievance constitutes, as the law stands, no cause of action. We do not mean that the law has *no* rule for these contingencies, but merely that we do not like the rule that the law directs the court to apply.[3]

It may be noted in this connection that that wide formulation, in Article 38 of the Statute of the Court, of the sources of international law has been adopted, almost as a matter of course, by other international tribunals[4] – although, once more, such adoption was no

[1] It is of interest to observe that in his *note doctrinale* in Lapradelle-Politis, I, 399, Asser, while referring to the possibility of *non liquet* in cases such as the award of the King of the Netherlands in 1831 (see above, p. 219, admitted that the prohibition of *non liquet* was a universally accepted principle of municipal jurisprudence. Anzilotti suggested that the provision of Article 38 (3) referring to general principles of law was dictated by apprehension lest the Court might be compelled to pronounce a *non liquet* owing to the absence of applicable rules of law (Anzilotti, I, 117).

[2] Note in Maine's *Ancient Law* (1920 ed.), p. 46.

[3] 'The General Act of Geneva', in *B.Y.* 11 (1930), 128.

[4] See, for example, the decision of the Special Arbitral Tribunal between Portugal and Germany in 1928 in the *Maziua and Naulilaa* cases (*Annual Digest*, 4 (1927–8), 466); in the *Lena Goldfields Arbitration* in 1930 (*ibid.* 5 (1929–30), 3); and, in particular, of the Special Arbitral Trinunal in 1928 between Roumania and Germany (*Goldenberg & Sons* v. *Germany*, *ibid.* 4 (1927–8), 542). In the Agreement of 5 May 1936 between France and Belgium concerning the *Interpretation of the Tardieu-Jaspar Agreement*, the two Governments in seeking an opinion from M. Limburg requested him to give it in accordance with the rules laid down in Article 38 of the Statute (*Annual Digest*, 8 (1935–7), 478). For an enumeration of a large number of general arbitration treaties which contain a provision of that nature to take effect in the absence of a relevant rule in the special agreement, see *United Nations. Systematic Survey of Treaties for the Pacific Settlement of International Disputes, 1928–48* (1948), pp. 117–19.

more than declaratory of previous practice. It is not easy to conceive of a rule or principle of international law to which the designation 'positive' could be applied with greater justification than the prohibition of *non liquet*. This is so irrespective of any apparent 'meta-legal' or other inarticulate major premise which may have inspired those who have elaborated the significance of its place in international judicial and arbitral settlement.

3

The constancy of international judicial and arbitral practice on the subject has made the rejection of *non liquet* appear as self-evident. Yet, but for the cogency of the general legal principle as stated, development might well have gone the other way. This is so having regard to the substantive and, on occasions, what may be described as ethical deficiencies of international law – those deficiencies which, at times, make writers cast a regretful and nostalgic glance at the potentialities of judicial or arbitral *non liquet* as a vehicle of justice and change. If development had gone the other way, the assumed admissibility of *non liquet* might have acted as an ever present, and occasionally effective, inducement to avoiding responsibility by way of declining jurisdiction or refusing to adjudicate in reliance on the fact – or the allegation – that the problem is one of novelty; that there is no law by reference to which it can be solved; and that the matter is therefore political and not legal. It would have acted in that way whenever the necessity of reaching a decision was politically embarrassing or inconvenient. It might have operated in that manner whenever a *non liquet* was deemed to provide an opportunity for opening up avenues for a desirable change of the law.

As stated, the inducements to act upon what in a municipal court is a legal heresy are particularly strong in the international sphere. The rarity of arbitral and judical settlement increases the potential number of cases *primae impressionis*. In vast areas – including those of apparent political and economic importance – the admitted disagreement of views and practice, even on matters of principle, is wide and fundamental. Frequently – perhaps normally – agreement on wide principle is not accompanied by a parallel concordance of views and practice in the matter of their detailed application. Of this, the entire field of jurisdictional immunities of States and their diplomatic representatives provides a striking example. The growth of custom as a source – or evidence – of law is difficult of ascertainment and surrounded by requirements of some stringency. This is shown clearly by the frequent refusal on the part of the International Court to give judicial imprimatur to an asserted existence of custom[1] and to its occasional disinclination to regard mere predominance of one practice over another as a sufficient hall-mark of a binding customary rule.[2] As against all these influences apt to work in the direction of *non liquet* there has asserted itself, in an unfavourable climate, the beneficence of the general principle of law on the subject. It has asserted itself through judicial and arbitral effort more active and more fertile than reliance upon the principle that in the absence of a restraining rule of law recourse must be had to the maxim that what is not expressly prohibited is permitted. That latter principle is of controversial doctrinal value and of limited practical utility. It often degenerates into a contest as to the distribution of the burden of proof.

These potential dangers of *non liquet* in the international sphere and the exploration of the methods by which they can be, and have been, overcome underlie to a considerable extent the prominence which the subject has acquired in the literature of international law. But there are two other factors which explain why, although the assumption of the completeness of the international legal order is a fundamental jurisprudential principle and although it is amply substantiated by arbitral and judicial practice, the problem of *non liquet* has loomed so large in the literature of international law.

One of these reasons is that the asserted admissibility of *non liquet* has lent colour to the current distinction between 'justiciable' and 'non-justiciable', or between 'legal' and 'political', disputes as it appears in treaties providing for compulsory arbitral and judicial settlement and as it has been rationalized by writers. The main – though not the only – explanation and justification of that distinction has been the belief, or the assertion, that owing to the possible absence of available legal rules there are disputes which are not capable of a legal solution and that such disputes are, therefore, outside the orbit of compulsory judicial or arbitral settle-

[1] As in *The Lotus* case (*P.C.I.J.* Series A, no. 10, pp. 28 *et seq.*); the *Reservations to the Convention on Genocide* case (*I.C.J. Reports* (1951), pp. 22, 31–42); the *Anglo-Norwegian Fisheries* case (*I.C.J. Reports* (1951), pp. 13 *et seq.*); the *Asylum* case (*I.C.J. Reports* (1950), pp. 276 *et seq.*); the *Rights of United States Nationals in Morocco* case (*I.C.J. Reports* (1952), pp. 200, 219).

[2] As in the cases of the *Reservations to the Convention on Genocide* and the *Anglo-Norwegian Fisheries* (see above, p. 221).

ment. Experience has shown that any such explanation or justification of 'non-justiciability' of disputes has no substance. As already stated, *non liquet* on account of absence, obscurity or uncertainty of the law is wholly unknown in the practice of international tribunals. Reasons have been given why, as a matter of both wider principle and positive law, it must remain so in the future.[1] Moreover, it does not appear that Governments have invoked that particular connotation of the distinction between legal and political disputes for challenging the compulsory jurisdiction of a tribunal upon which they have conferred jurisdiction in legal disputes. Thus no State that has accepted the Optional Clause of Article 36 of the Statute of the Court – which confers upon it jurisdiction in respect of specified categories of legal disputes – has on any occasion challenged the jurisdiction of the Court on the ground that a dispute, although falling within one of these categories, is not a legal dispute having regard to the insufficiency of the law.[2] Yet it was this particular explanation – one of the several conceptions of 'justiciability' of international disputes – which made it necessary to elaborate the view that, from that point of view, all disputes are justiciable and that, in so far as the possibility of a *non liquet* prompted that particular limitation of the undertaking of compulsory judicial or arbitral settlement, it had no foundation.

At the same time the examination of the question of *non liquet* by reference to the problem of justiciability of international disputes was bound to have effects more far-reaching than the elimination of an argument which was at variance with both principle and experience. For the reason stated above such examination[3] was bound to reveal, in particular in the international sphere, the beneficence of the notion of the completeness of the legal system – or, negatively speaking – of the prohibition of *non liquet.* It is thus possible that, in so far as there existed a danger, stimulated to some extent by the form of the instruments of arbitral and judicial settlement, of a *non liquet*, the critical analysis of the problem has assisted in the process of banishing that possibility as a problem of international jurisprudence. It did so at the risk of some misunderstanding to which it laid itself open – namely, the charge that it contemplated

[1] See above, pp. 215–23.

[2] It is not necessary here to attempt to answer the question whether both experience and the intrinsic meaning of that provision lend support to the view that the term 'legal' in this context of Article 36, far from signifying an additional qualification of these disputes, is merely descriptive of them.

[3] See, e.g., Lauterpacht, *The Function of Law*, pp. 52–135.

all disputes between States as a fit subject for judicial or arbitral determination. Yet its only object was to bring home the fact that once a State has agreed in advance to submit its disputes to adjudication by a legal tribunal it serves no useful purpose (and may be a source of confusion and evasion) to say that only legal disputes are submitted to it in the sense that they must be disputes capable of adjudication by rules of law and that among those left outside the obligation thus undertaken are those which cannot be so adjudicated because, on account of the possibility of *non liquet*, some disputes may not be capable of legal solution. There is no such possibility.

The second reason for the recurrent prominence of the question of *non liquet* is its association with the enduring problem of stability and change in international relations – a problem which in many respects is essentially that of the relation of law and justice. If, as is the case, the prohibition of *non liquet* is the paramount rule and if tribunals are invariably bound to give a decision regardless of any apparent insufficiency of the law – regardless of any 'gaps' in the law – then, the argument runs, it may not be possible in some cases to avoid the implications of the fact that the decision given may, owing to the absence of remedial action of an international legislature or other effective law-making process, constitute an injustice inimical to peace and progress. If this is so, is it not better, on that view, that international tribunals should be in the position to pronounce a *non liquet* – especially when the law is uncertain or controversial? If that is so, is not the prohibition of *non liquet* a retrogressive doctrine?

4

There is no warrant for rejecting with impatience these attempts at linking the problem of *non liquet* with that of international change. There is no good cause for such impatience even if we believe that the negation, on account of any possible injustice of the existing law, of the completeness of international law as ascertained by international tribunals is misguided. It may be all too easy to ignore the fact that it is especially from the point of view of so-called peaceful change that the problem, when coupled with the question of *non liquet*, of the possible adverse effect of the full compulsory jurisdiction of international tribunals has been a frequent feature of discussion by writers and Governments. For a time the preoccupation with that aspect of pacific settlement was so prominent as to make many oblivious to the advantages of the normal application of the law by international tribunals endowed with compulsory jurisdiction. There have been indications that that approach was being abandoned. Professor Brierly, who, while rejecting emphatically the notion of 'gaps' in international law'[1] was, for the greater part of his life, one of the most weighty exponents of the notion of the necessary limitation of the place of law in international relations, eventually recognized the dangers of such an attitude.[2]

Yet, as stated, there may – in turn – be an excess of simplification in leaving the matter altogether outside the orbit of our preoccupations. Can we be sure that we have exhausted all the relevant aspects of the situation if we say – as, indeed, we are entitled to say – that once a tribunal has been endowed with compulsory jurisdiction all disputes have become 'legal' in the sense that they can all be resolved, i.e., legally resolved, in terms of legal obligations and rights; that there can, therefore, never be any question of *non liquet*; and that legal tribunals cannot be concerned with any shortcomings – from the point of view of morals, politics or economics – of the law as declared or formulated by them?

It may be said, with much force, that it is not the business of tribunals to administer ethical justice or to give effect to what is socially desirable or politically conducive to the preservation of peace. Their business, it has been urged, is to administer the law and nothing else. The International Court of Justice has put on record, with deliberate clarity, that point of view in its Advisory Opinion on the *Status of South-West Africa*. After having expressed its inability to deduce from 'general considerations' underlying the instruments before it 'any legal obligation for mandatory States to conclude or negotiate' trusteeship agreements, it said: 'It is not for the Court to pronounce on the political or moral duties which these considerations may involve.'[3] Similarly, in the *de la Torre* case between Colombia and Peru, after having laid down that the asylum granted to the person concerned must end, but that there was no obligation to surrender the refugee, the Court, while noting that there was no contradiction between the two parts of

[1] See above, p. 222.

[2] He said, in 1946: '... If we want to have law we shall have to recognize that it is by its nature a conservative force; we shall have to accept a bias, and a strong bias, in favour of the *status quo*. But for my part I would go further than this and say that I think we have heard too much of the problem of peaceful change during the inter-war years.' 'International Law and Some Conditions of its Progress', in *International Affairs*, 22 (1946), 358.

[3] *I.C.J. Reports* (1950), p. 140.

that pronouncement, declared its inability 'to give any practical advice as to the various courses which might be followed with a view to terminating the asylum, since, by doing so, it would depart from its judicial function'.[1]

However, for the reasons stated, there is room for consideration whether a view of the judicial function which excludes from its orbit any expression of opinion other than that formulated in the binding decision and in the reasons directly leading thereto is an unavoidable consequence of the legal character of a tribunal. Is it in conformity with the judicial character of a pronouncement that, while leaving no doubt as to the law as declared by it and as indisputably binding upon the parties, it should – if it deems it necessary – draw attention to the shortcomings of the law thus declared and the necessity for its amendment? Is it consistent with its function that it should indicate directly – or indirectly by the manner of its reasoning – what ought to be the substance of any such change? Is it proper that, after it has clearly laid down the rights and duties of the parties, it should express an opinion as to how the successful party ought to conduct itself – by way of an act of grace, or neighbourliness, or accommodation – in agreeing to a modification of its legal rights in the interest of peace, or in accordance with moral duty, or having regard to the needs of a progressive international law? Is any such expression of opinion conducive to enhancing the authority of the legal pronouncement or is it bound to have the opposite effect? In the *Free Zones* case between Switzerland and France the Court seems to have acted on some such considerations when it said: 'The Court does not hesitate to express its opinion that if, by the maintenance in force of the old treaties, Switzerland obtains the economic advantages derived from the zones, she ought in return to grant compensatory economic advantages to the people of the zones.'[2]

In the case of the *Serbian Loans* the Court mitigated the rigour of the law which it applied by expressing a view as to the equities of the case. It refused to admit that the economic dislocations caused by the World War released the debtor State from its obligation – 'although', it added, 'they may present equities which doubtless will receive appropriate consideration in the negotiations'.[3] In the case of the *Société Commerciale de Belgique* the Court put on record the declaration made by Counsel for the Belgian Government on the

[1] *I.C.J. Reports* (1951), p. 83.
[2] *P.C.I.J.* Series A/B, no. 46, p. 169.
[3] *P.C.I.J.* Series A, no. 14, p. 40.

question of payments, with regard to which it was stated that 'it would have regard to the legitimate interests of the company, the ability of Greece to pay and the traditional friendship between the two countries'. That declaration the Court found to be in a general way in line with the Greek submission. This, it said, 'enables the Court to declare that the two Governments are, in principle, agreed in contemplating the possibility of negotiations with a view to a friendly settlement, in which regard would be had, among other things, to Greece's capacity to pay'. The Court added: 'Such a settlement is highly desirable.'[1]

There would thus appear to be a difference in the method as adopted in the Advisory Opinion, referred to above, on the *Status of South-West Africa* and that followed in the Judgment in the *Free Zones* case and, to some extent, in the cases of the *Serbian Loans* and the *Société Commerciale de Belgique*. Which method is preferable? The instances referred to above suggest that the problem is essentially the same in the matter of both contentious and advisory jurisdiction. It is not proposed in the present essay to attempt an answer to these questions. But it may be useful to draw attention to some relevant practice and to some general considerations underlying the question at issue.

There is no problem when the agreed submission by the parties authorizes or instructs the tribunal to make recommendations going outside the application of the existing law. This was the case in the Agreements, in 1892 and 1909 respectively, providing for the *Behring Sea Arbitration* and the *North Atlantic Fisheries Arbitration* between Great Britain and the United States of America. In these Agreements the Parties instructed the Tribunal to issue regulations or make recommendations should this become necessary as the result of the legal findings embodied in the award.[2] In both cases the Tribunals fully acted on the authorization of the instructions thus received – in the latter case in an ample manner going apparently outside the terms of the Agreement.[3]

[1] *P.C.I.J.* Series A/B, no. 78, p. 178.

[2] For details see Lauterpacht, *The Function of Law*, pp. 308–11.

[3] Article 4 of the Agreement provided that 'the Tribunal shall recommend for the consideration of the high contracting Parties rules and methods of procedure under which all questions which may arise in the future regarding the exercise of the liberties referred to may be determined in accordance with the principles laid down in the award'. In reliance on that Article the Tribunal, after having laid down the base line in respect of bays, admitted that the formula adopted by it 'is not entirely satisfactory as to its practical applicability, and that it leaves room for doubts and differences in practice' (Scott, *Hague Reports*, p. 188). It then proposed specific limits for particular areas. This

The question here under consideration arises when – and this is the normal occurrence – the instrument conferring jurisdiction upon the tribunal contains no express provision for any recommendation or expression of opinion on the duties of the parties other than those of a legal nature. It is of interest, before attempting to face the difficulties involved, to record the experience of an arbitral tribunal which functioned before and after the First World War, namely, the British-American Claims Arbitral Tribunal under the Convention of 1910. According to Article 7 of the Convention the Tribunal was authorized to decide the claims submitted to it 'in accordance with treaty rights and with the principles of international law and equity'. It invariably interpreted the latter phrase as meaning legally relevant equity[1] in the sense of being part of the law and not a derogation from it. Nevertheless, the Tribunal deemed it proper on a number of occasions to recommend to the parties a course of action going outside their legal duties as laid down in the award.

In the case of *Eastern Extension, Australasia and China Telegraph Co.*, it said by way of a general statement on the subject: 'If the strict application of a treaty or of a specific rule of international law conducts to a decision which, however justified from a strictly legal point of view, will result in hardship, unjustified having regard to the special circumstances of the case, then it is the duty of this Tribunal to do their best to avoid such a result, so far as may be possible, by recommending for instance some course of action by way of grace on the part of the respondent Government.'[2] The Tribunal did not find that in the case before it circumstances called for any recommendation additional to its award rejecting a claim of Great Britain for compensation in respect of the cutting of a cable by a belligerent. However, in a number of other cases it did act upon the principle thus enunciated.

In the *Cadenhead* case – a claim for compensation for the death of a British subject killed by a shot fired by a United States soldier at an escaping military prisoner on a public highway – the Tribunal disallowed the claim. However, in view of the fact that the regulations of the United States army on the subject 'may not have been altogether prudent' it 'ventured' to 'express the desire that the United States Government will consider favourably the payment

seems to go outside the 'rules and methods of procedure' as provided for in the Agreement.

[1] See, e.g., *Cayuga Indian Claims* case, referred to above, p. 219, n. 4.

[2] Award of 9 November 1923 (*U.N.R.I.A.A.* VI, 116).

of some compensation as an act of grace to the representative of Miss Cadenhead, on account of the unfortunate loss of their relative, under such distressing circumstances'.[1] The claim, as stated, was disallowed, 'with the above recommendation'.

In the case of the *Home Missionary Society*, the Tribunal rejected a claim by the United States in respect of loss of life and damage suffered by that Society in the course of a rebellion of the native population in the Sierra Leone Protectorate. However, in the circumstances of the case, the Tribunal put it on record that if the British Government 'can avail itself of any fund from which to repair so far as possible the losses sustained in the native revolt, it would be an act of grace which this Tribunal cannot refrain from recommending warmly to the generosity of that Government'.[2]

In the case of *Jesse Lewis* (*The David J. Adams*), the Tribunal disallowed a claim for the seizure and condemnation, which it considered to be in accordance with international law, of a fishing vessel. At the same time it recounted the circumstances of the case and the consequences of the confiscation, which it considered to be 'particularly unfortunate and unmerited'. It pointed to the distressing economic condition of the owner of the vessel, who appeared to have been innocent of the conduct of his master whom he had expressly prohibited from entering Canadian waters. In view of this the Tribunal thought it its duty to draw the attention of the British Government to the loss incurred by the owner of the vessel and 'ventured to express the desire' that that Government consider favourably an allowance as an act of grace for the loss of the vessel and the damage resulting thereform. 'That compensation, this Tribunal earnestly urges upon the attention of the British and Canadian Governments.'[3] With the above recommendation, the claim was disallowed.

In the case of *Adolf G. Studer*, the Tribunal rejected a claim put forward on behalf of an American citizen in respect of certain grants of land alleged to have been made by the Sultan of Johore prior to the assumption by Great Britain of international responsibility for that territory. The Tribunal dismissed the claim for lack of evidence and the unexplained failure to bring the matter before the courts of Johore notwithstanding an apparent offer made to that effect. Nevertheless, in dismissing the claim the Tribunal did

[1] *Ibid.* p. 41.
[2] Award of 18 December 1920 (*ibid.* p. 44).
[3] Award of 9 December 1921 (*ibid.* p. 93).

so 'subject to the following emphatic recommendation': 'This Tribunal earnestly recommends that this offer be renewed and accepted and that the courts of Johore in that event take the matter up in a liberal spirit without regard to legal refinements and technicalities.'[1]

The philosophy underlying that distinction between the operative part of the decision as based on law and the recommendation for tempering law with justice in cases – fortunately infrequent – in which the two do not coincide, was expressed early in the life of the Tribunal in a passage which merits quotation. In the case of the *William Hardman*, the Tribunal dismissed a claim for compensation for destruction of private property – in the interest of the preservation of health of the military forces – by the military authorities of the United States of America in Cuba during the Spanish–American Civil War. While disallowing the claim, the Tribunal said:[2]

> On the other hand, notwithstanding the principle generally recognized in international law that necessary acts of war do not imply the belligerent's legal obligation to compensate, there is, nevertheless, a certain humanitarian conduct generally followed by nations to compensate the private owner for losses as a matter purely of grace and favour, when in their own judgment they feel able to do so, and when the sufferer appears specially worthy of interest. Although there is no legal obligation to act in that way, there may be a moral duty which cannot be covered by law, because it is grounded only on an inmost sense of human assistance, and because its fulfilment depends on the economic and political condition of the nation, each nation being its own judge in that respect.

It is of interest to note that these principles and methods were adopted by a Tribunal presided over by M. Fromageot, a distinguished French lawyer of considerable experience who subsequently became one of the Judges of the Permanent Court of International Justice, and composed of other lawyers of distinction.

5

The series of awards surveyed above exemplifies, in conjunction with what has been said on the prohibition of *non liquet*, the possible significance of the part which international tribunals may play in the schemes of pacific settlement in addition to their primary function of deciding disputes in accordance with the law. At the same time, the distinctly narrow scope, political and economic, of the recommenda-

[1] Award of 19 March 1925 (*ibid.* p. 157). [2] *Ibid.* p. 26.

tions here surveyed brings to mind the limited and controversial nature of any such method. It may be said, with much force, that to decide disputes on the basis of law is the only legitimate task of a legal tribunal, and that any attempt to superimpose upon it other functions must prove inimical to the cause of international justice as based on law and that it ought therefore to be avoided. The refusal by the Permanent Court of International Justice in the *Free Zones* case to adjudicate *ex aequo et bono* in the absence of an unequivocal mandate by the parties to that effect demonstrates the force of these considerations. (This is so although the refusal to act in that capacity was reached only by the casting vote of the President and although, in its final Judgment, the Court did express a view on the moral duty of one of the parties[1] and although it made full use of the authority conferred upon it in the Special Agreement to settle all questions involved in the execution of the relevant provisions of the Treaty.)[2] If a tribunal, after having laid down the law, proceeds to elaborate the unsatisfactory nature of its legal finding from the point of view of humanity, moral obligation, convenience, reasonableness and similar considerations by reference to which it exhorts the parties not to insist rigidly on their legal right, is it not probable that any such proceeding must impair its authority and effectiveness? Is it not clear that the very standing of the tribunal as an organ created for judging according to law must suffer in consequence of such infusion of extra-legal considerations into the body of its pronouncements – even if that extraneous element is expressly stated to be without binding force? Is it not preferable that any necessary remedial action should be initiated by political and legislative bodies, or appropriate organs of conciliation, or by the parties themselves?

The force of these and similar questions is evident. If an attempt is made, in the lines which follow, to adduce considerations militating in the opposite direction, this is so not necessarily because the present writer subscribes to them without reservation, but because they merit attention as constituting one aspect of the abiding problem of the relation of law and justice and of its ever recurring concomitant, namely, the question of peaceful change. There is a close connection between these problems and the prohibition of *non liquet* which sets the seal of legal finality upon every dispute regardless of the nature of its complexities. This is so although the dis-

[1] See above, p. 228.
[2] *P.C.I.J.* Series A/B, no. 46, p. 172.

crepancy between law and justice, or law and reason, is an exception – and not a typical occurrence. For law, as has been often said in varying phraseology, is the expression of such justice as is socially obtainable; precepts of morality, such as those embodied in the injunction of fair dealing, good faith and the fulfilment of legitimate expectations, are part of the law. Yet, because in organized society morals act upon the conscience and because law is directed to external conduct, such discrepancies occasionally, and necessarily, arise. It may be a simplification to suggest that the law must ignore them. To do that is to run the risk of magnifying their incidence and importance. Like any other grievance, the sentiment of injustice feeds on the feeling that it is being ignored. As stated, the problem of peaceful adjustments in a system of law, endowed with a finality and inevitability as the twin result of the prohibition of *non liquet* and the absence of legislative agencies, has been a constant, though exaggerated, theme of international discussion. It has expressed itself in the recurrent, and impracticable, proposals for an International Equity Tribunal decreeing, with binding effect, changes in the legal position of the parties. It has found expression in the confused and confusing provisions of the Chapter on Arbitration in the General Act for the Pacific Settlement of International Disputes of 1928 which, after assuming that there are disputes which cannot be settled by law, provided for their solution by reference to rules of law as laid down in Article 38 of the Statute of the Court and, in the event that there exist no rules applicable to the dispute, for a solution *ex aequo et bono*.[1] It underlies the sporadic eruptions of disapproval of the established doctrine and practice of the completeness of the international legal system and the resulting prohibition of *non liquet*.

This being so, there would appear to be room for a re-examination of some of the questions pertinent to the issue. Is it inconsistent with the function of tribunals to express a view – negative, if necessary – on the adequacy of the law which it is their duty to administer? The highest municipal tribunals, whose subordination to the sovereignty of the existing law is uncontroverted, do it frequently

[1] Having regard to the criticism encountered by these provisions, the European Convention for the Peaceful Settlement of Disputes of 29 April 1957 provided, in the Chapter on Arbitration (Article 26), that 'if nothing is laid down in the special agreement or no special agreement has been made, the Tribunal shall decide *ex aequo et bono*, having regard to the general principles of international law, while respecting the contractual obligations and the final decisions of international tribunals which are binding on the parties'. No opinion is here expressed on the question as to whether the new formula has clarified matters. For the text of the first draft of the Convention see *Consultative Assembly*, 7th Session, First Part (1955), II, Doc. 356, 16.

and – on occasions – pungently. Their judgments have often constituted a direct invitation to a change in the law. It might be thought that if, when laying down the law binding upon the parties, a tribunal at the same time exhorts them to show readiness to abate their insistence on legal rights by reference to moral duty and political reason, it is adding to rather than detracting from the legally binding force of its pronouncement. It might be thought that although any such expression of opinion may weaken the moral authority of the particular legal rule which it administers, it adds to the authority of the law as a body of rules capable of development and adjustment. It would also appear that recommendations, which are not binding, for modifications in the legal position may more usefully come from a tribunal which, in the process of arriving at its legal conclusions, has the opportunity – on the basis of the written and oral argument submitted by the parties – to make itself fully acquainted with the intricacies of the problem before it.[1]

The fact that a tribunal is bound to apply the law does not necessarily mean that it must apply it uncritically. A legal rule or principle is not in need of all the virtues of excellence in order to claim the right – including the moral right – to be applied. The decisive consideration is that it is the rule or principle in force. But that fact does not mean that the tribunal, by ignoring any reference to the shortcomings of the law or the possibility of its emendation by the voluntary action of the parties, must follow a path of aloofness which is apt to create the impression of ethical indifference or relativism. This is so in particular when we consider that in many cases the preponderance of legal merit – as between the successful and the defeated party – is inconsiderable and that the decision, even if unanimous, might well have gone the other way. Both in the international and in the municipal sphere the position is seldom such that a clear legal right is opposed to a clear absence of legal right. As stated, the decision is brought about by a preponderance, however slight, of legal merit. A decision, final and authoritative, there must be; there must be no *non liquet*. But that does not mean that there is a sacrosanctity about it which precludes, in proper

[1] Of this, an interesting example will be found in the award given in 1921 by Walter D. Hines, Arbitrator, concerning *Cession of Vessels and Tugs for Navigation on the Danube.* After having rendered his decision on the substantive issue before him, the Arbitrator said in his Conclusions: 'Having disposed of the questions submitted for his determination, the Arbitrator now ventures to express two thoughts which are outside of his functions as Arbitrator, but which he regards as of great importance to all the countries upon the Danube.' He proceeded to elaborate these thoughts in some detail (*U.N.R.I.A.A.* 1, 97, at pp. 143–4).

cases, an expression of opinion on the desirability of a voluntary modification of the binding decision. There may be cases in which a party may welcome a recommendation of this kind as making it more easy for it, having regard to its own public opinion or the possible objections of its Treasury, to adopt an attitude of neighbourliness, generosity and accommodation. It may not be necessary for such recommendation to be formally expressed in the operative part of the pronouncement. It may figure, with an efficacy which is sufficient for many practical purposes, in the reasoning of the tribunal. No opprobium can justifiably attach to the refusal of a Government to act upon any such recommendation, wherever and however expressed. A party which insists on its legal right owes no apology for or explanation of its attitude. It is the best judge of its moral duties. Also, it may rightly attach importance to the degree of persuasive power of the reasoning of any such recommendation and to the majority by which it has been formulated. On the other hand, as stated, circumstances may arise in which some such recommendation may be found useful by both parties and pave the way for a settlement which, being based on the full agreement of the parties, partakes of a finality transcending that of a legal judgment.

6

It has been thought useful to present in this essay, without expressing a preference for either of the opposing views, the considerations militating both in favour of and against the propriety and justification of some such method of recommendation over and above a judicial or arbitral decision. They are intended as showing the propriety and justification of an examination of that question, which is intimately connected with the ever-recurrent question of the rationality of a system of compulsory jurisdiction of tribunals bound in every case to give a decision, irrespective of the shortcomings and uncertainties of the existing law, in a society in which ordinary legislative processes are conspicuous for their absence.

Subject to the desirability of a renewed examination of this question, it does not appear that a case has been made out for casting doubt upon the principle of the completeness of the international legal order and its corollary, namely, the prohibition of *non liquet*. Those principles lend themselves to the somewhat easy reproach of formalism and lack of realism. It may be wise not to attribute undue importance to that particular emanation of the jurisprudential tendency which describes itself as realistic. For those principles represent existing and, essentially, sound law. Neither is their force weakened on account of their possible or occasional inconsistency with a rational solution of a particular dispute in conformity with moral justice. The moral justice of the law – or of a particular law – is not necessarily determined by its approximation to moral justice in an individual case. At the same time, while the limits of the function of courts to secure results which are ethically, politically and socially desirable, as distinguished from their task to apply existing law, are narrowly drawn, this does not necessarily mean that the area within these limits is negligible. When properly ascertained and wisely observed, these limits may permit judicial or arbitral expression of opinion which might provide an accession of strength to the basic principle of the completeness of the law.

CHAPTER 10

DECISIONS OF MUNICIPAL COURTS AS A SOURCE OF INTERNATIONAL LAW

Editor's note This chapter originally appeared in the *British Year Book of International Law*, 10 (1929), 65–95.

I

The function of decisions of municipal courts as a source of international law has hitherto been obscured by four factors: by the current preoccupation with decisions of prize courts and their identification with decisions of municipal courts in general; by the rigid predominance of the positivist doctrine; by the so-called dualistic conception of the relation between international law and municipal law; and by the confusion enveloping the conception of sources of international law on the one hand, and the nature of the function of municipal judges on the other.

The fact that prize courts dispense international law on behalf of the territorial sovereign and that the law which they administer is ultimately determined by their national legislature and the imperative national interests in time of stress has had the result of creating a sceptical consensus of opinion to the effect that decisions of prize courts must necessarily be tainted by national bias and, as such, be of doubtful value for the creation of general international law. At a time when the laws of war occupied the major part of treatises on international law, this view tended to affect adversely the estimation of the value of decisions of municipal courts in other fields. They were either ignored or made to share the charge of unavoidable partiality levelled against prize courts. However, the proper approach to the question discussed here does not lie through a proof of the truly international character of those courts. Lord Stowell did much in this country to vindicate the independent position of British prize courts, and his judgments in *The Maria*, *The Recovery*, and *The Fox*[1] will certainly rank among the most eloquent efforts to impress their decisions with the character of pro-

[1] 1 C. Rob. 350, 6 C. Rob. 348, 1 C. Rob. 312, respectively.

nouncements emanating from free judicial agencies impartially administering international law. But those pronouncements should be read in the light of both the accompanying historical events[1] and the subsequent history of maritime warfare, including the period of the World War.[2] The share of prize courts in the development of international law, great as it is, has inevitably become so controversial that it is convenient to exclude it altogether from the scope of the present article, which, accordingly, is concerned only with such decisions of municipal courts as bear upon the international law of peace.

The exaggerations of the prevalent positivist doctrine acted as another obstacle in the way of a proper appreciation of the importance of decisions of municipal courts. According to that doctrine, extensions of the field of implied consent of States must not be presumed, and consent must not be deduced from the mere fact of uniform observance of certain rules by States and their organs. Such concordance, says the doctrine, merely brings about what may be termed uniform external law, which, if it is to create a binding rule, must be deliberate and accompanied by the will to act in a manner which binds the State for the future. According to the dualistic view, closely allied to the positivist doctrine, municipal and international law are separated from each other by a formal gulf, which is the result of a fundamental difference in the ways in which the law is created, in its subjects, and in its matter, so that municipal courts are formally incapable of applying and, in consequence, of developing or creating international law. This attitude of indifference towards decisions of municipal courts has been fostered by the separation of international customary law from its constitutive elements, which have been given the name of *evidence* of custom and subsequently separated from custom itself. The opinion has been largely accepted that, under a most favourable construction, municipal decisions are only evidence of customs but not a factor creating customary international law. Viewed

[1] The judgment in *The Maria*, in which the universality and the impartiality of the law administered by British prize courts was proclaimed for the first time and in a most solemn manner, was given on 11 June 1799. It will be observed that between the years 1796 and 1802 there sat in London, with considerable interruptions, the Mixed Commission under Article VII of the Jay Treaty, and that questions as to the finality and the character of the decisions of the British prize courts were among the main issues in the deliberations of the Commission. See Moore, *International Arbitrations*, I, 324 *et seq.*; *ibid.* III, 3161 *et seq.* (Opinion of Commissioner Gore in the case of *The Betsey*); and Lapradelle-Politis, I, 87 *et seq.*

[2] See Garner, *Prize Law during the World War* (1927), sections 126–37.

from a different angle, this attitude is the outcome of the rigid separation of the judicial from the legislative functions in the direction of totally divorcing the work of judges from law-making proper. As in any case, it is said, judges only apply existing law, their decisions are of little or no consequence for the creation of international law.

It is believed that the effect of this attitude has been harmful inasmuch as it has tended to create the impression that the interest in internationally relevant municipal case-law is a peculiarity of English and American international lawyers unduly generalizing their passion for case-law. It has deprived international law of a fruitful source of development, and has diminished the opportunities for taking advantage of the lessons of judicial treatment of international law in a world in which these opportunities are not frequent. As an unavoidable consequence, it has tended to impair in municipal judges administering international law the consciousness of being – on a higher plane – the organs and trustees of the international legal community bound to apply international law with the utmost care and impartiality in the spirit of that unity of international and municipal law which is the goal of legal development.

It is proposed here to examine the reasons underlying this attitude of indifference. The main purpose, however, of the present article is an inquiry into the actual extent of the contribution of municipal courts to the development of international law.

2. THE SCOPE OF DECISIONS OF MUNICIPAL COURTS AFFECTING INTERNATIONAL LAW

As stated, the discussion of decisions of prize courts lies outside the scope of this article. But, quite apart from judgments of prize courts, there is hardly a branch of international law which has not received judicial treatment at the hands of municipal tribunals.[1]

[1] Reasons of space do not permit an exhaustive enumeration of the more important cases decided by municipal tribunals of different countries on the questions mentioned in the text. Besides the decisions of British and American courts, there exist numerous valuable decisions of the highest courts of France, Germany, Italy, and other countries. The references in the footnotes which follow relate mainly to works or monographs where groups of cases are discussed or enumerated.

Reports of the non-English municipal cases bearing upon international law will be found in the official or private law collections of decisions like *Giurisprudenza Italiana*, *Entscheidungen des Reichsgerichts in Zivilsachen und Strafsachen*, the *Recueils* of Dalloz and Sirey, the *Pasicrisie Belge*, etc. But apart from the English–American collections of cases, mainly

Their judgments deal with the nature, the sources,[1] and the subjects[2] of international law, and with its relation to municipal law.[3] They define the position and requirements of the State as an international person,[4] including the problem of the beginning of its existence as such[5] and of its continuity in face of territorial changes.[6]

for the use of students, like those compiled by Pitt Cobbett, Scott, Bentwich, and Evans, there are no systematic or periodical collections of national decisions of interest for the international lawyer, although some periodicals of international law, in particular Clunet's *Journal du droit international*, frequently report such decisions. It is hoped that the gap will be filled to a certain extent by the publication of the *Annual Digest of Public International Law Cases*, edited by Dr McNair and the present writer, and frequently referred to in the course of this article.

On the other hand, copious references to case-law will be found in some text-books of international law, the foremost of which in this respect is Oppenheim's *International Law*, as recently edited by Dr McNair (4th ed. 1928); also, Pradier-Fodéré's treatise contains frequent references to decisions of municipal courts. Professor Anzilotti's *Il diritto internazionale nei giudizi interni* (1905) contains a useful enumeration of municipal decisions, especially on pp. 160–73. International case-law in the United States has been reviewed by Wright, *The Enforcement of International Law through Municipal Law in the United States* (1916), and Pergler, *Judicial Interpretation of International Law in the United States* (1928). Many monographs and works on special subjects are repositories of municipal case law on questions of international law. Here belong, in particular, in addition to works on extradition and nationality, the treatises of Praag, *Juridiction et droit international public* (1915), and of Travers, *Le droit pénal international*, 5 vols. (1920–2). Cf. here Dr J. B. Scott's *Cases on International Law* (1922), Preface, p. xvi, on the necessity for collections of decisions of national courts of various States.

[1] See here the English and American cases – some of them decided by prize courts – reported in Scott's *Cases*, pp. 1–18. See also *Thirty Hogsheads of Sugar* v. *Boyle*, 9 Cranch, 191, on the authority of municipal decisions ('The decisions of the courts of every country, so far as they are founded upon a law common to every country, will be received, not as authority, but with respect. The decisions of the courts of every country show how the Law of Nations, in the given case, is understood in that country, and will be considered in adopting the rule which is to prevail in this').

[2] Here belong, *inter alia*, numerous extradition cases, in which the courts have expressed opinions as to the right of individuals to invoke rules of international law. A large number of these cases are referred to in Anzilotti, *Il diritto internationale nei giudizi interni*, pp. 223 *et seq*. See also the *Spanish-German Extradition Treaty* case in *Annual Digest*, 3 (1925–6) for a repeated affirmation by the German Federal Court of the orthodox doctrine that international law does not confer rights upon individuals.

[3] This group comprises, *inter alia*, numerous cases connected with the enforcement of treaties and with their relation to statutory law. An account of them will be found in Picciotto, *The Relation of International Law to the Law of England and of the United States* (1915), pp. 315–26; Pergler, *Judicial Interpretation*, 8–18. But it also includes cases bearing upon the relation of customary international law to municipal law, such as the English cases of *Triquet* v. *Bath*, *Reg*. v. *Keyn*, and *West Rand Central Gold Mining Co. Ltd.* v. *Rex* – each of them a landmark in the flow of what Judge Moore (as he then was) called 'the majestic stream of common law, united with international law' (*The Lotus* case, *P.C.I.J.* Series A, no. 10, p. 75).

[4] See, for instance, *Cherokee Nation* v. *State of Georgia*, 5 Peters 1, and other cases on the status of Indian tribes referred to in the *Cayuga Indians Claim* case in 1926 before the British-American Claims Commission and reported in *Annual Digest*, 3 (1925–6), p. 237.

[5] See, for instance, a number of decisions of the highest tribunals in Czechoslovakia on the establishment of the Czechoslovak State, reported in *Annual Digest*, 3(1925–6), and strikingly reminiscent of an American decision *in pari materia*: *McIlvaine* v. *Coxe's Lessee*, 4 Cranch, at p. 212.

[6] See the decision of the Austrian Supreme Court in Civil Administrative Matters on

They define the legal status of various types of composite States and their State members,[1] of protectorates and other semi-sovereign States,[2] of Mandates,[3] of other territories or parts of territories under joint or international control or supervision,[4] of the Holy See before 1929.[5] They are the chief source of judicial authority on the nature, the conditions, and the effects of recognition of States, Governments[6] and belligerency,[7] as well as on questions of State succession and succession of Governments, not only in regard to private rights in their different aspects, but also on such matters as succession to obligations laid down in treaties.[8] Matters of jurisdiction or, rather, of restrictions upon the jurisdiction of the State, are their own peculiar province, and through it they decide a large number of questions of international law.[9] Under this heading comes the wide field of diplomatic immunities with its vast variety

the Austrian Republic as the continuation of the Austrian Empire in *Austrian Pensions (State Succession)* case and the decision of the District Court of Amsterdam on the Turkish Republic as the continuation of the Ottoman Empire, in *Roselius and Company* v. *Karsten*, both reported in *Annual Digest*, 3 (1925–6).

[1] Anzilotti, *Il diritto internazionale nei giudizi interni*, enumerates on p. 161, n. 1, numerous decisions on the legal status of the Austro-Hungarian monarchy, as well as of Switzerland, Germany, the United States, and other federal States.

[2] See, for instance, *The Charkieh*, L.R. 4 Adm. and Eccl. 59 and other cases on the international position of Egypt, Tunis, Bulgaria, and Congo, quoted by Anzilotti, *Il diritto internazionale nei giudizi interni*, p. 160, n. 1, and p. 162, n. 2.

[3] In addition to the much-discussed case of *R* v. *Jacobus Christian* (*B.Y.* 6 (1925), 211), see such cases as *Cape Law Society* v. *Van Aardt*, on the legal relations between the Mandatory Power and the Mandated Territory with reference to the execution of judgments given in the latter; the *Lebanon Expropriation* case and *District Governor, Jerusalem-Jaffa District and Another* v. *Suleiman Murra and Another*, on the rights and duties of the Mandatory in Lebanon and Palestine, respectively; and several cases on nationality in Mandated Territories – reported in *Annual Digest*, 3 (1925–6), at pp. 43, 44 and 46, respectively.

[4] Here belong, e.g., the decisions on the status of Bosnia and Herzegovina before 1908 (*Clunet*, 13 (1886), 461), or of the Moresnet territory (*Clunet*, 16 (1889), 494); on international leases (*United States* v. *P. W. Smith*, a case on the jurisdictional rights of the United States in Liaotung); on the legal status of the Governing Commission in the Saar Territory (*Saar Territory (Prussian Officials)* case); on the authority of the International Rhineland High Commission (*Rhineland Ordinances* case); on territories under the authority of a plebiscitary commission (*Czechoslovak Spirit Duty (Plebiscite)* case) – the last four cases reported in *Annual Digest*, 3 (1925–6), at pp. 118, 50, 9, and 109, respectively.

[5] See numerous cases cited in Praag, pp. 547–50.

[6] See here Henry, *Les gouvernements de fait devant le juge* (1927), *passim*; Oppenheim, *International Law* (4th ed. by McNair, 1928), 1, §75 *d, e, f*; Anzilotti, *Il diritto internazionale nei giudizi interni*, pp. 162, 163; and numerous cases in *Annual Digest*, 3 (1925–6), part II D.

[7] See Pergler, *Judicial Interpretation*, pp. 48–57; and the *Cía Minera Ygnacio Rodriguez Ramos* v. *Bartlesville* case (*Annual Digest*, 3 (1925–6), p. 67).

[8] See, for earlier cases, Anzilotti, *Il diritto internationale nei giudizi interni*, pp. 164–7, and Keith, *The Theory of State Succession* (1907), *passim*; see also Scott, *Cases*, pp. 74–115, and, for a large number of cases, *Annual Digest*, 3 (1925–6), part II, E and F.

[9] The comprehensive treatise of Praag, referred to above, constitutes a classical example of a treatment based on a conscientious consideration of municipal precedents. From this point of view Praag's work is an indispensable source of reference.

of detail, including the question of the diplomatic immunities enjoyed by persons other than diplomatic envoys proper – for instance, by State representatives permanently accredited to the League of Nations.[1] The extent of jurisdictional immunities of foreign States, their heads, and their property, including their public ships and armed forces, belongs to the same group.[2] In a variety of ways municipal courts illustrate both the working and the legal implications of the régime of capitulations.[3] The *Lotus* case before the Permanent Court of International Justice showed how extensively the parties and the Tribunal had to rely on municipal decisions in regard to the question of jurisdiction over foreigners for crimes committed abroad.[4] Here also belong questions of jurisdiction over foreign ships in ports, in territorial waters, at the maritime frontier, and on the high seas.[5] It is mainly, although by no means exclusively, through the medium of jurisdiction that questions as to the extent of State territory in respect of the breadth of the maritime belt and of bays are dealt with by municipal courts. They have been frequently called upon to decide problems of acquisition of territorial sovereignty through accretion, accession, discovery, prescription, and conquest,[6] or of restrictions upon it through servitudes[7] or occupation in time of peace. Of the positive aspects of jurisdiction the question of recognition of acts of recognized States and Governments, including the question of the extraterritorial effect of such acts, has been responsible for a considerable wealth of judicial precedent.[8] The various aspects of questions of nationality, like naturalization, double nationality, denationalization and statelessness, constitute

[1] See *Annual Digest*, 3 (1925–6), 325 (*V.* v. *D.*), for an instance of an action against the representative of Yugoslavia accredited to the League of Nations.

[2] See Praag, *passim*; Oppenheim, I (4th ed. by McNair, 1928), §115; Scott, *Cases*, pp. 265–85; Pergler, *op. cit.* pp. 101 *et seq.*

[3] See the cases enumerated by Anzilotti, *Il diritto internazionale nei giudizi interni*, p. 169, n. 2. The *Annual Digest*, 3 (1925–6), reports, *inter alia*, numerous cases decided by the Italian Court of Cassation.

[4] *P.C.I.J.* Series A, no. 10, pp. 28–30, 73–83, and Series C, no. 13–II, throughout, and in particular pp. 256 *et seq.*, 381 *et seq.*

[5] Jessup's treatise on *The Law of Territorial Waters and Maritime Jurisdiction* (1927) contains exhaustive references to municipal precedents in various countries.

[6] Numerous cases decided by the Supreme Court of the United States between the States of the American Union constitute here the main source of judicial authority. See Pergler, *Judicial Interpretation*, pp. 80–100; Scott, *Cases*, pp. 173–200, and the same, *Judicial Settlement of Controversies between States of the American Union* (1919), *Analysis*, pp. 390 *et seq.* And see below on the recent application of the doctrine of prescription in disputes between Michigan and Wisconsin, and Mecklenburg and Lübeck.

[7] See a judgment of the Cologne Court of Appeal in 1914, in *A.J.* 8 (1914), 907–13.

[8] See Oppenheim, I (4th ed. by McNair, 1928), 156, n. 1, and *Annual Digest*, 3 (1925–6), parts II A and IV A.

another wide field of application of international law. So do questions of extradition. That aspect of State responsibility which is connected with the duty of the State to prevent within its jurisdiction certain acts injurious to foreign countries is well represented in decisions of municipal courts.[1] The recent enlargement of the sphere of international protection of the individual through the minorities treaties has already brought forth a number of decisions forming a distinct contribution to this part of the law.[2] In the domain of treaties, municipal courts are constantly called upon to pronounce not only in regard to the operation of treaties in the municipal sphere and to the necessity for internal legislation, but also on the nature of treaties, the treaty-making power, the effect of treaties upon third parties, their termination and interpretation. Questions of law connected with the judicial settlement of international disputes lie naturally outside their scope, but even here we shall find decisions on such matters as the effect of an arbitral award.[3] There are decisions of municipal courts on certain effects of measures of redress short of war;[4] and although prize law, as already stated, lies outside the scope of this article, in other fields of the law of war the contribution of municipal courts cannot be ignored. It is sufficient to mention such questions as those of the beginning[5] and termination[6] of war, to the effects of the outbreak of war upon treaties, upon contracts with enemy persons, and upon the personal status and property of enemy persons. The numerous decisions of national courts on questions connected with the occupation of enemy territory afford another instructive example.[7]

The above enumeration of matters covered by municipal decisions is apt to leave the impression that there is hardly a branch of international law which they do not touch. Such an impression would not be entirely misleading. Undoubtedly, there are certain

[1] See the numerous cases discussed by the writer in *A.J.* 22 (1928), 105–30; Curtis, *ibid.* 8 (1914), 1–37, 224–52. But see also, on other aspects of State responsibility, Pergler, *Judicial Interpretation*, pp. 77 *et seq.*

[2] See, for instance, *Czechoslovak Language of Minorities* case, *Annual Digest*, 3 (1925–6), 313.

[3] See Anzilotti, *Il diritto internazionale nei giudizi interni*, p. 174, n. 2; Pergler, *Judicial Interpretation*, pp. 188, 189; Wright, *Enforcement of International Law*, p. 102.

[4] See Wright, *Enforcement of International Law*, pp. 28–30; Pergler, *Judicial Interpretation*, p. 193.

[5] See here the numerous cases reviewed by McNair in *Grotius Society*, 11 (1926), 46–9.

[6] See cases cited by Hudson in *H.L.R.* 39 (1925–6), 1039–44.

[7] A large selection of decisions connected with the law of war will be found in *Annual Digest*, 3 (1925–6), part XI (War and Neutrality).

matters which for obvious reasons are removed from the purview of municipal courts; for instance, questions of fact on which courts regard themselves as bound to accept as conclusive the statements of the executive department of their State. But this and similar exceptions merely confirm the general rule that there is scarcely a question or class of questions of international law of which it could be predicated in advance that it is incapable of treatment and decision by a municipal court. To say that municipal courts are restricted to questions of jurisdiction is, on the face of it, inaccurate. A limitation of a different nature has been suggested by Triepel[1] and developed in detail by Anzilotti. Their theory is that whereas international law can never, by reason of the fundamental fact that it applies only to relations between States, constitute the cause of action in so far as private persons are concerned, it may and ought to be applied to the determination of preliminary questions which are only incidental to the main issue. 'It happens', says Anzilotti, 'that in the course of a legal process governed by municipal law, and accordingly by municipal courts, it is necessary to take into account principles and rules of international law; such a necessity arises in the shape of questions preliminary (*pregiudiziali*) and incidental to the solution of questions not governed by international law.'[2] This, he appears to say, is not a case of individuals being governed by or invoking the Law of Nations, but of States applying it through their judicial organs. An example will illustrate this distinction: according to Anzilotti, the principle of immunity of diplomatic envoys is a duty prescribed by municipal law, whereas such questions as whether a particular grade of the diplomatic staff enjoys jurisdictional immunity, the beginning and the termination of the diplomatic mission, the effects of war upon it, and so on, are preliminary questions, which ought to be decided by international law.

Both the reasons underlying this distinction and its legal merits will be examined later. For the purpose of the present discussion it is sufficient to point out that the limitation to questions of an incidental character is of a merely formal nature and does not in fact restrict the scope of the application of international law. Even if it could be admitted that the function of municipal courts is thus confined to 'incidental' questions, it is clear that practically all matters of international law, as enumerated on the preceding

[1] *Völkerrecht und Landesrecht* (1899), pp. 438, 439.
[2] *Il diritto internazionale nei giudizi interni*, p. 159.

pages, are capable of coming and do come before municipal courts. It is these 'incidental' questions which constitute practically the wholy body of international law, seeing that its rules are as yet to a large extent of a jurisdictional character. To mention one instance: what remains, except a bare idea, of the law concerning diplomatic immunities, after the details of its application have been eliminated? The fact that the suggested limitation is merely a matter of terminology and that it does not actually restrict the scope of judicial application of international law would in itself be sufficient to render it somewhat theoretical. But it has deeply influenced the appreciation of the value of municipal decisions in the field of international law, and it is therefore impossible to ignore it in this discussion. Its roots lie to a large extent in the view that, as international law regulates only the relations between States, it also regulates only interests of States to the exclusion of private rights and interests. This view is in turn connected with the opinion that the proper and normal occasion for the judicial application of rules of international law is the existence of disputes between States. As a matter of fact, it is only by way of exception that they are thus applied. Normally, they are administered by the administrative and judicial authorities of States, partly because a great many of these rules regulate private rights of or duties either directly or as determining the jurisdictional competence of the State, and partly because private rights and duties are frequently in other ways dependent upon the answer to questions of international law. The Law of Nations certainly protects the rights of and imposes duties upon States as such, but it also shields private rights for the protection of which the State is responsible either to other members of the international community or – as, for instance, in certain cases of State succession, when the rights protected are those of its own subjects – to the impersonal authority of international law. Frequently private rights are protected in the interest of the foreign State, but that does not deprive them of their character as private rights. Neither is it true to maintain that international law regulates only the conduct of States. It is more accurate to say that it regulates such individual conduct of its subjects or its organs as is in international law attributable to the State and for which it is ultimately responsible. A broad rule can be laid down to the effect that wherever a right, private or public, is claimed, or a duty, private or public, is sought to be imposed by virtue of or by reference to a rule of international law, or whenever recognition of such rights and duties proves in the course of an action to be dependent upon questions of fact or law determined by international law, in all these cases there is room for judicial application of international law. Experience shows that the scope of such application is practically unlimited.

Finally, there should be mentioned in this connection a number of judicial decisions which lie on the border-line between municipal and international case-law. These are decisions by municipal courts settling disputes of a quasi-international character between member-States of composite States. This type of judicial settlement constituted the bulk of international arbitration among the City States of the various Greek federations in ancient Greece. It was revived and practised with considerable success in the second half of the Middle Ages between the cities of the numerous federations in upper Italy[1] and among the Swiss cantons.[2] In the Supreme Court of the United States, in its capacity as the judge in disputes between the sovereign States of the Union, it found an authoritative tribunal before which came important questions of international law.[3] Only three years ago, in a boundary dispute between Michigan and Wisconsin, the Supreme Court had occasion to apply the doctrine of prescription.[4] In the Judicial Committee of the Privy Council the members of the British Commonwealth of Nations have another high tribunal for settling disputes between them on the basis of international law when applicable.[5] Thus, to mention a recent instance, in the *Labrador Boundary* case in 1927, the Judicial Committee applied the doctrines of discovery and of the watershed.[6] The Swiss Federal Court exercises the function of the supreme judge between the members of the Swiss Federal State, and from this Court emanates one of the very few judicial pronouncements on the application of the *clausula rebus*

[1] See Frey, *Das öffentlich-rechtliche Schiedsgericht in Ober-Italien im XII und XIII Jahrhundert* (1928).

[2] See Usteri, *Das öffentlich-rechtliche Schiedsgericht in der Schweizerischen Eidgenossenschaft des XII–XV Jahrhunderts* (1925).

[3] See Scott, *Cases*, and the same, *Sovereign States and Suits* (1925); Smith, *The American Supreme Court as an International Tribunal* (1920); Warren, *The Supreme Court and the Sovereign States* (1924).

[4] 270 United States, 295; see also *Annual Digest*, 3 (1925–6), 113.

[5] There seems to be interesting evidence in support of the view which connects the origin of the Supreme Court of the United States with the familiarity of the authors of the Constitution with the work of the Judicial Committee, which had in the past advised the King in regard to boundary disputes between American colonies; see Warren, *The Supreme Court*, pp. 32, 33. And see, on this point and on the settlement of inter-State disputes by the Judicial Committee in general, Snow in *Proceedings of the American Society for Judicial Settlement of International Disputes* (1910), pp. 124 *et seq.*; Riddell, *ibid.* (1916), pp. 104–23; and Caldwell, in *A.J.* 14 (1920), 38–52.

[6] 43 T.L.R. at p. 294.

sic stantibus to relations between States.[1] The work, in recent years, of the German *Staatsgerichtshof* has shown how wide is the scope of the judicial application of international law in this field. In 1925, in a dispute between Lübeck and Mecklenburg-Schwerin, that Court issued a provisional injunction based on the fact of long undisturbed possession, and dealt in an affirmative way with the question whether one State may exercise sovereign rights over a part of the territorial waters of another.[2] In 1926 it dealt with a request of Bremen asking for the termination, by virtue of the *clausula rebus sic stantibus*, of certain treaties of exchange of territory concluded with Prussia before the World War.[3] In the following year it applied what it regarded as a rule of customary international law to a dispute between Prussia, Baden and Württemberg concerning the rights and duties of riparian States in respect of navigable rivers flowing through their territory.[4] In all these cases the Court availed itself of the provision of the German Constitution which declares international law to be an integral part of German federal law.

3. THE FORMAL NATURE OF INTERNATIONAL LAW ADMINISTERED BY MUNICIPAL TRIBUNALS

Can rules of international law administered by municipal tribunals be regarded as international law proper, or are they in fact rules of municipal law? The question seems at first sight to be of a purely theoretical character, but it has frequently occupied international lawyers, and it is of considerable importance for the appreciation of the value of municipal decisions as a source of international law. It can be dealt with briefly. It is settled law that English judges are bound to administer customary international law as part of the law of the land. The position is the same in the United States and, by virtue of the constitutional provision already quoted, in Germany, in regard to both customary and conventional international law. The laws of almost all countries incorporate by direct reference rules of international law on various kinds of topics. According to a widely held view, that reference to international law *eo nomine* is the result of a faulty terminology adopted by legislatures, judges, and writers, who ignore the fundamental difference between international and municipal law. This difference, it is said, consists: (a) in that

[1] See vol. 8, p. 57, of the decisions of the Federal Court.
[2] See *Annual Digest*, 3 (1925–6), 114. [3] *Ibid.*
[4] *Entscheidungen des Reichsgerichts in Zivilsachen*, vol. 116, Appendix.

international law emanates from the collective will of States, whereas rules of municipal law have their origin in the will of one State; and (b) in that rules of international law regulate the relations of co-ordinated and autonomous entities united in a community lacking a judicial and political organization, whereas in municipal law the opposite is the case. It results in the impossibility of a formal identity of rules of international law and municipal law. If one may be allowed to quote Anzilotti once more:

A rule of international law is by its very nature absolutely unable to bind individuals, i.e., to confer upon them rights and duties. It is created by the collective will of states with the view of regulating their mutual relations; obviously it cannot therefore refer to an altogether different sphere of relations. If several States were to attempt the creation of rules directly regulating private relations, such an attempt, by the very nature of things, would not be a rule of international law, but a rule of uniform municipal law common to several States. It is only by such rules that the private duty, as willed by international law, can be given effect.[1]

These objections, he says, do not apply to preliminary or incidental questions on the ground that they are decided by judges acting as organs of the State, which, as such, is bound to apply rules of international law. It has already been noted that incidental questions may cover practically the whole field of international law, and this fact tends to emphasize the doubtful value of the distinction. Apart from this, it is difficult to comprehend why judges should not be able to apply international law to principal questions while they are bound to do so in regard to incidental matters. Both types of question involve private interests. If in incidental questions judges may and must apply international law, that must necessarily mean that individuals have in regard to these questions the right to invoke the Law of Nations[2] – a factor which in itself would be sufficient to disprove the theory of the fundamental inapplicability of international law as such to the regulation of private rights and duties.

The theory here examined seems to be a good example of the consequences of extreme positivism, which frequently amounts to ignoring the positive law which it professes to recognize as the only source of authority. The only effective argument in support of that theory would be the negative proof that municipal law expressly eschews any direct reference to international law. Such a proof,

[1] *Il diritto internazionale nei giudizi interni*, p. 177.
[2] See on this point Diena, in *R.G.* 16 (1909), 57–70.

being obviously contrary to facts, is not practicable. The only alternative left to the doctrine is to explain away the existing law by maintaining that its terminology is unsuitable. It explains it away by asserting that, by the very fact of adoption, the rules of international law have lost their original character and become municipal law. But this reasoning is not accurate, or, at least, not wholly accurate. Reference, adoption, or delegation does not deprive the original source of its true character. The law merchant does not cease to be the law merchant because judicial precedent and custom have adopted it as a source of law. This negation of the international character of the rules of international law adopted by municipal courts is, particularly in Anglo-American literature, largely due to the aberrations of the discussion centring round the question of the supremacy of international law over the law of the land.[1] The formal supremacy of the law of the State has been defended with the help of the argument that rules of international law are valid in the municipal sphere not as rules of international law, but as rules of the law of the land. But it is submitted that recourse to this argument is unnecessary. The supremacy of municipal law, if there be such, is safeguarded by the fact that international law had to be adopted[2] before it acquired validity in the municipal sphere. The principle holds good that whenever, by implied or express delegation or reference to international law as a whole or to some of its rules, rights are conferred or duties are imposed, the rules thus adopted preserve their original character as precepts of international law notwithstanding their adoption as part of the law of the land.

4. REVIEW OF AUTHORITIES

The attitude of writers in regard to the question under discussion is largely determined by their attitude to the major issue outlined in the two preceding paragraphs. Positivist writers of the continental school deny to municipal decisions any direct law-creating effect in the sphere of international law, and the only concession which the more moderate among them are prepared to make is that such

[1] See, for instance, the exchange of views in the articles of Scott, in *A.J.* 1 (1907), 831–6, and Willoughby, *ibid.* 2 (1908), 357–65.

[2] The believer in the supremacy of international law will say, rightly it is submitted, that the adoption had taken place by virtue of a duty imposed by international law, and that the failure to adopt it would engage the international responsibility of the State which ultimately must yield to the higher authority of the Law of Nations.

decisions are either evidence of pre-existing customary law or may influence the creation of subsequent customary international law. On the other hand, there are writers who have no hesitation in regarding them as a source of international law proper. Reasons of space allow only a reference to the more representative writers. The attitude of both Triepel and Anzilotti, who have been among the leaders of the positivist movement in the last thirty years, is a negative one, and is based on grounds already indicated. According to Triepel, only the common will of sovereign States, consciously intent upon creating law, is able to produce international law. The will of a single State evidenced by its statutory law or its internal custom, judicial and otherwise, is unable to produce that effect. Secondly, as international law regulates relations between States only and exclusively, municipal law is formally incapable of becoming a source of international law.[1] Anzilotti has developed this view in more detail.[2] In addition to reasons based on the orthodox dualistic view, he points out that it is not sufficient for the creation of a rule of international law that the manifestations of the will of States should be of an identical content. These manifestations must be reciprocal, i.e., deliberately made to correspond to each other with a view to creating an obligatory norm in respect of the conduct in question. The law of a single State creates only external public law. It does not produce international law, and there is nothing to prevent the State from altering or repealing a law thus enacted, even if identical with that adopted by other States, so long as it has not become an objective rule of international law grounded in deliberate reciprocity. Professor Cavaglieri's recent treatise shows with what persistence scholars of authority adhere to this view.[3] Oppenheim's contribution to the controversy follows the same negative lines, although his estimate of the practical value of municipal case-law is illuminating and helpful.[4] He attaches decisive importance to the argument that judges are not law-makers in the technical sense. He stresses the rather obvious truth that isolated decisions of national courts cannot bind a foreign State or abrogate a rule of international law, and denies that they directly concern international law even to the extent of binding the Government of their own country. Both the manner of treatment and the negative

[1] *Völkerrecht und Landesrecht*, pp. 127, 128. See also pp. 28–32 and 99–101.

[2] *Il diritto internazionale nei giudizi interni*, pp. 197, 198, and 143–146. See also his *La teoria generale della risponsibilità dello stato nel diritto internazionale* (1902), pp. 30 *et seq.*

[3] Cavaglieri, pp. 56, 57.

[4] In *A.J.* 2 (1908), 336–41 (section entitled 'Appreciation of Municipal Case-Law').

results arrived at by Heilborn,[1] De Louter,[2] Fauchille,[3] and others show clear traces of Oppenheim's influence.

Praag accepts the negative view of these writers except in regard to such judicial decisions as influence the legal sphere of other States, that is, decisions on questions of jurisdiction – which, as it happens, constitute the subject-matter of Dr Praag's work and probably cover the major portion of the international law of peace. In this respect, he says, they form 'une source véritable pour la formation du droit international public'.[4]

However, there is a considerable weight of authority in favour of a more affirmative view. Westlake regards decisions of municipal courts as direct evidence of the consent of States, like treaties and other manifestations of the practice of States 'so far as in all these ways they have proceeded on general principles and not with a view to particular circumstances, and so far as their actions and the judgments of their courts have not been encountered by resistance or protest from other States'.[5] Rivier, who defines international custom as the manifestation of the juridical conscience of States operating through acts repeated *opinione necessitatis*, regards unilateral acts of the legislative and judicial authorities of the State as constituting international custom. He is clearly of the opinion[6] that concordant decisions of national tribunals are true manifestations of '*la conscience juridique internationale*'. Geffcken expresses a similar opinion in his note to Heffter, who regards national decisions as evidence of custom.[7] Of more recent writers Liszt (edited by Fleischmann),[8] Fenwick,[9] Kosters,[10] and, in part, Brierly[11] tend to accept the same view. Frequently writers include decisions of municipal courts in their enumeration of sources of international law, more often than not in the same breath with the decisions of prize courts – a circumstance which is responsible for the accompanying qualifications of the impartiality of municipal case-law and its law-creating effect

[1] *Grundbegriffe des Völkerrechts* (1912), pp. 70, 71, and in *Hague Recueil*, 11 (1926) (i), 51, 52.

[2] De Louter, I, 56, 57.

[3] *Traité*, I, part I, nos. 55–7.

[4] Praag, p. 24. See nos. 7 and 9.

[5] *Papers*, p. 83.

[6] Rivier, I, 35.

[7] Heffter, §8. So does Nys, I, 167, who, however, stresses the fact that they are only evidence of custom, not custom itself.

[8] Liszt, pp. 16, 17.

[9] *International Law* (1st ed. 1924), pp. 69, 70.

[10] 'Les fondements du droit des gens', in *Bibliotheca Visseriana*, 4 (1925), 241.

[11] *The Law of Nations* (1st ed. 1928), p. 41.

in regard to other States. Here belong, for instance, the works of Calvo,[1] Pradier-Fodéré,[2] and the recent treatise of Hyde.[3]

On the whole, it appears that the attitude towards municipal case-law is one of caution both on account of its association with prize courts and owing to the prevalence of the dualistic conception of international law. 'Without pausing to consider the value to be attributed to the judgment of municipal courts in connection with the establishment of a rule of international law',[4] the Permanent Court of International Justice proceeded, in *The Lotus* case, to examine at great length the relevant judicial decisions in various countries. That cautious attitude found expression also in Article 38 (4) of the Statute of the Court which provides that, subject to the provisions of Article 59, the Court shall apply 'judicial decisions and the teachings of the most highly qualified publicists of the various nations, as subsidiary means for the determination of rules of law'. However, the contention will be put forward later that the real *sedes materiae* of municipal case-law is to be found not in the passage just quoted, but in those parts of that Article which designate as direct sources of international law 'international custom, as evidence of a general practice accepted as law'.

5. DECISIONS OF MUNICIPAL COURTS AS A SOURCE OF CUSTOMARY INTERNATIONAL LAW

The basis of international law is the consent of States. Its sources are the facts and events showing the express or implied consent of the members of the international community. The implied consent deduced from these facts and events is the basis of international custom, which is the sum total of such acts of the organs of the State undertaken *opinione juris* as bear upon rights protected and duties imposed by international law. As courts are organs of the State, the rule may be formulated that decisions of municipal courts on matters of international law are a source of customary international law in so far as they are uniform and in regard to States the courts of which have participated in the creation of

[1] Calvo, I, § 34.

[2] Pradier-Fodéré, I, no. 30.

[3] *International Law* (1st ed. 1922), I, 6. There is no qualification of that kind in Phillimore, I, 55, who, while stating that 'the consent of nations is also evidenced by the decisions of prize courts, and of the tribunals of international law sitting in each country', is full of praise for the impartiality of prize courts.

[4] *P.C.I.J.* series A, no. 10, p. 28.

such uniformity. This rule, however, is far from being generally adopted.

The first question which arises in this connection is: Are these municipal decisions custom proper, or are they merely evidence of custom? There has been a tendency to attach importance to that distinction in the sense of accepting the latter alternative and rejecting the former. There is little to be said in commendation of that attitude. One of the reasons which complicate the issue under discussion is just that rigid separation of international custom as a source of international law from its various manifestations, namely, from the evidence of customary international law. There is no such distinction. International custom is nothing else than the sum total of concordant acts of States – 'States' meaning organs of States, executive, legislative, or judicial. These acts are the substance of the purely formal conception of international custom, which without them is a bare idea. It may be conceded that the same event may be regarded, according to circumstances, both as evidence of custom and as a constitutive element of custom. But custom, when permanently divorced from 'evidence of custom', is a legal conception as formal as consent when divorced from custom and treaty. When, therefore, the terms 'consent', 'custom', 'evidence', are being used, we must not think that we are dealing with altogether different matters. These terms are gradual materializations, in a descending order, of the same content. Consent is a formal source; it finds its partial materialization in custom and treaty which in relation to it are the material sources.[1] Custom, in turn, taken in itself is a purely formal source of law; it finds its materialization in the various manifestations of the practice of States which are called evidence of custom, and which in relation to custom are the material source. Very little useful purpose is served by hypostatizing these terms and setting them up into rigid categories.[2] Definitions, useful as they may be, must not become an obstacle to the recognition of the substance of things. If we halt for a moment and analyse the statement that a series of acts or declarations can be only evidence of custom, but not custom proper, we must see that such a statement amounts to a negation of customary law. Undoubtedly,

[1] See here Professor Higgins's *Studies in International Law and Relations* (1928), p. 98.

[2] The student of international law will note the periodical attempts 'to introduce clarity' into the use of the conception of sources. Both the urgency and the effectiveness of these well-meant efforts are perhaps open to question. See, for instance, the article of Professor Corbett in *B.Y.* 6 (1925), 20–30. It will be noted that Article 38 (2) of the Statute of the Permanent Court speaks of *custom* as *evidence* of the *practice* of States.

some acts may be only declarative of pre-existing custom, but it is clear that whenever there is an urgent necessity for referring to them for the purpose of evidence, the existence of custom as such is or has become doubtful, and the 'evidence' becomes the constitutive element of custom.

The law-creating effect of municipal decisions could be effectively denied only if it were possible to show: (a) that the requirements of international custom are different from those which, according to general legal principles, prevail in other fields of law; (b) that municipal courts cannot be regarded as the organs of the State called upon to act in the international sphere by producing binding effects in the domain of the creation of international law; (c) that the function of courts being limited to applying existing law, it is impossible to ascribe to them the function of *creating* customary law. No one of these propositions can be accepted.

(a) The opinion that uniformity of attitude on the part of State organs is not decisive so long as there is no express evidence of the will to enter a mutually binding obligation, has become very popular. It is not sufficient, says Professor Cavaglieri in his recent treatise, that the practice should be identical: 'It is necessary that the uniform acts should be reciprocal, that is, intended to meet and to merge into the correspondent acts of other States.'[1] What is the meaning of this qualification when applied to uniform legislative acts or to decisions of municipal courts? It is submitted that it is only a matter of speech. Judicial decisions are not political acts intended to produce results extraneous to the case before the court; their object is to pronounce judgments *opinione juris*, that is, in accordance with existing law or, when the law is not settled, in accordance with justice and with the nature of international law and relations. *Opinio juris* is the central requirement of custom, and it is in judicial decisions that this condition can be fulfilled in the international sphere in a spirit of detachment and impartiality free from considerations of immediate and important interests of States. Official expressions of views of Governments on matters of international law addressed to other Governments or made before international tribunals are frequently partisan assertions of claims. They come from

[1] Cavaglieri, pp. 56–7 ('occorre che gli atti uniformi siano *reciproci*, cioè diretti ad incontrarsi, a fondersi con quelli corrispondenti degli altri Stati'). See, to the same effect, Triepel, *Völkerrecht und Landesrecht*, pp. 28–32, 99–101; Anzilotti, *Il diritto internazionale nei giudizi interni*, pp. 143–6, 197, 198, and in *Corso di diritto internazionale* (2nd ed. 1923), I, 43; Diena, *Dritto internazionale* (2nd ed. 1914), p. 18; Heilborn, *Grundbegriffe des Völkerrechts*, pp. 70, 71; Praag, nos. 7, 9.

parties directly interested, and frequently change with circumstances. The arguments put forward by representatives of States before international tribunals illustrate this point very clearly. The attitude of this country and of the United States in the *Behring Sea Arbitration* on the question of admissibility in international law of damages for loss of profits was diametrically opposed to that adopted by them in the *Alabama Arbitration*. In the latter case, the views of this country on the question of the duties of neutrals were different from those adopted by her in the proceedings before the Commission sitting in 1796 under Article VII of the Jay Treaty. The views of the United States and of Great Britain, in arbitrations with each other and with other countries, on the respective merits of occupation and discovery as a title of acquisition of territorial sovereignty show an unusual degree of inconsistency. The persistent defence, for obvious reasons, of the natural law foundation of international law by the American counsel in the *Behring Sea Arbitration* would have proved a source of embarrassment for the American representative in many of the subsequent arbitrations. Although opposing counsel occasionally try to make capital out of such radical changes of attitude, an international tribunal has never, so far as we know, adopted it as a ground of decision. But the decisions of municipal courts on questions of international law before them are not opinions of an interested party eager to drive home an argument or to cloak a political claim with the garb of a legal rule. From the point of view, therefore, of intrinsic and lasting value, the pronouncements of courts are more important for the formation of international custom than those of other State organs.

It is only the apprehension, stimulated by an exaggerated regard for sovereignty, lest the State be bound by rules based on its implied, as distinguished from its express, will, that makes writers pile up these unnecessary conditions.[1] It is of the essence of custom that the binding force of its rules is based on implied, not express, consent, and a limitation – whatever it may mean – which requires an express intention that the rules announced should meet and merge into the corresponding rules laid down by the organs of other States, strikes at the very roots of customary law conceived as implied consent. For the essential conditions of international custom and municipal custom are the same. This applies also to the rule that custom

[1] It is to a large extent the theory, prevalent on the Continent, of international custom as based on contract or agreement (*Vereinbarung*) which is responsible for this tendency to limit the scope of implied consent as the basis of custom.

need not bind all members of the community; it may be partial and local, as in fact is the bulk of municipal custom in developed society. On the other hand, it is clear that the requirements of immemorial antiquity and of long repeated usage must be adapted to the fact that international law itself is of recent growth, and that, the opportunities for creating or acting upon a rule being comparatively rare, a usage will harden into custom after a comparatively short period of time and after comparatively few occasions have arisen for its application. The only essential condition is that there should be *opinio juris*.

(b) What has been said so far is, of course, subject to the acceptance of the view that the decisions of the courts of a State can properly be described as acts of the State itself. It is difficult not to accept this view. The State as such is an abstraction. As an acting entity it is cognizable only through the acts of its organs. Courts are organs of the State, and the State is responsible for such of their acts as fail to give effect to international law. 'It is an axiom in international relations that a sovereign State cannot speak with two voices'[1] – that of the executive and that of the courts. They are the same voice. The conclusiveness in relation to courts of statements by the Crown in certain matters bearing upon international law is in the majority of cases only the necessary corollary of this principle.

The question could be asked: Are *all* organs of the State in a position to participate on its behalf in the creation of rules of customary international law? Is it not, for instance, a well-established rule that in regard to the conclusion of treaties any obligation undertaken by an organ of the State not duly authorized by its Constitution has no binding effect whatsoever? The answer is that courts pronouncing upon questions of international law *do* act within their competence. Their judgments do not produce an express and immediate obligation in the same manner as a treaty does. They are not meant to do that. But their cumulative and indirect effect is to give expression to the *opinio juris* of the highest judicial organs of the State. This they cannot help doing, and no one who searches for the evidence of the legal conviction of States is at liberty to disregard the pronouncements of their courts.

(c) The view which denies to municipal decisions any part in the formation of customary international law on the ground that

[1] McNair, 'Judicial Recognition of States and Governments, and the Immunity of Public Ships,' in *B.Y.* 2 (1921–2), 65.

courts in general do not make law but only declare it, does not require elaborate refutation. It is now generally accepted that every application of a legal rule constitutes to a smaller or larger degree the creation of a rule for the individual case. It is equally generally admitted that although the nature of the law-creating activity of courts is different from that of the Legislature, it is nevertheless constantly in operation. In few matters has the departure from the tenets of the analytical school been so radical as in this respect – not only in England and America, where judicial custom has always enjoyed the authority of an independent source of law, but also on the continent of Europe.

It is perhaps necessary to refer in this connection to the persistent attempt to reduce the question here discussed to a somewhat trifling issue. Writers who otherwise do not show excessive solicitude for the supremacy of the Law of Nations, are in the habit of pointing out that it would mean the end of international law if the municipal courts of a single country could create international law.[1] The apprehension is groundless. No one suggests that an isolated municipal decision can *proprio vigore* create a rule of international law. The thesis here submitted is that such decisions, when forming a link in a chain of concordant decisions *in pari materia* on the part of courts of several States, participate in the creation of a customary rule of international law. It may be added that when the decisions in question originate from courts of a large number of States and relate to a matter which lies within the particular province of those States, they will create customary international law binding also upon such States as had no occasion to signify their adherence to this rule.[2]

It appears from the foregoing that uniform municipal case-law on questions of international law may well be regarded as forming part of 'international custom as evidence of a general practice accepted as law' referred to in the second paragraph of Article 38 of the Statute of the Permanent Court of International Justice. Such uniform municipal case-law is not included – or, at least, not wholly included – in the fourth section of this Article, which, subject to the provisions of Article 59, refers, *inter alia*, to judicial decisions

[1] See, for instance, Willoughby, *The Fundamental Concepts of Public Law* (1924), pp. 284, 285.

[2] See Oppenheim, in *Z.I.* 25 (1915), 8. If an instance taken from conventional international law may properly be used as an example, it was held by the Mixed Court of Appeal in Egypt that an international convention to regulate the question of salvage on the high seas adopted by almost all maritime States was applicable to Egypt, although she had never adhered to it (*Crichton* v. *Samos Navigation Company and Others: Annual Digest*, 3 (1925–6), 3).

as a subsidiary means for the determination of rules of law. Article 59 provides that 'the decision of the Court has no binding force except between the parties and in respect of that particular case'. This provision, as well as the entire history of that part of the fourth paragraph of Article 38, shows that the judicial decisions here referred to are in the first instance individual decisions of the Permanent Court itself, for which it was intended to secure all the persuasive influence of judicial precedent without adhering to the doctrine *stare decisis*. Possibly it refers also to individual decisions of municipal courts. But it is submitted that the true *sedes materiae* of uniform decisions of municipal courts in their cumulative effect as international custom is in the second paragraph of Article 38.

6. DECISIONS OF NATIONAL COURTS AS AN ELEMENT OF DEVELOPMENT OF INTERNATIONAL LAW

However strong may be the claim of municipal case-law to rank as a source of customary international law, its function in that capacity is limited owing to the fact that in many fields there is neither a sufficient number of precedents nor such a degree of uniformity as to warrant an affirmative conclusion as to the existence of a customary rule. But this limitation emphasizes the not less important part of municipal courts in developing and preparing the ground for the formation of rules of international law.

In the first instance, they bring into relief divergencies in the application of international law in different countries, and thus pave the way for the removal or reconciliation of such discrepancies as are of a merely accidental or formal character. These discrepancies are numerous, but it is rarely realized that, far from being rooted in any real conflict of interests, they are frequently grounded in the peculiar circumstances of place and time. It is only through a comparative study of these divergent decisions that the differences can be reduced to their proper proportions and ultimately eliminated for the sake of a uniform application of international law. Thus, for instance, it is clear that there are hardly any reasons of substance, from the point of view of the national interests involved, for the separate Anglo-American practice and the so-called French rule in regard to jurisdiction over crimes and offences committed on foreign merchantmen passing through the maritime belt. Moreover, a study of municipal decisions in this branch of law shows that the difference is one of approach only, and that in practice the courts of those countries deal with this question in much the same way. A study of municipal decisions will reveal that the practice of courts differs in regard to the question how far diplomatic immunity extends to acts not included within the field of the diplomatic functions of the envoy, but it will show at the same time how alien to any consideration of national interests are the reasons, if any, underlying this difference in treatment. These examples can be multiplied at will. It is mostly only a misplaced respect for the sovereignty of States which elevates these variations of practice to deeply rooted differences in the various systems of jurisprudence. Those acquainted with the work of international committees and conferences engaged upon the work of codification of international law know with what unenlightened loyalty delegates advocate the particular rule adopted in their States and how frequently this insistence wrecks the work of codification.

The part played by municipal tribunals in the development of international law appears even more clearly when we consider how largely international law is composed of definitions and abstract rules and principles. So far as application to the different situations and circumstances is concerned, there are in regard to many questions hardly any uniform customary rules in existence. There is either a divergence of views or a total lack of precedent. The law relating to the immunities of diplomatic envoys is a case in point. Who would be optimistic enough to maintain that there exist generally recognized customary rules in regard to such questions as the actual extent of immunities, the immunities of the subject of the receiving State, the immunities of persons combining diplomatic and consular functions, immunities in respect of immovable property and actions *in rem* in respect of movable property, immunities in actions brought in connection with the non-diplomatic activities, commercial and otherwise, of the envoy and of his retinue, the different aspects of express and implied renunciation of immunity, admissibility of execution, admissibility of counter-claim and set-off, immunity subsequent to the conclusion of the mission for acts committed prior to the termination of the mission, and many other questions? So far as rules of international law exist on these and similar points of detail, they are largely the product of the work of municipal courts. So far as they show divergencies, it is through the decisions of municipal courts that the divergencies are revealed. Their decisions are the substance which fills the frame of the general principles. And it is normally before municipal tribunals, not before international courts, that the judicial application, in all required detail, of these rules takes place.

While developing international law in its details, municipal case-law fulfils yet another function. It illustrates the practical difficulties inherent in some tendencies for reform in international law by revealing not only the inadequacies of existing rules, but also the difficulties connected with their total abolition. The question, much discussed in recent years, of jurisdictional immunities of public ships of foreign States may be mentioned as an example. It is not the popular tendency to attack the sovereignty of the State in its numerous ramifications which has been responsible for creating a movement for a change in the law on this matter, but, on the one hand, the absurdities and inconveniences shown as the result of cases which came before municipal courts and, on the other hand, the fact that courts in different countries continued to maintain different attitudes on the question. But this variety of practice has at the same time had the effect of showing the difficulties of the problem and of reducing to proper proportions some well-meant criticism. The reformer is frequently apt to see only the absurdity of some aspects of jurisdictional immunities. Well-reasoned decisions of municipal courts reveal in themselves the element of permanent necessity undiminished by occasional abuses or inconveniences.

The predominant tendency has been to disregard not only the function of municipal tribunals as a source of customary international law, but also as an element of development of international law. An attempt has here been made to show that persistence in this attitude must result in disregarding a large part of international law as actually practised. If one may paraphrase a saying of Mr Justice Holmes, international law, when washed with positivist acid, survives only as a bare skeleton of general principles. It is their application by courts which makes them live and develop. And as the opportunity of recourse to international courts is limited, the major part of the task devolves upon municipal tribunals. It is difficult to see how international law is to develop if, as the result of the insistence on the rule of unanimity, international legislation is as yet in a rudimentary stage, and if, at the same time, the barren union of sovereignty and of positivism frustrates any constructive use of customary international law, based on the practice of States and evidenced in the impartial work of their judicial organs.

7. MUNICIPAL DECISIONS AS A SOURCE OF PARTICULAR INTERNATIONAL LAW

We have been discussing so far the function of municipal tribunals in the creation and the development of universal or general customary international law. It is now proposed to consider how far their decisions are instrumental in bringing about binding rules of particular international law. This amounts largely to inquiring how far the fact that the courts of a State have adopted a definite attitude on a certain matter prevents that State from taking up a different position in the international sphere, for instance, before an international court. Writers seem to be disposed to agree that there is nothing to prevent a State from assuming an attitude opposed to that previously adopted by its legislative organs or its courts. In support of this view, it could be pointed out that whereas customary rules are not the result of a conscious and deliberate intention to enter a binding obligation, principle seems to demand that, apart from custom, an intention to incur an obligation should not be lightly presumed; that one must not forget that legislative acts frequently go beyond the minimum of duty imposed by international law; and that it would not be satisfactory to treat States as moving in a constant zone of danger in which they are continuously being presumed to create law against themselves. This view, although plausible, is not, on consideration, very convincing.

There is no escape from the fact that in a legal community where the opportunities for creating law are limited, the conduct of its members must to a certain extent occupy the place of a source of law. Acts of competent State organs must at least be treated as evidence of what the State from which they emanate acknowledges to be the rule of law. Phillimore says, in regard to formal declarations of Governments on matters of international law: 'These public documents furnish, at all events, decisive evidence against any State which afterwards departs from the principles which it has thus deliberately and solemnly invoked.'[1] If there is doubt as to the existence of a rule, it is appropriate to point out, as a matter of evidence, that the State itself acknowledged it by having acted upon it. These considerations apply with special force to judicial decisions, which as a rule confine themselves in an impartial manner to the domain of law, except when they act at the instance of the Executive

[1] Phillimore, I, 54.

or the Legislature – in which case it is again the will of the State which is responsible for their decisions.

The opinion must therefore be rejected that a State is always at liberty to go back upon a rule sanctioned by its own Judiciary. The position is different when such departure does not adversely affect the interests of foreign States. But when a State seeks to modify, to the detriment of other States, the law embodied in the pronouncements of its courts, it is not justified in pleading that it never entered into a binding obligation. This is not the issue. The point is what, in a detached manner and in the normal course of affairs, it regarded as the law. The question is not of unfairly burdening the State with risks, but of not allowing it to throw overboard a rule which it suffered its courts to pronounce and of which it implicitly approved by not resorting to legislative measures to have the judicial pronouncement set aside. It is in the long run impossible to maintain a position which attaches decisive importance to the will of the State as a source of international law, and at the same time reduces to a minimum the opportunities for giving expression to that will. The obligation in the case under discussion is not one of general customary international law, but of particular international law; it is not evidence of the existence of a general rule of international law (although it may be that at the same time), but of a rule of particular international law brought about by the implied consent of the State to adopt the law as laid down by its courts. The State may, of course, plead that the law thus laid down is bad law, but the presumption will be against it and the burden of rebuttal will rest upon it. And that negative proof will not be an easy one in view of the presumption that States and their organs act in accordance with a rule of international law. The following rule, for which there exists no judicial authority, may therefore be submitted. In case of a dispute as to the existence or otherwise of a rule of international law, the fact that the rule in question has been recognized and acted upon by the courts of a State will be regarded as proving *prima facie* the existence of that rule so far as that State is concerned. In regard to that State the rule will be looked upon as having the effect of a customary rule of particular international law. And there is at least one case in which it is even doubtful whether a State would be free to prove the existence of a rule of customary international law opposed to that hitherto acted upon by its own courts. In all cases in which a foreign State has relied upon the existence of a legal rule adopted by the courts of its neighbour, and, in particular, if, as the result, it has altered its situation for the worse, justice requires that that foreign State should be prevented from advocating an entirely different rule. Thus, for instance, if a foreign State has been induced by the constant practice of the courts of another country to adopt a restrictive interpretation of its own rights or to accord specially favourable treatment to the subjects of that country, the latter will be estopped from going back upon the rule thus adopted. Estoppel is not merely a procedural, but also an equitable, rule of evidence not foreign to international practice.[1]

Lastly, decisions on matters of international law given by the courts of a country, are, in a very real sense, a source of particular international law for the courts, the practising lawyer and the student in States in which judicial precedent is a material source of law. If a question of international law is covered by judicial precedent the judge will rely on it, frequently to the extent of quoting the precedent, and not the relevant rule of international law. This does not mean that, once called to life, precedents become permanent and immutable and, as such, block the path of development. They are followed like any other precedent, which means that if need be they are consciously adapted to new conditions and, when antiquated, 'distinguished' out of existence. Accordingly, although the lawyer is on safe ground when he turns in the first instance to the judicial interpretations of international law by the courts of his country in order to know how these courts will act in the future in similar cases, he must not treat them as immutable and as an invariably accurate interpretation of international law. The science of international law and the decisions of foreign courts, which frequently supply a much-needed corrective of the purely national point of view, should be regarded as a subsidiary source, for they influence in the long run the development of judicial precedent on matters of international law. It should also be noted that the authority of municipal decisions is not altogether negligible in countries where the function of judicial precedent is limited. The decisions of the highest courts, if not binding, are certainly of a persuasive character in those countries. So are, to a smaller extent, the decisions of courts of other foreign countries. It is not only as between English and American courts, but also between those of other countries, that the decisions of foreign courts on matters of international law are frequently referred to – an important step in the process of 'internationalizing' internationally relevant municipal case-law.

[1] See Lauterpacht, *Analogies*, pp. 202–6; and McNair, in *B.Y.* 5 (1924), 34.

8. THE TASK OF MUNICIPAL COURTS

The wide scope of the function of municipal judges administering international law and its importance for the international lawyer appear clearly from what has been said in the last three sections in regard to their part in creating general rules of customary international law, in developing the substance of international law, and in formulating rules of particular international law binding upon their State and applicable in it as law endowed with formal validity. It is proposed to consider in this concluding section the obligations which the performance of this function imposes upon municipal courts.

For one who chooses to confine himself to the field of municipal law, judges administer in all these cases the law of their own country, and nothing else. But one who looks at the substance of things rather than at their form must realize that, when acting in that capacity, municipal judges are the organs of the international legal community. In their decisions, perhaps only in them, the unity of international and municipal law reveals itself. Although their judgments are given in the name of the territorial sovereign, when questions of international law are concerned they must be rendered in accordance with the international duties of their State as bound by the rules of a more comprehensive and legal community. It is true that they are bound even by such statutory law of their State as is contrary to international law, but they are under a duty to interpret it so as to reduce the possibilities of conflict. This may be impossible on occasions, and courts are then compelled to comply with the will of the State. But the effect of the judgments thus given is provisional and subject to such changes as may be dictated by the international duties of the State enforced before an international forum.[1]

However, if the hope of a learned writer, expressed thirty-six years ago, that in the future 'municipal courts may become the trusted mouthpieces of international law as local divisions of the great High Court of Nations'[2] is to become a reality, then their decisions must be not only studied, compared, and criticized, but also the work of the judges must be scrupulously impartial and thorough. It must be done with that special care and devotion which flows from the consciousness that States, on whose behalf they administer international law, are the guardians of the international legal order which is as yet in a stage of minority, as it were. This

[1] See, on this point Hyde, *International Law* (1st ed. 1922), I, 12.
[2] Walker, *Science*, p. 49.

position of trust imposes upon them the duty of strict impartiality whenever the interests of their country are concerned. Lord Stowell's words about his court being a 'Court of the Law of Nations, though sitting here under the authority of the King of Great Britain', of its belonging 'to other nations as well as to our own', and of foreigners having 'a right to demand from it . . . the administration of the Law of Nations simply, and exclusively of the introduction of principles borrowed from our municipal jurisprudence'[1] are applicable, with special force and with more real opportunity for strict observance, to decisions of municipal courts in time of peace. The treatment of foreign States and their subjects with the utmost courtesy and consideration of their legitimate interests should be a duty deliberately adhered to in times of crisis and national tension. There is a special occasion for this spirit of independence revealing itself in all cases affecting the national treasury. The record of municipal tribunals in this respect has not always been satisfactory, as is shown for instance by their practice in matters of State succession. Whereas they adhere to the doctrine that the State succeeds to the rights of its predecessor, they show at times a conspicuous reluctance to recognize the same rule in regard to the obligations contracted by the predecessor. The courts of the European successor States after the World War have pursued the same policy. The only instance in the post-war period of a court expressing itself in a pronounced way in favour of succession to obligations is the decision of the German Federal Court in 1926 in which it saddled the South African Mandatory Government with responsibility for certain sums deposited with the former German administration.[2] The manner in which certain courts have alternated in accepting and rejecting the 'Daimler' test[3] in respect of corporations and their shareholders is another illustration of this tendency. We find the French Court of Cassation applying the 'Daimler' test in cases where the State seeks to seize the assets of former enemy subjects in their character as shareholders in a neutral corporation,[4] but the same Court applied the orthodox doctrine of *siège social* when a subject of an associated Power asked for exemption from confiscation of his assets in a company registered in a former enemy country.[5]

[1] *The Recovery*, 6 C. Rob. 349.

[2] *State Succession* (*Windhuk in South West Africa*) case (*Annual Digest*, 3 (1925–6), 75).

[3] *Daimler Co. Ltd.* v. *Continental Tyre & Rubber Co.* [1916] 2 A.C. 307.

[4] See *Liquidation de la Société des Transports Internationaux* v. *Séquestre de la Société des Transports Internationaux*, Sirey (1925), part 1, p. 225.

[5] See *Wilkens* v. *Lagarde et Procureur de la République près le Tribunal de Papeete*, *ibid.* (1926), part 1, p. 268.

Another duty flowing from the realization of the international task imposed upon municipal courts is that of thorough acquaintance with and equally thorough treatment of the questions of international law underlying their judgments. Some of these decisions are monuments of patient investigation and learning. Judgments like those delivered by Mr Justice Hill in *The Jupiter*[1] cases on the limits of recognition of acts of recognized Governments, or of the German *Staatsgerichtshof* in 1927 in the dispute between Prussia, Baden and Würtemberg on the rights and duties of riparian States, certainly rank with the best international arbitral awards.[2] But this is not always so, and there are decisions of national courts in which superficiality of treatment is only thinly veiled by references to authors of treatises on international law.

By not availing themselves to the full of the lessons of municipal decisions international lawyers have debarred themselves from access to a rich source of development of international law. In the long run, such an attitude cannot fail to impair in those called upon to render these decisions the sense of responsibility for a comprehensive and scientific treatment of international law. It would be of advantage if judges could know that their decisions on matters of importance to international law are studied not only by the lawyers of their own country, but also, through a system of easily accessible reports, by scholars and students abroad, intent upon learning from judges conscious of the international character of their functions. From this point of view, one may consider the possibility of a development in which the highest national tribunals will prefer to ask competent international tribunals, preferably the Permanent Court of International Justice, sitting in its full strength, for an opinion on difficult or unsettled questions of international law which do not involve national interests. In a more integrated stage of international organization – which is still far off – this request for an opinion might assume the form of leave to appeal against the decision of the national court on a point of international law. It is not unusual for inferior municipal courts to invite an appeal from their own decision on questions of legal interest on which the opinion of the highest organs of the Judiciary is felt to be desirable. However, a formal application, emanating from the highest judicial authorities of the country and addressed to the Permanent Court, for a ruling on any important question of international law pending before the municipal

[1] *The Jupiter*, no. 1 and no. 3 [1924] P. 236, and [1927] P. 122, 250 (*Annual Digest*, 3 (1925–6), 136).

[2] *Entscheidungen des Reichsgerichts in Zivilsachen*, vol. 116, Appendix.

court would constitute a less radical step. Such a procedure, being a voluntary one in form and substance, would derogate neither from the sovereignty of States nor from the authority of their highest tribunals; it would testify that these tribunals regard themselves as the organs of the international community when administering international law, and it would give the Permanent Court, whose main work consists at present in interpreting treaty provisions, the opportunity of developing international law in much-needed directions. A suggestion of a procedure of this kind naturally raises a number of questions, such as the right of the Court to deal under its present constitution with matters referred to it in this way, and the necessity of appropriate changes in the Statute; the desirability of reserving to the Court the right to decide whether the matter raised in the application for an opinion is important enough to put into motion the machinery of the Court; the definite obligation, moral rather than legal, on the part of the municipal court in question to give effect to the ruling of the Permanent Court. These are questions of detail which need not be discussed here.[1] But it is believed that such an innovation would bring into relief the deep significance of the fact that international law is the only branch of law containing identical rules professedly administered as such by the courts of all nations.

[1] Professor Anzilotti discusses the possibility of municipal courts refraining in the future from dealing with questions involving matters of international law and referring them to specially instituted international tribunals. He dismisses this suggestion as a '*volo di fantasia*', but regards as more practicable the establishment, within the State, of special tribunals competent to adjudicate on questions of international law (*Il diritto internazionale nei giudizi interni*, p. 193). See also, for a suggestion on lines similar to those in the text, Bisschop, in *B.Y.* 4 (1923–4), 131 *et seq.*

CHAPTER II

CODIFICATION AND DEVELOPMENT OF INTERNATIONAL LAW

Editor's note The first British member of the International Law Commission was Professor J. L. Brierly, who had retired from the Chichele Chair of International Law at Oxford in 1947. In 1951 he resigned from the Commission and Lauterpacht was elected in his place. Lauterpacht remained a member till his election as a Judge of the International Court of Justice in 1954. He thus served during four sessions of the Commission. In 1952 he became Special Rapporteur on the Law of Treaties and prepared two Reports on that subject in 1953 and 1954 respectively. (These will be printed in a later volume in this series.) In 1953 he acted as Rapporteur of the Commission and, as such, was primarily responsible for the preparation of the Commission's report for that session – a more substantial document than any previously produced. During his period of service he was one of the most active and influential members of the Commission. His experience is reflected in this article, written prior to, but published after, his election to the International Court, in the *American Journal of International Law*, 49 (1955), 16–43.

The object of the present article is to survey the problems and to assess the achievements and prospects of the codification of international law within the United Nations in the light of the experience of the first five years of the activity of the International Law Commission. The Charter, in Article 13, imposes upon the General Assembly the obligation to 'initiate studies and to make recommendations . . . for the purpose of encouraging the progressive development of international law and its codification'. In pursuance of that Article the General Assembly set up the International Law Commission and adopted a Statute regulating its functions and organization. The first session of the Commission took place in 1949. Since then, it has been meeting in yearly sessions lasting between eight and eleven weeks. In the intervals of the sessions, some of its members, acting as Rapporteurs, have studied and submitted reports on selected topics. The Commission itself has adopted and laid before the General Assembly a number of draft declarations, conventions and articles.[1]

[1] See below, p. 301, n. 1.

Normally the results of an effort extending for five years would warrant an attempt to review the achievements of an organ of the United Nations in what was hoped would become an important field of its activity. This is so, although, from one point of view, it might appear doubtful whether the time has arrived for any such assessment. As in the case of many other aspects of the Charter, the political climate has not been propitious for revealing the full potentialities of the objects of the United Nations. However, such endeavour as has been possible in the conditions prevailing in the first decade of the existence of the United Nations has helped to draw attention to some more general features of codification. Accordingly, alongside the discussion concerned with the general revision of the Charter of the United Nations, it may be desirable to consider any necessary improvements in the methods and the constitution of its organ entrusted with the codification and progressive development of international law. That there is room for a very substantial difference of opinion on the subject of the prospects and importance of codification may be seen from a comparison of the following views expressed, respectively, prior to the commencement of the activity of the International Law Commission and after what may be regarded as the initial experimental period of its work. In 1947, the author of a penetrating analysis of the problem of codification of international law and of the task of the Commission in the light of its Statute, expressed his considered view that 'it is surely evident that the implementing of Article 13 of the Charter is a task the urgency and importance of which yield place to none of the other problems that face the international lawyer to-day'.[1] In 1953, a former Judge of the International Court of Justice committed himself to the opinion that attempts to codify international law within the larger community of the United Nations constitute a clear menace to the development of international law and that 'the prospects of codification of international law on a universal plane are nil'.[2] As will be suggested later,[3] this drastic estimate on the part of a lawyer not usually given to extreme statements does not necessarily bear the pessimistic interpretation which appears on the face of it. However, it is a statement which calls for reflection.

[1] Jennings, in *B.Y.* 24 (1947), 329.
[2] Charles de Visscher, *Théories et realités en droit international public* (1953), pp. 177, 181.
[3] See below, p. 297.

I. THE ABSENCE OF AGREED LAW AND THE MEANING OF CODIFICATION

In the first instance, the experience of codification under the United Nations fully confirms the lesson of past attempts to the effect that there is very little to codify if by that term is meant no more than giving, in the language of Article 15 of the Statute of the International Law Commission, precision and systematic order to rules of international law in fields 'where there already has been extensive State practice, precedent and doctrine'. For, once we approach at close quarters practically any branch of international law, we are driven, amidst some feeling of incredulity, to the conclusion that although there is as a rule a consensus of opinion on broad principle – even this may be an overestimate in some cases – there is no semblance of agreement in relation to specific rules and problems. Thus, for instance, with regard to the law of treaties, perhaps the only principle of wider import as to which there is no dissent is that treaties ought to be fulfilled in good faith. Even that statement is accurate only if we reduce the emanations of the so-called *rebus sic stantibus* doctrine to the manageable confines of a general principle of law applied by an international tribunal at the instance of the State which claims to be released from the treaty on account of a change in vital circumstances. Apart from that general and unavoidable acceptance of the basic principle, *pacta sunt servanda*, there is little agreement and there is much discord at almost every point.

By way of example, reference may be made to one portion of the law of treaties which the writer of this article had recent occasion to investigate in some detail, namely, their conclusion and validity. There is a difference of opinion on the very notion of the treaty in relation to the question of who may be parties thereto. Can public international organizations, i.e., organizations of States, be parties to treaties? They seem to have concluded a great many of them – between themselves, with the United Nations (which is itself a public international organization) and with States (both Members of the United Nations and others). But the International Law Commission adopted in 1951 a provisional article in which the definition of a treaty covered States only, as distinguished from organizations of States. About one-third of international agreements are at present concluded by way of exchanges of notes. However, in the course of its initial consideration of the subject, the Commission decided provisionally, by a bare majority, that exchanges of notes do not come within the purview of the law of treaties. On both these questions the Report on Treaties which the Special Rapporteur submitted in 1953 to the Commission reached contrary conclusions.[1] The legal meaning of the signature of the treaty is contested. Is it no more than a clerical act of authentication which implies no legal rights and obligations and which the signatory States are entitled to ignore at will? Or is it an act which connotes some, if imperfect, obligations such as abstention, in the period between signature and ratification, from conduct aimed at impairing the effectiveness of the substantive provisions of the treaty; a measure of obligation to submit the treaty to national authorities for confirmation or rejection; and perhaps the duty to ratify a treaty confirmed by the competent legislative authority? There is an even sharper controversy as to the necessity for ratification of treaties which are silent on the question whether they require such action or not. Is it a condition of the validity of treaties that they must be ratified unless they contain a specific provision exempting them from the requirement of ratification? Or is such exemption to be implied from the nature of the compact in the sense, for instance, that some types of agreement do not require ratification? Or is it the rule that no ratification is required unless the treaty expressly provides for it? There is a wide and unresolved divergence of views and practice as to the effect of the disregard of constitutional limitations on the part of the organ which ratifies or otherwise accepts a final treaty obligation on behalf of the State. Is that State bound by the treaty; or is it free to repudiate it; or is it bound in certain circumstances, for instance, if it has acted upon it or derived benefits from it; or, while not bound, is it in some contingencies under a duty to pay compensation to the other contracting party? Varying answers have been given to these questions.[2] With regard to accession to treaties, there are conflicting views and practices on the question whether accession can take place prior to the treaty entering into force or only subsequent to that event – with the result that treaties which might enter into force if the first alternative is adopted, may never materialize if the second

[1] Report on Treaties, by H. Lauterpacht, U.N. Doc. A/CN.4/63, Articles 1 and 3.

[2] The position is illustrated, in the sense suggested above, by the fact that although Mr Fitzmaurice (as he then was), writing in *B.Y.* 15 (1934), 113, adopted, in a searching analysis, a more definite attitude in respect to some of them and although he adhered to the same view in 1948 in his lectures at the Hague Academy, after stating what he considered to be the law, he added the following words of caution: 'these excellent precepts are unfortunately only too often honoured in the breach' (*Hague Recueil*, 73 (1948) (ii), 357, n. 1).

view is allowed to prevail. If the treaty provides, as do the Hague Conventions of 1907, that accession may be effected only by agreement of the contracting parties, does that mean all the contracting parties or merely the majority of them? Are the 'Contracting Parties' in this connection the original signatories or also those who have subsequently validly acceded to the treaty? On the important subject of reservations to multilateral treaties[1] it has become doubtful whether there is now any generally agreed law at all.

The same lack of certainty or agreement envelops the law relating to the validity of treaties from the point of view of reality of consent, legality of subject-matter, and compliance with requirements of form. Has the prohibition or limitation of the right to have recourse to war or force rendered obsolete the rule of traditional international law which disregards the vitiating effect of duress? Is the vitiating effect, if any, of duress absolute or only in relation to the guilty State in the sense that a treaty imposed by that State is invalid? Conflicting answers have been given to these questions. The same uncertainty prevails as to the limits of the principle that a treaty is void if its performance involves an act which is illegal under customary international law. There is an even more pronounced difference of view as to the illegality of treaties inconsistent with previous treaty obligations binding upon one or both of the parties – a problem which raises a host of questions, including that of the validity of the Charter of the United Nations itself. There is conflicting or ambiguous judicial and arbitral authority as to the requirement of written form as a condition of validity of treaties. The exact meaning of the provisions of the Charter of the United Nations in the matter of enforceability of non-registered treaties in relation to Members and non-Members is far from commanding a uniform answer.

It would be possible to continue that sorry tale in relation to the entirety of the law of treaties and, indeed, of most of international law.[2] The fact, which is both disquieting and chastening, speaks for itself. There is, upon reflection, nothing astonishing about it. How could it be otherwise in a society in which judicial settlement is sporadic, in which there is no legislative activity in the accepted sense, and in which custom is slow of growth and controversial in

[1] See below, p. 275.

[2] See 'Survey of International Law in Relation to the Work of Codification of the International Law Commission' (Memorandum by the Secretary-General, 1949), p. 7 [printed in these *Collected Papers*, I, 445 *et seq.*].

interpretation and application? It is probably a fact that the absence of agreed rules partaking of a reasonable degree of certainty is a serious challenge to the legal nature of what goes by the name of international law. That circumstance alone supplies cogent proof of the justification, nay, of the urgency, of the task of codification of international law. The matter is not merely one of *elegantia juris* and of a 'better expression of international law' in the sense that it evokes 'a somewhat vague and distant interest of States'.[1] Clarity and certainty are not mere embellishments of the law. They are, particularly in the international sphere, of its essence. Within the State obscurity and uncertainty of the law are a drawback, but a drawback which is provisional inasmuch as the uncertainty can be removed with regard to a particular controversy by the decision of a court endowed with compulsory jurisdiction. This is not the position among States. The jurisdiction of international tribunals is still voluntary. The compulsory jurisdiction of the International Court of Justice under the Optional Clause of its Statute is not universally accepted. Even in relation to those States which have accepted it, it has been weakened in many cases by reservations to the point of being nominal. There have been instances, among enlightened States bound by the Optional Clause, of differences as to clearly legal rights and obligations being settled by recourse not to the International Court of Justice but to reprisals.[2] As the result, the uncertainties, gaps, and obscurities of the law are not merely perpetuated. They feed and grow on their own evil inasmuch as they are kept alive and magnified by the conflicting and extreme assertions of the parties to disputes. The call for codification is therefore not the product of legal perfectionism. It is an imperative need of international society, and it is only on account of more pressing problems assailing its very existence that the consciousness of the urgency of codification has been relegated into the background.

It may, of course, be said that the seriousness of the challenge can be exaggerated; that, after all, tribunals applying international law have not felt themselves frustrated by the absence of agreed rules of law; that there is in the background that vast reservoir of creative judicial decision applying general principles of law now elevated to the status of one of the main sources of international law; and that

[1] Charles de Visscher, *Théories et realités*, p. 180.

[2] It was reported in 1953 that the French Parliament enacted, apparently as a measure of reprisals against the United States, legislation compelling certain categories of foreign nationals resident in France to perform military service there. It was alleged that the United States was acting on legislation identical in substance.

there is therefore no danger that, even if such contingency were admissible (or, indeed, conceivable), an international tribunal might be compelled to decline to render a decision on account of the absence of a rule of law directly bearing upon the issue before it. The comfort to be derived from these and similar considerations is deceptive. This is so not only for the reason of the absence, in principle, of compulsory jurisdiction of international tribunals. Even apart from that fact, the anomaly of international tribunals having to resort to judicial legislation, under the respectable guise of the application of general principles of law, instead of applying existing legal rule, is obvious and needs no elaboration. (It is significant that one of the principal recommendations of the Committee of Jurists who in 1920 framed the Statute of the Permanent Count of International Justice was that the Council of the League of Nations should proceed with the task of codification of international law. They assumed that the absence of clear and agreed rules of law and the corresponding latitude or discretion of international tribunals are not likely to assist in inducing Governments to undertake the commitments of obligatory judicial settlement.)

Moreover, experience has shown that, on occasions, decisions of international tribunals themselves, far from supplying the missing element of completeness, may infuse an element of doubt and uncertainty where hitherto there existed relative clarity and agreement. Two examples will illustrate that point. Prior to the Advisory Opinion of the International Court of Justice on *Reservations to the Convention on Genocide*,[1] it was thought that the principle of unanimous consent is the generally accepted rule of international law on the subject, namely, the principle that ratification or any other method of accepting a multilateral treaty is void if accompanied by reservations not agreed to by all the other parties to the treaty. The Court declined to hold that the principle of unanimous consent constituted, as a matter both of existing practice and of the reason of the thing, the rule of international law. It laid down novel principles of its own to which, if it may be said with respect, it is difficult to deny qualities of statesmanship and reasonableness. These principles are based on the test of compatibility of the reservations with the object and the purpose of the treaty. However, in the absence of legal rules and procedures ensuring the application of these principles, that test is no more than a subjective and necessarily abstract standard which in itself can provide no working solution of the difficulty. It is probable

[1] *I.C.J. Reports* (1951), p. 15.

that the traditional rule of unanimity affords no such solution of the problem, and that alternative procedures must be envisaged. That such modifications of the rule of unanimity are feasible is shown by the attitude adopted in 1953 at the General Assembly by the United Kingdom, notwithstanding the fact that it considered the unanimity rule to be the established rule of international law.[1] However, as stated, the Opinion of the Court on *Reservations to the Convention on Genocide*, while denying the existence of a binding rule on the subject and while formulating a new general test of admissibility of reservations, left in abeyance the question of its practical application. Thus on occasions judicial activity, far from supplying the missing link of certainty and clarity, may achieve the opposite effect. It may do so in two directions: it may disturb or do away with the conviction, hitherto operative, of the existence of an agreed rule of law; after having done that, it may accentuate the anomaly by laying down a principle which is incomplete and which requires further elaboration if it is to be of practical value. Such absence of complete solution may be due to the legitimate disinclination to strain the processes of judicial legislation. However, while considerations of that order explain the resulting gap, they do not fill it.

Another example in the same category was provided by the Judgment of the International Court of Justice in the *Anglo-Norwegian Fisheries* case.[2] Prior to that Judgment, the rule that the base line of territorial waters runs parallel to the sinuosities of the coast and that the ten-mile line across the mouth of the bay is the base line in regard to bays, had not been universally accepted. But it had been generally accepted. The Court declined to view it in that light. It considered that there was no such agreed practice on the subject as to warrant its recognition as a rule of law. After having held that, it proceeded to lay down principles of a general and subjective nature, which need more detailed formulation before they can become a working rule of law.

Enough has been said to draw attention to what probably is a fact, namely, that the task of codifying international law, if it is to mean anything, must be primarily one of bringing about an agreed body of rules rather than introducing systematic order and precision into

[1] An attitude which Sir Gerald Fitzmaurice subsequently elaborated in constructive detail in an article in *I.C.L.Q.* 2 (1953), 1, and which was given practical application by the representative of the United Kingdom in the Human Rights Commission in 1954 in connection with the Final Clauses of the proposed Covenant of Human Rights (Doc. E/CN.4/L.345 and Add. 1). The British proposals substituted for the principle of unanimity the requirement of consent by a substantial majority of the parties.

[2] *I.C.J. Reports* (1951), p. 116.

legal rules already covered by customary or conventional agreement of States. At present the area of such agreement is small in the extreme. To put in into different words: There is little substantive meaning or practical purpose in the definition, already referred to, of codification given in Article 15 of the Statute of the International Law Commission, namely, 'precise formulation and systematization of [existing] rules of international law in fields where there already has been extensive State practice, precedent and doctrine'. For the existence of a rule of international law does not necessarily follow, as that definition seems to assume, from the existence of 'extensive State practice, precedent and doctrine'. These may demonstrate the non-existence of an agreed rule of international law. The fact that, because of the absence of agreed law, codification in the sense of making the law precise and systematic has little or no actual application in relation to international law, has been recognized by practically all writers and, generally, by those who have become actively engaged in the work of codification at international conferences and otherwise.[1] It is inconvenient and it is a cause of confusion that that fact has been ignored in the Statute of the International Law Commission and that the task of making the – non-existent – agreed law

[1] See, e.g., Professor Brierly's statement as Rapporteur, in 1947, of the Committee on the Progressive Development of International Law to the effect that any work of codification reveals gaps and uncertainties, and that 'if you were to disregard these uncertainties and these gaps and simply include in your code rules of existing law which are absolutely certain and clear, the work would have little value' (A/AC.10/30, pp. 2, 3); 'Survey of International Law in Relation to the Work of Codification' (Memorandum by the Secretary-General, 1949): 'It is clear that if the task of the International Law Commission were confined to fields with regard to which there is a full measure of agreement among States, the scope of its task would be reduced to a bare minimum'; Flournoy, in *A.J.* 24 (1930), 468: 'Early in the discussions at the recent Hague conference it was realized that there was little international law on the subject of nationality which could be codified, if "codification" is to be limited to the reduction to writing of rules of law already generally agreed upon by States'; as to the London Conference of 1909, see Jennings, in *B.Y.* 24 (1947), 307. In its reply to the inquiry of the League of Nations subsequent to the Hague Conference of 1930, the British Government expressed the view that the work of that Conference would have been more useful if it had been recognized from the outset that its function was one of legislative codification, and it expressed doubts as to 'the likelihood of important branches of international law being found to which the application of consolidating methods would be useful' (League Doc. A. 12. 1931). The same view was expressed with all requisite clarity by Senator Elihu Root as far back as 1911. He said: 'To codify municipal law is to state in systematic form the results of the law-making process already carried on by a nation through its established institutional forms. To codify international law is primarily to set in motion and promote the law-making process itself in the community of nations in which the institutional forms appropriate for the carrying on of such a process have been so vague, indistinct, uncertain and irregular that they could hardly be said to exist at all' (*A.J.* 5 (1911), 579). He gave expression to the same view, in almost identical terms, in 1925, *ibid.* 19 (1925), 681. It is of interest to note that this generally acknowledged and most conspicuous feature of international codification finds no expression in the language of the Statute of the International Law Commission.

precise and systematic was there made to constitute one of the two principal features of the work of the Commission.

2. REASONS FOR ABSENCE OF AGREED LAW

There would normally be little object in a pedantic analysis of a definition of codification in the Statute of the International Law Commission – a definition which might have been arrived at rather hastily amidst the pressure of business of the General Assembly. However, the matter is more than one of definition. For, as stated, Article 15 of the Statute of the Commission, especially when taken in conjunction with the definition of 'development of international law' as contained there, would seem, unless explained to the point of being disregarded, to exclude from the purview of the activity of the Commission practically the entire field of codification in its large sense. For the area of international law in which no more is needed than 'precise formulation and systematization', i.e., codification in the apparent sense of Article 15, is insignificant. For that reason a more accurate definition of the work of the Commission must concentrate not on the task of giving precision to, or systematic formulation of, existing agreed law, but on bringing about agreement where so far there exists only conflict of views and practice. However, if that is so, it is essential for the better understanding of the task of codification thus conceived to realize that it, in turn, has two aspects.

There are, in the first instance, situations where there exists a divergence of views and practice but where the reasons for the absence of agreement are intrinsically of little moment and where one group of States can afford, or can reasonably be held to be able to afford, a change in their views or practice for the ostensible reason that no substantial interest of their own is involved. Let us consider, for instance, from this point of view the question, already referred to, of the requirement of ratification in cases in which the treaty is silent on the matter. There are impressive arguments in favour of either of the two solutions as summarized above. The discussion on the subject has been learned and vigorous. However, on reflection, it does not really matter much, in terms of actual interests of States, which solution is adopted. This is so particularly if it is borne in mind that the difference between the two points of view on this question is a matter of emphasis. Thus those who urge that, in the absence of provisions to the contrary, a treaty is not binding unless ratified, admit of broad exceptions not only in case of the wide range of exchanges of notes and intergovernmental agreements, but also by reference to the previous practice of the parties and other attendant circumstances. Moreover, the importance of the subject appears in proper perspective if it is recalled that in fact practically all treaties regulate the matter one way or another: they either lay down that the treaty shall be ratified or they provide that it shall enter into force upon signature, that is to say, that it need not be ratified. This being so, the proper task of the work of codification (and of the work connected therewith) is to bring authoritatively to light the modest dimensions of the issue involved and the absence of any important national interest militating against the adoption of an agreed uniform solution. These factors do not diminish the necessity for codification. For the justification of a legal rule does not depend upon the frequency of the situations which give rise to its application or the weight of the interest involved.

The same considerations apply to other questions, jurisprudentially more complicated, such as the relevance of the disregard of constitutional limitations or of inconsistency with previous treaty obligations, questions in which the doctrinal and juridical issue is real and in which there is no obvious preponderance of argument in favour of one solution. It is perhaps unimportant, in this connection, whether the solution in one sense is juridically obvious or whether it can be reached only after a laborious balancing of relevant considerations. What *is* important is that such solution – whatever it may be – does not affect any weighty or vital national interest. From that point of view it is, for instance, of little consequence whether the law as eventually codified will prescribe that a treaty must be in the form of a written document or whether it will endow with valid effect obligations assumed by way of an oral undertaking. Undoubtedly, it is preferable that a rule should be adopted which is juridically sound and workable. But no one – no person and no Government – ought to be so sure of his position, in matters not affecting interests of significance, as to permit disagreement on the merits of a rule of that category to perpetuate a situation in which there is no agreed rule at all. The absence of an agreed rule is a greater evil than the adoption of a rule which is perhaps not as good as the one which could have been adopted.

We have been concerned so far with that wide – by far the widest – area of divergence in which agreement and uniformity could be achieved by a mutual process of accommodation in a sphere which is predominantly not one of conflicting interests but of doctrine and juridical controversy. However, this is not the most important aspect of the problem which confronts the task of codification. For there is, secondly, that source of disagreement which *is* due to conflicting interests and claims in the political, economic and strategic spheres. Of this, the present position of the law relating to the limits of territorial waters provides an instructive example. It may, of course, be contended, not altogether inaccurately, that notwithstanding the various claims to a wide limit, the traditional rule of customary international law on the subject is still law; that it is so regarded by the principal maritime Powers whose aggregate tonnage comprises by far the largest part of the tonnage of the world's shipping; that there has been no agreement to displace that rule; and that claims, whether exorbitant or not, going outside it have, in general, met with protests. However, although this may be so, it cannot be denied that the traditional rule has been widely and actively challenged in practice. What can the work of codification by lawyers do in this field? Or can it be said that the problem here is political in nature? It is so, though not exclusively so. Whenever the absence of an agreed rule is due to a divergence of interest, the function of codification is, in a distinct sense, no less political than that of legislation generally. However, it is clear at the same time that in this context political, economic, and cognate factors are also factors of legal relevance. It is the business of codification, after revealing fully the extent of the divergence in all its implications, to use these factors as legitimate components of an eventual legal rule.

The manner in which the International Law Commission has approached this subject illustrates the potentialities of this method of approach. The Commission has refrained from proposing solutions by way of a mechanical compromise in the nature of an average of the various figures of mileage claimed by various States. It has attempted, in the first instance, to take the rough edges off the problem by formulating, in 1953 and in preceding years, in precise language the widely adopted practice of contiguous zones, not exceeding twelve miles, in connection with customs, immigration, fiscal or sanitary regulations.[1] There have been, so far, no indications that the principal maritime nations will feel bound to resist such indirect approach to the problem. On the direct issue of the limit of territorial waters a proposal was laid by the Rapporteur before the

[1] Report by M. François on the Régime of the Territorial Sea (U.N. Doc. A/CN.4/53), p. 11.

Commission in 1953, startling and extreme at first sight, but on closer scrutiny deserving of consideration as showing one of the possible methods of codification in relation to a subject of this character. The proposal was in substitution for that submitted in 1952 in which it was laid down, by way of an attempt at a compromise, that the breadth of the territorial waters should be fixed by the coastal State but that it may not exceed six marine miles. In 1953 it was proposed that the maximum breadth of the territorial waters to be fixed by the coastal State may not exceed twelve miles, subject, in addition to guarantees of the right of innocent passage, to the limitation that the coastal State may only claim exclusive fishing rights for its nationals up to three miles.[1] No expression of opinion is here called for as to the propriety or wisdom of the proposal for a twelve-mile limit as a basis of future discussions, even if the sting has been taken out of it by excluding fisheries from the operation of the sovereignty of the coastal States in the zone outside three miles. But the proposal is indicative of the possibilities of meeting the difficulty by way of a combination of the claims of the coastal State to an extended limit with the essential features of the freedom of the seas, of which unimpeded freedom of navigation, not referred to in the proposal, must be regarded as fundamental. Some such combinaion may, upon analysis, prove identical with the notion of contiguous zones and thus provide a solution of a problem which otherwise may become a source of serious weakness to the authority of international law. For its authority is bound to be impaired by the fact that, while the principal maritime States uphold the traditional rule as a fully valid principle of international law, a considerable number of States have legislated and acted in defiance of that principle. In a further report, submitted in 1954, the Special Rapporteur outlined yet another possible solution. He proposed (1) that the breadth of the territorial sea shall be three nautical miles measured from the base line of the territorial sea, but (2) that the coastal State may extend the territorial sea up to a limit of twelve nautical miles from the base line, subject to the following conditions: (a) that there shall be a guarantee of free passage in the territorial sea, as provided in the draft; (b) that the coastal State may claim exclusive fishery rights for its nationals only up to a distance of three nautical miles measured from the base line of the territorial sea; that beyond this limit fishing in the territorial sea may be regulated by the coastal

[1] Second Report by M. François on the Régime of the Territorial Sea (U.N. Doc. A/CN.4/61), p. 10.

State solely for the purpose of protecting the resources of the sea and without any discrimination against foreign nationals;[1] and that the validity of the measures adopted for these purposes by the coastal State must be submitted to conciliation or, if no agreement is reached, to arbitration.[2] These successive hesitating and apparently contradictory reports and alternative proposals reveal the intricacy of the problem involved and the nature of the task required for its solution. In this and similar cases the task of codification, confronted with an acute divergence of practice in a matter affecting important interests of States, calls for a combination of legislative activity with measured adherence to a legal rule sanctioned by tradition and by considerations of unimpaired validity. For the validity of the principle of the freedom of the sea is far from spent. However, that principle can be preserved only by dint of its being adjusted to the reasonably conceived interests of the coastal State and, in relation to the high seas proper, through the adoption of rules which will prevent the freedom of the seas from becoming a régime of anarchy and waste. It is in this light that the articles finally drafted by the International Law Commission in 1953 in the matter of fisheries and the continental shelf[3] must be viewed.

These, then, are the two aspects of codification in relation to matters on which there has either never been agreed law or on which there is no longer agreed law. In relation to one aspect, the business of codification is to bring about uniformity by persuasion and instruction pointing to the absence of any substantial reason for continued disagreement. In relation to the other aspect, its task is more exacting; it is to bring about an agreed rule of law where the source of divergence *is* due to a substantial conflict of interests and claims and where no less persuasion and instruction, coupled with attempts at a practical and statesmanlike reconciliation of opposing principles and considerations, are required as a condition of the emergence of an agreed rule. In neither case is the task one of a purely academic order. Governments do not take well to intimations, when coming from outsiders, that no substantial interest of their own is involved. Thus, in connection with the preparation of draft conventions on

[1] An apparently liberal provision which may hide pitfalls of substantive discrimination inasmuch as measures of conservation may affect exclusively methods employed by aliens for catching fish (for instance, trawl-fishing) but not methods used by inshore fishermen (e.g., line fishing).

[2] Third Report by M. François on the Régime of the Territorial Sea (U.N. Doc. A/CN.4/77), p. 5.

[3] Report of the Fifth Session (1953), General Assembly, 8th Sess., *Official Records*, Suppl. no. 9 (A/2456), pp. 12–19; *A.J.* 48 (1954), Suppl. pp. 27–43.

elimination or reduction of statelessness, they have shown impatience with the argument that deprivation of nationality by way of punishment serves either no national interest at all or an interest of a sentimental nature so questionable as hardly to outweigh the more general objections against deprivation of nationality resulting in statelessness. Neither, in cases of a genuine conflict of claims and interests, are they easily amenable to a counsel of moderation and accommodation emanating from scholars and external agencies. Yet it is a fact that such evaluation of national interests and their reduction to a common denominator of national and international interest is of the essence of codification. These considerations have a distinct bearing on the character of the work of codification and of the organs engaged on it.[1] To this subject we will return presently.

3. CHANGE AND DEVELOPMENT OF EXISTING LAW

We may now turn from codification in matters where there is no agreed rule of law to those in which the existing law is agreed, undisputed, and amply covered by precedent and doctrine but in which a change – a development – is felt to be called for by considerations of progress, of mutuality of enlightened economic interest, of international interdependence, of good faith, of morality, of the rights of man. There is no question here of 'progressive development of international law' as meaning the preparation of draft conventions on subjects which, in the somewhat unhelpful language of Article 15 of the Statute of the Commission, 'have not yet been regulated by international law or in regard to which the law has not yet been sufficiently developed in the practice of States'. Two subjects on which the International Law Commission produced drafts in 1953, namely, those on elimination and reduction of statelessness and on arbitral procedure, provide an instructive example of this aspect of its activity. Thus there is, so far as the existing law is concerned, general agreement on the subject of statelessness. According to international law, States are fully at liberty to adopt legislation resulting in statelessness, e.g. by not conferring nationality at birth or by depriving persons of their nationality by way of penalty or otherwise. The matter is regulated, and abundant though often melancholy practice has grown around it. But, to paraphrase the language of the Preamble of the Draft Convention on Elimination of Statelessness, that practice is productive of much hardship offensive to the dignity

[1] See below, p. 292.

of man; it provides a cause of international friction; and it is inconsistent with the more general principles of international law according to which nationality is an essential link between the individual and the Law of Nations. It is a change in the existing agreed law and practice that is here the proper object of codification.

The same applies to the main aspect of the Code of Arbitral Procedure as drafted by the Commission. Its purpose is to do away with an existing feature of the law of arbitral procedure which often renders somewhat nominal the obligation to settle a dispute by arbitration. Thus, according to existing law, if the parties cannot agree on the choice of arbitrators or if the arbitrators are unable to agree on the selection of the umpire, then, in the absence of provisions on the subject in the treaty of arbitration, the entire procedure collapses and with it the obligation to settle the dispute by arbitration. Similarly, if one of the parties maintains that the award is null and void on account of excess of jurisdiction on the part of the tribunal, there is, as the law stands at present, no obligatory judicial or other machinery for resolving the dilemma. By asserting that there has taken place excess of jurisdiction a party to the dispute may, in effect, avoid the fulfilment of its principal obligation. Here again, in a field covered by the practice of States, change and development are felt to be desirable having regard to the requirements of good faith and to the effectiveness of international obligations.

The States participating in the Hague Codification Conference of 1930 fully realized that codification could not be confined to a registration or systematization of existing law. The Assembly of the League of Nations, in laying down in 1927 the broad principles which were to govern the work of the conference to be convened, adopted a recommendation that 'the Governments which might be invited to the Conference should be informed that the codification effort to be undertaken by the first Codification Conference must aim at adapting existing rules to contemporary conditions'.[1] The drawbacks and dangers resulting from any deliberate limitation of the task of codification to a mere restatement of the existing law were illustrated in a revealing manner in the report submitted in 1951 by the International Law Commission on the question of reservations to multilateral treaties. That report was, apart from certain suggestions of procedural innovations, confined to a restatement of the traditional rule based on the principle of the unanimous consent of all contracting parties to reservations appended

[1] *L.N.O.J.* (1927), Special Suppl. no. 55. And see above, p. 277, n. 1.

by States. This was so although the Commission was invited by the General Assembly to study the question 'both from the point of view of codification and from that of the progressive development of international law'. The International Court of Justice, when called upon to give an advisory opinion on substantially the same question, made in effect a pronouncement which was in the nature of a progressive development of this aspect of international law.[1] The somewhat strange result was that, while the organ called upon to *apply* international law made a contribution to its *development* on the subject in question, the International Law Commission, whose competence is less narrowly drawn, confined itself to restating the existing position as it saw it. It is equally significant that it was the view of the Court rather than that of the Commission which commended itself to the large majority of the States represented at the General Assembly. The feature of the situation thus created, which calls for comment, is that the Commission in its desire to confine itself to a restatement of the existing law was inclined in its report to regard that law as satisfactory. No such virtue can reasonably be attributed to the rule of unanimity in the sphere of reservations – and elsewhere. It is probable that that approval of what was considered the traditional doctrine stemmed from the conviction that where there exists a clear and easily ascertainable rule of law, its alteration is outside the province of the codifying body. Any such view misrepresents the true task of codification. Even within that very limited field where there is both agreement and considerable practice, the work of codification cannot discard *a limine* the legislative function of developing and improving the law.

4. THE DISTINCTION BETWEEN CODIFICATION AND DEVELOPMENT IN THE STATUTE OF THE INTERNATIONAL LAW COMMISSION

It follows from the preceding observations that, unlike codification in other fields, the codification of international law must be substantially legislative in nature. It must consist essentially in inducing Governments (or some Governments) to accept new law. This is so primarily in all cases in which their practices and views are in articulate conflict, both where the conflict does not correspond to an actual divergence of interests and where it does so correspond. This is so, secondly, where views and practices agree, but where a pro-

[1] See above, p. 275.

gressive change in the law is considered desirable. Somewhat strangely, these, by far the widest and typical areas of codification, are not in fact covered by the Statute of the International Law Commission. For, as mentioned, the Statute provides only (a) for codification (in the sense of introducing precision and systematization) in cases in which there exists essential agreement evidenced by long practice, precedent and doctrine, and (b) for 'development' where there is as yet no regulation of international law and no sufficient practice, precedent or doctrine. It does not provide for codification where there exists practice but no agreement; neither does it provide for development where existing practice calls for a change. It is probable that the result thus achieved is due to an oversight in drafting; it is so drastically out of keeping with experience and with the views persistently expressed on the subject[1] that it cannot be regarded as intentional. It is not surprising that the relevant Article 15 of the Statute of the Commission has been disregarded in practice. It must be so left out of account in the future unless the work of both codification and development is to be reduced to nominal dimensions.

For these and other reasons it has proved impracticable to pay attention to the emanations, formulated in various articles of the Statute of the Commission, of the distinction thus conceived between codification and development of international law – articles which bear both on the methods of preparing drafts and on action to be taken upon them by the General Assembly. There is no good reason for deploring this departure from the letter of the Statute. In most cases the work of the Commission on a given topic partakes of the nature of both codification and development. The Draft Code of Arbitral Procedure constitutes a conspicuous procedural innovation – a development – in providing machinery of a binding character intended to prevent the frustration of the original undertaking to arbitrate. At the same time, in the words of the report of the Commission on the subject, the Draft Code 'must be considered as being primarily in the nature of codification of existing international law' inasmuch as it is based on the autonomy of the parties (which is the basis of the traditional law on the subject) with regard to the composition of the tribunal, the determination of its competence as well as of its law and procedure, and, above all, the respect for the sovereignty of both parties as expressed in their agreement, voluntarily undertaken, to settle the dispute by arbitration. The purpose of the

[1] See above, p. 277, n. 1.

Draft Code is to give effect to the sovereignty of both parties and to protect it against being rendered nugatory by the unilateral will of one of them.

The Draft Convention on Statelessness constitutes 'development' – a change in the law – in the sense that it limits the freedom of States, hitherto forming part of the law, to create and augment causes of statelessness. At the same time it constitutes codification in a double sense: (a) the proposed change in the law gives expression to the policy of many States, as already expressed in their legislation, to reduce or eliminate causes of statelessness; (b) the very change as proposed is in accordance with the wider principle of existing international law according to which nationality is the link between the individual and international law. The Draft Articles on the Continental Shelf seem naturally to fall within the orbit of 'development' inasmuch as they cover a situation of obvious novelty and formulate new rules calculated to shape that situation by reference to the existing principle of the freedom of the sea. From a different point of view they may be said to codify and consolidate that existing principle by reference to the problems created by the claims to the continental shelf put forward by various States and not challenged by others, with the result that these claims may now be fairly held to constitute part of international practice. The Draft Articles on Fisheries, providing as they do for obligatory regulation by an international authority, clearly went outside the existing law. But the Commission, while stating that the articles fall generally within the category of development of international law, attached importance to noting that they are not altogether in the nature of a drastic departure from the principles of international law. This was so on account of their admitted connection with the prohibition of abuse of rights, a doctrine which the Commission considered to provide a satisfactory legal basis for the rules formulated by it.[1] Undoubtedly, it is useful and desirable that in its drafts the Commission should state in what respects and in what parts its work constitutes essentially a re-affirmation – a codification – of existing law and how far it amounts to development. As the report adopted in 1953 shows, the Commission has attempted in most cases to perform that task. There is all the difference between doing that and treating a topic as a whole as being exclusively in the nature of codification or exclusively

[1] Sec. 100 of the Report of the Commission of 1953. This report, which, like other reports of the Commission, is published also in *A.J.* 48 (1954), Suppl. pp. 1–70, provides an instructive illustration of the submissions in the text.

in the nature of development and adopting different procedures for the elaboration of its drafts and bringing it to fruition by way of governmental action. In this respect, too, it is to be hoped that an early opportunity may be taken to eliminate the shortcomings of an experimental Statute.

In the light of the preceding observations and of the experience of codification under the League of Nations and the United Nations, the following submissions in relation to some main general problems of codification seem to be appropriate.

5. PRIVATE AND OFFICIAL CODIFICATION

In the first instance, the codification of international law can have but little justification and but slender chances of success, in terms of eventual acceptance by States, if it is confined to purely private effort, however scholarly and thorough. Mere academic restatement of the law, however competent and impartial, cannot hope to answer the real need. For, as already suggested, the field of agreed law to be restated is severely limited. The main need is for agreeing on the law and, in some cases, for changing it. From this point of view it is probable that the work of codification, if it is to achieve its primary purpose, must take place under the auspices of Governments, acting, if possible, through and within the United Nations; that there must be constant co-operation with Governments, and that the eventual, though not immediate, result of codification must be envisaged in the form either of conventions ratified by States or drafts and pronouncements enlisting the support of Governments, not necessarily of all Governments, in diverse other ways falling short of the conventions envisaged in Article 23 of the Statute of the International Law Commission. That Article enumerates the various courses open to the Commission in respect of drafts finally submitted by it to the General Assembly.[1] The Commission may recommend to the General Assembly that it in turn recommend the report to the Members with a view to the conclusion of a convention or that it convene a conference to conclude a convention. But, according to that article, the Commission may consider that it will be sufficient to recommend that the General Assembly take note of the report or adopt it by resolution, or even that no action be taken, the report having already been published. Whatever the proposal of the Com-

[1] Although that article refers to 'codification', it is clear—and this has been the practice of the International Law Commission—that it applies also to 'development'.

mission, the General Assembly may adopt any of these courses. These provisions, envisaging as they do diverse stages of official codification, are capable of elastic application.

Codification thus conceived, as distinguished from restatement of the law by private scientific effort, has been exposed to much trenchant and weighty criticism.[1] Thus it has been said that codification under governmental auspices undertaken with the view to concluding conventions, far from achieving its object, tends to retard progress by revealing divergencies where none had been expressed or anticipated before; that it imparts a political character to what might otherwise be a purely scientific process; and that, by giving to any actual or assumed discrepancy a rigid complexion of finality, it impairs such prospects of success as may otherwise exist. These objections are perhaps less persuasive than they appear at first sight. They seem to leave out of account the view that, unless the work of codification is thought of in terms of eventual acceptance by Governments, it has little meaning;[2] that the making of the law – and codification of international law is to a large extent within that category – is necessarily a political process; that the disclosure of disagreement must constitute the first step towards agreement; that little is gained by nursing the illusion that all is well; that Governments have been able in the past to reach agreement on many matters; that such agreement need not be unanimous; that even if reached between a number of States, not necessarily the majority of them, it may still, in proportion to its intrinsic merits, constitute an achievement and provide a legal standard of regulation available for acceptance by others in the light of the experience of its actual working; and that it does not therefore necessarily follow that the result of official codification will be to reduce its content to a level determined by the most obstructive and least progressive Governments. Such result might be inevitable if codification were conceived only as *universal* codification whose *raison d'être* lies in acceptance by all Governments. This, as will be submitted presently, is by no means the case. There is an element of over-simplification in the apprehension that attempts

[1] See, in particular, the paper contributed in 1946 by Sir Cecil Hurst in *Grotius Society*, 32 (1946), 135, and the report of a committee, under the chairmanship of Sir Arnold McNair (as he then was), in *International Law Association Report*, 42 (1947), 64.

[2] 'It does not require great perception to see that a mere restatement of existing law, however elegantly and liberally accomplished, would be ludicrously inadequate to meet the needs of contemporary international society, and it would be tragic if the comparative ease with which this process could be set in motion were to blind us to the need of something much more radical in the way of law-making. Radical law-making can only be done in time by the vehicle of the multipartite treaty' (Jennings, in *B.Y.* 24 (1947), 329).

at codification may leave things in a condition worse than they were before by casting doubt upon principles hitherto generally accepted and by enabling some Governments to cloak political claims for a change of the law in the garb of existing legal rules as they purport to see them.[1]

Some caution, it may be stated in this connection, may usefully be shown in describing the Hague Codification Conference of 1930 as a failure. There is room for the view, which cannot be elaborated here in detail, that the conference and the preparatory work which preceded it were a success, even if they were not immediately successful. Its main Convention on the Conflict of Nationality Laws entered into force and gave the impetus, in particular with regard to nationality of married women, to radical legislative changes on matters previously described as forming unalterable and fundamental features of national systems of law.[2] Its preparatory work and the deliberations concerning territorial waters must provide, as shown in the reports and discussions of the International Law Commission, the starting-point of any future attempts in this direction. It is often forgotten that the results of the Conference of 1930 would have been more spectacular if its conveners had chosen the easy path of selecting for codification technical and other subjects unlikely to raise controversy, rather than three topics fraught with conflict already both latent and apparent prior to the conference.[3]

Undoubtedly, the international composition of the official organs engaged in the work of codification must, because of the unavoidable infusion of the political element implicit in the consideration of national interest, tend to blur the element of scientific detachment. However, this is not a drawback limited to official efforts at codification. As experience shows, there is no assurance that that element can be entirely eliminated from the deliberations of scientific bodies which, although of a private character, are international in their

[1] Judge de Visscher, after apparently associating himself with such apprehension, admits that the divergencies revealed at the Hague Conference of 1930 were due less to the desire of Governments to resume their liberty of action at the expense of existing law than to disagreements of substance due to the various not sufficiently clarified aspects of the problems involved and that 'ce rappel à certaines réalités de la réglementation internationale . . . a rapproché le droit de la vie internationale envisagée dans sa diversité et sa croissante complexité' (*Théories et realités*, p. 181).

[2] See, e.g., the statement of the Commissioner in the *Elise Lebret* case, decided by the French–American Commission under the Treaty of 1880, to the effect that the rule of automatic change of the nationality of a wife in consequence of a change in the nationality of the husband was part of the 'public law of the world'. Reported in Wilson, *The International Law Standard in Treaties of the United States* (1953), p. 57.

[3] Professor Brierly, writing in 1931, observed that 'the results of the Hague Conference, such as they are, are greater than we were entitled to expect' (*B.Y.* 12 (1931), 6).

composition. Neither can the political element be ruled out if the task of the codifying body acting under the auspices of Governments or of the United Nations is limited to a mere 'restatement' as distinguished from an effort aiming at producing conventions. For its work is bound to be influenced by the belief that somehow such restatement is likely to be of practical application and corresponding political importance. Rigid detachment from political and economic factors underlying divergent legal conceptions when practised by bodies which, unlike judicial tribunals, are called upon to shape the law of the future, may often be achieved only at the price of the diminished practical value of the solutions formulated by them. Above all, it is difficult to disregard what is probably the paramount factor in the situation, namely, that the ultimate need is not for a collective treatise or encyclopaedia restating the existing agreed law, but a legislative process of codification improving, completing and developing international law.

Once this has been realized, so-called private codification assumes its proper place as a desirable aid and stimulus to official activity in this field. The work of the Harvard Research, the most important and successful in the sphere of private codification, has shown the wide possibilities of such effort in which the devotion and the competence of individuals, unhampered by claims of geographical representation, can achieve results with an economy of expense and time which cannot be expected from official bodies of international composition. There is room for the resumption, on an enlarged scale and on a broader basis, of the endeavour thus begun in order, after a quarter of a century, to bring up to date the topics already covered, to complete the prodigious undertaking of the Harvard Research by the inclusion of subjects which it had left on one side, and to keep alive, as a permanent effort, the task of continuous and encyclopaedic presentation and periodic scrutiny and revision of the entire body of international law. As in the past, such activity cannot be in the nature of a mere restatement of the existing law. The Drafts of the Harvard Research, while giving an exhaustive account of existing practice, at the same time indicated what, in the absence of an agreed or satisfactory practice, ought to be the law of the future. This they did with regard to practically every subject which they covered. Unlike the case of the Harvard Research, while discarding the hampering artificialities of rigidly conceived geographical representation, such efforts need not be limited to groups of scholars from one country. There are compelling reasons in support of the view not only that 'there is room' for the resumption of the constructive and creative work of private codification thus conceived, but that there may be a measure of urgency in picking up the threads of an imposing endeavour interrupted by the cataclysm of the Second World War. So long as the official work of codification under the aegis of the United Nations is of nominal dimensions, owing to the limited resources at the disposal of the codifying agency and to the rudimentary character of the machinery provided by the General Assembly for examining and for bringing to legislative fruition the drafts and reports prepared by the International Law Commission, codification by non-official bodies must be deemed to be an urgent task worthy of general support. In the sphere of constructive and far-sighted promotion of ideas of international peace and the rule of law, it is not easy to think of objects of enlightened private munificence more worthy of assistance than non-official codification as here described. Pending realization of the desirable developments in the field of official codification, this may be the main instrument for furthering and keeping effectively in being a prominent object of the Charter of the United Nations.[1]

6. THE INDEPENDENCE OF THE CODIFYING AGENCY

While it is imperative that the task of codification should be attempted, alongside of any other methods, under the auspices of Governments, and that the body entrusted with that task should be an organ of the United Nations, it is of equal importance that it should be independent of Governments not only in its composition but also in other relevant aspects. Thus it is essential for the success of codification that the reports and drafts as finally put before Governments and the General Assembly should express, with all requisite and, if need be, uncompromising clarity, the views of the codifying agency as to the solution which is accurate *de lege lata* and desirable *de lege ferenda*. This is so, although, as stated, the task of codification must be approached with the view to its eventual adoption within the framework of positive international law as distinguished from its value as a scientific exposition, however full and informative. Although account must be taken of the attitude of Governments, there is little or no merit in proposals of codification

[1] Sir Arnold McNair, in two lectures delivered at the Law Center of New York University and published in 1954 under the title, 'The Development of International Justice', has given the weight of his authority in support of this aspect of codification of international law (see, in particular, pp. 24–31).

which anticipate, to the extent of regarding it as decisive, the possible opposition of Governments and which are couched in terms of the lowest common denominator of probable general acceptance. Governments are composed of human beings and they must be credited with the capacity for being influenced by the intrinsic merits of drafts as finally elaborated. Experience has shown that Governments are often less 'realistic' than pessimism or lassitude makes them out to be. Undoubtedly, the proposals put before them must take into account the not unnatural reluctance of Governments to consent to changes which may amount to a modification or an abandonment of their law and practice and necessitate complicated amendments in their legislation. Admittedly, codification must be the result of a laborious process of adjustment of, and compromise between, conflicting interests of States. But once the codifying agency, which is not composed of representatives of Governments, has reached the conclusion that a draft is desirable and dictated by the interests of the international community, by the rationally conceived interest of States and the requirements of a progressive development of international law as an instrument of international co-operation and as the protector of the rights of the individual conceived as the ultimate subject and beneficiary of all law, then it must take the risk that the General Assembly will do no more for the time being than take note of the report which has been published. A report adopted after mature consideration and after taking into account the views expressed by Governments, is bound to exercise an influence and to rally around it the support of enlightened States.

Of such possibilities the Draft Convention on the Elimination of Statelessness, tentatively formulated in 1953, provides an instructive example. Some States, such as the United Kingdom, could subscribe to that convention practically without a change, or any significant change, in their legislation.[1] Some countries may see in it no more than an embodiment – startling at first sight because of its completeness – of their own deliberately pursued legislative policy on the subject. On the other hand, States such as the United States of America with its Nationality and Immigration Law enacted in 1952, would have to be prepared, at an appropriate time, to abandon provisions of municipal law which, enacted in what was considered to be a period of acutely felt danger and crisis, disregard the avowed general tendency not to augment causes of statelessness. It is not

[1] See below, pp. 294–5

improper for a codifying body not composed of representatives of Governments to urge that no vital national interest is involved in such renunciation of a national practice, however emphatic and however recently adopted. There can be no question of the dignity and sovereignty of States being involved in the expression, on the part of the codifying body, of the view that deprivation of nationality by way of punishment is, upon impartial examination, unrelated to any national interest of importance; that it has been abandoned, either formally or in practice, by many States without obvious detriment to their safety and well-being; and that the absence of national interest in its retention is coupled with a clear international interest in its abandonment. In particular, no impropriety can reasonably attach to any insistence, on the part of the codifying agency, on the essential irrelevance of the consideration, conceived as an exclusive consideration, that a specific product of codification necessitates changes in the national law. For clearly any codification, unless in the exceptional case of a restatement of the law agreed by all States, must necessitate changes in the law of some States. The same applies, more obviously, to codification which consists in a development of the law. In fact, the task of legislative codification of international law must remain sterile and lacking in moral authority unless it becomes axiomatic that the international interest – the interest of international society as such – is a legitimate factor in the situation, not only as a means of reconciling divergent national interests but also as an end in itself. This may not be the view of some of the States intent upon perpetuating any particular practice. The time may therefore be distant when the Draft Convention on the Elimination of Statelessness will be adopted generally or even by the majority of States. This circumstance does not affect its intrinsic justification and eventual influence. It is not only of interest to note that the first Great Power – the United Kingdom – which formulated its attitude toward the far-reaching proposals of the Commission on the subject, expressed its approval of the principal article of the more drastic Convention on the Elimination of Statelessness in preference to that on the Reduction of Statelessness.[1] What is of equal significance is the preparedness of some States to adopt an attitude toward proposals for a change in international law on this subject, not by reference to the fact that such changes are inconsistent with their existing legislation, but in the light of the intrinsic merits of the proposals in question. Thus the Norwegian Govern-

[1] U.N. Doc. A/CN.4/82, p. 11.

ment, after drawing attention to the fact that the adoption of the Conventions on Reduction or Elimination of Statelessness would necessitate drastic changes in Norwegian law, continued as follows:

> Considering the important humanitarian aspects of the matter and the importance of demonstrating some liberality in the international co-operation aimed at relieving statelessness, the Norwegian Government will not be adverse to the idea of seeking to effect the necessary changes in the law provided there is some prospect of general adherence to one of the draft conventions on the part of Governments.[1]

Undoubtedly, it is useful for the codifying body to be informed of the state of the law in the countries concerned, but there is a distinct element of unhelpfulness in a reply which views the existing legislation of the State as the exclusive relevant factor in the situation. There is little object in creating an agency for codification and then confronting it with the existing anomalies and divergencies in the law as the factor of decisive relevance.

While it is of the essence of the successful accomplishment of the task of the codifying agency that Governments should respect its independence by not treating it as a body confined to a registration of the existing municipal legislation and other practices of States, it is of equal importance that the International Law Commission should preserve its independence of Governments not only, in the manner as here indicated, with regard to the character of its proposals, but also with regard to its own methods and procedure. The Commission is an organ of the United Nations. But it is an organ *sui generis*. It is not a political body and there may be a measure of incongruity in its procedure and deliberations being governed by technical and rigid rules appropriate to committees of the General Assembly, for instance, that a majority of two-thirds shall be required for a reconsideration of any decision taken during any session of the Commission. These considerations apply generally to the wider aspects of the activity of the Commission. The influence of its work must in a large measure depend upon the product having the support of the substantial majority of its members. Unlike other bodies where the necessity for action calls for decisions by a majority, however slender, the authority and effectiveness of drafts prepared by a codifying agency must be decisively impaired if formulated under the impact of the hazards and alignments of voting. For similar reasons it is desirable, contrary to the existing practice, that the

[1] U.N. Doc. A/CN.4/82/Add. 1. See also the reply of the Dutch Government conceived in the same spirit (Doc. A/CN.4/82/Add. 6).

reports of the Commission should give as full publicity as is practicable to opposing or supplementary views of the minority or of individual members. The reasons which have prompted the recognition of the right of the judges of the International Court of Justice to append dissenting or separate judgments or opinions apply with no less cogency to the work of the International Law Commission.[1]

7. THE PROBLEM OF THE UNIVERSALITY OF CODIFICATION

Codification constitutes a need of international society at large, and it is in accordance with its purpose that it should be undertaken within the orbit of the general organization of States represented within United Nations and that it should aim at universal acceptance. While this appears to be the ultimate objective, the universal character of codification cannot, in the light of experience, mean more than that all States should be given an equal opportunity of participating in the work of codification and of associating themselves with its results. In particular, it cannot mean that the values of codification ought to be judged by the degree of generality of its acceptance or that its content should be allowed to be influenced decisively by any desire to approximate to universality. From this point of view, so long as there exists no international legislature able to impose upon all members of the international community the law as formulated by a majority of States after due consideration of the national and international interests involved, the scope of codification in the international sphere must differ from that within the State. As a rule, universal acceptance of the results of codification can be achieved in the international sphere only at the risk of making it nominal and retrogressive. This is so in particular in periods when political divisions in the world and the conflict of some fundamental notions of law as between groups of States render impracticable, in most matters, any attempt to achieve a generally agreed statement or development of the law. International law, whether codified or not, implies essentially a restriction of the sovereignty of States

[1] Any diminution of that right, for reasons of possible abuse, is not in keeping with the scientific character of the Commission, and is, on more general grounds, indefensible. The authority of the decisions and drafts of the majority of the Commission is grounded in their intrinsic merit, as distinguished from the formal fact of their being the result of a majority vote. As a rule, it cannot be impaired—it stands to gain—by an accompanying expression of the view of the minority. Where the persuasive force of a report of the majority is in fact in danger of being impaired by an accompanying expression of dissent, it may perhaps be desirable that it should thus be impaired.

whose relations it governs. It is in the nature of things that States wedded to an uncompromising maintenance of their sovereignty cannot view with favour attempts at effective codification. The deliberations of the International Law Commission on the subject of nationality and statelessness provided an instructive example of that difficulty arising from the fact that some of the members of the Commission were opposed to the codification of that subject on the ground that regulation of nationality is a matter which is exclusively within the domestic jurisdiction of States. There can therefore be no objection to accepting as accurate the statement, referred to above,[1] of Judge Charles de Visscher to the effect that the prospects of a codification of international law on *a universal plane* are at present non-existent. It is not necessary to impart to that view a degree of pessimism going beyond the apparent intention of its author.

For the fact that universal codification is not practicable or, perhaps, in the existing circumstances, desirable, does not warrant sweeping conclusions in relation to codification as such. On the contrary, the reality of codification, its effectiveness, and its ultimate beneficence must be enhanced if it is envisaged, in the first instance, as extending to a limited circle of States. Drafts and conventions, formulated as part of the systematic codification of international law and approved by the General Assembly or subsequently adopted at a conference by a limited number of States, must be regarded as amply fulfilling, in the first instance, the purposes of codification as generally understood and as contemplated by the Charter. When formulated after prolonged and mature study and when supplemented by scientific comment and accompanying materials giving an exhaustive account of governmental and judicial practice, they are bound to constitute, even when they enter into force only between a restricted number of States, all that can be legitimately expected and all that is objectively required in the first stages of codification of international law. The fact that the Hague Convention on the Conflict of Nationality Laws has entered into force only among a small number of States, has not impaired its authority and its influence. Products of codification, even if initially approved or accepted only by a limited number of Governments, constitute a positive and tangible achievement and a starting-point for a gradual extension of their operation. The very fact that their authors, having discarded the spurious inducements of immediate universal par-

[1] See above, p. 270.

ticipation and the resulting artificialities or retrogression of diplomatic compromise, have framed them so as not to sacrifice the reality of the context to an appearance of universality, must add to their value.

Undoubtedly, as stated, in the work of codification under the aegis of the United Nations, all States must be given the opportunity of participating in the preparatory work of codification even if there is doubt as to the genuineness of their attachment to that task and the prospects of their ultimate association with its results. Their views must be listened to with the respect to which they are entitled. Patience, tolerance and statesmanship will find means of reducing the danger of the stature and results of codification being impaired in the course of preparation by those who in any case are unlikely to subscribe to it. For there may be little object in meeting the views and interests of States which are in any event likely to keep aloof. On the other hand, in view of the potential general character of codification, means ought to be considered for associating with it States which are not at present Members of the United Nations. Such an association has proved practicable in the case of the International Court of Justice.

8. THE PART OF GOVERNMENTS

As experience has shown, the task of codification is impossible of achievement unless aided by co-operation on the part of Governments at every stage. Such collaboration entails heavy commitments of more than an administrative nature. In the first instance, it involves the discharge of the delicate and often difficult task of securing an adequate composition of the codifying body. While the Statute of the International Law Commission provides in Article 2 that 'the Commission shall consist of fifteen members who shall be persons of recognized competence in international law', it also lays down in Article 8, as a consideration to be borne in mind by the electors, that although the members of the Commission should individually possess the qualifications required, 'in the Commission as a whole the representation of the main forms of civilization and of the principal legal systems of the world should be assured'. It may be possible to take account of these two sets of considerations without doing violence to the letter and spirit of the Statute, but this may not be feasible in all cases. Apart from the undeniable necessity of making the codifying body as representative as possible, the nature of the task to be fulfilled by it is not without relevance in this connection. In an organ which is concerned not only with the restatement of existing law but also with its change and development, qualities of statesmanship and experience may legitimately count for no less than expert knowledge. In this respect the requirement of expert composition of the Commission need not necessarily follow the exacting conditions laid down in the constitutions of some other international bodies.[1] At the same time, it is clear that an adequate proportion of membership fulfilling the requirements of Article 2 of the Statute of the Commission is an indispensable condition of the proper fulfilment of its task. The care and conscientiousness with which Governments discharge that function, in this and similar spheres, is a touchstone of their sense of responsibility to the international community. Obviously, it is also an essential factor in the adequate fulfilment of the objects entrusted to any particular organ. A Government which proclaims its devotion to an object of international endeavour and co-operation and which at the same time fails in its duty to make the best contribution, so far as lies with it, to the membership of the organ concerned, lays itself open to a charge of contradictory conduct inimical to international interest. It is probable that this aspect of governmental action or omission constitutes, as a matter of moral duty and international trust, one of the crucial problems of international organization in general.

Secondly, the collaboration of Governments involves, as an important condition of the success of the work of codification, the furnishing of information as to the existing law and practices of the State concerned, a burdensome task for an already overburdened department of Government. Such information is not a mere product of research. Insofar as it expresses the official view of a State as to its understanding of the law, it may be relied against it in the future to some extent. As such, the supply of information is a task of some complexity. It is a task which, unless performed perfunctorily and unhelpfully, constitutes a considerable addition to the responsibilities on a high level, of Governments. The provision of such information cannot be delegated exclusively to subordinate officials. The same applies, more conspicuously, to comments on drafts prepared by the codifying organ. Such comments may require interdepartmental consultation and decisions on a high level of governmental responsibility, in a manner often approaching decisions preliminary to the

[1] Such as the Universal Postal Convention or the International Telecommunications Convention.

assumption of international obligations. For, as already noted, this is not only a question of supplying information as to legislation and other practice in the past; it may be a question of a State agreeing in advance to a change in its law. Yet it is clear that without such collaboration the work of codification, operating in a vacuum, must remain unreal. This being so, codification, conceived as a systematic long-range effort and as distinguished from attempts of limited scope, may require the creation of something in the nature of a special section in legal departments of foreign offices. It is bound to add to the responsibilities of the foreign offices as such. In the absence of some special machinery created for that purpose, no sustained collaboration on an adequate scale can reasonably be expected from them. For their normal business is with matters of immediate practical concern and urgency.[1] It follows that, unless within the foreign offices of the Members of the United Nations machinery is devised on a larger scale than exists at present for assisting the work of codification and shaping effectively a constructive attitude towards the drafts and proposals put forward by the International Law Commission, its activity must continue to remain within a restricted orbit. For, severely circumscribed as that activity has been, owing to its constitution and the resources available to it, its output has probably been as great as Governments have been able to cope with. There can be no appreciable advance in the sphere of official codification unless Governments are in the position to make it part of their own effort. Similar considerations apply to the machinery established within the General Assembly – at present through its Legal Committee – for assessing and acting upon the drafts and reports of the International Law Commission.

It is not surprising that there may be a reluctance on the part of

[1] This aspect of the situation was cogently commented upon by Senator Elihu Root as far back as 1911. See *A.J.* 5 (1911), 580.

In answer to the request of the Commission to be supplied, in accordance with Article 19(2) of its Statute, with 'texts of laws, decrees, judicial decisions, treaties, diplomatic correspondence and other documents relevant to: (1) treaties; (2) arbitral procedure, and (3) the régime of the high seas', the French Government replied that it 'unfortunately cannot consider communicating all the documentary material which has appeared on these three classic topics, representing as it does several tons of its archives', but that it was 'prepared to supply the Commission with such of these texts as it possesses and as are requested in conformity with Article 19, paragraph 2' (U.N. Doc. A/CN.4/19, p. 27). Article 19(2) refers to a 'detailed request'. The request could have been made 'detailed', without undue effort, by compiling, within the three topics mentioned, an exhaustive catalogue of subjects. Yet it is clear that Governments may be unable to comply with a request of this nature, essential to the scientific fulfilment of the task of the Commission, without considerable research conducted by staff deputed for that purpose. There also arises the question whether the Commission, with the resources available to it, is in the position to make full use of the material thus supplied.

Governments to undertake extended responsibilities in the sphere of codification at a time when the state of international relations claims their urgent attention in other directions and when the very task of codification appears, by comparison, to partake of a measure of unreality. However, these conditions are not inevitably permanent. If and when international relations enter, or revert to, channels of legality and orderliness, codification of international law in the wider sense as here described will claim more persuasively than it can do at present that it is an urgent function of organized international society; that it is of importance for the authority and effectiveness of international law and international judicial and arbitral settlement; and that organs entrusted with the task of codification must be endowed with a constitution and resources commensurate with its place in the scheme of the Charter. For it is only by way of exception that ideas are stronger than men and agencies charged with their translation into reality. Thus viewed, the progress and the fortunes of codification under the auspices of the United Nations must to a large extent be determined by the following considerations:

In the first instance, in time of stress – and international society has been living through times of stress in the first decade of the existence of the United Nations – it may be provident, for the sake of continuity and preservation of future possibilities, to maintain what is no more than a token force in this and other spheres. Such token forces and their limited achievements need not be regarded as fully expressive of the potentialities of the major purpose of their being. If this is so, then there is no reason to view with dismay the fact that in the initial period of its existence the organization of the Commission has been rudimentary and its achievements correspondingly limited.[1] Thus it may be held that any development in the

[1] 'The Survey of International Law in Relation to the Work of Codification of the International Law Commission', prepared in 1948 and published as Memorandum submitted by the Secretary-General, expressed, on p. 17, the optimistic view that 'in two decades or so' the work of the Commission may 'cover practically the entire field of international law'. It seems, in the light of the first five years of the activity of the Commission, that having regard to the resources open to it by virtue of its Statute and the time available for its periodic meetings, the completion of that task may require several generations. By that time the first products of its labours would necessarily have become obsolete. A general survey of the results of the first five years of the activity of the Commission illustrates this aspect of the situation. In 1949 the Commission adopted a Draft Declaration of Rights and Duties of States. In 1950 it drafted its 'formulation of the Nürnberg Principles'. In 1951 it adopted a tentative 'Draft Code of Offences against the Peace and Security of Mankind' and a Report on Reservations to Multilateral Treaties. It finally adopted the Draft Code in 1954. In 1953 it submitted a final draft code on certain aspects of arbitral procedure. Of the three major topics—treaties, régime of the high seas,

direction of transforming the Commission into a continuously functioning body may not be practicable in the absence of conditions enabling Governments to provide it with membership of unchallenged efficacy in conformity with Article 2 of its Statute,[1] and unless appropriate machinery, as indicated above, is devised within the framework both of the foreign offices and of the General Assembly for taking action on the reports and drafts prepared by the Commission. These considerations may, for a time, be decisive. On the other hand, it is arguable that the evolution of the Commission as an effective instrument of acknowledged competence may in itself pave the way for the changes, deemed desirable, with regard both to the character of its membership and the attitude of Governments and the General Assembly towards the work of the Commission and its products. The difficulties surrounding the realization of this aspect of the Charter are not inherent in it; they lie outside it. The rational assumption, which admittedly is an assumption of faith, is that these difficulties may be of a transient character.

Secondly, while some of the objects of the Charter of the United Nations are such that their realization in a particular period must be impeded or halted by the unfavourable realities of the political situation or constitutional limitations such as the requirement of unanimity, these factors are not necessarily relevant to all spheres of activity of the United Nations. They are not decisive in connection with codification, which is outside the purview of the rule of unanimity. There may be wisdom and foresight in the resolve to use to the full the opportunities already available with respect to some needs of the international community without waiting until it is practicable to bring nearer to fruition all the purposes proclaimed in its constitution.

Thirdly, there are disadvantages in permitting an important and, in a wider perspective, urgent object of the United Nations and of the international community in general to be fulfilled, for an in-

and nationality—of its systematic programme of codification none was within sight of completion at the end of the first five years' period of its activity except for isolated subjects, namely, the Articles on the Continental Shelf and the Draft Conventions on Elimination and on Reduction of Future Statelessness and the incomplete Draft Articles on the Régime of the Territorial Sea. The Commission also submitted, in 1954, proposals for the reduction of existing statelessness.

[1] There is room for considering to what extent the requisite expert element in the composition of the Commission may be effectively secured by a method of election—or appointment—differing from that adopted in its Statute as formulated in 1948. Such method might consist in appointment by separate or joint action, possibly with or without association with the General Assembly, of other organs of the United Nations, such as the Secretary-General or the International Court of Justice.

definite or prolonged period, by 'token forces'. For once the scope and the stature of the task of codifying and developing international law have been reduced to dimensions out of keeping with its true significance, it may be difficult to alter the initial pace and character of the endeavour thus begun and to restore to it the momentum and dignity commensurate with the true merits of its original purpose.

IV

THE WRITERS AND DOCTRINE OF INTERNATIONAL LAW

CHAPTER 12

THE GROTIAN TRADITION IN INTERNATIONAL LAW

Editor's note From conversations which my father had with me, I know that he regarded this article as probably the most important that he ever wrote. Certainly, I can recall the immense amount of labour that he put into it. The article was published in the *British Year Book of International Law*, 23 (1946), 1-53.

The tercentenary of the death of Grotius – he died on 29 August 1645 – passed almost unnoticed in the literature of international law.[1] When compared with the solemn prominence accorded twenty years before to the three hundredth anniversary of the appearance of *De Jure Belli ac Pacis*, that absence of remembrance of a life so rich in fame and achievement is significant. It coincided with a period in which international law, after having survived the fiercest assault ever made upon it, proved as yet unable to impose its authority over the essentials of the new international system.[2] At no time was it therefore more necessary than after the Second World War to sustain hope by drawing inspiration from works in which principle has asserted itself against makeshifts. It is believed that instruction of this kind may still be derived from the ideas which Grotius bequeathed to international law and which supply the key to the attraction and the influence of his treatise in the course of centuries. This is so although the principal work on which his fame rests may be faulty in its method, pretentious in its learning, and, unless it is studied with a sense of historical perspective, unreadable in the twentieth century. The object of this essay is to attempt to supply that perspective through an estimate of his teaching in the light of the enduring problems of international law. A survey of that nature is bound to show that the contribution of Grotius is more than a mere link in the evolution of thought; that there is about it a unity and a consistency which transcend its evasions and contradictions; that it is

[1] Professor Lee's article in *L.Q.R.* 62 (1946), 53–7, is a notable exception.

[2] It was with some difficulty that the authors of the Charter of the United Nations were persuaded to assign to international law a place within the scheme of the United Nations. The view is widely held that, conceived in the spirit of realism, the Charter in many respects preferred order to law.

representative of the main problems with which international law has been confronted since its inception; and that, upon final analysis, the true value of his teaching is bound to assert itself over the repetitious and often uncritical adulation which has threatened to obscure the true import of his work.

Admittedly, the significance of his achievement has been, and probably will remain, a subject of controversy. Although criticism is unlikely to reach the low level of vituperation adopted by Rousseau[1] and some lesser writers,[2] it is by no means a relic of intolerance or hasty reading. Thus we find a distinguished modern author referring in the following terms to the principal work of Grotius:

> That learned medley, *De Jure Belli ac Pacis*, which, however valuable as a first attempt to lay the foundations of international law – and even here it is vitiated by a perpetual confusion between fact and Right – is, for all speculative purposes, a nest of sophistries and contradictions.[3]

There is no reason to assume that he was ignorant of the fervent advocacy of Grotius's merits by writers of no mean calibre such as Sir James Mackintosh,[4] Hallam,[5] and Whewell.[6] Grotius himself, when at the close of his days he surveyed the achievements of a lifetime, may well have had his doubts. In a very real sense he was one of the greatest international figures of his age – a prodigy, almost a miracle, of learning; an intimately familiar name to all interested in religious controversy at a time when questions of religious dogma and polemics were in the very centre of public attention; a brilliant literary scholar; the acknowledged greatest exponent of the Law of Nations. It would be necessary to go back to Erasmus to find a figure who was as much a household name wherever learning and culture reached. But we can well understand the doubts which beset Grotius as he lay on his death-bed in the town of Rostock, in Pomerania. He was then on his return journey from Stockholm, where he had gone to tender what was in fact his enforced resignation as Swedish Ambassador to the French Court and to attempt to obtain a diplomatic appointment of comparable

[1] *Contrat Social*, book I, chs. ii and iv. He reproaches Grotius with favouring tyrants and says: 'His constant way of reasoning is to establish law by reference to the facts' (ch. ii). See below, p. 356.

[2] See, e.g., Dugald Stewart's outspoken criticism expressed in his first *Dissertation on the Progress of Philosophy*, and answered by Hallam, *Introduction to the Literature of Europe* (1839), III, 439 *et seq.*

[3] Vaughan, *Studies in the History of Political Philosophy* (1925), I, 22.

[4] *Discourse on the Study of the Law of Nature and Nations* (ed. of 1828), pp. 23 *et seq.*

[5] *Introduction to the Literature of Europe*, III, ch. iv.

[6] See his Preface to the Abridged Translation of *De Jure Belli ac Pacis* (1853).

dignity and usefulness. No such offer materialized. There he lay, shattered in body by a storm which made his ship a total wreck, and broken in spirit, his long and varied career unfolding itself before his mind's eye. According to a report, as to the authenticity of which there has been some controversy, among his closing words there was the exclamation of despair: 'By undertaking many things I have accomplished little.'[1]

Posterity has successfully challenged that self-deprecatory judgment. Yet he may well have had reasons for his doubts, for the final estimate of his work is not so self-evident as the lavish praise often bestowed upon it may lead us to assume. This is so not because of the fact, which possibly was foremost in his mind in August 1645, that his diplomatic career was not an unqualified success. He had had to contend with difficulties which any ambassador of Sweden, then allied with France, would have had to meet at that time. For French diplomacy oscillated, with transparent unscrupulousness, between the desire to extract the maximum of help from the subsidized ally and the determination to prevent Sweden from establishing herself as a dominant Power in Europe. But it is probable that he did not feel strongly about the set-backs in his diplomatic career, which for him was merely a source of livelihood. It is not even certain that international law had been or remained the centre of his interest. He was busy with the successive editions of *De Jure Belli ac Pacis*. But the mysteries of the doctrines of Atonement and of Transubstantiation were more real to him than the work on which his fame eventually rested. What affected him more deeply was the failure of his persistent efforts, through writings and otherwise, to promote the unity of the Church – a unity conceived as an aim praiseworthy in itself and as a pre-eminent instrument of peace.[2] He was not primarily a man of affairs, and his powers as a negotiator were impaired rather than enhanced by the range and the conviction of his scholarship. His main literary activity – which was not in the sphere of international law but of poetry, literary criticism, religious dogma, and biblical exegesis – has proved of ephemeral value. There are very few, if any, who now draw their inspiration or knowledge from these writings.

What is perhaps more important is that the merits of that very work which has secured for him a permanent place in history are not by any means above controversy. The view is widely held that

[1] As quoted by Knight, *The Life and Work of Hugo Grotius* (1925), p. 289.

[2] See below, p. 359.

as an exposition of international law – or even as a presentation of a jurisprudential system – *De Jure Belli ac Pacis* is in many respects a somewhat superficial, hasty, and pretentious production. It is impossible to brush aside that view with astonished impatience. That monumental work is a dazzling exhibition of learning, but much of that learning creates the impression of being irrelevant. This is so not because he overwhelms the reader with a mass of ancient authorities while neglecting those nearer home. For this was the custom of the time. Witness, for instance, the way in which Machiavelli, the realist, relied almost exclusively upon the experience of antiquity. Hobbes, the atheist, devotes a substantial portion of the *Leviathan* – a secular work if ever there was one – to a discussion of the Scriptures. The principles and practice of the Greeks and Romans were used as the basis of the revival of the study of military science in the seventeenth century. This also was the case with political science and constitutional law. Neither is there more substance in the facile criticism pointing to Grotius's promiscuous reliance on what appears to the modern eye to be the exotic authority of poets, philosophers, schoolmen, scholastic writers, the Holy Scriptures and their innumerable commentators. For he is at pains to prove not only the Law of Nations – the evidence of which he sought in unbroken custom and the testimony of those skilled in it[1] – but also the law of nature in its diverse connotations. For the latter purpose it was legitimate for him to draw upon a manifold variety of opinions. The impression of irrelevancy is largely due to the ostentatiousness and prolixity in the piling up of authorities. The unwieldy mass of authorities cited from various periods other than the coeval with his own and from most diverse spheres of human thought almost seems to suggest that Grotius had never outgrown the mentality of the precocious youth who at the age of fifteen had published work to his credit and had joined a Dutch diplomatic mission to Paris, where he was greeted by the King of France as the miracle of Holland.

However, this somewhat exhibitionist learning is not limited to the method of spectacular assembling of authorities. It seems to extend to the treatise as a whole. For one-half of the work is concerned with matters which, to all appearance, have no connection with international law. That part of the treatise includes a general jurisprudential theory of the law of property, of contract, and of reparation; in part it comprises also a general theory of constitutional law, especially in relation to such questions as sovereignty and the

[1] Book II, ch. i, § xiv. 2.

social contract. It may not be difficult to find an explanation – and a justification – of what thus appears to be something in the nature of a patchwork. The explanation is that as, according to Grotius, the main cause of a just war is a threatened or actual violation of a legal right[1] or the refusal of reparation, it was necessary to give an account of the substantive law which may be affected by a breach of legal duty. The explanation may appear to some far-fetched. Thus it may not be easy to see the relevance of the chapters on the rights of parents over children, of the husband over the wife, and of the master over the slave; or those on the law of wills and succession; or that on the right of sepulchre (which follows immediately upon the chapter on the right of legation). Another explanation of the somewhat patchy character of the work is the circumstance, for which there now appears to be substantial evidence,[2] that while composing it Grotius made use of a great deal of material assembled many years before in a work entitled *De Jure Praedae Commentarius*, written about 1604 in connection with a case in which he appeared as counsel for the Dutch East India Company. Of that work discovered in 1864 and published in 1868, only one part – *Mare liberum* – had previously been published in 1609.

To that seemingly deficient and artificial construction of the treatise there must be added a defect of method which, apparently, has no redeeming feature. That defect does not consist in the fact that it is impossible to classify Grotius as belonging to any of the accepted schools of thought in the matter of sources of international law. He is not a pure positivist – a mere chronicler of events laboriously woven into a purely formal pattern of a legal system. Neither is he a naturalist pure and simple for whom an irresistible law of nature is the overriding – or the only – rule of conduct. We cannot even consider him as what is usually described as a 'Grotian' who has accomplished a workable synthesis of natural law and State practice. The fact seems to be that on most subjects which he discusses in his treatise it is impossible to say what is Grotius's view of the legal position. He will tell us, often with regard to the same question, what is the law of nature, the Law of Nations, divine law, Mosaic law, the law of the Gospel, Roman law, the law of charity, the obligations of honour, or considerations of utility. But we often look in vain for a statement as to what is *the* law governing the matter. Occasionally

[1] Book II, ch. i, § ii.

[2] See Scott's Introduction to the translation of *De Jure Belli ac Pacis* in the 'Classics of International Law' (1925).

we obtain a glimpse of how useful the treatise would be if Grotius had adhered to these distinctions for the practical purpose of indicating the existing legal rule. Thus in discussing unjust causes of war he distinguishes between strictly legal obligations and those arising from generosity, gratitude, pity, or charity, which obligations must not be enforced by war any more than they can be enforced in a court of law.[1] But this is an exception rather than the rule. With regard to the crucial aspect of the work, namely, the law of war, it is often well nigh impossible to elicit what is the law on the subject. Thus Grotius asserts the legality, under the Law of Nations, of killing of enemies or of devastation. But these permissive rules he qualifies by the statement that such things are permissible not for the reason that they can be done 'without violence to right conduct and rules of duty, but because among men they are not liable to punishment'.[2] It is not easy to decide whether that distinction is of legal relevance or not. Things, he says, which are permissible – i.e. lawful – may not be consistent with justice[3] (which on some occasions he identifies with honour) or with what he describes as moral justice or internal justice.[4] Yet, on the other hand, conduct, though consistent with 'justice', may not be in conformity 'with goodness, with moderation, with high-mindedness'[5] or with 'equity and goodness'.[6]

There is almost a touch of levity in this indiscriminate and confusing eclecticism in the use of sources. Thus, after giving an account of the unmitigated rigours – of which he occasionally seems to approve – of the law of war in the light of actual practice, i.e. of the Law of Nations, he says in a passage entitled 'With what meaning a sense of honour may be said to forbid what the law permits':

I must retrace my steps, and must deprive those who wage war of nearly all the privileges which I seemed to grant, yet did not grant them. For when I first set out to explain this part of the Law of Nations I bore witness that many things are said to be 'lawful' or 'permissible' for the reason that they are done with impunity, in part also because coactive[7] tribunals lend to them their authority; things which, nevertheless, either deviate from the rule of right (whether this has its basis in law strictly so

[1] Book II, ch. xxii, § xvi.

[2] Book III, ch. iv, § ii. 1–3. *Ibid.* § v. 2 ('We must not understand such a law as would free what is done from all blame, but such immunity from punishment as I have mentioned').

[3] Book III, ch. x, § i. 1.

[4] Book III, ch. xi, § ii.

[5] Book III, ch. xi, § vii.

[6] Book III, ch. iii, § xv. 1.

[7] The original text uses the expression *judicia coactiva*. Possibly 'enforceable judgments' conveys more accurately the intention of the author. The quotations in the present article are taken, unless otherwise stated, from the translation by Kelsey in the 'Classics of International Law' (Carnegie Endowment for International Peace, 1925).

called, or in the admonition of other virtues), or at any rate may be omitted on higher grounds or with greater praise among men.[1]

By way of explaining[2] the meaning of the passage he quotes with approval Agamemnon's answer to Pyrrhus in Seneca's *Trojan Women.* While the latter invokes the law as laying down the victor's full power over the captive, Agamemnon's retort is that such conduct although permitted by law may be contrary to our sense of justice and therefore forbidden. Upon which Grotius's comment is that 'in this passage the sense of shame signifies not so much a regard for man and reputation as a regard for what is just and good, or at any rate for what is more just and better'. This appeal from law to justice is made, we are told, only with regard to things which are done in an unjust war though undertaken in a lawful way.[3] In such a war 'all acts which arise therefrom are unjust from the point of view of moral injustice' (*interna injustitia*). What are we to make of all this? The distinction between just and unjust wars is clear enough. Grotius repeatedly explains it in the treatise: it is a legal distinction and various legal consequences follow from it.[4] But we have not been told so far that it affects the legal quality of the acts of those engaged in an unjust war. On the contrary, Grotius asserts the opposite view.[5] What is meant by the statement that they are now to be 'deprived' of all the privileges which the author 'seems' to have granted to them? Is that denial of privileges and rights a precept of law or a dictate of morals or of the law of nature which is paramount over all? His explanation does not help us: '. . . in consequence, the persons who knowingly perform such acts, or co-operate in them, are to be considered of the number of those who cannot reach the Kingdom of Heaven without repentance'.[6] Neither does his insistence that 'true repentance . . . if time and means are adequate, absolutely requires that he who inflicted the wrong, whether by killing, by destroying property, or by taking booty, should make good the wrong done'.[7] We are thus uncertain, once more, whether we are in the realm of law or morals.

Neither should we be appreciably better off if we were to have more definite guidance on the subject, for it is possible – we are not altogether sure – that considerations of moral justice (*justitia interna*) enter the province of the ultimately binding law of nature. If it

[1] Book III, ch. x, § i. 1.
[2] Book III, ch. x, § i.
[3] Book III, ch. x, § iii.
[4] See below, p. 348.
[5] See below, p. 349.
[6] Book III, ch. x, § iii.
[7] *Ibid.*

were otherwise, what is the meaning of the statement that he is now about to deprive those who wage war of nearly all the privileges which he seems to have granted them, and yet has not granted them? Nor are we always certain, in the important chapters on moderation in a just war, at what point precepts of 'goodness, moderation, and high-mindedness' merge into the relentlessly binding law of nature – a confusion which is especially apparent in the chapter on moderation in punishments, where he speaks of the precepts of 'justice and of the law of nature';[1] or when he insists that 'nature does not sanction retaliation except against those who have done wrong';[2] or when he gives expression to his desire to 'restrict the unrestrained licence of war' in the matter of devastation to 'that which is permitted by nature'[3] (although, apparently, there is little limit to it according to the Law of Nations). The fact is that we are often at a loss as to the true meaning which he attaches to the law of nature. It is true that he gives a seemingly exhaustive definition of the law of nature as 'a dictate of right reason which points out that an act, according as it is or is not in conformity with rational nature, has in it a quality of moral baseness or moral necessity; and that, in consequence, such an act is either forbidden or enjoined by the author of nature, God'.[4] He explains also with some clarity what is the proper evidence of the law of nature, namely, either abstract reasoning showing the necessary agreement or disagreement of a rule 'with a rational and social nature' or *a posteriori* proof by reference to general belief[5] – the kind of evidence which is mainly responsible for the dazzling exhibition of learning displayed in the treatise. But we have only to go back to the *Prolegomena* to find that the law of nature thus defined is identical with law in general as determined by the necessity to maintain the social order and by human nature in general. The law of nature, it appears from the *Prolegomena*, is the law which is most in conformity with the social nature of man and the preservation of human society – a law of nature in its 'primary sense', which includes the duty of refraining from appropriating what belongs to others, restoration of what belongs to them, the obligation to fulfil promises, reparation of injury, and the right to inflict punishment.[6] With that natural law there is connected, as equally arising from nature, the inclination of man 'to follow the direction of a well-tempered judgment, being

[1] Book III, ch. xi, § xvi, 1.
[2] *Ibid.* § xvi, 2.
[3] Book III, ch. xii, § viii. 1.
[4] Book I, ch. i, § x. 1.
[5] Book I, ch. i, § xii, 1.
[6] *Proleg.* 8–10.

neither led astray by fear or the allurement of immediate pleasure, nor carried away by rash impulse'.[1] There is another kind – or consequence – of natural law which causes us to discriminate between and show preference 'now to him who is more wise over the less wise, now to a kinsman rather than to a stranger, now to a poor man rather than to a man of means'.[2]

This uncertainty as to the meaning of natural law is not relieved by the fact that in both parts of the treatise – in the *Prolegomena* and in book I – there is a significant attempt to place the law of nature upon a secular basis. The law of nature, he says in a frequently quoted passage of the *Prolegomena*,[3] 'would have a degree of validity even if we should concede that which cannot be conceded without utmost wickedness, that there is no God, or that the affairs of man are of no concern to Him'.[4] That alternative he is unwilling to accept. For such disinterestedness on the part of the Divinity is, he says, contrary both to reason and to all experience, and the duty of obedience to God follows therefore with absolute cogency. Accordingly, he concludes that in addition to the law of nature there is another source of law, namely, the will of God, to which absolute obedience is due and to which the law of nature must be attributed.[5] Similarly, when subsequently defining the law of nature, he asserts that it is 'unchangeable – even in the sense that it cannot be changed by God'.[6] For 'measureless as is the power of God, nevertheless it can be said that there are certain things over which that power does not extend. . . Just as even God . . . cannot cause that two times two should not make four, so He cannot cause that that which is intrinsically evil be not evil.'[7] But here, once more, he retreats from his position by an ingenious piece of dialectics. It may happen, he says, that while the law of nature is unchangeable the object which it regulates has undergone a change: 'So if God should command that any one be slain, or that the property of any one be carried off, homicide or theft – words connoting moral wrong – will not become permissible; it will not be a case of homicide or theft, because the deed is done by authority of the Supreme Lord of life and property.'[8]

[1] *Ibid.* 9. [2] *Ibid.* 10. [3] *Ibid.* 11.
[4] *Ibid.* [5] *Ibid.* 12. [6] Book I, ch. i, § x. 5.
[7] *Ibid.* This separation of the law of nature from theology was already foreshadowed by Suarez in *De Legibus ac Deo Legislatore* (1612), book II, ch. xiv: 'God does not, properly speaking, grant dispensations with respect to any natural precept; but He does change the subject-matter of such precepts or their circumstances, apart from which they themselves do not possess binding force. . .' And see Troeltsch, *The Social Teaching of the Christian Churches* (English transl. by Wyon, 1931), II, 636, for an interesting comparison of Grotius's rationalism as compared with Calvin's *stat pro ratione voluntas*. And see below, p. 365, n. 1.
[8] Book I, ch. i, § x. 6.

While he thus leaves the reader uncertain – there is no question of abandoning the position altogether – as to his determination to emancipate the law of nature from the shackles of theology, it is by no means clear that the law of nature, as used by him, invariably fulfils a humanizing function in the cause of alleviation of suffering and of progress conceived as an assertion of the liberty of man. Undoubtedly, more often than not he resorts to the law of nature as a mitigating factor, as, for instance, in the matter of the treatment of prisoners; he contrasts the more severe rules of the Law of Nations with the principles of the law of nature.[1] But on other occasions his conception of natural law approaches very much that of Hobbes's notion of the right of nature and of a law of nature as expressive of physical laws rather than ethical and juridical norms.[2] Most of the harshness of the law of war he deduces from the law of nature thus conceived. There are, according to it, no limits to the right to kill, to destroy, and to plunder. Thus the law of nature, though not the Law of Nations, permits the killing of the enemy by poison.[3] By the law of nature, though not by Mosaic law or the law of the Gospel, it is permissible to kill a person in defence of property.[4] But this is not consistent with his basic view of the law of nature as determined by the social nature of man. There is reason to believe that Grotius oscillated between these two conceptions of the law of nature and that, when in difficulty, he resorted to God for assistance. Thus while he admits that according to the law of nature a man who is in imminent danger of receiving a blow or a similar injury has the right to prevent it by killing the enemy, he denies that this is so by the law of the Gospel, which is the law of God; and he asserts that God's will is paramount in the matter: 'For God, the creator of nature, is also able to act freely outside the realm of nature, and has the right to lay down laws for us even concerning those matters which are by nature free and undetermined; even greater is His right to make

[1] Book III, ch. xvi, § ii. 3.

[2] 'The Right of Nature, which writers commonly call *jus naturale*, is the liberty each man hath, to use his own power, as he will himself, for the preservation of his own nature; that is to say, of his own life; and, consequently of doing any thing, which is his own judgment, and reason, he shall conceive to be the aptest means thereto' (*Leviathan* (1651), ch. xiv); 'A Law of Nature, *lex naturalis*, is a precept or general rule, found out by reason, by which a man is forbidden to do that, which is destructive of his life, or taketh away the means of preserving the same; and to omit that, by which he thinketh it may be preserved' (*ibid.*).

[3] Book III, ch. iv, § xv. 1. There seems to be much substance, from this point of view, in Montesquieu's criticism of the manner in which Grotius referred to the law of nature as justifying the rights and cruelties of war; for, says Montesquieu, the essence of the law of nature is preservation, not destruction (*Esprit des Lois*, x. 3).

[4] Book II, ch. i, §§ xi–xiii.

obligatory what by nature is honourable, even though not obligatory.'[1] On the whole we are probably right in assuming that the most frequent use of the notion of the law of nature by Grotius is what we should describe as general principles of law arrived at by way of a generalization and synthesis of the principal systems of jurisprudence.

The treatise abounds in laborious and elaborate distinctions between diverse kinds of justice and various categories of law, but it is not always clear what object these distinctions are intended to serve. Commentators and biographers have made interesting attempts to explain these classifications and bring them within the systematic orbit of modern terminology.[2] But there is not much in the treatise which lends itself, with any substantial accuracy, to these well-meant attempts. He distinguishes between the volitional law[3] (including statutory and, generally, positive law) and the law of nature which is unchangeable and impervious, it would seem, even to the will of God – a position which, as has been suggested,[4] he does not find it possible to maintain with uniform consistency.[5] The volitional law is divided into human and divine, the first being in turn subdivided into municipal law and the Law of Nations (which derives its obligatory force from the will of all nations or many nations), the latter into universal divine law and divine law peculiar to a single people.[6] Occasionally he distinguishes between the Law of Nations and the law of the better nations.[7] He differentiates clearly between the Law of Nations improperly so called, i.e., rules of private law which are common to all or some nations and which any people is entitled to change without consulting others and, on the other hand, the Law of Nations in the strict sense of the word which affects the mutual society of nations in relation to one another.[8]

[1] Book II, ch. i, § x. 1.

[2] See, in particular, Westlake, *Papers*, pp. 39–47, and Lee, *Hugo Grotius* (Annual Lecture on a Master Mind, British Academy, 1930), pp. 53–6.

[3] Book I, ch. i, § ix.

[4] See above, p. 315.

[5] See also, with regard to Punishments, Book II, ch. xx, § x. 1, where he points out that there is nothing strange in the fact that conduct which is permissible according to the law of nature and municipal law is forbidden by divine law 'since this is most perfect and sets forth a reward greater than human nature; to obtain this reward there are justly demanded virtues which surpass the bare precepts of nature'.

[6] Book I, ch. i, §§ xiv–xv.

[7] Book III, ch. iv, § xix. 1.

[8] See, for repeated references to that distinction, ch. viii of book II (on such questions as acquisition of property in animals *ferae naturae* and on the law relating to islands and alluvial deposits). For a clear distinction between international law proper and *jus gentium* see book II, ch. viii, § i.2: 'Hoc autem non est jus illud gentium proprie dictum; neque enim pertinet ad mutuam gentium inter se societatem, sed ad cujusque populi tranquillitatem; unde ab uno populo aliis inconsultis mutari potuit.' And see *Proleg.* 1.

In a different sphere he distinguishes between *jus aequatorium* (i.e., law applying in the relations of persons on a footing of equality such as citizens or allies) and *jus rectorium*[1] (i.e., law applying to relations of persons on a footing of inequality such as master and slave, or king and subject). He attaches even greater importance to the old Aristotelian distinction between expletive justice (*justitia expletrix*) which, apparently, is concerned with legal rights proper, rights to one's own, with *facultas* (which, again, he divides into private and public), and attributive justice (*justitia attributrix*) which is concerned with aptitudes (*aptitudo*)[2] – something to which a person may be entitled as a matter of 'generosity, compassion, and foresight in matters of government'. Probably this latter distinction figures more prominently in the treatise and is more consistently applied than any other. Thus, for instance, only the violation of a perfect right, of a *facultas* (as distinguished from an imperfect right, an aptitude), legitimately gives rise to a just war[3] and, generally, to enforcement by processes recognized by the law. However, on the whole the various distinctions are unhelpful for the purpose of assisting the student or the statesman in discovering what is the legal rule on the subject. There is no hierarchy of legal norms to assist the seeker after the correct rule of law. There is often little to guide us as to whether in case of conflict the law of nature (in its various and often contradictory meanings) is to prevail over the Law of Nations, or conversely. Often it is clear enough that in Grotius's view the law of nature has yielded to the Law of Nations,[4] but we cannot always be sure that this is his opinion. He supplies a partial clue to the solution of the difficulty by explaining that natural law is unchangeable only with regard to matters which it expressly prohibits and enjoins, but not with respect to those which it merely permits.[5] However, this fact does not explain the various other departures from natural law. The result is that for some purposes the latter appears to act *pro foro interno* only – as a kind of moral law.[6] And yet the supposedly unchangeable law of nature is claimed to be superior to God Himself. Westlake[7] summarizes the position by suggesting that according to Grotius *justitia*

[1] Book I, ch. i, § iii. 2. [2] Book I, ch. i, §§ vii, viii. I. [3] See below, p. 347.

[4] See e.g., book III, ch. ii, §§ i, ii, to the effect that although according to the law of nature no one, except the heir, is bound by an act of another, this is not so according to the Law of Nations—with the result, *inter alia*, that the goods of subjects may be seized in respect of the debts and obligations of their rulers and states; or book III, ch. iii, § vi, to the effect that although a declaration of war is not necessary according to the law of nature, it is required by the Law of Nations. [5] Book I, ch. ii, § v. I.

[6] See, for an analysis to the same effect, Basdevant in *Les Fondateurs du droit international* (1904), pp. 237–9, and Lee, *Hugo Grotius*, p. 55. [7] Westlake, *Papers*, p. 40.

attributrix (distributive justice) operates in international relations as natural law and that, therefore, in this sphere there is to that extent in the Grotian system no difference between moral and legal rights. This reading of Grotius is probably unwarranted – witness, for instance, Grotius's emphatic insistence that only perfect rights given by *justitia expletrix*, which is determined also by the law of nature, are a legally justifiable reason for war[1] – but the fact that this was the interpretation put on it by a careful scholar like Westlake is symptomatic.

Somewhat similar difficulties arise in connection with the use Grotius made of Roman law. He often treated it as evidence of the law of nature. But on occasions he was at pains to show that specific rules of Roman law found no confirmation in the Law of Nations[2] and could not therefore properly be adduced as a valid rule of international law. In general, his reliance on Roman law is less frequent and less emphatic than is generally assumed.

These conspicuous defects of method are not the only feature of *De Jure Belli ac Pacis* which invites criticism. For the principal part of the treatise, namely, the presentation of the laws of war, is, on the face of it, vitiated by the abandonment of the main object which the author set himself out to achieve. That purpose, which was the humanization of the conduct of war, he expressed in the frequently quoted passage:

> Fully convinced . . . that there is a common law among nations, which is valid alike for war and in war, I have had many and weighty reasons for undertaking to write upon this subject. Throughout the Christian world I observed a lack of restraint in relation to war, such as even barbarous races should be ashamed of; I observed that men rush to arms for slight causes, or no cause at all, and that when arms have once been taken up there is no longer any respect for law, divine or human; it is as if, in accordance with a general decree, frenzy had openly been let loose for the committing of all crimes.[3]

This was the avowed object of the treatise. Actually, in the view of many, it is a negation of that purpose. This is so not because of the fact that Grotius elaborates and defends the lawfulness of war[4] with much zeal and learning by reference to the law of nature, to history, to the law of the Gospel, and to arguments drawn from

[1] See below, p. 347.

[2] See, e.g., as to alluvial deposits, or islands in a river, or dried-out beds (book II, ch. viii, § viii). And see his frequent references to the 'errors' of Roman law, e.g. in book II, ch. xi, § xiii; book II, ch. xvi, § xi; *ibid.* § xxxi.

[3] *Proleg.* 28.

[4] Book I, ch. ii.

Holy Writ and the practice of the early Christians. To deny the lawfulness of war from the very outset and in all circumstances would have rendered meaningless the object of the treatise as apparently conceived by the author. What is more difficult to understand is that he seems to elevate that 'lack of restraint in relation to war, such as even barbarous races should be ashamed of' to the dignity of a rule of the Law of Nations. The Law of Nations gives the right to kill or injure all those who are in the territory of the enemy.[1] The same right is given with regard to the subjects of the enemy wherever they may be found.[2] Captives taken in war may be killed. So can those who surrender but whose surrender is not accepted.[3] Water may be polluted, though not by poison.[4] Both by the Law of Nations and by the law of nature it is permissible to use assassins.[5] In general, by the Law of Nations anything is permissible as against an enemy.[6] Enemy property may be destroyed and pillaged, including sacred property.[7] The same Law of Nations permits the enslavement of those captives with regard to whom the captor does not avail himself of his right to kill them – a rule which he regards as justified and, on the whole, beneficent as being an inducement to the captors to 'willingly refrain from recourse to the utmost degree of severity, in accordance with which they could have slain the captives, either immediately or after a delay'.[8] All this appeared to some, perhaps not without plausible reason, as lending support to the inhuman conduct of warfare by conceding to it the character of law – an effect which seems to be enhanced rather than diminished by his attempts, in the *temperamenta*, to suggest a mitigation of what he considered to be rules of law.

There are various possible explanations of this somewhat surprising outcome. The obvious explanation is that, without in the least approving that practice, Grotius believed it to be part of the customary Law of Nations – although, if that be so, it may not be easy to see why, in the *Prolegomena*, he spoke of them as evidencing a lack of restraint of which even barbarous races should be ashamed. It is possible that he adopted the device of *reculer pour mieux sauter* by pointing to the inhumanity of the existing practices as an irresistible argument in support of those precepts of humanity, charity, and honour which he developed in the *temperamenta* with so much zeal and fervour. It may also have occurred to him that his exhortations

[1] Book III, ch. iv, § vi.
[2] *Ibid.* § viii.
[3] *Ibid.*, § xi.
[4] *Ibid.* § xvii.
[5] *Ibid.* § xviii.
[6] *Ibid.*
[7] Book III, ch. v, §§ i, ii.
[8] Book III, ch. vii, § v. 1.

to moderation might appeal to statesmen and commanders in the field only if they knew that the appeal came from a writer acquainted with the realities of warfare and not altogether unwilling to consider the actual practice as a source of legal rules – imperfect as they might be. Neither can the possibility be dismissed that the treatise which he was writing – an exile without private means to support himself and his large family – was being prepared with an eye to diplomatic employment and that, for that purpose, it would have been of advantage to gain the reputation of a lawyer who takes fully into account the practice of States.

On the other hand, in estimating the probable humanizing influence of *De Jure Belli ac Pacis* we must not disregard the possibility that it may have been influential in the opposite direction. When a commanding general finds it laid down in the leading treatise that the killing or enslavement of prisoners of war or devastation of cities is part of the Law of Nations, he may be disinclined to decide that it is his imperative duty to act upon a different rule. He may, with some justification, disregard the exhortation which Grotius addresses to generals that 'it is the duty of the highest authorities and commanders, who wish themselves to be regarded as Christians, both by God and by men, to forbid the violent sack of cities and other similar actions'.[1] They may have considered that their calling was not a proper occasion for exhibiting the virtues of Christian charity – kindly and humane as they may have been as individuals. We recall the extraordinary episode of Tilly – the general commanding the troops who sacked Magdeburg on 17 May 1631, when 24,000 inhabitants lost their lives – riding amid the confusion of the burning city, clumsily nursing a baby which he had plucked, alive, from the arms of its dead mother.[2] There may be substance in the report that Gustavus Adolphus, King of Sweden, carried with him a copy of *De Jure Belli ac Pacis* wherever he went during his German campaign.[3] He was a devout Christian and, as was his wont, he prayed in front of his troops on the day on which the bullet of the enemy – or was it the hand of an ally? – cut short the span of a gallant life. But he could have used Grotius's work for an opposing variety of

[1] Book III, ch. xiii, § viii. 4. Sir Henry Maine (*International Law* (1st ed. 1887), p. 23) expresses the view that the effects of *De Jure Belli ac Pacis* in this respect were 'exceedingly prompt', but this is a matter of conjecture which was not substantiated by the subsequent course of the Thirty Years War.

[2] Wedgwood, *The Thirty Years War* (1938), p. 288.

[3] Miss Wedgwood apparently accepts the report as authenticated in Oxenstierna's writings (*The Thirty Years War*, p. 271).

purposes. It is not certain that he did not. His practice of systematically devastating the countryside through which his troops passed is a matter of history. This he did as part of the practice – which was then general – of depriving the enemy of the possibility of feeding his armies. The savagery of the concluding phases of the Thirty Years War – at a time when repeated editions of *De Jure Belli ac Pacis* were making their appearance – had not diminished by the time the struggle had reached a drawn-out end of futility and exhaustion. There is no doubt that the conduct of war at the beginning of the eighteenth century marked a distinct mitigation of practice as compared with the Thirty Years War, but more evidence than is as yet available would be necessary to justify us in assuming a connection between that improvement and the teaching of Grotius.

Finally, while the treatise has appeared to some to fail in the achievement of its avowed object in respect of the law of war, it has drawn upon itself vehement condemnation as a servile and reactionary instrument of justification of established authority. The doctrine of the law of nature has been exposed to the reproach that it has served more often as a bulwark of the existing order of things than as a lever of progress. Grotius seems to have given a semblance of support to that view. He justifies slavery by reference to the law of nature – a proceeding supported by a venerable array of authority from Aristotle to Locke. Although the social contract is an important component of his political theory, he attributes equal weight to the original acquisition of sovereignty by conquest on the part of the ruler. It is in this sphere that he has been denounced, in intemperate terms, as confusing law and fact.[1] He explicitly refuses to commit himself to any unqualified affirmation of the sovereignty of the people. He expressly rejects the view that 'everywhere and without exception sovereignty resides in the people so that it is permissible for the people to restrain and to punish kings whenever they make a bad use of their power'.[2] He supports his opinion by an elaborate and lengthy argument the gist of which is that any person may voluntarily enslave himself to anyone he pleases for private ownership.[3] For this reason he denies that the subjects are always entitled to regain their liberty – even if they lost it as the result of force. For, he says, subjection though due originally to force may receive subsequent confirmation by tacit acceptance: 'The will of the people, either at the very establishment of sovereignty or in connection with a later act, may be such as to confer a right which for the future is

[1] See above, p. 308. [2] Book I, ch. iii, § viii. I. [3] Book I, ch. iii, § viii.

not dependent on such will.'[1] In the same line of thought he denies the right of active resistance.[2] This view is qualified, as we shall see,[3] not only by the affirmation of the right and duty of passive resistance in face of orders contrary to the law of nature and the commandments of God,[4] but also by vast and significant categories of exceptions. Viewed in proper perspective, the denial of the right of resistance and the support for the sovereignty of the ruler appear less damaging to the character of the treatise than their intransigence suggests.[5] Yet they are not accidental; neither is the uncompromising expression with which they are affirmed. They are not, as we shall see, due to a perversity of thinking which makes us shrug our shoulders with incredulous astonishment. But they do not add to the greatness of *De Jure Belli ac Pacis*.

These faults of method and substance which we have traced in *De Jure Belli ac Pacis* are such that, indirectly, they suggest qualities so great and so permanent as to give the very fullest measure of compensation for these defects and to explain the enduring influence of that work in the realm of human thought in general and of international law in particular. We are concerned here only with the latter. The standing of *De Jure Belli ac Pacis* as an authority relied upon in judicial decisions, national and international, has been higher and more persistent than that of any other of the founders of international law. This can be seen, for instance, in the lengthy pleadings and arguments before and by the various Claims Commissions established by the Jay Treaty of 1794 between Great Britain and the United States, the first modern treaty of arbitration.[6] What is even more impressive is the reverent recourse to his treatise by the four greatest writers in the field of international law in the century which followed, namely, by Pufendorf, Bynkershoek, Wolff, and Vattel – even when, as often happens, they disagree with him. Undoubtedly, the general picture of international relations in the two centuries which followed the publication of *De Jure Belli ac Pacis* was not one pointing to any direct influence, in the sphere of practice, of the essential features of the Grotain teaching. But the view that, for that reason, Grotius's work was during that period consigned to

[1] Book II, ch. iv, § xiv. 1.

[2] Book I, ch. iv, § ii. 1. He denies that the ruler who maltreats an innocent person by that fact necessarily ceases to be a ruler (book II, ch. i, § ix. 2).

[3] See below, p. 357. [4] Book I, ch. iv, § i. 3. [5] See below, p. 356.

[6] See, e.g., *International Adjudications* (ed. by Moore), IV (1931), Mixed Commission under Article VII of the Jay Treaty, pp. 357, 384–6, 413–15 (on carriage of contraband), pp. 232–7, 269–79, 282–3 (on enemy character), pp. 246–7, 251–2 (on reprisals and exhaustion of legal remedies), pp. 419–21 (on measure of damages).

oblivion[1] is unwarranted and pessimistic. If it were so, there would have been no reason why Grotius should have been the first target of criticism in the opening chapters of *Contrat Social.*[2] Rousseau would have hardly thought it worth while to select for that purpose a writer who had become a dim memory. Voltaire, who, he said, was bored by Grotius's learned quotations masquerading as argument, would not have troubled to read him.[3] De Saint-Pierre's *A Project for Settling an Everlasting Peace in Europe* would not have its title-page adorned with a passage from *De Jure Belli ac Pacis* recommending the holding of international conferences for the purpose of settling disputes.[4] Between 1680 and 1780 there were thirty editions of the work in Latin; nine in French; four in German; three in English.[5] An English historian of international law writing in 1795 attributed to him a lasting influence not only upon the science but also on the practice of international law.[6] In the nineteenth century his authority, in the writings of jurists and in State Papers, remained unimpaired. When in 1925 jurists of many nations united in celebrating the tercentenary of the publication of *De Jure Belli ac Pacis*, it was manifest that the inspiration which for three centuries emanated from that treatise had by no means become a thing of the past.

There are a number of factors which, in a sense, are external to the substance of Grotius's teaching and which had a share in securing its contemporaneous success and its place in the succeeding centuries. The first is its timeliness. At the time that *De Jure Belli ac Pacis* was published the historic process of the disintegration of European political society as hitherto known and the rise of the territorial sovereign State were being consummated. The Thirty Years War, which, to all appearances, was a war of religion, actually began and continued as a war of secular claims and ambitions of dynasties and nations. The rivalry between France and Spain had been a problem of European politics for three centuries. It had been kept in check by the overriding unity of religion. The Thirty Years War, when Catholic France allied herself with the Protestant cause in opposition

[1] See Van Vollenhoven, 'Grotius and Geneva', in *Bibliotheca Visseriana*, 6 (1926), 15, 16, 30–4.

[2] Book I, ch. ii.

[3] *Dialogues et entretiens philosophiques* (Œuvres complètes, 1824), XXXVI, 232.

[4] Book II, ch. xxiii, § vii. 4 (English transl., 1714).

[5] For an exhaustive list see *De Jure Belli ac Pacis* (transl. in 'Classics of International Law', 1925), pp. 877–86.

[6] Ward, *An Enquiry into the Foundation and History of the Law of Nations in Europe from the Time of the Greeks and the Romans to the Age of Grotius* (1795). He says: 'We may probably be safe in assuming that it is to his comprehensive mind and learning that the law, as construed at present, has chiefly owed its distinguishing regularity' (II, 604).

to the dynastic ambitions of the Habsburgs and when the Pope, for similar reasons, stood aloof at a time of deadly peril for the Catholic party, showed clearly the implications of the change. In a different sphere, the demise of the feudal system gave a new and higher significance to the territorial State. The need for a system of law governing the relations of the independent States to replace the legal and spiritual unity of Christendom had thus become urgently obvious. If it is accurate to say that Grotius is the founder of modern international law, it is equally true that the necessity for an international law secured to the work of Grotius a place which otherwise it might not have acquired. Of that necessity the lessons of the Thirty Years War were a most compelling reminder. The *temperamenta* may have proved a vain hope so far as the actual conduct of the war was concerned. But its experience proved their urgency up to the hilt. The sacredness of the plighted word of treaties, one of the cornerstones of Grotius's teaching, may have had to stand the mocking test of the treachery of the politics of the Thirty Years War – the State whose interests Grotius represented diplomatically in Paris was bound with France and Saxony by treaties of alliance to which, taught by experience, it attached an importance not superior to that of a precarious armistice with a treacherous foe – but that very experience tended to emphasize the meaning of the fundamental rule *pacta sunt servanda.*

Secondly, however incomplete – when judged by reference to the present scope of international law – *De Jure Belli ac Pacis* may appear to be, it was the first comprehensive and systematic treatise on international law. Grotius was not the first writer on the Law of Nations. Belli in 1563,[1] Ayala in 1581,[2] and, above all, Gentilis in 1598[3] wrote learnedly on the laws of war; Vittoria about 1532[4] and Suarez in 1612[5] laid the foundations of the jurisprudential treatment of the problem of the international community as a whole. But no one before Grotius attempted the treatment of the subject in its entirety. There is in *De Jure Belli ac Pacis* a great deal of matter which is not and never has been within the proper sphere of international law, but there is in it all the international law that existed in 1625.

Thirdly, the very circumstance that a substantial portion of the treatise was devoted to matters which had little to do with what is

[1] *De re militari et bello tractatus.*
[2] *De jure bellico; De officiis bellicis; De disciplina militari.*
[3] *De jure belli libri tres.*
[4] *De Indis; De jure belli* (published in 1557).
[5] *Tractatus de legibus et Deo legislatore.*

generally regarded as belonging to international law proved a weighty contributory factor in the success which it achieved. For *De Jure Belli ac Pacis* is to a large extent a general treatise of law in its wide meaning (including constitutional law, the theory of the State, and the basis of legal and political obligation) and of jurisprudence. International law proper forms merely a part – though the most important part – of a wider system. The reason assigned by Grotius, and by others, for that prolixity is that that peripheral matter was necessary as an exposition of the rights which might be affected by unlawful action providing a legitimate reason for war.[1] But Grotius, himself spoke of the treatise as one pertaining to philosophy of law.[2] There is no doubt that, on balance, what many critics regarded as pretentious irrelevancy proved to be an invaluable asset. For there was presented to the world an exposition of international law woven into the structure of a general system of law and jurisprudence – a significant affirmation of the unity of all law and of the final place of international law in the general scheme of legal science. The effect was to enhance the authority of the treatise and of its main theme, namely, the Law of Nations.

Finally, the probability ought not to be discounted that the contemporaneous success of the work was to some extent determined by the already great reputation of its author. In 1625 Grotius was a European figure in his own right. His name added lustre to and helped to launch a work which in the course of centuries became synonymous with his fame.

However, all these factors – the timeliness of the treatise, its comprehensiveness as an exposition of international law, its wide jurisprudential background, and the already considerable reputation of its author – are, in a sense, circumstances external to the work. While they may account for its success at the time of its publication and the period immediately following it, they do not explain the powerful and sustained influence of what may be called the Grotian tradition in international law. They do not explain why *De Jure Belli ac Pacis* has been in the history of modern international law more than a mere symbol. Undoubtedly, the treatise is no longer a readable work for the purposes of current instruction. Its usefulness as an authority for any specific legal proposition is questionable. Writers and advocates still attach importance to supporting their thesis by reference to a passage from Grotius, but the persuasive

[1] *Proleg.* 33–5.

[2] *Ibid.* 30.

power of such arguments is, except for the purpose of historical illustration, distinctly limited. It is doubtful whether any ambitious attempt to rewrite the treatise would impart to it an air of modernity or any appreciable degree of usefulness. Yet the fact is that the impact of *De Jure Belli ac Pacis* is not spent; that the 'father of international law' is still a teacher; and that the significance and the potentialities of the guiding ideas of the treatise as a moulding force are such as to preclude it from being consigned to the province of mere legal history.

What are the aspects of the teaching of Grotius which, notwithstanding shortcomings of method and defects of substance, lift his work above the plane of a mere episode, however important, in the history of international law and of its development as part of jurisprudence? There has been controversy whether Grotius could justly claim to be the 'founder' of international law or whether others, especially Gentilis and Vittoria, cannot more accurately be regarded as having laid the foundations of the modern Law of Nations. But the dispute is, in essence, one of words. For no one denies to Grotius the representative quality of pre-eminence. What, once more, is the reason? What permanent qualities have prompted eulogies such as that by a great man of letters and a wise statesman who referred to *De Jure Belli ac Pacis* as one of the 'cardinal books in European history'[1] and as being, together with Adam Smith's *Wealth of Nations*, among the dozen products of literature which have been 'wide spreading acts', not books?[2] The answer is that the principal and characteristic features of *De Jure Belli ac Pacis* are identical with the fundamental and persistent problems of international law and that in nearly all of them the teaching of Grotius has become identified with the progression of international law to a true system of law both in its legal and in its ethical content. These main features of the Grotian tradition will now be considered.

1. *The subjection of the totality of international relations to the rule of law*

In the first instance, Grotius conceives of the totality of the relations between States as governed by law. This is the central theme of the treatise and its main characteristic. There are no lacunae in that subjection of States to the rule of law. Modern international law recognized for a long time the existence of gaps which obliterated altogether the border-line between law and lawlessness in inter-

[1] Viscount Morley, *Politics and History* (1912), in *Collected Works* (1921), IV, 57. And see below, p. 365, n. 1, for Lord Acton's view.
[2] *Ibid.* p. 13.

national relations. Of these gaps the admissibility of war as an absolute right of States, requiring no other legal justification, is the outstanding example. In laying down the distinction between just and unjust war Grotius rejected the claim to any such right.[1] Neither did he concede to States the absolute faculty of action in self-preservation – a right which, till recently, writers coupled with the legal power of the State to determine, with finality and to the exclusion of any outside tribunal, the justification of action in self-defence.[2] The emphasis with which Grotius denies the absoluteness of the right to act in self-preservation is deeply impressive. That denial of an unqualified right of self-preservation was not a seed which fell on totally barren soil. For we find the same idea expressed in pregnant words two and a half centuries later by Westlake. Self-preservation, he says, does not constitute a principle. It is rather 'a primitive instinct, and an absolute instinct so far as it has not been tamed by reason and law, but one great function of the law is to tame it. . . In principle we may not hurt another or infringe his rights, even for our self-preservation, when he has not failed in any duty towards us.'[3] In the same line of thought Grotius challenged the right of a State to go to war in order to ward off an anticipated attack.[4] There is no trace in his treatise of the suggestion that the regulative power of international law is limited to matters of small

[1] See below, p. 347.

[2] Thus writers have interpreted the various declarations accompanying the General Treaty for the Renunciation of War and reserving to the Parties the right both of resorting to war in self-defence and of determining when such action is necessary as meaning that the Parties have the exclusive and ultimate right to pronounce upon the legitimacy of the action said to have been taken in self-defence. No such right is implied either in the Treaty or in the reservations thereto. The State which believes itself to be in danger is entitled to determine, in the first instance, whether action in self-preservation is necessary. The ultimate determination of the legitimacy of the action taken is a matter for decision by an impartial body. See the Judgement of 31 August 1946 of the International Military Tribunal at Nuremberg: 'It was further argued that Germany alone could decide, in accordance with the reservations made by the many Signatory Powers at the time of the conclusion of the Briand–Kellogg Pact, whether preventive action was a necessity, and that in making her decision her judgment was conclusive. But whether action taken under the claim of self-defence was in fact aggressive or defensive must ultimately be subject to investigation and adjudication if international law is ever to be enforced' (*Transcript of the Proceedings*, p. 16, 853).

[3] Westlake, *Papers*, p. 112. He says in the same chapter: '. . . although it is certainly indispensable for the welfare of men that they should be associated in some State tie, it does not follow that their welfare imperatively requires the maintenance in its actual limits, and with resources entirely unimpaired, of the actual State tie in which they happen to be engaged' (*ibid.* p. 113). And see Green, *Principles of Political Obligation* (1895), § 166, who says that a State that 'needs to defend its interest by action injurious to those outside it . . . by no means fulfils its purpose . . . it might perhaps be swept away and superseded by another with advantage to the ends for which the true State exists'.

[4] See below, p. 348.

import – a view which has gained currency in relation to the question of the compulsory jurisdiction of international tribunals[1] and, more recently, of the function of international law as a whole.[2]

Although he did not achieve the impressive solemnity of the language of Suarez in the affirmation of the unity of mankind[3] and of the existence of a community of nations, he put the recognition of the interdependence of States and of their subjection to law in the forefront of the treatise.[4] Negatively, he interpreted the juridical solidarity of nations as implying that every State is entitled to inflict punishment upon the wrongdoer, who by his very transgression puts himself in a position of inferiority to other States.[5] It may also be noted in this connection that he did not limit the orbit of international law to the States of Christian civilization. He recognized the binding force of treaties concluded with infidels. There was no room in his system for wars of religion – though he considered that there was a duty incumbent upon Christian States to defend one another against aggression by infidels.

2. *The acceptance of the Law of Nature as an independent source of international law*

With the affirmation of the rule of law as extending to the totality of the relations of States there is connected the second feature of the Grotian tradition, namely, the view that the law thus binding upon States is not solely the product of their express will. Grotius accepted as self-evident the proposition that the sovereign – the State – is bound by the law of Nations and the law of nature.[6] The Law of Nations proper – *jus gentium voluntarium* – is, of course, the product of consent as manifested in the practice of States. Grotius's *jus gentium* thus conceived is not synonymous with public international law. It is distinguished from municipal law (*jus civile*),

[1] The existing limitations upon the jurisdiction of international tribunals—limitations expressed in specific reservations and implied in one of the many connotations of 'legal' disputes—assume that these tribunals cannot properly be entrusted with compulsory jurisdiction affecting vital interests of States. For an analysis of the underlying theory see Lauterpacht, *The Function of Law*, pp. 183–201.

[2] See Brierly in *B.Y.* 21 (1944), 51–7, and in *International Affairs*, 22 (1946), 353–6. And see below, p. 345.

[3] 'Mankind, though divided into numerous nations and States, constitutes a political and moral unity bound up by charity and compassion; wherefore, though every republic or monarchy seems to be autonomous and self-sufficing, yet none of them is, but each of them needs the support and brotherhood of others, both in a material and a moral sense. Therefore they also need some common law organizing their conduct in this kind of society' (*Tractatus de Legibus ac Deo Legislatore* (1612), book II, ch. xix, § 5).

[4] See below, p. 340.

[5] Book II, ch. xx, § iii. 1; *ibid.*, § xl. 1.

[6] Book I, ch. iii, § xvi. 1.

which emanates from the civil power of one State; it embraces all law – public and private, international and other – which has been sanctioned by the practice of all nations or of many nations.[1] It is one of the component parts of international law, but not the whole of it – a fact which seemingly escaped some of the early critics of Grotius such as Pufendorf and Barbeyrac, who reproached him with basing all international law on consent. Similarly, though a great deal of international law proper rests on consent, much, but not all,[2] of it follows from the precepts of the law of nature. In a wider sense, the binding force even of that part of it that originates in consent is based on the law of nature as expressive of the social nature of man.

It would be a mistake to judge the importance of the part played by the law of nature in *De Jure Belli ac Pacis* by reference to its use in relation to matters affecting international law proper, such as treaties between States, the law of diplomatic immunities, and, above all, the law of war. For, as Grotius points out in the opening passages of the chapter on the Right of Legation,[3] in these matters he relies largely on the 'voluntary' Law of Nations as evidenced by international practice. The significance of the law of nature in the treatise is that it is the ever-present source for supplementing the voluntary Law of Nations, for judging its adequacy in the light of ethics and reason, and for making the reader aware of the fact that the will of States cannot be the exclusive or even, in the last resort, the decisive source of the Law of Nations.

This aspect of the system of Grotius has become an integral part of the doctrine and of the practice of the modern Law of Nations – a part more real than the accepted terminology in the matter of sources of international law has accustomed us to assume. For who are the positivists of whom it may be said, with any approach to accuracy, that they regard the will of sovereign States as the exclusive source of international law? Bynkershoek, generally regarded as the typical positivist of his period, not only repeatedly invokes custom and reason as a source of the Law of Nations.[4] When confronted with an apparently uniform chain of treaties and municipal enactments cited in support of a view which he considered unreasonable, he refused to accept them as an authority for an asserted legal rule on

[1] Book I, ch. i, § xiv.

[2] There is probably no sufficient warrant for Sir Henry Maine's view (*Ancient Law* (1920 reprint), p. 103) that Grotius identified *jus gentium* and *jus naturae*.

[3] Book II, ch. xviii.

[4] *Quæstionum juris publici libri duo* (1737 ed.), book I, ch. vi. p. 46; ch. viii, p. 66; ch. x, p. 77.

the ground that 'the Law of Nations cannot be deduced from these, for reason, the preceptress of the Law of Nations, will not permit a general and indiscriminate interpretation of these practices'.[1] Hall, the leading British positivist, who appears to limit the sources of international law to usage and treaties,[2] actually bases international law on the natural law foundation of postulates and assumptions. 'The ultimate foundation of international law is an assumption that States possess rights and are subject to duties corresponding to the facts of their postulated nature.'[3] What is that assumed nature? 'It is postulated of those independent States which are dealt with by international law that they have a moral nature identical with that of individuals, and that with respect to one another they are in the same relation as that in which individuals stand to each other who are subject to law.'[4] Kelsen, who denounces natural law as being both unscientific and, historically, an instrument of reaction, assumes as the basis of international law the same jurisprudential maxim on which, in substance, Grotius made it to rest, namely, the rule *pacta sunt servanda* – the difference being that for Grotius the rule *pacta sunt servanda* is a precept, perhaps the main precept, of natural law while for Kelsen it is a 'meta-legal' initial hypothesis. The methodological difference may be considerable, but we cannot be sure of its practical relevance.

The fact is that while within the State it is not essential to give to the ideas of a higher law – of natural law – a function superior to that of providing the inarticulate ethical premiss underlying judicial decisions or, in the last resort, of the philosophical and political justification of the right of resistance, in the international society the position is radically different. There – in a society deprived of normal legislative and judicial organs – the function of natural law, whatever may be its form, must approximate more closely to that of a direct source of law. In the absence of the overriding authority of the judicial and legislative organs of the State there must assert itself – unless anarchy or stagnation are to ensue – the persuasive but potent authority of reason and principle derived from the fact of the necessary coexistence of a plurality of States. This explains the pertinacity, in the international sphere, of the idea of natural law as a legal source. With modern writers that search

[1] Book I, ch. xii, p. 95 (Tenney Frank's transl. in 'Classics of International Law', 1930).

[2] *A Treatise on International Law* (3rd ed. 1890), Introduction, p. 7.

[3] *Ibid.* § 7 (p. 44).

[4] *Ibid.* § 1 (p. 18).

for a legal source supplementing the ordinary sources of positive law expresses itself in the doctrine of implied acquiescence of any single State confronted with the fact of general consent.[1] Implied consent in this sphere is, upon analysis, a recognition of the law-creating result of the existence of a society of States, of the 'reason of the thing' inherent in that fact, of the natural law of international relations. The same necessity has found expression in treaties laying down the rules of law to be applied by international tribunals[2] and, in particular, in Article 38 (1) (*c*) of the Statute of the International Court of Justice which enumerates among the sources of law to be applied by the Court 'general principles of law recognized by civilized nations'. Neither is that view absent from judicial decisions. Of these, Mr Justice Story's Judgment in *La Jeune Eugénie* is one of the most lucid and most uncompromising assertions of this aspect of the Grotian tradition. He refused to admit 'that no principle belongs to the Law of Nations which is not universally recognized as such, by all civilized communities, or even by those constituting what may be called the Christian States of Europe'. 'It may be unequivocally affirmed', he said, 'that every doctrine, that may be fairly deduced by correct reasoning from the rights and duties of nations, and the nature of moral obligations, may theoretically be said to exist in the Law of Nations; and unless it be relaxed or waived by the consent of nations which may be evidenced by their general practice and customs, it may be enforced by a court of justice whenever it arises in judgment.'[3] This may appear to some an exaggerated affirmation of the authority of the higher law – of the law of nature – in the international sphere. It is not suggested that it is in accordance, in all its challenging rigour, with the predominant view on the subject. But the gist of it expresses accurately that particular aspect of the Grotian tradition which, in broad outline, has become part and parcel of modern international law. We are not concerned here with the controversy as to the merits or otherwise of the law of nature. Undoubtedly the law of nature has often been resorted to in support of causes dubious and retrogressive. But this ambivalance of the ideology of natural law is only slightly relevant in the field of international law. There, by and large, it has

[1] See, e.g., Westlake, I, 16. Professor Borchard says: 'The rules [of international law] rest partly on the assent of States and partly on generally approved practice, assent to which is either presumed or, in respect of a single State declining adherence, immaterial' (*Encyclopædia of the Social Sciences* (1932), VIII, 167).

[2] For a survey of these treaties see Lauterpacht, *Analogies*, § 26.

[3] 2 Mason 409, 448.

acted as a lever of progress.[1] The law of nature has been rightly exposed to the charge of vagueness and arbitrariness. But the uncertainty of the 'higher law' is preferable to the arbitrariness and insolence of naked force. These considerations explain the significance of this aspect of the Grotian tradition in the history of the Law of Nations. He secularized the law of nature. He gave it added authority and dignity by making it an integral part of the exposition of a system of law which became essential to civilized life. By doing this he laid, more truly than any writer before him, the foundations of international law.

3. *The affirmation of the social nature of man as the basis of the law of nature*

The place which the law of nature occupies as part of the Grotian tradition is distinguished not only by the fact of its recognition of a source of law different from and, in proper cases, superior to the will of sovereign states. What is equally significant is Grotius's conception of the quality of the law of nature which dominates his jurisprudential system. It is a law of nature largely based on and deduced from the nature of man as a being intrinsically moved by a desire for social life, endowed with an ample measure of goodness, altruism, and morality, and capable of acting on general principles and of learning from experience.[2] He admits that man is an animal, but one different in kind from other animals. That difference consists in his impelling desire for society – not for society of any sort, but for peaceful and organized life according to the measure of his intelligence. It is a difference the essence of which is the denial of the assertion that 'every animal is impelled by nature to seek only its own good'.[3] There is perhaps no political writer in whose system that conception of the nature of man is more prominent. The theme is, of course, one of the persistent problems – perhaps *the* problem – of political thought. For Machiavelli and Hobbes man is essentially selfish, anti-social, and unable to learn from experience; *homo homini lupus* is the fundamental truth; human nature does not change; pessimism as to the potentialities of its improvement is of the essence of sanity; the basis of political obligation is interest pure and simple; the idea of a sense of moral duty rising supreme over desire and pas-

[1] On the part of the law of nature as a pioneer of reform see Gierke, 'Die Staats- und Korporationslehre der Neuzeit', in *Das deutsche Genossenschaftsrecht* (1913), IV, 276.

[2] *Proleg.* 5–9.

[3] *Proleg.* 6. He says elsewhere: 'If other ties are wanting, the tie of a common human nature is sufficient. Nothing belonging to mankind is indifferent to man' (Book II, ch. V, § ii. 1 (Whewell's transl.)).

sion is a figment of imagination fatal alike to action and to survival. This is the typical realistic approach of contempt towards the 'little breed' of man. On that line of reasoning there is no salvation for humanity but irrevocable subjection to an order of effective force which, while indifferent to the dignity of man, yet contrives to prevent his life from being 'solitary, poor, nasty, brutish, and short'. The approach of Grotius and – to mention a writer as distinguished and as influential – Locke is diametrically different.

One of the salient characteristics of *De Jure Belli ac Pacis* is not only the frequency of the reliance on and appeal to the law of love, the law of charity, of Christian duty, of honour, and of goodness, and to the injunctions of divine law and the Gospel; the element of morality and the appeal to morality are, without interfering decisively with the legal character of the exposition, a constant theme of the treatise. An equally persistent feature is Grotius's faith in the rational constitution of man and his capacity to see reason and to learn from experience. This aspect of *De Jure Belli ac Pacis* goes a long way towards explaining the force of the Grotian tradition in the international sphere. For there, more than anywhere else, the implications of the pessimistic estimate of human nature reveal themselves in all their paradoxical and depressing clarity. Writers and statesmen dwell lucidly and persuasively upon the incongruity and absurdity of the fact that modern civilized States live in a primitive state of nature in their mutual relations. They admit that the resulting situation is such as to threaten not only the rational growth of States but, in the age of scientific weapons, their very existence. They concede that only effective submission to a comprehensive rule of law and a corresponding curtailment of the sovereignty of States may avert these dangers. But after having thus diagnosed the evil and after having disclosed the remedy, they lay down the pessimistic proposition that Governments and peoples are unlikely to agree to any such solution. That renunciation of faith in the sovereignty of the rational human will shows itself in the widely adopted view that the great events and trends of history, including the phenomenon of war, are impervious to and outside the conscious and responsible volition of man and that the 'irresistible march of events' is the ultimate arbiter of human fate.[1] This lack of faith in the power of man conceived as a rational social being manifests itself not only with respect to the crucial aspect of international relations, but also

[1] For a philosophical refutation of this view see Viscount Samuel's *Belief and Action* (1937), pp. 194–9.

with regard to specific questions of international organization. Thus it is generally admitted that international legislation, conceived as a process of enacting binding rules of law by competent organs of international society, is a vital condition of the normal functioning of international law and of the compulsory jurisdiction of international tribunals which, in default of an international legislature remedying and developing existing law, may have to render judgments inconsistent with progress and dangerous to peace. Yet those who propound and admit the force of that view point with resignation to the improbability of States ever acquiescing in the limitation of sovereignty implicit in a true legislative competence of the international community.

Now it is characteristic of that pessimistic school of thought with respect to the social and moral nature of man that it has applied itself consistently only to the international relations of human beings. Within the State, it has advanced means for overcoming the evils of strife and anarchy. Thus, according to Hobbes,[1] it is a law of nature that the individual, by giving up in the social contract his right to do all things, should achieve a relative degree of security; and it is a law of nature that the contract be kept (so long, at least, it appears, as the security which it gives is effective). No such law of nature, in either sense, is asserted to be in operation among States; they are – and apparently can[2] and must remain – in the true and original state of nature. We are thus confronted, in addition to the double standard of morality as expressed in the doctrine of 'reason of State', with what may not inaccurately be described as the double standard of reason and foresight. There is no room for either in the system of Grotius. In fact, much of the appeal and potentialities of the Grotian tradition lies in the lesson which can be drawn from his conception of the social nature and constitution of man as a rational

[1] *Leviathan*, ch. xiv.

[2] In fact, Hobbes, Spinoza, and Vattel – who may not inaccurately be described as belonging to the 'state of nature' school of international law – seem to have faced the problem in that way. They did not ignore it. They arrived at the conclusion that the dangers which beset the individual and which call for his submission to law do not threaten independent States. Vattel, who, notwithstanding his disapproval of the 'paradoxes' and the 'detestable principles' of Hobbes, followed him closely, is explicit on the subject. 'Individuals', he says, 'are so constituted that they could accomplish but little by themselves and could scarcely get on without the assistance of civil society and its law. But as as soon a sufficient number have united under a government, they are able to provide for most of their needs, and they find the help of other political societies not so necessary to them as the State itself is to individuals' (Preface to *The Law of Nations and the Principle of Natural Law* (1758), Fenwick's transl. in 'Classics of International Law' (1916), p. 9 *a*). He gives reasons, characteristically plausible, why the mutual intercourse of States can be sufficiently regulated by natural law.

being in whom the element of moral obligation and foresight asserts itself triumphantly over unbridled selfishness and passion, both within the State and in the relations of States.

4. *The recognition of the essential identity of States and individuals*

That all-pervading element of morality and rationality which is the result of Grotius's conception of law as based on the social nature and the intrinsic goodness of man is not limited to the conduct of individuals. It extends to the conduct of nations and of rulers acting on their behalf. In fact, one of the most decisive features of the teaching of Grotius is the close analogy of legal and moral rules governing the conduct of States and individuals alike. 'Populi respectu generis humani privatorum locum obtinent'[1] – this is a pregnant and persistent theme in the teaching of Grotius. This analogy of States and individuals has proved a beneficent weapon in the armoury of international progress. It is not the result of any anthropomorphic or organic conception of the State as being – biologically, as it were – assimilated to individuals, as being an individual person 'writ large'. The analogy is much more simple, more direct, and more convincing. The analogy – nay, the essential identity – of rules governing the conduct of States and of individuals is not asserted for the reason that States *are like* individuals; it is due to the fact that States *are composed of* individual human beings; it results from the fact that behind the mystical, impersonal, and therefore necessarily irresponsible personality of the metaphysical State there are the actual subjects of rights and duties, namely, individual human beings.[2] This is the true meaning of the Grotian analogy of States and individuals. The individual is the ultimate unit of all law, international and municipal, in the double sense that the obligations of international law are ultimately addressed to him and that the development, the well-being, and the dignity of the individual human being are a matter of direct concern to international law. Vattel, writing in 1758, apparently gave emphatic and lucid expression to the analogy, thus conceived, of States and individuals; though, *more Vatteliano*, this was mere meaningless lip-service to the 'natural

[1] *Mare liberum*, ch. v. See also *De Jure Belli ac Pacis*, book II, ch. xv, § xii. 1.

[2] In the Judgment given on 31 August 1946 by the International Military Tribunal at Nuremberg we find an illustration of the practical implications of the problem. The Tribunal said: 'It was submitted that international law is concerned with the actions of sovereign States, and provides no punishment for individuals . . . these contentions must be rejected. . . Crimes against international law are committed by men, not by abstract entities, and only by punishing individuals who commit such crimes can the provisions of international law be enforced' (*Annual Digest*, 13 (1946), 221).

Law of Nations' destined to yield to another natural law, that 'which declares every nation free and independent of all other nations'.[1] At the end of the nineteenth century Westlake was propounding, without compromise or circumlocution, the same doctrine as a matter of sound international law and of international morality. 'The society of States', he says, '. . . is the most comprehensive form of society among men, but it is among men that it exists. States are its immediate, men its ultimate members. The duties and the rights of States are only the duties and the rights of men who compose them.'[2] Hall's similar view has already been noted.[3]

Undoubtedly, international law is primarily – though not exclusively – a body of rules governing the relations of States, i.e., of individuals organized as a State. But this circumstance cannot affect decisively the moral content of international law and of the dictates of reason and of the general principles of law which underlie it. It may be true to say that 'after all' States are not individuals; but it is even more true to say that 'after all' States are individuals. For this reason there can be no insuperable difficulty in applying generally recognized principles of law to the conduct of individuals acting as members of a State and on behalf of their State. There are psychological factors which explain the tendency towards the relaxation of the moral code of conduct of individuals acting in a group. But these inducements do not partake of the immutability and of the necessity of a physical law.[4] Like other manifestations of desire and instinct, they can be regulated and curbed by reason, by the impact of moral ideas, by law. Moreover, in a group association which, like the State, is to a large extent the artificial product of law and

[1] *Le Droit des gens ou principes de la loi naturelle appliqués à la conduite et aux affaires des Nations et des Souverains*, Introduction, §§ 7, 9. The 'natural' or 'necessary' Law of Nations, he says, 'contains those precepts which the natural law dictates to States, and it is no less binding upon them than it is upon individuals. For States are composed of men, their policies are determined by men, and these men are subject to the natural law under whatever capacity they act' (§ 7). Yet he proceeds to lay down—in § 9—that that natural Law of Nations is, in fact, valid only as an inner law of conscience. 'The liberty of a nation would not remain complete if other nations presumed to inspect and to control its conduct; such a presumption would be contrary to the natural law which declares every nation free and independent of all other nations' (Gregory's transl. in 'Classics of International Law'). [2] Westlake, *Papers*, p. 78. [3] See above, p. 331.

[4] It has become a hall-mark of what is considered to be the realistic approach to expatiate on the lower morality of States as compared with that of individuals. See, for instance, Niebuhr, *Moral Man and Immoral Society* (1933), and, in particular, Carr, *The Twenty Years' Crisis 1919-1939* (1939), ch. 9. There is an advantage in drawing attention to factors which impair the strength of moral obligation in individuals acting on behalf of the State. On the other hand, the theme lends itself to exaggeration. In particular there has been a tendency to ignore the factors which operate in the opposite direction and to represent the existing manifestations of the 'double standard of morality' as inescapably inherent in State action in the international sphere.

force rather than of the more direct and intimate interplay of crowd emotions, there is even less justification for treating as permanent and inevitable the factors which tend to weaken moral restraints in the collective activities of men. The modern State is not a disorderly crowd given to uncontrollable eruptions of passion oblivious of moral scruples. It is, as a rule, governed by individuals of experience and ability who reach decisions after full deliberation and who are capable of forming a judgment on the ethical merits of the issues confronting them. Admittedly that judgment is often warped by the notion, inculcated or excused by theoreticians of 'reason of State', that rulers of States, being trustees of interests other than their own, are not entitled to act invariably upon the precepts of the moral code as generally recognized.

In stressing the practical analogy of States and individuals Grotius derived substantial assistance from the fact that in the century in which he wrote the emerging territorial State was a creature of personal rule. The history of Europe could still, to a large extent, be conceived as a history of dynasties and dynastic ambitions. The three hundred-odd independent sovereignties in Germany were a living example, in a variety of forms, of the patrimonial conception of the State. Marriage settlements and testamentary dispositions continued to be an important medium of territorial changes. The policy of the State was the policy of the ruling prince. The rules of conduct binding upon States were deemed to be rules binding upon their sovereigns. They were rules of law and morality governing the conduct of individual human beings. In the middle of the eighteenth century we find one of the leading treatises – that of Vattel – indicating in its title that the law which it propounds is one relating to the conduct of nations and sovereigns.[1] 'The Law of Nations is the law of sovereigns', says the author in the Preface. Yet, essentially, the situation did not change radically with the disappearance of the patrimonial theory and practice. That event had an effect on the rules which assimilated State territory to private ownership of land, and the like. It was not relevant to the more general question of subjects of the obligations of international law. For whatever may be the form of the government of the State, those who rule it and act on its behalf are individual human beings, and it is to them only that, upon final analysis, rules of law are addressed.

Thus the analogy of States and individuals which is one of the

[1] See above, p. 337.

crucial aspects of Grotius's teaching was the twin result of two distinct causes. One, which was of a transient character, was the patrimonial character of a considerable number of European States. The other, more enduring, was the realization of the true nature of rules of international law as addressing themselves to individual human beings acting on behalf of the State. The cumulative effect of these two causes was to further the scientific development of international law and to emphasize the moral content of its rules. Largely on account of the recognition of that fundamental analogy, the door was wide open for the enrichment and advancement of international law with the help of rules of private law, Roman and other, as expressive of the general principles of law recognized by civilized States. Critics of the positivist complexion have frequently raised doubts as to the propriety of that process of borrowing from private law. Even if that criticism had been justified – and it is not believed that it was – it was a lament after the event. There have been few branches of international law which have remained unaffected by the influence of private law. We have only to think of Grotius's contribution, by reference to private law, to the development of the rules of law relating to acquisition of territorial sovereignty, the principle of the freedom of the seas, and the law of State responsibility. The very notion of sovereignty, which Grotius conceived, like property, as dominion held under law, helped to deprive it of the character of absoluteness and indivisibility.[1] Neither was it a process confined to the exposition of international law by writers; Governments and international arbitrators relied upon it frequently and effectively. If we were to ignore or to underestimate these 'illicit borrowings' we should be depriving ourselves of the possibility of understanding what is perhaps the major part of international law. To discard them as a matter of future practice is impossible. To do so would mean to jettison a substantial part of positive international law in which the rules derived by analogy have become crystallized. It would mean challenging the purpose of that significant provision of the Statute of the International Court of Justice which constitutes the general principles of international law as recognized by civilized nations one of the three principal sources of the law to be applied by the Court. To discard them as a matter of principle would mean to abandon the view, which is amply justified by experience, that

[1] This is probably one of the reasons why Grotius never advocated the principle of absolute equality of States. See Dickinson, *Equality of States in International Law* (1920), pp. 34–67.

upon the continued vitality of this aspect of the Grotian tradition depends the progressive approximation of international law to a system of legal rules worthy of that name.

5. *The rejection of 'reason of State'*

The recognition of the social and moral nature of man as the principal source and cause of law explains, when coupled with the persistent affirmation of the analogy of States and individuals, the fifth characteristic of the Grotian tradition, namely, his denial of the 'reason of State' as a basic and decisive factor of international relations. That denial of the principle of double morality is for Grotius so obvious and so fundamental that he regards it, it would seem, as below the dignity of his work to engage in the then customary argument *ad hominem* on the subject. A startling feature of *De Jure Belli ac Pacis* is the absence not only of any polemics, but of all reference to Machiavelli. Bynkershoek, in discussing the observance of public agreements, refers with contempt to 'the master of iniquity [who] in his *Principe* teaches that treachery is lawful for princes' and to the '*ratio status*, a monster of many heads which almost no prince resists'.[1] Elsewhere he speaks of 'that *monstrum horrendum, informe, ingens, cui lumen ademptum*' which we call 'reason of State' and observes that 'if nations will yield to this beast . . . it will soon be useless to argue further about the principles of international law'.[2] Grotius's disapproval is one of silence. There is simply no mention of the great realist. The flood of books and pamphlets on the 'reason of State', which at that time assumed the dimensions of a torrent, is ignored.[3]

But although he does not mention Machiavelli by name, he takes up the issue of 'reason of State' at the very beginning of the treatise. After remarking upon the usefulness of a knowledge of the law 'which is concerned with the mutual relations among States or rulers of States',[4] he points to the special necessity of studying that branch of law. For, he says, there are 'in our day' persons who view it with

[1] *Quæstionum Juris Publici Libri Duo*, book II, ch. x (p. 190 in the 'Classics' transl.).

[2] *Ibid.* book I, ch. xxv (*in fine*).

[3] At the time when *De Jure Belli ac Pacis* was in preparation, the famous – and notorious – Machiavellian tract, attributed to Father Joseph, the *éminence grise* behind Richelieu, was being composed: *Discours des Princes et Estats de la Chrestienté plus considérables à la France, selon leurs diverses qualitez et conditions.* It was published in 1624. The no less famous *De l'intérest des Princes et Estats de la Chrestienté* by Prince Henry de Rohan was not published till 1638, and Naudé's *Considérations politique sur les coups d'état* appeared in 1639. Both were able expositions of the Machiavellian doctrine and they testified to the wide interest which the subject evoked at the time. There is no trace of all this in *De Jure Belli ac Pacis*.

[4] *Proleg.* 1.

contempt as having no reality; who consider that for a king or a State nothing is unjust which is expedient; and that the business of the State cannot be carried on without injustice.[1] He sees an intimate connection between the rejection of the ideas of 'reason of State' and the affirmation of the legal and moral unity of mankind. He insists that if no association of men can be maintained without law, 'surely also that association which binds together the human race, or binds many nations together, has need of law'.[2] This means, he says, quoting Cicero with approval, that shameful acts ought not to be committed even for the sake of one's country.[3] It means also that the hall-mark of wisdom for a ruler is to take account not only of the good of the nation committed to his care, but of the whole human race.[4] 'The name of Minos became odious to future ages for no other reason than this, that he limited his fair dealing to the boundaries of his realm.'[5] While denying that law is based on expediency alone,[6] he was ready to meet the theorists of 'reason of State' on the ground of their own choosing, namely, that of advantage. He records the fact that, according to many, the standards of justice applicable in the relations of individuals within the State do not apply to a State or the ruler of a State. The reason usually given for that assertion of a double standard of justice is, he says, that law is indispensable to individuals who, taken singly, cannot protect themselves, while great States, which dispose of everything needed for adequate protection, are in no need of law. Grotius rejects this view. Such, in his opinion, is the impact of economic interdependence or military security that there is no State so powerful that it can dispense with the help of others.[7]

Grotius's rejection of the ideas of *raison d'état* finds more direct expression in relation to concrete issues. It expresses itself in the denial of the right to resort to war unless in pursuance of a good legal cause;[8] in the rigid limitation of the right of self-defence (including the right of war in order to ward off an anticipated attack); in the concession of the right—indeed, in the injunction of the duty—of passive resistance against orders and laws contrary to the law of nature and the law of God;[9] in the concession to the subject of the right—and, again,

[1] *Ibid.* 3. [2] *Ibid.* 23. [3] *Ibid.*
[4] *Ibid.* 24. [5] *Ibid.* [6] *Ibid.* 5, 22, 57.
[7] *Ibid.* 21, 22. See also *ibid.* 18: 'For just as the national, who violates the law of his country in order to obtain an immediate advantage, breaks down that by which the advantages of himself and of his posterity are for all future time assured, so the State which transgresses the laws of nature and of nations casts away the bulwarks which safeguard its own future peace.' And see above, p. 333, n. 3, and p. 335, n. 2.
[8] See below, p. 347. [9] See below, p. 357.

in the injunction of the duty—to refrain from participation not only in unjust wars but also in wars the justice of which is doubtful;[1] in his stressing of the sacredness of the principle *pacta sunt servanda*.[2] There is in the treatise a challenging absence of recognition of anything approaching the ideas of reason of State directly or – as, for instance, in the case of Pufendorf[3] – indirectly. In this rejection of *raison d'état* Grotius went further than Bodin – although Bodin, to whom Grotius was perhaps more indebted than is generally assumed,[4] had gone far in that direction. There are, indeed, in Bodin's writings passages reminiscent of the 'reason of State' when he says that 'nothing can be shameful which is connected with the well-being of the State',[5] but these are not typical of the treatise. On the contrary, although known principally as one of the main architects of the modern theory of the sovereignty of the State, he subjected that sovereignty to the precepts of the law of God and of the law of nature.[6]

There is a symbolic significance in this rejection of *raison d'état* by the founder of modern international law. For there is an inherent antagonism between international law, which, except when conceived as an empty and contradictory 'law of co-ordination', which means restraint upon freedom of action, and the idea of 'reason of State', which means freedom from restraint. It would be mere speculation to attempt to assess the influence of Grotius on curbing the

[1] See below, p. 349. [2] See below, p. 352.

[3] Thus we find the latter saying that it is the duty of the Prince to subordinate entirely his personal life and his personal inclinations to the interest of the State (*De jure naturae et gentium*, book VII, ch. 8, §§ 1–3); or that compacts of Princes possess validity only for so long as they are not inconsistent with the interest of the State (*ibid.* ch. 6, § 14; ch. 9, § 5).

[4] See, for instance, the close resemblance between the insistence on the part of Grotius on the duty of submission and obedience when the struggle against triumphant power seems hopeless (see below, p. 356), and Bodin's emphatic advice to the same effect (book V, ch. 5). And see Chauviré, *Bodin* (1914), pp. 279 *et seq.* [5] Book V, ch. 5.

[6] He approved with emphasis Seneca's maxim 'Caesari dum omnia licent, propter hoc minus licet' (see book I, ch. 8). 'The Prince', he taught, 'must not overstep the limits which God Himself, of whom the Prince is the living and breathing image, has set up through the enduring laws of nature' (*ibid.*). The prince is bound by the principles of good faith to observe compacts both with other States and with his own subjects, for 'good faith is the foundation of all justice. Good faith holds together not only States but the entire human society.' God Himself is bound by His promises. As the prince is the guarantor and the avenger of right and good faith within the State, he must himself observe them even at the cost of his interests. He condemns sharply the numerous examples, cited in the chapter on the Law of Nations (*De jure feciali*, book, 5, ch. 6), of breaches of treaties and of treachery. Treaties must be kept even if loyalty to them threatens the existence of the State, except when what has been promised 'is by nature iniquitous or which is impossible of performance'. Neither need compacts be kept which are 'so shameful that they cannot be kept without committing a crime or confirmed by oath, without wickedness' (*ibid.*). He was unsparing in his repeated condemnation of Machiavelli, that '*homo levissimus ac nequissimus*'. (See also Chauviré, *Bodin*, p. 276.) At the same time he was expressing the view that law common to all nations is binding although it may not coincide with the law of God or nature (book I, ch. 8).

profane outlook which drew its inspiration from Machiavelli – just as it may be difficult to estimate the actual impact of *The Prince* upon the practices of international politics and diplomacy. It is immaterial that the succeeding four centuries witnessed the unprecedented ascendancy of the ideas of 'reason of State'. To attribute that phenomenon to any substantial degree to Machiavelli is to simplify the issue and to ignore the decisive factor, namely, the rise of the territorial State and of the dogma of its unlimited sovereignty. After all, Cesare Borgia was not the product of *The Prince*; he was his prototype. Machiavelli provided a philosophy, an explanation, a rationalization which was in keeping with the inductive and secular temper of the Renaissance. That does not mean that he supplied an indispensable inducement. What must remain a subject for reflection is not the merits of the teaching of Machiavelli as a scientific foundation of rules of conduct. For seldom has a doctrine been propounded which fails more obviously in the primary test of a scientific rule, namely, its capacity to serve as a general canon of behaviour. Neither need we take seriously its shallow and naïve claim to exclusive realism – to seeing things as they are, and not as they ought to be. What is disquieting in the matter is the continued fascination, in one form or another, in the science of history and in the literature of international law, of the basic idea of 'reason of State' and the apparent difficulty experienced by those who condemn it to cut themselves adrift from it wholly and unequivocally. Witness, for instance, the embarrassed hesitation, on the part of a shrewd writer, between the emphatic condemnation of the Machiavellian doctrine; the admission that there *is* a difference between public and private morality; the exhortation not to treat as iniquitous selfishness the statesman's regard for the existence, safety, and strength of his country; the view that certain actions of Bismarck which can be neither admired nor condoned 'must be treated more leniently than any dereliction of his cardinal duty, devotion to his people'; and the consummation of the elaborate argument in which he concedes that such actions are blameworthy but that they are to be regarded as the natural faults of the politician.[1] A more recent treatment of the subject on the part of a distinguished historian follows the same inconclusive lines.[2] He associates himself fully with the general condemnation of the basic idea of *The Prince*. But he attaches importance to qualifying his condemnation: a private

[1] Figgis, *Studies of Political Thought from Gerson to Grotius* (1907) (reprint of 1931), pp. 87, 88.

[2] Gooch, 'Politics and Morals', in *Studies in Diplomacy and Statecraft* (1942).

individual, he says, when confronted with a conflict between survival and moral duty, may choose to sacrifice his life. 'A State cannot and must not make such a sacrifice, for it is the trustee of generations to come. If brutally attacked or summoned to surrender its independence, its duty, I believe, is to resist.'[1] The argument, which is often used in this connection,[2] injects, it is submitted, a somewhat artificial element of controversy into the fundamentally simple question of what Lord Morley called the 'awful difference'[3] between good and evil. It has not been customary for critics of the ideas of '*raison d'état*' to urge that a State, when attacked, should sacrifice its independence. The State's right of self-defence or existence is not in question. But the manner in which distinguished historians, such as those mentioned, have approached the subject is symptomatic of the lure of relativism also on that issue. Lord Acton, one of the greatest and perhaps the most majestic figure in historical science, stands practically[4] alone in uncompromising condemnation of crime clad in the garb of 'reason of State .[5]

The great issue of 'reason of State' is still with us and, while it will continue to be an absorbing dilemma of historical science, it is one of the main problems of international law – perhaps the central problem if by law we understand restraint and if by 'reason of State' we mean rejection of any substantial restriction upon the freedom of action of sovereign States in matters which are of significance. The '*raison d'état*' may no longer present itself in the international sphere in the cruder forms of treacherous violence, of brazen perfidy, and of outright deceit – although recent history has shown that species of *ratio status* to be not altogether obsolete. Modern formulae, such as that international law is possible only as a 'law of co-ordination' effected by agreement of sovereign States, express ideas of distinct affinity

[1] Gooch, *Studies in Diplomacy*, p. 322. See also, for a similar trend of argument, Lindsay, *The Modern Democratic State*, I (1943), 98, 99.

[2] See, for instance, Meinecke, *Die Idee der Staatsräson* (1924), pp. 531 *et seq.*—a laborious and somewhat fatalistic affirmation of the idea of 'reason of State'.

[3] Morley, *Machiavelli*, Works (ed. of 1921), IV, 115.

[4] Lord Morley and Thomas Arnold are in the same category. The majority of historians have deemed it incumbent upon them to refrain from passing moral judgment. The serene detachment of Ranke, of Prescott, and of Bishop Creighton is typical of that attitude, although it did not descend to the level of justifying crime or explaining it away so as to bring them within Lord Acton's bitter dictum of the strong man with the dagger being followed by the weak man with the sponge.

[5] Yet the almost legendary grandeur of his personality is due largely to the rigid consistency of his attitude on this vital problem of politics, national and international. There is no conclusive evidence that at the very end of his life Acton retracted from the fanaticism of his judgment on the subject. Nothing short of conclusive evidence can, in the circumstances, be regarded as sufficient for assuming as proven a departure from a lifelong attitude.

with those of 'reason of State'. For there is probably more truth than exaggeration in the view that uncompromising insistence upon the unlimited rights of State sovereignty in contempt of the interests of other nations, of the interdependence of States, and of the public opinion of the world, is one of the manifestations of the spirit of ruthless egotism which has become associated with the idea of *raison d'état*.[1] The claim of sovereign States – a claim fully admitted by existing law – to be entitled to deny to other members of the international legal community the benefit of judicial determination of disputed legal rights belongs, essentially, to the same category. So does the practice – reminiscent of the Machiavellian doctrine of the virtues of the pretence of virtue – of cloaking the refusal to limit the State's full freedom of action in the garb of pretentious phrases and purely nominal declarations implying some such submission.[2] So does the assertion, which is an attempt at a rationalization of the existing practice, that the subjection of States to the rule of law in the international sphere is and ought properly to be limited to matters which are not 'political' and which do not affect their vital interests.[3] It may be difficult to form an estimate of the influence of *De Jure Belli ac Pacis*

[1] These aberrations are embedded in international practice. They are, essentially, part of existing international law. As such they have acquired a degree of respectability. It is, therefore, to be expected that some may decline, with impatient surprise, to regard them as manifestations of 'reason of State'. Such reaction, which is a natural product of habit, does not mean that the description is arbitrary or far-fetched.

[2] Of these the most prominent are the various types of undertakings of compulsory judicial settlement which leave to the State concerned the legal power to determine the extent of its own obligation.

[3] One of the reasons recently adduced in support of this view is that even within the State it is difficult, if not impossible, to enact and enforce laws in opposition to organized groupings of vast numerical strength, such as powerful trade unions, and that the proper approach to the regulation of their interests is therefore 'political'. See, in particular, the illuminating discussion of the problem by Professor Brierly, above at p. 329, n. 2. However, while compromise is of the essence of true democracy in the sense that the majority ought not to ride rough-shod over the interests of the minority, once a decision has been reached in accordance with constitutional practice it is enforced and, as a rule, obeyed by groups however powerful. Witness, for instance, the enactment in England, against the resentful protest of the Trade Union movement, of the Trade Disputes Act of 1927. The subjection of States members of a Federation to federal law is another example. Neither does the fact that the normal subjects of international law – i.e., sovereign States – are few in number import a decisively 'political' character to the social regulation of their conduct and of their interests. A very substantial number of statutes in a modern State is concerned with problems and interests affecting particular groups – social, professional, geographical, and others. Probably the argument, in its entirety, is intended to show that Great Powers cannot properly be expected to submit to an outside body in matters affecting their vital interests. Under the Charter of the United Nations all Members other than the Great Powers are under a legal obligation to abide by a decision, reached without their consent, of the Security Council which may involve them in war or which may determine disputed points affecting their vital interests. There may be a disadvantage in expressing in terms of general principle the attitude of all or some Great Powers at any particular period.

in curbing the spirit of *The Prince*. But there ought to be no doubt as to the place which the rejection of the ideology of *raison d'état* occupies in the Grotian system – a repudiation significant both in the absence of direct reference to Machiavelli and, more particularly, in Grotius's attitude to the questions which 'reason of State' has pretended to solve in its crude and realistic fashion.

6. *The distinction between just and unjust wars*

In the assertion of 'reason of State' and of the double standard of morality, the claim to an unrestricted right of war, though not the most conspicuous, is the most important. It is not the dagger or the poison of the hired assassin or the sharp practice of the realistic politician which expresses most truly, upon final analysis, the ideas of *raison d'état*. It is the infliction, without a shadow of a specific right and without a claim to any particular right, of the calamities and indignities of war and of the territorial mutilation and the very annihilation of statehood following upon defeat in war. Prior to the changes introduced by the Covenant of the League of Nations, the Pact of Paris of 1928, and the Charter of the United Nations, that central idea of 'reason of State' formed part of international law. States claimed – and had – the right to resort to war not only in order to defend their legal rights but in order to destroy the legal rights of other States. In the sphere of political theory Machiavelli put the position with his usual terseness: 'That war is just which is necessary.'[1] And he added, by way of explanation: 'The people will complain of a war made without reason.'[2] Bacon, who did more than anyone else to transplant the ideas of *The Prince* to English soil, and who praised Machiavelli for seeing 'things as they are', expressed similar views in holding that while a civil war is like the heat of a fever, a foreign war is like the heat of exercise, and helps to keep the body in health. To this set of ideas Hegel, Treitschke, and other nineteenth-century German theoreticians of 'reason of State' may have added the nebulous and arrogant pretentiousness of philosophical jargon; in fact they added little.

But although this particular – and most important – manifestation of 'reason of State' became and for centuries continued to be part of international law, it was not an unchallenged doctrine. It was opposed by the parallel and powerful current of opinion that distinguished between wars which, in law, were just and those which

[1] *Thoughts of a Statesman*, ch. ii. [2] *Ibid.*

were not. That current of opinion is represented by yet another aspect of the Grotian tradition, namely, his denial of the absolute right of war and his consistent differentiation between just and unjust wars. Grotius did not invent that distinction. It was part of the heritage of the Middle Ages; it was fully discussed and adopted by scholastic writers and other forerunners of Grotius. Saint Augustine elaborated in detail the notion of a just war and limited it to action taken for the punishment of wrong-doing and to restoration of property taken away.[1] Isidore of Seville wrote on similar lines in the seventh century. The *Decretum Gratiani* gives elaborate definitions of a just war. In Giovanni da Legnano's *De Bello, De Repraesaliis, et De Duello*, written in 1360, there was a detailed disquisition on the subject. But it was in the works of the two great scholastic writers, Franciscus de Vittoria[2] and Suarez,[3] that the doctrine of just war – as the only war permissible in law – was developed with a juridical acumen and a moral fervour hardly surpassed by Grotius himself. Like some of their predecessors they held that, because of 'invincible ignorance', a war may be legally just on both sides.[4] They both denied the right to wage war on infidels for reasons of religion only.

In the elaboration of the causes of just war Grotius made no obvious advance upon the already elaborate treatment of the subject by his predecessors. The merit of his own contribution lies in the clarity and in the emphasis with which he treated the subject. For a war to be just there must exist a legal cause for it – a reason which would be recognized by a court of law as a cause of action. As he points out, war begins where judicial settlement ends. It follows that a war undertaken to enforce a claim which 'is not an obligation from the point of view of strict justice'[5] is not a just war. He devotes an entire chapter to an enumeration, by way of example, of various kinds of unjust war.[6] On the other hand, the causes of just wars are limited to defence against an injury either actual or immediately threatening,[7] to recovery of what is legally due, and to inflicting punishment. He definitely excludes wars undertaken in order to

[1] *Quæstionum in Heptateuchen*, lib. vi. 10.

[2] *De jure belli* (about 1541).

[3] *Opus de triplici virtute theologica* (1621).

[4] A conclusion rejected by Ayala, *De Jure et Officiis Bellicis et Disciplina Militari Libri III* (1582), but approved by Gentilis, *De Jure Belli* (1589), provided that there is reasonable doubt as to the justice of the war. And see *De Jure Belli ac Pacis*, book II, ch. xxiii, § xiii.

[5] Book II, ch. xxii, § xvi.

[6] Book II, ch. xxii.

[7] Book II, ch. i, § ii. 1; § v; § xvi. In the latter paragraph he permits a State to forestall an act of violence not actually present but threatening from a distance. But even in this case he excludes direct action – which he considers unjust – and limits it to obtaining satisfaction for a delinquency begun but not yet consummated.

weaken a neighbour who is a potential threat to the security of the State. He says, with regard to such a war, in a passage typical of the temper of the work in its challenging rejection of *raison d'état*: 'That the possibility of being attacked confers the right to attack is abhorrent to every principle of equity. Human life exists under such conditions that complete security is never guaranteed to us. For protection against uncertain fears we must rely on Divine Providence, and on a wariness free from reproach, not on force.[1] He says in another part of the book: 'That defence may be just, it must be necessary; and it cannot be this, except there be clear evidence, not only of the power, but also of the *animus* of the party; and such evidence as amounts to moral certainty.'[2] By way of example he discusses the case of the justice – which he denies – of a war undertaken against a neighbouring State on the ground that it engages in building a fortress or fortifications which might prove a source of danger. Against such apprehension, he says, the proper remedy is to build counter-fortifications, not to resort to arms.[3] The relevant section of book II[4] – the shortest paragraph in the treatise – consists of one sentence, significant and impressive in its brevity, referring to the causes of war: 'Advantage does not confer the same right as necessity.' He also denies that there is any question of a justifiable war of defence in the case of those who deserved the war waged against them.[5]

But it was in the drawing of the practical consequences from the distinction between just and unjust wars that Grotius went beyond anything taught by his predecessors. This applies not only to the all-important question of neutrality,[6] or to such matters of detail as the rule that a State bound by treaties of alliance with States engaged in war ought to give preference to that engaged in a just war, for 'there is no obligation to undertake unjust wars';[7] that a treaty of alliance is not binding in relation to a State waging an unjust war;[8] or that a State engaged in a just war may, under certain strictly defined conditions, take possession of a place situated in a neutral country;[9] or, though apparently only as a matter of *interna justitia*, with regard to restoration of property taken in an unjust war;[10] or even to the assertion of the right of the belligerent fighting an

[1] *Ibid.* § xvii.

[2] Book II, ch. xxii, § v. 1. (The translation is from Whewell's edition as it seems, on this point, more precise than that in the 'Classics of International Law'.)

[3] Book II, ch. xxii, § v. 2.

[4] Ch. xxii, § vi.

[5] *Ibid.* ch. i, § xviii.

[6] See below, p. 350.

[7] Book II, ch. xv, § xiii. 1.

[8] Book II, ch. xxv, § iv. He regarded as not permissible military alliances concluded without regard to the cause of the war in which the ally may be involved. Book II, ch. xxv, § ix. 1.

[9] *Ibid.* § x. 1.

[10] Book III, ch. x, § iii. 1.

adversary waging 'a very unjust war' to inflict capital punishment upon those carrying contraband.[1] It applies to the more fundamental question of the duty of the subject to serve in a war which is unjust or doubtful, an aspect of his teaching which is of particular significance in view of the respect – some thought servile respect – with which Grotius treated established authority and with which he discouraged any thought of rebellion. He is emphatic that the subject when ordered to take up arms in a clearly unjust war ought to refrain from doing so.[2] Moreover, after much careful deliberation and weighing of authorities, he considers that the obligation is the same when the justice of the war is doubtful. He admits the dangers of disobedience, but he is content to take the risk: 'For when either course is uncertain that which is the lesser of two evils is free from sin; for if a war is unjust there is no disobedience in avoiding it. Moreover, disobedience in things of this kind, by its very nature, is a lesser evil than manslaughter, especially than the slaughter of many innocent men.'[3] The only concession that he is prepared to make is that in the case of a doubtful war the ruler may impose an extraordinary tax upon those refusing to carry arms.[4] At the same time, in conformity with the view which has remained unchallenged and which is in accordance with the humanitarian character of his treatise, he lays down that the question of the justice or injustice of the war is irrelevant for the purpose of observing the rules of warfare as between the belligerents.[5] Any other rule would add to the inherent evils of war the horrors of unrestrained licence and cruelty accentuated by what must often be an unverified *ex parte* claim to wage a just war.

International law, in the three centuries which followed *De Jure Belli ac Pacis*, rejected the distinction between just and unjust wars. War became the supreme right of sovereign States and the very hallmark of their sovereignty. To that extent international law was deprived of a reasonable claim to be regarded as law in the accepted sense of the word. The law on the subject has now undergone a fundamental change. War has ceased to be a supreme prerogative of States. The Grotian distinction between just and unjust war is once more part of positive international law. Factors more potent and more irresistibly compelling than the influence of any single writer

[1] *Ibid.* ch. i, § v. 3. [2] Book II, ch. xxvi, § iii 1.

[3] *Ibid.* § iv. 5; *ibid.* § iv. 8. With this may be compared the view of Pufendorf, book VIII, ch. i, *in fine*, who points to the dangers of destroying civil sovereignty and advises the citizen to 'leave the supreme sovereign accountable to God for the injustice of his war'.

[4] Book II, ch. xxvi, § v. [5] Book III, ch. iv, § iv.

have had a share in that achievement. Yet, among the imponderables which have worked in that direction, the Grotian tradition occupies a high place.

7. *The doctrine of qualified neutrality*

It followed from the emphasis on the distinction between just and unjust wars that no affirmation of absolute impartiality on the part of neutral States in relation to a State waging an unjust war was to be expected in a legal treatise in which the element of moral obligation was as prominent as in *De Jure Belli ac Pacis*. It is theoretically possible for international law to declare that some wars are illegal and criminal and yet to lay down that the neutral States not involved in the war must act with absolute detachment in relation both to the aggressor and to his victim. The legal consistency of such a system of international law would be questionable; its ethical impropriety would be obvious. In any case such a solution would not have been in keeping with the spirit of *De Jure Belli ac Pacis*. Grotius's view on the subject is expressed tersely in the brief chapter on neutrality entitled 'On those who are of neither side in war'.[1] He says: 'It is the duty of those who keep out of war to do nothing whereby he who supports a wicked cause may be rendered more powerful, or whereby the movements of him who wages an unjust war may be hampered.'[2] It will be noted that these duties do not include the positive obligation to assist actively the State waging a just war. But they clearly imply a right to do so. The duty not to hinder may in practice not always be distinguishable from the right to give assistance. There are various passages in the treatise in which Grotius applies in detail that principle of qualified neutrality. Thus he states that the right of passage ought to be granted to a people which is seeking to recover by a just war what is due to it.[3] He is equally emphatic that the right of passage can be refused to a State commencing an unjust war.[4] He is not prepared to attach decisive importance to the fears and even the safety of the State through the territory of which passage is requested. In particular, he says, fear of the ruler against whom a just war is being waged is not a valid reason for refusing passage. 'My right is not extinguished by your fear.'[5]

While in elaborating the distinction between just and unjust wars Grotius was following a centuries-old tradition, in propounding the

[1] Book III, ch. xvii.
[2] *Ibid.* § iii. 1. But he counsels impartiality in doubtful cases.
[3] Book II, ch. ii, § xiii. 1. [4] *Ibid.* § xiii. 4. [5] *Ibid.*

principle of qualified neutrality he was breaking new ground. As may be surmised from the passages just referred to, he was aware of the dangers in which the application of the doctrine of qualified neutrality involved small States and principalities interested in avoiding any pretext for being dragged into the struggle. Principle seemed to him, in this matter as in others, more important than 'reason of State'. Over a hundred years later Christian Wolff, in a somewhat involved exposition, affirmed the right to neutrality when the justice of the war is doubtful or when it is in the interest of the State to remain neutral, 'for every right of a people by nature should be determined by the purpose of the State'. Yet he had no doubt that by the law of nature it was illegal to give aid to a State waging an unjust war.[1] Vattel followed Grotius closely. In one respect, though subject to an important qualification, he went further. He says: 'It is lawful and praiseworthy to assist in every way a Nation which is carrying on a just war; and such assistance even becomes a duty for every Nation which *can give it without injury to itself*. But no assistance may be given to one who wages an unjust war.'[2] Again following Grotius, he was also of the opinion that every treaty of alliance is subject to the implied reservation that it is not operative in cases in which the ally wages or is about to wage a war which is manifestly unjust, of which question the other ally is the only judge 'because you owe it no assistance except in so far as its cause is just and it is convenient for you to give it help'.[3] Even Bynkershoek, who impatiently rejected Grotius's view that the character of neutral duties must be determined by considerations of the justice of the war, admitted that the question becomes relevant in the matter of the fulfilment of treaties of alliance.[4] In general, the right of neutrals to form a judgment on the legal justice of the war waged by belligerents and to adopt discriminatory treatment in accordance with that judgment was generally recognized in the eighteenth century under the influence of Grotius.

The doctrine of qualified neutrality was rejected in the nineteenth century – with perfect logical consistency – by the overwhelming majority of writers. If every war is, in law, just, then neutrality must be an attitude of absolute impartiality. Occasionally writers of authority expressed their disapproval of neutrality thus conceived as being morally intolerable.[5] But that denunciation of neutrality was in

[1] *Jus gentium methodo scientifica pertractatum* (1740), § 674.
[2] *Les Droits des gens*, book III, ch. vi, § 83.
[3] *Ibid.* § 86.
[4] *Quaestionum Juris*, book I, ch. ix.
[5] See, in particular, Westlake, II, 90.

fact a condemnation of a system of international law, fully in operation at that time, in which resort to war was an unlimited right of sovereign States.

With the drastic limitation of the right of war as adopted in the Covenant of the League of Nations and in the General Treaty for the Renunciation of War, the law restored the historic foundations of the doctrine of qualified neutrality as taught by Grotius. The Covenant of the League, in permitting neutrality and in obliging the Members to resort to sanctions and other measures of discrimination against the Covenant-breaking State, was, in this respect, based on the principle of qualified neutrality. When in 1940 and 1941 the United States committed itself to a determined departure from the customary and conventional rules of absolute neutrality as they obtained in the nineteenth century, it invoked, among others, the argument that with the general renunciation and condemnation of war as an instrument of national policy, the right, asserted by the founders of international law, to discriminate against the aggressor was fully restored. Grotius's teaching on the subject was adduced in support of the attitude thus adopted.[1]

Under the Charter of the United Nations neutrality is no longer an absolute right. Members of the United Nations are bound, if called upon to do so by a valid decision of the Security Council, to resort to war against a State waging an aggressive, an unjust, war. But it is possible that the call made upon them may fall short of a summons to resort to war. In that case, the principles of qualified neutrality would once more be applicable. It is, of course, highly questionable whether in a system of collective security – such as that set up by the Charter of the United Nations – in which force has been renounced, there is properly room for any neutrality at all, qualified or otherwise. We may be able to appreciate the legal and ethical merits of this aspect of the Grotian tradition – and the service which it has rendered – without holding it applicable in an international society which claims to have made a radical advance along the path both of the prohibition of unjust war and of the fundamental obligation to suppress it by collective action.

8. *The binding force of promises*

The denial of the right of war, unless for a cause recognized by law, and the principle of qualified neutrality constitute the main application, with regard to the law of war, of Grotius's rejection of the

[1] See the speech of Attorney-General Jackson on 27 March 1941 (*A.J.* 35 (1941), 351).

ideas of reason of State. In the sphere of the law of peace, that same tendency expressed itself most conspicuously in the emphasis which he placed upon the binding force of promises and the obligation of good faith in their fulfilment. The subject is treated at great length in the six chapters of book II on Promises, on Contracts, on Oaths, on Promises of those holding Sovereign Power, on Public Treaties and Sponsions, and on Interpretation.[1] In addition, the five concluding chapters of the treatise are devoted to the subject of promises and good faith in war.[2] The last exhortation, in the final chapter of the treatise, is an appeal to the sacredness of good faith.[3] To Grotius the obligation to abide by pacts is not only the basis of municipal law and of civil society; it is of the essence of the social contract.[4] Without it the social contract is meaningless.[5] As such, the obligation to keep promises is the principal tenet of the law of nature. It is an obligation which binds the ruler in relation to the contract which he has entered into with his subjects; they derive a clear legal right under it. And this, he adds, 'holds even between God and man'.[6] It is not surprising that to him the binding force of treaties is the basis of international law. They must be kept even in relation to pirates and tyrants, in peace or in war;[7] they may be made, according to the Christian law and otherwise, with infidels,[8] and faith must be kept even with them.[9] He lays down the modern and, in the circumstances, unexceptional rule that promises made during war or for the purpose of terminating a war are valid even if extorted by fear.[10] The reason for this seemingly repulsive qualification is that unless this rule were adopted most wars would be incapable of termination.

This categorical affirmation of the sanctity of promises – even in relation to God Himself – had a pointed meaning at a time when the Pope claimed the right to release rulers from the binding obligation of oaths and treaties, by way of interpretation or express dispensation,[11] and when the view was widely adopted and acted upon that there is

[1] Chs. xi–xvi.

[2] Book III, chs. xix–xxiii.

[3] Book III, ch. xxv, § vii.

[4] *Proleg.* 15.

[5] This explains why he is prepared to base the right of punishment on implied contract (book II, ch. xx, § ii. 3).

[6] Book II, ch. xiv, § vi. 2.

[7] Book III, ch. xix, § ii. 1, 2.

[8] Book II, ch. xv, § x. i.

[9] Book III, ch. xix, § xiii. 1. Although he advises caution in concluding treaties of alliance with infidels, he regards such alliances as permissible and, above all, as binding (Book II, ch. xv, § ii).

[10] *Ibid.* § xi—unless such duress is, in turn, contrary to the Law of Nations, as, for instance, in the case of a promise extorted from a captured ambassador (*ibid.* § xii).

[11] For numerous examples of such releases see Laurent, *Histoire du droit des gens* (1865), x, 432–9.

no binding force in treaties concluded not only between Christians and infidels but also those between Catholics and Protestants. But its significance goes considerably beyond that. It supplies a scientific basis – that of the law of nature and of the social nature of man – for the 'volitional Law of Nations', i.e. international law based on agreement, whether expressed in a treaty or implied by custom. In modern terminology, the rule *pacta sunt servanda* is the initial hypothesis of the Law of Nations. Some prefer to consider it as being in itself of an extra-legal character for the reason that the validity of the ultimate source of legal obligation cannot, logically, be explained in terms of law; Grotius grounded its binding force in the law of nature. As suggested above, the difference is perhaps not so profound as may appear at first sight. What is important is that at a period of European history when the authority of the pledged word of treaties had become a byword – a phenomenon which was destined to become a recurrent phase in international relations – he made it the very pivot of his teaching.[1]

9. *The fundamental rights and freedoms of the individual*

There is one perplexing aspect of the work of Grotius which appears to be alien to the spirit of his teaching as outlined so far, and which calls for careful examination, namely, his attitude to the question of the freedom of the individual in his relation to constituted authority. The importance of this subject is not confined to the field of political theory. In many ways it is closely connected with international law. It has given rise to scornful and impatient reprobation of Grotius's work as a whole. What is the reason for this exception – if exception it is – to the otherwise uniformly progressive trend of the treatise? On the face of it the record is disillusioning. Grotius justified slavery and claimed to have found support for it in the immutable canons of the law of nature. He rejected the idea of the sovereignty of the people.[2] He denied the right of resistance to oppression by the ruler.[3] He did not see why, if an individual can voluntarily sell himself into slavery, a whole people should not be able to do so collectively. He attributed an irrevocable legal effect not only to collective voluntary

[1] It is interesting to note that in his chapter on Observance of Public Agreements (book II, ch. x) Bynkershoek refers with some disapproval to the numerous exceptions and qualifications, laid down by Grotius, of the binding force of treaties. These exceptions and qualifications, though they may have been abused by others for the purposes of specious pleading, testify to the thoroughness of Grotius's treatment of the subject. See below, p. 361.

[2] Book I, ch. iii, § viii.

[3] See in particular book I, ch. iv, §§ i–vii.

submission, but also to conquest. He completed this chain of reasoning by including in his examples of unjust wars a contest waged by an oppressed people in order to regain its liberty.[1] It is not easy to fit all this into the general pattern of the treatise. The matter becomes even more obscure when we consider the personal circumstances of its author. Here was a refugee who escaped from the sentence of a political court set up by an arbitrary decree. Yet he deprecated resistance to oppressive rule. Here was a Dutchman, the loyal son of a people which half a century before had by force thrown off the yoke of the Spanish oppressor and which, at the very moment when *De Jure Belli ac Pacis* was being written, was preparing war against the United Provinces to reimpose upon them the tyranny of alien rule. Yet Grotius considered to be unjust a war waged by an oppressed people for the sake of its freedom.

What is the explanation of these views, so foreign to the spirit of his teaching and to his personal condition? It is true that, writing as he did in a country under an absolute monarch, to whom he dedicated the treatise, who bestowed a pension upon him, and from whom he might have expected the favours of a remunerative appointment, he could hardly write in the vein of *Vindiciae contra Tyrannos*. It is possible that, in view of the intransigence with which the right of resistance was advocated, both in the latter tract – which appeared in 1579 but which had not by any means fallen into oblivion – and in Hotman's *Franco-Gallia*, published in 1573, he felt it incumbent upon himself to give to the matter a special argumentative emphasis. But this in itself is an inadequate explanation. What is much more to the point is that this frowning upon rebellion and the favouring of authority were in accordance with what were considered to be the essential needs of the times. The horrors of civil war were foremost in the minds of political thinkers. There was not, in this respect, much difference between Hobbes and Bacon on the one side, and Hooker, Gentilis, and Bodin on the other. They discussed in detail the right of resistance; they all rejected it. So, perhaps with less justification, did Pufendorf.[2] At a time of general uncertainty and of loosening of traditional ties of society, national and international, order was looked upon as the paramount dictate of reason. In the period preceding the Thirty Years War the territorial sovereign State which emerged from the dissolution of the feudal system of society on the continent of Europe had hardly taken over the functions of the feudal lord; the resulting vacuum accentuated the necessity for stability

[1] Book II, ch. xxii, § xi.

[2] Pufendorf, Book VII, ch. 8, §§ 5, 6.

even at the expense of freedom.[1] Considerations of this order must have weighed heavily with one in whose work the desire for peace was the dominant motive and the ever-recurring theme. This particular feature of Grotius's outlook appears clearly from his unheroic advice given to defeated peoples, to yield to fate rather than to engage in a suicidal fight for liberty, for, he says, reason prefers life to freedom.[2] Strange as it may sound, his attitude towards slavery was to a large extent determined by humanitarian considerations. Enslavement of those captured in war was an alternative preferable to the unlimited power – including the right to kill – which, in his view, the customary Law of Nations and, probably, the law of nature gave to the captor. His treatment of the institution of slavery is permeated throughout by a spirit of charity and mercy.[3]

What is more important than these explanations is the fact that behind the façade of general disapproval of the right of resistance there lay qualifications so comprehensive as to render the major proposition almost theoretical. Thus, according to Grotius, there is a right of resistance in cases in which the ruler, by virtue of an original or subsequent contract, is responsible to a free people (as was the case in Sparta);[4] against a king who has renounced his authority or has manifestly abandoned it;[5] who attempts to alienate his kingdom (but only so far as is necessary to prevent the transfer);[6] who openly shows himself the enemy of the whole people – an elastic and formidable exception;[7] who attempts to usurp that part of the sovereign power which does not belong to him;[8] and, finally, where the people have reserved the right of resistance in certain cases.[9] These exceptions as laid down by Grotius were relied upon as an authority for the justification of the resistance to and deposition of James II.[10] If Rousseau had concentrated on the reality of these

[1] He says, after stating that by nature all men have the right of resistance in order to ward off an injury: 'As civil society was instituted in order to maintain public tranquillity, the State forthwith acquires over us and our possessions a greater right, to the extent necessary to accomplish this end. The State, therefore, in the interest of public peace and order, can limit that common right of resistance' (book I, ch. iv, § ii. 1).

[2] Book I, ch. ii, § xxiv. 6. See also *ibid.* § vi. 5, and *ibid.* ch. iii, § xxv. 4. Grotius, who in 1643 read *De Cive*, expressed agreement with Hobbes's view on political authority though he was unable to agree with the bases of the Hobbesian argument: 'Librum de Cive vidi, placent quae pro Regibus dixit. Fundamenta tamen quibus suas sententias superstruit, probare non possum. Putat inter homines omnes a natura esse bellum . . .' (*Epistolae quotquot*, 1687, Appendix No. 648).

[3] Book III, chs. vii and xiv.

[4] Book I, ch. iv, § viii.

[5] *Ibid.* § ix.

[6] *Ibid.* § x.

[7] *Ibid.* § xi.

[8] Book I, ch. iv, § xiii.

[9] *Ibid.* § xiv.

[10] An interesting illustration of this recourse to Grotius will be found, for instance, in an anonymous pamphlet published in 1689 in London by 'A Lover of the Peace of his Country' under the title *The Proceedings of the Present Parliament Justified by the Opinion of the most*

exceptions rather than on the appearance of the general proposition he would have found less reason for vituperation.[1] It is unlikely that one or more of these exceptions did not recall to the mind of the reader the various articles of the Dutch Act of Abjuration against Philip of Spain.

Finally, in this connection we must bear in mind other indications of Grotius's true attitude. Thus it is significant that, notwithstanding his reluctance to sanction recourse to war, he considers as just resort to war to prevent the maltreatment by a State of its own subjects. In such cases, he says, if a ruler 'should inflict upon his subjects such treatment as no one is warranted in inflicting, the exercise of the right vested in human society is not precluded'.[2] This is, on the face of it, a somewhat startling rule, for it may not be easy to see why he permits a foreign State to intervene, through war, on behalf of the oppressed while he denies to the persecuted themselves the right of resistance. Part of the answer is, perhaps, that he held such wars of intervention to be permitted only in extreme cases, which coincide largely with those in which the king reveals himself as an enemy of his people and in which resistance is permitted.[3]

However that may be, this is the first authoritative statement of the principle of humanitarian intervention – the principle that the exclusiveness of domestic jurisdiction stops where outrage upon humanity begins. The doctrine of humanitarian intervention has never become a fully acknowledged part of positive international law. But it has provided a signpost and a warning. It has been occasionally acted upon, and it was one of the factors which paved the way for the provisions of the Charter of the United Nations relating to fundamental human rights and freedoms. In that development the teaching of Grotius has some share. Neither must we forget that although he denied – with substantial qualifications – the right of active resistance, he permitted and enjoined the right of passive resistance;[4] that he safeguarded the conscience and the freedom of the individual in

Judicious and Learned Hugo Grotius; With considerations thereupon. Written for the Satisfaction of some of the Reverend Clergy who yet seem to labour under some Scruples concerning the Original Rights of Kings, their Abdication of Empire, and the People's inseparable Right of Resistance, Deposing, and of Disposing and Settling of the Succession to the Crown. The author invoked Grotius the famous Civilian . . . because of the great Credit and Authority he has obtained in the world, especially amongst the Clergy, and is above all other of his Faculty, most tender of the Rights and Prerogatives of Crowned Heads' (at p. 6).

[1] The same applies to the observations of Dr Figgis on the subject (*Studies of Political Thought*, at p. 185).

[2] Book II, ch. xxv, § viii. 2. See also *ibid.* ch. xx, § xl. 1.

[3] See above, p. 356. But this would not apply to the cruel treatment of a minority.

[4] See above, p. 323.

such matters as the right to refuse to carry arms in an unjust, and even doubtful, war;[1] and that he championed the cause of such claims of the individual as the right of expatriation, the rights of economic freedom, and the right to share, through a plebiscite, in the decision to transfer part of national territory.[2]

10. *The idea of peace*

The tenth – and not the least important – aspect of the Grotian tradition is his pacifism. He does not deny that war is a legal institution. On the contrary, he is at pains to show that war is not inconsistent with the law of nature and with many other kinds of law. There were good reasons – in addition to the recognition of a patent fact – for this initial legitimation of war. It would not be feasible to attempt to introduce a measure of legal regulation into a relation not recognized by law. A corresponding method suggested itself – and was adopted – with regard to the contents of the rules of warfare. Thus Grotius's treatment of the laws of war seems to be open to the charge that, after setting out to humanize rules of war, he gives the *imprimatur* of law to rules of pronounced inhumanity.[3] His answer to any such criticism would probably have been that the proper course was not to deny the character of law to practices which apparently had secured a wide degree of acceptance, but to urge a mitigation of their rigours. Ayala went as far as Grotius – and farther – in treating these practices as law, but he did not propose anything in the nature of *temperamenta*.

In general, there breathes from the pages of *De Jure Belli ac Pacis* a disapproval, amounting to hatred, of war.[4] There is nothing in that work reminiscent of the Baconian conception of war as a healthy exercise. Grotius is clear that where the question of legal right is doubtful, a State ought to refrain from war.[5] He proposes various methods of settling disputes, including negotiation[6] and arbitration.[7] He suggests that 'it would be advantageous, indeed in a degree necessary, to hold certain conferences of Christian powers, where those who have no interest at stake may settle the disputes of others, and where, in fact, steps may be taken to compel parties to accept

[1] See above, p. 349. [2] See below, p. 361.

[3] See above, p. 320.

[4] It is the same overriding desire for peace which explains the extraordinary passage in which, with some uneasiness, he elaborates the view that a State may surrender to an enemy an innocent subject in order to avoid a greater danger (book II, ch. xxv, § iii).

[5] Book II, ch. xxiii, § vi. [6] *Ibid.* § vii.

[7] Book II, ch. xxiii, § viii.

peace on fair terms'.[1] He devotes a whole chapter to 'warnings not to undertake war rashly, even for just causes'.[2] Elsewhere, he distinguishes between justifiable wars, namely, those for which there is a true legal cause, and those in which the law is but a pretext. These latter he describes simply as wars of robbers.[3] He fully approved of the view of St Augustine that aggressive wars of conquest are nothing but 'wholesale robbery'.[4] And he cited other distinguished authorities in support of the same opinion.[5] It is probable that his persistent striving towards the unity of the Christian Church and the appearance of leanings towards Catholicism[6] were the outcome of the realization that no other basis was as yet possible for the international organization and preservation of peace.

11. *The tradition of idealism and progress*

The pacifist strain which runs through the entire work of Grotius is only one feature of the more general aspect – the last to be here considered – of the Grotian tradition, namely, what may not inappropriately be called the tradition of progress and idealism. He initiated or gave his support to progressive ideas in various fields in the sphere of international relations. He was one of the first to assist the cause of international co-operation in the suppression of crime by urging extradition of criminals as a matter of legal duty.[7] He did

[1] *Ibid.* § viii. 4.

[2] Book II, ch. xxiv.

[3] *Ibid.* ch. xxii, § iii, 1.

[4] Book II, ch. xxii, § iii. 2.

[5] Book II, ch. i, § i. 3.

[6] There seems to be no warrant for the suggestion that before his death, prior to leaving France on his journey to Sweden, he expressed the desire to become a Roman Catholic. That possibility is discounted by the most judicious of his biographers: see De Bourigny, *The Life of the Truly Eminent and Learned Hugo Grotius* (transl. from the French, 1754), pp. 300 *et seq.* See also Hanshagen, in *Z.V.* 23 (1939), 13–48, and, in particular, the illuminating Preface of Schulte to Broere's *Hugo Grotius' Rückkehr zum katholischen Glauben* (1871). However, the legend of Grotius's Catholicism dies hard. See, e.g., Pastor, *Geschichte der Päpste*, XIII (1929), 783. The source of the belief, occasionally expressed, that Grotius was converted to Catholicism lies probably in the fact that much of his theological doctrine was in the nature of an approximation to or, at least, of a sympathetic understanding of the Catholic point of view. To what extent that tendency was, in turn, due to his desire to assist in bringing about the unity of the Christian Church must remain a matter of conjecture. In any case, it was that practical problem which constituted the main preoccupation of his life from the time that he entered the public service of his own country till his death. That cause he served with a sustained fervour and ability which reveal a stature more impressive than that of an essentially academic person who had never grown into full practical maturity—a picture presented by some biographers. See on this aspect of his life: Krogh-Tonning, *Hugo Grotius und die religiösen Bewegungen seiner Zeit* (1904); Schlüter, *Die Theologie des Hugo Grotius* (1919); Wernle, *Der schweizerische Protestantismus im XVIII. Jahrhundert*, I (1922), 471 *et seq.* See also von Luden, *Hugo Grotius nach seinen Schicksalen und Schriften dargestellt* (1806), and Knight, *The Life and Works of Hugo Grotius* (1925), pp. 245–90.

[7] Unless the State of refuge itself chooses to mete out punishment (book II, ch. xxi, §§ iii, iv. 3).

more than any of the other founders of international law in developing the theory and elucidating the practice of diplomatic immunities. He supplied the basis of the modern law of State responsibility founded on fault as distinguished from absolute liability[1] and thus helped to displace the undiscriminating and anarchic practice of reprisals as a normal means of redressing grievances. He urged, and laid down as a rule of law, the principle of freedom of navigation on international rivers and canals.[2] His share in the evolution of the principle of the freedom of the seas needs no elaboration. In all these matters his teaching became part of international practice, wholly or in part. In others, although it has remained a mere postulate of reason, it is not without significance.

Thus in matters of economic freedom he spoke the language of uncompromising free trade expressed in terms of legal right. Men are entitled to obtain things without which life cannot comfortably be lived. And although this is an imperfect right inasmuch as the owner retains the power of disposition, no obstacles to the free acquisition of the necessaries of life must be raised by 'law or by conspiracy'.[3] To do that, he says, quoting Ambrose, is 'to separate men from relation with their common parent, to refuse fruits freely produced for all, and to do away with the community of life'.[4] He reiterates that 'all men have the right to buy such things at a fair price unless, as in time of extreme scarcity of grain, they are needed by those from whom they are sought'. As if in anticipation of some modern monopolistic practices, he inquired, in this connection, whether it is permissible for one people to make an agreement with another to sell to it exclusively products which do not grow elsewhere. He thought this permissible and not inconsistent with the law of nature provided the latter people was prepared to re-sell at a fair price.[5]

It will be noted that these various claims are not postulates of mere ideal justice. They figure in the part of the treatise which is concerned with the causes of war – one of which is 'injury actually received',[6] 'an injury to that which actually belongs to us'.[7] He was clearly in advance of his time when he urged that refugees driven from their homes have the right to acquire permanent residence in another country provided they submit to the Government in authority;[8] that deserted and barren portions of national territory be given to immigrants who ask for it, and that they are entitled to take possession,

[1] Book II, ch. xvii, § 20; ch. xxi, § 2.
[2] Book II, ch. ii, § xiii.
[3] Book II, ch. ii, § xviii.
[4] *Ibid.*
[5] *Ibid.* § xxiv.
[6] *Ibid.* § i.
[7] *Ibid.*
[8] *Ibid.* § xvi.

subject to the sovereignty of the original people, of uncultivated land;[1] that a State is bound to grant freedom of passage through its territory to a people which has been forced to leave its country and is seeking unoccupied lands, or desires to carry on commerce with a distant nation;[2] that freedom of passage for the purpose of carrying on commerce extends, as a matter of right, not only to persons but also to merchandise;[3] and that such freedom of passage includes freedom from taxation unless in return for services rendered.[4] He urged with emphasis the right of the individual to expatriate himself from his country of origin,[5] and he acknowledged the right of self-determination to the extent of requiring the consent of the population to a transfer of national territory.[6]

Some of these proposals appear to be chimerical; others have been partly adopted in practice. But they all illustrate the temper of the treatise and explain much of its attraction throughout the centuries. There is about it an atmosphere of strong conviction, of reforming zeal, of moral fervour. These qualities were typical of Grotius himself. This does not mean that the argument in *De Jure Belli ac Pacis* is not often specious and involved. Some of the apparently tortuous character of his exposition is explained by the fact that elaborate qualifications are often of the essence of a conscientious presentation of the legal position. Thus Grotius's detailed treatment of the exceptions to the binding force of promises – a subject as to which his integrity was above suspicion – elicited some caustic remarks from Bynkershoek on the ground that it was abused for the purpose of denying in practice the validity of treaties.[7] Yet this is clearly one of the cases in which a simple statement of the legal position may be neither convincing nor accurate. The same applies to other examples of apparent casuistry as, for instance, the section entitled 'The question whether a war may be just from the viewpoint of both parties, with many qualifications',[8] or to his submission that although a belligerent must not resort to assassination he may accept an offer to that effect,[9] or that though waters must not be poisoned they may be polluted.[10] Some of the tortuousness of the argument must be put to the account of the anxiety not to offend religious feeling. Thus the secularization of the law of nature and the assertion of its supremacy over God Himself was hedged round by highly strained pieces of

[1] *Ibid.* § xvii.
[2] *Ibid.* § xiii. 1.
[3] *Ibid.* § xiii. 5.
[4] Book II, ch. ii, § xiv.
[5] *Ibid.* ch. v, § xxiv.
[6] *Ibid.* ch. vi, § iv.
[7] See above, p. 354, n. 1.
[8] Book II, ch. xxiii, § xiii. 1.
[9] Book III, ch. iv, § xviii.
[10] *Ibid.* §§ xvi, xvii.

casuistry such as that if God should command a person to be killed this would not render murder lawful, but that the act having been commanded by God, the Supreme Lord of Life, it would cease to be murder.[1] His efforts to reconcile the apparent denial of the right of resistance with a measure of popular sovereignty have already been noted.[2] Although he considered the contract between subject and king to be binding upon the latter, he was of the view that the contract cannot be enforced.[3] Neither was he invariably above altering his views in deference to the changed political situation – witness the modification in *De Jure Belli ac Pacis* of the rigidity of the principle of the freedom of the seas as advocated in *Mare Liberum*.[4] And examples may be found of straining the meaning of an event to fit a purpose, as in the suggestion that the citizens of Rome are inheritors of the Roman Empire – a piece of special pleading which could be used as a link in the chain of argument in favour of the unity of the Church within the general framework of Catholicism.[5]

These intrusions of opportunism and realism did not decisively influence the character of *De Jure Belli ac Pacis*. But they are symbolic of the perennial problem with which the science of international law has been confronted almost from the outset. It has been exposed to the inducement to supply a rationalization of inferior and irrational

[1] Book I, ch. i, § x. 6.

[2] See above, p. 356.

[3] Book II, ch. xiv, § vi. 2. This mixture of evasiveness and elaboration in the matter of the mutual rights of the ruler and the subject is, of course, typical of the age. See, e.g., the way in which Pufendorf set out to prove that supreme authority was not necessarily unlimited (as summarized by Gierke, *Natural Law and the Theory of Society*, 1500–1800 (transl. by Barker, 1934), I, 142, 143).

[4] Probably these modifications are not so far-reaching as appears at first sight. The seas, he says, cannot be appropriated. However, not inconsistently with the reason for the freedom of the seas, namely, that they cannot be physically occupied, Grotius holds that part of the sea can be acquired by him who holds the shore on both sides, as in the case of bays or straits, 'provided that the part of the sea in question is not so large that, when compared with the land on both sides, it does not seem a part of them' (book II, ch. iii, § viii). This applies, generally, by the law of nature to parts of the seas which are shut in by land (*ibid.* § x. 1–2) – although, in this as in other respects, 'universal customary law, by a kind of common understanding', may prohibit what is permitted by the law of nature (*ibid.* 3). Moreover, such possession of parts of the seas must not impede unarmed and innocent passage (*ibid.* § xii). He devotes a long section, backed by numerous authorities, to showing that although ownership over the seas cannot be acquired, that limitation does not apply to jurisdiction in the nature of *imperium*. 'Ut autem solum imperium in maris partem sine alia proprietate occupatur, facilius, potuit procedere: neque arbitror, jus illud gentium de quo diximus obstare' (*ibid.* § xiii. 1). He does not explain the nature of the distinction, for this purpose, between *proprietas* and *imperium*. However, the illustrations which he adduces of the consequences of such *imperium* suggest that they merely embrace such rights as taxing foreign shipping in order to obtain compensation for expenses incurred in connection with protecting navigation and making it safe by providing lighthouses and buoying shoals (*ibid.* § xiv).

[5] Book II, ch. ix, § xi. And see above, p. 359.

practices; to confuse, in the name of realism, the function of chronicling events with that of a critical exposition of rules of conduct worthy of the name of law; to furnish a philosophy of the second best; and to represent the transient manifestations of immaturity and anarchy in international relations as resulting necessarily and permanently from the nature of States the mutual relations of which, it is said, may be regulated by voluntary co-operation but not by a rule of law imposed and enforced from above. Grotius did not succumb to that tendency. This fact explains much of the influence which he has wielded. For, in the history of political ideas and human progress, it will be found that the attraction of the short cuts of sound realism is matched – and surpassed – by the appeal to faith and to principle.

These then are the principal features of what has here been called the Grotian tradition in international law. They may be conveniently enumerated by way of conclusion. They are: the subjection of the totality of international relations to the rule of law; the acceptance of the law of nature as an independent source of international law; the affirmation of the social nature of man as the basis of the law of nature; the recognition of the essential identity of States and individuals; the rejection of 'reason of State'; the distinction between just and unjust war; the doctrine of qualified neutrality; the binding force of promises; the fundamental rights and freedoms of the individual; the idea of peace; and the tradition of idealism and progress. Some of these elements of the Grotian tradition have now become part of the positive law; others are still an aspiration. But they all explain why Grotius's work has remained an abiding force and not merely an episode, however important, in the literature of international law. They explain why writers and statesmen have turned to Grotius not only as a source of evidence of the law as it is, but also as a well-spring of faith in the law as it ought to be. Grotius did not create international law. Law is not made by writers. What Grotius did was to endow international law with unprecedented dignity and authority by making it part not only of a general system of jurisprudence but also of a universal moral code. To many, indeed, it may appear that *De Jure Belli ac Pacis* is more a system of ethics applied to States than a system of law. This would not inevitably imply a condemnation of the work. For it may be held that at that time – as, indeed, at any time – it was important that the relations of States should be conceived and taught as part of ethics as well as part of law. Grotius's great merit is that he performed both tasks in one work. This combination of functions resulted in much methodological confusion offensive to the purist, who is in danger of forgetting that in the seventeenth century eclecticism was as important as systematic accuracy. *De Jure Belli ac Pacis* is pre-eminently a treatise which must be judged not by reference to its method, but by its influence on the doctrine and on the practice of the Law of Nations. It satisfied the craving, in jurist and layman alike, for a moral content in the law. In stressing and, on the whole, maintaining the distinction between law and morality, it vindicated the place of the Law of Nations in legal science. Last – but not least – it became identified with the idea of progress in international law.

These considerations may help to answer, to a large extent, the question whether *De Jure Belli ac Pacis* is still a proper medium of study and instruction in international law. The reply is clearly in the negative if what we have in mind is assistance in the search for a legal rule which we may assume an international court would now apply in a case before it. From this point of view most text-books and treatises are obsolete. But *De Jure Belli ac Pacis* may nevertheless have its uses not only for the legal historian or for the writer or advocate anxious to embellish a quotation or strengthen an argument by reference to a passage from Grotius. It cannot be rewritten or modernized by the simple device of omitting quotations from the ancient authorities.[1] To do that, as Whewell did in the abridged version of his translation, is to run the risk of depriving the treatise of one of its characteristic features by reducing it to a body of dry propositions unsupported by the ripe wisdom of antiquity. It is not necessary for the average student to examine the whole of *De Jure Belli ac Pacis*, which ought to disappear, as a mere ornamental item, from reading-lists. But selected portions of the treatise may still be read with advantage as an instance of juridical method typical of the seventeenth century; as a fairly accurate statement, on any given subject, of international law in its formative period; and, above all, as expressive of the various aspects of the Grotian tradition. However, the significance of the subject transcends that of one item in the educational curriculum of international lawyers. In gaining an understanding of the Grotian tradition as a whole – this has been the main object of the present article – we may not only fathom the secret of its influence upon generations of scholars and men of affairs. We may, and that is no less important, obtain an insight into the

[1] For an interesting discussion of this and cognate questions see Sandifer in *A.J.* 34 (1940), 459–72.

persistent problems of international law in the past, in the present, and, probably for some long time to come, in the future. It is a measure of the greatness of the work of Grotius that all these questions should have found a place in his teaching and that he should have answered them in a spirit upon the acceptance of which depends the ultimate reality of the Law of Nations as a 'law properly so called'.[1]

[1] For an appreciation of some aspects of the teaching of Grotius in relation to the development of international law see Bourquin in *R.I.* 3rd ser. 7 (1926), 86–125; Vlugt in *Hague Recueil*, 7 (1925) (ii), 397–506. See also Hearnshaw, *Some Great Political Idealists of the Christian Era* (1937), pp. 81–104; and Pound, 'Philosophical Theory and International Law', in *Bibliotheca Visseriana*, 1 (1923), 71–90. And see Klee, *Hugo Grotius and Johannes Selden* (1946).

It appears from the notes left by Lord Acton that he considered Grotius a pivotal figure in the history of freedom conceived as the emancipation of human thought from the shackles of theological dogma and the ideas of reason of State. (The relevant bundle of notes – No. 5434 – is part of a large collection in Lord Acton's handwriting deposited in the Cambridge University Library. I am indebted to my son, Mr E. Lauterpacht, of Trinity College, for drawing my attention to them.) Lord Acton seems to have believed that some of Grotius's influence may have been due to the fact that his competence and reputation extended to the fields of both theology and law. He says: 'The literature of divines had little influence on the world. The jurists . . . walked independently of theology. To bring the ideas of the divines and of civil law into combination the man was required who was as much a divine as a jurist. This was Grotius' (5434/76). Lord Acton remarks that before Grotius most writers were touched with denominational prejudices. Grotius, while not an enemy of religion—he was deeply religious, was independent of any Church. He made morals independent of religion and, therefore, above religion. He made them a test of the best religion. His object was to advocate principle rather than principles; not to promote certain truths, but to see that truth should prevail over interest (5434/45, 53, 88). Elsewhere Lord Acton remarks on 'Grotius's notion of a code distinct from the moral law, yet obliging conscience; not the work of the Church, but requiring the obedience of the Church; not given by God, but claiming to exist even if there is no God, and to precede the law that He gives; taking away the results of 1,000 years of Christian civilization' (5434/104). He compares Grotius with Copernicus as the herald of a new scientific era. Grotius's attitude, discussed above (at pp. 340–6), to the ideas of 'reason of State' may have prompted the observation, intimately in keeping with Acton's teaching, that 'there is no State so sacred or so necessary that it must not be sacrificed to a more universal obligation and a higher cause' (5434/99).

There are repeated reference in Lord Acton's notes to the great contribution of Grotius to the secularization of the law of nature and of political thought generally. (See above, pp. 315, 361, on Grotius's submission, rendered more emphatic by its verbal qualifications, that the law of nature would be valid even if there were no God.) The importance of that contribution is not affected by the circumstance that Grotius was actually not the first to assert the independence of the law of nature. See Maitland's note in Gierke, *Political Theories of the Middle Age* (Maitland's transl. 1900), p. 174, quoting from Gierke's *Johannes Althusius* that 'already medieval schoolmen had befriended the saying, usually attributed to Grotius, that there would be a law of nature discoverable by human reason and absolutely binding, even if there were no God'. In that work Gierke cites a passage from Gabriel Biel's *Collectorium Sententiarum* (1501) strikingly reminiscent of Grotius's phraseology. And see above, at p. 315, as to Suarez. See also Professor Hazeltine's Introduction to Ullmann, *The Medieval Idea of Law* (1946), at p. xxx, where he refers to Hemmingius, *De lege naturae apodictica methodus* (1562), Q. 9, as yet another example of the attempts, prior to Grotius, to emancipate jurisprudence from theology.

CHAPTER 13

SPINOZA AND INTERNATIONAL LAW

Editor's note This chapter is the first article which Lauterpacht contributed to the *British Year Book of International Law*. It appeared in vol. 8 (1927), at pp. 89–107, and represented the beginning of an association which was to continue almost until his death in 1960. During that time, Lauterpacht published fourteen articles in the *Year Book* and from 1944 until 1956 was its Editor.

I

Spinoza's contribution to international law does not exceed one thousand five hundred words,[1] and its direct influence on the science of international law in the following centuries appears to have been altogether negligible. Von Ompteda, the first scientific bibliographer of international law, mentions him, amidst some indignation at his doctrine,[2] in his enumeration of post-Grotian writers, but it is obvious that the reference is one for the sake of completeness only.[3] He assigns to him a place even inferior to that occupied by Robert Sharrock, an author who wrote a few passages on the law of war in his exposition of the law of nature, but whose chief merit lies in championing Boyle's scientific discoveries and in having published a treatise on the *Propagation and Improvement of Vegetables by the Concurrence of Air and Nature* (1669). By asserting that international law owes to Spinoza next to nothing Ompteda was not merely giving vent to his disapproval of Spinoza's teaching. For there is no evidence to show that (with the possible exception, to be discussed later, of Pufendorf

[1] Even this is a liberal computation considering that what he said on this subject in the third chapter of the *Tractatus Politicus* (cited here as *P.*) is largely a repetition of the view previously expressed by him in the sixteenth chapter of the *Tractatus Theologico-Politicus* (cited here as *T.P.*). Spinoza was born in 1632; he died in 1677.

[2] *Litteratur des gesammten, sowohl natürlichen als positiven Völkerrechts* (1785), p. 265.

[3] Ompteda's own words on the subject may usefully be quoted: 'Among other philosophical and theological paradoxes, he also expressed some altogether detestable opinions on international law. He wrote namely a Theological-Political Treatise in which he attempted to undermine both natural law and the Law of Nations. With regard to the first he maintained that according to natural law a man may do everything that is in his power. By applying this view to relations between States he did not hesitate to hold that a State may, if it is only strong enough, attack its neighbours, and also, if it thinks it to be of advantage, dissolve at will its treaties of alliance and assistance. And, in order to show how far an otherwise sensible thinker may be led astray by the desire to propagate novelties, I shall cite the very words in which he puts forward those shameful doctrines.'

and some writers of minor importance[1]) international lawyers knew of his existence, or, if they knew, that they cared to quote or to refute him. Bynkershoek, his countryman, while writing exhaustively[2] on a subject on which Spinoza's views were not only diametrically opposed to his own, but also clear and emphatic, ignored him completely. His views on international law shared the fate of his political theory which was totally overshadowed by the acute controversy centring round his philosophical and theological doctrines.[3] The nineteenth century, during which much of the prejudice surrounding his teaching was swept aside, could not, in the very nature of things, bring any appreciable change in this particular respect. There was no prejudice to be overcome as far as his international doctrine was concerned. As it happened, the worst that could be said about it was not far off the mark. No wonder that text-books do not refer to him and that he has remained unknown to the student of international law.[4] On the other hand, those of his admirers who were engaged in expounding his political theory could not well pass over the embarrassing utterances, and, especially in this country, attempts were made to put on the much denounced passages a construction calculated to vindicate for them some semblance of inherent accuracy.[5] It even came to pass that a very competent commentator of Spinoza, while discussing his relation to international law, allowed himself to be led astray by an inaccurate translation of a crucial passage in the *Tractatus Politicus* and to maintain, on the strength of it, that Spinoza recognized an obligation of faith in international compacts.[6]

However, in spite of the negative results of the above survey of Spinoza's influence, it is believed that the attention paid to this aspect of his teaching may not be altogether without advantage for the student of the history and the theory of international law. There are several reasons which seem to justify such a belief.

The beginning of the nineteenth century witnessed the elevation of

[1] Cf., for instance, Schmauss, *Neues Systema des Rechts der Natur* (1754), p. 270.

[2] *Quaestiones Juris Publici* (1737), vol. II, ch. 10.

[3] This is well illustrated by the fact that Frederick II, the author of the well-known anti-Machiavellian treatise, while referring to Spinoza in the preface of his book, is obviously of the opinion that the latter's negative influence extended to the field of religion only: '"The Prince" of Machiavell'—thus begins the Preface—'is with regard to morality, what Spinoza's work is with regard to religion' (*Examen du Prince Machiavel avec des notes historiques et politiques* (1741)).

[4] Rivier, in Holtzendorff, I, 435, refers to him casually in his bibliographical article.

[5] Menzel, 'Spinoza und das Völkerrecht', in *Z.V.* 2 (1908), 17–22. Professor Wolf, writing in *Chronicon Spinozanum*, II (1922), 11–12, goes to the length of maintaining that Spinoza was 'a believer in the essential unity and solidarity of mankind', and that he saw in reason 'the surest means of international conciliation'.

[6] See below, p. 376.

the doctrine of Machiavelli, notably of his conception of international relations, from the level of what had previously been a byword and a widely resented challenge to the moral sense of man, to the dignity of an organic part of a comprehensive system of political theory. The separation of morals from politics and the identification of power with right – both constituted the main feature of Spinoza's theory of the State – began to permeate European political thought. At the same time Spinoza's general philosophy, hitherto the centre of barren controversies, became finally recognized as one of the foundations of philosophical endeavour. Is there any ground for holding that the simultaneousness of these achievements was one not only of time, but also of intimate connection? Did the general acceptance of his philosophy have the effect of facilitating – by making them appear fit to form part of an imposing ethical and political system – the adoption of international doctrines which would otherwise have been rejected with scorn and abhorrence? It will be of interest to examine whether and how far Spinoza's views on international relations became part of those great systems of political theory which, although international lawyers of the nineteenth century remained ignorant of Spinoza himself, influenced the subsequent development of international law.

For the relation between political theory and international law is of a more pervading character than is commonly assumed. It is the ultimate results of the theory of the State which are resorted to by international lawyers as the foundation of their systems. A political doctrine based on the omnipotence and glorification of the State as an end in itself will naturally result, and has usually resulted, in the negation of the Law of Nations as a body of rules which, both in its binding force and in its creation, is independent of the will of the State. The present, still rudimentary, stage of international law is in no small degree due to the prevalence of this type of doctrine. And the time seems as yet far off when the legal – and, of necessity, also the political and sociological – theory of the State will turn to international law as the necessary starting-point of a truly scientific inquiry. Nevertheless, the philosophical bases of international law and its position among cognate social and legal sciences cannot be better illustrated than by disclosing the manner in which representative systems of thought ended in the treatment of the problem of the relation of States to humanity, i.e. of their relations to one another. Of them Spinoza's views are the more instructive as he made it a point to apply here *more geometrico* the fundamental principles of his ethical and political doctrine.

Finally, there is, with regard to Spinoza, a special reason which adds interest to such an investigation. His negative attitude in matters of international law is to all appearance so pronounced that the student acquainted with the little ways of his method is inclined to suspect some hitch lurking in the background. Spinoza was a thinker who, it may seem, found delight in not leading his reader straight to the point. He wrote the *Tractatus Theologico-Politicus* with the avowed object of vindicating the ideals of political freedom and religious toleration, but he did it with such an acumen that the chief task imposed subsequently upon his commentators was to prove that the treatise was not a plea for despotism.[1] His political theory is to a large extent based on the identification of power with right, and, consequently, on conceding to the State a measure of authority over the citizen which is co-extensive with its power – a very doubtful way to establish the principles of freedom. It is only a subtle turn that saves the cause which he champions from being condemned out of his own mouth. The State's power, he says, and accordingly its rights, are limited by the nature of its commands. The State cannot, and therefore has not the right to, enact laws the enforcement of which entirely escapes its control. The success of his thesis was thus made to hinge on a dialectical device which, upon analysis, proves highly deficient in convincing power and utterly meaningless as a rule of action. For an attempt on the part of the governed to give, if need be, effect to this principle, is, according to Spinoza, a revolutionary act of war and of return to the state of nature – an act which he is all but eager to advise. And yet he was content to let his main contention rest on a foundation as frail as that. Is it probable that also with regard to what he said on relations between States there should be only one step between a mischievous idea and a constructive approach to a solution of the problem? Spinoza never expressly made this final step, but it will be of more than passing interest to inquire exactly how far he went in the right direction.

2

Three main features may be distinguished in Spinoza's doctrine of international relations. The first is the broad assertion that the mutual condition of States is that of the state of nature with all its implications. The second is the special emphasis laid upon one of the incidents of the state of nature, namely, upon the absence of any

[1] See, e.g., Pollock, *Spinoza, His Life and Philosophy* (2nd ed. 1912), p. 292.

obligation to observe treaties. The third is the clear formulation of that set of ideas which is commonly given the name of 'reason of State': the notion that the State in its dealings with its neighbours is not bound by the canons of morality and good faith observed either between the individuals who compose it, or between itself as the Government and its own subjects.

The state of nature

The necessity of preserving their existence and promoting their welfare forces men to abandon the state of nature and to establish, through the social contract, the reign of law in the form of a civil government. This, however, does not abolish the state of nature altogether; it only shifts it to a higher plane, so to speak. For as in the state of nature the right of the individual is co-extensive with his power, so also is that of the civil government thus established. In fact it could not be otherwise considering that what really has taken place is that from the numerous individual units of the state of nature one huge unit of the state of nature has been created.

The right of the supreme Government is nothing else than the right of nature, which is determined not by the power of each individual, but by that of the multitude, guided, as it were, by one mind; that is as each individual in the state of nature, so likewise the body and mind of the commonwealth have just so much right as they have power.[1]

States are now typical specimens of units living in the state of nature. Here, however, the analogy stops. There is apparently no need for those aggregates of men to unite in order to ward off dangers, to dispel fear and to co-operate for common purposes. Spinoza feels here that he ought to explain why that should be so, and he does it by pointing out that the State is able to guard itself from oppression by its neighbours, which men in the state of nature cannot do, weighed as they are daily by sleep, suffering from disease and old age, and liable to other natural troubles from which the State rests immune.[2] Having thus answered the most embarrassing question, he is not slow to draw the necessary conclusions. States being in the state of nature and retaining all rights of the state of nature, they are mutual enemies. Hence the unlimited right of war and conquest, accompanied if necessary by the total destruction of the settlements of the defeated adversary and by the transplantation of the inhabitants to the territory of the victor.[3] 'If', he says, 'one State wishes to bring

[1] *P.*, ch. iii, 2. [2] *P.*, ch. iii, 11. [3] *P.*, ch. vi, 35; ch. ix, 13.

war on another State and resorts to extreme means to bring it under its jurisdiction, it can by right do so since it needs but the bare will of the commonwealth for war to be waged.'[1] This does not necessarily mean that there obtains a permanent condition of actual hostilities between nations. For they may conclude agreements which for a time constitute the basis of their mutual relations. But, again, however numerous and enduring, such compacts form in principle an exception to the natural state of enmity. And, as we shall see presently, they are of a highly precarious nature.

The obligation of treaties

The treaty, urges Spinoza, lasts so long as the cause which produced it. When this inducement disappears, there is a perfect right, vested in either contracting party to disengage itself from the obligation.[2] For in the state of nature it is clearly understood by both parties from the very beginning that fear of a threatened injury or hope of gain are the bases, and the sole bases, of contractual relations. In addition – and here we have what appears to be perhaps the first modern formulation of the *clausula rebus sic stantibus* in international law – 'no one makes a contract for the future except on the hypothesis of certain preceding circumstances. But when these change, the reason underlying the whole position also changes; accordingly every contracting party retains the right to consult its own interests.' Curiously enough he found it advisable – quite unnecessarily from the point of view of the formal requirements of his method – to prove the compatibility of this principle with ethical and religious considerations. In the *Tractatus Politicus* he appeals to reason and religion in support of the assertion that the obligation to keep promises is not an absolute one. Thus, he says, faith need not be kept with a thief who has entrusted stolen property to another man's custody.[3] In the *Tractatus Theologico-Politicus* he invoked *pietatem et religionem* in aid of the same contention. It would be nothing short of a crime if the ruler insisted on observing promises injurious to his subjects; he must not break faith with those who have entrusted their welfare to him. We are thus brought face to face with the third canon of his international doctrine, namely, with the principle known as 'reason of State'.

'Reason of State'

The State is not altogether without moral obligations. If it has none towards its neighbours, it certainly has distinct duties as regards the

[1] *P.*, ch. iii, 11. [2] *T.P.*, ch. xvi; *P.*, ch. iii, 14. [3] *P.*, ch. iii, 17.

individuals who compose it, or rather as regards itself in the capacity of guardian of the interests of those who have confided themselves to its care. There is indeed a law, which governs it to the exclusion of all other considerations: the prosperity of its own Government. *Imperii salus summa lex.* A State – says Spinoza – which expects its neighbours to abide by a treaty that has ceased to be advantageous, expects it to do a thing which is not only foolish, but also dishonest because involving a breach of the original and implied contract made with its own subjects.[1] This is a typical exposition of 'reason of State', a principle which, while affirming obligations of faith and duty in one sphere of action, deems it possible and necessary to exclude them from another.[2]

3

It is of importance to note at this stage that, just as Spinoza's political theory is deeply rooted in that of Hobbes, so also are his views on international relations. Hobbes's real teaching on this subject is obscured by his occasional identification of the Law of Nations with the law of nature,[3] a circumstance which led some writers to regard him as a precursor of Pufendorf in the naturalistic affirmation of the Law of Nations. As a matter of fact, however, his law of nature as applied to States is not a law at all in the sense of a legal or moral precept. It is a right of nature, *jus naturale*, i.e. 'the liberty each man hath to use his own power, as he will himself, for the preservation of his nature . . . and of doing anything which in his own judgment and reason he shall conceive to be the aptest means thereto'.[4] The true meaning of this right of nature as applied to States is fittingly illustrated by what he understood to be the state of nature in which States are placed. It is a state of war. We remember the picturesque passage in the *Leviathan* in which he refers to the condition of States which 'because of their independence, are in continual jealousies and in the state and posture of gladiators having their weapons pointed and their eyes fixed on one another, which is the posture of war'.[5] The same trend of thought is given eloquent expression in several passages of the *De Cive*.

The state of independent Governments with respect to one another is a state of nature, that is of hostility. Nor, if they cease to fight, is it therefore

[1] *P.*, ch. iii, 14.

[2] On this aspect of Spinoza's teaching cf. Meinecke, *Die Idee der Staatsräson* (1924), pp. 270–80.

[3] *Leviathan*, ch. xxx.

[4] *Ibid.* ch. xvi. This is in contradistinction to what he calls the law of nature, *lex naturalis*, which is a binding precept of law and reason, but which he does not apply to relations between States.

[5] *Leviathan*, ch. xiii (*in fine*).

to be called peace, but a breathing time; in which each adversary, watching the motions and countenances of the other, judges his security, not from compacts, but from the force and councils of his adversary.[1]

'Not from compacts', for covenants of mutual faith made in the state of nature are – with one solitary and truly Hobbesian exception[2] – vain and invalid. There is no obligation of faith in relations between nations.[3]

On all these points Spinoza follows Hobbes very closely. The differences between them are mainly formal. To Hobbes, who was preoccupied, to the exclusion of all other considerations, with proving a very difficult thesis, the question of relations between States was one to be dealt with for the purpose of illustration and ingenious argument. To Spinoza it was an independent part of his system, and he dealt with it more fully. Secondly, Hobbes, for a very good reason of his own, conceived of the state of nature as a truly horrible condition of incessant physical fear, if not of actual war – an urgent inducement to form a State under quite specific stipulations. Spinoza's conception of the state of nature prevailing between individuals, although similar in kind, differed from it in degree. The life of the individuals thus placed is indeed an 'almost brutish' one, but their wretchedness is not one of wild terror, only, it seems, of impossibility of peaceful development for higher human purposes. This conception of the state of nature gave him thus the advantage of a less pessimistic and more constructive approach to the problem. The gulf between the state of nature as understood by him and the idea of a community of nations under the reign of law was not so wide as to convert the latter into a Utopia unrelated to facts. However, before discussing the advance made by him on Hobbes, it is necessary to inquire in what do the shortcomings of his own teaching consist.

4

Throughout his treatment of the problem under discussion, Spinoza is at pains to apply to the relations of States the principles which stood the test so well in the case of individuals. One gains the impression that he is merely copying himself without taking the trouble to alter words. What, for instance, he says on the continued validity of treaties is nothing else than a well-nigh literal repetition

[1] Ch. xiii, 7; see also ch. x, 7.

[2] Promises extorted by fear are, according to him, binding, for otherwise 'promises which reduced men to civil life . . . might likewise be of none effect' (*De Cive*, ch. ii, 12, 16).

[3] *Ibid.* ch. ii, 11.

of the views previously expressed on the binding force of contracts in the state of nature, including the hypothetical contract establishing the civil government.[1] Examples of this kind could be multiplied at will. However, he breaks off the chain of analogy at the most vital point. In dealing with the individual man he was not content to limit himself to his conception of natural right as identical with *potentia*. There is another law, the law of reason, the rational principle of human welfare, which is altogether different from and frequently opposed to the right of nature. The latter, he says, prohibits nothing except what no one desires or no one can obtain, but it does not prohibit strife and hatred. But reason, human reason, whose supreme command is peace and by which nature as a whole is not bound – man is only 'one atom' in the eternal order of creation – abhors them.[2] And yet it is this law of reason which is the dynamic and truly creative element in Spinoza's political theory. Man must be compelled to live according to dictates of reason if he does not do so by his free will.[3] The principle of reason is the guiding motive of the two treatises. It is throughout a command of the conscious human will led by a conception of definite ends, and on its account Spinoza is not content to accept the State as it is, but searches after the *good* State. The man is free who lives, not according to the right of nature, but according to reason. And it is liberty achieved through obedience to reason which is the ultimate object of the State.[4] However, all this is thrown to the winds when he comes to deal with relations between States. The law of reason retires to the background; the *jus naturae* asserts itself unfettered and undisturbed. Few statements are, in this connection, more open to question than that which explains the unsatisfactory results of his international doctrine by the circumstance that he applied here the same principle as he did in his political theory.[5] The very opposite is the case. A fatalistic determinism here took the place of his reliance upon the power of reason. Why should not the same motive which prompts men to live under the reign of law apply to whole nations? Are not the perils which beset them equally great? The function of the law, says Spinoza, is to protect the individual before his lower self. Are States less in need of such protection? Are collective passions less strong or less dangerous? And is not, with collective units, the teaching of experience less productive of results? There is no attempt on Spinoza's part to deal

[1] Cf. *P.*, ch. ii, 12, and the respective passage of *T.P.*, ch. xvi.
[2] *P.*, ch. ii, 8; *T.P.*, ch. xvi. [3] *P.*, ch. xi, 3. [4] *P.*, ch. ii, 11.
[5] Vaughan, *Studies in the History of Political Philosophy* (1925), I, 82.

with these matters in a manner worthy of the magnitude of the problem. The only approach to an explanation is contained in the paragraph, already mentioned, of the *Tractatus Politicus* with which he opens his discussion of international relations. The State is self-sufficient; it can defend itself from oppression whereas the individual labouring under physical disabilities and infirmities cannot. This reasoning is, of course, grossly naïve. The possible range of physical inequality – and that is what mainly matters in the state of nature – is incomparably greater between States than between individuals where intellectual superiority may counterbalance physical prowess. In the mere state of nature, no amount of foresight, good government, or sacrifice can save a small State from the clutches of a powerful neighbour should the latter wish to annihilate it. The inducement to leave the state of lawlessness is here, in the long run, not smaller than in the case of individuals.

No doubt, explanations might be forthcoming as to why Spinoza stopped short of what seems to be the natural consummation of his argument. The foremost of them would be the fact that the political condition of Europe in the seventeenth century was not such as to bring home to him the feasibility of a juridical organization of States, and that the signs of an order emerging with the Westphalian Treaty from the state of general disorder were still of a rudimentary and problematic nature. The fate of his own country at the time when he wrote the *Tractatus Politicus* was to him a telling example of the remoteness of the *civitas maxima*. It is also possible that with him, as with Hobbes, the picture of nations living in an anarchical state of nature was resorted to for the purpose both of emphasizing the absolute character of State sovereignty – international law has frequently been used as a scapegoat in this manner – and of providing an illustration of the consequences involved in the dissolution of the bond of the civil State. But these explanations cannot do away with the fact that the master's hand lost its cunning when he set himself to deal with relations between States.[1] The breadth of vision of the pantheistic thinker who embraced the universe here narrowed down to the frontiers of a single State, and the principle of expediency which animates his political theory was jettisoned. The fault lay not in this principle, but in Spinoza's failure to extend it beyond the State. And it would be equally off the mark to maintain that his

[1] Suarez (*De Legibus ac Deo Legislatore*) wrote in 1612 on the necessary interdependence of States and on the consequent restriction of national sovereignty in a manner that would do honour to a most advanced modern believer in the League of Nations.

avowed business was to take things as they are and not as they ought to be. His avowed business was *to draw conclusions* from things as they are, and this he did to excellent purpose in his political theory. He failed to do it in the field of international relations, and thus gave to a necessarily transient state of imperfection the character of finality.

Neither is it possible to regard his refusal to acknowledge the binding force of treaties as something other than a consistent application of the view that there is no law above or between States. It is difficult to follow those jurists and political writers who deem it necessary to emphasize their admiration for the great thinker by defending as inherently accurate this aspect of his doctrine.[1] They point out that neither law nor equity make it an unbreakable rule that promises should be kept at all costs. This is certainly true, but it is irrelevant so far as Spinoza's conception of the *clausula rebus sic stantibus* is concerned. For what he taught was that no compacts need be kept unless they continue to be advantageous. This is a very different proposition from the view that it is not always right or fair or permissible to exact the fulfilment of a contract. It is the very essence of the law of contract that it compels a party to fulfil the obligation also after it has ceased to be interested in the maintenance of the *vinculum juris*. To maintain, as does Spinoza, that the contract is valid so long as the will, prompted by the hope of gain, lasts, is to proclaim that the contract is not binding at all. It is a hopeless task to defend such a proposition as a rule of law or equity. Its author himself did not view it as such; it was to him one of the incidents of the law of nature, i.e. of the absence of law between nations. In fact, in so far as the application of the *clausula* is dependent upon the discretionary will of one of the parties, its essence is illegality, and such elements of right and justice as it may otherwise contain are necessarily ineffective. It has never been recognized as a rule of positive international law, although it may become so when resorted to by an authoritative judicial tribunal applying generally recognized principles of law and intent upon giving effect either to the will of the parties or to higher considerations of the common international good. But this Spinoza did not think.

5

However disappointing may be the sudden turn which diverted a promising trend of Spinoza's argument to a passive recognition of a

[1] Sir Frederick Pollock in *Chronicon Spinozanum*, I (1921), 48; Vaughan, *Studies*, pp. 83, 84.

state of anarchy between nations, there are several elements in his teaching which lessen considerably the criticism directed against it.

In the first instance, the fact – already referred to – should be noted that he travelled almost the whole distance along the road which he finally abandoned, fascinated by the assumed self-sufficiency and majesty of the State. It is impossible to read and to understand the crucial paragraphs of the third chapter of the *Tractatus Politicus* without being struck by the almost pathetic vacillation between the purely Hobbesian conception of international relations and the idea of a comprehensive federation of states as the most efficacious means of securing peace. This in fact is a significant advance made in the *Tractatus Politicus*, written at the close of his days, upon the *Tractatus Theologico-Politicus*. We see here repeated attempts on his part to avail himself of the same fruitful line of thought which was of decisive merit in his plea for the establishment of a civil society. The natural right of man, he says, so long as its realization rests upon the individual in the natural state of isolation, is of a mere conceptual character. It consists *magis opinione quam re*. Only through a combination of powers, otherwise rendered nugatory by fear, can the natural right be realized.[1] 'If two come together and unite their strength, they have jointly more power, and consequently more right, over nature than both of them separately, and the more there are that have so joined in an alliance, the more right they all collectively possess.'[2] He applies exactly the same principle to States: 'We cannot at all doubt that if two States are willing to offer each other mutual help, both together are more powerful, and therefore have more right than either alone.'[3] Fear being the great destroyer of might and right, 'the more commonwealths there are which have contracted a joint treaty of peace, the less each of them is an object of fear to the remainder'.[4] We feel that he has traversed the whole road, and that what was left was to draw the conclusion which he had just drawn in the analogous case of individuals. Instead, doubts of an altogether different order arise to obscure the argument and shift the issue. Such an alliance, he says, makes the State less *sui juris* because more dependent on others for the preservation of its rights; it diminishes its faculty to go to war; it binds it to observe the conditions of peace and to submit itself to the joint will of the confederates. Unfortunately he leaves us quite in the dark as to his final opinion on the subject. Are these restrictions of national sovereignty following upon comprehensive treaties of alliance such as to render their con-

[1] *P.*, ch. ii, 18. [2] *P.*, ch. ii, 13. [3] *P.*, ch. iii, 12. [4] *P.*, ch. iii, 16.

clusion dangerous or undesirable? Or are these drawbacks merged in the higher advantage accruing from such additional security? He is non-committal and refrains from stating that this dependence is only provisional and, according to his own argument, the fundamental condition of the realization of a more valuable right. And it seems that he is unwilling to say it, considering that the insistence on the precarious nature of treaties of alliance thus concluded dominates the whole argument. But it is apparent at the same time that he is wrestling to find a new approach to the problem.

These considerations suggest also that it would be a mistake to identify his general attitude with one of glorification of war. The necessity for peace is the starting-point and the regulative principle of his political system *pro foro interno*; to it he is occasionally prepared to sacrifice the ultimate aim of the civil society, namely, the liberty of the subject. It would be strange if the internal peace thus secured were to be frustrated by continuous war coming from outside. In fact, Spinoza is constantly in search of safeguards against the dangers of war. A democratic form of government is one remedy;[1] the abolition of paid armies another.[2] And we find in the *Tractatus Politicus* a detailed plan designed to enhance the chances of peace in an aristocratically governed community. He proposes that the senators be awarded a hundredth or a fiftieth part of the total value of the imports and exports as an inducement to preserve peace and not to protract war. For the foreign trade during war being reduced to a minimum, the senators will naturally feel inclined to diminish the evils of war. The possible objection that such a tax would constitute too great a burden upon the citizen, Spinoza meets with the argument that 'peace cannot be bought at too great a price'.[3]

This pronounced affirmation of the necessity for peace seems also to suggest that, however strongly worded his conception of the *clausula* may have been in theory, his view on the relations between States was not one of Governments breaking their engagements at the slightest provocation. For if, by hypothesis, the state of war is the only alternative to a condition regulated by treaty, it is not to be supposed that indiscriminate violation of treaties was regarded by him as a normal course of action. In addition, the passages in the two treatises in which he sets forth his views on the question of the binding force of treaties convey the impression that the treaties to

[1] *P.*, ch. vi, 10, 31; ch. vii, 12, 17, 22, 28.
[2] *T.P.*, ch. xviii; *P.*, ch. vii, 5.
[3] *P.*, ch. viii, 31. See also *P.*, ch. vii, 7.

which he refers are political conventions in the strict meaning of the word, namely, treaties of peace and alliance. There is as a matter of strict law no reason for making distinctions between this type of convention and others. Nevertheless their position has ever since been regarded as a peculiar one, and many writers who put the rule *pacta sunt servanda* in the foreground of international law think it necessary to make an exception in point of alliances.[1] Thus, if it is alliances which he had in mind, then, except for the poignancy of the statement, there is not much to choose between him and no less a person than Grotius.[2] Moreover, quite apart from treaties of alliance, the father of international law himself gave to the *clausula* a blessing more hesitating in form than in substance. (It is of interest to note here the similarity of the instances quoted in this connection by Grotius and Spinoza. Both refer to deposits which need not in certain circumstances be returned.[3] This similarity may be accidental but, if it is not, it throws some light on the controverted question of Spinoza's acquaintance with the writings of Grotius.)[4]

6

It was inevitable that Spinoza's influence should rest not on the hesitating undercurrent which we have been tracing, but on the apparent content of his teaching. Accordingly he was more than once drawn upon by those who either denied international law, or attempted to introduce into it disintegrating elements in the form of a vague and comprehensive *clausula rebus sic stantibus* or 'reason of State'. Pufendorf may be referred to here as an instructive instance. Stripped of its contradictions and of its meaningless appeals to generosity, Pufendorf's statement on the binding force of treaties strikingly resembles that of Spinoza: He does not expressly mention him in this connection, although elsewhere he criticizes his political doctrine in scathing terms.[5] The main points of his discussion of the subject are the same as those dealt with by Spinoza. There is the same insistence upon the obligation ceasing to be binding if found inconsistent with the interests of the State, and upon the precedence of the sovereign's duty to his subjects to whom he is bound by the

[1] See, e.g., Lammasch, *Das Völkerrecht nach dem Kriege* (1917), pp. 159–71.

[2] *De Jure Belli ac Pacis*, book II, ch. XXV, § 4. He maintains here, *inter alia*, that an ally is not bound to render assistance if the common effort is not likely to be crowned with success. See also book II, ch. XVI, § 27 (1).

[3] Grotius, book II, ch. XXVI, § 25 (2); *P.*, ch. iii, 17.

[4] Cf. here Sir Frederick Pollock in *Chronicon Spinozanum*, I (1921), pp. 47, 48.

[5] Pufendorf, book II, ch. ii, § 3; book III, ch. iv, § 4.

original promise embodied in the social contract. Like Spinoza he points out that a limitation of this kind is implied in every promise of aid and assistance, and that an ally who puts his faith in a treaty which is not equally advantageous to the other contracting party is a fool and has himself to blame for his improvidence.[1] The trend of reasoning and the very terms employed in this connection by Pufendorf and Spinoza are so similar that the latter's direct influence does not appear to be a matter of pure conjecture.[2]

It is probable that the general influence exercised in this respect by Spinoza was that of having imparted to some of the doctrines of Machiavelli the authority and detachment of an imposing philosophical system. The development of certain political doctrines in Germany in the first half of the nineteenth century provides a good example of this process. The student of the history of 'reason of State' and of its bearing on the science of international law will notice, not without interest, that men like Herder, Fichte and Hegel were admirers of both Spinoza and Machiavelli. This may be a coincidence, but it is highly probable that it is not. They all saw in the Italian writer, not the great challenger of morality in the domain of man's collective action, but the patriot offering to a prince of divided Italy wise counsels on how to save the fatherland. In contemporaneous Germany they saw a sad analogy with the State of Italy in Machiavelli's time, and longed for men and principles able to promote their country's liberation from the yoke of the oppressor and from internal dissension. However, an abnormal political

[1] Pufendorf, book VIII, ch. vi, § 14, ch. ix, § 5.

[2] That, on the other hand, Spinoza's parallel line of reasoning envisaging a comprehensive confederation of States might not have passed altogether unnoticed, is rendered probable by the study of those writings of Kant and Rousseau in which they deal with international law and the problem of eternal peace. Kant does not refer here directly to Spinoza. Yet it is sufficient to compare the relevant chapter in *Metaphysical Principles of the Science of Law* (1797, para. 54) – it is entitled 'The Elements of International Law' – in order to note how both deal in the same manner with the same questions. Kant, like Spinoza, emphasizes that States are by nature in a non-juridical condition; that this condition is a state of war in which the right of the stronger prevails; that an alliance is an adequate means for mutual protection, and that the federation thus created is revocable on any occasion. There is one fundamental difference between them, inasmuch as Kant took the step which Spinoza shrank from taking. This natural position of potential war, says Kant, is wrong in itself in the highest degree, and States are mutually under the obligation to pass out of it. It will also be observed that Kant too attaches considerable importance to the abolition of standing armies and to a republican form of government as guarantees of peace.

Rousseau, *A lasting Peace through the Federation of Europe* (1756), and his plan of a confederation are obviously based on the proposals of Abbé de Saint-Pierre, but those passages of the essay (see p. 47 of Vaughan's transl. of 1915) in which he speaks of the natural state of war between nations, of treaties constituting only a provisional truce and changing with the change of circumstances, again bring to mind the corresponding passages of the *Tractatus Politicus*.

situation would have been hardly sufficient to secure general acceptance for doctrines which even Frederick II deemed it necessary to refute page by page and sentence by sentence. It was necessary to show that the Machiavellian teaching was not a bundle of cynical statements and ingenious devices concocted in order to ensure success in doubtful enterprises, but one of the consequences of an organic theory of the State. The probability that it was Spinoza's teaching that did much to lift the odium resting on Machiavelli cannot be lightly dismissed.

Of all these writers – perhaps of *all* political and philosophical writers – Hegel's influence on the theory of international law is by far the profoundest and the most clearly demonstrable. Bodin's theory of sovereignty had left unimpaired the State's subjection to the higher rule of the law of nature and nations. Hobbes's teaching on international relations remained on the whole without influence, and so far as it was noticed it was effectively dealt with in the numerous 'refutations of Mr Hobbes'.[1] But Hegel's theory of sovereignty and of the supremacy of the State has become for many writers the starting-point for their exposition of international law. It is therefore not without significance that Hegel was within the circle of men to whom Spinoza was all but unknown. That he was conversant with Spinoza's writings is amply confirmed both by his enthusiastic acknowledgement of Spinoza's place in philosophy, and by his casual disparagement of his doctrine. The differences between the political systems of Spinoza and Hegel are no doubt profound, but they are not productive of any such practical consequences as is the idea which is common to both, namely, the identification of right and power as the basis of the State.[2] Hegel's saying, 'the real is the rational, and the rational the real', is only another formulation of Spinoza's conception of the *jus naturale*. In no part of Hegel's writings is this affinity of views more striking than where he deals with relations between States. Consider, for instance, the well-known passages in his *Philosophy of Right* which bear the title 'International Law'. Freed of their cumbersome language, they read like a paraphrased version the of corresponding passages of the *Tractus Politicus*. We find here the same conception of States as being in the state of nature;

[1] Cf. here especially Cumberland's *A Treatise on the Law of Nature* (1672); Maxwell's translation appeared in 1727, where in paras. 54 and 55 of the fifth chapter, after an exhaustive analysis, the international doctrines of Hobbes are described as conducive to 'the greatest inconvenience of mankind', as contrary to experience and altogether monstrous.

[2] Cf. here Heller, *Hegel und der nationale Machtstaatsgedanke in Deutschland* (1921), pp. 54–67.

the same statement – after lip-service has duly been paid to the proposition that the rule *pacta sunt servanda* is the basis of international law – that, States not acknowledging a superior power over them, the obligation to observe treaties is a purely formal one, adapting itself to the changed circumstances and resulting, if need be, in the total voidance of the treaty;[1] and, finally, the opinion that, in default of an agreement of the particular wills of the interested States, a dispute between them can be settled by war only.[2]

Hegel was following in this respect the lead given by Fichte, the man who first attempted the task of incorporating the idea of *Machtstaat* in the working moral order of the universe, and who in his essay entitled 'Machiavelli as a Writer' has done much to complete the task, begun by Herder, of vindicating Machiavelli in Germany. Here again the decisive argument bears a striking resemblance to the third chapter of the *Tractatus Politicus*. At the same time the fact must be borne in mind that Fichte also belonged to the group of men with whom Spinoza's influence gradually superseded that of Kant. It is, of course, difficult, in the absence of direct reference to Spinoza's political writings,[3] to claim for this and similar instances of his influence a degree of cogency which is not warranted by irrebuttable evidence. But it is submitted that as a result of a comparison between the corresponding passages – a task which reasons of space do not allow me to attempt here – the element of doubt is considerably reduced. This may also be said of Rosin's scholarly and guarded essay[4] on Spinoza's influence over Bismarck, the man whose recourse to Machiavelli's methods in the welding of a great Empire left a visible impress upon the development of international relations during the fifty years preceding the World War. But the influence of the conception of international relations and sovereignty as propounded by Fichte and Hegel was not restricted to Germany, although it found ready acceptance there. Its spirit underlies to a large extent the international law of the nineteenth and twentieth centuries. Spinoza's indirect part in this development does not, in the light of the preceding observations, appear to be altogether negligible. This is well illustrated by the

[1] § 333. [2] § 339.

[3] Such direct reference to Spinoza will be found in the well-known monograph of Lasson, *Prinzip und Zukunft des Völkerrechts* (1871), pp. 152, 153. He was a convinced denier of international law. See also Menzel in *Schmoller's Jahrbuch*, 31 (1907) (ii), 45 *et seq.*, on Spinoza's influence on Seydel and other prominent German jurists whose attitude towards international law was a negative one.

[4] 'Bismarck und Spinoza', in *Festschrift für Otto Gierke* (1911), pp. 383–420.

manner in which Bernard Bosanquet, one of the leading exponents of English idealistic philosophy, who in his *Philosophical Theory of the State*[1] voiced with almost convincing eloquence the Hegelian principle of the absence of law between States, reminded his readers that this Machiavellian principle has in its support the great authority of Spinoza.

7

It is not necessary to summarize here in the usual manner the conclusions reached in the preceding sections of this article. Only one fact should, it is believed, be specially referred to; a fact which explains why Spinoza, of all men,[2] should have lent himself to preaching the doctrine of lawlessness in the relations of States. The inclinations of his personal life; the importance he attached to the necessity of securing peace as the primary task of Governments; the spirit of formal unity which pervades his work – all these factors pointed to a different solution. The explanation, as we have seen, is that he failed to apply to international relations the principles of the method of which he and Hobbes were the precursors, if not the founders, and which under the influence of men like Bentham on the one hand, and of the historical school on the other, gained in the nineteenth century general recognition. It is the method of dealing with human relationships on a rational basis and by means of inductive inquiry. This does not mean that the science of man thus conceived abdicates the function of consciously promoting social ends, or that man is to it no more than a lifeless object of nature. It means only that it is content to be judged by the standards of scientific method; that it is intolerant of contradictions within the systematic exposition of the subject; that it avoids unnecessary fictions and personifications. For a variety of reasons this manner of treatment has so far been only imperfectly applied to that aspect of social life which is embraced by relations of independent States. The theory of international law still operates with the conception of a plurality of States of which every one is the highest; with the idea of rights not grounded in an objectively binding rule of law; with the doctrine of duties addressed, not to human beings, but to impersonal, although personified, States; with the assumption that States are self-sufficient.

[1] (3rd ed. 1920), Preface, p. xiv. Similar is the attitude of Duff, *Spinoza's Political and Ethical Philosophy* (1903), pp. 457–61.

[2] Hallam, *Introduction to the Literature of Europe* (5th ed. 1885), IV, ch. iv, § 76, who expresses indignant disapproval of Spinoza's international doctrine, refers to him as a virtuous and benevolent man, and comments on the slight connection between theoretical principles and personal conduct.

It is now generally admitted that these and similar notions are unable to bear the test of critical examination from the point of view of either juridical logic or economic facts or cultural needs. And yet they are firmly embedded in the theory of international law, and influence constantly the actions of Governments. It is therefore not merely of historical interest to investigate how far this state of affairs is a heritage from writers like Hobbes and Spinoza, who, while laying the foundations for the scientific study of human society, refrained from applying it to international relations. In the present article an attempt has been made to show how this elimination of the inductive method and of the principle of expediency worked in Spinoza's mind, and how it was unsuccessfully opposed by a more constructive line of thought.

CHAPTER 14

WESTLAKE AND PRESENT DAY INTERNATIONAL LAW

Editor's note This chapter appeared in *Economica*, vol. 5 (November 1925), at pp. 307–25. It was Lauterpacht's first article published in English, two years after his arrival in England and making his first spoken acquaintance with the language. (See the recollections of Lord McNair in the *International and Comparative Law Quarterly*, 10 (1961), 5.) The original typescript of the article, found amongst Lauterpacht's papers, bears a note in his hand: 'Typescript of my first article, kindly corrected by O. H. Mootham, printed in *Economica*'. Mootham, then a young research student at the London School of Economics, later achieved distinction as a judge in India and was for six years Chief Justice of Allahabad.

If events have justified Hall's gloomy prediction that the next great war would reveal the weakness of many rules of international law, it may be said that the other part of his prophecy, that this 'will be followed by a reaction towards increased stringency of law',[1] is now being fulfilled. This is true not only with regard to that part of international law which aims at the limitation of the hitherto unrestricted right to go to war and at the gradual enlargement of the scope of judicial settlement of international disputes.[2] Whatever the character of the League of Nations may be, supernational or international, and whatever its imperfections, the overwhelming majority of States has now, through it, embarked upon an attempt at some kind of international government. The pre-war institutions and organs of international co-operation have been revived, almost in their entirety, and their number enlarged by new conventions providing for economic and cultural co-operation. Both in Europe and in America the tendencies towards the codification of international law, so frequently shelved both by the friends and the enemies of a legal

[1] Hall, Preface to the 3rd edition.

[2] It is, perhaps, not sufficiently realized how radical is the change brought about in this respect by the Covenant of the League, especially by Articles 10–17. Cf. Baker, *The Geneva Protocol* (1924), p. 27. Although the Protocol has fallen to the ground, there is no doubt that that part of it which forbids a war of aggression is expressive of a growing rule of international law. The Assembly of 1925 reaffirmed, by a unanimous resolution, the principle that a war of aggression is an international crime.

ordering of interstate relations, seem at last to enter into a phase of gradual realization.[1] Together with these changes in conventional international law there goes a searching investigation into the problems of its theoretical foundations; the problems of sovereignty, of its subjects, and of its sources. I purposely use the expression 'theoretical', although the student acquainted with the history of international relations in the last hundred years will deny that these problems are purely of such a character; on the contrary, he will insist that they have shaped in detail not only legal theories but also, in the last resort, political events. But be it as it may, it is evident that there is a move in the ranks of international lawyers towards creative activity in terms of the urgent needs of the international society. International law is no longer a servile *ancilla regnorum* registering the practice of States and supplying a scientific justification of the dogma of sovereignty. This changed attitude, furthered no doubt by the general trend of legal philosophy, slowly eliminating the exclusive domination of the analytical and historical method, is due largely to important modifications in post-war international society. International lawyers cannot help being influenced by these facts. There is indeed every indication that they are now determined in their turn to influence events.

It is perhaps not inappropriate, in view of these changes, to venture a modest attempt at restating the principles of the teaching of one whom some regard as 'England's greatest international scholar',[2] and who, at any rate, is the philosopher amongst English international lawyers. Although it is true that the fine precision of Westlake's style, and the abstract manner of his exposition, render him not easily accessible, except to the expert student, he is eagerly resorted to by authors of monographs and text-books whenever an authoritative statement is sought. To bring to light his attitude to international law as a whole and to contrast it with the current tendencies of international law, is the purpose of this paper.

In February 1928 one hundred years will have elapsed since John

[1] The Fifth Assembly of the League unanimously adopted a resolution requesting the Council to convene a committee of jurists which would undertake the preparatory steps towards a codification of those parts of international law which are 'sufficiently ripe'. The Committee met at Geneva in April 1925 and selected a provisional list of subjects submitted for further consideration by eleven sub-committees. (See the Monthly Summary of the League of Nations (April 1925), p. 106.) The Governing Board of the Pan-American Union of twenty-one republics is at present engaged in the preparation of the work of a Commission composed of two representatives from each of the American republics and charged with the codification of international law, both public and private (See Garner and Scott, in *A.J.* 19 (1925), 327, 333; also Finch, *ibid.* pp. 534–42).

[2] See Gregory, in *A.J.* 8 (1914), 695.

Westlake was born. There is no reason to doubt that Cambridge will pay worthy tribute to – I am using Oppenheim's words – 'one of her most illustrious sons', and that international lawyers will celebrate in an adequate manner the memory of the jurist who occupied the Whewell chair for twenty years. This might, in part, be done by arranging for a new edition of his treatise, an edition adapted for today's use and thus rendered more useful to the student.

I

Three questions were always, and are now, in the centre of international law. There is, first, the problem of sovereignty in its different aspects: independence, equality, self-preservation – the crux of international law. There is, second, the question of the sources of international law, a problem which ten years ago seemed to be removed from the scope of useful discussion in view of the undisputed domination of the positivist method, but which now occupies international lawyers with an ever increasing intensity. There is, third, the problem of the subjects of the Law of Nations, a problem the importance of which will increase in the measure in which the scope of interests regulated by international law becomes larger. We shall discuss the three questions, comparing in each case the present state of the respective doctrines with the principles adopted by Westlake. We begin with the third problem.

The subjects of international law

The predominant doctrine is well known. It flows – says this theory – from the very conception of international law as a law between States that these only are the subjects of international law.[1] Neither individuals nor corporations other than States can ever come into direct contact with international law. Their rights, if any, grounded in international law, are not rights of international law, and their duties, if any, originating from international law, are not duties imposed by international law; these rights and duties must be *transformed* into rights and duties of municipal law in order to be enjoyed by or to be binding upon individuals. They have no *locus standi* in international law; this only States have. This is the doctrine. In the science and in the practice of international law the question occurs incessantly: the relation between international and municipal

[1] See Oppenheim, *International Law* (3rd ed. 1920), I, 18, 456–60; Hatschek, *Völkerrecht* (1923), p. 20; Anzilotti, *Corso di diritto internazionale* (1923), p. 67.

law, the position of heads of states and of diplomatic agents, the position of insurgents recognized as belligerents, of pirates, of blockade-runners, of war criminals (e.g. of commanders of submarines acting in contravention of the provisions of the Washington Conference of 1922), of private parties befoıe an international court, of individuals and associations in connection with acquisition of territory by occupation, of international unions, bureaux and commissions, of the British Dominions, of the Holy See, of the League of Nations. It is not possible to discuss here every one of these problems. Their mere existence speaks *prima facie* against the accepted doctrine which, however, while admitting that some of them constitute an exception to the general rule, apparently succeeds in explaining the other cases. For a long time its task was made easy by the fact that the only opposition challenging its reign came from a doctrine which, although inspiring by its high moral standard, must needs have remained ineffective because of the unpopular naturalist savour attaching to it. This theory sees in international law the world-embracing law of humanity conferring its benefits and protection directly upon the individual. 'Man must be considered as a person of the *civitas maxima*; as such he is a subject of law in his relations with international law,' says Fiore.[1] The ideal underlying this conception is, no doubt, high; for it postulates the vindication of the rights of human personality, the ending of a situation in which a stateless person is legally a *homo lupinus*. But, then, it is not the only ideal which the positivist doctrine brushes away by the simple statement that it is not in accordance with the practice of States.

The answer seemed so conclusive that the defeated opinion found no courage to inquire whether the opposing assertion corresponded with the facts. Had it done so, it would have found strange things. For the answer given by the positivists was *not* taken from the facts of international life. It was gained merely by way of a deduction from an arbitrary definition of international law. But instead of arriving at that conception by inquiring, in an inductive way, who is a subject of law, that is, to whom does international law grant rights, for example, the right of legation, or upon whom does it impose duties, for example, the duty of observing the laws of war, the leading writers constructed a definition into which, Procrustes-like, they endeavoured to fit actual facts. They thought – quite unnecessarily even from the positivist point of view – that if States

[1] Fiore, *Code*, no. 66; for a more recent exposition of the doctrine see Fauchille, I, part I, 210–12, and *Annuaire*, 28 (1921), 220, 221.

only create international law – which no one denies – they must remain the only subjects of international rights and duties. Ingenious reasoning is applied in order to avoid the obvious difficulties. The manner in which the theory deals with the position of the blockade-runner, of diplomatic agents, of international commissions and other international organs affords class-room examples of dialectic. But this reasoning cannot be applied in all cases, and avowed positivists are now forced to recognize as subjects of international law the League of Nations, the Dominions, the Holy See, and insurgents recognized as belligerents. It is impossible to explain away Article II of the Convention for the Establishment of a Central American Court of Justice: 'This Court shall also take cognisance of the questions which the individuals of one Central American country may raise against any of the other contracting Governments, and other cases of an international character; no matter whether their own Government supports said claim or not.'[1] Neither is it possible to ignore the fact that in some States international treaties or international custom or both become *per se* binding upon individuals and courts – without the intervention of municipal legislation. Of course, the argument that in the United States an Act of Congress may derogate from a previous treaty is quite irrelevant. It proves only that municipal courts are not competent to recognize the supremacy of a rule of international law in view of a conflicting statute.[2]

It is not surprising, therefore, that the conception, hitherto predominant, of States as the only possible subjects of international law is now being abandoned by positivist writers as being both at variance with facts of international life, and as incapable of grasping the new

[1] *A.J.* 2 (1908), Suppl. p. 231.

[2] This is also the opinion of Hyde, *International Law* (1st ed. 1922), p. 12. New light on the question – so far as the derogatory effect of a conflicting statute upon the provisions of a previous treaty is concerned – is thrown by Potter, in *A.J.* 19 (1925), 315–27. The outspoken provisions of the new German (Article 4) and Austrian (Article 9) constitutions are for themselves a clear refutation of the orthodox doctrine. As to the position in Great Britain there is no doubt that the continental positivist school (especially Triepel) succeeded in impressing upon British writers the conviction that the classical rule of international law being a part of the law of the land is no longer valid in this country. Mr Picciotto's monograph on the subject (*The Relation of International Law to the Law of England and of the United States* (1915)) is a valuable attempt at an independent treatment of the problem, although the author seems to yield much to Oppenheim's positivist influence. It will be necessary, in the future, to pay more attention to the fact that the usual 'act of transformation'—the enabling act of Parliament—fulfils here not so much the function of transformation of a rule of international law into that of municipal law, but rather that of a political ratification rendered necessary by the right of the executive to conclude a binding treaty. There is no reason why the classical English doctrine which is of fundamental importance from the point of view of the ultimate unity of international and municipal law should be removed from the field of international law.

institutions of international organization. The recent writings of Strupp and Anzilotti, the leading positivists of today, are strikingly illustrative of this change of opinion. Says Anzilotti, pointing to the uncritical attitude hitherto adopted by publicists: 'Instead of demonstrating that States *are* subjects of international law, it is being maintained that only States may become subjects of international law' – an assertion which he refuses to accept.[1] Says Strupp, with even greater clearness: 'The opinion is to be rejected that according to the conception of international law (*begrifflich*) States only can be subjects of international law. Such an opinion is the logical consequence of the wrong premise that international law is only law between States, whereas what is true is that until now States only are the organs of international legislation.'[2]

It is not possible to dwell here in detail upon the effects which this change in the doctrine is bound to produce. It is enough to bring to mind some of the subjects mentioned above in order to see that it is not only the text-books which are affected.[3] The old doctrine is to a great extent the result of an unnecessary application of that conception of sovereignty which would not suffer supreme sovereign States being put on the same level with entities of lesser value, and in especial with individuals supposed to be merged for all international purposes in the all-embracing Leviathan. But there is one aspect of the question to which, in view of our occupation with Westlake, special attention must be given: Are commands of international law addressed to impersonal sovereign States, or are the legal and moral responsibilities of international life imposed upon men of flesh and blood? It is a question which in the last resort resolves itself into the problem of the admissibility of a double morality for states and for the men of whom they are composed. And here, and last, we turn to Westlake.

Westlake admits that international law is a body of rules prevailing

[1] *Corso*, p. 67; see especially Cavaglieri, in *Rivista* (1925), 18–32, 168–87.

[2] *Grundzüage des positiven Völkerrechtes* (1923), p. 37. There are, of course, writers who still adhere to the orthodox theory. See Strisower, in *Z.ö.R.* (1924), 272–98, and Koster, in the *Bulletin Instit. Interm. Internat.*, 9 (1923), 1, who quotes a recent decision of the Swiss Federal Court (17 July 1923; *ibid.* pp. 31–51) as fully accepting the view of the predominant doctrine. Similar is the provision of Article 34 of the Statute of the Permanent Court of International Justice. But it is instructive that in the course of the discussions in the Commission of Jurists charged with the drafting of the statute international lawyers of the authority of Professor Lapradelle and Loder strongly urged the necessity of the Court being open to private parties. However, the arguments based on the principle of sovereignty prevailed. See *Proceedings of the Commission*, pp. 196 *et seq.*

[3] The question of the legal status of national minorities is here, for example, of paramount importance.

between States, but only in the meaning that *States are the authors of international law.* It would be pedantic, he says, to deny that the pirate and the blockade-runner are subjects of international law; although, he adds, 'it is only by virtue of rules prevailing between States that they are so'.[1] This view is clearly brought to light in his theory of neutrality, where he discusses the position of individuals with regard to blockade and contraband. '... To say that an individual so left to himself is incapable of interfering in a war, and that his acts can receive no legal qualification unless they are first carried up to his State and then down again to himself, is purely arbitrary.'[2]

This clear distinction, however, between the authors of international law and the subjects of international rights and duties – a distinction which it took the positivists a generation to arrive at – is for him more than a postulate of scientific exactitude. It will be observed that he defines international law as a science 'of what a State and *its subjects* ought to do, or may do, with reference to other States and their subjects'.[3] 'International law deals with all human action not internal to a political body.'[4] This is one of the main principles upon which his teaching of international law is based. It is clearly expressed in his *credo*, in the 'Introductory Lecture' in 1888 at Cambridge. He has no sympathy with those writers who, by stressing the artificial entity of the State draw a sharp distinction between the latter and its subjects.[5] He deprecates the evil influence of such a trend of thought.

> It may weaken the sense that the action of the State is the action of those within it who help to guide it...; nay, that in a lesser degree it is also the action of those who suffer the other to guide it. The influence of the same tone of thought will again be evil if it allows us to forget that not only is the action of our State that of ourselves, but that those towards whom it is taken are also men like ourselves, though they may be veiled from our eyes by the interposition of another artificial entity.

It is unusual to find in a modern leading international lawyer this insistence on personal responsibility without which 'there can be neither sound international law nor sound international politics'.[6]

This conception of men as subjects of international law is one of the most impressive parts of Westlake's teaching. Again and again are we confronted with it. Consider his attitude towards the question of the relation of individuals to war. His criticism of the famous

[1] Westlake, *Papers*, pp. 1–2.
[2] Westlake, II, 197.
[3] Westlake, *Papers*, Preface, p. xix.
[4] *Ibid.* p. 412.
[5] *Ibid.* p. 411.
[6] *Ibid.*

saying of Rousseau that 'War is not a relation of man to man but of State to State' is unsparing. 'The levity of mind displayed by such a passage is extraordinary, even for a man of Rousseau's character,' is his scathing comment.[1] He condemns 'the claim that men, acting in groups not subject to regulation by a superior, can repudiate their personal responsibility, and leave outsiders to seek their only satisfaction from the means which they have chosen to clothe the group'.[2] However, although he is explicit in pointing out that the same applies with even greater force to the modern State where the responsibility for the war can reasonably be attributed to the masses composing the States,[3] he does not go to the length of maintaining that there exists a direct active relation of war between all the individual subjects of the belligerent States. He assumes – in an analogy to private law and in agreement with the generally adopted view – a subsidiary responsibility of non-combatants. But to exclude such responsibility altogether is, to his mind, to act unreasonably and unjustly. He again expresses the same opinion while opposing the proposal to abolish the belligerents' rights at sea with regard to the enemy's mercantile flag.[4] 'In natural justice there is no power for individuals to form themselves into a group and disclaim responsibility for the actions of that group.' It is the same view which enabled him to write in a truly great manner on the Hague Conference called upon to diminish the irresponsibility of international action,[5] on the dangers of an abused plea of necessity corrupting and degrading those who urge it,[6] or on the relation between English and international law. He endeavours to bridge what is believed by some to be a chasm between international and municipal law, and he arrives in conclusion at a lucid restatement in a modern form of the old principle of international law being a part of the law of the land.[7] Among the eighteen 'Principles of international law,' the first is this: 'The society of States . . . is the most comprehensive form of society among men, but it is among men that it exists. States are its immediate, men its ultimate, members. The duties and rights of States are only the duties and rights of men who compose it.' It is to be regretted that international writers, while accepting or rejecting, as the case may be, his arguments with regard to pirates and blockade-

[1] *Ibid.* p. 266.
[2] *Ibid.*
[3] *Ibid.* p. 618.
[4] *Ibid.* p. 617.
[5] *Ibid.* p. 532. 'To bring that action under some responsibility is the object of a great cry which goes up from modern Europe, a cry based on no new spiritual vision, but wrung from suffering and fear.'
[6] *Ibid.* p. 282.
[7] *Ibid.* pp. 498–503.

runners, paid no attention to the broader aspect of his views on which I have tried to throw some light. It is well that they regard it now as compatible with the positivist doctrine to adopt the opinion to which Westlake was attaching so much importance. And it may be added that not only professional international lawyers, but also leading jurists, who work in the field of general philosophy of law and whose influence is by no means insignificant, strongly urge the same view. Duguit, Kelsen, and Krabbe may be mentioned in this connection.[1]

2. *The sources of international law*

As there is nothing in the current doctrine of sovereignty which should lead us to adopt the rule that States only are subjects of international law, so there is nothing in it which should compel us to adopt the purely positivist view in the controversy touching the sources of international law. And yet this has been done. If States are sovereign, it needs must be their will, express or tacit, and nothing else, to which rules of international law may be traced. Hence the rigid positivist formula: Only custom and treaty are sources of international law. There is no doubt that the extreme positivist view was in the ascendant in the last fifty years, and that Oppenheim's dogmatic statement to the effect that 'We know nowadays that a law of nature does not exist', and that 'Only a positive Law of Nations can be a branch of the science of law', were but a correct expression of the prevailing attitude. But it is at least doubtful whether they are true today. The 'Renascence of natural law' has found its way from legal philosophy and from municipal law into the domain of international law, where the influence of the new ideas was facilitated by the depressing consciousness, strengthened by bitter experience, of the practical inadequacy of positivist international law. Of course, it is not the old law of nature; it is rather the modern 'natural law with changing contents', 'the sense of right', 'the social solidarity', the 'engineering' law in terms of promoting the ends of the international

[1] 'International law', says Krabbe (*The Modern Idea of State*, English transl. 1919, p. 240), 'lays obligations upon those individuals or groups of individuals – judges called upon to give effect to a treaty, the legislature which must appropriate money for the execution of a treaty – who by the constitutional law of their country are entrusted with the care of the respective interests.' At the same results arrive Duguit (*Droit constitutionnel* (1921), I, 560) and Kelsen (*Der Begriff der Souveränität und die Theorie des Völkerrechtes* (1920), pp. 130–4, 162–7); the first from the standpoint of the negation of the juridical personality of the State, the second on the basis of that identification of State and law which lies at the bottom of his teaching.

society. But, be that as it may, the old dogmatic positivism is no longer expressive of the general attitude. In fact, rather is it surprising that it should have been accepted for so long a time and without serious challenge. No municipal law can, in the long run, afford to dispense altogether with sources of law other than those expressed in the terms 'custom' and statute. And if this is the case in municipal law – where the legislative machinery can as a rule be resorted to in order to fill a gap – how much more urgent is the need within the international society with its rudimentary undeveloped law, and with its heavy legislative machinery, if any. In fact, numerous arbitration treaties and awards, as well as the practice of States, prove abundantly that 'natural justice', or 'equity' or 'general principles of law' are regarded as a source of law called upon to *interpret and to supplement* existing rules of international law.[1] Also the theoretical objections raised against the positivist doctrine are by no means negligible.[2] But – I must not forget that this is a paper on Westlake.

It is sufficient, for the purpose of illustration of the present position, to refer to a recent inquiry instituted by Professor Niemeyer. In a circular letter addressed to a number of eminent international lawyers he asked for an opinion on whether the law of nature conception of international law as taught by Grotius is valid today; that is, whether it may be resorted to by international tribunals as a source of decision for the purpose of supplementing and interpreting the customary and conventional international law.[3] Now it is significant that out of forty-one answers which have so far reached the editor, only eleven were in the negative, whereas seventeen may be regarded as in the affirmative. There are, in addition, eight answers which, although adhering formally to the positivist principle, give in fact an affirmative reply to the question. Of course, such

[1] *Cf.* Koster, 'Les fondements du droit des gens', in *Bibliotheca Visseriana*, 4 (1925), 180–190; Verdross, *Die Einheit des rechtlichen Weltbildes* (1923), pp. 120–5; Castberg, in *R.G.* 32 (1925), 170; see Article 38 (3) of Statute of Permanent Court of International Justice; Article 7 of the Hague Convention concerning the creation of an International Prize Court (1907) provides: 'In the absence of such provisions the Court shall apply the rules of international law. If no generally recognized rule exists, the Court shall give judgment in accordance with the general principles of justice and equity'; see also: Article 7 of the Treaty of September 1794 between Great Britain and the United States; Article 7 of the Arbitration Agreement of August 1910 between the same countries; Article 1 of the Arbitration Agreement of February 1903 between the United States and Venezuela; the Arbitration Treaty of December 1921 between Germany and Switzerland; and Article 1 of the Arbitration Agreement of October 1922 between the United States and Norway.

[2] See Krabbe, *The Modern Idea of State*, pp. 249–69; Kelsen, *Der Begriff der Souveränität*, pp. 204–31; Nelson, *Die Rechtswissenschaft ohne Recht* (1917), *passim*.

[3] *Z.I.* (1925), pp. 113 *et seq.*

questions are not decided by being put to a vote. But these numbers are illustrative of the fact that the dogmatic positivism as advocated ten or fifteen years ago in an exaggerated application of the doctrine of sovereignty is no longer predominant. For the ayes Professor Weiss says: 'My answer is quite in the affirmative. . . . To my mind this natural law which should serve to interpret and, when necessary, to supplement the positive law, is before all identical with international morality.' For the noes Lord Phillimore says: 'It would be dangerous for international tribunals of any kind to resort to this theory in order to interpret or supplement international law actually in force, or in order to search here for new maxims of jurisprudence.' And he adds confidently: 'The field of international jurisprudence is today totally covered by positive rules.' Of the third group the answer of Professor de Louter, the author of the well-known treatise on *Positive International Law*, will be found interesting: 'Only in cases where there is no rule or where the law is silent or uncertain is it competent for the judicial authority . . . to decide upon grounds of higher justice – provided always that the source of decision is expressly mentioned.' The answer is so far quite in the affirmative. The restriction which follows is of a more technical character: 'Thus a permanent jurisprudence will gradually evolve which, however, will become law proper only through custom or treaty.'

'Custom and reason are the two sources of international law', says Westlake, adding Roman law as a subsidiary source.[1] By reason he means, first of all, the source of international law 'for the seekers of international right', as he says. It is Westlake's habit – and indeed more than habit – to invoke the idea of right underlying international law, and he has no hesitation in using the unpopular expression 'natural justice'. This is nowhere clearer than in the Introductory Lecture where he stresses the fact that 'a tolerable approximation to an embodiment of international right' is a condition of the continued validity of international law.[2]

It will be observed that he is repeatedly at pains to distinguish between juridical right and ethical right. This insistence should guard him against the possible misunderstanding that he simply identifies law and morality. But further than this his caution does not go. Custom, no doubt, is the primary evidence of what international law is, and as such is a source of international law. But in contradistinction to the habit of filling international law with fictions in order to

[1] Westlake, I, 14. [2] Westlake, *Papers*, p. 407.

preserve the positivist formula, he does not shrink from basing international law on 'natural justice', on 'the sense of right' or on the 'social nature of man' whenever the recourse to consent is unable to explain things. A new State enters the family of nations. It asks for recognition and receives it. Is it bound by the rules of international law to which it never consented? The positivists accept – by way of fiction – that in the mere request for recognition there is impliedly contained the will to be bound by the rules of existing international law. Westlake deprecates strongly this straining of interferences 'from incidents in which we may be sure that nothing of the kind was thought of when they occurred'. He sees the source of the obligation in the fact that the action of a State being the action of men who compose it 'there is not in natural justice a right for men to sink their individual responsibilities by forming associations at their free pleasure'.[1] The State is new, the masses of men are the same. We see how strongly his conception of the subjects of law influences the other parts of his teaching. He bases, for instance, the authority of the opinions of international publicists on the fact that as a rule they represent the general consent of men, their reputation proving that they represent many persons besides them.

There is, in his Introductory Lecture, a remarkable passage, in which he dwells upon the necessarily inductive method to be applied in international law. But what constitutes the elements of the inductive process? Only the external historical fact? Together with the external fact, answers Westlake, the tendency which is no less a fact, has to be taken into consideration.[2] I should like to draw special attention to this passage. The definition of the sources of rules of international law as historical events to which their establishment can be traced, is, I think, correct; but there is no reason to restrict these historical events to those only which are evidenced by acts of statesmen or written documents; the legal conviction and the sense of right of masses of men is a historical fact of no less force. No one is nearer to such a conception than Westlake.[3] As to the use of 'reason' as a subsidiary source, his answer is in the affirmative. It must be applied, says Westlake, (a) for the purpose of interpretation and extended application of rules already established; (b) international law being a rudimentary and undeveloped law, reason may supply new rules which ought to be acted on provisionally 'and

[1] Westlake, I, 49. [2] Westlake, *Papers*, p. 410.
[3] Cf. his review of Oppenheim's *International Law*, in *L.Q.R.* 21 (1905), 433.

ultimately adopted or rejected as may be determined by experience';[1] (c) as a test of the value of the existing rules.[2]

Equal independence of thought is shown by Westlake by his adoption of Roman law as a subsidiary source of international law. Roman and private law are indiscriminately rejected by the positivist doctrine as mischievous and destructive of the independent and scientific character of international law. It cannot here be pointed out in detail how much harm is being done to international law by dogmatic insistence on the fundamental difference between the two systems of law. The bonds which connect international and private law are not of a merely historical character. They are grounded in the fact that, although the subjects of legal relations in the two spheres of law are different, there is in many cases an identity or at least a close analogy of legal relations, an analogy calling for application of analogous rules. A closer investigation shows that in many cases the modern – and not only the 'patrimonial' – practice of States and of international tribunals follows this path of analogy,[3] and that, frequently, the analogous application of a principle of private law is conducive to the vindication of – if one may say so – the legal character of international law. Westlake does not share the positivist prejudices, and he himself has shown in his masterly treatment of the theory of succession how fruitful and stimulating a moderate and critical application of private law may be.

3. *The dogma of sovereignty*

It is not necessary to expatiate upon the present state of the doctrine of sovereignty. Its foes are many. It is attacked as constituting one of the main obstacles in the way of political and legal organization of the international community; as rendering abortive, through the doctrine of equality of States, every attempt at creating a working international legislation; as being logically in irreconcilable opposition to the conception of independent States with mutually limited scopes of competence; as being out of accord with the political and economic realities of international life. It is not possible to discuss here any one of these aspects, but it may safely be stated, once more, that the condition of things obtaining not so long ago, namely that

[1] Westlake, I, 15.

[2] *Ibid.*

[3] For a striking instance of this tendency see the award in the *Russian Indemnity* case (The Hague, 1910); Scott, *Hague Reports*, p. 297.

of international lawyers engaged in a systematic development of the theory of sovereignty as the basis of international law, is no longer existent. There is a growing reluctance among international lawyers to use the term at all, and although it is not to be expected that the text-books will drop it altogether, much seems to point to a development in which the conception of sovereignty will assume the meaning of a sum of rights given by international law to the State, of a scope of competence granted to it by international law. But sovereignty will lose the character of something standing fundamentally above the law,and tolerating international law only so far as it is deemed by the State to be conducive to its self-preservation and development.

The doctrine of sovereignty does not figure among Westlake's eighteen 'Principles of International Law'. He regards sovereignty, for all practical purposes, as identical with independence. And it is not independence of law, only lack of control by other States, that he has in mind. Independence is this freedom of action which is, by international law, left to the State.[1] The State is, in principle, subject to law, and no appeal to its character as State is allowed to interfere with its duty as a member of the international society. This frame of mind is clearly expressed in his attitude towards the so-called right of self-preservation. There is, according to him, no absolute right of self-preservation. Not only because it is impracticable, resulting as it does in the last resort in a clash of equal claims, there being no superior to judge the respective merits of the alleged rights;[2] and not only because the international society cannot be considered 'as having consented to an absolute right of self-preservation'.[3] It does not constitute a principle, it is rather 'a primitive instinct, and an absolute instinct so far as it has not been tamed by reason and law, but one great function of the law is to tame it . . . In principle we may not hurt another or infringe his rights, even for our self-preservation, when he has not failed in any duty towards us.' The predominant doctrine, influenced as it is by the Hegelian teaching of the absolute value of the State not amenable to moral and legal standards as obtaining between individuals, denies that this principle can be applied to States. This is not Westlake's view. The State has even less reason for pushing the right of self-preservation to an extreme. 'Although it is certainly indispensable for the welfare of

[1] Cf. Westlake, *Papers*, p. 116. He distinguishes clearly between internal and external sovereignty (Westlake, I, 20) and shows that the analogy between the two terms is mainly an historical one.

[2] Westlake, I, 307.

[3] Westlake, *Papers*, p. 113.

men that they should be associated in some State tie, it does not follow that their welfare imperatively requires the maintenance in its actual limits, and with resources entirely unimpaired, of the particular State tie in which they happen to be engaged.'[1] These words, so strikingly reminiscent of a similar passage in T. H. Green's *Principles of Political Obligation*,[2] do, I think, great honour to John Westlake. It may be added that he approves of a right of self-defence in exceptional cases expressly allowed by law.[3] But he denies that such a right is given by the mere fact of the internal growth of a neighbouring State,[4] or of the danger of contagion of revolution. 'The international society to which we belong, is not for the mutual insurance of established Governments.'[5]

He clearly admits of political action by a State when a rule of international law is wanting, or when, in the absence of a legislative authority adapting old rules to changed circumstances, the State is called upon to frame a new rule, or when a hitherto undefined 'imperfect' international rule has to be applied.[6] But he is quite emphatic in rejecting the idea that in such cases it is only the interests of the acting State which should guide its action. For even then the State acts in lieu of the international legislator – till 'the parliament of man' becomes a fact. Its actions must be within the domain of right and of distributive justice. 'When a State has to act, although a rule is wanting, it ought as far as possible so to act that a rule might be framed on the precedent.'[7]

Neither does sovereignty extend to an unrestricted right of making war. I do not know of another modern writer of authority who more approaches the letter and the spirit of Grotius's conception of *justum bellum*. It is criminal to stand aloof when unjust war is waged. 'Neutrality', says Westlake, 'is not morally justifiable unless intervention in war is unlikely to promote justice, or could do so only at a ruinous cost to the neutral', because 'the general duty of every member of society is to promote justice'.[8] 'If the tendency to this interference', he says in another place, 'died out, if even it did not increase, all hope would be at an end that a regular international tribunal could ever be established which might submit disputes to its judgments and reduce war to an affair of police against a recalcitrant

[1] Westlake, *Papers*, p. 113; Westlake, II, 194 ('Defeat in war is not necessarily inconsistent with self-preservation').

[2] P. 173.

[3] Westlake, *Papers*, pp. 115–21.

[4] *Ibid.* p. 123.

[5] *Ibid.* p. 124.

[6] Westlake, I, 300.

[7] Westlake, *Papers*, p. 79.

[8] Westlake, II, 90.

disputant.'[1] Neither does he shrink – once more in opposition to the current opinion – from recommending benevolent neutrality when justice is at stake.

4

An attempt has been made here to show that in the three questions underlying every system of international law Westlake's views are in accord with the present trend of opinion. It is submitted that the principles applied by him in order to answer these questions constitute a distinct element of progress in international law. About thirty years have elapsed since his *International Law* was written, and the supervening changes are greater than anyone could foresee. His treatise naturally requires modification. But it is only alterations in detail that are required. The structure of his system remains as solid as before, or rather stronger when compared with the new facts and opinions. For his *International Law* is written not as an illustration of the static principle of sovereignty; it is written rather in terms of a development towards an organized society of nations. 'We are in the presence of the first stages of a process which in the course of ages may lead to organized government among States, as the indispensable condition of their peace, just as organized national government has been the indispensable condition of peace between private individuals.'[2] This practical and undogmatic attitude enables him to view with equal independence such questions as that of equality of States – for which he shows no exaggerated sympathy[3] – or of the legal character of war, to which he denies the character of an institution of international law.[4] His rejection of commercial blockade may still prove a valuable point of departure.[5]

If the contents of Westlake's teaching render him supremely useful for the study of international law in its actual tendencies, there is especially one quality about him which is, I think, of value, and which will endear him to those who combine the theoretical study

[1] Westlake, *Papers*, p. 377. At a time when the international community, unanimous in declaring as unlawful the war of aggression, is striving, amidst great difficulties, to define the duties of States called upon to suppress wars of aggression, these words are of special significance.

[2] Westlake, I, 322.

[3] *Ibid.* p. 323.

[4] *Ibid.* II, 3. Nys obviously misunderstands him when he writes (*Memories*, p. 55) that 'Westlake is forced to state that in the actual phase of civilization war is a means of enforcing law.' Nothing is further from his intention.

[5] See, for example, the resolution of the *American Institute of International Law* of January 1917, demanding the total abolition of commercial blockade. It is a mistake to assume (see Oppenheim, II, 513, n. 3) that Westlake withdrew later his opposition to commercial blockades (see Westlake, *Papers*, p. 615).

of international law with the personal inclination to see the reign of law established in the international society. It may be put thus: There are even among international lawyers 'impatient pacifists' who, despairing of the realities of international life, concern themselves mainly with suggestions for the future. There are, on the other hand, writers who, while believing themselves to be giving a true account of these realities, deny the reality of international law. But there is a third type to which the majority of writers belong. They certainly share the desire to see a real development of international law, but they have, on the other hand, a full appreciation of the forces working against it. They are positivists, not because they approve of what is, but because they think that even an unsatisfactory law is better than no law at all; and that imagining what ought to be, instead of what is, is likely to damage the not yet firmly established authority of international law. Who will listen to international lawyers whose books are full of pious wishes unrelated to facts? Perhaps some day a historian of international law will arise who will write the history of this science in terms of a deep conflict in the hearts of many of its expounders. Men of broad internationalism and of best intentions striving against heavy odds to impress the character of law upon rules of conduct sometimes as different from the unstrained conception of law as a primitive society from a modern State. *Virtutem credant habere et habebunt.* Only let the international society believe that the actual rules are true law and the rest will come.

Such a work requires faith. It is with a confession of faith that Oppenheim ends his classical exposition of the positivist method. 'For ours is faith that removeth mountains . . .'[1] But this method is fraught with danger. There is always the possibility that not only will the practice of States be taken as an unquestionable rule of law, but that the philosophy underlying this practice will be regarded as a true expression of the tendencies and the possibilities of the international society. An example will illustrate this: The *civitas maxima* with a central government has certainly no place in the international law of today. But there are two ways of putting it. It is possible to say that a central political and legal organization, although far off, is the necessary goal which we are slowly approaching, and which alone will ensure the undisturbed working of an effective international law; but it may be said – to use Dean Pound's expression – in the way of a 'plan of the traditional international law drawn in an ideal

[1] *A.J.* 2 (1908), 356.

picture of itself' – that such a superstate runs counter to the very conception of international law and that its achievement would result in the destruction of international law.[1] It is a frame of mind such as is expressed by the latter argument which is characteristic of pre-war international law. It renounces every attempt at directly influencing the development of international law, except so far as it stresses the legal character of rules governing the conduct of States. Thus it results in being a weighty element in perpetuating an all but perfect state of affairs. Many a mischievous phrase derives its authority from well-meaning international lawyers. The post-war cry for the renovation, in the spirit of its founder, of the creative activity of international law, seems to have much in its favour.

Westlake's method is different. There is scarcely a writer who takes more notice of the realities of international life. His method is in this sense thoroughly positivist, and his practical attitude towards current international events is well known. But with these qualities he combines an idealistic temper which renders his teaching of international law a source of inspiration and a vehicle of real progress. He has no hesitation in discussing individual questions from the point of view of the *civitas maxima*. International law is to him the march towards the Great Design, 'the Parliament of Man, the Federation of the World'. 'I should guard myself against being supposed to imply that the ultimate destiny of civilization will not be in this direction.'[2]

International law based on consent, the rules of which are interpreted, modified, and applied by recourse to reason, to the sense of right, and to private law applicable to the given case; international law, the commands of which are directed not to impersonal States, but to men and women charged with international responsibilities; international law built not upon the deification of the State, but upon the law's function of regulating the mutual conduct of self-governing entities called States and marching towards the 'federation of the world' – these are the principles of the teaching of John Westlake. An attempt has been made here to show that it is in essential accord with today's tendencies of international law. But this is no more than a suggestion which may be rejected or adopted according to the weight one attaches to the changes introduced since the end of the war by conventional international law or to the new spirit in an ever-

[1] See Oppenheim, *The Future of International Law* (1911), pp. 16, 21; also, by the same author, *The League of Nations* (1918), p. 32.

[2] Westlake, I, 352; see also Westlake, *Papers*, pp. 376–7.

growing body of publicists. What is urged with some confidence is that it contains the main elements of a system of progressive international law culminating in a legally organized international society. The missing links of this system can easily be supplemented – *more geometrico*, one would say[1] – by building on the foundation of the three principles to which attention has been drawn in this paper. Perhaps they do not sufficiently come to light in Westlake's writings. For it must not be forgotten that he is at the same time an expounder of the prevailing practice – which is not always illustrative of these principles. It is the purpose of this paper to present them as a whole. I think that his *International Law* – after new facts have been worked in and after the principles which are less abstract now than they were fifteen years ago have been illustrated by the recent developments within the international society – will not only continue to be indispensable for the expert, but will become a guiding and inspiring book for the less experienced reader. Let us hope that a disciple of Westlake – perhaps one of the Whewell scholars of his training – will, by undertaking the responsible task of re-editing his treatise, combine a notable service rendered to the cause of a progressive international law with an act of homage paid to the memory of the Master on the hundredth anniversary of his birth.

[1] Attention may be called here to a recent article by Professor Baker ('The Obligatory Jurisdiction of the Permanent Court of International Justice' in *B.Y.* 6 (1925), 68) as an example of such a method, and also as an intimation that even in cases where Westlake's statement is no longer in accordance with existing international law, his fundamental principles may still be used as an illustration of the new developments.

CHAPTER 15

KELSEN'S PURE SCIENCE OF LAW

Editor's note 'Kelsen's Pure Science of Law' was one of a series of ten lectures given mainly by members of the staff of the London School of Economics and Political Science in 1932 and published under the title of *Modern Theories of Law* (Oxford, 1933). The names of Morris Ginsberg, Harold Laski and Ivor Jennings, who were amongst the participants in the series, give some indication of the intellectual vigour and distinction which contributed to the endowment of the School with the special reputation which it has so long enjoyed.

Lauterpacht was a student at the University of Vienna during the period when Kelsen was professor of Public Law and Philosophy of Law there. During this period, Lauterpacht devoted much time to the study of continental legal philosophy – the results of which are strikingly demonstrated not only in this individual study of Kelsen but also in Lauterpacht's major work, *The Function of Law in the International Community*, published in the same year.

For Kelsen's recollections of Lauterpacht, see *International and Comparative Law Quarterly*, 10 (1961), 2–3.

I. NORMATIVE SCIENCES AND THE 'FUNDAMENTAL RULE'

The final estimate of Kelsen's place in legal philosophy and jurisprudence is likely to be – if this submission may be made at the *beginning* of the lecture – that his work constitutes a powerful contribution to legal thought.[1] But so destructive has been his assault upon most of the accepted doctrines that what leaps to the eye is not the imposing edifice of an original legal system for which he has become responsible, but the negative irreverence of the iconoclast. There is hardly a leading doctrine or conception of modern jurisprudence that he has not assailed. It is sufficient to mention the sovereignty of the individual State, the juxtaposition of State and law, the distinction between private and public law, the distinction between juristic and physical persons, the conception of subjective rights, and the current assumption of a rigid distinction between the legislative and the judicial processes. This *prima facie* impression of a purely negative effort is accentuated by Kelsen's insistence on the formal character of his analysis of the positive law and the absence of any political or

[1] For a list of Kelsen's works, see p. 429.

ethical tendency in the 'pure science of law'. It is a pure science of law and State, i.e. a science whose sole object is to comprehend State and law in their juridical reality, to grasp them notionally, to analyse their structure, to explain their interrelations. It refrains painfully from making science an ideology of politics or an instrument in the struggle for power. Nothing is more abhorrent to it than the attempt to cloak partisan interests in the garb of legal science. Kelsen insists repeatedly that only a purely analytical approach to law can be regarded as scientific. He is impatient of the cry that jurisprudence must serve the needs of life. The needs of life, he says, can also be served by helping to comprehend objectively the nature of things, including the nature of the State and of the law.[1] Throughout his work he adheres to the formal and analytical method with a consistency which, he claims, surpasses that of the great philosopher whom he professes to follow.

For his method and approach to law are essentially those marked out by Kant. After Professor Ginsberg's most lucid exposition of this method as followed by Stammler[2] it is not necessary for me to repeat in what it consists. However, while Stammler went beyond Kant in developing what has been called the supplemental categories, Kelsen does not follow Kant all the way. He does not follow him for the reason that, in his opinion, Kant, a personality deeply rooted in Christianity, abandoned in his capacity as legal philosopher the transcendental method of his critical idealism to the point of making his *Metaphysic of Morals* a perfect expression of the classical natural law doctrine.[3] But he fully accepts and transplants to the domain of law the basis of Kant's method, namely, the view that knowledge is not merely a passive picture of the objective world, but that it creates its objects according to its inherent law from the material given by the senses. Kelsen's conception of law is such a creation. Contrary to Stammler, he does not regard the law conceived as the sum total of legal rules as a will. Neither does he regard it as a command or a psychological process or even a social reality. It is the product of a mental operation. It is a phenomenon in the category of essence (*das Sollen*) as distinguished from the category of existence

[1] See his article entitled 'Juristischer Formalismus und reine Rechtslehre' (1929), p. 18. And see *ibid.*, pp. 16–17, where he points out that at least that aspect of his theory which is based on the doctrine of the gradual crystallization of the law (see below, p. 410) is of pre-eminently practical importance inasmuch as it amounts to the incorporation of the principles of the 'free law' school on the subject of judicial activity.

[2] See *Modern Theories of Law* (1933), p. 38.

[3] See *Philosophischen Grundlagen der Naturrechtslehre und des Rechtspositivismus* (1928), pp. 75–7.

(*das Sein*); which is an abstract way of saying that the science of law is a branch of normative sciences as distinguished from natural sciences; which is still another abstract way of saying that the legal rule is concerned with what the positive law says shall be, and not with the question why positive law is obeyed or what the positive law ought to be. The legal rule itself is logically a hypothetical judgment. It says: If a person becomes responsible for a certain state of facts through commission or omission, compulsion shall be applied against him. There are in the legal rule two sets of facts: the legal cause and the legal effect. But the connection between them is not one of cause and effect in natural science. It is a normative connection. The law does not say that if *X* (commission or omission) happens *Y* (compulsion) will happen. It says that if *X* happens *Y shall* happen. The relation is determined not by the category of causation, but by the equally fundamental category of norms. The connection between the two sets of facts is not one of causation but of attribution. We attribute the legal effect to the legal cause. The attribution is effected through the instrumentality of the legal rule.

The insistence on the character of legal science as a normative science distinguished from natural science is an essential feature of Kelsen's pure science of law. It is, therefore, of importnace to realize clearly the difference between these two branches of knowledge.[1] Any concrete law in the domain of natural science is a specific application of the general law of causality. It shows a certain event as the necessary consequence of another. It explains to the human mind the actual occurrences in nature. In normative sciences the word 'law' is used in an entirely different sense. It lays down rules which prescribe right conduct. The rules of logic, grammar, ethics, aesthetics, and law are normative rules. They do not predicate what actually happens; their existence is not impaired by the fact that they are disregarded in individual cases. The rules of English grammar will survive anything that may be said in this lecture. But the law of gravitation would not survive if it were demonstrated beyond possible doubt that on a single occasion an object failed to behave in accordance with that law.

From the fact that what is and what shall be — the category of causation and the category of norms – are two distinct modes of thinking, it follows directly that one cannot be derived from the

[1] The distinction between natural and normative sciences is put very clearly in what may now be regarded as a classical chapter in *Hauptprobleme*, pp. 3–33. See also *Staatsbegriff*, pp. 75–81.

other. A norm cannot be explained by reference to a fact in the domain of existence. The question why a legal rule is obeyed, is a question in the domain of individual or social psychology and is, as such, outside the domain of legal science. The question why a legal rule is binding is properly a question to be answered by the lawyer. But it can only be answered by reference to another – higher – legal rule. The answer to the question why a ruling of an administrative authority shall be obeyed is that there is a higher legal rule, for instance, that embodied in an Act of Parliament, which lays down that the law as prescribed by the administrative authority shall be obeyed. Why must the law as laid down by Parliament be followed? The answer is that there is a fundamental rule of the Constitution to the effect that the law of Parliament shall be obeyed. The validity of a legal rule can thus logically never be understood by reference to a fact in the domain of existence but only by reference to what shall be, i.e. by reference to a fact of a higher order in the domain of norms. This relation of delegation is one of the principal features of Kelsen's system. Of course, ultimately the question arises why shall the Constitution be obeyed. The answer is: because we have adopted, as an initial hypothesis of the legal system, the fundamental norm (*die Grundnorm*) that the Constitution shall be obeyed. The reasons which prompt us to accept the validity of the fundamental rule are in themselves meta-legal. The jurist goes back to the fundamental rule; he does not go beyond it. It is an assumed, hypothetical validity.

Undoubtedly, the choice of the initial hypothesis is not an arbitrary matter. We must be careful in choosing it seeing that it has to be the basis of a structure enclosing a complicated variety of norms. We have to choose it so as to be able to include, by reference to it, as much as possible of the actual experience[1] of positive law as habitually obeyed in a given society. There would be no use in choosing as the initial hypothesis a rule to which nothing or little corresponds in actual experience.[2] The axioms of mathematics on which the theorem of Pythagoras is based exist independently of whether they are recognized by more or less individuals, but an initial hypothesis

[1] See *Souveränität*, pp. 85–101.

[2] For a lucid presentation of the purpose and the limitations of the 'fundamental norm' see *Staatsbegriff*, pp. 95 *et seq.*, and *Die philosophischen Grundlagen der Naturrechtslehre und des Rechtspositivismus* (1928), pp. 12–14, 66–72. For a criticism of it see Verdross, in *Juristische Blätter* (25 October 1930); Walz, in *Archiv des öffentlichen Rechts*, new series, 19 (1930), pp. 1 *et seq.*; Ross, *Theorie der Rechtsquellen* (1929). The initial hypothesis is not, of course, a speculation confined to continental writers. The attention of the English student may perhaps be drawn to Salmond's formulation of the idea of the fundamental norm. He says: 'It is requisite that the law should postulate one or more first causes, whose

which would make it impossible to explain and to include within a uniform system the actual operation of legal rules within the State would be of little value. It would, for instance, be absurd to try to comprehend the present Russian State with the help of the initial hypothesis which could be assumed before the Revolution of 1917, namely, that the will of the Tsar shall be obeyed. There must be a certain parallelism between what is and what shall be. The tension between the factual and the normative must not be too great (if the fundamental rule is to retain its usefulness), just as it ought not to be too small (if law is to remain a normative as distinguished from an explicative science). It will be noted how dangerously near the realm of norms approaches the realm of mere fact – a danger which has led many to base law on might or to identify the two. Kelsen attaches the greatest importance to keeping them apart. The initial hypothesis is certainly influenced by facts, including the paramount element of might. It can even be said that it transforms might into law. However, once adopted it constitutes the beginning of an autonomous system governed by its own specific – not by causal – laws. That these laws are autonomous and altogether specific may be seen from the fact that the revolution constitutes an absolute break in the legal order and that the new legal order can never be comprehended by reference to the old one but only by dint of the adoption of a new fundamental hypothesis. The very fact that there is such a thing as a revolution in the legal order shows that its laws are different from causal laws. There are no revolutions in the natural order governed by natural laws. There is only evolution, i.e. relations of cause and effect.

Enough has been said to indicate that the 'fundamental norm' is not only the juridical basis of the legal system as construed by Kelsen. It is indicative of Kelsen's approach and legal philosophy in general. The norm which lies at the basis of his system, although not arbitrary, is purely relativist and hypothetical. There is in it no such absolute element which it would necessarily contain if it were grounded in a

operation is ultimate, and whose authority is underived. In other words there must be found in every legal system certain ultimate principles, from which all others are derived, but which are themselves self-existent. . . Whence comes the rule that Acts of Parliament have the force of law? This is legally ultimate; its source is historical only, not legal. No Statute lays it down. It is certainly recognized by many precedents, but no precedent can confer authority upon precedent. It must first possess authority before it can confer it. If we inquire as to the number of these ultimate principles, the answer is that a legal system is free to recognize any number of them, but it is not bound to recognize more than one. From any one ultimate legal source it is possible for the law to be derived, but one such there must be' (*Jurisprudence* (8th ed. by Manning, 1930), § 48 ('Ultimate Legal Principles')).

material ethical value, for instance, in that of justice. The initial hypothesis is an act of human intelligence. It is not a dictate of a higher power. It is not a deduction from an immutable principle of justice; it is an assumed hypothesis glorying in its realistic relativism. Kelsen claims for his initial hypothesis that it transforms might into law. However, this claim is in itself morally indifferent. Frequently such transformation will prove ethically repugnant. The fundamental norm is a methodological instrument pure and simple. It certainly substantiates Kant's dictum of 'the method creating its objects'.

2. SOME PRACTICAL ASPECTS OF THE PURE SCIENCE OF LAW

Subjective rights and legal personality

It would be a mistake to assume that this formal basis of Kelsen's science of law divorces Kelsen's approach altogether from legal problems of practical importance. In order to dispel a misleading assumption of this kind it may be necessary to show – before proceeding with the exposition of Kelsen's doctrine of the identity of State and law – that there is a direct relation between his analytical method and some pre-eminently practical problems of law. This may be seen, for instance, from his treatment of the question of rights, especially of subjective rights. In Kelsen's view the legal duty is the central and only essential element of the legal system. For it is of the essence of an ordering, in particular of a compulsory ordering, that it binds those subjected to it. This fact of being bound is best expressed through the conception of duty. The legal duty is nothing else than the legal norm related to the concrete conduct of the given individual. A legal norm lays down that a person is bound to obey a given rule of conduct only in so far as the norm posits the contrary conduct as a condition for an act of compulsion conceived as the consequence of the wrong. Every legal rule necessarily lays down a legal duty. It may contain a legal right if the putting into effect of the consequence of the disregard of the legal rule is made dependent upon the will of the person who has an interest in the sanction of the law being applied. The subjective right does not confront the objective law as something independent, for there is a subjective right only in so far as it is laid down in objective law. The subjective right is one of the possible and by no means necessary tools of legal technique. It is the specific technique of a society which is built upon the basis of private property and therefore pays particular attention to individual interests.[1] But even in that society modern criminal law has overcome that technique inasmuch as in the place of the injured person (who in the primitive stage of legal development was the subject of the right to claim the realization of the legal sanction) the State itself puts in motion the procedure which realizes the consequences of the legal wrong. The understanding of the central position occupied by the legal duty helps us to overcome the dualism between subjective right and objective law. We see clearly that the subjective right is not different from the objective law. It *is* the objective law.

The result thus reached has in turn certain practical consequences. Once we have rejected the conception of subjective right as an independent element in law we have little difficulty in recognizing that the conception of a subject of law or of the person – conceived as an entity independently confronting the law – is only an artificial device which juristic thinking has adopted in order better to comprehend certain objects of legal knowledge. A 'person' is merely an expression for the personified unity of a bundle of legal duties and rights. Moreover, from this denial of the reality of the subject of the law there follows the rejection both of the reality of the juristic person[2] and of any material distinction between the latter and the physical person. Juristic and physical persons are essentially on the same plane. The physical person is the personification of the sum total of legal rules applicable to one person. The juristic person is the personification of the sum total of legal rules applicable to a plurality of persons. The rights and duties of juristic persons – including the juristic person of the State – are thus conceived as the rights and duties of human beings and of nothing else.[3]

The doctrine of the gradual concretization of the law

As Kelsen's attitude in the matter of subjective rights and legal persons follows largely from the conception of the legal system as the sum total of norms ordering compulsion, so the other basic principle of the pure science of law, namely, the phenomenon of delegation from the fundamental hypothesis, results in a specific attitude in the

[1] See 'Allgemeine Rechtslehre im Lichte materialistischer Geschichtsauffassung', in *Archiv für Sozialwissenschaft und Sozialpolitik*, 66 (1931), pp. 491 *et seq.*

[2] It is easy to guess that Kelsen also rejects the reality of groups not only as juristic persons but as psychological entities on the ground that psychology in its sphere has been guilty of the same hypostatizing process as legal science in regard to the juristic person. How important this aspect of his teaching is, especially for international law, will be seen from what will be said later on the theory of the identity of State and law.

[3] See *Staatslehre*, pp. 47–71.

matter of the relation between the creation and the application of the law. Kelsen denies that there exists a difference of kind between the two processes. He accepts and develops the doctrine, introduced by other German and Austrian writers, of the 'gradual concretization of the law' (*die Lehre vom Stufenbau des Rechts*). There is, according to that doctrine, a descending process of delegation from the Constitution to legislation, administration, judicial decisions, and private transactions. Legislation is only relatively law-creative; it applies the fundamental rule of law embodied in the Constitution, just as administration applies the law laid down in statutes. The process of the creation of the law is not concluded in legislation. It is continued in administration, in judicial decisions laying down the concrete rule, in private transactions – grounded in and validated by the higher rule of law – laying down the rules by which the parties will be bound in the future. If the doctrine of the gradual concretization of the law is accepted then there follow from it two practical consequences. One is that it is no longer possible to maintain that the subjective private law sphere of the contractual creation of law is, in contradistinction to legislation, politically indifferent. If we regard the private contract as the crystallization of the more general rule of law which establishes the institution of private contract, which defines it and renders it binding, then, of course, the contract establishing the subjective and private right is no less the instrument of political domination than the objective and impersonal law laid down by statute or administrative decrees. Kelsen quotes with approval a distinguished socialist commentator[1] to the effect that the right of the capitalist, grounded in contract, is nothing else than public power blindly delegated to the advantage of the class in power. From this point of view freedom of contract in a number of relationships becomes a fiction.

The other – more general and less controversial – consequence of the doctrine of the gradual concretization of the legal order is that it facilitates the acceptance of the principles of the 'free law school' in the matter of judicial activity. As the statute is recognized as the mere frame to be filled by the activity of judges or administrators continuing in a more concrete sphere the function of the legislator, it follows that within the orbit of the statute there exist a multitude of possible decisions to be arrived at by the exercise of judicial discretion within the four corners of the law.

[1] Renner, *Die Rechtsinstitute des Privatrechts und ihre soziale Funktion*, p. 55. And see Kelsen in *Archiv für Sozialwissenschaft und Sozialpolitik*, 66 (1931), p. 495.

The distinction between private and public law

Once we realize that the difference between the creation and the application of the law is less pervading than is commonly supposed, then the way is open to a new approach to the question of the distinction between private and public law. Kelsen rejects this distinction. He regards it as liable to abuse, in a manner contrary to positive law, in the interest of persons and groups in authority and as one which has actually been so abused. He denies the accuracy of that test of the distinction which is based on the alleged difference of interests protected by private and public law respectively. The very fact that the legal order protects a private interest shows that it is a matter of public interest to protect that private interest. The fact that the law contains private law rules concerning the sale of goods shows that there is a collective interest in the regulation of this particular transaction. Any rule of criminal or administrative law – commonly included within public law – can ultimately be traced to the individual person or persons in whose interest it has been created.[1]

Neither is there, according to Kelsen, any foundation for the traditional distinction based on the theory that while private law governs the relations between equal and co-ordinate persons, public law governs the relations between the State authority and the subjects subordinated to it. That theory attributes to certain persons, notably the person of the State, a legal value higher than that attributed to other persons. However, this legal *Mehrwert* disappears when we consider analytically in what that alleged higher value consists. It is supposed to consist in the fact that certain persons are legally bound to obey the commands of other persons endowed with attributes of rulership, i.e. that in case of disobedience the person issuing the command may apply force against the recalcitrant. The

[1] In this, as in many other respects, the approach and the results of Kelsen's analytical method show a striking resemblance to those of Austin: 'Any injury cognizable by the law of England will be found to be an injury to some person or body of persons. Public nuisances for instance; offences against *bonos mores*, etc., which seem to be violations of obligations to which there are no corresponding rights in any given person or persons; and which may be called public offences, by reason of the injury being entirely contingent, and being liable to fall upon *any* of the whole heterogeneous mass which is called the Public. In all other cases of international or negligent violation, there is the same contingent evil, but there is also a past injury done to some assignable individual, either in his own right or as trustee for others' (Austin, *Jurisprudence*, II (4th ed. by Campbell, 1873), pp. 786–7). See also *ibid.* pp. 783–4. 'By "the Public" (where it means anything) we mean all the individuals who compose the community, governors as well as governed. In which sense of the word public, *all Law is public*; whether we look to the *persons* in whom rights and obligations reside, or whether we look to what is, or at least ought to be, the *end* of law; that end being the good of all.'

position is said to be different in the relation of private persons. The duty to observe certain conduct is here grounded not in the unilateral will of one person, but in agreement; moreover, in case of a breach of the legal duty thus created, compulsion issues not from the other party, but from the State. The difference seems to be substantial. It disappears when we consider that in law the duty to obey the command of a 'person in authority' is ultimately not grounded in the will of that person just as legal duties of a private nature are not ultimately grounded in the private agreement. The command of the person in authority is not a source of law: it is a condition which the law posits for the creation of duties of other persons just as the private agreement is a condition for the validation of a more general rule of law relating to the observance of contracts. In the one case the law says to the individual: Act in a manner prescribed by a certain individual acting in his capacity as the official of the State. In the other case it says: Act in a manner agreed upon in the contract. In both cases the expression of will – as commanded or as agreed upon – constitutes a concretization of the general rule of law. It cannot even be said that there is a substantial difference between the two relationships inasmuch as in the one case the State is the agency which issues the command and which applies the sanction in cases of disobedience, while in the other case the rule is enforced by a person other than the one who is entitled to insist on the fulfilment of the legal duty. For as a rule even in so-called public law the organ which fulfils the condition creating the legal duty and the organ which enforces it are not the same. However, it is impossible to discuss here the various theories of public law.[1] It is sufficient to say that, in addition to its theoretical interest, the problem is – like other aspects of Kelsen's teaching – of a pre-eminently practical importance. Kelsen attacks the orthodox distinction for the reason, *inter alia*, that it has always tended to confer upon State organs, particularly in their higher ranks representing definite partisan interests, a standing higher than that to which they are entitled by positive law. The same distinction, whose origin can be traced to the autocratic legal principle of ancient Rome, *princeps legibus solutis*, supplies the theoretical basis for the immunity of the State organs from the normal operation of the law. It is the foundation of Machiavelli's *ragione di stato* which was essentially a number of postulates coined by the ruling autocracy against the traditional rule of law.

[1] This aspect of Kelsen's teaching is put clearly and concisely in *Staatslehre*, pp. 80–91, where the various theories of public law are discussed.

It is the justification of the theory which liberates the 'State' – i.e. those who rule it – from the bonds not only of positive law but also of morality. In a different sphere it is responsible for the widespread assumption that it is inadmissible to treat problems of public law by analogy with private law – a view which has had particularly disastrous effects in international law by depriving it, in actual defiance of the practice of States, of a fruitful source of development.[1]

3. THE IDENTITY OF STATE AND LAW

The most conspicuous and one of the most original aspects of Kelsen's teaching is probably the doctrine of the identity of State and law. The negative proof of this identity Kelsen shows to lie in the fact that other sciences cannot dispense with the legal conception of State and take it for granted. This can be said particularly of sociology. The State unity which sociology assumes as existing is a unity posited by legal science. The fact that an individual forms part of the State is one which sociology accepts not as the result of an investigation governed by causal laws, but by assuming the existence of a given legal ordering. Sociology does not inquire by means of an empirical investigation of psychological actions and reactions in society whether a person forms part of the State. Empirical sociology has never maintained that certain individuals belong to a certain State juridically but not sociologically, or sociologically but not juridically. Sociology assumes that all individuals – including children, lunatics, and, generally, persons who have no consciousness of their association with others in the State – comprised within the juridical unity of the State, participate in the psychological process which is the basis of the inward association of a unity in the sociological sense. But the assumption of such a psychological unity within the legally defined territorial borders of a State is no more than a fiction.[2]

However, it is not necessary to rely on a mere negative proof to demonstrate the identity of State and law. The direct proof of this proposition consists in demonstrating that the State is a normative ordering coextensive with the normative ordering of the legal system. Only by contemplating the State as a system of norms is it possible to understand the current conception of the State as an authority

[1] See Lauterpacht, *Analogies*, §§ 30–4.

[2] See *Staatsbegriff*, pp. 4–74, for a discussion of the various sociological theories of the State.

which renders the relation between the individual and the State one of subordination. It is impossible to understand the nature of the State without realizing that duties issue from the State, that persons who form part of the State are bound to observe certain rules of conduct. By the same token, the State can be thought of as an authority only inasmuch as it is an ordering consisting of norms binding the individual. It is true that we speak of the authority of nature and of the subjection of things to natural laws. This form of speech, however, is only an inaccurate analogy which is due to the fact that natural science has taken over the terminology of human thought in the matter of the relation of man to God and State.

This affirmation of the normative character of the State is substantiated by a more empirical approach. Within a territorially defined unit called 'State' there presents itself to the eye an infinite variety of human actions. What is the criterion which leads us to qualify certain of these actions as actions attributable to the State? For the individual participates in the existence of the State only with a fraction of his personality. Not everything that he does is attributable to the State. What is the test which bids us attribute certain actions not to the person responsible for them but to an ideal subject, the State? For purely empirical consideration there exist only acts of individuals; empirically there are no State acts. One arrives at the idea of the State only by means of a mental operation which attributes certain acts to the ideal entity of the State. The State as the subject of State acts is the central point of attribution. But the only possible criterion which permits the imputation of certain acts to the State is that these actions are in a specific fashion in accordance with a valid ordering, that they are posited in the norms of this ordering, and are reducible to a unity of this ordering. The State is nothing else than the personified expression of this unity. It exists owing to the mental operation of the assumption of a valid ordering to which we attribute certain human actions out of a multitude of others. Just as the conception of law, so also the conception of the State is made possible by the concept of attribution. In both, the latter constitutes the central element. The identity of State and law is finally established when we consider that the State is not the only normative ordering. For so are many other social groupings. The State differs from them by being an ordering of compulsion. Its norms posit compulsion to be applied under certain conditions by one individual against another. If a person behaves in a certain way, that is, if he becomes responsible for an act of omission or commission, another person –

the organ of the State – shall apply compulsion in the form of punishment or execution. The definition of the State as the personified unity of norms ordering compulsion proves to be identical with that of the law. The apparatus of compulsion, called State, is identical with the legal order. The norms, of which the State ordering is composed, are legal norms. The legal norm is the rule through which there takes place attribution of acts to the State. It consists of two elements: the condition posited by the law (i.e. the conditioning fact) and the legal consequence (i.e. the conditioned fact). The legal consequence in the form of compulsion is the specific reaction of the law; it is at the same time the specific action of the State.[1]

The view that the State is a normative ordering is frequently confronted with the assertion that the State is a power, a force, a tangible being. One points to the typical manifestations of State power: its guns, ships, fortresses, prisons, and gallows. But these – the pure science of law retorts – are inanimate and indifferent objects. They derive their significance from the fact that they are used by men for certain purposes. And they are so used as the result of ideas dominating men, the idea, that is to say, that they ought to act in accordance with the law and that these acts are valid as State acts only in so far as they conform to the law. When one speaks of the power of the State, one necessarily refers, therefore, to the actuating force of ideas whose content is the objective ordering of the State.

This being so, what is, according to Kelsen, the explanation of the predominant view of the dualism of State and law? The answer is that the State is the product of a process very frequent in the history of human thought, namely, the process of personification.[2] Human thinking finds it inconvenient to deal unaided with the unity of the legal system and to visualize the complicated mechanism of a multitude of abstract norms. As a measure of convenience, the totality of legal rules is represented through the more expressive metaphor of a human being whose essential quality is a 'will'. This urge to personification, which is identical with the tendency to

[1] The *normative* (as distinguished from the factual) *validity* of the State constitutes, as mentioned, its specific existence. However, it is important to remember that the State ordering is not only normatively valid, it is also actually operative. It not only shall be obeyed; it *is* more or less obeyed. But – and this is equally important for the understanding of the pure science of law – that does not mean that the *norm* is operative. It is the fact that the individual conceives the norm as valid – it is this fact which induces him to obey the norm. A person feels tempted to steal. He is reminded of the norm: 'thou shalt not steal', and refrains from theft. The norm itself is not a psychological phenomenon. It is a logical category *sui generis*. The *perception* of the norm – not the norm itself – is a psychological act. And it is the perception which is operative.

[2] *Staatsbegriff*, pp. 206 *et seq.*

comprehend objects by analogy with the human ego, is deeply rooted in man's mind. At the same time, however, there is a tendency to hypostatize these instruments of thinking and to transform them into real entities. The instrument of perception is changed into an object of perception. The objects are thus duplicated. The 'State', created for the purpose of comprehending and better expressing the unity of the law, becomes an independent being standing in a variety of relations to the law and even regarded as the transcendent creator of the law. This process of duplicating objects of knowledge is a general phenomenon in science – to mention only the conception of force in physics, of the soul in psychology, and of substance in natural science. But as modern physics tends to eliminate from its system the conception of force and substance as different from qualities and relations of things, and as modern psychology tends to ignore the soul as distinct from individual psychical acts, so also, according to Kelsen, legal theory must abandon the conception of the State as an entity different from the legal order.

Already in 1913 Kelsen gave clear utterance to the view that the State is only the expression for the logical completeness and the inner consistency of the system of legal norms.[1] He pointed out that this personification is the result of a mental process similar to that which has led to the conception of a world deity as the personification of the unity of norms governing the universe in so far as they can be thought of in terms of a purposeful and self-consistent system. The implications of this phenomenon Kelsen subsequently developed in a magnificent analogy between the theologist's conception of God and the jurist's conception of the State. He shows how theology, as the result of its insistence upon the transcendence of God in relation to Nature, has become entangled in the same difficulties which beset the juridical theory of the State in regard to the asserted meta-legal character of the State. Knowledge aims at unity, and the avenues by which the deeply rooted urge towards unity of knowledge achieves its objects are strangely uniform. This may be seen from the way in which both theology and the juridical theory of the State try to overcome the dualism in their respective domains. Christian theology has developed the doctrine of God limiting his infinite power by subjecting himself, in the person of the god-son, to the order, both moral and natural, of the world. God's freedom in relation to the physical world expresses itself in the conception of the

[1] 'Über Staatsunrecht', in Grünhut's *Zeitschrift für das private und öffentliche Recht der Gegenwart*, 40 (1913), 1–114.

miracle. The orthodox juridical theory of the State, says Kelsen, has a miracle of its own, in the shape of the theory of the self-limitation of the State – of that entity which is supposed to be different from the law and at the same time inconceivable without the law. The State, it is said, establishes the legal order and after having established it subjects itself to the law. The same questions with which pantheistic thinkers overwhelmed orthodox theology are put by critical legal theory to the doctrine of the self-limitation of the State. How can God, omnipotent, in His essence indefinable and unbound, be at the same time subject as man to the laws of the world, be born, live, suffer, die, be subject to moral law? How can the State, whose essence is power as distinguished from law, be legally bound by its own law? If the State can *ex hypothesi* do everything it has the power to do, how can it be maintained that it can do only what it is legally entitled to do? There is no answer, says Kelsen,[1] to these questions. The problems created by the process of personification cannot be solved; they can only be dissolved by the abandonment of the personification.

The doctrine of the identity of State and law is not merely of theoretical importance inasmuch as it does away with confusing problems of the relation of State and law such as whether the State preceded the law or vice versa, or whether the State is subject to law or conversely. It is of practical value for a variety of reasons. The dualism of State and law lends itself easily to political abuse. It has degenerated into a dualism of two divergent systems of norms, of which one, under the designation of 'State', 'reason of State', 'State interest', or 'public interest', is frequently put forward as claiming priority wherever positive law leads to consequences which are unpalatable to those who happen to be in control of the State. Much of the distinction between public and private law is reducible to this source. It is undesirable to perpetuate the conception of a tangible State distinct from the law so that it can be said – as it has in fact been said – that the law is for the State (so that it may break it whenever convenient) and not the State for the law. It is undesirable to perpetuate the conception of a tangible State which even if it acknowledges the binding force of the rule of law divorces that law from the qualities and the moral substance inherent in the general principles of law governing relations between individuals. The

[1] The analogy between God and Nature, on the one side, and Law and State, on the other, has been developed by Kelsen in *Staatsbegriff*, pp. 219–47, and in *Logos*, 2 (1922–3), 261–84.

elimination of the real entity of the State as distinguished from the law helps to effect the attribution of legal and moral responsibility to human beings who alone are subjects of legal rights and duties. These results lie already more in the international than in the municipal sphere. So also does the last consequence of the doctrine of the identity of State and law. If the State is only an expression for the unity of the legal system and if international law is recognized – as admittedly it is – as a body of rules of law binding upon States independently of their will, then, from a purely legal point of view, there is already in existence a State over and above the national sovereignties. The term 'super-State' is usually an easy prey for arguments, of controversial relevance, on the merits of nationalism and internationalism, and on the practical difficulties of international government. A truly legal treatment of the conception of the *civitas maxima* will be greatly facilitated by the realization of the essential identity of law and State.

4. INTERNATIONAL LAW

The possibility of a legal construction of an already existent *civitas maxima* is only one of the incidental consequences, in the international sphere, of the doctrine of the identity of State and law. The bearing and influence of the pure science of law on international law is of a more direct and more general nature. In no other branch of law is legal theory more self-contradictory and less mindful of the necessity of the unity of the legal system than in international law. It is in this domain that Kelsen's criticism has been most vigorous and destructive. But it is also here that his contribution has been of a truly creative nature and of generally admitted effectiveness. It is sufficient to refer to his analysis of the problem of the relation between international law and municipal law, to his criticism of the doctrine that the will of States is the only source of international law, to the application of the theory of the fundamental norm, in the form of the rule *pacta sunt servanda*, to international law, and to his criticism of the conception of sovereignty as an essential and specific attribute of the territorial State. It cannot be the object of this lecture to give a detailed account of Kelsen's discussion of these questions,[1] but his treatment of the problem of sovereignty – the *fons et origo mali* – requires consideration. It is not that Kelsen rejects the conception of

[1] See *Das Problem der Souveränität und die Theorie des Völkerrechts* (1920).

sovereignty altogether. For sovereignty is the expression of the unity and exclusiveness of the legal system. The assumption of such a unity is essential for law as a science and as a normative reality. It is, in a sense, identical with the positive character of the law as underived from a source higher than itself. But this sovereignty need not and must not be the sovereignty of a single State. For the sovereignty of the State, while implying that the legal order of the State is independent, self-existent and self-sufficing, necessarily asserts the exclusiveness of that individual sovereign entity. It implies that in relation to it other similar sovereign systems exist only in so far as they have been recognized. Such recognition necessarily means nothing else than that the foreign legal system has been included within the legal order of the recognizing State. It is also clear that the sovereignty of the individual State excludes the possibility of a legal order above national sovereignties. But the more immediate and insoluble difficulty is that the sovereignty of one State, conceived – as in juridical logic it must be – as the highest power, is inconsistent with the sovereignty of any other State. These are startling but inescapable consequences of juridical analysis, and writers anxious to stress the binding force of international law but reluctant to abandon the accepted conception of sovereignty have taken refuge in transforming it from a merely formal quality of highest underived power to an aggregate of attributes called fundamental rights. This conception, which has all the drawbacks of the conception of subjective rights and which is fact presupposes the existence of an objective international law, is frequently the expression of the subjective wishes and pretensions of a given writer or State. It is an instructive example of the anarchy of legal science which cloaks political postulates and desires in the garb of subjective rights.

These are the consequences of the doctrine of the sovereignty of the State which – in the international sphere – is identical with the assumption of the primacy of municipal law over international law. The alternative assumption is that of the primacy of international law. According to this view, the legal system of the individual State is a partial legal system derived by way of delegation from the legal orde of the *civitas maxima*, which in turn is based on the fundamental rule *pacta sunt servanda*. This world legal order is already in being as the result of the existence of international law, and its existence is not affected by the absence of law-creating and law-enforcing agencies such as are found in a developed society. If such agencies were established they would not add essentially to what already exists.

States would not be subordinated to a tangible super-State or to its political organs; they would continue to be subordinated to the same rule of law to which they are in principle subordinated today. There are other consequences of this approach. If the law of the State is regarded as delegated from a higher legal authority and not as the highest sovereign power, then there disappears at one stroke the asserted difference of kind between the State and the territorial and other associations within its borders. The difference becomes one of degree. It will be seen at once that this result has a bearing not only on the position of the State in international society. It is of equal importance for the question of the relation of the State to national associations. The rights of associations have – particularly in this country by writers like Maitland, Figgis, and Laski – been vindicated by dint of the emphasis on the real personality of groups. However, the doctrine of the real personality of associations is not only highly controversial: it is impossible to assert the real personality of associations without claiming the same in regard to the comprehensive association of the State itself – a doctrine upon whose unsatisfactory consequences in the international order it is not necessary to expatiate. The theory of the primacy of international law subordinates the State to a higher authority and thus achieves at the same time the result of depriving it of the element of absolute superiority over other corporate entities within its territorial limits.

Kelsen admits that the assumption of the primacy of international law is, from the point of view of a single State, not the only possible juridical hypothesis. In juridical logic it is possible to conceive of a system of law in which the national State appears as sovereign and other States and international law appear as delegated subordinated systems of law included through recognition within the law of the particular sovereign State. But then, of course, from the point of view of that State the other States would not be sovereign. They would be recognized; which means that they would be delegated; which means that they would be subordinate. Thus while the primacy of the State law is possible as a juridical construction of the positive law of a single State, it is incompatible with the ultimate unity of legal knowledge. That unity abhors the conception of over sixty sovereignties of which each is at the same time the highest in its capacity as the recognizing and delegating authority, and of which each forms at the same time a delegated legal order, part of the sovereign legal system of the fifty-nine other States. The primacy of municipal law is incompatible with the generally accepted notion of international law as regulating the relations of co-ordinated and equal States. The very conception of co-ordination and equality logically presupposes the existence of a higher authority establishing and realizing the relation of equality. In addition, the primacy of municipal law is inconsistent with many generally accepted rules and principles of international law, including the generally recognized rule of the continuity of the State notwithstanding the legal break through revolution – a continuity which can be secured only by dint of assuming the existence of the primacy of international law bridging the gap between the old and the revolutionary legal order.

However, although the sovereignty of the individual State is a bad fundamental rule, it is, as mentioned, a possible one. Kelsen himself leaves no doubt as to his preference for the hypothesis of the primacy of international law, not only for the reasons stated but also because the initial hypothesis and the choice between the primacy of international law and that of the law of the State are in the last resort a matter of one's philosophy of life and because he has no hesitation in expressing his preference for a particular philosophy of life. The doctrine of the primacy of municipal law – a doctrine which regards the national sovereign State as the source of all legal authority and the other States as delegated and recognized by it – is like that of the subjective theory of knowledge in epistemology and ethics, which, in order to comprehend the world, begins with the ego and regards nature as the ideal creation of the individual and the world of values merely as the product of his will. The theory of the primacy of international law is like the objectivistic philosophy of life, which, in order to reach the individual unit, begins with the world as a whole by presupposing an objective reason; the willing and perceiving individuals are merely the ephemeral expression of that objective reason. But just because they are the emanation of the highest world reason they confront one another not as estranged and incomprehensible one to another but as co-ordinate and uniform personalities before that World Being who alone is sovereign. Kelsen does not urge the student to accept his philosophy of life, but he shows that the legal fundamental rule which is based on subjectivistic philosophy leads eventually to the negation of law and of the possibility of legal science, just as the primacy of State law leads to the negation of international law and to the affirmation of mere force.

5. NATURAL LAW AND POSITIVISM

Critics have pointed out that Kelsen's predilection, in deference to a definite philosophy of life, for the theory of the primacy of international law constitutes an acceptance of natural law pure and simple. Kelsen, to whom natural law is anathema, answers that he has recognized the juristic possibility of the alternative doctrine. However, it is permissible to doubt whether the recognition of the alternative possibility is more than verbal. To say: 'You may adopt the sovereignty of the State as the initial hypothesis; you may even, at the cost of being illogical and ignoring principles which you yourself profess, build a legal system on this basis; but your approach ultimately makes legal knowledge impossible and amounts to an affirmation of force' – to say this is not to leave to an intelligent mind much scope for choice. One is therefore apt to inquire whether there has not, by a back door as it were, crept into the cast-iron logic of the system the ghost of natural law. Kelsen would deny it. For, as already stated, the rejection of natural law is the ever-recurring theme of his teaching. It is the argumentative starting-point; it is the test of the purity of the pure science of law. Natural law, as Kelsen conceives it, is based on the assumption of a natural order whose rules – unlike those of positive law – are valid not because they are made by a human authority, but because they originate from God, Nature, or reason, and are therefore just and adequate. The validity of the norm of natural law is thus absolute; the validity of the norm of positive law is assumed inasmuch as it is based on the hypothetical fundamental rule. Juridical science can assume the validity of only one of these systems. On no account can it regard both as valid. Juristic knowledge cannot accept a position in which the same conduct is governed by a rule of positive law which says '*a* shall be' and by a rule of natural law which says 'non-*a* shall be'. The logical rule of contradiction applies also in the normative sciences. The two systems are so fundamentally heterogeneous that Kelsen doubts whether there is even possible between them a relation of delegation without the delegated legal system losing in the process its specific characteristics. But the rejection of natural law is the result not only of the striving for methodological purity. It is deeply rooted in his relativist and secular philosophy of life. It is the result of the conviction that natural law is due to the tendency, ever dear to the human mind, to duplicate the objects of knowledge by picturing entities – 'the thing in itself' – existing behind the objects of actual experience and independent of human reason and senses. This tendency of metaphysical-religious dualism is in Kelsen's view the result of man's lack of confidence in his own powers. It bids him regard the direct objects of experience as an imperfect picture of a reality which is for ever inaccessible to his perceiving knowledge. The same tendency exists in the sphere of values. As the metaphysical philosophy of nature pictures the world of experience as an inaccurate rendering of a transcendent reality, so the natural law philosophy of State and law regards positive, valid, and true law not as a free creation of the human legislator and judge but as an imperfect attempt at reproduction of the law in itself, of a natural law above the positive law. The rejection of natural law is for Kelsen tantamount to the affirmation of the dignity and autonomy of man.[1]

The scope of this lecture has not permitted any detailed attempt at a critical examination of Kelsen's doctrines, but an exception may fittingly be made in the matter of his attitude to natural law. The reason for this exception is that this aspect of his teaching is, it is believed, a theory superadded to the main structure of his doctrine – principally for the sake of argumentative advantages, but ultimately to the disadvantage of the whole system. It is of importance that the prominence which he gives to his rejection of natural law should not be regarded as the outstanding feature of the system of the pure science of law.

It is somewhat surprising to find that although Kelsen discusses the problem of natural law with great learning and acumen he does not say what is the substance of natural law, as distinguished from its formal attributes. These formal qualities of natural law are – Kelsen tells us – that it is not posited deliberately by man, but finds its validity in God, Nature, or reason; that, therefore, it needs no compulsion for its realization; that its validity is absolute, whereas that of positive law is hypothetical and assumed with the help of the fundamental norm which itself has not and cannot have a legal foundation; that, whatever may be the claims of a 'natural law with changeable contents', it is in its essence unchangeable and eternal; and so on. But Kelsen makes no attempt to analyse what is natural law and what are the problems and incidents of its application and incorporation in the body of positive law. Is it natural justice? Or

[1] For a most stimulating presentation of the problem see his monograph entitled *Die philosophischen Grundlagen der Naturrechtslehre und des Rechtspositivismus* (1928).

the reason of the thing? Or general principles of law distinct from concrete positive rules? Or public policy? Or morals generally? Or those regulative principles of legislation and administration of justice variously conceived by various schools of law, like the securing of freedom, or of cultural development, or of a maximum of needs? Kelsen does not answer these questions. But, it is submitted, an attempt to answer them would necessarily have shown that the significance of the idea of natural law is not only that it can be abused for political reasons or that it disturbs the purity of legal science.

It would show that the rejection of natural law may not always be consistent with the positivist idea. As a matter of legal experience there takes place constantly a process of incorporation of natural law by positive law. Kelsen argues that, given the absolutely heterogeneous nature of the two systems, such a delegation is not possible. Like Zeno's paradox on the Moving Arrow, his reasoning may be difficult to analyse. However, dismissed it must be as contrary to experience. Positive law refers to and incorporates, in various forms, extra-legal rules which, but for the fear of flouting suspiciously general disapproval, we might find it quite convenient to call by the name of natural law. This process of delegation will be found in the codes of many a country expressly referring the judge, in the absence of applicable provisions of the law, to natural justice, to principles of good faith, or to general principles of law.[1] The Swiss Civil Code lays down expressly in its first Article that when neither positive law nor custom provide in the opinion of the judge a sufficient basis for decision he ought to decide the case as if he were a legislator, and, in doing so, to be guided by tradition and recognized legal doctrine. But Kelsen tells us that 'positivism rejects decisively the specifically natural law view that legal science is a source of law'.[2] This is a typical instance of positivism ending in disregard of positive law – an occurrence which is as frequent in municipal as in international law. However, it is not in specific statutory provisions that this process of delegation manifests itself most conspicuously. In the daily activity of courts homage is paid to the fact that law is the realization of socially obtainable justice – which means of the socially obtainable natural law. We may have abandoned the theory that statutes repugnant to natural justice are void, but that does not mean that we have ceased to shape positive law and to interpret it, sometimes

[1] See, for instance, Article 7 of the Austrian Civil Code.

[2] *Die philosophischen Grundlagen der Naturrechtslehre und des Rechtspositivismus* (1928), p. 70.

out of recognition, by ideas for which the term natural law is an elastic and convenient expression.

In so far as positivism disregards this phenomenon it becomes a dogma divorced from its own premises and from actual practice. It also becomes divorced from the general trend of legal thinking. The manner in which judges have recourse to the 'law above the law' or to the 'law behind the law' in order to obliterate the gap between law and justice has been for a long time the persistent and central theme of legal philosophy not only in England and America, but also on the continent of Europe. This is the problem of reconciling the antinomy of rule and discretion, of security and justice, of stability and change. But it is a problem which is outside the range of Kelsen's writing. He disposes of it summarily by saying that the rules and principles resorted to by the judge in the exercise of judicial discretion are not rules of positive law and therefore are of no interest to the pure science of law.[1] But is it not true to say that by authorizing judicial discretion positive law has incorporated in advance the indeterminate body of rules and principles upon which the judge falls back in the exercise of his function? In any case there is no compelling reason for reducing legal science to a logical analysis of the existing legal materials. There is no justification for denying the name of legal science to the investigation of the relationship between law and justice, or – and this is the same thing – between natural justice and positive law. There is no watertight demarcation between the science of law and philosophy of law as Kelsen would have it. The dynamics of law – i.e. the processes of its creation and application – are as important and as suitable for scientific investigation as the law conceived as a concrete product. A legal purist like Austin regarded the science of legislation as a juridical science *par excellence*.

Pure positivism is self-contradictory for the simple reason that it takes into account only one part of legal reality. In so far as the initial hypothesis of a positivist system claims to be divorced entirely from the element of natural law, the claim is not justified, seeing that that element is contained in the existing law and that the initial hypothesis is admittedly framed so as to embrace as much as possible of actual legal experience.[2] Kelsen himself admits that some natural law – although only the barest minimum of it – is contained in the very idea of the initial hypothesis, i.e. in the postulate of a self-

[1] *Juristischer Formalismus und reine Rechtslehre* (1929), p. 17.
[2] See above, p. 407.

consistent order. He chooses to call it a transcendal-logical natural law for the reason that it is devoid of any element of material justice. Perhaps it would not be difficult to argue that the very assumption of a unity of the legal ordering involves an element of justice, be it merely the justice of a peaceful order. This latter consideration is probably at the basis of the positivist recognition of the existing legal authority as actually obeyed. It would be difficult otherwise to comprehend Kelsen's proud insistence that the initial hypothesis transforms power into right. But for its peace-creating effectiveness the achievement would be of doubtful value. If there existed an effective international order it might be possible to secure in the fundamental hypothesis of municipal law some element of material justice by the simple means of international law refusing to recognize a municipal system which is lacking in certain minimum standards of justice. At present there is no such international authority, and, recognition being a matter for each individual State, international law recognizes a State, i.e. its legal order, on the sole basis of actual power, that is to say, of habitual obedience to the successful authority. Peace and authority and government are in any case better than anarchy. This *désintéressement* of the international society in the quality of the bases of the municipal system is not necessarily permanent. It is a function of the degree of integration of the international community. But in the meantime an initial hypothesis transforming power into right undoubtedly constitutes, juridically, the basis of a peaceful order.

Kelsen's choice of the fundamental hypothesis in international law shows that some measure of ethical postulate may be unavoidable. The gap between the principle *pacta sunt servanda* and the actual practice of States is too wide to permit the unqualified statement that there is a close correspondence between the fundamental hypothesis and the typical manifestations of international life. For, however large may be the measure of observance of international obligations in time of peace and in minor matters in a society in which freedom of action is the rule and legal regulation an exception, in questions of importance the rule *pacta sunt servanda* is still a postulate. On the other hand, the formulation of the fundamental hypothesis is open to criticism inasmuch as it seems to confine international obligations to the express will of States as manifested in *pacta*. While it thus bases the binding force of international law as a whole in an objective rule independent of the will of States, it is still in the chains of the orthodox positivist theory which refuses to recognize any source of international obligations other than the clearly expressed will of States.

Kelsen's dislike of natural law is largely influenced by the view that natural law may be and has been abused for political purposes in a manner not always consistent with progress or justice. We must respectfully decline to follow Kelsen in this respect. Undoubtedly, like everything else, natural law lends itself and has lent itself to abuse. Historically, it has more often than not served as a justification of the existing legal order; it has justified not only private property but also slavery and war. Those who look forward to a natural law revival of international law ought to temper their enthusiasm by remembering that, after all, natural law has produced not only Grotius but Vattel. It was Vattel's book and not that of Grotius which supplied the text for the practices and dispatches of chancellories and foreign offices in the last two centuries. But Vattel's treatise was entitled *Le Droit des gens, ou principes de la loi naturelle appliqués à la conduite et aux affaires des nations et des souverains*. However, exaggeration and abuse ought not to determine the fate of an otherwise beneficent idea. *Ab abusu ad usum non valet consequentia*. We would rather retain natural law with its possible abuses than cut off the branch of law from the tree of justice. We would rather err in pursuit of a good life for all than glory in the secure infallibility of moral indifference. It is true that justice is invoked by selfish interests, but that is a poor reason for dispensing with it altogether. It is true that the 'general good' – another expression for natural justice – is frequently appealed to by partisan interests, but that is not a reason for denying its existence or for asserting that the conception of a legal order realizing the general good of a community on the basis of solidarity of interests is natural law incarnate. It may be that – as Kelsen assumes – the content of a positive legal order is only a compromise between conflicting group interests of which ultimately none is fully satisfied and none totally defeated, but if this is so it is because natural law and natural justice have consciously or subconsciously played their part. The positive legal order is not the result of a physical balance of forces. We may sympathize with Kelsen's insistence on the dignity of man – this is one of the philosophical reasons underlying his attitude to natural law – but, to say the least, we may doubt whether human dignity is involved at all. Affirmation of the autonomy of man need not necessarily result in ethical agnosticism. And frankly, it is not suggested that Kelsen aspires to or succeeds in maintaining his moral relativism. There is, throughout his writings, behind the dialectical and abstract form of the pure science of law, a prophetic pathos – from what other source could there have sprung an iconoclasm so powerful and so creative – which will remain an abiding source of inspiration and which suggests that his ethical relativism is in itself dictated by the moral idea.[1] Kelsen insists that he has always kept his legal science apart from his moral *Weltanschauung*. But we doubt whether this is so as a matter of fact and whether it ought to be so as a matter of method.

I have dealt with this point at some length because there is a danger that this aspect of Kelsen's doctrine may deprive his teaching of the effectiveness to which it is entitled. Kelsen's criticism of the established doctrines is effective not because he has shown them to be natural law, but because he has proved that they are inconsistent with the admitted and necessary assumptions of law. This is the reason why he ought to be able to dispense with the doubtful weapon of the imputation of natural law to anything he disapproves. He finds himself in company which he may otherwise not find congenial. But a slight retreat would strengthen the position as a whole. He has only to admit – as every positivist lawyer ought to do in justice to himself – that positive law has always incorporated and does incorporate ideas of natural law and justice. There would, on our part, be no difficulty in admitting that natural law thus incorporated has ceased to be an independent system and has become part and parcel of positive law. We do not mind if natural law has served a good cause at the expense of its separate existence. But we will mind if a purely negative attitude towards the perennial source of legal justice succeeds in diminishing the effectiveness of a great contribution to the cause of law and – we may say this as Kelsen is not here to correct us – to the cause of justice.

Hans Kelsen was born in 1881 at Prague. In 1911 be became lecturer (*Privatdozent*) at the University of Vienna. In 1919 he was appointed to the Chair of Public Law and Philosophy of Law in that University. Since 1930 he has been Professor of Public and International Law at the University of Cologne.

His principal works are:

Hauptprobleme der Staatsrechtslehre (*entwickelt aus der Lehre vom Rechtssatz*) (1st ed. 1911; 2nd, unaltered, ed. 1923, with a new Preface): cited here as *Hauptprobleme*.

[1] For a confirmation of this view the student is invited to read the concluding pages of his *Vom Wesen und Wert der Demokratie* which, it is submitted, are among the best that political literature has produced.

Das Problem der Souveränität und die Theorie des Völkerrechts (1st ed. 1920; 2nd ed. 1918): cited here as *Souveränität.*

Der soziologische und juristische Staatsbegriff (1st ed. 1922; 2nd ed. 1928): cited here as *Staatsbegriff.*

Allgemenine Staatslehre (1925): cited here as *Staatslehre.*

The following of the more important monographs and articles may be mentioned:

Die Staatslehre des Dante Alighieri (1905).

Über Grenzen zwischen juristischer und soziologischer Methode (1911).

Die Verfassungsgesetze der Republik Deutschösterreich (1919, 1920).

Vom Wesen und Wert der Demokratie (1st ed. 1920; 2nd, revised, ed. 1929).

Österreichisches Staatsrecht (1923).

Sozialismus und Staat (1923).

Die Bundesexekution (1927).

Der Staat als Integration (1930).

'Les rapports de système entre le droit interne et le droit international public', *Hague Recueil,* 14 (1926) (iv), 231–331.

'Über Staatsunrecht', in *Zeitschrift für das Privat- und Öffentliche Recht der Gegenwart,* 40 (1913), 1–114.

'Zur Lehre vom öffentlichen Rechtsgeschäft', in *Archiv des öffentlichen Rechts,* 31 (1913), 53–98, 190–249.

'Die Rechtswissenschaft als Norm- oder als Kulturwissenschaft', in Schmoller's *Jahrbuch,* 40 (1916), 1181–239.

'Zur Theorie der juristischen Fiktionen', in *Annalen der Philosophie,* 1 (1919), 630–58.

'Sozialismus und Staat', in *Archiv für die Geschichte des Sozialismus und der Arbeiterbewegung,* 9 (1920), 1–129.

'Das Verhältnis von Staat und Recht im Lichte der Erkenntniskritik', in *Z.ö.R.* 2 (1921), 453–510.

'Gott und Staat', in *Logos,* 2 (1922–3), 261–84.

'Marx oder Lassalle', in *Archiv für die Geschichte des Sozialismus und der Arbeiterbewegung,* 9 (1924), 261–98.

Das Problem des Parlamentarismus (1925).

Die philosophischen Grundlagen der Naturrechtslehre und des Rechtspositivismus. (Publications of the Kant Society, 1928).

'Allgemeine Rechtslehre im Lichte materialistischer Geschichtsauffassung', in *Archiv für Sozialwissenschaft und Sozialpolitik,* 66 (1931), 449–521.

And see, for an exhaustive bibliography of Kelsen's writings, Métall, in *Gesellschaft, Staat und Recht. Festschrift gewidmet Hans Kelsen* (1931), pp. 417–41.

CHAPTER 16

BRIERLY'S CONTRIBUTION TO INTERNATIONAL LAW

Editor's note Lauterpacht had the great ability to take a synoptic view of the work of an author in the field of international law and to present a comprehensive and constructive assessment of his mark on the subject. We have already seen three illustrations of this technique in the present section, of which the most important is 'The Grotian Tradition in International Law' (see above, p. 307). In this chapter a comparable technique is applied to the work of J. L. Brierly, who held the Chichele Chair of International Law and Diplomacy at Oxford, from 1922 to 1947.

It is a reflection of Lauterpacht's great concern that nothing which was worth while should be lost or overlooked that in 1958 he joined Brierly's successor in the Oxford Chair, Humphrey Waldock, in preparing a volume of Brierly's collected papers under the title of *The Basis of Obligation in International Law and other Papers*. The essay printed here served as an introduction to that volume (pp. xv–xxxvi), having originally been published as a tribute to Brierly in the *British Year Book of International Law*, 32 (1955–6).

I

Brierly's most significant – and perhaps most lasting – contribution to international law lies in the fact that during a period of transition and reassessment of values he threw the weight of his writing and teaching in the scales of what may properly be regarded as a progressive conception of international law. From the outset he dissociated himself from the still predominant doctrines of rigid positivism. He had no hesitation in pointing to the beneficent potentialities of a revived law of nature as one of the main elements of the moral foundation of international law – for, upon final analysis, he saw no other basis for it. Largely for the latter reason, he stressed the limitations of the view that States only, as distinguished from individuals, are subjects of international law. He affirmed, in opposition to the dualistic school of thought, the essential unity and identity of international and municipal law. He challenged, as being incompatible with the very notion of international law, the current conception of the international sovereignty of the State. On all these matters he did not aspire to have discovered new truths. All pretentiousness was alien to him. He did not claim to have founded sociological or similar schools of thought. Yet there are few writers on modern international law who have exhibited a greater capacity for searching painstakingly, at the risk of inconclusiveness and of creating occasionally the impression of contradiction, for some unifying element amidst the perplexing social reality of the relations of States – of States which, as he said, are civilized but for the primitive nature of their mutual relations.

The period which began at the end of the First World War, approximately at the time when Brierly was commencing his career as teacher and writer, witnessed the advent of radical changes in the doctrine of international law. In many ways these incipient changes were no more than expressions of developments in actual practice – to which extent they were truly positivist – but they nevertheless bore the mark of novelty. Those who attempted to give them expression in terms of basic notions of international law were still looked upon as innovators. At the time when the present assessment of Brierly's contribution is being written, these apparently doctrinal difficulties seem to have received a quietus. With regard to many of them, their approximation to actual practice has become too manifest to permit of doubt. Thus, having regard to the widely extended scope of international law and to other developments, it is now generally acknowledged that there remains little substance in the view – previously almost uncontested – that States only and exclusively are subjects of international law. The same applies to the rigidly conceived notion that the will of States is the only source of international law. This has also been the fate of the dogma that international and municipal law are fundamentally different and disparate – a dogma whose validity has become particularly doubtful at a time when the constitutional law of many countries has formally incorporated international law as part of the law of the land.

In these – as in some other – respects, what in 1924 was iconoclastic has become almost orthodox. This is so although the reality of the changes which have been accomplished tends to be obscured by the more immediate reality of the insecurity and the precariousness of the international political scene. However, after the First World War, when Brierly was embarking upon his career as an international lawyer, the attack on positivism and its offshoots in their various manifestations had only begun. Brierly's adherence to the challenge, and the manner of his adherence to it, gave to the new tendencies a sustained accession of strength and authority. It is in this sense that

Judge Charles de Visscher has recently referred to 'les écrits à la fois profonds et mesurés de J. L. Brierly'.[1] It is also from this point of view that it is intended to survey here the principal aspects of Brierly's contribution: the rejection of positivism, the affirmation of the moral foundation of international law, the recognition of the individual as a subject of international law, the vindication of the unity of international and municipal law, and his criticism of the notion of the international sovereignty of the State.

Rejection of positivism

Brierly's rejection of positivism dates back to the very beginning of his work. Already in his inaugural lecture delivered in 1924 he deplored the fact that 'international law lost the most faithful seed of development that it has ever had when, far too early for the health of the system, though doubtless inevitably, its foundation in natural law was undermined'.[2] He deplored it, on that occasion, for the reason that the divorce from natural law, in depriving international law of a fruitful source of development, affected adversely the possibility of peaceful change – a subject which, as we shall see, became a recurring and somewhat laboured theme of his writings. However, his attitude to natural law was determined by more weighty reasons. It went to the roots of his legal and political philosophy. Thus at the conclusion of his lectures, delivered in 1928, on 'The Basis of Obligation in International Law', we find him saying that, if we wish to go on living and acting, we are all bound to act as if we were convinced of the reality of an objective order, physical and moral. This, he said, amounts to a belief in a law of nature, but, he added, 'I confess that to me the modern resurgence of natural law theories seems to open a vista full of hope for legal science.'[3]

He developed in his text-book[4] the same theme at greater length and by reference to its principal implications. He recognized the limitations and possible dangers of some of the doctrines of the law of nature inasmuch as they connote an immutability of its content or introduce the 'anarchical principle' which claims for natural law the power to overrule positive law in case of conflict. These valid criticisms did not, in his view, affect the 'paramount truths' in the con-

[1] *Théories et réalités en droit international public* (2nd ed. 1955), p. 448.

[2] 'The Shortcomings of International Law', in *B.Y.* 5 (1924), p. 9.

[3] 'Le Fondement du caractère obligatoire du droit international' (hereinafter cited as 'Fondement'), in *Hague Receuil*, 23 (1928) (iii), 549.

[4] Brierly, *The Law of Nations*, pp. 20–5.

ception of the law of nature – one of which truths is the emphasis upon the purpose and the ends of law, differently formulated in different times and places, as distinguished from law conceived as the will of the sovereign or as a mere conglomeration of principles mechanically applied by courts. Similarly, it is the law of nature – natural justice – which supplies the substance of decision in case of apparent gaps in the law in order to meet novel problems or situations. Thus viewed, such gaps are only apparent. In fact, it was largely owing to the place which he assigned to the law of nature that Brierly had no doubt about accepting the completeness of the legal order as a principle of administration of international justice.[1]

As in practically everything that he wrote, he did not weaken the force of his argument by a refusal to qualify it when necessary. Thus he recognized the service rendered by positivism inasmuch as it assisted in drawing more sharply the line between law and ethics.[2] Similarly, he had no hesitation in rejecting the doctrine of fundamental rights notwithstanding its association with doctrines of natural law and the service which it rendered in the formative period of international law.[3]

The moral foundation of international law

It is not surprising, having regard to the place which he assigned to the law of nature, that he should have sought in ethics the ultimate foundations of international law.

> We are too often tempted to forget that the link between law and morals is much more fundamental than the difference between them and that the ultimate basis of the obligation to obey the law can only be a moral one. The problem of the binding nature of international law is only one aspect of the binding character of law in general, in the same way as the latter is no more than an aspect of the wider problem of obligation in general. And this is a problem of ethics.[4]

This, he was at pains to explain, does not mean that legal and moral obligations are of the same nature, or that in case of a conflict we are entitled to disregard the legal obligation in deference to what we conceive to be our moral duty. For we must always bear in mind such compensatory factors as the prospect of obtaining a modification of the law, the social evil resulting from the refusal to obey the law, and the possibility that we may be erring in our judgment as to the moral aspect of a particular rule. What the assumption of the ethical

[1] See below, p. 449. [2] 'Fondement', p. 547.
[3] *Ibid.* p. 476; and see below, p. 439.
[4] 'Fondement', p. 547 (the translation is the writer's).

foundation of the law means, in the first instance, is that no other answer is possible to the question why it is that we must obey the law for no other reason than that it is the law.

However, it is clear that that assumption signified for him more than a formal statement that, as a matter of logic, the basis of international law must be non-juridical inasmuch as it is not possible to ground it exclusively on the consent or in the will of States – just as, as a matter of logic, the binding force of the highest and fundamental rule of law within the State cannot itself be based on a legal rule. In fact, one of the main reasons for his rejection of positivism was that its result 'has been to secularize the whole idea of law and thus to weaken the moral foundation which is essential to the vitality of all legal obligation'.[1] We shall see presently what were some of the practical consequences which he deduced from his view of the moral basis of international law.[2] In the present context, it is sufficient to say that that view determined his entire approach to the practical application and the teaching of international law as when, in urging the rightful place of international law in the study of the law, he pointed to the close connection between law, morals and politics, and the consequent importance of international law for the philosophic study of the law, as well as the importance of the study of politics by the lawyer;[3] or when he elaborated the theme of international law as an instrument of welfare operating by consent rather than as a system of coercion;[4] or when he stressed, in relation to international law, 'the right of private judgment according to the guidance of each man's conscience' – a right whose ultimate validity only a philosophy of totalitarianism could deny.[5]

For he was emphatic that as the law exists for the sake of the individual living in society, its final appeal must be directed to the individual and not to a non-existent collective conscience.[6] No system of law, he insisted, partakes of an absolute value; there is no rule, either of law or of ethics, which is absolutely independent of the situation in which the individual is called upon to act. It is this aspect of his philosophy which largely explains his affirmation of the position

[1] Brierly, p. 45.

[2] See below, p. 440.

[3] 'International Law as a Subject of Education', in *Journal of the Society of Public Teachers of Law* (1926), p. 5.

[4] *The Outlook for International Law* (1944), p. 106 (hereinafter cited as *Outlook*).

[5] 'Vitoria and International Law', in *Dublin Review* (July 1947), p. 11. In the same line of thought, although he believed that order precedes law—and not conversely—he was clear that 'although Hitler could probably have given order, or a sort of order, to Europe . . . he would never have given it law' (*Outlook*, p. 74).

[6] 'Fondement', p. 548.

of the individual human being as a possible subject of international law, and his disinclination to concede that only States can be its subjects. This also made it wholly unnecessary for him to attach any importance to the view – heavily relied upon by some adherents of the modern realistic school in international relations – that as the collective conscience is untrammelled by the restraints of private morality, the moral content of international law and, correspondingly, the efficacy of international law as such, must be correspondingly reduced. For the question hardly arises if international law is conceived as being addressed, ultimately and actually, to individual human beings.

The individual as a subject of international law

However, while Brierly's recognition of the place of the individual in international law was due in large measure to his acceptance of the moral basis of international law, this was not the only reason for his attitude in the matter. There were other reasons. In particular, in addition to the fact that international law had already recognized in many ways the procedural capacity of individuals, he saw that some such developments in other directions corresponded to the realities of international life. Thus, although the State is in some ways an expression of the unity of its subjects, it is not true that they have no other interests, including international interests, except those represented by their State.[1] From this point of view, the rule that States are subjects of international law is no more than a rule of convenience; there is no sacrosanctity about it. On the contrary, considerations of utility may militate in favour of the return to the Grotian conception of the international community being not an association of *civitates*, but a community of *genus humanum*. Thus he pointed out that there may be a measure – though only a measure – of convenience in the abandonment of the orthodox practice which, by rendering the national State a necessary and exclusive party to proceedings arising out of an injury to an individual, tends to impart a political complexion to every attempt to vindicate his rights.

He uttered warnings against adopting the extreme of the opposite solution. For – and here he seems subsequently to have somewhat modified his attitude – 'it seems to be the case that the nature of international society, and in particular its vastness and heterogeneity, imposes, as a rule which it is nearly always convenient to adhere to, the practice that international law should touch the individual not

[1] 'Fondement', p. 529.

directly, but only through the State to which he belongs'.[1] Yet it is not certain that this manner of placing the emphasis represented his final conclusions on the matter. He had previously challenged, as being strained and artificial, the view that in espousing the cause of its nationals before an international jurisdiction the State actually defends its own right to insist on respect for international law in relation to the person of its nationals[2] – a view which is based on the assumption that the individual as such has no rights under international law. Eventually, notwithstanding his customary restraint, Brierly was prepared to go to the length of accepting and urging the view that the contrary is the case, and that upon final analysis it is only the individual who is a subject of international rights and duties.[3] This is so although as a rule States are the immediate members of international society. The subjects of law are the same in international and municipal law.

These two systems of law differ, in fact, in their technique and their procedure, not in their essence. When we say that a rule of international law imposes an obligation upon a State, what we actually intend to say – unless we wish to utter an absurdity – is that although that obligation must, like any other, be performed in the last resort by one or more individuals, international law leaves it to municipal law to designate the individual or individuals in question.[4]

The unity of international and municipal law

It is in the light of this approach to these questions that Brierly arrived at the affirmation of the essential unity and identity of international and municipal law and the rejection of the then still predominant dualistic view. He deprecated the customary exaggerations of the absence of sanctions of international law and the laxity of its observance. He suggested that, in normal periods of peace, international law is probably more regularly observed than municipal law – though he admitted that the regularity of its observance stems largely from the fact that its obligations, being limited in scope, weigh only lightly upon Governments.[5] The difference between the two systems, he urged, lies not in the realm of principle but in that of organization. 'It is right that international lawyers should not blind themselves to the defects of the existing international order, but candour does not require of them to take refuge in a doctrine which

[1] 'The Rule of Law in International Society', in *Nordisk T.A.* 7 (1936), 18.

[2] 'The Theory of Implied State Complicity in International Claims', in *B.Y.* 9 (1928), 42–9. And see, for a restatement of this view, 'Règles générales du droit de la paix' (hereinafter cited as 'Règles Générales'), in *Hague Recueil*, 58 (1936) (iv), 45.

[3] *Ibid.* p. 47. [4] *Ibid.* p. 40. [5] 'Fondement', p. 532.

makes of these defects a specific and paramount quality of that order.'[1] It is also for this reason that, after a restrained and critical analysis of actual practice, he summed up as 'beneficial' the so-called doctrine of incorporation – namely, the doctrine according to which courts apply international law, *per se*, as being part of the law of the land. It is, in his view, beneficial not only as showing that municipal courts apply international law as authoritative in its own right, but also 'because by asserting that it is part of the law of the land we deny that it has any specific quality which distinguishes it from that law'.[2] The doctrine of incorporation has constituted one of the main contributions of the common law to international legal tradition. Its significance as such has occasionally been obscured by dicta on the part of judges when actually engaged in giving effect to it, or by writers intent upon stressing the specific character of international law and its subjects and the view that it is therefore incapable of forming *per se* part of municipal law – a purely doctrinal approach rendered even more theoretical by the almost general trend of modern constitutions declaring international law to be part of the law of the land.

The independence and the sovereignty of States

Finally, the denial of any specific character of international law led Brierly, as it has led others, to an emphatic rejection of the validity, in the international sphere, of the notion of sovereignty as the supreme will not subordinated to any overriding legal obligation. Such a notion he conceived to be inconsistent with the very concept of international law. His criticism of the theory of self-limitation as an explanation of the source of international legal obligation was trenchant and unqualified.[3] He distinguished sovereignty, thus conceived, from independence, i.e. absence of dependence upon other States. That notion of independence he regarded as legitimate – though, like Westlake, he refused to believe that it is entitled to any quality of absoluteness. He denied, in particular, any 'natural right' to independence. To assert any such right would be to suggest that for an independent State to pass from the condition of independence to that of dependence necessarily involves a moral loss 'instead of a mere change of legal status to be judged according to the circumstances of the case'.[4] No moral loss accompanied the merger

[1] *Ibid.* p. 535.
[2] Brierly, p. 90.
[3] 'Fondement', p. 483. See below, p. 449, n. 5.
[4] Brierly, p. 122.

of the American States into the Union – an example not without significance for the possibilities of international integration.

It is also for that reason that he frequently availed himself of the opportunity of challenging the doctrine of fundamental rights which – being an expression of extreme individualism – treats as immutable the present status of independent sovereignties in international society.[1] It is for the same reason that, again closely following Westlake, he considered self-preservation to be not a right but an instinct which is liable to, and in need of, regulation by law.[2] In its current absolute connotation as identical with irresponsible will, the international sovereignty of States was to him no less objectionable than the internal sovereignty – including that of the majority in the democratic State. To adhere to that notion of sovereignty was, in his view, to render inescapable the conclusion that 'international law is nothing but a delusion'.[3] He had no hesitation in criticizing, with his customary restraint, certain expressions of the Permanent Court of International Justice in the case of *The Lotus* which, when taken in isolation, were liable to be misunderstood as giving undue prominence to sovereign States as a source of law.[4] He looked forward to the time when these terms will become no more than an honorific epithet.[5] Neither did he limit his criticism of sovereignty to its express manifestations. Thus, inasmuch as it is clear that the extreme application of the doctrine of equality of States is no more than an offshoot of the claim to a fundamental right emanating from sovereignty, he rejected it in emphatic terms as being no more than 'a quite spurious application of a nominally democratic principle'[6] and as misleading, mischievous and obstructive of progress.

At the same time, his capacity and his desire not to overstate his

[1] 'Fondement', p. 473.
[2] Brierly, p. 295.
[3] *Ibid.* pp. 15, 16.
[4] 'Règles Générales', p. 147.
[5] The following passage from a paper read in 1945 may aptly be quoted in this connection: 'Mais si nous voulons être les maîtres et non pas les esclaves des termes politiques que nous trouvons convenables d'user, alors nous pouvons au moins espérer qu'au fur et à mesure que le droit international exercera une influence progressivement plus forte dans les relations internationales, nous n'oublierons pas que, en appliquant l'épithète de souverain à un État, nous voudrons dire tout simplement qu'il s'agit d'un État indépendant, d'un État qui n'est pas subordonné à aucun autre, et rien que cela, et par là nous n'impliquerons absolument rien quant à sa position par rapport au droit international. En parlant des États comme souverains, comme je ne doute pas que nous continuerons à en parler, nous pourrons même parvenir à sentir et à nous rendre compte que ce terme n'est rien de plus qu'un épithète honorifique conventionnel, plus ou moins comme chez Homère Ulysse est toujours "rusé" et chez Virgile Énée est toujours "pieux"' ('La doctrine de la souveraineté dans le droit international moderne', in *Academia das ciências de Lisboa* (1945), pp. 24, 25).
[6] Brierly, p. 124.

case and to give a complete picture of the problem involved caused him repeatedly to draw attention to the fact that the place which the doctrine of sovereignty held in the doctrine of international law was no mere aberration of logic. It was an expression of the overriding reality of the actual power wielded by States.[1] An analysis which ignored that factor was bound to be incomplete.

2

In the preceding pages an attempt has been made to give an account of Brierly's approach to the basic aspects of international law. It is now proposed to draw attention to what is perhaps the most characteristic – as it is the most persistent – feature of his teaching in this respect, namely, the use to which he put his emphasis upon the moral and spiritual content of the law. It is this feature which explains his repeated insistence on the inherent limitations of the range of international law. This feature, coupled with a high intellectual integrity, made him impatient of easy solutions which treat the law, or the mere formulation or formal acceptance of it, as a panacea. Law is to him an organic thing; it is no mere piece of machinery. The efforts of lawyers cannot create the ground for its full operation – though they can stimulate its growth once we have obtained clarity on the restricted scope of our endeavour. Such clarity – a theme which he developed in many a context – consists in the realization that law never creates order, but is its product.[2] Law depends on international organization; the more comprehensive that organization, the more fully will there be established the primary condition of the growth and of the effectiveness of the law. It is largely – though not exclusively – for that reason that he was critical of exclusive reliance on the acceptance of international obligations of judicial and other methods of pacific settlement and on the mere formulation of the law. Considerations of that nature apparently weighed with him when he expressed scepticism concerning the current proposals to establish an International Criminal Court.[3] It is possible – perhaps probable –

[1] See, for example, 'International Law: Some Conditions of its Progress', in *International Affairs*, 22 (1946), 353, and the lucid comment on this aspect of the problem by Charles de Visscher, *Théories et réalités*, p. 87.

[2] See, in particular, *Outlook*, pp. 74 *et seq.*; and in *International Affairs*, 22 (1946), 359.

[3] 'Do we need an International Criminal Court?', in *B.Y.* 8 (1927), 81–8. For the same reason he also expressed doubts as to any excess of confidence in the effectiveness of imposed solutions in the matter of settling international disputes. 'The truth is that government with the consent or at least with the acquiescence of the governed and in particular of those among the governed whom a measure particularly affects is not a mere ideal, but

that his suspicion of imposed or ready-made solutions caused him to exaggerate, or misjudge, the importance of the question of priority in the relations of law and order. It would seem that he did not attach sufficient weight to the effect which the law, albeit extraneous and artificial in its inception, gradually exercises upon the habits and the thinking of society; that he did not give full scope to the possibility that law and order may be established *pari passu*; and, above all, that he may have failed to realize that order is in a large measure no more than a system of legal obligations for respecting and ensuring respect for and observance of order. Moreover, as we shall see, in the course of the final development of his thought he came to realize the limitations of this approach to the problem and the necessity for its revision.

But there was one aspect of his emphasis upon the limitations of the scope of law to which Brierly devoted particular attention, which is a recurrent topic in practically every one of his major contributions, and which he apparently never abandoned. This is the view that having regard to the fact that the membership of the international community is distinctly limited in comparison with the multitude of individuals composing the national society, the content of international law must necessarily be restricted in the matter of general principles. Within the State the law governs large numbers of individuals possessing identical qualities; it can disregard the differences seeing that, on the whole, these are outweighed by similarities. In international society, where 'every state is unique', stress must be laid not on the qualities which they have in common, but on the features and interests which are particular to them.[1]

Brierly did not claim originality in propounding this theme. In particular, he often acknowledged his indebtedness in this respect to the writings of Professor Schindler.[2] He could have claimed earlier authority – that of Maitland[3] – in support of that view. However, he

one of the basic conditions upon which the smooth and efficient working of modern government depends' ('The Essential Nature of International Disputes', in *Virginia Law Review*, 16 (1930), 543). He suggested that the true analogy lies rather in the field of settling disputes, especially of an economic nature, between powerful groups within the State, where the typical method is that of conciliation or of legislation aiming at balancing conflicting interests.

[1] 'The Rule of Law in International Society', in *Nordisk T.A.* 7 (1936), 9, 10; *Outlook*, pp. 40 *et seq.*; 'Règles Générales', pp. 17, 18.

[2] *Hague Recueil*, 46 (1933), (iv), 265.

[3] 'In my view the great difficulty in obtaining a body of international rules deserving the name of law lies in the extreme fewness of the 'persons' subject to that law and the infrequency and restricted range of the arguable questions which arise between them' (letter to Henry Sidgwick (11 December 1888), printed in Fisher, *Frederic William Maitland* (1910), p. 48).

found a considerable following on the subject[1] and it may not be out of place to re-examine it critically. In the first instance, any mischief resulting from the inapplicability of general principles may be tempered by the application of specific rules and exceptions – a factor which constitutes an argument in favour of, not against, the elaboration of the law. The circumstance that such specific regulation is not easy of achievement and that it may require the consent of the interested States points to the difficulty of the task, not to its lacking urgency or justification. There may be a measure of deceptiveness and oversimplification in entrusting it to international tribunals which possess no compulsory jurisdiction. Moreover, in so far as international tribunals may play a legitimate part in this connection, they must – unless their task is to be one of regulation of interests or of outright judicial legislation – be assisted by general principles either already existing or specifically adopted. Thus, for instance – an example on which Brierly frequently relied – it is true that no two international rivers are the same. But, as he himself admitted,[2] there exist general principles of law not infrequently acted upon by international tribunals which in most cases may provide a satisfactory solution, such as the principle of prohibition of abuse of rights or of equitable apportionment of legitimate interests. It is a matter of machinery whether the application of these principles is entrusted to international courts or river commissions. Above all, in most spheres of international law[3] – such as diplomatic immunities or the law of treaties – detailed regulation is feasible and desirable provided that existing divergences are not elevated to the rank of fundamental differences of national interest and outlook.

Neither is it easy to accept another of his reasons for the limitation of the place of legal regulation in the international sphere, namely, the alleged fact of the limited scope of contacts between States.[4] For, as he himself admitted, the international contacts of individuals have conspicuously tended to increase. Modern international law has been conspicuous for the manner in which these contacts have tended to be governed by general multilateral conventions concluded between Governments.[5]

[1] See, for example, Charles de Visscher, *Théories et réalités*, pp. 171, 195.

[2] 'Règles Générales, p. 187.

[3] As shown, for instance, in the volumes of the Harvard Research on Codification and the Report submitted in 1956 by Sir Gerald Fitzmaurice to the International Law Commission and embodying a detailed code on some aspects of the law of treaties.

[4] See, for instance, 'The Function of Law in International Relations', in *Problems of Peace* (1929), p. 284.

[5] See Jenks, 'The Scope of International Law', in *B.Y.* 31 (1954), 1–48.

However, that may be, the frequent reliance on the argument of the 'fewness of the members of the international community' considerably influenced Brierly's views not only on the inherent limitations of the place of law in international society but also on particular questions, such as that of the codification of international law. This was probably the main reason why, notwithstanding – or, perhaps, because of – direct personal experience in that sphere, he assigned but a narrow function to the work of codification. He was inclined to limit it to what is occasionally described as restatement of those parts of international law with regard to which there is general agreement and no actual divergence of practice. In so far as codification amounts to creating new law with the view either to meeting new conditions or reconciling actual and important conflicts of national interests, he was of the opinion that a task of that nature was more suitably within the province of Governments and politicians.[1] It is not necessary here to express an opinion upon the justification of that view. It stemmed largely from the conviction, already noted, of the limitations of legal regulation in the international sphere. But it sprang also from a discipline of thought and an integrity of method reluctant to sanction easy solutions and to confuse machinery with substance.[2]

It was also this inclination to assign but a limited field to legal regulation which, coupled with his recognition of the moral basis of international law, explains the persistence, for a long time, of the theme of peaceful change in his writings. Law which is static tends not only to be inadequate; it must increasingly be lacking in moral content. That aspect of international relations was predominant in his mind when, in particular with regard to the problem of obligatory pacific settlement, he returned repeatedly to the dictum that 'law is not a panacea'. He had already given expression to these views in his

[1] See, for example, 'The Future of Codification', *ibid.* 12 (1930), 1–12, especially at p. 8.

[2] In his article, written in 1948, on 'The Codification of International Law', in *Michigan Law Review*, 47 (1948), p. 4, he said: 'We are tempted to think of codification as a cheap method of establishing international order, as something that lawyers could easily do for the world if only they could be brought to see how badly it needs doing. But that is a complete delusion. The responsibility cannot be shifted in this light-hearted way on to the shoulders of the lawyers. Lawyers can help; they can do the donkey work, but the responsibility belongs to all of us, and of course particularly to the leaders of our nations. For international law can only be codified if and so far as sovereign nations will agree among themselves on what the lawyers are to put into the code, and we have only too much evidence of the difficulty of getting agreements of that kind. The ambiguity of the word codification, its use to describe two processes which differ so widely both in their objects and in the techniques that they require, has had most unfortunate effects; it has disguised the real difficulties and induced men to think of codification as a means of international progress that can be adopted without any important concessions being made by our nations. It is something very different from that.'

inaugural lecture;[1] he did not modify them until the Second World War.[2] Occasionally he came near to finding, on that score, a justification of war as an instrument of change;[3] he found it difficult to concede without reservations the illegality of war, which, he thought, fulfils in the international sphere the same function as revolution within the State. Both aim at effecting changes which cannot be achieved within the limits and according to the forms of the law – the only difference being that whereas municipal law does not envisage the contingency of a revolution and does not regulate it in advance, international law possesses a system of rules governing the conduct of war.[4] He attached importance to reiterating that an international dispute is not necessarily 'settled' merely because it has received a legal quietus.[5] A survey of the literature of this and the following period shows the full extent of his influence in this respect.[6]

His over-emphasis of the question of peaceful change was probably an error of judgment on his part, and he realized and admitted it in the end. The antinomy of stability and change is an abiding problem of all law, both in the administration of justice and otherwise. For obvious reasons it may be particularly acute in the international sphere having regard to the absence of a Legislature amending, with binding effect, the existing law. It does not follow that we are right in underestimating, on that account, the normal beneficence of the observance and the enforcement of law – especially if, at the same time, we proclaim the impracticability of alternative solutions such as the establishment of an international Legislature decreeing any necessary changes of the *status quo*. This being so, it is not surprising that in the course of time Brierly came to revise his views on the subject. Writing in 1942, he pointed to past exaggerations of the problem of peaceful change. He recalled the fact that many wars – and, in particular, most wars in his lifetime – could not have been prevented by the existence of an international authority decreeing reasonable changes of the law.[7] These wars were not due to demands which could be related to any properly conceived problem of peaceful change and which could have been satisfied by offers made in

[1] 'Shortcomings of International Law', in *B.Y.* 5 (1924), 16; *ibid.* 11 (1930), 130–2 (in relation to the General Act of 1928); *ibid.* 12 (1931), 134.

[2] See below, p. 445.

[3] 'International Law and Resort to Armed Force', in *Cambridge Law Journal*, 4 (1930–2), 318.

[4] 'Règles Générales', pp. 117, 118.

[5] Brierly, p. 289.

[6] See, once more, Charles de Visscher, *Théories réalités*, p. 411, and, in particular, the writings of Sir John Fischer Williams and E. H. Carr.

[7] 'Law, Justice and War', in *Czechoslovak Year Book of International Law* (1942), p. 19.

accordance with reason or justice. Later on he elaborated this development of his thought in a separate chapter of *The Outlook for International Law*[1] – a chapter to which he apparently attached so much importance that he incorporated it in the last edition of *The Law of Nations*.[2] Eventually, he went the full length in abandoning a point of view which, under his influence, had gained considerable currency. The relevant passage merits quotation:

We are sometimes told that to put security first would be to stabilize the *status quo* and that that would be neither practicable nor just. I think there is more than one answer to that objection. For one thing, if we want to have law we shall have to recognize that it is by its nature a conservative force; we shall have to accept a bias, and a strong bias, in favour of the *status quo*. But for my part I would go farther than this and say that I think we have heard too much of the problem of peaceful change during the inter-war years.[3]

It is a measure of Brierly's intellectual integrity that he should have so fully and emphatically turned his back upon what seemed formerly to constitute one of the pillars of his creed.

Brierly's main contribution and influence lay in the field of philosophy of international law and its impact upon international relations. In his introductory text-book he could touch but lightly upon substantive questions of international law. Yet on those occasions on which he discussed in detail a particular question of international law, he showed, with valuable results, the qualities of his analytical mind. Thus there has been wide acceptance of his criticism of the traditional view that, in the field of State responsibility, the interest of the individual is fully merged in the formal interest of his State.[4] There was more than a suggestion of a shift of emphasis, on the question of termination of treaties on account of a change of circumstances, when he urged the analogy of the rule of English law on the subject, namely, that the contract is not dissolved by a change of circumstances as such, however vital, but only by an implied term of the contract itself in the sense that it is to be dissolved when the event in question has occurred.[5] On the intractable problem of the validity of treaties imposed by force, he contributed the valuable suggestion that it is preferable to regard instruments of that nature as legislative

[1] (1944), ch. viii. [2] Brierly, pp. 265–72.

[3] 'International Law: Some Conditions of its Progress', in *International Affairs*, 22 (1946), 358. [4] See above, p. 437, n. 2.

[5] 'Some Considerations on the Obsolescence of Treaties', in *Grotius Society*, 11 (1925), 16, 17; see also, to the same effect, 'Règles Générales', p. 215.

acts rather than compacts based on the consent of the parties.[1] His essay on 'Domestic Jurisdiction',[2] although bearing mainly on the Geneva Protocol for the Pacific Settlement of International Disputes, sheds instructive light on the subject. His article on 'The Nature of War Crimes Jurisdiction'[3] elucidated in a helpful manner the basis of the jurisdiction of municipal courts, as distinguished from that of international tribunals, to adjudicate upon war crimes. In particular, he pointed out that as the jurisdiction of municipal courts in the matter is grounded in the law of war, it need not take into account all the limitations of municipal law, operating in normal times of peace, such as the prohibition of retroactivity or the principle of territoriality, likely – in the circumstances – to defeat the ends of justice.

3

There is one feature of Brierly's work which pertains to the domain of method rather than of substance, but which can nevertheless properly be regarded as being in the nature of a distinct contribution to the science of international law. That contribution lay not so much in the solutions which he propounded – for he often admitted, or implied, that there was no solution or no easy solution – as in the way in which he pointed to the difficulties involved and, after apparently propounding an answer to them, proceeded to develop the theme of the deceptiveness and the insufficiency of the answer thus given. It would almost appear that what weighed with him was not the result of the search, but the search itself; that he was content to be an exponent of difficulties and not a provider of solutions; and that it did not matter to him that in fact he left the problem unresolved. It is this intellectual integrity, which chooses the more arduous method and which is content with raising the question without aspiring to propound a clear-cut or a fully satisfying solution – where in all conscience none is believed to exist – which may well be among his most notable achievements. On occasions that tendency to hesitation, to inconclusiveness, and to piling qualifications upon qualifications may seem unsatisfying and perplexing. But there is at least room for the view that in the sphere of international law and international relations the appearance of complete solutions may be deceptive and confidence in them misplaced. This may not be a method which recommends itself to everyone, but it seems fair to say that inter-

[1] *Ibid.* p. 208.

[2] In *B.Y.* 6 (1925), 8–19.

[3] In *The Norseman*, 2 (1944), 2–8.

national law has been enriched by the way in which Brierly pursued it.

He stressed the place of order as an essential prerequisite of and antecedent to law. But order implies, if necessary, coercion and the obligation to take part in coercion. Yet he insisted repeatedly that States, being powerful groups, cannot normally be coerced, and that the duty to participate in the coercing of an aggressor ought to be undertaken only if we are sure that, when the time comes, we shall be willing and that we shall be in a position to comply with that obligation. But of that, he urged, we cannot be sure. He himself was not certain whether, having regard to the fact that Governments are the trustees not of their consciences but of the transcending interests of their States, any such promises covering necessarily unforeseeable contingencies ought to be given at all. So while he conceded the importance of precise commitments as an element of international order, he doubted whether they ought to be made at the risk of uncertainty whether they will be honoured.[1] While he was prepared to counsel the acceptance at least of the precise obligation not to help an aggressor, we are not sure that he was willing to go to the length of the precise obligation to leave to an outside body the legal power to determine the aggressor. Yet eventually he was inclined to admit that the very interest of the State may require, in modern conditions, the adoption of the principle of the indivisibility of peace – which he questioned on occasions – and the consequent recognition of the deceptiveness of neutrality as a principle of policy. The latter was probably the view which, in the end, he was inclined – with hesitation, occasional oscillation, and qualifications[2] – to accept.

We have seen how, by degrees, Brierly came to relegate the problem of peaceful change from the central position which it originally occupied in his thought. He did not abandon it altogether, and he deemed it incumbent upon him to examine the possibilities of machinery appropriate for that purpose.[3] But investigation suggested to him that specialized machinery – such as an equity tribunal or legislation brought about by an international authority – was neither necessary nor desirable, and that the most promising

[1] *Outlook*, p. 87.

[2] His exposition of the subject in *Outlook*, pp. 79–85, is no more than a marshalling of opposing arguments. See also, in the same vein, his paper on 'The Existence, Basis, Scope and Consequences of the Prohibition of War in International Law', in *Report of the International Law Conference* (1943), pp. 23–32. And see 'Law, Justice and Peace', in *Czechoslovak Year Book of International Law* (1942), p. 20, for an unqualified expression of the view that 'force must be organized'—which consummation is hardly possible without specific binding obligations undertaken in advance.

[3] *Outlook*, pp. 131–40.

approach was to provide avenues for organized influence by third States. However, upon further study, he doubted whether such influence could really be effective unless within the framework of collective security – as to which for a long time he entertained serious doubts.

He felt it his duty to discuss the current proposals for a system of international protection of human rights through judicial supervision and otherwise. His conclusions seemed to be negative – largely owing to what he conceived to be insurmountable difficulties in the judicial interpretation and application of an international bill of rights.[1] But they were not altogether negative. For he proceeded to envisage a right of intervention in cases of gross inhumanity on the part of the State. However, he considered such intervention to be dependent upon the authorization of an international authority. Yet he viewed without enthusiasm the notion of an international authority proceeding by way of legally effective decision binding upon a dissenting State.

In the field of judicial settlement of disputes he considered the existing freedom of States to refuse to other States the benefit of adjudication based on law to be 'entirely indefensible'.[2] But he found some justification for it both in the absence of machinery of peaceful change and in the fact of the existence of vital interests of States. In view of this he seemed to lend his support to the method of the Optional Clause of the Statute of the International Court of Justice, based on the principle of compulsory jurisdiction with regard to expressly enumerated classes of disputes.[3] At the same time, he doubted whether it would not be going too far to include in that enumeration disputes relating to customary international law as provided in the Statute of the Court. However, even if thus attenuated, the system of enumeration – under which Governments can reduce to conspicuously nominal proportions the scope of disputes thus specified – merely raises a new problem.

That tendency to conscientious qualification – bordering on indecision – exhibited itself not only in his approach to international organization. It went to the roots of his legal philosophy and of his treatment of specific questions of international law. In his discussion of natural law he considered that 'a rational universe, even if we cannot prove it to be fact, is a necessary postulate of thought and action'.[4] But on the preceding page he pointed to the exaggerations

[1] *Ibid.* p. 117.

[2] Brierly, p. 268.

[3] *Outlook*, p. 117.

[4] Brierly, p. 21.

of the medieval conception of natural law in its belief in the rationality of the universe. To give an example in the field of detail, while in one place he asserted positively that international law does not require that immunity be extended to foreign public ships engaged in commerce,[1] he thought – in the same chapter – that the principle of complete jurisdictional immunity of foreign States is a workable and desirable rule of law.[2] There is not necessarily a contradiction between these statements. They are examples of scholarly circumspection – such as will be found, for instance, in his analysis of the Judgment of the Permanent Court of International Justice in *The Lotus* case[3] and his reports to the Committee for Progressive Codification of International Law on Extradition and Territoriality of Jurisdiction. It is the same temper which made it possible for him to abandon or modify, whenever he felt impelled to do so in the light of experience or further reflection, some of the apparently rigid aspects of his teaching. Of this, his attitude to the problem of peaceful change and collective security and neutrality has already been noted. The same may be said of the readiness with which, after initial hesitation prompted by his preoccupation with peaceful change, he fully adopted the view of the completeness of international law[4] for the purpose of international judicial settlement and the absence of any element justifying, on that score, the distinction between justiciable and non-justiciable disputes – a distinction which, as in the end he had no hesitation in admitting, has often been no more than a device resorted to for explaining the claim of Governments to remain judges in their own cause.

Similarly, while he disdained any tendency to polemics – I have found in his writings no instance of his engaging in disparaging controversy with individual modern writers[5] – his exacting standards of

[1] *Ibid.* p. 193.

[2] *Ibid.* p. 211.

[3] 'The "Lotus" case', in *L.Q.R.* 22 (1928), 154–63.

[4] Brierly, pp. 68, 69; 'Règles Générales', p. 74. The doctrine, which is believed to express accurately the legal position, of the completeness of international law (as, indeed, of all law) is occasionally—though without sufficient justification—interpreted as meaning that international law can settle satisfactorily every dispute and conflict. The possible injustice or inadequacy of the existing law is a legitimate subject of preoccupation by lawyers. From this point of view the admissibility of *non liquet* is not without attraction. See, for example, in connection with the problem of *non liquet*, the valuable analysis by Professor Stone, *Legal Controls of International Conflict* (1954), pp. 153–64. However, it is doubtful whether any moral or political insufficiency of the existing law points conclusively to its incompleteness *qua* law in a manner calculated to affect the jurisdiction, validly accepted, of international tribunals.

[5] But see his outspoken criticism of the theories of auto-limitation in 'Fondement', pp. 483 *et seq.* He used language of some pungency in relation to Hegel, whose influence upon international law he considered to have been most devastating: 'for even cynicism

rectitude caused him on occasions to express views of pronounced emphasis on what he considered attempts by Governments, in particular his own, to represent mere formulas as achievements or concessions of substance. Thus, after recounting the British reservations to the General Act for the Pacific Settlement of International Disputes, he observed: 'After this it seems almost indecent to dissect the absurd little mouse that has been born.'[1] There was a trenchancy, bordering upon impatience, in his criticism of what he considered the purely nominal advance achieved by the Charter of the United Nations as compared with the Covenant of the League of Nations.[2] Notwithstanding his deep faith in the International Court, he found no reason for refraining from giving expression to surprise at the brevity of the Court's reasoning in the Advisory Opinion on the *Austro-German Customs Union* – an Opinion which, he suggested, gave the impression that as the result of a clerical error entire pages had been omitted in the crucial part of the Court's pronouncement.[3] However, as a rule, what appeared at first sight as a remark tinged with sarcasm was no more than an outright statement of fact, such as the frequent observation that the normal observance of obligations of international law by Governments may be largely due to the fact that these obligations, being limited in scope and intensity, weigh but lightly upon States.[4] He was quick to correct occasional exaggerations, as when, after expressing – under the impact of the experience of the Second World War – strong doubts as to the prospects of the humanizing effects of the law of war, he proceeded to admit its importance.[5]

What, however, is perhaps most impressive in his contribution – and this seems to be a fitting theme on which to conclude this essay – is that, amidst his restraint, his apparent inconclusiveness, his disillusionment born of the experience of a period of unprecedented retrogression, and his disapproval of easy solutions, there asserted itself a fervent and constructive hope. While he was sceptical of

may be refuted by argument and observation of facts, but that is hardly possible in relation to mysticism' (at p. 510).

[1] In *B.Y.* 12 (1931), p. 133. And see *ibid.* 11 (1930), 119–33, for his trenchant criticism of that instrument.

[2] Brierly, pp. 281–7; 'The Covenant and the Charter' (Sidgwick Memorial Lecture, 1946).

[3] 'The Advisory Opinion of the Permanent Court of International Justice on the Customs Régime between Germany and Austria', in *Z.ö.V.* 3 (1933), 71.

[4] See, for example, 'Fondement', p. 532; *B.Y.* 5 (1924), 5; *International Affairs*, 22 (1946), 353.

[5] 'The Law of War', in *The Background and Issues of the War*, by Fisher and others (1940), pp. 129, 132.

radical schemes of world government, of constraint and of rigid legal obligations, he went beyond mere negation and mere questioning. The solution, he taught, lies in evolving an international order based on collaboration, on institutions, on consent, on international administration, on – he would have said if he had been less averse to pretentiousness of expression – functional international government.[1] To these he pinned his faith. 'There is one solid ground for hope . . . We have begun to see . . . that though the problem of world community remains essentially a moral problem, it is also in part a problem of statesmanship, and that international society needs institutions through which its members can learn to work together for common social ends.'[2] It was a faith rooted in a fundamental optimism – even if that optimism was no more than an assumption. For he knew, from experience and otherwise, that the fate of institutions depends upon the persons to whom they are entrusted and that, in the sphere of action, ideas may not be more potent than the individual human beings called upon to realize them. He believed, perhaps, that the transcending power of these ideas is bound, in turn, to enhance the very stature of the persons into whose charge they have been committed. There may be a moral duty to cherish some such hope. That optimism expressed itself also in his readiness to assume that, notwithstanding the principle of unanimity, international legislation is already a fact[3] and, above all, that a fundamental identity of inerests – and not a conflict between them – is the main underlying reality of international relations.[4]

As constructive hope born of the travail of exacting search is, in the long run, of greater power than negation or confident assertion, there are good reasons for the belief that there is an even more convincing testimony to the importance and the permanence of his contribution than the fact that his introductory textbook has gone through more editions and has been translated into more languages than any other comparable work in this field. His was a luminous influence persuasive in its sanity and tolerance. He gave expression, in language of dignity and simplicity, to the perplexing and persistent problems of international law – not only of his own time but probably also of some considerable time to come.

[1] See, in particular, Brierly, pp. 45, 46.
[2] *Ibid.* p. 45.
[3] 'Règles Générales', pp. 97, 100.
[4] *Ibid.* pp. 231, 233.

CHAPTER 17

THE SO-CALLED ANGLO-AMERICAN AND CONTINENTAL SCHOOLS OF THOUGHT IN INTERNATIONAL LAW

Editor's note A further reflection of Lauterpacht's early interest in the theory of international law is provided by this chapter which originally appeared in the *British Year Book of International Law*, 12 (1931), 31–62.

I

The view that there exist in international law two different schools of thought, the Anglo-American and the Continental, is one which has gained wide acceptance in many countries, and in particular in Great Britain and in the United States. It has recently been given prominence in connection with the question of obligatory arbitration and the justiciability of disputes. Thus it has been widely maintained in Great Britain that, as there exist on many vital questions of international law rival doctrines of these two schools of thought, to confer upon a permanent international tribunal jurisdiction in all questions of international law would amount to subjecting this country in advance to decisions of a tribunal the great majority of which is bred in and wedded to the Continental doctrine. This was, for instance, the view propounded by Lord Hailsham, the then Lord Chancellor, when replying, on 1 May 1929, in the House of Lords to a motion concerning the signature of the Optional Clause.[1] The view may be said to have found the support of some of the leading international lawyers in this country. Thus – to mention only some of the recent authorities – Professor Pearce Higgins, writing in 1929 in connection with the Optional Clause, remarked that 'it is well-known that on some questions of prize law there is a fundamental divergence between the views of the Anglo-American and the Continental prize courts, e.g. the meaning of "enemy property"'.[2] When writing two years before that date, he ascribed a much more fundamental character to the 'divergence of outlook and method of

[1] 74 *H.L. Deb.* 5s., cols. 303–4.
[2] *British Acceptance of Compulsory Arbitration under the 'Optional Clause' and its Implications* (1929), p. 15.

treatment between lawyers of the Anglo-American school and those trained in the Continental schools of law'.[1] Sir John Fischer Williams has lent his support to a similar view of the 'latent conflict between the Continental and the Anglo-Saxon conception of international law'.[2] Professor Brierly has spoken generally of 'a further cause of uncertainty peculiar to international law' which 'lies in the persistence of two traditions, the Anglo-American and the Continental, which often assert conflicting rules on the same matter'.[3]

What are these matters in which 'conflicting rules' are 'often' asserted by the 'two traditions'? When writers refer to the difference between the Anglo-American and Continental conceptions of international law they may be referring to three different matters: they may mean that on certain specific subjects of international law of war or peace there is a definite cleavage of opinion, for instance, on the question of enemy property, or on the question of jurisdiction over foreign ships in national ports; or they may have in mind certain specific rules of municipal jurisprudence – like the doctrine of consideration, or the rules of evidence, or the doctrine of merger of previous negotiations in the contract – which are different on the Continent and in Anglo-American countries, and which may become relevant in the international sphere; or, finally, they may think of the general difference of approach and method underlying the two systems of municipal law and necessarily influencing the solution of any particular question put before an international court. It is proposed here to consider each of these three meanings of the supposed difference between the 'two schools of thought'. We say 'supposed', for it will be submitted in the present article that the current statements on the alleged contrast between Anglo-American and Continental schools of thought in international law in any of the above meanings of the term find no support either in the existing rules of international law, or in the practice of international tribunals, or in the general jurisprudential considerations on which they profess to be based.

[1] Quoted below, p. 467. [2] Quoted below, p. 468.
[3] Brierly (1st ed. 1928), p. 55. See also *ibid.* p. 189.

2. DIFFERENCES BETWEEN THE 'TWO SCHOOLS OF THOUGHT' ON SPECIFIC MATTERS OF INTERNATIONAL LAW

The law of peace

The most practical approach to an examination of this aspect of the question is to survey the whole field of international law, and to ascertain on what questions there exist differences of view and practice. Such a survey, when undertaken, shows that the whole international law of peace has produced only one doubtful instance of divergence of practice, namely, that relating to jurisdiction over foreign ships in national waters. Even this single individual divergence has been shown to be a matter of form rather than of substance.[1] The lawyer surveying this part of international law will be impressed both by the large measure of uniformity with which its rules are understood and applied throughout the world and by the fact that such differences as exist, far from being reducible to a clash of Anglo-American and Continental ideas, owe their origin and preservation to altogether different reasons. Thus it has happened that in recent years the courts of some European countries, like France and Italy[2] (but not Germany), in estimating the right to jurisdictional immunities of diplomatic envoys or of public ships, have been inclined to attach importance to the question whether the activities in regard to which jurisdiction is invoked are of a public or

[1] See Oppenheim, I (4th ed. by McNair, 1928), § 190 c. And see Jessup, *The Law of Territorial Waters and Maritime Jurisdiction* (1927), pp. 115–92, who, after a detailed examination of the legislation and judicial practice of various countries, arrives at the conclusion that 'as a matter of practice there seems to be little actual divergence between the action of American and British courts on the one hand and French and Italian courts on the other'. As to the frequently quoted case of the *Amiral Hamelin* between Great Britain and France, both Jessup, *The Law of Territorial Waters*, p. 150, and Charteris, in *B.Y.* I (1920–1), 83, point out that the attitude of the French Government in this case was not altogether consistent with some leading pronouncements of French courts in the matter. It will also be noted that the British-American attitude is shared by a number of Continental countries. Thus it appears that the courts of Soviet Russia claim jurisdiction in regard to disputes arising out of a contract of service on board a foreign vessel in a Soviet port. See the case *Reznokov* v. *Ships Arcos*, referred to in the Russian reply to the questionnaire sent in connection with the proposed codification of international law in the matter of territorial waters (League Doc. C.74 (b), M. 39 (b), 1929, v).

[2] But see the case of *Lurie* v. *Steinmann*, decided on 26 January 1927 by the Court of Rome, in which it was held that the rules of international law as to diplomatic immunities apply precisely to transactions made in the diplomatic person's private capacity, as his transactions in his public capacity are covered not by diplomatic immunities but by the much wider jurisdictional immunity of foreign states as such. See *Annual Digest*, 4 (1927–8), p. 364.

private character, whereas British and American courts do not consider the character of the particular State activity as relevant.

Or, to give another example, it happens that English and American law does not assume jurisdiction over aliens in respect of crimes committed abroad, whereas the law of Italy, Turkey, China, and Mexico does. But the Anglo-American law is in this matter the same as that of Germany, Spain, France, The Netherlands, and other countries,[1] and it is therefore difficult to speak here of an Anglo-American view as distinguished from the Continental. How inappropriate are any generalizations in this field may be seen, in regard to the question of jurisdictional immunities of States, from the fact that whereas English and American courts have proceeded in this matter by way of a somewhat rigid logical deduction from the principle of the immunity of States from jurisdiction,[2] the Continental courts have differentiated in a practical manner between the various manifestations of State activity – a rather startling gloss on the view, stressed by the upholders of the doctrine of 'two schools of thought', that it is Continental law which proceeds by way of methodical elaboration of abstract principles in contradistinction to the more practical approach of Common Law courts.[3] Differences of this nature are not even the result of conflicting interests, as is, for instance, the case in regard to the divergence of views on the questions of State responsibility in cases in which there is no discrimination between the national and the alien, or on the matter of the extent of territorial waters.

The law of war

A more substantial reason for the current assumption of a difference between the Anglo-American and Continental conceptions of international law lies in the divergences of opinion and practice in regard to the rules of warfare. It must be admitted that in regard to the laws

[1] In respect of crimes and offences as distinguished from contraventions, see the dissenting opinion of Judge Altamira in *The Lotus* case (*P.C.I.J.* Series A, no. 10, pp. 100–1) for a discussion of the law on the subject in various countries.

[2] See, for instance, the reasoning of the Supreme Court of the United States in *Berizzi Brothers* v. *Steamship 'Pesaro'*, 271 U.S. 562; *Annual Digest*, 3 (1925–6), p. 186.

[3] The writer thought for a time that this divergence might perhaps be due to the attitude of Anglo-American law as expressed in the immunity of the Crown (or, in the United States, of the Government) from suit, and to the application of this principle to foreign States. However, the fact that German courts, where the civil responsibility of the governmental agencies in internal law is a recognized principle, follow the practice of English and American courts, shows that there is no connection between the two sets of facts. See *The Ice King* case, finally decided on 10 December 1921, by the German *Reichsgericht* and discussed by Feine in Strupp, *Wört.* 1, 543. See also Garner, in *B.Y.* 6 (1925), 133 *et seq.*

of war there existed before 1914 a marked divergence of theory and practice on a considerable number of points, although even here the views of Great Britain and the United States were frequently shared by several other states. Some of these differences had reference to matters of minor importance. Thus, for instance, according to the British and American (and also Japanese) practice, a blockade-breaking vessel was liable to seizure when the master had actual or constructive knowledge of the blockade; while according to the Continental view only an actual attempt to break the line of blockade justified the infliction of punishment. English and American practice was ready to assume that a breach of blockade had been committed when a vessel which, according to her papers, was not destined for the blockaded port, was found near it and steering to it; while more direct evidence of the intention to break the blockade was necessary according to Continental opinion. Views differed as to the penalty for the breach of blockade, as to the determination of the destination of contraband goods, as to the penalty for carrying contraband, as to rules governing the transfer of merchant vessels to a neutral flag, and on many other matters. In the course of the World War most of these differences shrank into insignificance as the result of the wide application of reprisals, and of those two radical levellers of divergences, the doctrine of continuous voyage and the extension of the list of contraband goods. Whereas the policy of reprisals may, at least theoretically, be regarded as having been dictated by special circumstances of the war of 1914–18, the wide and uniform application of the doctrine of continuous voyage and the inclusion of nearly all the principal foodstuffs and commodities in the list of absolute contraband were a manifestation of the lasting change which has occurred in the character of modern warfare. This change in the nature of war, which has ceased to be a mere trial of strength of the combatant forces *stricto sensu* – a change which is new and fundamental notwithstanding the fact that a similar development has been asserted to have taken place during the Napoleonic wars[1] – has deprived most, if not all, divergences between the Anglo-American and Continental doctrines of any but historical importance.

This change has decidedly influenced, to the point of obliterating it, that aspect of the difference between the 'two schools of thought' which is connected with the question of the subjects of the relation of war. When, in February 1928, a bill was passed by the French Parliament which provided for the conscription of the entire man-

[1] See Moore, *International Law and Some Current Illusions* (1924), p. 27.

power in time of war, the reason for it being – to quote the words of the Rapporteur to the Senate – that the efforts of nations in modern war 'can no longer be limited to the action of armed forces, but that they must be ready to throw into the battle . . . the totality of their forces and their resources',[1] this law, passed as it was in a country in which, through the resounding maxims of Rousseau and Portalis, the Continental doctrine of the State as the sole subject of the relation of war found its clearest expression, was only a logical consummation of the abandonment of a theory which had become utterly divorced from the realities of modern warfare. The actual change had begun long before the World War. No account of it was taken in the numerous provisions of the Hague Conventions conceived in the atmosphere of unreality which surrounded much of the work of the Hague Conferences. But there is little doubt that this aspect of the distinction between the Continental and Anglo-American schools of thought – and it was the principal subject of the distinction, most of the others being mainly its derivatives – has now become a thing of the past. It was virtually abandoned by the Continental countries, in all relevant matters, in their practice during the World War. Thus in France and Germany the inviolability of private enemy property on land survived in name only under the cumulative impact of the policy of sequestration, frequently amounting to liquidation, and of reprisals.

The question of 'enemy character of private property' may be mentioned as another concrete example of the fate which has befallen the difference between the 'two schools'. This subject has, as we have seen, been recently described by a leading British authority as still constituting a substantial point of difference between the Anglo-American and Continental views. Undoubtedly, there existed before the War a cleavage of opinion on this matter. While Great Britain, the United States, Japan, The Netherlands, and Spain insisted that both nationality and domicil must be taken into consideration for the purpose of determining enemy character, France, Germany, Austria–Hungary, Italy, and Russia made the character of goods dependent upon the sole test of the nationality of the owner. Article 58 of the Declaration of London was in effect limited to a statement of this disagreement.[2] However, whereas, in view of the character of the measures adopted by Great Britain by way of re-

[1] Quoted from Toynbee, *Survey*, 1927 (1929), p. 3.

[2] It provided that 'the neutral or enemy character of goods found on board an enemy vessel is determined by the neutral or enemy character of the owner'.

prisals and otherwise, the question of enemy character lost much of its importance in relation to liability to capture, it remained important in regard to municipal legislation concerning trading with the enemy. It was in this respect that both France and Great Britain, the representative countries of the 'two schools', abandoned their respective positions held before the War, and cumulated the two tests. France, in September 1914, forbade, *inter alia*, trade with non-enemy subjects residing in an enemy country. British legislation applied the prohibition to, among others, persons of enemy nationality or enemy association.[1] Legislation concerning trading with the enemy is essentially a question of municipal law, but it is not without a bearing on the question of enemy property as a whole. This may be seen from a passage, which may be usefully quoted here, in a communication addressed in this matter in October 1916, by Sir Edward Grey to the American Ambassador in London:

> As the United States Government are well aware, the Anglo-American practice has in times past been to treat domicil as the test of enemy character, in contradistinction to the Continental practice, which has always regarded nationality as the test. The Anglo-American rule crystallized at the time when means of transport and communication were less developed than now, and when in consequence the actions of a person established in a distant country could have but little influence upon a struggle. To-day the position is very different.[2]

It is submitted that whereas the view as to the existence of two schools of thought on definite subjects in international law has never been in accordance with facts so far as the international law of peace is concerned, in regard to the international law of war it has ceased to be so and has become a matter of history. In so far as it subsists in minor details, it has become unreal when compared with major developments which have taken place.

3. ANGLO-AMERICAN AND CONTINENTAL RULES AND DOCTRINES OF MUNICIPAL LAW OF POSSIBLE RELEVANCE IN INTERNATIONAL LAW

Questions of municipal law before international tribunals

It might be maintained that whatever may be the fate of the doctrine of 'two schools of international law' in regard to discrepancies of view on individual questions of international law of peace and war,

[1] See Garner, *Prize Law* (1927), pp. 433 *et seq.*, and the same, *International Law and the World War* (1920), vol. 1, § 155.
[2] *A.J.* 11 (1917), Suppl. p. 45.

there are nevertheless situations possible in which differences in the municipal law of the two groups of countries may prove of importance for the decision of international questions. Thus, common law rules of evidence differ substantially from those adopted in the countries whose legal systems are based on Roman law; and it is argued that, as the large majority of judges on permanent international tribunals like the Permanent Court of International Justice are trained in the Roman law systems of law, the probability is that they would tend to apply the rules of evidence obtaining in their own legal systems and disregard those applied by common law courts. The same applies to the question, which is partly one of evidence, of the admissibility of so-called preparatory work and of the consideration of negotiations as an element in the interpretation of treaties. The same difficulty is said to occur in regard to the question of nationality, inasmuch as in some countries the *jus soli* plays a decisive part in determining nationality, whereas in others the emphasis rests on the *jus sanguinis*. In general the problem may also be said to arise whenever an international tribunal is called upon to decide a question of private law in regard to which the two systems of law differ.

The first observation that ought to be made in connection with this class of case is that its application is of limited scope. The fact that the rules of municipal law in one group of States differ from those in another group is on the whole irrelevant for the purposes of international law. International law is not concerned with matters of municipal law; it is concerned with relations between States. This does not mean that international tribunals are not on occasions called upon to determine matters of municipal law. Frequently, in particular in regard to disputes arising out of claims of private individuals, they are called upon to decide, as a question of private international law, which municipal law is applicable, or even, in some cases, to interpret and to apply a rule of municipal law. Thus, for instance, in the case concerning the payment of various Serbian loans issued in France, the Permanent Court had to determine whether the obligations entered into by Serbia were governed by Serbian or French law, and also what law governed the question of the currency in which the payment must or might be made in France.[1] In nearly every case in which the responsibility of the State is claimed to be engaged on account of denial of justice, international tribunals are called upon to review the application of municipal law.[2] But there

[1] *P.C.I.J.* Series A, no. 20.

[2] The detailed judgment of 30 December 1896 of the President of the Swiss Con-

is in fact in such cases no question of international tribunals having to choose between two rules of international law, the choice between which may be influenced by the fact that some judges are trained in one system of law and the others in another. The question in such cases is, to put it at its highest, one substantially of private international law, and, after this question has been decided, of applying the relevant rule of municipal law as chosen in accordance with a rule of private international law.[1] Thus in the above-mentioned case of the Serbian loans, the Court, after having decided that French law was to govern the question of currency, proceeded to decide the meaning and scope of the relevant French law by reference to French legislation and to French judicial decisions interpreting that legislation.[2]

The position is essentially the same in regard to those numerous cases in which treaties include disputed terms of municipal law,[3] for instance when a number of treaties concluded by Japan contained a provision to the effect that subjects of certain European Powers should enjoy freedom from taxation in respect of *leases in perpetuity* held by them.[4] The question in such cases is not that of determining the content of the disputed term by its direct interpretation in a manner which may be influenced by the Anglo-American or Continental law conceptions of the judges. The problem in such cases is to find, by reference to the intention of the parties, which of the two systems of municipal law represented by the contracting parties is applicable for the determination of the rights and duties involved, and then to decide the dispute by the application of that particular

federation in the *Fabiani* case between France and Venezuela (Lafontaine, *Pasicrisie Internationale* (1902), pp. 344–68) is a good illustration of this type of case. See also *P.C.I.J.* Series A, no. 7, pp. 19, 42, on the consideration of municipal law by the Court, and the *Georges Pinson* case, *Annual Digest*, 4 (1927–8), p. 9.

[1] It is, of course, possible that the rules of international private law in the States which are parties to the dispute are in conflict, in which case an international court may have either to choose between them or to proceed to apply a kind of supernational international private law. See on this matter Zitelmann, *Internationales Privatrecht* (1897), 1, 19 *et seq.*

[2] *P.C.I.J.* Series A, no. 20, p. 46 *et seq.* And see, in general, on the application of local legislation, Ralston, nos. 146–7, 255–9.

[3] See on this subject the scholarly article of Ruegger in *Z.I.* 28 (1919–20), 426–502.

[4] See below, p. 461.

Such questions do not occur in connection with the interpretation of treaties only. Thus, for instance, in the *Casablanca* case, decided by the Permanent Court of Arbitration, Germany maintained that the contract of service of the German members of the Foreign Legion was a private law contract which, according to German law, i.e. § 1381 of the Civil Code, was contrary to good morals and, as such, invalid, whereas France contended that it was a contract of public law and, as such, valid in all places, including foreign occupied territory, in which the Legion was present. See French *Contre-Mémoire*, pp. 25 *et seq.*

municipal law. In a great number of cases the conventions remove, by giving a clear definition of the relevant conceptions of municipal law, any doubts as to the law to be applied. In particular, in conventions of a technical character and in arbitration treaties, there may be found a long list of definitions similar to those encountered in British Acts of Parliament. In other cases the conventions refer to the law of the State within which the relevant legal event takes place, or, as is often done in extradition treaties, to provisions common to the law of both contracting parties. Frequently, the choice of the *termini technici* shows which law the parties wish to be applied, for instance, when the treaty refers to *wakufs* of Ottoman law.[1] But even when no such express reference to a definite source is available, it is not the unhampered discretion of judges which decides which law is applicable, but general rules like the one that relations affecting immovable property are governed by the law of the country within which it is situated; or by reference to the principle that the treaty should be interpreted with a close approximation to the legal system of the country within which it takes effect; or, finally, by reference to the most general and overriding principle that effect is to be given to the intention of the parties. Thus in the *Japanese House Tax* case, the Permanent Court of Arbitration refused to discuss by reference to 'principles of civil law' the question whether the leased properties referred to in the treaties between Japan and the European Powers included buildings erected on land or were confined to the land alone;[2] it based its decision on the manifestations of the intention of the parties to these treaties. Even municipal courts when interpreting treaty provisions are reluctant to have recourse to rules of interpretation and legal doctrines peculiar to their own country and not having a sufficient degree of generality, such as – in the case of English or American courts – the doctrine of *cy-près*[3] or the doctrine of an equity of redemption outstanding in the mortgagor.[4]

[1] See, e.g., Article 12 of the Berlin Act of 13 July 1878, Martens, N.R.G. 2nd series, III, 449, and other examples cited by Ruegger, *op. cit.*, p. 477, n. 93.

[2] Japan denied the applicability of the common and civil law principle of accession, according to which the buildings shared the legal position of the land on which they were erected, and appealed to the old Japanese custom of dualism of land and building. See *Japanese Statement of Objections*, p. 43, and *Reply to Objections*, p. 23.

[3] *The Amiable Isabella*, 6 Wheaton 1.

[4] *Josef Inwald Actien Gesellschaft* v. *Pfeiffer and Another*, 43 *Times Law Reports*, p. 399; *Annual Digest*, 4 (1927–8), p. 557. And see *Adams* v. *Akerlund*, 168 Ill. 632, 48 N.E. 454 (cited by Moore, V, 255) for an even more striking example of an American court interpreting a treaty between the United States and Sweden by holding that the term 'effects' should be interpreted by having regard to the fact that it was represented in the French draft of the Treaty by the word '*biens*', which, in civil law, includes immovables as well as movables.

It is true that, apart from these cases of determining subjective rights and obligations grounded in definite conceptions of municipal law, international tribunals are frequently confronted with questions of international law proper which, by virtue of their analogy to corresponding situations in private law, may be deemed to raise the dilemma of a choice between two systems of law and of a possible preponderant influence of one of them. Such situations do necessarily arise in international law,[1] but, by the very nature of these relations, the rules governing them cannot be rules of municipal law. They are created and applied having regard to the necessities of international life and to the general principles of law which underlie them, although it may happen that the rule of international law finally adopted will approximate or even be identical in form[2] or in substance with a rule of law as adopted by a particular municipal system of law. So long as the rule thus adopted is known in advance and so long as an international tribunal does not arbitrarily give preference to one set of rules, it does not matter which is ultimately established as a rule of international law. There is no inherent and absolute merit in any particular rule of national municipal law such as to make its incorporation in international law a matter of national interest or honour.

Anglo-American and Continental rules of evidence

The question of rules of evidence applied by international tribunals shows not only that this aspect of the problem causes little difficulty, but also that international judicial settlement may be relied upon to produce, independently of any particular system of law, rules appropriate to its own requirements and circumstances. Thus, the history of international arbitration shows that whatever may be the merits of the strict common law rules regulating the admissibility of evidence and of burden of proof, it is not practicable to follow them in international litigation. They are not followed there; in fact, they have been expressly repudiated. There are therefore in this matter no longer two schools of thought in international law; there is one rule of international law on the subject, which, as it happens, does

[1] See Lauterpacht, *Analogies*, *passim*.

[2] Thus, for instance, the common law rule of estoppel is frequently applied by international tribunals (see Lauterpacht, *Analogies*, §§ 87, 88), and it appears that the Permanent Court in the *Serbian Loans* case (*P.C.I.J.* Series A, no. 20, p. 38) considered the argument as to estoppel on its merits. But the doctrine of estoppel is only in form a common law doctrine. It has its roots in Roman law (see Riezler, *Venire contra factum suum* (1912)), and some of its elements will be found, e.g., in Articles 307–9 of the German Code and 1350–2 of the French *Code Civil*.

not coincide with that which common law courts apply in actions brought before them. No particular national interest, including national self-esteem, is thereby injured. For the practice of international tribunals in this matter is known and established, and consequently no legitimate expectations are disappointed. In fact, as we shall see, this practice was adopted with approval by English and American judges acting as international arbitrators; it has not been opposed by Great Britain or the United States when appearing as parties. As to the inherent merits of the present common law rules of evidence, it may be sufficient to say that many English lawyers of authority are of the opinion that there is little rational justification for their complexities and technicalities; that they are an undesirable remnant of the formalism of the older law of pleading; and that any system which trammels judicial discretion in the admission or exclusion of evidence may not be beneficial to the purposes of justice.[1]

Apart from the rules of permanent tribunals like the Permanent Court of Arbitration or the Permanent Court of International Justice, no specific rules as to evidence and proof have so far evolved in international arbitration. But there has been a general tendency, sanctioned by a long series of arbitral pronouncements, to disregard elaborate restrictions upon the admissibility of evidence and to accept the principle that no evidence should be excluded *a limine* and that it should be left to the judge to appreciate the weight and persuasiveness of the evidence put before him. This tendency has been given emphatic expression in the *Parker* case decided, in March 1926, by the American–Mexican Mixed Claims Commission, where the Commissioners expressly refused to be bound by restrictive and purely technical rules of proof and evidence.[2] The same view was expressed by Professor Huber, acting as the sole Arbitrator in the *Island of Palmas Arbitration* between the United States and Holland. The United States contended that statements without evidence to support them cannot be taken into consideration by an international arbitrator, and that evidence is not only to be referred to but is also

[1] See Sir John Salmond in his Introduction to the *Science of Legal Method* in the *Modern Legal Philosophy Series* (1921), p. lxxviii: 'There is no other form of human inquiry in which the inquirer is not at liberty to seek guidance from any source which seems good and sufficient to him. Why then should the inquiries of courts of justice be conducted on any different principle?' And see Admiralty Short Cause Rules (1908), according to which the parties may agree that the Judge shall be at liberty to receive, call for, or act upon, such evidence, whether legally admissible or not, as he may think fit (*The Annual Practice* (1931), p. 2404). And see *ibid.* p. 2402, the Commercial Causes Notice of 1895.

[2] *A.J.* 21 (1927), 174; *Opinions of Commissioners*, 1927, p. 35; *Annual Digest*, 3 (1925–6), p. 240.

to be laid before the tribunal. One of the Dutch contentions was that statements made by a Government in regard to its own acts are evidence in themselves and have no need of supplementary corroboration. The arbitrator dealt in detail with these contentions,[1] which he rejected. He pointed out that it would be 'contrary to the broad principles applied in international arbitrations to exclude *a limine*, except under the explicit terms of a conventional rule, every allegation made by a party as irrelevant if it is not supported by evidence', that 'it is for the arbitrator to decide both whether allegations do or . . . do not need evidence in support and whether the evidence produced is sufficient or not', and that 'such liberty of weighing the merits of the evidence produced is essential to the arbitrator'. These pronouncements, referring as they do to established arbitral practice, are in fact in keeping with the emphatic views expressed on this subject by a long series of arbitrators – most of whom came from England or America.[2]

Preparatory work as an element of interpretation of treaties

The question of recourse to preliminary negotiations for the purpose of interpreting treaty provisions is in a sense a question of evidence. It has recently become a matter of special interest in connection with the circumstances accompanying the signature and ratification of the Paris Pact for the Renunciation of War. It is particularly in this connection that it has been adduced as yet another instance of the diversity of Anglo-American and Continental methods. Thus it is contended that, whereas Continental law favours the interpretation of treaties by recourse to preliminary negotiations, such interpretation is contrary to a clear common law rule of interpretation. Reasons of space do not allow of a detailed consideration of this aspect of the doctrine of two schools of thought, but it is submitted that such an examination, if undertaken, would show that the doctrine has found no support in the attitude adopted by Great Britain or the United States when appearing as parties before international tribunals;[3]

[1] See pp. 19, 20, of the original award, and *Annual Digest*, 4 (1927–8), 479 *et seq*. See also the *Georges Pinson* case, *ibid.* p. 481.

[2] See, for instance, the *Pelletier* case (Moore, *International Arbitrations*, II, 1752); the *Lasry* case (Ralston, *Venezuelan Arbitrations*, p. 38); the *Faber* case (*ibid.* p. 602 and the authorities there cited on pp. 600 and 601).

[3] See, for instance, as to the dispute concerning the *Interpretation of the Treaty of Ghent* and the award of 1822, Moore, *International Arbitrations* I, 352–6; as to the *Behring Sea Arbitration*, see *Argument of Great Britain*, U.S. no. 4 (1893) (Cd. 6921, p. 19); *Counter-Case of Great Britain*, U.S. no. 3 (1893) (Cd. 6920, p. 27); and see the *Case of the United States*, U.S. no. 6 (1893) (Cd. 6949, p. 53); as to the *North Atlantic Fisheries Arbitration*, see pp. 163, 166, 177, 184, and 190 of the award as printed in Scott, *Hague Reports*; as to the *Alaskan*

that, whatever may be the law in the matter of interpretation of statutes and contracts, it is not shared by the courts of these countries in regard to interpretation of treaties;[1] and that it is unknown to the practice of international tribunals which, far from assimilating treaties to either statutes or contracts, attaches considerable although merely corroborative importance to negotiations preceding the conclusion of treaties.[2] The consideration of preparatory work is only in

Boundary Dispute, see Argument of Mr Christopher Robinson, *Proceedings of the Alaskan Boundary Tribunal*, U.S. Senate Doc. no. 162, 58th Congress, 2nd Session, p. 502; *ibid.* pp. 503, 507, 557.

With this should, for instance, be contrasted the attitude of France questioning before the Permanent Court of International Justice the admissibility of this means of interpretation in the *Case concerning the competence of the International Labour Organization in regard to international regulation of the conditions of labour of persons employed in agriculture* (*P.C.I.J.* Series B, no. 2). See Additional Observations of Professor de Lapradelle, *P.C.I.J.* Series C, no. 1, p. 187. See, in addition to the three British-American arbitrations referred to above, the *Kummerow* and *Aroa Mines* cases (Ralston, *Venezuelan Arbitrations*, pp. 526 and 358); the award of the Swiss Federal Council of 1 December 1900 in the boundary dispute between France and Switzerland concerning French Guiana (Lafontaine, *Pasicrisie Internationale*, p. 573); the awards of the Permanent Court of Arbitration in *Japanese House Tax* and *Venezuelan Preferential Claims* cases (Scott, *Hague Reports*, pp. 83 and 66 respectively). The recourse to preparatory work by the Mixed Arbitral Tribunals established by the Peace Treaties of 1919 and by the Treaty of Lausanne has constituted a constant feature of their activities. See *Annual Digest*, 4 (1927–8), for numerous references.

[1] See *The Jeanne*, in Trehern, *British and Colonial Prize Cases*, II (1918), 302, in which Sir Samuel Evans relied on the deliberations of the London Conference of 1908 and 1909; *The Lucia*, *ibid.* I, (1916), 226; *Porter* v. *Freudenberg*, [1915] 1 K.B. at p. 876, in which the Court of Appeal, while regarding the text of the relevant Hague Convention as decisive, devoted a passage to the consideration of the changes made in the original draft. And see the British Order in Council of 20 August 1914 adopting the general report of the drafting committee of the Conference as an authoritative statement of the meaning and of the intention of the Declaration of London. On the other hand – and this again is an interesting gloss on the alleged difference between the English and Continental practices – the French *Conseil d'Etat* repeatedly refused to accept the report of the drafting committee as an authoritative interpretation of the Declaration. See *The Federico*, in Fauchille, *Jurisprudence française en matière des Prises maritimes*, p. 287, and Garner, *Prize Law* (1927) §§ 115, 449.

As to the practice in the United States, see the recent case of *Nielsen* v. *Johnson*, 279 U.S. 46, decided by the Supreme Court on 18 February 1929, in which it was held that 'recourse may be had to the negotiations and diplomatic correspondence of the contracting parties'. See on this case Hyde, in *A.J.* 23 (1929), 826–8; a report of the case is also printed *ibid.* p. 422.

[2] The study of the work of the Permanent Court seems to justify the submission that, although there is no occasion to have recourse to preparatory work when the meaning of the treaty is clear, the Court will not refuse to consider previous negotiations for the purpose of dispelling and answering such doubts as have been raised by either of the parties by reference to such preparatory work. See, for instance *The Mavrommatis Palestine Concessions* (*P.C.I.J.* Series A, no. 2, p. 24); the *Lotus* case (*P.C.I.J.* Series A, no. 10, pp. 16–17); *Exchange of Greek and Turkish Populations* (*P.C.I.J.* Series B, no. 10, p. 22); *Interpretation of Article 3, paragraph 2, of the Treaty of Lausanne* (*P.C.I.J.* Series B, no. 12, pp. 19, 22, 23); *Jurisdiction of the European Commission of Danube* (*P.C.I.J.* Series B, no. 14, pp. 28–31). And see in particular the recent judgments, in the form of Orders, in the French–Swiss Free Zones dispute. In the Order of 10 August 1929 (*P.C.I.J.* Series A, no. 22, p. 21), the Court stated that its view was 'corroborated by the facts relating to the drafting of Article 435 of the Treaty of Versailles'; in the Order of 6 December 1930

exceptional cases essential for the purpose of interpretation. International tribunals are amply served by the ordinary rules and methods of interpretation, and their preoccupation with the question of preliminary negotiations is mainly due to the abundance of forensic argument in the matter.

Nationality

The subject of the frequently alleged difference between the common law and Continental law principles in the matter of nationality requires only very brief mention. The question is not a matter of international law, the determination of nationality being, subject to the existing international obligations of the state, left to its municipal law. Apart from this, however, the difference between the *jus soli* and *jus sanguinis* is, of course, not one between the Anglo-American and Continental conceptions of law. It was only after the beginning of the nineteenth century that, following upon the example of the *Code Napoléon*, the *jus soli* was replaced by the *jus sanguinis*. At present there is no State in existence whose law is based solely on the *jus soli*. The predominant rule is a combination of the two systems; the difference is one of emphasis. It appears that in over twenty States the law is based principally upon *jus sanguinis* and partly upon *jus soli*, while in about an equal number of States the emphasis is reversed. Great Britain and the United States belong to the latter group. To speak here of a manifestation of a difference between the Anglo-American and Continental conceptions is to use a phrase which, if it is not meaningless, is inaccurate. In so far as the question assumes an international aspect, that is, when there is a conflict of nationalities, international tribunals tend to evolve a rule of international law which, differing in its formulation from each of the systems of municipal law, is based on the criterion of effective nationality.[1]

(*P.C.I.J.* Series A, no. 24, p. 11), it again relied on 'the history of the negotiations which have taken place between the Parties with a view to concluding the agreement provided for by Article 435, paragraph 2, of the Treaty of Versailles'. This reluctance of the Court to commit itself to an elimination of preparatory work is emphasized by its refusal to consider it in some specific sets of cases, for instance, when reference is made to confidential negotiations (*P.C.I.J.* Series B, no. 14, p. 32), or to negotiations in which one or more of the parties to the dispute did not participate (*P.C.I.J.* Series A, no. 16, p. 8, and Annex 3, pp. 41, 42), or when conclusions are being drawn from offers and declarations made in the course of abortive negotiations (*P.C.I.J.* Series A, no. 17, p. 51).

[1] See the case of *Baron Frédéric de Born* v. *Yugoslavian State*, in which the Tribunal considered that when a person was entitled to claim one nationality in one country and another nationality in another country 'it was the duty of the Tribunal to examine in which of the two countries existed the elements essential in law and in fact for the purpose of creating an effective link of nationality, and not merely a theoretical one' and that in solving the conflict of nationalities the Tribunal ought to consider where the claimant was

4. GENERAL DIFFERENCES IN LEGAL APPROACH AND LEGAL PHILOSOPHY

The Continental and Anglo-American legal traditions

It has been submitted in the preceding sections that there is no substance in the doctrine of 'two schools of thought' from the point of view either of differences on specific questions of international law or of discrepancies in rules of municipal law in so far as they may become relevant in the field of international law. The opinion is, however, widely held that, apart from any such specific differences, there still remains a substantial divergence in the domain of legal philosophy and in the juridical method and approach, which, it is said, are the consequence of a fundamental difference in legal thinking and jurisprudence between the common law and Continental countries. It is pointed out that this difference in legal upbringing and outlook may not only become of importance when international judges are called upon to have recourse to general principles of law, as envisaged, for instance, in Article 38 of the Statute of the Permanent Court, but also that it may exercise an influence on the manner of deciding any question of international law put before them. A comprehensive statement of these fundamental differences, in relation to international law, was made by Professor Pearce Higgins, and it may therefore be useful to quote part of it:

In dealing with questions of International Law it will be found that the systems of law in which men have been trained and under which they live exercise a very marked influence on their outlook and methods of treatment. It is not sufficiently realized even by lawyers, much less by the mass of mankind, how much their outlook on all matters involving legal principles and methods is influenced by the legal atmosphere in which their special national civilization has developed. There is a marked divergence of outlook and method of treatment between lawyers of the Anglo-American school and those trained in the Continental schools of law. The former are in the habit of dealing with facts by the aid of principles extracted from a long series of cases decided by their courts administering the common law or that branch of law which originally came into being to modify its too great rigidity and to which the name of Equity is applied in England and the United States. The states of the continent of Europe and the peoples of the New World who derive their jurisprudence from

domiciled, where he conducted his business, and where he exercised his political rights. (*Annual Digest* 3 (1925–6), p. 277). See also the case of *Barthez de Montfort* v. *Treuhänder Hauptverwaltung* (*ibid.*, p. 279), in which the Franco-German Mixed Arbitral Tribunal applied the doctrine of active nationality *eo nomine*.

them, have been brought up under the system of codified rules of law, primarily those of the Roman Law, and in more recent times the codes which they have respectively enacted. France, Germany, Switzerland, Italy, and Austria, to name a few of such States, are in this position, and the tendency of such peoples is to seek for clear-cut definitions and concise statements in the code for the guidance of judge and people.[1]

We find, even more recently, Sir John Fischer Williams giving expression to the same view. He speaks of premature or ambitious attempts at codification as likely to raise 'the latent conflict between the Continental and the Anglo-Saxon conception of international law, between the conception, that is, of law as a complete structure of right and justice legally ordered and commanded by authority, the high idea incorporate, and the conception of law as the slow elaboration of custom, the gradual adjustment of things to the demands of practical reason, the interpretation and the rationalization of the fact'.[2] This particular approach to the supposed divergence between the Continental and Anglo-American conceptions of international law is widespread, frequently voiced, and received with a respect which is somewhat out of keeping with the distrust with which the English lawyer is inclined to confront general statements of an abstract nature.

There is, so far as the writer is aware, in English or American literature, no comprehensive presentation of the supposed fundamental difference between the Anglo-American and Continental jurisprudence and legal philosophy as distinguished from the difference in individual legal rules or doctrines.[3] There are mainly general references and vague statements on the subject. Thus the student will find a report of Austin commenting upon the rigour and abstract character of his own exposition by saying that he ought to

[1] *International Law and Relations* (1928), pp. 30–1.

[2] Fischer Williams, *Chapters*, p. 58. Sir John Fischer Williams makes this statement while discussing the attitude of the two countries on the matter of codification. Reasons of space do not permit of an examination of this aspect of the 'two schools of thought', but perhaps Austin's 39th lecture, which is a powerful plea for codification as against some Continental arguments against it, will suggest the drawbacks of broad generalizations also in regard to this particular matter. See also, to the same effect, Keith in Wheaton, *International Law* (6th ed. 1929), I, 34.

[3] For some aspects of the matter see Pound, in *H.L.R.* 36 (1922–3), 645–52. There is also a remarkable dearth of presentations of the individual differences on a comparative basis. However, Kuhn's *Grundzüge des Englisch-Amerikanischen Privat- und Prozessrechts, besonders im Vergleiche mit den Systemen des europäischen Kontinents* (1915), will be found useful. See also Walton, *The Egyptian Law of Obligations* (2nd ed. 1920), 2 vols., which is an admirable commentary on the differences, so far as this part of the law is concerned, between the *Code Civil* and the Common Law. And see Anglin, in *The Canadian Law Review*, I (1923), 33 *et seq.*; Mignault, *ibid.* 3 (1925), I *et seq.*; Rinfret, *ibid.* 4 (1926), 68 *et seq.*; Laverty, *ibid.* 9 (1931), 13 *et seq.*

have become a German professor.[1] He will read Salmond's warning that the reader who ventures into the region of Continental legal philosophy will find himself 'a stranger in a strange land, where men speak to him in an unknown tongue'.[2] As a rule his attention will be drawn to the difficulties and the dangers of the confusion resulting from the fact that on the Continent the term law (*Recht*, *droit*, *diritto*) covers not only positive law properly so-called, but also ideas of right and justice, whereas the English term 'law' 'means law and nothing else'.[3] It is pointed out to him that this difference in terminology is expressive of a difference in legal method consisting in the fact that the Anglo-Saxon approach is more realistic and pragmatic; and that, being concerned with what the law is and not with what it ought to be, it is pervaded by a scientific unity lacking in the Continental presentation and treatment of the law which, it is said, constantly confuses the idea of law with the idea of right. This inclination to abstract reasoning and logical deduction from general principles obtaining on the Continent is regarded both as the cause and the effect of the absence of judge-made case law as expressed in England and America in the binding force of judicial precedent as a source of law. It is this last feature of Anglo-American law which has impressed itself most upon the minds of international lawyers not only in this country, but also on the Continent, where there has otherwise been no such pronounced tendency to insist on the existence of fundamental differences between the two schools of thought.[4] The

[1] See the Preface (of 1861) of Sarah Austin to *Lectures on Jurisprudence* (ed. by Campbell, 1911), I, 12.

[2] *Jurisprudence*, § 4.

[3] See Salmond, *Jurisprudence*, § 4. Holland, *Jurisprudence* (6th ed. 1893), p. 13, according to whom the continental *Recht* or *droit* covers law, rights, and justice; Fischer Williams, *Chapters*, p. 16.

[4] Another supposed peculiarity of the common law which has attracted the attention of Continental international lawyers is English equity as representing the broad, humane, and generous approach to and application of rules of law. Thus Professor Anzilotti, at that time President of the Permanent Court of International Justice, when paying a tribute to the memory of Lord Finlay, and when reviewing the contribution which Lord Finlay made to the work of the Court, said: '... What Lord Finlay truly represented in this Court, as it was his duty to do, was the legal system in which he was brought up. It is in particular thanks to him that certain principles and institutions of Anglo-Saxon law, particularly as regards procedure, which seem best destined to meet the requirements of international justice have, with the appropriate limitations and modifications, found a place in the Rules of Court. And there is no need to add that in the course of the sometimes difficult tasks which we have to fulfil, he never failed to help us with those ideas of flexibility and of equity which are the basis and almost the life-breath of the English legal system and which in certain respects are so well suited to fill the gaps and make good the imperfections that exist in international law.' (The first public sitting of the XVI (extraordinary) Session on 15 May 1929, *P.C.I.J.* Series E, no. 5, pp. 22–3.) It is interesting to note how, alongside the view prevalent in this country that Continental jurisprudence is on the whole an idealistic and philosophical disquisition as to what law ought to be, there is among Continental writers a tendency to look to English equity

scope of this article neither permits nor calls for any systematic attempt at an examination of the major aspects of the differences between Anglo-American and Continental jurisprudence and legal philosophy. It is therefore intended to limit this inquiry to the two aspects of the question which, as we have seen, have been made the object of particular attention by international lawyers emphasizing the fundamental differences between the Anglo-Saxon and Continental conceptions of international law. They are, firstly, the differences in the conception of law; secondly, the differences in the function of judicial precedent.

Recht, droit, diritto versus *law*

It would be interesting to inquire who first propounded the view, which has now become an axiom with English lawyers, that the terms *Recht, droit, diritto* – in so far as they correspond to the English term 'law' – are on the Continent confused with and frequently indistinguishable from the conceptions of right and justice. While the elucidation of the origin of this belief may be left to the student of the history of legal thought, the fact remains that leading English authorities, like Salmond and Holland, have held it, and that it is at present widely accepted and frequently repeated. But, it may be asked, from what representative Continental writings have English lawyers gained this notion, unless indeed they have relied on Ulpian's definition of jurisprudence as '*rerum divinarum atque humanarum notitia, justi atque injusti scientia*', or on Celsius' definition of law as '*ars boni et aequi*'? In the conception and definitions of law in modern Continental jurisprudence, the distinction between law and morals and between the existing and postulated law is consistent and clear beyond doubt. Definitions of law – on the Continent and elsewhere – do, of course, vary. They may lay emphasis on the source of the legal obligation, for instance, on the fact that it is a rule emanating from the State; they may have regard to one or more functions of the law, for instance, the securing of freedom, or of social needs or of the socially enforceable maximum of ethics or of the development of human personality; or they may be based on the coercive and

as containing the element of justice, generosity, and adaptation which the Continental lawyer misses in the rigid application of the existing law under his own system of law. The pronouncement, quoted above, of Professor Anzilotti, is a good illustration of this view. The Continental jurist who sees in the English equity jurisdiction the embodiment of the equitable treatment and application of the law, will be somewhat surprised to find English writers urging the abandonment of the dualism of common law and equity in favour of the Continental system in which *aequitas* forms part of the positive law without there being assigned a special jurisdiction for its application.

heteronomous nature of legal norms. But in the flux of definitions there is, among jurists, the constant phenomenon of the realization of the difference between law and morals[1] and between what the law is and what it ought to be. The only substantial difference between the Continental and Anglo-American terminology is that whereas in English usage the term law signifies either the legal order as a whole or a specific manifestation of it, on the Continent it connotes both the sum total of existing law and the subjective legal right of the individual derived from the positive law. Thus we find in Planiol's treatise a clear distinction between the two meanings of the term *droit*:

Les emplois très variés qu'a reçus le mot *droit* se ramènent à deux sens principaux. Dans son sens fondamental, le mot *droit* désigne *une faculté, reconnue à une personne par la loi, et qui lui permet d'accomplir des actes déterminés.* Tels sont: le *droit de propriété*. . . Dans un autre sens, le mot droit désigne *l'ensemble des lois*, c'est-à-dire les règles juridiques applicables aux actes des hommes. Ainsi on peut dire que les *droits* des individus sont déterminés par le *droit*. Dans cette phrase le mot droit est pris successivement dans les deux sens qui viennent d'être indiqués.[2]

The same distinction is even more current in Germany, whence it has indeed been taken by French writers.

There is nothing to warrant the view that 'in Continental languages law and justice are called by the same name',[3] just as nothing would justify the Continental lawyer in assuming that there is in Anglo-American law a confusion between the two provinces because the term 'right' serves the purpose of describing both a legally protected interest and a moral judgment, or because of the current usage referring to courts of justice when courts of law are meant,[4] or because the term 'wrong' has a double connotation inasmuch as it may refer to a legal or to a moral wrong. In some way or other there have survived in different languages traces of the original identification of law, custom, and justice.[5] There is no reason to deplore this linguistic phenomenon. It is as a rule clear from the context in which sense a term is used. There is no confusion when we say 'it is not right that X should have a right against Y', as there is no confusion

[1] See an interesting paragraph on *Le Droit et la Morale* in the Introduction to the treatise of Colin and Capitant referred to below, p. 474, n. 1.

[2] *Traité élémentaire de droit civil* (1st ed. 1899), § 2.

[3] See Salmond, *Jurisprudence*, § 4.

[4] See, for instance, Ross, *Theorie der Rechtsquellen* (1929), p. 80.

[5] In Ihering's *Der Zweck in Recht*, the reader will find an interesting exposition of the historical identity of these terms in the various derivations of the Greek δίκη and the Latin *mos*. See on this point Somlo, *Juristische Grundlehre* (2nd ed. 1927), § 41.

when the German '*Recht*' is used with the same double meaning. In fact the question hardly arises for the lawyer at all. For, as a rule, lawyers use these terms in their legal sense only. The English reader will in general be on safe ground if, having regard to the context, he translates as a matter of course the terms *Recht*, *droit*, *diritto* as connoting either law pure and simple, or a legal right. In so far, therefore, as the supposed confusion in Continental jurisprudence between existing law and postulated law rests on the belief that the Continental term for law has a double meaning, it proves to be non-existent.

Apart from questions of terminology, the view that the science of jurisprudence and of legal philosophy on the Continent is distinguished by its confusion of what law is with what it ought to be, shows merely an imperfect acquaintance with Continental legal thinking. Has not the powerful 'free law' movement in Germany been primarily directed against the predominance of positivist tendencies throughout the nineteenth century? Has not Ihering, even long before the 'free school' movement, poured his scorn upon the positivist 'jurisprudence of concepts' (*Begriffsjurisprudenz*)? Has not the French *école de l'exégèse*, which was predominant in the epoch following upon the adoption of the *Code Civil* and which reduced the judicial function to one of formal logical deduction, been successfully challenged by writers like Geny,[1] Lambert, and Saleilles? It is difficult not to gain the impression that English jurists have raised certain transient and historically conditioned characteristics of Continental legal method in the first three-quarters of the nineteenth century to the authority of a permanent quality of Continental legal thought. The international lawyer who is acquainted with the fact that it is from the Continent – in particular from Germany and Italy – that has come the rigid and frequently uncompromising positivist school in international law, will be specially inclined to treat with appropriate caution the accepted view of the nature of Continental jurisprudence. Probably the main reason which led writers like Salmond and Holland to speak of 'strange lands' and 'law in the air' in the field of Continental legal science is – apart from misconceptions due to the barrier of language – the fact that, for historical reasons, the preoccupation on the Continent with the problems of legal philosophy, especially in regard to the purpose of the law and the nature of the judicial function, has been more intensive than in

[1] See in particular the chapter entitled 'Exposé analytique de la méthode traditionnelle', in his *Méthode d'interprétation et sources en droit privé positif* (2nd ed. 1919), I, 17–60.

this country and, until recently, in the United States. The output of this aspect of legal thinking has been so large as to give to the casual observer the misleading impression that that is the whole of Continental legal thinking, and to cause him to attribute to the latter a confusion into which the observer alone has fallen.

The authority of judicial precedent

The second argument most frequently adduced in connection with the supposed fundamental difference between Anglo-American and Continental legal thought is the one bearing upon the relative authority of judicial precedent and the resulting differences in the process of making and applying the law. The fact that in one group of countries judicial precedent constitutes a source of law whereas in others its formal authority as a source of decision in future cases is excluded either expressly or impliedly, is regarded by some as pointing not only to a mere difference in legal tradition and in judicial *technique* but also as showing a fundamental difference of legal approach, a difference between a pragmatic and practical approach based on former judicial experience and one relying on abstract reasoning from general principles. To some writers the whole question of the difference between the two systems of law reduces itself in fact to the difference in the function of judicial precedent.[1]

It is submitted that this view as to the fundamentally different function of judicial precedent under the two systems of law is based more on a consideration of appearances and of legal formulae than of the substance of legal life. It disregards the fact that, on the one hand, no formal provision of the law and no form of judicial organization can prevent judicial precedent from constituting a powerful factor of positive law, and that, on the other hand, the power of judicial precedent is in the long run not greater than the inherent value of the legal substance embodied in it. No legal doctrine and no express legal provision can do away with the fact that judges actually do, within their sphere, make law; that the legal principles or views enunciated in and underlying judicial decisions do inevitably influence judges in future cases *in pari materia*; that such influence is due not only to the natural reluctance of courts to admit they were wrong in the past, but more particularly to the fact that these former decisions embody a volume of legal experience which is persuasive in itself; that judicial decisions, particularly when published, become

[1] See, for instance, Lévy-Ullmann, *Eléments d'introduction générale à l'étude des sciences juridiques*, II, *Le système juridique de l'Angleterre* (1928), 33–44.

part and parcel of the legal sense of the community; and that adherence to them, within the limits of justice, is imperative if the law is to fulfil one of its primary functions, i.e. the maintenance of security and stability as expressed in the ensuring of the fulfilment of legitimate expectations prompted by judicial decisions once given.

As mentioned, no express legal provision can prevent judicial precedent from exercising this function. In France, judges are forbidden, by virtue of Article 5 of the Code Civil, to lay down principles 'par voie de disposition générale et réglementaire sur les causes qui leur sont soumises'. This is perhaps the reason for the laconic precision of the great majority of the decisions of French courts, for the corresponding exuberance of the commentators, and for elaborate provisions calculated to secure some unity in the administration of justice by ensuring the binding effect upon inferior courts of the decisions of the Court of Cassation after the same case has come before it for the second time. But all this notwithstanding, and in spite of the fact that French courts are not bound either by their own decisions or by decisions of superior courts, it is hardly possible to doubt the actual authority and influence of judicial precedent in France. The volume of law reporting in France, the scope of annotations and comment upon them, and the weight attached to *jurisprudence* in daily practice, make it impossible to eliminate judicial precedent from any accurate account of the forces actually operating in the shaping of French law.[1]

The same applies to Germany, where a whole series of the provisions of the Civil Code has been interpreted out of existence in consequence of the activity of the courts.[2] In the decisions of the Reichsgericht, in particular in recent years, one finds elaborate references to previous judgments of that Court; not infrequently this

[1] See on this subject Colin and Capitant, *Cours élémentaire de droit civil français* (4th ed. 1923), I, 35–36. In the domain of administrative law the activity of French courts, in particular of the *Conseil d'Etat*, in regard to the existing law is to a large extent built upon *jurisprudence*. See Hauriou, *La jurisprudence administrative de 1882 à 1929* (nouveau tirage, 1930), 3 vols. The following observations of an English lawyer speaking from practical experience are of interest: '... The impression which prevails in England to the effect that in interpreting the Code the French Courts do not recognize the doctrine of *stare decisis*, and are not influenced by the authority of precedent, is greatly exaggerated, if indeed it is not truer to say that it is simply mistaken. In point of fact great respect is paid in France to the authority of decided cases; indeed it is sometimes said that things have come to such a pass nowadays, that counsel no longer need display any knowledge of legal principle, since all that judges will listen to is an exposition of the *jurisprudence*, as it is called' (Amos, 'The Code Napoléon and the Modern World', *J.C.L.*, 3rd ser. 10 (1928), 225). And see, to the same effect, Pound in *H.L.R.*, 36 (1922–3), 646, 647.

[2] See the illuminating article of Professor Jung entitled 'Das sogenannte Gewohnheitsrecht als Grundfrage der Rechtsquellenlehre', in *Archiv für Rechts- und Wirtschaftsphilosophie*, 22 (1928–9), 227–59.

enumeration concludes with the word '*daran ist festzuhalten*' ('this must be adhered to'). The way in which German courts have in the post-war period 'adapted' the civil code law of mortgages to the extraordinary requirements of the inflation time offers a good illustration of the place of judicial decisions in the actual working of the law. There exists in France and in Germany a judge-made case law, and the authority of judicial precedent is not alien to those countries. It is not, however, the authority of single cases and precedents which is decisive, but their cumulative and growing weight. It is customary in this country to contrast the pragmatic method of English case law with the deductive and theoretical nature of the Continental approach. It would not be surprising to find Continental lawyers insisting on the pragmatic character of their own case law as contrasted with that obtaining in England.

While a study of the actual working of the administration of justice on the Continent must necessarily lead the English lawyer to revise his view as to the insignificance of the part played by courts and judicial precedent in the development of the law, the Continental lawyer, beginning the investigation from the other end of the road, must soon learn that the binding force of precedent in the common law countries is, to say the least, not higher than that of the written law in his own country. It is the inherent value of the law contained in a given precedent and the considerations of stability of legal relations embodied in the institution of precedent as a whole which are the soul of its vitality. Once these powerful factors supporting its formal authority have departed, the days of its operation are numbered.[1] There is in this respect a difference of degree only between, on the one hand, so-called precedents of absolute authority, i.e. decisions of superior courts which are absolutely binding upon inferior courts, and of the House of Lords and the Court of Appeal, each of which is absolutely bound by its own decisions, and, on the other hand, precedents of 'conditional authority', which, as Sir John Salmond puts it, may be disregarded if they are wrong decisions, i.e. if they are contrary to law or contrary to reason.[2] Any disposition to

[1] This is not always realized by the Continental student of English law. As in other matters, there is here a tendency to attach exaggerated importance to formal legal doctrines without taking into account the actual operation of law. See, for instance, Lambert, *La fonction du droit civil comparé* (1903), as translated in *The Science of Legal Method* in *Modern Legal Philosophy Series* (1921), pp. 265–70, and, to the same effect, Gerland, 'The Operation of the Judicial Function in English Law', *ibid.* pp. 229–50, who points to the 'fundamental weakness of the English system' consisting in the fact that 'every legal proposition, once authoritatively enumerated, becomes a legal rule' which 'is no longer capable of further transformation, of further elaboration' (at p. 249).

[2] *Jurisprudence*, §§ 57–9.

disregard a precedent must necessarily be tempered by the consideration that the disturbance of certainty and stability resulting from such disregard may be more disadvantageous to the social purpose of the law than the apparent improvement in the soundness and justice of the rule achieved thereby. But no legal doctrine can save a precedent based on bad or obsolete law from being disregarded directly or by the less conspicuous but equally effective process of distinguishing. And, as Professor Allen has convincingly shown,[1] even the absolutely authoritative precedent is not immune from this process of distinguishing, in which free judicial activity necessarily asserts itself as it does on the Continent in respect of the written law.

Thus while under one legal system artificial limitations of the function of judicial precedent have necessarily given way to the requirements of legal stability and consistency in the administration of justice, under the other the authority of precedent as a formal source of law is and has always been limited by the requirements of justice, convenience, and reasonableness.[2] Undoubtedly there still remains the cleavage in legal theory consisting in the fact that under the common law a single judicial decision constitutes a binding precedent, whereas this is not its function under the Continental systems of law. This may be true, but it appears from what has been said above that the difference is one of legal theory only, and that in essence it is unable to affect either the latent possibilities of judicial precedent in one system of law or its necessary limitations in the other. An increased mutual understanding of the actual working of the administration of justice in the Anglo-American and Continental countries must, it is believed, show how inappropriate, particularly in the domain of judicial precedent, is the exaggeration of the idea of fundamental differences in the law in the two groups of countries. In this process of reducing the discrepancies to their proper propor-

[1] *Law in the Making* (1927), pp. 164, 165.

[2] When speaking of the wide differences obtaining between the two systems of law in the matter of the weight attached to the decisions of courts, Holland remarked that 'there have been of late some symptoms of an approximation between the two theories' and that 'while on the Continent judicial decisions are reported with more care, and cited with more effect, than formerly, indications are not wanting that in England and in the United States they are beginning to be somewhat more freely criticized than has hitherto been usual' (*Jurisprudence*, p. 60). Evidence of this approximation was not lacking throughout the nineteenth century. In any case his forecast has been substantiated in the last thirty years by a whittling down of the authority of judicial precedent in the United States (see on this subject Goodhart, 'Case Law in England and America', *Essays in Jurisprudence and the Common Law* (1931), pp. 50–74) and by an equally marked development in the opposite direction in the Continental countries.

tions, international judicial settlement is destined to play a prominent part.

There are two principal reasons why the lesson which international judicial settlement affords on the question of the authority and function of precedent is specially instructive. The first is that the development of the law here takes place unhampered by artificial and traditional restrictions of any particular system of municipal law. The second is that in the field of international arbitration there have repeated themselves on a higher and different plane the causes which had a decisive effect in shaping the fate of judicial precedent within the State. Article 5 of the *Code Civil*, which forbids judges to lay down rules of general application to govern future cases, has its apparent counterpart in Article 59 of the Statute of the Permanent Court which lays down that 'the decision of the Court has no binding force except between the parties and in respect of that particular case'. The rule of the *Code Civil* was inspired by the doctrine of separation of powers and of the sovereignty of the people. The judge was expected to be merely 'la bouche qui prononce les paroles de la loi'.[1] It was regarded as derogatory to the sovereignty of the people to subject the citizen, not to the law of the State, but to the magistrate's personal judgment as to what was right. In the same way the positivist doctrine in international law has been insistent on interpreting Article 59 of the Statute as signifying a limitation of the power of judicial precedent in the international sphere, on the ground that international tribunals owe their very existence and such jurisdictional powers as they possess to the will of States whose sovereignty would be impaired by raising judicial decisions to the authority of a source of law.

This negative attitude was, however, bound to prove ineffective, not only for the reasons which caused judicial precedent to maintain itself in the sphere of municipal law even in the face of express legal prohibitions, but also because in the international society judicial decisions constitute one of the not too numerous manifestations of the rule of law, as well as a powerful instrument for the crystallization of the abstract rules of international law. In the prevailing scarcity of agencies and opportunities for declaring and developing existing international law, no source is so poor that it can be ignored altogether; and the decisions of international tribunals are not the poorest of the sources. That is the reason why international tribunals are full of evidence of recourse to former decisions *in pari materia*,

[1] Montesquieu, *Esprit des Lois*, I, 6, ch. iii.

regardless of whether such tribunals are composed of Continental or common law judges. No student of international arbitration can fail to notice the eagerness of such recourse to previous arbitral decisions, an eagerness which is both conspicuous and, in view of the scarcity of the available material, almost pathetic. The Permanent Court of International Justice itself has referred to 'principles recognized by the jurisprudence of international tribunals', in addition to the references to individual arbitral decisions, for the purpose of distinguishing or corroborating its own decisions.[1] This the Permanent Court is entitled to do by virtue of Article 38 of its Statute, which provides that the Court shall apply 'subject to the provisions of Article 59, judicial decisions...' as a subsidiary means for the determination of rules of law. Thus it would appear that while the decisions of international tribunals in general may be relied upon as a subsidiary source without any limitations, the decisions of the Permanent Court may only be relied upon in future cases subject to Article 59. The result would be strange, if Article 59 were to be read literally and as referring deliberately to the doctrine of judicial precedent. It is submitted that it cannot be so read.

Does Article 59 of the Statute amount to an acceptance of the Continental Doctrine?

The history of Article 59 shows that it was not originally intended to refer to the major aspects of the question of the authority of judicial precedent. In the draft of the Statute submitted by the Committee of Jurists of 1920, the present Article 59 did not appear at all. It was inserted by the Council of the League, acting on the strength of the so-called Brussels Report. This report leaves little doubt that the addition of the present Article 59 had no reference to the question of the authority of precedent. It arose in connection with the right of intervention as laid down in the present Article 63 of the Statute, which provides as follows:

Whenever the construction of a convention to which States other than those concerned in the case are parties is in question, the Registrar shall notify all such States forthwith.

Every State so notified has the right to intervene in the proceedings:

[1] See, for instance, *P.C.I.J.* Series A, no. 17, p. 57, in which the Court 'in accordance with the jurisprudence of arbitral tribunals' refused to take into account possible but contingent and indeterminate damages. And see the discussion, in *P.C.I.J.* Series B, no. 11 (at p. 30), of the problem of *res judicata* by reference to the award in 1902 of the Permanent Court of Arbitration in *Pious Funds of the Californias* case, or, in *P.C.I.J.* Series A, no. 10 (at p. 26), of the *Costa Rica Packet* case.

but if it uses this right, the construction given by the judgment will be equally binding upon it.

In connection with this Article there must be read the provision of Article 62, which lays down that should a State consider that it has an interest of a legal nature which may be affected by the decision in the case, it may submit a request to the Court to be permitted to intervene as a third party, it being for the Court to decide upon this request. This was also the substance of Article 61 of the Draft. The reason for inserting the article as to intervention was, in the opinion of the Drafting Committee of 1920 and of the Brussels Report, to prevent situations from arising in which an apparently unimportant case between two States might, without other States having had an opportunity to put their view as to the legal position before the Court, result in a decision laying down certain principles of international law which might be inconsistent with the views held by other States. This, it was thought, applied in particular to the interpretation of multilateral conventions. It appears from the Brussels Report that the present Article 59 was inserted merely *ex abundanti cautela* in order to give a more explicit formulation to the provision that if a State uses its right of intervention, the construction given by the judgment shall be binding upon it in the same measure as it binds the original parties to the dispute. The Report says:

This last stipulation establishes, in the contrary case, that if a State has not intervened in the case the interpretation cannot be enforced against it. No possible disadvantage could ensue from stating directly what Article 61 indirectly admits. The addition of an Article drawn up as follows can thus be proposed to the Assembly: the decision of the Court has no binding force except between the parties and in respect of that particular case.[1]

The close connection between Articles 59 and 63 – indeed the fact that the former is supplementary to the latter – appears clearly from the fact that in Article 84 of Hague Convention no. I of 1907 for the Pacific Settlement of International Disputes (and in the corresponding Article 56 of the Convention of 1899) the two provisions were placed side by side. Article 84 was as follows:

The award is binding only on the parties in dispute. When there is a question as to the interpretation of a convention to which Powers other than those in dispute are parties, the latter shall inform all the signatory Powers in good time. Each of these Powers is entitled to intervene in the

[1] *Documents Concerning the Action taken by the Council under Article 14 of the Covenant*, p. 50. See also *Procès-Verbaux* of the meetings of the Committee of Jurists of 1920, p. 776.

case. If one or more avail themselves of this right, the interpretation contained in the award is equally binding of them.

And a study of the proceedings of the Hague Conferences on this matter confirms the opinion that it was merely with this object in view that Articles 84 and 56 were inserted. In fact the very phrase now used in Article 59 of the Statute was proposed at one of the Committees of the Second Hague Conference in connection with the question of interpretation of multilateral treaties.[1]

While an examination of the origin and the antecedents of Article 59 of the Statute shows that that provision has little to do with the adoption of the Continental, as distinguished from the Anglo-American, treatment of judicial precedent, a survey of the work of the Permanent Court in regard to the authority of its own decisions shows that the alleged clash between Continental and Anglo-American conceptions has been disregarded, and that the problem is being solved, not by reference to particular national decisions, but on the basis of the inherent value and the inescapable influence of judicial precedent. Express reference to its previous pronouncements constitutes a constant feature of the activity of the Court. It is in this way that a considerable number of questions in the field of substantive international law and of arbitral procedure have now become crystallized as rules whose application by the Court in future similar cases may be safely assumed. This is shown by the way in which the Court has consistently discouraged the argument that treaty obligations imposing limitations upon the sovereignty of States ought to be interpreted restrictively; in which it has followed an independent line of practice in considering preparatory work as an element of interpretation of treaties; in which it has asserted its right to give declaratory judgments; in which it has judged itself competent to assume jurisdiction by virtue of the implied consent of the parties and unhampered by defects of form in their submissions; in which it has asserted the international character of disputes in which a case has been taken up by a State on behalf of its nationals; and in

[1] See, for instance, the proposal of the so-called Fusinato Committee at the Second Hague Conference (*Actes et Documents*, II, 436), where the passage occurs: 'Que la sentence arbitrale n'oblige que les parties en litige, et pour ce litige seulement.' And see also on this point the deliberations of the Institute of International Law, in *Annuaire*, 16 (1897), 115 *et seq.*, *ibid.* 19 (1902), 333 *et seq.*; and *Actes et Documents*, II, 457 *et seq.*, 515 *et seq.*, 569; and on the whole question Lammasch, *Die Rechtskraft internationaler Schiedssprüche* (1913), pp. 97–124. Any other explanation of the present Article 59 would be utterly unintelligible seeing that the necessity of providing for a tribunal developing international law by its own decisions had been the starting-point for the attempts to establish a truly permanent international court as distinguished from the Permanent Court of Arbitration.

numerous other questions.[1] To this constant and express reference to previous decisions there must be added the eagerness of the Court to explain any apparent inconsistencies between its various pronouncements.[2] The lack of hesitation in this reliance upon previous decisions is conspicuous, as may be seen from some of the typical forms of such reference: 'As the Court has said in Judgment no. 12';[3] or 'Nothing has been advanced in the course of the present proceedings calculated to alter the Court's Opinion [as expressed in Advisory Opinion no. 6] on this point';[4] or, more generally, 'As the Court has had occasion to state in its previous Judgments and Opinions';[5] or, simply, 'Following the precedent afforded by its Advisory Opinion no. 3'.[6]

Does the Court refer to its previous Judgments merely by way of illustration? Or does the reference imply that it feels itself bound by its previous decisions? Or is it merely to emphasize the element of continuity in the work of the Court? These are idle questions. They tend to reduce the problem to the plane of national jurisprudential differences from which it has been lifted by the constant practice of the Court. This practice shows that if Article 59 was intended to stultify the task of the Court of developing international law by its own decisions and to prevent it from availing itself of the fruits of such development, then, with the concurrence of all the judges representing various systems of municipal jurisprudence, it has remained a dead letter. However, it has been submitted that it was not so intended. The practice of the Court amply corroborates this submission. Without adopting the common law doctrine as to the binding force of the single precedent, and while disregarding formal prohibitions reminiscent of legal provisions in individual Continental Codes, the practice of the Court has become an instructive manifestation of the intrinsic merits – inevitably revealing themselves under every system of law – of judicial precedent.

[1] See, here, for a very useful synopsis of the relevant cases, *P.C.I.J.* Series E, no. 3, pp. 217, 218; *ibid.* no. 4, pp. 292, 293, and *ibid.* no. 6, p. 300. See also *Annual Digest*, 3 (1925–6), 430, and *ibid.* 4 (1927–8), part X.B.

[2] See, e.g., *P.C.I.J.* Series A, no. 9, p. 24; or, as to Advisory Opinion no. 12, *P.C.I.J.* Series E, no. 3, p. 226, where reference is made to a pronouncement made by the Court at the public sitting; or *P.C.I.J.* Series A, no. 2, p. 16; or *P.C.I.J.* Series A, no. 15, p. 24.

[3] *P.C.I.J.* series A, no. 17, at p. 37; see also *ibid.* p. 33; *P.C.I.J.* Series A, no. 7, p. 19; *P.C.I.J.* Series A, no. 15, p. 24; *P.C.I.J.* Series B, no. 9, p. 36.

[4] *P.C.I.J.* Series A, no. 7, at p. 31.

[5] *P.C.I.J.* Series B, no. 14, at p. 36.

[6] *P.C.I.J.* Series B, no. 16, at p. 15.

CONCLUSIONS

It is submitted that the results of the investigation here undertaken justify the conclusion that there is no substance in the view that there exist two schools of international law – the Anglo-American and Continental – either in regard to specific questions of international law, or in respect of differences in those questions of municipal law which are of possible relevance in international law, or in the matter of general legal approach and method. The work of international tribunals shows that international judicial settlement, far from being impeded by the alleged existence of 'two schools of thought', is not actually confronted with the problem. An analysis, which reasons of space do not permit to be undertaken here, of the work of the Permanent Court in general and of the dissenting opinions and observations appended to its Judgements and Advisory Opinions would show that the question has not arisen there at all.

There have been various causes which furthered both the wide acceptance and the continuation of the belief in the existence of an Anglo-American and a Continental conception of international law. For some it is the outcome of a generalization of divergent although, as has been shown, transient interests of different groups of belligerents; for others, it has become one of the expressions of an attitude of caution in regard to obligatory arbitration; with others still it is largely the consequence of a vague feeling, born of the lack of acquaintance with foreign law and lying largely in the domain of sentiment, that there *is* a fundamental difference, whose consequences reveal themselves with fatal necessity in inter-State relations, in the various systems of law. It is submitted that an abandonment of this deeply-rooted belief is desirable. This is so not only on the ground that as a matter of legally relevant facts the two conceptions of international law do not exist and that it is therefore imperative to discard it on the ground of scientific accuracy. There is an additional and not unimportant reason for doing away with what is essentially no more than a phrase.

The idea of the existence of two schools of thought in international law, in so far as it is based not on differences in respect of specific subjects of international law, but on a fundamental divergence of approach and outlook, is an undesirable idea from a more general and – if the term may be used here with due apology – humanitarian point of view. It suggests, as between the nations of today, differences in legal thinking of so fundamental a nature as to manifest themselves even in a field of relations distinct from those regulated by municipal law. Only a pedant would see any danger or undue inconvenience in the maintenance of traditional national differences in legal terminology, institutions, or regulation of specific aspects of conduct. But to elevate these divergences to the authority of fundamental differences in legal thinking likely to influence substantially judicial activity on matters of international law, i.e. on matters other than those directly affected by the differences of national jurisprudence, is to question that ultimate uniformity of the sense of right and justice which is the foundation of the legal ordering of the relations between States. In the future, when the exclusiveness of the conception of States as the sole subjects of the Law of Nations will have become a matter of the past, international law will coincide with *jus gentium* as originally conceived by Greek philosophers, by Roman jurists, by scholastic writers and by the father of international law, that is to say it will become again the common law of mankind – a conception which is probably much older than that of *jus naturæ*. That time is still far off. But present day international law at least constitutes a successful attempt at a common law of mankind, of relatively intensive and pervading universality and uniformity, in the limited field of relations between sovereign States. This is in itself no mean achievement. There is no good reason why it should be imperilled for the sake of traditional notions of doubtful legal value.

V

THE SUBJECTS OF INTERNATIONAL LAW

CHAPTER 18

THE SUBJECTS OF THE LAW OF NATIONS

Editor's note This chapter was originally published in two parts in the *Law Quarterly Review*, 63 (1947), 438–60 and 64 (1948), 97–119. It reflects an important period in Lauterpacht's work. In 1945 he had published *An International Bill of the Rights of Man* (Columbia University Press, New York) which was, in effect, the first edition of the book which appeared in 1948 as *International Law and Human Rights* (London, Stevens and Sons Limited). In addition, between 1944 and 1946 he was actively associated with the preparations for the trials of the major German war criminals. This had led him to publish in the *British Year Book of International Law* in 1944 an article on 'The Law of Nations and the Punishment of War Criminals'.

These two categories of interest caused him to re-examine in detail the question of the subjects of international law and in particular to develop the theme that neither in practice nor in theory was there anything in international law to prevent the individual being a direct subject of international rights and duties. Although most of the article on 'The Subjects of the Law of Nations' was later used in the opening four chapters of *International Law and Human Rights*, I have nonetheless considered this would be an appropriate case in which to depart from the working rule of excluding from these volumes those articles which had previously been incorporated within books published by Lauterpacht.

The question of the subjects of international law has been discussed in the past largely from two aspects. It has been debated, in the first instance, as part of the controversy whether not only States but also individuals are subjects of the Law of Nations. With regard to individuals, the discussion has centred largely on the question whether they possess or can possess rights given to them directly by customary international law and treaties. In particular, much attention has been devoted to the problem of the direct access of individuals to international tribunals and other international agencies. The issue of the so-called fundamental rights of the individual recognized and protected by international law as against the sovereign power of the State has underlain, though in a somewhat inarticulate form, much of the discussion.

All these are questions of significance. But there have been other factors which have imparted to the discussion a degree of urgency unusual in a seemingly theoretical controversy. One of them has been the position of individuals as subjects of international duties. In the first instance, the proposition that individuals can be subjects of international rights necessarily involves the corollary that they can be subjects of international duties; the cogency of the claim to the former gains by an admission of the latter. Secondly, it has been increasingly realized that to limit the operation of the duties prescribed by international law to the impersonal entity of States as distinguished from the individuals who compose them and who act on their behalf is to open the door wide for the acceptance, in relation to States, of standards of morality different from those applying among individuals. Experience has shown that 'different' standards mean, in this connection, standards which are lower and less exacting. Thirdly, upon final analysis it is difficult to escape the conclusion that unless legal duties are accepted as resting upon the individual, they do not in practice and, to some extent, in law obligate anyone. These apparently theoretical considerations received illuminating comment in the Judgment given on 30 September 1946 by the International Military Tribunal established by the Four-Power Agreement, and the Charter annexed thereto, of 6 August 1945. The Tribunal said:

> It was submitted that international law is concerned with actions of sovereign States, and provides no punishment for individuals . . . these contentions must be rejected. . . Crimes against international law are committed by men, not by abstract entities, and only by punishing individuals who commit such crimes can the provisions of international law be enforced.[1]

This statement was in the nature of an explanatory gloss upon the provision of Article 6 of the Charter which laid down that there shall be individual responsibility of the defendants for the acts within the jurisdiction of the Tribunal. The joint effect of the Charter and the Judgment was to bring to mind with particular emphasis the fact that the question of the subjects of international law is not one of mere theory. However, this is only one aspect of the wider problem which it is intended to discuss in the present article. It will be submitted: (a) that the doctrine that States are the only subjects of international law is not an accurate statement of the actual legal position; (b) that the modern development of international law, from

[1] *Annual Digest*, 18 (1946), 221.

a system of procedural and ceremonial rules regulating the external intercourse of States and delimiting their jurisdiction to a body of law concerned with substantive interests of States and their nationals, has rendered the traditional positivist doctrine on the subject obsolete and unworkable; and (c) that the time is now ripe for assessing the significance of these changes in the substantive law and in the functioning of organized international society.

I. THE TRADITIONAL DOCTRINE AND THE PRACTICE OF STATES

The orthodox positivist doctrine has been explicit in the affirmation that only States are subjects of international law.[1] In those cases in which individuals seem to derive benefits under international law, the predominant view has been that such benefits are enjoyed not by virtue of a right which international law gives to the individual but by reason of a right appertaining to the State of which the individual is a national. The right is a right of the State; the individual is the object of that right. Thus, while it is an established principle acted upon by international tribunals that the alien resident within the territory of a State is entitled to be treated in accordance with a minimum standard of civilization, the traditional theory has been that, in strict law, it is not the alien who is thus 'entitled', but only his State. His membership of the State – his nationality – is an

[1] That traditional doctrine is now rejected by the great majority of those who have devoted special study to the matter – though it continues to linger in some repetitious statements in text-books. Dr Knubben, in the most exhaustive work yet published on the subjects of international law – *Die Subjekte des Völkerrechts* (1928) – reaches the conclusion that the traditional view is antiquated and no longer tenable. He defines international law as 'a law regulating the mutual relations of States and the international relations of other subjects, in particular those of States and of entities other than States' (at p. 527). Professor Spiropoulos, in an important essay published in the same year and anticipating more recent developments such as an International Bill of Human Rights—*L'individu en droit international*—arrives at the same view. So, in 1927, did the author of the present article: Lauterpacht, *Analogies*, pp. 73–9; Politis, *Les nouvelles tendences du droit international* (1927), pp. 55–93; Segal, *L'individu en droit international* (1932); Ténékidès, *L'individu en droit international moderne* (1933); Siotto-Pintor, 'Les sujets du droit international autres que les Etats', in *Hague Recueil*, 41 (1932) (iii), 251–357. More recently, Professor Jessup, in a series of articles which are to form part of a more comprehensive work, has shown both the decisive inroads which practice has made upon the established doctrine and the further possible impacts of the change resulting from the fact that the individual—and, generally, persons and bodies other than States—have acquired a status in international law; see Jessup, 'Responsibility of States for Injuries to Individuals', in *Columbia Law Review*, 46 (1946), 903–28; 'The Subjects of a Modern Law of Nations', in *Michigan Law Review*, 45 (1947), 383–408; and 'Law of International Contractual Agreements', in *A.J.* 41 (1947), 380–405. In fact, what has been considered the established doctrine is no longer 'established'.

essential condition of the jurisdiction of international tribunals when resorted to for the purpose of redressing wrongs alleged to have been suffered by him. Much of the existing practice, in the form of the rule of 'nationality of claims' and otherwise, seems to lend support to that view. Thus, when confronted with the so-called Calvo Clause, international tribunals have held that it is not competent for an alien to sign away, with an effect binding upon his Government and the tribunal, his right to appeal for the protection of his State in case of a denial of justice amounting to a violation of international law – the reason being that the faculty to vindicate the violated rule of international law is the right of his State, not a right of his own. For a similar reason the traditional theory has denied the possibility of any direct relation between international and municipal law. If individuals can never be subjects of international rights and duties then, according to that view, the rules of international law can have no immediate effect, without a previous act of transformation, upon the municipal law of the State. On that theory the classical English doctrine of the Law of Nations being part of the law of the land – a doctrine which has become part of the law of many States – is merely a deceptive and inaccurate form of words. For the same reason, it has been asserted that so-called fundamental rights of the individual recognized by international law are not only non-existent but also impossible in principle, as being inconsistent with the structure of international law conceived as a law between States only. Similarly, if individuals have no rights under international law, it seems to follow that they have no *locus standi* before international tribunals and other international agencies, though occasionally it has been argued that they are not subjects of international law *because* of their procedural incapacity before international tribunals. Finally, it has been denied, for essentially the same reason, that international public bodies of a political and administrative character, created by agreements between States, possess an international juridical personality of their own and are as such subjects of international law in their own right.

This dualism of subjects, of international law and municipal law respectively, has been stressed with particular emphasis by the exponents of the positivist school of thought. It is not surprising that this should have been so. In the first instance, in so far as the positivist doctrine is identified with the extreme assertion of State sovereignty, it is natural that it should have viewed with disapproval the notion of private persons, or even of public international bodies, being placed in the same elevated category as sovereign States. Secondly, inasmuch as the conception of fundamental rights of the individual represents him as a subject of international rights irrespective of the law of the State, it amounts to a rejection of the doctrine that the will of States is the exclusive source of international law. If, according to the positivist doctrine, States themselves can become subjects of international law only by virtue of recognition granted, with constitutive effect, by already existing States acting in the free and unfettered exercise of their discretion, how much more is this the case with regard to individuals and other persons. Even those positivist writers who have admitted the possibility of persons other than States being subjects of international law insisted that this could be so only as the result of express agreement by States. It is thus probable that the criticism of the accepted doctrine in the matter of the subjects of international law cannot be separated from the challenge to the twin positivist doctrine of international law as emanating exclusively from the will of States.

Like various other tenets of the positivist creed, the doctrine that only States are subjects of international law is unable to stand the test of actual practice. This is so although some of the criticism directed against it under this head has been of controversial value and confined to matters of limited compass. Thus the rules of international law in the matter of piracy have often been referred to as confuting the predominant doctrine. It has been pointed out that inasmuch as every State is entitled to exercise jurisdiction over a pirate, piracy is a crime not only under municipal law but also under international law and that, therefore, pirates are subjects of the Law of Nations. Yet it is possible that the rule in question amounts in effect to no more than a reciprocal concession of jurisdictional rights over an alien for a crime committed abroad, as is the case, for instance, in the matter of the jurisdiction over aliens conceded in the Convention of 1929 on the Suppression of Counterfeiting Currency[1] or in the (unratified) Convention of 1937 for the Prevention and Punishment of Terrorism.[2] For while some countries, such as Great Britain, in assuming jurisdiction over pirates refer to piracy as defined by the Law of Nations, others assume jurisdiction over piracy as defined by their own law. On the other hand, when – as in the Nyon Agreement of 1937 relating to piratical acts of submarines in the Mediterranean in the course of the Spanish Civil War of 1936–9

[1] Hudson, *Legislation*, IV, 2692.

[2] Hudson, *Legislation*, VII, 862.

— States claim to assume jurisdiction over offenders of whatever nationality, we are confronted with the direct subjection of individuals to international law in a manner which cannot be interpreted as a mutual concession of jurisdictional rights.

Similarly, it is controversial whether it can be accurately maintained that a blockade-runner penalized by a belligerent is a subject of the Law of Nations inasmuch as he is being punished for a violation of a rule of international law. There is probably no rule of international law prohibiting individuals from breaking a blockade or carrying contraband. The penalty for such acts is inflicted by the belligerent in conformity with his own law, though subject to an authorization laid down and qualified by international law. The rules of international law in the matter of contraband and blockade are binding upon States in the sense that they circumscribe their freedom of action in interfering with and suppressing the activities of nationals of other States.

Somewhat strangely, insufficient attention has been paid, in this connection, to the fact that the operation of the law of war constitutes a decisive refutation of the view that States only, and not individuals, are subjects of international duties. For it is an accepted principle of law that individual members of the armed forces of the belligerent are criminally responsible for violations of the law of war and that the enemy State is entitled to punish them for war crimes committed by them. The controversy, which is now somewhat unreal, whether they are thus liable for acting in obedience to superior orders is irrelevant in this connection. For it is universally agreed that in any case persons who have ordered the commission of war crimes are liable to punishment for the violation of rules of warfare. It is clear that in this vital respect the apparently established doctrine breaks down altogether. The law declines, in this matter, to accept the artificial distinction between the State and those acting on its behalf. The fact that the offender acts on behalf of the State is irrelevant. He is bound personally by rules of international law whether he is acting in his personal capacity, in order to satisfy private greed or lust, or as an organ of the State.

Neither can it be said that, in the criticism of the doctrine that only States are subjects of international law, full use – or, indeed, any use – has been made of the fact that, according to the law of many States, rules of international law form part of their domestic law. This is so in particular in Great Britain, in the United States of

America, and in other common law countries where the doctrine of the incorporation of international law as part of the law of the land must be regarded as firmly established – at least with regard to customary international law. There has been occasional hesitation on the part of English courts to acknowledge the full operation of the doctrine of incorporation, but there ought to be no doubt as to its validity, its general effectiveness and its significance.[1] It constitutes perhaps the most important contribution of common law to the cause of the Law of Nations. It has been expressly adopted by a number of countries; it is probable that, without express adoption, it has been acted upon by others.[2]

Now, the principle that international law is, without an express act of transformation, part of municipal law means in effect that rights and duties created by international law are directly applicable to individuals through the instrumentality of municipal courts and that, to that extent, individuals are subjects of the Law of Nations. Writers of the positivist complexion have denied the operation of that principle by resorting to the simple device of begging the question. International law, they have maintained, cannot act directly in the municipal sphere for the reason that the subjects of the two systems of law are fundamentally different. Actually the alleged difference of subjects is disproved by the fact that, according to the positive law of most States, international law is a direct source of rights and obligations of individuals enforceable by municipal courts. The wide acceptance of that practice has imparted to it a degree of generality which has made it approximate to a customary rule of international law. For the uniformity of municipal law and legislation in matters affecting international law is in itself evidence of international custom.

[1] See *Lauterpacht*, in *Grotius Society*, 25 (1939), 77–84. [Printed at p. 537 below.]

[2] For an emphatic affirmation of the doctrine of incorporation of international law, both customary and conventional, as part of Swiss law, see Guggenheim, part 1, pp. 34–6. Swiss law goes further in this direction than that of Great Britain or the United States. In case of a conflict between a treaty and a subsequent Swiss law, the former prevails: *ibid.* p. 36. Article 2 of the French Constitution of 1946 provides that 'diplomatic treaties duly ratified and published possess the force of law even if contrary to French municipal statutes'; Article 28 lays down that as such treaties are superior to French statutory law they cannot be abrogated, modified or suspended except by virtue of express denunciation. It will be noted that in the United States a statute can validly alter, in relation to municipal courts, the provisions of a binding treaty. For the provisions of other constitutions based on the doctrine of incorporation see Oppenheim, 1 (6th ed. by Lauterpacht, 1947), 41. And see generally, on the subordination of constitutions to rules of international law, Blondeau, in *Revue de droit public* (1932), 579 *et seq.* As to the position in Latin-America see Accioly, *Traité de droit international public* (transl. by Goulé), 1 (1940), 18–20.

2. ENTITIES OTHER THAN STATES AS SUBJECTS OF INTERNATIONAL LAW

It is predominantly in international practice proper, as distinguished from municipal law, that we must look for guidance on the question of subjects of international law – 'predominantly', for there is no escape from the fact that, in this as in other matters, certain principles follow from the very existence and the assumed purposes of international society. International practice shows that persons and bodies other than States are often made subjects of international rights and duties; that such developments are not inconsistent with the structure of international law; and that in each particular case the question whether a person or a body is a subject of international law must be answered in a pragmatic manner by reference to actual experience and to the reason of the law as distinguished from a preconceived notion as to who can be subjects of international law. Before discussing the position of international public bodies as subjects of international law, brief reference may be made to the following three examples of international legal capacity of bodies other than States:

(i) *Insurgents recognized as belligerents*

These – although not States – are, in law, entitled to exercise belligerent rights in relation to the recognizing States and their nationals. They are bound by the obligation to conduct hostilities in accordance with the rules of international law. This, indeed, is an acknowledged condition of recognition of belligerency. Moreover, substantial practice supports what is probably the accurate view on the subject, namely, that insurgents are entitled as a matter of law to recognition of belligerency provided that the requisite conditions of fact are present. This view has been frequently challenged on the ground that insurgents, not being subjects of international law, cannot possess a legal right to recognition. However, that challenge begs the question. It assumes that unrecognized insurgents are not and cannot be subjects of international rights and duties, including the right to recognition of belligerency. There is no sufficient warrant for any such assumption. Moreover, it is also clear that unrecognized insurgents may, without having acquired a specific status of belligerency, be admitted to various forms of intercourse with outside States. Such intercourse, which involves the application of international law by and in relation to the insurgents, may include the conclusion of agreements, diplomatic and consular relations, and recognition of the insurgent authority as a Government.[1] Of these possibilities, the relations between Great Britain and the Nationalist Government of Spain in the concluding stages of the Spanish Civil War of 1936–9 afford an interesting example. It would therefore appear that not only insurgents recognized as belligerents, but also insurgents not recognized as such, may be subjects of international rights and duties.

(ii) *The international position of the Holy See in the years 1871–1929*

In the period between the annexation of the Papal State by Italy in 1870 and the restoration of its temporal sovereignty in the Lateran Treaty of 1929, the Holy See concluded treaties (in the form of concordats) and entertained diplomatic relations with the great majority of States. It was to that extent a subject of international law without being a State in the accepted sense of the term.

(iii) *The British Dominions prior to the achievement of full international personality*

The present position of the British Dominions is indistinguishable from the full international status of normal statehood. Prior to the recent developments the British Commonwealth of Nations was represented in the international sphere by Great Britain alone. In that period the Dominions exercised treaty-making powers and maintained diplomatic relations. Though not States, they were subjects of international law. This attribution of international rights and duties to States which are not fully sovereign entities was not a novel development. Thus the Heads and Governments of British protectorates and protected States have been treated as entitled to the jurisdictional immunities which international law concedes to sovereign States. In general, protected States, though deprived of full international capacity, have been regarded as international persons, as subjects of international law.

International public bodies as subjects of international law

It is now generally agreed that international public bodies created by agreement among States are capable of possessing an international personality distinct from that of the States which compose them. These bodies include the United Nations; the specialized agencies brought into relationship with the United Nations, such as the

[1] It is occasionally maintained that a measure of intercourse on that scale constitutes implied recognition of belligerency. There is no warrant for that assertion.

International Labour Organization, the International Civil Aviation Organization, the Food and Agriculture Organization of the United Nations, the United Nations Educational, Scientific and Cultural Organization, and the International Refugee Organization; various other international administrative unions which have achieved a requisite degree of distinctness and cohesion; and a variety of other agencies ranging from International River Commissions to – to mention a somewhat exotic example – the International Commission for the Cape Spartel Lighthouse.[1] Whether in any particular case the international public body in question does in fact possess a distinct international personality of its own is a matter of law as laid down in the relevant international agreements (though, as will be suggested, it is arguable that this also is a question of principle independent of any specific legal provision). Some of these bodies have been accorded a distinct legal personality under the municipal law of various States. Thus, in Great Britain, under the Diplomatic Privileges (Extension) Act, 1944, the Crown was given power to provide by Order in Council that an international organization shall have the legal capacities of a body corporate. Various conventions creating international agencies stipulate that the contracting parties shall accord to the international agency in question a legal personality under their law.[2]

However, there has been hesitation in expressly conferring full international capacity upon these bodies. Thus, the Constitution of the Food and Agriculture Organization of the United Nations provides that 'The Organization shall have the capacity of a legal person to perform any legal act appropriate to its purpose which is not beyond the powers granted to it by this Constitution.'[3] The Constitution of the International Refugee Organization, approved by the First General Assembly in December 1946, lays down that 'The Organization shall enjoy in the territory of each of its members such legal capacity as may be necessary for the exercise of its functions and the fulfilment of its objectives.'[4] It is arguable that these and similar provisions amount to the conferment of international personality – some of the consequences of which must be implemented by municipal legislation, whenever necessary – upon these organizations and that they were not intended to be limited to the

[1] For a detailed bibliography on the international personality of these bodies see Jenks, in *B.Y.* 22 (1945), 267, n. 1.

[2] For examples see Jenks, *B.Y.* 22 (1945), 268, n. 2.

[3] Article XV (1).

[4] Article 13. An identical wording was adopted in Article 66 of the Constitution of the World Health Organisation signed on 22 July 1946.

municipal sphere. But the hesitation, which is to a large extent the result of the traditional view that States only are the subjects of international law, is significant. It contrasts with the explicit language of other instruments, such as the Agreement of 1946 concerning the establishment of a European Central Inland Transport Organization which, in addition to providing for the capacity to perform legal acts appropriate to the objects of the Organization, includes the express undertaking by member States 'to recognize the international personality and legal capacity which the Organization possesses'.[1] The relevant Article 104 of the Charter of the United Nations is conspicuous for its restraint on the subject. It provides that 'The Organization shall enjoy in the territory of each of its Members such legal capacity as may be necessary for the exercise of its functions'. As suggested above, it is possible that the result of that Article is to confer upon the United Nations a legal personality the incidents of which are to be implemented by municipal legislation in those countries in which the provisions of the Charter are not self-executing. Yet it appears from the history of the drafting of Article 104 that the omission of an express reference to *international* personality was not accidental. It is stated in the official report of the President of the United States that 'The committee which discussed this matter was anxious to avoid any implication that the United Nations will be in any sense a "superstate".'[2] It was not explained in what way the express conferment of international personality could have that effect.

Nevertheless, an international public body – such as the United Nations – may possess or acquire international personality by virtue of facts other than formal attribution of such capacity. Such result may be brought about by the fact of that body being entrusted with or exercising functions compatible with or implying international personality. Thus the United Nations must be deemed to possess that quality by virtue of the treaty-making power conferred upon it by the Charter or otherwise actually exercised by it.[3] The United

[1] Article VIII (13). The Convention of 1944 on the Inter-American Institute of Agricultural Sciences contemplates the substitution of an international status for the previous incorporation of the Institute under the laws of the District of Columbia. And see Jenks, *B.Y.* 22 (1945), 272 and 273, n. 1, for other examples.

[2] *The Charter of the United Nations, Hearings before the Committee on Foreign Relations* (1945), p. 135.

[3] See, e.g., Article 43 of the Charter, which provides for the conclusion of agreements between the Security Council and Members of the United Nations concerning the armed forces and other forms of assistance to be contributed by them for the maintenance of international peace and security; and Article 62 concerning agreements between the Economic and Social Council with specialized international agencies brought into relationship with the United Nations. Such agreements have been concluded in 1946

Nations may exercise jurisdictional and legislative powers with regard to such Trust areas as, according to Article 81 of the Charter, may be placed under the administrative authority of the United Nations. Moreover, it is vested with residuary sovereignty over Trust Territories. For it is axiomatic that these territories are not under the sovereignty of the Trustee Powers. For similar reasons the League of Nations was considered to possess a distinct international personality of its own. The contractual capacity of some of the international public bodies has been expressly recognized. They have made agreements with the United Nations, with one another, and with Governments. Thus the International Labour Organization has concluded an agreement with Switzerland defining the privileges and immunities of the Organization in that country.[1] This agreement is also conspicuous by reason of the fact that it provides for the submission to the International Court of Justice of disputes arising out of it. Moreover, some specialized agencies have been accorded a substantial degree of independent procedural capacity by being given authority to ask the International Court of Justice for an advisory opinion.[2] Even prior to the setting up of the United Nations, the amended Statute of the Permanent Court of International Justice, following the rules of the Court previously enacted and applied in practice, permitted international organizations to take part in the written and oral proceedings before the Court when acting in the exercise of its advisory jurisdiction.[3] In particular, on a number of occasions representatives of the International Labour Organization

with the International Labour Organization, the United Nations Educational, Scientific and Cultural Organization, the Food and Agriculture Organization, and the International Civil Aviation Organization. The First General Assembly adopted a draft Convention between the United Nations and the United States in connection with the establishment of the seat of the United Nations in that country.

[1] Protocol of 11 March 1946.

[2] Article 96 of the Charter provides that advisory opinions may be asked of the Court by the General Assembly or by the Security Council on any legal questions. Paragraph 2 of this Article lays down that 'other organs of the United Nations and specialized agencies, which may at any time be so authorized by the General Assembly, may also request advisory opinions of the Court on legal questions arising within the scope of their activities'. On 11 December 1946 the General Assembly authorized the Economic and Social Council (Assembly Doc. A/201), as one of the principal organs of the United Nations, to request advisory opinions on all legal questions within its scope, including legal questions concerning mutual relationships of the United Nations and the specialized agencies. As regards the specialized agencies, the General Assembly on 14 December 1946 authorized the following to request advisory opinions of the Court: the International Labour Organization (Assembly Doc. A/72), the United Nations Educational, Scientific and Cultural Organization (*ibid.* A/242), the Food and Agriculture Organization (*ibid.*), and the International Civil Aviation Organization (*ibid.* A/106).

[3] Article 73 of the Rules; Articles 66 and 67 of the Revised Statute.

addressed the Court.[1] Occasionally, international public bodies have been endowed with the capacity of resorting to tribunals of an international character. Of these, the powers given to the Reparations Commission – a body the international legal personality of which has been asserted by writers of authority[2] – under the London Agreement of 1924 are conspicuous. A number of interesting cases were decided under these provisions.[3] Nor are instances lacking of international arbitral decisions in cases in which one of the parties has been a public or private corporation opposing a State.[4]

Finally, apart from express attribution of international personality or the implied conferment or acquisition thereof as the result of actual exercise of rights in conformity with international law, it is probable that the international personality of these bodies follows from the fact of their being autonomous entities created by international agreement and distinct from the States which have created them. Their separate personality is not in doubt. It is only because of the aberrations of the doctrine of the exclusive international personality of States that there has been a tendency to question their separate international personality. Yet to subject them to the law of any single State is, in effect, to allow that State to assume jurisdiction over the States responsible for their creation. These were the reasons for which the Italian Court of Cassation, in holding in 1931 that the International Institute of Agriculture was an 'international legal person . . . free . . . from interference by the sovereign power of the States composing the Union', overruled the Court of Appeal of Rome, which had held that the Institute 'was not a subject of international law, seeing that it did not exercise sovereignty over a fixed territory and a population'.[5]

The international personality of international public bodies not only constitutes additional evidence of the inaccuracy of the traditional doctrine according to which States are the exclusive subjects of

[1] See, for a detailed account, Hudson, *The Permanent Court of International Justice, 1920–1942* (1943), pp. 400–2.

[2] See Sir John Fischer Williams, in *B.Y.* 9 (1932), 9–38, and in *A.J.* 24 (1930), 665.

[3] See *Dawes Plan Interpretation* (*Commissioner of Controlled Revenues*) case, between Germany and the Reparations Commission (*Annual Digest*, 3 (1925–6), 208); *Social Insurance* (*Upper Silesia*) case, between Germany and the Reparations Commission (*ibid.* p. 349); *Standard Oil Company Tankers* case, between the Reparations Commission and the United States (*ibid.* pp. 231 and 475); *Reparations Commission* v. *German Government* (*ibid.* 2 (1923–4), 334 and 341).

[4] *Lena Goldfields Arbitration* (*Annual Digest*, 5 (1929–30), p. 3); *Société des Quais de Smyrna* v. *Greek Government* (*ibid.* p. 495); *Sopron Köszeg Local Railway Company* case (*ibid.* p. 57); *Radio Corporation of America* v. *National Government of China* (*ibid.* 8 (1935–7), 26).

[5] *International Institute of Agriculture* v. *Profili* (*Annual Digest*, 5 (1929–30), 413).

international law. It shows its inadequacy in meeting the developing needs of international society. A purely formal international law concerned with war, with delimitation of jurisdictional competence and with ceremonial, could limit itself to the narrow and selected circle of sovereign States. In modern international society the interests to be protected and regulated can no longer be entrusted exclusively to States. These interests call for the recognition of new subjects of rights and duties conceived as the rational means of international social welfare. In this sense the question whether international public bodies are subjects of international law is not one of mere doctrine. Nor is it merely a question of making them capable of enjoying jurisdictional immunities,[1] or of securing for them the benefits of a uniform legal régime.[2] The problem is rather one of not permitting the dead hand of an obsolete theory to continue to lie heavily upon the development of international organization. It is a question of meeting satisfactorily the requirements of an expanding and developing law not limited to the niceties of international intercourse but concerned with the well-being of individuals as the ultimate units of human society and with the adequacy of the instruments which serve their needs. We can hope to gain an accurate approach to an understanding of the nature of modern international law only if we discard the notion that it regulates exclusively the relations of States and realize that it is concerned with interests which are in need of regulation on account of the existence of independent States constituting the international society. These interests are not co-extensive with the external relations of States.

3. INDIVIDUALS BEFORE INTERNATIONAL TRIBUNALS

Recognition of the procedural capacity of individuals

Important as may be the question of the international personality of communities not recognized as States and of international public bodies, it is in relation to the position of the individual that the question of the subjects of international law has been discussed with particular vigour. The significance of the problem has been somewhat obscured by the excessive concentration on the question of the

[1] For this result can be equally well achieved by the argument that the international public body, being a body of representatives of sovereign States, enjoys the jurisdictional immunities to which these States are entitled: see *Goodman* v. *Winterton*, decided in 1940 by the English Court of Appeal – a case involving an action against the Inter-governmental Committee for Refugees (*Annual Digest* 11 (1919–42), 205).

[2] See on this point Friedmann in *Modern Law Review*, 4 (1943), 203–5.

access of individuals to international tribunals and other agencies. For the traditional doctrine in the matter of subjects of international law has derived much support from the rule that only States have a *locus standi* before international tribunals. That rule has found terse expression in Article 34 of the Statute of the International Court of Justice, which lays down that 'Only States may be parties in cases before the Court'. However, the importance of this provision of the Statute, in relation to the question under discussion, ought not to be exaggerated. It is a provision defining the competence of the Court. It is not intended to be declaratory of any general principle of international law. No such principle prevents States, if they so wish, from securing to individuals and international public bodies access to international courts and tribunals. International arbitral law on the subject is not static. Some arbitration conventions, while in fact permitting individuals to put forward claims before the commission or tribunal, leave to the national agents of the States concerned full discretion as to the presentation of the claim and the conduct of the case. These conventions include, for example, that of 8 September 1923 between the United States and Mexico providing for the setting up of a General Claims Commission.[1] In this and similar conventions[2] the State retains full control of the claim which it espouses.[3] Agents and counsel are appointed by Governments. It is expressly laid down that all claims must be filed by Governments or their agents and that no statements, documents or evidence are to be received unless presented by agents. However, even in these cases there is an incipient recognition of some measure of independent status of the individual claimant, in particular with regard to the duty of the State to hand over to the claimant the amount awarded in respect of the claim made on his behalf.[4]

[1] For the text of the Convention see Feller, *The Mexican Claims Commission* (1923), pp. 321 *et seq*. And see *ibid*. pp. 83–90, for a lucid exposition of the position of the individual claimants before the Commission.

[2] See, e.g., the British–Mexican Claims Commission established by the Convention of 19 November 1926 (*L.N.T.S.* 85, 51).

[3] For a clear and somewhat emphatic affirmation of full State control over claims adjudicated upon by an international tribunal see the decision given in 1940 by the Court of Appeals for the District of Columbia in *Z. & F. Assets Realization Corporation et Al*. v. *Hull, Secretary of State, et Al*. (*Annual Digest*, 10 (1941–2), p. 424).

[4] See *American-Mexican Claims Bureau, Inc*. v. *Morgenthau, Secretary of the Treasury*, decided in 1939 by the United States District Court for the District of Columbia (*Annual Digest*, 9 (1938–40), 336). See also *Administrative Decision No. V* by Parker, Umpire, United States–German Mixed Claims Commission (*Consolidated edition of Opinions*, p. 190), to the effect that when an award is made on a specific claim, 'the fund so paid is not a national fund in the sense that the title vests in the nation receiving it entirely free from any obligation to account to the private claimant'. And see Parker, Umpire, in *Administrative Decision no. I* in the Tripartite Claims Commission, 1927: 'While the nation's

In other cases the independent *locus standi* of individuals before international tribunals has been more clearly recognized. This was the position under the provisions of Articles 297 and 304 (*b*) (2) of the Treaty of Versailles and of the corresponding provisions of the other Peace Treaties. In particular, the former Article gave the nationals of the Allied Powers the right to put forward claims for compensation, in their own name, against the German State. Some writers have attempted to qualify the significance of these provisions by suggesting that the Mixed Arbitral Tribunals were in fact joint national courts of the States concerned entrusted with the task of applying their respective municipal law which incorporated the relevant articles of the Treaty.[1] These explanations cannot be accepted as expressing the correct legal position. Although the claimants could avail themselves of the assistance of the agents appointed by their Governments, there was nothing to prevent them from pursuing their claims unaided.[2] Neither were the provisions of these Treaties unprecedented. In the statute of the proposed international prize court as adopted in Convention no. XII at the Second Hague Peace Conference, it was laid down that individual claimants shall have a right of appeal to the court against judgments of national prize courts. In the Treaty of 1907 between the five Central American Republics establishing the Central American Court of Justice, individuals were given direct access to the Court.[3]

Developments have gone beyond securing to individuals direct access to international tribunals in actions against a foreign State. In the Upper Silesian Convention of May 1922 between Germany and Poland, the contracting parties provided for a tribunal which, in effect, was given jurisdiction to entertain actions brought by nationals of either party against their own State. The innovation was so revolutionary that in the case of *Steiner and Gross* v. *Polish State* – an action brought against Poland by two of her nationals – the Polish agent contended that the Convention could not mean, in this

absolute right to control a private claim espoused by it is necessarily exclusive, because of the national interest that may be or become involved, nevertheless the private nature of such claim continues to inhere in it and the claim only in a very restricted sense becomes a national claim' (*Annual Digest*, 4 (1927–8), 262). See also, to the same effect, the Opinions of Van Vollenhoven, Umpire, United States and Mexico General Claims Commission, in *William A. Parker* case (*Annual Digest*, 3 (1925–6), 243), and in *North American Dredging Company of Texas* case (*ibid.* p. 244).

[1] See, e.g., Anzilotti, I, 136.

[2] A course apparently not always conducive to the efficient working of the tribunals: see Blühdorn in *Hague Recueil*, 41 (1932) (iii), 174–6.

[3] For an account of *Diaz* v. *Guatemala* (1908), an action for false arrest, imprisonment and expulsion, see Hudson, *Legislation*, p. 54.

respect, what on the face of it it said. The Tribunal rejected that contention.[1] It would thus appear that there is nothing inherent in the structure of international law which prevents individuals and, generally, persons other than States from being parties to proceedings before international tribunals. The matter is one of machinery and of the determination of Governments in any given case. For this reason it is probable that Article 34 of the Statute of the International Court, far from declaring an immutable rule of international law, has gone to an excessive length in giving countenance to what was assumed to be one of the consequences of the view that States only can be subjects of international law. It would have been proper and practicable for the Statute to provide that the Court shall have jurisdiction only in cases in which at least one party is a State. A provision of that nature would not have given individuals any *right* to bring a State before the Court – unless in pursuance of a previous agreement. At the same time it would have made the machinery of the Court available for the solution of major controversies between States and private individuals and corporations – as well as between States and public international bodies wherever States, in pursuance of a general or an *ad hoc* agreement, deem it convenient and desirable to acquiesce in such a course. The availability of such machinery would be specially appropriate in a period in which the economic activities of States tend to increase. Provision could be made for cases of that description – in particular disputes arising out of contracts with or injuries to aliens – being adjudicated upon by a special chamber or chambers of the Court. For this reason it is to be hoped that at a not distant date the present rigid formulation of Article 34 of the Statute will yield to a less uncompromising and more practical definition of the jurisdiction of the Court.

The problem of the obligatory jurisdiction of international tribunals in claims by private persons

On the other hand, there is no good reason for confusing the question of the status of individuals as subjects of international law with the question of their access to international courts as a matter of right whenever they deem their rights under international law to have been violated by a foreign State. Undoubtedly, any such consummation would have obvious advantages. These have been repeatedly

[1] *Annual Digest*, 4 (1927–8), 291. The Tribunal said that the Convention conferred in unequivocal terms jurisdiction upon the Tribunal irrespective of the nationality of the claimants, and, the terms of the Convention being clear, it was unnecessary to add to it a limitation which did not appear from its wording.

stated.[1] It would provide a remedy in cases in which the private individual's own State is unable or unwilling to take up the claim; in which no remedy is available for the reason that there does not exist an instrument conferring compulsory jurisdiction upon the Court; and in which the claimant is a stateless person or otherwise debarred from assistance by a State by reason of the operation of the rule as to nationality of claims. In all these cases the provision of a remedy by way of the automatic jurisdiction of the Court would promote justice and divest the foreign State of the character – some will say, of the stigma – of a mere instrumentality of power. Moreover, it would remove a source of international friction inasmuch as it would direct private claims into the normal channels of ordinary judicial process. At present the espousal of a claim by the State tends to impart to the complaint the complexion of political controversy and of unfriendly action. However, to state the advantages of any such general access of individuals to international tribunals is not to present the case in its entirety. For to confer upon individuals the general right to invoke the jurisdiction of international tribunals whenever they feel themselves aggrieved by a foreign State would be to introduce, in a wide field of international relations, the principle of obligatory arbitral and judicial settlement which States have so far refused to accept and which, in so far as they have accepted it, they have circumscribed by comprehensive reservations, especially those relating to matters which are exclusively within the domestic jurisdiction of the State. Questions which may be the subject of an appeal by an individual to an international tribunal are as a rule those which normally fall within the description of matters of domestic jurisdiction. A survey of the activity of international tribunals, in particular of that of the Permanent Court of International Justice, would disclose that the majority of cases which have come before them have been cases involving private interests of aliens. There are probably decisive reasons in favour of acceptance of the general principle of the obligatory jurisdiction of international courts in disputes between States, but so long as that principle has not been adopted it is impracticable to expect that States will adopt it indirectly without reservations and without any assurance that the right thus granted to individuals would be exercised with the restraint and sense of responsibility which Governments exhibit in this sphere.

[1] See Hurst, in *B.Y.* 6 (1925), 61–7. And see generally, for the extensive literature on the question, Oppenheim, I (6th ed. by Lauterpacht, 1947), 581, n. 4; and II (6th revised ed. by Lauterpacht, 1944), 51, n. 2.

For the espousal of a private claim by a Government is usually preceded by a thorough examination, on the part of the department concerned, of the legal merits, and of the propriety from other points of view, of the claim in question.

Secondly, if we accept the rule that individuals can, without any limitations, hail a State, against its will, before an international tribunal in order to assert their rights under international law, it is not easy to see why that faculty should be confined to aliens – unless we assert with finality the view that individuals can never possess as against their own State rights under international law enforceable, at their own instance, before international tribunals. Yet to urge, in the present state of international organization, a reform of this kind is to advance a proposition which many will regard as impracticable in itself and unlikely to secure acceptance by States.[1] A development of this nature is not, it may be added, impossible. It would become a reality if fundamental human rights and freedoms were to acquire the undoubted character of international rights proper by virtue of an International Bill of Human Rights made enforceable before international judicial agencies.

Procedural capacity and the quality of a subject of law

Important as is the recognition of the procedural capacity of aliens – and of individuals generally – before international tribunals, there is no reason to exaggerate its bearing on the question of the subjects of international law. The two questions are not synonymous. The existence of a right and the power to assert it by judicial process are not identical. In the municipal sphere there are persons, such as minors and lunatics, who though endowed with rights are unable to assert them by their own action. If States were to declare, solemnly and without equivocation, that they recognize certain inalienable rights of the individual – as they have to some extent in the Charter of the United Nations – that declaration would amount to constituting individuals subjects of international law even if it were not accompanied by a concession to individuals of the faculty of independent action to enforce these rights. There is a clear distinction between procedural capacity and the quality of a subject of law.

Moreover, the denial of full procedural capacity may be accompanied by the creation and recognition of remedies falling short of a

[1] See Lauterpacht, *An International Bill of the Rights of Man* (1945), pp. 184–93. On the other hand, see the cogent observations of Brunet, *La garantie internationale des droits de l'homme* (1947), pp. 313–32.

right of independent action. In the Minorities Treaties concluded after the First World War certain linguistic, racial and religious minorities were made beneficiaries of rights guaranteed by the Treaties. How far did these Treaties constitute the minorities in question subjects of international law? In strict law and according to the accepted doctrine, they created rights and duties as between the contracting parties only. The practice of the Council of the League of Nations, under whose guarantee the Treaties were placed, denied the minorities any independent right of enforcing the benefits grounded in the Treaties. Yet this restrictive interpretation of their provisions hung on the slender thread of the accepted doctrine according to which individuals are not subjects of international law and do not benefit directly from international treaties. Both these assumptions are debatable. In particular, as is noted below, the view that a treaty cannot in any circumstances confer rights upon individuals has failed to secure endorsement on the part of the Permanent Court of International Justice. The same considerations apply to the rights created in the mandates and trust agreements in favour of the populations of the territories in question.

Moreover, as these instruments have shown, it is not necessary that the espousal of interests created by treaty in favour of individuals should be limited to the State of which they are nationals.[1] Such benefits can be made the subject of judicial proceedings by any State which is a party to the treaty in question. The rule as to nationality of claims – a rule according to which an international tribunal has no jurisdiction to entertain a claim unless the person or corporation concerned was a national of the claimant State at the time of the alleged injury up to the presentation of the claim – does not necessarily apply. Nationality is no longer the only link between the individual and international law. The State invoking the provisions of the treaty in favour of an individual who is not its national no longer acts on behalf of its own particular interest; it acts on behalf of the international interest in the welfare of the individual or groups of individuals concerned and of its own general interest

[1] Thus the Minorities Treaties of 1919 provided that any of the Allied and Associated Powers or any other Power a member of the Council of the League of Nations should be entitled to bring, as being a dispute of an international character, before the Permanent Court of International Justice any difference of opinion as to questions of law or fact arising out of the Articles of the Treaty (Article 12 of the Treaty with Poland). The various mandates provided for submission to the Court of any dispute between a Mandatory and any other Member of the League relating to the application or interpretation of the provisions of the mandate (see, e.g., Article 26 of the Mandate for Palestine). The rule as to 'nationality of claims' could not be invoked in relation to any of these provisions.

in the maintenance of respect for treaties. Emphasis is thus given to the direct relation between the individual and the international interest. The same applies to treaties which regulate the condition of stateless persons. Here, once more, the parties entitled to invoke the treaty are States which, by definition, are not the home States of the persons concerned. For these have no home State. In all these treaties the right to espouse a claim is not dependent upon the nationality of the person concerned. This relaxation of the rule of nationality of claims signifies a landmark in the assertion of the international personality of the individual.[1] The international enforcement of his claim ceases to be dependent upon his membership of a particular State.

The voluntary jurisdiction of international tribunals in respect of private claims

While there are weighty objections to the recognition of the right of individuals to bring States before international tribunals independently of their consent, there would appear to be no decisive reason why individuals should not be able to exercise a right of this nature within the framework of such obligations of compulsory arbitral and judicial settlement as may be undertaken by States. Thus, when States subscribe to the obligations of the Optional Clause of Article 36 of the Statute of the International Court of Justice there is no intrinsic reason, save that of the traditional doctrine in the matter, why the reciprocal undertaking in question should not enure to the benefit of the nationals of the States concerned by conferring upon them a right of action in respect of the four categories of 'legal' disputes enumerated in Article 36. However, that doctrine is nothing but a technical rule grounded in the dogma that individuals can have no rights under international law. If they have no such rights, then, clearly, there is nothing which they can assert in their own name before international tribunals. Once the cobwebs of that antiquated doctrine have been swept aside, the procedural incapacity of individuals is deprived of its logical foundation. In particular there disappears the reason why, in the case of two States bound by the

[1] It is probable that the rule of nationality of claims is open, in its present rigid formulation, to legitimate criticism on grounds other than that it no longer accords with international practice in all respects. There is no cogent reason why a State should not be able to espouse a claim of its national for the mere reason that at the time of the injury that person did not possess the nationality of that State—unless it be the reason that a person by deliberately assuming, *in fraudem legis* as it were, the nationality of a powerful State might be able to secure more effective protection than if he had remained the national of a weak State.

obligations of compulsory judicial settlement, the competence of the Court should not be concurrent in the sense that it should be open either to the States concerned or to their nationals to invoke the jurisdiction of the Court within the framework of the commitment of judicial settlement. In substance the States in question would not, as the result, undertake a wider obligation. They would merely make it possible for the same claim to be put forward either by the private party aggrieved or by its State (or, in special circumstances, by both). It is true that, in theory, the result would be an increase in the number of potential claims inasmuch as private individuals might not exercise the same degree of restraint which States have on occasions exercised in this connection. It is also possible that at times the new procedural right conferred upon individuals might be abused in order to cause embarrassment or to gain notoriety. Such contingencies are remote. On the other hand, the heavy cost of international litigation would act as an effective deterrent against rash or malicious recourse to the machinery put at the disposal of private persons.

It may thus be found that the recognition of the right of access of individuals to international tribunals, in cases covered by a general commitment of obligatory settlement, would not cause a cumbersome addition to the work of the Court. The difficulties of any appreciable increase in its activity could be met by the creation of special chambers of the International Court of Justice combining the advantages of an authoritative decision and the preservation of the continuity of the law with the requirements of expeditious disposal of claims. The practical advantages of any such reform of the law have already been alluded to. There is no doubt that it would be a powerful contributory factor in fostering appreciation of the place of justice in international relations and in defeating the suspicion that private persons and corporations are being denied their legal rights because of transient considerations of governmental policy. Above all, it would administer the *coup de grâce* to the obsolete and inaccurate notion, of which it is both the cause and the effect, that individuals can have no procedural or substantive rights under international law. To make that consummation feasible the Statute of the International Court of Justice must, as suggested, be freed from the shackles of the present wording of Article 34 so as to make it possible for States to agree, either *ad hoc* or by virtue of undertakings of a general nature, to appear as defendants at the instance of private individuals or corporations of foreign nationality in all cases in which, under international law, their State would possess the right to espouse their claim. Article 34 would then run as follows:

The Court shall have jurisdiction:
(1) in disputes between States;
(2) in disputes between States and private and public bodies or private individuals in cases in which States have consented, in advance or by special agreement, to appear as defendants before the Court.

It is not improbable that some States would make use of that innovation, in the same way as they have availed themselves of the possibility of a simple and unqualified signature, subject to reciprocity, of the Optional Clause.[1] A significant departure in the substantive and procedural law would thus take place without affecting any vital interest of States. In the meantime, Article 34 of the Statute of the Court must, in its present formulation, be regarded as out of keeping with the needs and tendencies of international law. The discussions in the Committee of Jurists who drafted the Statute of the Court in 1920 showed how strongly the adoption of Article 34 was influenced by the dogma that States only can be subjects of international law. The developments of the three decades which followed might have suggested a reconsideration of that Article when the Statute was revised in 1945. As it is, its adaptation to a more modern conception of international law and of international society must be kept in the forefront of any future attempts to amend the Statute of the Court. There is no justification for its retention in the present wording. If the present article does nothing else than draw attention to the propriety and necessity of that reform, it will well have served its purpose.[2]

Any developments on the lines suggested may pave the way for a change even more far-reaching. That change would consist in conceding a right of appeal before the highest international authority to the State's own nationals against any violations of their rights under international law. A truly revolutionary change of that nature would presuppose one even more radical and fundamental – the previous acknowledgment of rights enjoyed by the State's own subjects as

[1] See, for the text of the declarations made in 1946 by China, Norway and Denmark, *A.J.* 41 (1947), 13.

[2] The exercise of jurisdiction in disputes between States and private persons and bodies other than States would not be inconsistent with the limitation of the Court's function to the administration of international law in accordance with Article 38 of its Statute. For it is not suggested that the Court should adjudicate on all disputes between a State and private individuals or corporations. The extended jurisdiction should cover normally only such disputes as raise an issue of international law, such as denial of justice, State succession, interpretation of a treaty involving private rights, and the like.

originating in international law. We are not at liberty to regard such a development as purely chimerical. The recognition by the international society of fundamental human rights and freedoms is not a chimera. It is, in essence, part of the existing law as expressed in the Charter of the United Nations. It is as yet an imperfect law, deliberately shorn of direct means of enforcement. But the Charter is only the first step in the inauguration of a new period in the mutual relations of the State, the individual and the international society. It may be followed by an international bill of the rights of man, which may go a step further in translating the declaratory provisions of the Charter into a more effective rule of international law. Admittedly, this is a development the fruition of which is dependent upon a more radical change in political and moral conceptions than can be contemplated in the immediate future. By contrast, the recognition of the full international capacity of aliens, on a footing equal to that of their States, is a measure of reform which is largely procedural in nature and which is open to an objection no more serious than that it runs counter to an obsolete doctrine.

4. THE INDIVIDUAL AS A SUBJECT OF INTERNATIONAL RIGHTS

Individuals as subjects of rights under treaties

It has been suggested[1] that there is a distinction between the recognition, in an international instrument, of rights enuring to the benefit of the individual and the enforceability of those rights at the instance of the private person. The fact that the beneficiary of rights is not authorized to take independent steps in his own name to enforce them does not signify that he is not a subject of the law or that the rights in question are vested in the agency which possesses the capacity to enforce them.[2] Thus, in relation to the current view that the rights of the alien within foreign territory are the rights of his State and not his own, the correct way of putting the matter is not that the State asserts its own right but that it enforces the right of the individual who is incapable of asserting it in the international sphere. Conversely, there seems to be no warrant for the disposition

[1] See above, p. 505.

[2] The following observation of the Permanent Court of International Justice, made in a different connection, may be noted: 'It is scarcely necessary to point out that the capacity to possess civil rights does not necessarily imply the capacity to exercise those rights oneself' (*Peter Pázmány University* case, *P.C.I.J.* Series A/B, no. 61, p. 231).

to allow the question of enforceability of rights to be influenced by the doctrine that individuals cannot be subjects of international law. The question whether individuals in any given case are subjects of international law and whether that quality extends to the capacity of enforcement must be answered pragmatically, by reference to the given situation and to the relevant international instrument. That instrument may make them subjects of the law without conferring upon them procedural capacity; it may do both these things.

The legal position in the matter is well illustrated by the question whether individuals can acquire rights directly by treaty independently of municipal legislation. Prior to the Advisory Opinion of the Permanent Court of International Justice in the case concerning the *Jurisdiction of the Courts of Danzig* in the matter of Danzig railway officials,[1] that question was generally answered in the negative – though even then some caution would have been indicated having regard to the law of some countries, such as the United States, in which duly ratified treaties are a self-executing part of municipal law.[2] Similarly, there had already existed treaties – such as that establishing the Central American Court of Justice, the provisions relating to the Mixed Arbitral Tribunals in the Peace Treaties of 1919, and the Polish-German Upper Silesian Convention[3] – which conferred upon individuals direct rights of international action. However, it was the Advisory Opinion, given in 1928, in the case concerning the *Jurisdiction of the Courts of Danzig*,[4] which dealt a resounding blow to the dogma of the impenetrable barrier separating individuals from international law. In that case Poland contended that the agreement between her and Danzig, regulating the conditions of employment of Danzig officials whom she had taken over into her railway service, was an international treaty which created rights and obligations as between Poland and Danzig only; that, as that agreement had not been incorporated into Polish municipal law, it did not create rights and obligations for individuals; that Poland's responsibility was limited to that owed to Danzig; and that therefore Danzig courts, before which the officials had brought an action in the matter, had no jurisdiction. The Court rejected this contention.

[1] See below.

[2] Possibly it could have been argued, in reply, that this was so only by virtue of municipal law and not of international law – an argument the relevance of which is open to question. It could also have been said, with more justification, that in some of these countries, as in the United States, a subsequent statute can make inoperative a conflicting treaty. This is not possible under the new French Constitution: see above, p. 493, n. 2.

[3] See above, p. 502.

[4] *P.C.I.J.* Series B, no. 15, pp. 17–21.

It said:

It may be readily admitted that, according to a well-established principle of international law, the *Beamtenabkommen*, being an international agreement, cannot, as such, create direct rights and obligations for private individuals. But it cannot be disputed that the very object of an international agreement, according to the intention of the contracting parties, may be the adoption by the parties of some definite rules creating individual rights and obligations and enforceable by the national courts. That there is such an intention in the present case can be established by reference to the terms of the *Beamtenabkommen*.[1]

This pronouncement is among the most important rendered by the Court. On the first occasion on which it was directly[2] confronted with the traditional argument, it rejected it – though with the courtesy due to a doctrine which for a long time enjoyed undisputed ascendancy.[3] It laid down, in effect, that no considerations of theory can prevent the individual from becoming the subject of international rights if States so wish. That affirmation by the Permanent Court of International Justice of the right of individuals to acquire rights directly under treaties was not an isolated event. It was followed – and the coincidence is significant – by other judicial decisions pointing in the same direction.[4]

[1] At p. 17.

[2] The Judgment of the Court in the *Mavrommatis Palestine Concessions* case (*P.C.I.J.* Series A, no. 2) gave some indication of the possible attitude of the Court. In that case the Court attached decisive importance to the fact that, although no negotiations had taken place between the Greek Government and Great Britain, negotiations sufficient for the purpose of the jurisdiction of the Court had taken place between Great Britain and the Greek national concerned.

[3] Less than a quarter of a century prior to the opinion of the Court, Anzilotti (in 1927 a judge of the Court) wrote, 'It is inconceivable that there should exist subjects of international rights and duties other than States' (*Il diritto internazionale nei giudizi interni* (1905), p. 44).

[4] See, e.g., the decision of the District Court of Amsterdam of 16 October 1925 in the *Wirbelauer* case, to the effect that the Hague Convention of 1905 concerning Procedure in Civil Cases conferred directly rights upon Russian nationals in Holland irrespective of recognition of the Soviet Government by Holland (*Annual Digest*, 4 (1927–8), 59, and the Note bearing on the subject); the judgment of the Amsterdam Court of Appeals of 13 March 1928 in the *Papadopoulos* case, to the effect that the Treaty of Lausanne was binding not only upon the parties thereto but also upon individuals (*ibid.* p. 414); the decision of the German Reichsgericht of 29 March 1928 in the *German Railways* (*Most-Favoured Treatment*) case, laying down that the provisions of Article 365 of the Treaty of Versailles could be invoked 'without the necessity of further measures in the sphere of international or public law' by German subjects against the Reich (*ibid.* p. 406); the decisions of the Egyptian Summary Tribunal of Port Said in 1931 and 1932 in the *Noujaim* case, to the effect that the protection of the International Telegraph Convention of 1875 enured to the benefit not only of the contracting parties but also of private companies (*ibid.* 6 (1931–2), 413); the decision of the Danzig High Court on 16 January 1934 in the *Zoppot Street-Crossing* case, applying expressly the principle laid down by the Permanent Court of International Justice in its Advisory Opinion no. 12 (*ibid.* 7 (1933–4), 269). See, on the

Individuals as subjects of international law in the matter of jurisdiction and extradition

The way in which the Permanent Court of International Justice – and other courts – have clarified the rules of international law bearing upon conferment of rights upon individuals by treaty suggests that, in this and other matters, the question is not one of reliance upon preconceived notions but of investigation whether positive international law as embodied in custom or treaty has that effect, having regard to the intention of States or to the reason of the thing. On some of these questions practice is still under the influence of the traditional doctrine. Thus, for instance, municipal courts have held occasionally that such protection as extradition treaties stipulate in favour of individuals is not based on rules of international law which they are entitled to invoke in their own right.[1] Municipal courts have occasionally assumed jurisdiction over persons brought before them in disregard of existing extradition treaties.[2] The reasons for that practice do not lie exclusively in the influence of the traditional doctrine in the matter of subjects of international law, but it

other hand, the decisions of the German Reichsgericht of 29 March 1928 in the *Liquidation of German Property* (*Treaty of Versailles*) case (*ibid.* 4 (1927–8), 408) and of 14 March 1928 in the *High Treason* (*Treaty of Versailles*) *in Germany* case (*ibid.* p. 11); the *Martini* case between Italy and Venezuela, 3 May 1930 (*ibid.* 5 (1929–30), 153). See also *Civilian War Claimants' Association, Ltd* v. *The King*, 46 T.L.R. 581; 47 T.L.R. 102; [1932] A.C. 14 (*Annual Digest*, 6 (1931–2), 237). In this case the Court held that in concluding a treaty the Crown is not acting as trustee or agent for the subject. See *ibid.* for the observation of Lord Atkin that when the Crown is negotiating a treaty it is inconsistent with its sovereign position that it should be acting as agent for its nationals, but that there is nothing to prevent it from acting as agent or trustee if it chooses deliberately to do so. See also *Administrator of German Property* v. *Knoop*, [1933] Ch. 439 (*Annual Digest*, 6 (1931–2), 240). But see the decision of the Anglo-American Mixed Arbitral Tribunal of 13 December 1923 in *Lederer* v. *German State*, in which the Tribunal rejected the contention of the British Government that it was the sole beneficiary of the provisions of Article 297 of the Treaty of Versailles in the matter of compensation (*Recueil des Decisions des Tribunaux Arbitraux Mixtes*, 3 (1924), 762). The Tribunal said: 'the right to compensation granted by the Treaty is granted as compensation to the national of an Allied and Associated Power. It is granted to him as a facultative right, that is to say, a right of which he may or may not make use' (at p. 768). Referring to the wording of Article 297 (*h*) (2), the Tribunal observed that the very fact that the individual nationals were mentioned, in the first instance, as the persons to whom proceeds of liquidation and cash assets were to be paid immediately, showed that these persons were actually those who were entitled to payment, and 'that the Government in such a case can only be an intermediary to receive and hand over the said proceeds of liquidations' (at p. 769). As the result of a careful analysis the Tribunal refused to attach a literal interpretation to the wording of Article 297 (*h*) according to which the proceeds of liquidation were to be credited to the State of which the owner was a national through the Clearing Offices established by the Treaty.

[1] See, for instance, the decision of the German Reichsgericht of 8 May 1929 (*Extradition* (*Germany and Italy*) case: *Annual Digest* 5 (1929–30), 270).

[2] See, e.g., *United States* v. *Insull* (8 F.Supp. 310; *Annual Digest*, 7 (1933–4), 188).

is probable that the doctrine has had some share in the result.[1] The same circumstance explains, to some extent, why the principle of non-extradition of political offenders, which has become a constant feature of modern international practice as expressed in treaties, is not as yet a principle of international law on which the individual can rely as a matter of course. This is also the explanation of the practice of the courts of some countries in the matter of their jurisdiction over persons brought before them in violation of international law.[2] Apparently in these cases the courts were not of the view that such persons were entitled to rely in their own right on rules of international law. Otherwise, it is difficult to see how courts could consider themselves entitled to exercise jurisdiction.

The Charter of the United Nations and the position of the individual as a subject of international law

The position with regard to treaties, extradition and jurisdiction acts as a reminder that the answer to the question as to the status of the individual as a subject of rights under international law must be sought, in the first instance, by reference to the actual development of the law. This applies also to the question whether international law recognizes fundamental rights of the individual independent of the law of his State. Prior to the Charter of the United Nations the question of the existence of such rights was controversial. Their international recognition manifested itself in the precarious doctrine of humanitarian intervention in cases in which a State maltreats its subjects in a manner which shocks the conscience of mankind. That doctrine was advocated by writers, beginning with Grotius. It was honoured in theoretical recognition rather than in practice. There was a conflict between the defence of human rights through external intervention and considerations of international peace threatened by such intervention. That conflict was, in the long run, more apparent

[1] The main reason has probably been the fact that out of the two principal functions of the law of extradition – that of the protection of the accused and of international co-operation in the suppression of crime – the latter has been more prominent. Witness, for instance, the way in which some courts construed the requirement of 'liberal interpretation' as implying a construction favouring the accused (*Valentine* v. *United States* (1936) (299 U.S. 5; *Annual Digest*, 8 (1935–7), 352)), while others considered 'liberal interpretation' as necessitating an interpretation favouring the effectiveness of international co-operation in the suppression of crime (*Factor* v. *Laubenheimer* (1933) (290 U.S. 276)).

[2] See, e.g., *Ex p. Lopez* (6 F.Supp. 342; *Annual Digest*, 7 (1933–4), 190). It is particularly difficult to follow the reasons for that practice in States, like the United States of America, which are committed to the doctrine of incorporation of international law as part of the law of the land. See, on the other hand, *Re Jolis*, decided in 1933 by a French court (*ibid.* p. 191).

than real. For, ultimately, peace is more endangered by tyrannical contempt of human rights than by attempts to assert, through intervention, the sanctity of human personality. However, Governments are not invariably in the habit of taking a long-range view in matters involving the peace of the peoples entrusted to their care. As a result, humanitarian intervention has remained sporadic and infrequent. Yet there has been occasional recognition of fundamental human rights in treaties providing for religious freedom and the cultural and political rights of minorities. Of these, the Minorities Treaties concluded after the First World War provide an outstanding example.

It is in the Charter of the United Nations that the individual human being first appears in his full stature as endowed with fundamental human rights and freedoms. We shall fail utterly to realize the full significance of that innovation if we permit our understanding of it to be blurred by the fact that these rights are not, so far as the Charter is concerned, fully enforceable at the instance either of the individual or of the Members of the United Nations. Covered as they are by the express denial of the right of intervention, they would appear to amount to no more than a political declaration. This, it is believed, is a pessimistic view of the legal value of these provisions. The Charter of the United Nations is a legal document; its language is the language of law, of international law. In affirming repeatedly the 'fundamental human rights' of the individual, it must of necessity be deemed to refer to legal rights – to legal rights recognized by international law and independent of the law of the State. These rights are only imperfectly enforceable, and, in so far as the availability of a remedy is the hall-mark of a legal right, they are imperfect legal rights. Yet in the sphere of international law the correlation of right and remedy is not so close as within the State. Even if we assume that the prohibition of intervention as expressed in paragraph 7 of Article 2 of the Charter extends to fundamental human rights and freedoms – an assumption which cannot be made without qualification – the weapon of discussion and recommendation, which under the Charter is fully available for the protection of fundamental human rights and freedoms, may not be altogether without potency. Moreover, irrespective of the question of enforcement, there ought to be no doubt that the provisions of the Charter in the matter of fundamental human rights impose upon the Members of the United Nations the legal duty to respect them. In particular, it is clear that any Member of the United Nations who is guilty of a violation of these rights commits a breach of the Charter. There may be no international tribunal endowed with compulsory jurisdiction to ascertain the fact of such violation, but international tribunals have, as a rule, no compulsory jurisdiction in the matter of the fulfilment of international duties in general. This fact does not deprive them of their legal character. Moreover, in so far as the Charter forms part of the municipal law of the Members of the United Nations, it may be enforceable as such. While the law of the State is supreme so far as its courts are concerned, there is no reason why they should not resort to the Charter as a direct source of law in this respect. Within several months of the adoption of the Charter of the United Nations, a Canadian court set aside a restrictive covenant in a private contract on the ground that it discriminated, on racial grounds, against one section of the community. In the view of the Court, to uphold the contract would have run counter to the obligations undertaken by Canada under Articles 1 and 55 of the Charter to promote universal respect for, and observance of, human rights and fundamental freedoms for all without distinction as to race, sex, language or religion.[1]

It would therefore appear that, to the extent to which the Charter incorporates obligations to respect the fundamental human rights and freedoms, it amounts to recognition of individuals as subjects of international law. These obligations and the methods of their implementation are more effective than is commonly assumed.[2] In turn, their effectiveness will depend to some extent on the final abandonment of the doctrine of the inherently inferior status of individuals in the sphere of international law.

Crimes against humanity and fundamental human rights

Since the Second World War, the acknowledgment of fundamental human rights has taken place – indirectly, but most significantly – through the recognition of so-called crimes against humanity in Article 6 of the Charter annexed to the Four-Power Agreement of 8 August 1945, providing for the establishment of the International Military Tribunal for the Prosecution and Punishment of the Major War Criminals of the European Axis.[3] In addition to the crimes of planning and waging wars of aggression and war crimes, the Tribunal was given jurisdiction in the matter of 'crimes against humanity'. That Article of the Charter conferred upon the Court jurisdiction with regard to '(c) Crimes against humanity: namely, murder,

[1] *Re Drummond Wren* ([1945] O.R. 778; [1945] 4 D.L.R. 674; *Annual Digest*, 12 (1943–5), 178).

[2] See above, p. 515.

[3] Treaty Series no. 7 (1946), Cmd. 6903.

extermination, enslavement, deportation, and other inhumane acts committed against any civilian population, before or during the war; or persecutions on political, racial or religious grounds in execution of or in connection with any crime within the jurisdiction of the tribunal, whether or not in violation of the domestic law of the country where perpetrated.' As the result of a subsequent amendment, embodied in the Berlin Protocol of 6 October 1945, and substituting a comma for the semicolon in the section quoted above, the scope and the significance of the Article were reduced from the outset inasmuch as all the crimes against humanity enumerated therein were made punishable only in so far as they were ancillary or subsidiary to other criminal acts within the jurisdiction of the Tribunal. This limitation was adopted owing to the apprehension – probably unfounded – that to give the Tribunal jurisdiction, without qualification, over crimes against humanity as defined in the Charter would be tantamount to confronting it with a multitude of charges and dangerously complicating a task in itself of unprecedented magnitude. The Judgment of the Tribunal contained a further limitation which is not apparent from the terms of the Charter. The Tribunal, partly in disregard of the terms of the Charter which gave it jurisdiction in respect of crimes against humanity 'before or during the war', declined, it would appear – though this is not quite clear from the Judgment – to treat acts committed prior to the war as crimes against humanity within the meaning of the Charter.[1]

Notwithstanding these qualifications, the Charter and the Judgment of the Tribunal, in so far as they recognize in principle crimes against humanity, have a direct bearing on the question of recognition, in the international sphere, of fundamental rights of the individual. Crimes against humanity are crimes regardless of whether they were committed in accordance with and in obedience to the national law of the accused. Such acts were deemed to violate the sanctity of human personality to such a degree as to make irrelevant reliance upon the law of the State which ordered them. To lay down that crimes against humanity are punishable is, therefore, to assert the existence of rights of man grounded in a law superior to the law of the State. Thus, upon analysis, the enactment of crimes against humanity in an international instrument signifies the acknowledgment of fundamental rights of the individual recognized by inter-

[1] The Tribunal expressly refused to make a general delaration that such crimes were crimes against humanity. No such general declaration was required from the Tribunal. In so far as it refrained from treating crimes committed before the war as crimes against humanity, the Judgment finds no warrant in the terms of the Charter.

national law. It is possible that this result did not occur to the authors of the Charter nor, perhaps, to the Tribunal which applied it. Yet, unless the Charter is conceived as an *ad hoc* piece of vindictive legislation enacted by the victor against the vanquished, this is its inevitable and logical result. In terms of law, to the conception of crimes against humanity there must correspond the notion of fundamental human rights recognized by international law and, as a further result, of an international status of the individual whose rights have thus been recognized.[1]

The enactment, in the Charter of the International Military Tribunal, of crimes against humanity was not an isolated act. It was repeated in Article 5 of the Charter of the International Military Tribunal for the Far East, established on 19 January 1946, by a Proclamation of the Supreme Commander for the Allied Powers in the Far East. The Paris Peace Treaties of 1947 with Italy, Roumania, Hungary, Bulgaria and Finland provided for the surrender, *inter alios*, of persons accused of crimes against humanity. Above all, the Four Powers in occupation of Germany enacted legislation providing for the prosecution of crimes against humanity committed in Germany before and during the War (and probably also after the War and during the period preceding the assumption of power in Germany by the National-Socialists),[2] without stipulating for any connection of these crimes with war crimes or crimes against the peace.[3] These enactments have a significance transcending the occasion which gave rise to them. They have become a weighty precedent binding upon all. The principle which they enunciate is among those which the First General Assembly of the United Nations accepted, alongside the other principles of the Charter of 8 August 1945 and the Judgment of the Nuremberg Tribunal, as the basis of the codification of international law on the subject.[4] In an indirect but compelling manner the enactment of 'crimes against humanity' constitutes the recognition of fundamental human rights superior to the law of the sovereign State.

[1] For an exhaustive treatment of the question of crimes against humanity see Schwelb in *B.Y.* 23 (1946), 176–226.

[2] See *ibid.* pp. 216–18.

[3] Control Council Law no. 10 of 20 December 1945. See also the special Ordinance, passed in the British Control Zone of Germany in pursuance of Law no. 10, authorizing German courts to exercise jurisdiction with regard to crimes against humanity committed by persons of German nationality against German nationals or Stateless persons. Similar Ordinances were passed in other Zones.

[4] See Resolution of the General Assembly of 11 December 1946 in which it 'affirms the principles of international law recognized by the Charter of the Nuremberg Tribunal and the Judgment of the Tribunal' (*Journal of the General Assembly*, no. 75, p. 945).

5. THE INDIVIDUAL AS A SUBJECT OF INTERNATIONAL DUTIES

So-called offences against the Law of Nations

As in the case of subjects of international rights, so also in the matter of international duties the accurate approach to ascertaining the legal position is to rely not on preconceived notions as to the capacity of individuals to be subjects of international law but, primarily, on the practice of States in both the international and the municipal sphere. In the first instance, there must be considered the cases in which international law imposes directly, i.e. without recourse to State legislation, duties upon individuals when not acting as organs or on behalf of States. The rules relating to piracy can be interpreted to this effect – though, as pointed out above,[1] they may be explained as a mutual concession of jurisdiction by States over their subjects. On the other hand, the operation of rules of warfare is, as suggested,[2] a clear example of the direct effect of rules of international law upon individuals. A soldier who, for the satisfaction of private gain or lust, is guilty of murder or plunder in occupied territory or, generally, in the theatre of operations, is guilty of a war crime *jure gentium*. In so far as, according to the law of many States, international law is part of the law of the land, the obligations of international law are directly binding upon individuals. In *Respublica* v. *De Longchamps*,[3] McKean, Chief Justice of Pennsylvania, in sentencing the accused for an assault upon the Consul-General of France, said:

[1] See above, p. 491.

[2] See above, p. 492. There is no warrant for the suggestion recently advanced by Professor Kelsen that national tribunals, military and other, in applying Hague Convention no. IV to the punishment of war criminals, administer their own municipal law, into which the Hague Convention has been transformed, as distinguished from international law (*International Law Quarterly*, 1 (1947), 160). Any such contention amounts to an assertion, which cannot be accepted, that municipal tribunals do not administer international law. A contention of that nature is expressive, at best, of the purely dialectical proposition that rules of international law incorporated into municipal law cease to be rules of international law. See *Grotius Society*, 25 (1939), 85. Professor Kelsen seems to have drastically abandoned the view which he advanced, correctly, in 1944 (*Peace through Law* (1944), p. 77). He then said: 'The military court, by punishing the acts, executes international law even if it applies at the same time norms of its own military law. The legal basis of the trial is international law, which establishes the individual responsibility of the person committing the act of illegitimate warfare.' The innovation, such as it was, introduced by the Charter of the International Military Tribunal of 1945, was not the declaration of individual responsibility for criminal violations of international law but its application to the crime of aggressive war—an innovation which is not surprising seeing that prior to the developments culminating in the Kellogg–Briand Pact aggressive war was not a criminal act under international law as it then existed.

[3] (1784) 1 Dallas' Report 111.

The first crime in the indictment is an infraction of the Law of Nations. This law, in its full extent, is part of the law of this State. . . The person of a public minister is sacred and inviolable. Whoever offers any violence to him, not only affronts the sovereign he represents, but also hurts the common safety and well-being of nations – he is guilty of a crime against the whole world. . . You then have been guilty of an atrocious violation of the Law of Nations.

The criminal and, generally, the municipal law of various countries contains direct references to offences against the Law of Nations. The Constitution of the United States gives Congress the right to define and punish, *inter alia*, 'offences against the Law of Nations'.[1] It has been often maintained that, notwithstanding the terminology used, individuals are in such cases subject to the obligations of their own municipal law as distinguished from the Law of Nations. There is a distinct element of artificiality in that distinction.

Individuals as organs of the State. Contractual and tortious liability

However, what is much more important from the point of view of both principle and practice is the question as to who is the subject of international duties – who is the subject of international law – in the case of individuals acting not in their private capacity but on behalf of and as an organ of the State. The view has been gaining ground that even in this sphere of action the subject of duty and responsibility is in every case the individual human being. It is probable that this aspect of the question has influenced the doctrines of Duguit,[2] Krabbe[3] and, more recently, Professor Scelle,[4] who have urged not that individuals can also be subjects of international law, but that they are the only subjects of the Law of Nations. These opinions cannot be lightly brushed aside as assertions of pure theory. The State is composed of individual human beings. Its rulers and those responsible for its actions are individual human beings. Moreover, there is cogency in the view that unless responsibility is imputed and attached to persons of flesh and blood, it rests with no one. There is, finally, the consideration, which has most far-reaching consequences, that unless the subject of international duties is thought of

[1] Article 1, sec. 8, cl. 10. For an interesting case applying that clause to counterfeiting within the United States of notes and securities of other States see *United States* v. *Arjona*, 120 U.S. 479. For numerous other examples of municipal legislation on the same lines see Triepel, *Völkerrecht und Landesrecht* (1889), ch. 3, § 13 (1). He disapproves of that terminology: 'If, as we have demonstrated above, the individual can only be the object and not the subject of international law, then it is inconceivable that a "norm" of international law should be violated by an individual.'

[2] *Traité de droit constitutionnel* (3rd ed. 1927), I, 713 *et seq.*

[3] *Die moderne Staatsidee* (1919), p. 273.

[4] Scelle, I, 42–4.

as identical with the individual human being as distinguished from the mystical entity of the State, we open the door wide to that dualism of moral standards which, under the guise of 'reason of State', has proved a disintegrating and destructive factor in the sphere of international morality and peace.

On the other hand, it must be borne in mind that the State is a corporation, a juristic person, and that reasons of convenience and justice require that, in the normal course of affairs, the collective entity of the State should be the subject of responsibility. In that sense international law is primarily a law between States. Thus, for instance, when there is a question of the duties of the State in fulfilling the normal obligations of treaties or of customary international law in matters of commerce, finance, or international administration, while it is true that these duties are ultimately the duties of the human agencies, it is just and proper that, in law, responsibility should be imputed to the State as a whole and that the State should appear exclusively as the subject of international law for the purpose. Independent political societies function in the form of the corporate entity of the State, and it is appropriate that the general principles of law applicable to juridical personality and to the corporate capacity for action should apply also in the case of States. The legal structure of a limited liability company is as necessary in the relations of States as in private life. It is clear that for the purposes of redress, in terms of economic compensation, for violation of treaties, and of customary international law, the State as a whole is, from the practical point of view, the proper *situs* of attribution of responsibility.

The position is similar, though not identical, with regard to what may be called tortious responsibility, for instance, in relation to the question of responsibility for denial of justice to aliens. As a rule such tortious liability implies – and may be satisfied by – finanical compensation. In practice, the subject of international liability in the matter of tort has been the State – even if that liability has on occasions assumed the form of penal damages.[1] But there is intrinsically nothing – save the traditional doctrine on the question of the subjects of international law – to prevent the tortious responsibility of the State from being combined, in the international sphere, with the responsibility of the organs directly liable for the act or the omission in question. It is proper and desirable that an official who is responsible for causing serious injury to an alien by way of denial

[1] See, e.g., the *Janes* case, decided by the American–Mexican Claims Commission (*Annual Digest*, 3 (1925–6), 218).

of justice or otherwise should not personally escape reprobation at the hands of an international tribunal. This, clearly, is not the existing position in international law. But there is room for envisaging an improvement of the law in the matter. The law, when thus improved, will provide that the subject of the duty to treat aliens in accordance with the minimum standard of civilization (and, generally, in accordance with international law) is not only the corporate entity of the State, but also the individual organ acting on its behalf. There would appear to be no reason why the person or persons responsible should not be made jointly liable with the State. Moreover, it may well be in such cases that what – so far as the State is concerned – is a mere tortious responsibility, may in the person of the organ concerned assume an international criminal responsibility. A corrupt or criminally minded judge who has inflicted upon an alien, through a deliberate or negligent miscarriage of justice, an unjust sentence of death or imprisonment; an official who has permitted the murderer of an alien to escape; a military officer who when called on to shield an alien from the fury of a mob joins in the murderous attack – all these persons could, consistently with principle, be held to have transgressed not only the law of their country but also a rule of international law directly binding upon them. Systems of municipal law which recognize a clear distinction between contractual and tortious responsibility admit in appropriate cases the liability in tort of persons acting on behalf of the corporate entity – in addition to the tortious liability of the corporation as a whole.[1]

Criminal responsibility

Similar considerations apply to the question of the subjects of criminal responsibility under international law. In the field of contract and, to some extent, of tort, the requirements of justice and of international peace can be met by making the corporate entity of the State mainly, if not exclusively, the subject of responsibility. This is not so in the field of criminal acts performed by the State, i.e. by persons acting on behalf of the State and under the colour of the authority of the State. In this sphere the analogy of municipal law must fully apply. The primary subject of the international duty is

[1] See, as to English law, Salmond, *The Law of Torts* (7th ed. by Stallybrass, 1928): 'But it is undoubted law that the servants or agents by whom a corporation commits a tort are themselves personally liable in the same case and to the same extent as any other servants or agents who commit torts in the service or on behalf of their principals or employers' (at p. 79).

the human agency which puts into motion the criminal act; the criminal responsibility of the State is of a subsidiary character. Thus it is futile to maintain that if a cabinet minister, fully endowed with governmental authority, orders the massacre of the nationals of a foreign State, the subject of international responsibility is his State only, and not he himself. The futility of that attitude has often been emphasized by the parallel doctrine that States, because of their sovereignty, cannot be subject to criminal responsibility. Both these views must now be regarded as exploded. The question of the criminal responsibility of States is outside the present discussion.[1] But we are concerned with the view that individuals cannot be subjects of criminal responsibility in the international sphere for the reason that they are not subjects of international law. This view, it has been shown here,[2] is not in accordance with the law. When the Charter annexed to the Agreement of 8 August 1945 setting up the International Military Tribunal laid down that there should be individual liability of the defendants for criminal acts which they committed as organs and on behalf of the German State, the only innovation which it introduced was to give the formal imprimatur of a general international treaty – for it was a treaty signed or adhered to by the vast majority of the nations of the world and subsequently endorsed by the First General Assembly of the United Nations – to the abandonment of a doctrine which had loomed large in the writings of publicists but which had no foundation in the principles and necessities of international law. That doctrine was that individuals, not being subjects of international law, cannot be subjects of international duties in the criminal or any other sphere. The Judgment of the Nuremberg Tribunal treated the provision of the Charter laying down the individual responsibility of the accused for acts committed on behalf of the State as a self-evident rule of international law, as a matter both of principle and of the effectiveness of the Law of Nations.[3]

It is not likely that the express rejection of the view that individuals cannot be directly subject to international duties will remain an isolated event in international practice. The greater the heinousness

[1] See Oppenheim, I (6th ed. by Lauterpacht, 1947), § 156*b*.

[2] See above, p. 519.

[3] See above, p. 488. In view of this it is not easy to follow Professor Kelsen when he says that 'what really impairs the authority of the judgment is that the principle of individual criminal responsibility for the violation of rules of international law prohibiting war has not been established as a general principle of law, but as a rule applicable only to vanquished States by the victors' (*International Law Quarterly*, I (1947), 170). The language of the Judgment on the subject is studiously general.

of the act and the graver the danger to international peace, the more difficult it is to accept the artificial divorce between the State and individuals acting on its behalf. In the Resolution of the First General Assembly of the United Nations of 13 December 1946 concerning the condemnation and prohibition of genocide, the Assembly affirmed that genocide is a crime under international law which the civilized world condemns and for the commission of which principals and accomplices – whether private individuals, public officials, or statesmen, and whether the crime is committed on religious, racial, political, or any other grounds – are punishable.[1] The international regulation and control of atomic energy as a potential weapon of war has raised the question of the necessity of attaching criminal responsibility to individuals.[2] Unless not only the State as such but also its organs are made personally responsible for complying with the measures laid down by the international authority, the effectiveness of the international regulation of this vital problem will be considerably impaired. The magnitude of the interests involved requires that that liability should be of a criminal character.

Three other considerations of a general nature must be noted in connection with the developments which mark more clearly than ever before the emergence of the individual as a subject of international duties: the first is that the evolution of an international law in which the individual is the subject of duties imposed by international law is a corollary of the attribution to him of rights grounded in international law. It is difficult to urge and justify the existence of the former without admitting the operation of the latter.

The second relevant consideration is that, in the sphere of criminal responsibility, the recognition of the individual as a subject of international duties tends to diminish the necessity for and the scope of collective punishment of States. Such necessity cannot always be avoided; neither is it inherently unjust, especially if it can be effected without the indiscriminate infliction of physical harm upon the

[1] *Journal of the United Nations*, no. 58, Supp. A-A/P.V. 55.

[2] In the First Report of the Atomic Energy Commission to the Security Council of 31 December 1946, the Commission suggested that the proposed convention should include provisions 'setting forth such violations [of the convention] as shall constitute international crimes, and establishing the nature of the measures of enforcement and punishment to be imposed upon persons and upon nations guilty of violating the terms of the treaty or convention' (*United Nations Atomic Energy Commission*, Special Suppl., Report to the Security Council, p. 19). In the Russian proposal of 19 June 1946 the violation of the provisions of the convention was declared to be 'a most serious international crime against humanity' (*Atomic Energy Commission, Official Records*, no. 2, p. 27).

individual members of the guilty State. Moreover, although individuals may have been innocent of a particular criminal act attributable to the organs of the State, they have a share in endowing that organ with power or in tolerating its rule. If the criminal act is successful they may all reap the fruits of transgression. However, collective responsibility is, at best, a rough instrument of justice, and there are compelling reasons for reducing the scope of its operation. It can be so reduced by the effective recognition of the individual as a subject of international duties. This is essentially the position in the constitutional theory of the Federal State, where Federal execution against the member States as such is in the nature of an exception. A violation of the national Constitution by a member State is, as a rule, treated as a violation of the Federal law by the individuals responsible. They, and not the corporate entity of the member State, are the subjects of responsibility. It is not likely that the gradual integration of international society in the direction of a supra-national Federation of the World – a development which must be regarded as the ultimate rational postulate of the political organization of man – will be achieved by sudden and drastic changes in the legal organization of mankind. But it may be brought nearer to realization by the gradual adoption of the fundamental principles of Federal Government. Of these, the direct subordination of the individual to Federal law, in his capacity as a subject of the law of the Federation, is a vital link. Here lies the deeper significance of the affirmation of the principle that the individual is a subject of international law in the domain both of rights and of duties.

Finally, the full and effective acceptance of the principle that individuals are subjects of international duties has a direct bearing on the evolution of international morality. The tendency to affirm and tolerate a double standard of morality in international relations – a tendency to assert that the individual acting as the organ of the State is not bound by the universal code of ethics which obtains in the relations of individuals – has in the past received nourishment from the notion that the obligations of international law do not rest upon the individual members of the State, but upon 'the State'. The unavoidable outcome must be the impairment of that moral factor which is the backbone of all law.[1] It is not necessary to expatiate upon the consequences of the resulting position in relation to the

[1] This phenomenon must be distinguished—though the distinction may appear to be a subtle one—from the operation of the doctrine of 'reason of State'. The latter does not necessarily rule out the individual as a subject of legal and moral obligation. It asserts different standards of obligation.

effectiveness of international law – for the two questions are interconnected. When in 1928 the German Reichsgericht upheld the conviction of a German national sentenced for publishing certain plans of the Reichswehr, it rejected the plea of the accused that he had acted in order to uphold the disarmament provisions of the Treaty of Versailles which was part of German law. The Court said: 'The Reichsgericht must reject the view that the conviction of the accused would violate the rule of international law which lays down that treaties must be fulfilled in good faith. For this rule binds only the contracting parties, not individuals.'[1]

Conclusions. The subjects of international law and the doctrine of sovereignty

It is now possible to summarize the position with regard to the status of the individual as a subject of international law, i.e. as a subject both of rights granted and of duties imposed by international law. There is no rule of international law which precludes individuals and bodies other than States from acquiring directly rights under customary or conventional international law and, to that extent, becoming subjects of the Law of Nations. The question is largely one of ascertaining what is the intention – and, generally, the practice – of States in each particular case. The conferment of such rights may cover either particular rights or the so-called fundamental rights of the individual in general. With regard to the latter, there is room for the view that having regard to the inherent purposes of international law, of which the individual is the ultimate unit, he is in that capacity a subject of international law. Apart from the controversial doctrine of humanitarian intervention, practice did not, until recently, follow that view. However, recent developments have introduced a decisive change also in this respect. The Charter of the United Nations, in recognizing the fundamental human rights and freedoms, has to that extent constituted individuals subjects of the Law of Nations. The question whether that innovation is constitutive or merely declaratory of a pre-existing higher law is of interest but not of decisive importance. The significance of that change is not impaired by the fact that it is not accompanied by the concession of independent procedural capacity. Finally, the express enactment of crimes against humanity must be regarded as an indirect recognition of fundamental rights of human personality independent of the law of the State and enforceable by international law. The absence of

[1] *High Treason* (*Treaty of Versailles in Germany*) case (*Annual Digest* (1927–8), 11).

such capacity reduces the status of the individual as a subject of international law; it does not negative it. International law as a whole provides a persuasive illustration of the fact that the conception of law is not a rigid notion admitting of no gradation. The same applies to the conception of subjects of international law.

Similar considerations apply to the question of subjects of duties imposed by international law. In this sphere also, no support for the traditional doctrine can be found in the practice of States, both international and municipal. The provisions of recent treaties – in particular in connection with the prosecution of war crimes and crimes against the peace – are to a large extent declaratory of previous practice. While, in the sphere of tortious responsibility, the liability of the individual must continue to be predominantly subsidiary, his primary responsibility for crimes against international law is becoming increasingly recognized.

What have been the reasons which have prompted these changes in the matter of subjects of international law, with regard both to international rights and to international duties? These causes have been numerous and manifold. They have included, with reference to the recognition of the individual as a subject of international rights, the acknowledgment of the worth and of the function of the individual as the ultimate unit of all law; the realization of the dangers besetting international peace as the result of the denial, by the absolutist and totalitarian State, of fundamental human rights; and the attention paid to those already substantial developments in international law in which, notwithstanding the traditional dogma, the individual is in fact treated as a subject of international rights. Similarly, in the sphere of international duties there has been an increasing realization that the direct subjection of the individual to the rule of international law is an essential condition of the strengthening of the ethical basis of international law and of its effectiveness in a period of history in which the destructive potentialities of science and the power of the machinery of the State threaten the very existence of civilized life. Above all, with regard to both international rights and international duties, the decisive factor has been the change in the character and the functions of modern international law. The international law of the past was to a large extent of a formal character. It was concerned mainly with the delimitation of the jurisdiction of States. Substantial portions of it were devoted to immunities of States, their diplomatic representatives and their property. In so far as it was concerned with substantive law, it was mainly concerned with the law of war. There is not much difference in this respect between the treatises of the early publicists and of modern writers. In traditional international law the individual played an inconspicuous part because the international relations of the individual and his contacts across the frontier were rudimentary. This is no longer the case. The interdependence of States which requires regulation is the interdependence of the individuals who compose them. An international law which disregards that fact is bound to be artificial. There is a growing tendency to take that fact into account. Of this the tripartite character of the constitution of the International Labour Organization provides an instructive example. The Charter of the United Nations empowers the Economic and Social Council to 'make suitable arrangements for consultation with non-governmental organizations which are concerned with matters within its competence'; it also lays down that 'Such arrangements may be made with international organizations and, where appropriate, with national organizations after consultation with the Member of the United Nations concerned.'[1] Steps were subsequently taken to implement that provision, and organizations such as the World Federation of Trade Unions, the International Co-operative Alliance, the American Federation of Labor, and the International Chamber of Commerce were given consultative status in relation to the Economic and Social Council.[2] The Committee which framed the rules governing the attribution of consultative status was careful to emphasize that the non-governmental organizations thus admitted should not be given the same rights as States which are not members of the United Nations or as governmental specialized agencies, but the innovation is significant.[3] At the same time the constitutions of a number of governmental specialized agencies, such as the European Central Inland Transport Organization,[4] the International Bank for

[1] Article 71.

[2] See *Report of the Economic and Social Council*, p. 67 (Doc. E/43/Rev. 2). See also *Journal of the Economic and Social Council*, no. 29, pp. 484–6.

[3] Given the disposition to descend from the purely governmental plane, there are possibilities, even within the eixisting Charter, for the closer association of non-governmental agencies with the work of the Economic and Social Council. Thus it has been suggested that a select number of non-governmental agencies should be given the right to have their communications distributed directly to the members of the Council without waiting for a request from them, that there should be a standing committee of the Council for consultation with such organizations accessible to them throughout the session of the Council, and that consultants should be called in at the recommendation of the Standing Committee whenever required. See *Journal of the Economic and Social Council*, first year, no. 27 (15 June 1946), pp. 414–18 (proposals of Mr Winant). And see *Resolutions adopted at the Fourth Session* (February–March, 1947), pp. 46–50.

[4] Article VII (2).

Reconstruction and Development,[1] the World Health Organization,[2] and the International Civil Aviation Organization,[3] made provision for consultation with and advice by private organizations. In a different sphere, international co-operation has provided interesting instances of the relinquishment of the idea that only sovereign States may constitute the membership of international governmental organizations. Thus the authors of the Constitution of the World Health Organization, set up in 1946, provided for associate membership of the Organization on the part of territories or groups of territories, such as protectorates, colonies and trust territories, which are not responsible for the conduct of their international relations.[4] The Charter of the International Trade Organization, accepted in 1947, lays down that, in addition to the membership of fully sovereign States, full voting rights and the consequent status of a Member of the Organization may be accorded to separate customs territories invited by the United Nations Conference on Trade and Employment or proposed by the Member having responsibility for the conduct of its diplomatic relations.[5] The Convention of the Universal Postal Union signed at Paris on 5 July 1947 provides for membership as 'countries of the Union' or 'administrations of the Union' on the part of specifically enumerated postal territories the status of which is that of a colony or protectorate.[6] This, in fact, had been the

[1] Article V, s. 6 (*a*).

[2] The Constitution enjoins upon the Organization to establish co-operative relations with other organizations, both governmental and non-governmental, national and international, which are concerned with any phase of the work of the Organization. Provision is made for consultative arrangements with national organizations subject to the consent of the Government concerned (Articles 70 and 71).

[3] Article 79 of the Chicago Convention of 1945 provides: 'A State may participate in joint operating organizations or in providing arrangements, either through its Government or through an airline company or companies designated by its Government. The companies may, at the sole discretion of the State concerned, be State-owned or partly State-owned or privately-owned'. It was the practice to invite unofficial organizations to send representatives to the Regional Air Navigation meetings organized by the Provisional International Civil Aviation Organization. Thus the South American meeting held at Lima in June 1947 was attended by representatives of the States concerned and the Fédération aéronautique internationale (F.A.I.), the International Air Transport Association (I.A.T.A.), and (as an observer) the Pan-American Institute of Geography and History. The South Atlantic Regional meeting, held in July 1947, included representatives of the I.A.T.A., the F.A.I., and the International Meteorological Organization (I.M.O.). The Meteorological Division of the I.C.A.O. includes representatives of the I.A.T.A. and the I.M.O. (see *Monthly Bulletin* of the I.C.A.O. (Section on Relations with other Organizations)).

[4] Article 8. Application for such membership must be made by the Member of the Organization or other authority entrusted with the conduct of international relations.

[5] Article 5 (3) and (4). Provision is made for the extension of rights and obligations of membership to Trust Territories and to the Free Territory of Trieste.

[6] Articles 3 and 8.

practice of the Universal Postal Union and the International Telecommunications Union for some time. In all these international agencies the non-sovereign units are for most practical purposes contracting parties and full members of the Organization. The sovereign State is thus no longer the exclusive person of organized international intercourse based on treaty.[1] Administrative convenience and economic efficiency rather than the principle of 'sovereign equality' provide the test of membership. The preamble to the Charter of the United Nations opens with the words 'We the peoples' of the United Nations – a significant form of words which, after some discussion, received general approval at San Francisco 'although no other treaty among nations had thus thought to speak for the peoples of the world instead of merely for their Governments'.[2] These developments are only indirectly germane to the question of the position of individuals as subjects of international law, but they show, in conjunction with the other changes outlined above, how antiquated is the conception of international law confined to sovereign States and their purely governmental agencies.[3]

[1] See the illuminating observations of Fawcett, in *B.Y.* 24 (1947), 376, in a note on the International Trade Organization, and Jessup in *A.J.* 41 (1947), 380–5.

[2] The Charter of the United Nations, Report of the Secretary of State to the President of the United States, *Hearings before the Senate Committee on Foreign Relations*, p. 51. However, it will be noted that the concluding paragraph of the preamble refers to Governments as agreeing to the Charter.

[3] How out of date, in comparison with the recent developments and trends of international law, appear, for instance, the dogmatic statements made in 1904 by Anzilotti, an international lawyer of distinction, that 'it is inconceivable that there should exist subjects of international rights and duties other than States' (*Il diritto internazionale nei giudizi interni* (1905), p. 44), and again in 1912 that 'it follows from the very notion of international law as the body of rules established by the collective will of States for the regulation of their mutual relations that the subjects of that law are States and States only' (*Corso di diritto internazionale*, I (1912), 69). But in 1929 the same author warns the student against the mistake of affirming that States only can be subjects of international law. He suggests that, instead, we ought to direct our attention to showing that in fact only States are subjects of international law (*ibid.* revised ed. transl. by Gidel (1929), p. 123). No such proof is possible consistently with the facts. But the learned author still believes it possible to adhere to the traditional view by suggesting that when we say that States only are subjects of international law we refer to 'States' not as understood in other disciplines and in municipal public law, but to organisms which are States in the contemplation of international law – the fact that they are States in this sense being proved by the circumstance that international law treats them as subjects of rights and duties (*ibid.* p. 125). This reasoning amounts, it is believed, to an abandonment of the original position. With regard to individuals as subjects of fundamental rights recognized by international law Anzilotti still maintains the traditional doctrine on the ground that there does not exist a juridical system of humanity as such and that there are no fundamental rights of the individual generally recognized (*ibid.* pp. 122–3). That view, too, must be regarded as antiquated. Note, for instance, the enactment of crimes against humanity (see above, p. 516), the recognition of fundamental human rights and freedoms in the Charter of the United Nations, and the proposed definition of human rights in an International Bill of the Rights of Man.

It is probable that in order to comprehend fully the meaning and the potentialities of these changes it may be necessary not only to revise the traditional conception of the subjects of international law. We may have to become more conscious than we are now of the justification and the practical beneficence of proceeding on the basis of a conception of international law as being not the law of the society of States[1] but the law of international society in all the diversity of its manifestations requiring and admitting of legal regulation by rules other than the municipal law of States.

The issue has the appearance of a purely theoretical question, and impatience is occasionally expressed at what is believed to be the disproportionate amount of argumentative effort expended upon it.[2] The appearance is deceptive. Witness, for example, the rigid and decisive reliance on the doctrine of the exclusiveness of States as subjects of international law in the discussions preceding the present formulation of Article 34 of the Statute of the International Court of Justice;[3] in the determination of the question of the legal personality of international governmental agencies, including the United Nations itself;[4] in the approach to the problem of the legal personality of private international organizations;[5] in the restrictive interpretation of the procedural remedies for the implementation of the fundamental human rights and freedoms under the Charter of the United Nations; and in the denial of individual responsibility for criminal violations of international law.[6] The other direct practical implications of the problem have already been indicated.[7] In all

[1] A definition given by Westlake, I, 1.

[2] See, for instance, the observations of M. Ricci Busatti and M. Fernandez adducing the orthodox doctrine in support of the opposition to conferring upon individuals the faculty of appearing as parties before the Court (*Procès-Verbaux of the Committee of Jurists*, pp. 208 and 311 respectively).

[3] See, e.g., Briggs, *The Progressive Development of International Law* (lectures delivered at the Faculty of Law of Istanbul in 1947), p. 29, who points out that the question whether the individual is a subject or an object of international law is immaterial so long as he actually receives the benefits stipulated on his behalf by international law. The answer is that the traditional doctrine, by emphasizing the procedural limitations and otherwise, has often served as a factor impeding the full utilization of the benefits thus conferred upon the individual. It has also frequently obstructed the development of international law in that direction. A more recent Italian writer (Ziccardi, *La costituzione dell'ordinamento internazionale* (1943), p. 364) maintains that no isolated developments constituting the individual a subject of international rights and duties justify the abandonment of the traditional doctrine. This can be done, he says, only following upon 'una congrua modificazione di tutta la struttura organizzativa dell'ordinamento'.

[4] See above, p. 497.

[5] See on this subject the illuminating report by Politis to the Institute of International Law, in *Annuaire*, 30 (1923), 120–56.

[6] See above, p. 522.

[7] See above, p. 528.

these the repetitive statements to the effect that 'individuals are only objects but not subjects of international law' and that 'sovereign States only are subjects of international law', have played a part.

For it is in relation to State sovereignty that the question of subjects of international law has assumed a special significance. Critics of the traditional theory have treated it as an emanation of the doctrine of sovereignty. In their view it is State sovereignty – absolute, petty, and overbearing – which rejects, as incompatible with the dignity of States, the idea of individuals as units of that international order which they have monopolized and thwarted in its growth. It is the sovereign State, with its claim to exclusive allegiance and its pretensions to exclusive usefulness, that interposes itself as an impenetrable barrier between the individual and the greater society of all humanity. This charge, which cannot be regarded as altogether unfounded, explains much of the acerbity of the criticism. For human dignity and considerations of utility alike rebel against the idea of the State as the sole guardian of the interests of man. The purpose of the State is to safeguard the interests of the individual human being and to render possible the fulfilment, through freedom, of his wider duty to man and society. Some of these interests can be effectively safeguarded by the State in the international sphere. But it is inadmissible that the State should claim, in the conditions of the modern world, that it is the best instrument for protecting all these interests and that it is entitled to exclude from this legal sphere individuals and non-governmental bodies which may be created for that purpose. Any such claim, which is an accompaniment of the current pretensions of sovereignty, lacks justification and is a legimate cause of resentment. But there is an even deeper connection between the two doctrines. State sovereignty – the incarnation of the supreme will of the State as the exclusive source of the law – must disdain the idea of persons owing their quality as subjects of the law to a source independent of the will of States.[1] That source is the fact that, in relation to both rights and duties, the individual is the final subject of all law. To that extent the practice of States, inasmuch as it expressly confers rights and imposes duties upon the individual – important as it is in showing the

[1] 'C'est le développement de la notion de la souveraineté absolue et incontrôlable qui a conduit à la doctrine à ne voir dans les rapports internationaux que les États. Soumis à leur omnipotence, les individus en furent totalement éclipsés' (Politis, *Les nouvelles tendances du droit international* (1926), p. 58).

artificiality and the inaccuracy of the established doctrine in the matter – must be regarded as essentially declaratory. This view, too, is incompatible with the notion of sovereignty as ordinarily conceived. It does not follow that it is a view which is not beneficent in practice and not in accordance with the true purpose of international law.

VI

THE RELATION OF INTERNATIONAL LAW TO MUNICIPAL LAW

CHAPTER 19

IS INTERNATIONAL LAW PART OF THE LAW OF ENGLAND?

Editor's note The question which is the subject of this chapter interested Lauterpacht from the moment of his first arrival in England. Some years before his death we found in the attic of his house the remains of a mouse-eaten copybook in which it was still possible to decipher a few lines of manuscript. Lauterpacht identified it as the notebook in which he had written his first essay for his supervisor at the London School of Economics, Dr Arnold McNair (as he then was); and the subject was 'Is international law part of the law of England?'.

The present chapter was a paper read at the Annual Meeting of the Grotius Society on 25 May 1939. It was subsequently published in the *Transactions* of the Society, vol. 25 (1939), pp. 51–88.

The object of this paper is to examine the present position of what has been often described as the classical doctrine of English law in the matter of the relation of international law to the law of England – the doctrine according to which the Law of Nations is *per se* part of the law of the land. In particular, it is proposed to inquire to what extent that doctrine has withstood the onslaught of positivist theories and their corollaries which until recently lay so heavily on international law. While a considerable number of writers have on that question yielded to the impact of the torrential current of positivism, fed in some cases from the channels of the Austinian tradition, the concessions made to it by English judicial practice have been insignificant and belong to the domain of form rather than of substance. This fact constitutes yet another ground for re-examining the arguments put forward against the predominant English view of the relation of the two systems of law. Within the limits of this paper that task can be attempted only in a summary fashion. For the same reason no reference can be made to the repeatedly affirmed application of international law by prize courts or by ordinary courts deciding matters particularly within the province of international law, such as piracy *jure gentium*. Similarly, no special account can be taken of the law and the judicial practice of the United States.[1]

[1] As to which see, in particular, Scott, in *A.J.* 1 (1907), 831; Wright, *The Enforcement*

These have, with regard to the subject under discussion, developed on the same lines – and more emphatically so – as the common law of England, to which they have in this matter repeatedly acknowledged their indebtedness and allegiance. Accordingly, much of what will be said in this paper has a bearing upon the same problem in the United States.

I. JUDICIAL AFFIRMATION OF THE DOCTRINE OF ADOPTION

The established doctrine on the relation of international law to the law of England has often been described as expressing the classical view for the reason, if there be no other, that it is of long standing. For it was in 1765 that Blackstone gave eloquent and solemn expression to the doctrine of adoption or incorporation – to the doctrine, that is to say, that the Law of Nations is adopted to its full extent as part of the law of England. He said, in the fifth chapter of the fourth book of his *Commentaries on the Laws of England*:

> The Law of Nations (whenever any question arises which is properly the object of its jurisdiction) is here adopted in its full extent by the common law, and is held to be a part of the law of the land. And those acts of parliament, which have from time to time been made to enforce this universal law, or to facilitate the execution of its decisions, are not to be considered as introductive of any new rule, but merely as declaratory of the old fundamental constitutions of the kingdom; without which it must cease to be a part of the civilized world.

(In referring to the Law of Nations Blackstone apparently had in mind the *jus gentium* in its wider meaning as understood by many in the eighteenth century, for he included in it the law merchant and maritime law on such matters as freight, demurrage and insurances. But in the chapter mentioned, in which he expounded the law relating to offences against the Law of Nations, he was concerned with questions of public international law proper.)

The statement that the Law of Nations is to its full extent incorporated in the law of England was not a picturesque generalization of the first Vinerian Professor of English Law in the University of Oxford. The author of that great treatise was also a practising lawyer. He was Solicitor-General to Her Majesty; and he was counsel in the first case in which the unity of the common law and the Law of

of International Law through Municipal Law in the United States (1916), and in *A.J.* 11 (1917), 1; and Dickinson, referred to below, at p. 550.

Nations was emphatically asserted by Lord Mansfield, one of the greatest English judges. In 1764, in *Triquet* v. *Bath*,[1] Lord Mansfield fully associated himself with the view expressed in 1737 by Lord Talbot in *Buvot* v. *Barbuit*[2] (a case in which Lord Mansfield, then Mr William Murray, acted as counsel) to the effect that 'the Law of Nations, to its full extent, was part of the law of England'. He re-affirmed that view in subsequent cases. In 1765, in *Lockwood* v. *Coysgarne*,[3] he held that the 'Statute of 7 Ann. was only declaratory of the Law of Nations, and that the Law of Nations was in full force in these kingdoms'. In 1767, in *Heathfield* v. *Chilton*,[4] he said with regard to the privileges of public ministers and their retinue that they 'depend upon the Law of Nations; which is part of the common law of England' and that 'the Law of Nations will be carried as far in England, as any where'. As pointed out below,[5] it is controversial whether in laying down the rule that international law was part of the law of the land Lord Mansfield and Blackstone were giving expression or intending to give expression to an actual rule of English law obtaining at the time, or whether they were formulating a principle whose rationality appeared to them obvious and irrefutable regardless of its historical accuracy. However that may be, the principle thus formulated proved an exposition of the law as it was applied in the 170 years that followed. For the rule that the Law of Nations is part of the law of England has not remained a mere form of words. It has been acted upon in circumstances revealing that the Law of Nations was regarded as a living source of the law of the land. Principles of international law have been drawn upon in order to fill what was an admitted gap in the law. Remedies, hitherto unknown, have been given on the ground that they clearly followed from the Law of Nations. Jurisdictional immunities have been accorded for the reason that they were grounded either in the Law of Nations or in the common law of which the Law of Nations must be deemed to be a part. It is convenient to recall some of the leading cases in the nineteenth century illustrating the thorough application of what must now be regarded as a well-established principle.

In *Viveash* v. *Becker*,[6] the leading case on consular immunities,

[1] 3 Burr. 1478. [2] Cas. T. Talb. 281. [3] 3 Burr. 1676.

[4] 4 Burr. 2015. Similar language was used in 1769, in *Darling* v. *Atkins*, 3 Wils. 33 (where the Court refused to grant diplomatic privilege to the purser of an English ship of war who was at the same time Secretary to the Envoy from the Elector of Bavaria): 'To be sure Courts of law will protect the ambassadors or public ministers of foreign princes or States, and their servants, from being arrested; it is the Law of Nations; but we must not confound the right of protection with the abuse of that right.'

[5] See below, p. 551. [6] 3 M. & S. 284.

decided in 1814 and involving the question whether a person appointed as consul was entitled to immunity from arrest, it was argued on behalf of the defendant that, as the Act of Queen Anne was merely declaratory of the Law of Nations, the consul was entitled to immunity under the Law of Nations although no reference to such privilege was made in the Act. Lord Ellenborough regarded it as improbable that this should be so in the case of an Act designed to deal comprehensively with the privileges of persons standing in any relation to foreign States, but he was quite prepared to decide the matter on that footing and he proceeded to inquire at length into the opinions of writers on the question of consular privilege. He said: 'If we saw clearly that the Law of Nations was in favour of the privilege, it would be afforded to the defendant; and it would be our duty rather to extend than to narrow it.'

In *De Wutz* v. *Hendricks*[1] – an action decided in 1824 and arising out of the plaintiff's attempt to raise a loan for the Greek insurgents who rose in rebellion against Turkey – Best, C. J. was clearly of the opinion 'that it was contrary to the Law of Nations (which in all cases of international law is adopted into the municipal code of every civilized country) for persons in England to enter into engagements to raise money to support the subjects of a Government in amity with our own, in hostilities against their Government, and that no right of action could arise out of such a transaction.' A year before, in *Novello* v. *Toogood*,[2] Abbot C. J. said with regard to the Act of Queen Anne that 'the Act itself was only declaratory and in confirmation of the common law, of which the Law of Nations must be deemed a part'. (The acknowledgment of the doctrine of incorporation by means of the more limited statement to the effect that the Act of Queen Anne was merely declaratory of the common law – of which international law is a part – has been a constant feature of judicial pronouncements.)[3]

The case of *The Duke of Brunswick* v. *The King of Hanover*,[4] decided in 1844, is remarkable for the directness of its recourse to international law as a source of decision on the ground that the Law of Nations is part of the law of England. Strangely enough, this was the first case

[1] S. C., 9 Moore 586; 2 Bing. 317.

[2] 1 B. & C. 361.

[3] See, e.g., in addition to the other cases here cited, *Hopkins* v. *De Robeck* (1789), 3 T. R. 80; *Service* v. *Castaneda* (1845), 2 Coll. 56; and, more recently, Lord Maugham in *The Cristina*, [1938] A. C. at p. 516 (*Annual Digest*, 9 (1938–40), 250); *The Amazone*, *The Times* newspaper, 9 May 1939 (*ibid.* p. 417).

[4] 6 Beav. 1.

which raised the question of the immunity of foreign sovereigns from suit. The Court said:

The question upon the demurrer is one to be determined by that which may be thought to be the Law of Nations applicable to the case... There is no English law applicable to the present subject, unless it can be derived from the Law of Nations, which, when ascertained, is to be deemed part of the common law of England.

The same view was expressed in 1851 in *De Haber* v. *The Queen of Portugal*, a novel case relating to the property of a foreign sovereign. The Court held that 'to cite a foreign potentate in a municipal court, for any complaint against him in his public capacity, is contrary to the Law of Nations',[1] and that to insist on the appearance of the sovereign thus indirectly impleaded would be 'a further violation of the Law of Nations'.[2] In *Magdalena Steam Navigation Co.* v. *Martin*[3] it was admitted by the Court that 'it has not hitherto been expressly decided that a public minister duly accredited to the Queen by a foreign State is privileged from all liability to be sued here in civil actions', but the Court thought 'this follows from well established principles'. These principles were 'the immunity which the Law of Nations gives to ambassadors'. So firmly had the doctrine of Blackstone and Mansfield become entrenched by that time that in these and other cases[4] it was simply acted upon without the accompanying explanatory statement referring to international law being part of the law of England.[5] But such references did not disappear altogether. Thus in the case of *The Emperor of Austria* v. *Day and Kossuth*,[6] an important example of a remedy granted by direct and exclusive reference to international law, the Court, in issuing an injunction restraining the defendants from printing money on behalf of the revolutionary Government of Kossuth in derogation of the public

[1] 17 Q.B. 170, 208.

[2] At p. 214. See also *Wadsworth* v. *The Queen of Spain* (17 Q.B. 218), where the Court said: 'Judicial procedure in England would have been liable to great reproach had it not afforded a prompt and effectual remedy at once to put an end to actions brought in perversion of the ancient and laudable custom of foreign attachment in the City of London, and in violation of the universal law by which the civilized nations are bound' (at p. 220).

[3] 2 Ellis and Ellis Reports 94.

[4] See, e.g., *The Parlement Belge*, 5 P. D. 197, a case *primae impressionis* on the immunity of foreign public ships, decided almost exclusively by reference to applicable rules of international law.

[5] See also Lord Ellenborough's judgment in *The Duke of Montellano* v. *Christin* (1816), 5 M. & S. 503. The Lord Chief Justice said: '... considering that an ambassador is the immediate representative of the crowned head, whose servant he is, it would hardly be respectful, in the first instance, to exact such security, unless there were pregnant reasons for believing it necessary'. And see Lord Ellenborough's judgment in *Wolff* v. *Oxholm* (1817), 6 M. & S. 92 – a striking application of the doctrine of adoption.

[6] (1861), 2 Giff. 628.

rights of the Emperor, said: 'A public right, recognized by the Law of Nations, is a legal right; because the Law of Nations is part of the common law of England. These propositions are supported by unquestionable authority.'[1] The Court relied fully on the doctrine of adoption as enunciated by Blackstone, to which it referred as one of 'unquestionable authority' and one which had always been acted upon by English courts.

That persistent tradition of incorporation was continued in the twentieth century. In 1905 the doctrine of Lord Mansfield and Blackstone was reaffirmed in the much-quoted judgment of Lord Alverstone in *West Rand Central Gold Mining Co.* v. *The King*[2] – a significant pronouncement, for it rejected by implication the deductions which hasty readers were inclined to draw from *The Franconia* case, to which we shall refer presently.[3] The Lord Chief Justice said:

> whatever has received the common assent of civilized nations must have received the assent of our country, and that to which we have assented along with other nations in general may properly be called international law, and as such will be acknowledged and applied by our municipal tribunals when legitimate occasions arise for those tribunals to decide questions to which doctrines of International Law may be relevant.[4]

In 1918, in *Re Suarez*, the Court, confronted with a novel point in the matter of diplomatic immunities, insisted once more that the Act of Queen Anne must 'be construed according to common law, of which the Law of Nations must be deemed a part'.[5] In 1928 we find Lord Phillimore in *Engelke* v. *Musmann*[6] and Lord Finlay in his dissenting opinion in *The Lotus* case, using the same language.[7] It will be shown that, notwithstanding some deprecatory and hesitating language, this has also been the view of judges in some recent important decisions.[8]

The doctrine that international law is part of the law of the land has in addition found expression in two subsidiary rules, one of which is a rule of construction and the other a rule of evidence. The rule of construction is that, while Acts of Parliament are in every case of overriding effect, they must, if only possible, be interpreted so as not to be in conflict with international law; they must be interpreted against the background of international law in the same way as they

[1] At p. 678.

[2] [1905] 2 K. B. 391.

[3] See below, p. 545.

[4] At p. 406.

[5] [1918] 1 Ch. 176, at p. 192.

[6] [1928] A. C. 433, at p. 449 (*Annual Digest*, 4 (1927–8), 362).

[7] *P.C.I.J.* Series A, no. 10, p. 54 (*Annual Digest*, 4 (1927–8), 5); See also *P.C.I.J.* Series A, no. 10, p. 75, for the reference by Judge Moore to 'the majestic stream of the common law, united with international law'.

[8] See below.

must be construed by reference to the principles of international law. 'It is a sound rule', said Byles J. in *R.* v. *Morris*, 'to construe a statute in conformity with the common law rather than against it, except where and so far as the statute is plainly intended to alter the course of common law.'[1] The same principle has been consistently applied to international law,[2] which also in this respect has been put on the same footing as the general body of the common law. The practical effects of this rule of construction have been considerable; it has been applied almost as frequently as the major doctrine of incorporation itself. The absolute superiority of Acts of Parliament, even when they conflict with international law, has indeed been repeatedly and emphatically affirmed.[3] But this has been a theoretical affirmation having the probably not unintended effect of stressing the duty of judges to do their utmost to interpret statutes so as not to impute to the Legislature the intention of disregarding international law. It is easier to interpret away a provision of an Act of Parliament on the face of it inconsistent with international law if previously due obeisance has been made to the supremacy of the Legislature. This, in fact, has been the normal sequence of judicial declarations on the matter.[4] Probably there are no cases on record – not excluding, perhaps, the frequently cited case of *Mortensen* v. *Peters*[5] – in which a Court has interpreted a statute in such a way as to acknowledge

[1] (1867), L. R. 1 C. C. R. 90, at p. 95.

[2] See, e.g., Blackburn, J., in *R.* v. *Dudley* (1884), 14 Q.B. 273, 284; Sir R. Phillimore in *R.* v. *Keyn* (1876), 2 Ex. D. 63, at p. 85.

[3] See, e.g., Cockburn, C.J., in *R.* v. *Keyn* (1876), 2 Ex. D. 160, 210, and other authorities there cited; Dr Lushington in *The Amalia* (1863), 1 Moore P. C. (new series) 471, 474; the same in *The Zollverein*, 2 Jur. (new series) 429. And see *Cope* v. *Doherty*, 4 K. & J. 374. And see below, n. 4.

[4] See, e.g., Dr Lushington in *The Annapolis. The Johanna Stoll*, Lush. 308: 'The Parliament of Great Britain, it is true, has not, according to the principles of public law, any authority to legislate for foreign vessels on the high sea, or for foreigners out of the limits of British jurisdiction, though if Parliament thought fit so to do, this Court, in its instance jurisdiction at least, would be bound to obey. In cases admitting of doubt, the presumption would be that Parliament intended to legislate without violating any rule of international law, and the construction accordingly.' See also *Croft* v. *Dunphy*, [1933] 1 D. L. R. 225; [1933] A. C. 156; *The Johannes*, Lush. 189; and the numerous cases in which British enactments relating to slave traffic have been held inapplicable to aliens abroad.

[5] It will be noted that nowhere in the judgment did the Court assert or admit that the Act in question was in violation of international law. On the contrary, it pointed out that 'there are many instances to be found in decided cases where the right of a nation to legislate for waters more or less landlocked or land-embraced, although beyond the three-mile limit, has been admitted'. The matter was debated at length in the House of Lords on 21 February 1907. Lord Fitzmaurice, the Under-Secretary of State for Foreign Affairs, while repudiating any intention to criticize the decision, pointed out that the British attitude in previous cases of that nature had been that the expression 'any person' was 'an expression commonly used in British statutes dealing with crimes and misdemeanours, and was never applied except to persons owing obedience to the British Parliament' (169 *H.L. Deb.* 4s., p. 990).

clearly that the statute as intended by the Legislature was in violation of international law or that it inevitably had that effect independently of the intention of the Legislature. The presumption that Parliament did not intend to commit a breach of the Law of Nations has been a powerful weapon wielded with a determination which on occasions has come near to a denial of the supremacy of Parliament.[1]

The second subsidiary rule is the rule of evidence to the effect that international law need not be proved in the same way as foreign law or any other fact must be proved[2] – apparently for the reason that it is not foreign law. Judicial notice is taken of it as of Acts of Parliament or of any branch of the unwritten law, although having regard to the frequent absence of direct authority the range of judicial inquiry is wider and, on occasions, more laborious than in the case of ordinary rules of municipal law. In *Re Piracy Jure Gentium*[3] we find the Lord Chancellor saying: 'In considering such a question, the Board is permitted to consult and act upon a wider range of authority than that which it examines when the question for determination is one of municipal law only.'[4] The reliance upon and citation of legal writers are nearly as prominent a feature of decisions bearing upon international law as they were in the eighteenth and nineteenth centuries.[5]

[1] See, e.g., Lord Stowell in *The Le Louis*, 2 Dods. 210, 251, 254: '. . . no nation can privilege itself to commit a crime against the Law of Nations by a mere municipal regulation of its own . . . the Legislature must be understood to have contemplated all that was within its power, and no more'. Similar language was used by Sir William Grant in *The Amedie* (1810), 1 Acton 240, 250. In *Lopez* v. *Burslem* (1843), 4 Moore 300, 305, we find Lord Campbell affirming that 'the British Parliament certainly has no general power to legislate for foreigners out of the dominions and beyond the jurisdiction of the British Crown', although in the same case he left no doubt that the Court was bound by an Act of Parliament.

[2] This is clearly stated in a number of American cases: 'Foreign municipal laws must indeed be proved as facts, but it is not so with the Law of Nations' (*The Scotia* (1875), 14 Wall. 170, 187); *The New York* (1899), 175 U.S. 187. English judicial practice is the same, but I have not been able to trace any judicial pronouncement bearing directly on the matter.

Mr Picciotto states on pp. 103–5 of his monograph (referred to below, p. 546) that international law must be proved as a question of fact like any other foreign law. This is not believed to be an accurate statement.

[3] [1934] A. C. 586 (*Annual Digest*, 7 (1933–4), 213); Viscount Sankey added the following, somewhat controversial, observation: 'Speaking generally, in embarking upon international law, their Lordships are to a great extent in the realm of opinion, and in estimating the value of opinion it is permissible not only to seek a consensus of views, but to select what appear to be the better views upon the question.' See also Brett J.A., in *R.* v. *Keyn* (1876), 2 Ex. D. 63, at p. 142: '. . . In my opinion, a general consent of recognized writers of different times and different countries to a reasonable proposition is sufficient evidence of a general consent of nations to that proposition.'

[4] At p. 588.

[5] See, e.g., *Chung Chi Cheung* v. *The King* (1938), 55 *T.L.R.* 184 (*Annual Digest*, 9 (1938–40), 264), and *Re Piracy Jure Gentium*, above, n. 3.

There has been only one remarkable departure – and even this one is more apparent than real – from the doctrine of incorporation which English courts have acknowledged for more than a century and a half. The exception in question is the frequently quoted case of *The Franconia* (*R.* v. *Keyn*).[1] In that case a bare majority of an authoritative English tribunal decided that, in the absence of a clear rule of international law to that effect, English courts had no jurisdiction to try a foreigner for manslaughter committed in British territorial waters. A closer examination of this case suggests that its relevance to the question of the relation of international law to municipal law has been exaggerated. The main issue in *The Franconia* was not the question whether international law is part of the law of the land, in the sense that it can be enforced without an Act of Parliament or other municipal act of transformation authorizing its enforcement. The issue was the existence and the content of a rule of international law in the matter of jurisdiction in territorial waters. The majority judges based their judgment on the ground that 'by the principles of International law the power of a nation over the sea within three miles of its coast is only for certain limited purposes; and that Parliament could not, consistently with these principles, apply English criminal law within those limits'.[2] Although some of the majority judges insisted on the requirement of an act of transformation in every case, most of the judges who contended for the necessity of such special legislation did so not because they maintained that international law could never be enforced without an Act of Parliament, but merely on the ground that international law on the matter of jurisdiction in territorial waters was not settled. There is a significant passage in the principal judgment given in that case, namely, that of Cockburn C.J. After stating the divergent views of writers on the question, the Chief Justice proceeded as follows:

> Looking to this, we may properly ask those who contend for the application of the existing law to the littoral sea independently of legislation to tell us the extent to which we are to go in applying it. Are we to limit it to three miles or to extend it to six? Are we to treat the whole body of criminal law applicable to it, or only so much as relates to 'police and safety' . . .? What is there in these conflicting views to guide us, in total absence of precedent or legal sanction, as to the extent to which we may subject foreigners to our law?[3]

[1] (1876), 2 Ex. D. 63.

[2] *Ibid.* p. 63 (from the headnote).

[3] At pp. 192, 193. In *The Charkieh* (1873), 8 Q.B. 197, Cockburn C.J., said: 'The questions raised relate to international law, which is recognized by the municipal law of this country.'

It would seem, therefore, that the insistence on the necessity for an Act of Parliament was due not to the desire to challenge the established doctrine as formulated by Blackstone, but to the uncertainty of international law on the subject. Moreover, even if the rule of international law concerning territorial waters had been clear and undisputed it would not necessarily have followed that, as the result of the doctrine of incorporation, English courts would automatically have been entitled to exercise jurisdiction. In a permissive jurisdictional rule it is reasonable to expect a special authorizing pronouncement of national organs. Thus, for instance, international law does not deny to States the right to punish their nationals for offences committed abroad. It does not follow from this permissive rule that, in the absence of legislation or a clear common law rule, English courts possess such jurisdiction with regard to any particular crime. This being so, it is submitted that the case of *The Franconia* cannot accurately be quoted as diverting into an altogether different channel what has been called 'the majestic stream of the common law, united with international law'.[1]

In view of the impressive uniformity of practice in the application of the doctrine enunciated by Blackstone and Lord Mansfield, what is the explanation of the criticism, or at least of the hesitation, with which it has met in some quarters in the last thirty years? In the previous editions of Professor Oppenheim's treatise – I have, in the fifth edition, taken the responsibility of substituting my own view – the doctrine of incorporation was described as inaccurate.[2] Professor Oppenheim's opinion was subsequently elaborated in some detail by Mr Picciotto, who, however, while criticizing the traditional formula, admitted that international law, although it is not part of English law, is a source of it.[3] A similar view has been expressed by Professor Brierly.[4] Sir William Holdsworth has recently put it on record that there have always been two schools of thought on the subject of the accuracy of the doctrine of incorporation.[5] What, once more, are the reasons which have prompted this opposition to and this hesitation concerning what many regard as a beneficent and progressive legal tradition?

[1] Judge Moore in the *Lotus* case (*P.C.I.J.* Series A, no. 10, p. 75).

[2] Oppenheim, *International Law* (4th ed. by McNair, 1928), §§ 20–1.

[3] *The Relation of International Law to the Law of England and of the United States of America* (1915), pp. 105, 106.

[4] In *L.Q.R.* 51 (1935), 31.

[5] *A History of English Law*, x (1938), 373. See also Jennings and Young, *Constitutional Laws of the British Empire* (1938), pp. 5–7.

2. THE SIGNIFICANCE OF THE DOCTRINE OF ADOPTION

Before attempting to answer this question it is proper at this stage to try to explain why the expression 'beneficent and progressive' is widely regarded as fittingly characterizing the notion of incorporation of international law as part of the law of the land.

The subjects of international duties and the effectiveness of international law

In the first instance, that notion has commended itself to many as beneficial for the progress of international law inasmuch as it is based, upon analysis, on the view that the rules of international law must not only be respected in the external relations of States as conducted by their Governments, but that they also regulate the conduct and the obligations of individuals in matters affecting the international relations of the State. They are rules binding directly upon the individual acting as such and not only as the representative of his State.[1] They are so binding regardless of whether they have been previously adopted in any particular case by the action of the Government, the Legislature, or of any other organ of the State. In this sense the doctrine of incorporation is intimately connected with the idea which is believed to be one of the most vital principles of an effective Law of Nations – a principle which Westlake expressed in a precise but pregnant *dictum*: 'The duties and the rights of States are only the duties and rights of the men who compose them.'[2] It is a progressive principle because in its final implications it signifies the abandonment of what has been the greatest evil of modern international law and relations, namely, the dualism of moral and legal standards applicable to individuals acting singly and to individuals grouped in collective units in the form of States. This connection of the doctrine of incorporation with the problem of enhancing the reality of rules of international law explains perhaps why Westlake felt specially attracted by the question of the relation of international

[1] It is of interest to note that this point is apparently stressed by Blackstone in the place where he enunciated the doctrine of adoption, namely, in the fifth chapter of the fourth book of his *Commentaries*. While admitting that offences against the Law of Nations 'are principally incident to whole States or nations', he insisted on the importance of the rule of international law being binding upon individuals. 'But where the individuals of any State violate this general law, it is then the interest as well as the duty of the Government under which they live, to animadvert upon them with a becoming severity, that the peace of the world may be maintained. For in vain would nations in their collective capacity observe these universal rules, if private subjects were at liberty to break them at their own discretion, and involve the two states in war.'

[2] Westlake, *Papers*, p. 78.

law to the law of England. In an article published in 1906 and whose title I ventured to borrow for the present paper, he affirmed, in guarded language, the full validity of the doctrine enunciated by Blackstone.[1]

The subjects of international rights

Secondly, inasmuch as the doctrine of adoption signifies that the benefits of customary international law may accrue directly to the individual without an express act of transformation by an organ of the State in any particular case, it contributes to the development in which the position of the individual as the ultimate unit of international law – as, indeed, of all law – is recognized to a substantial degree. The State is the normal subject of international law for the reason that normally international law regulates the conduct of individuals organized as and acting through States. The State alone has, as a rule, full procedural capacity before international tribunals. But the doctrine of incorporation reminds us that the exclusiveness of the State as the subject of rights conferred by international law is relative and not absolute. It reminds us that there is a sphere in which the law, both international and municipal, recognizes individual rights independently of the direct and specific approval of the State.[2] Such independence is conceded by the State and is revocable at its instance, but so long as it lasts it is expressive of a legal phenomenon whose significance is greater than any particular benefit conferred upon the individual as a result of its operation.

Voluntary submission to international law. The unity of international law and municipal law

Thirdly, and perhaps even more significantly, the doctrine of incorporation gives expression to the view that the external relations of States, in so far as they come before English courts in connection with the adjudication of private rights, are normally under the sway

[1] *L.Q.R.* 22 (1906), 14. The article was written as a commentary on *West Rand Central Gold Mining Company* v. *The King*, a case affirming in principle that English courts will enforce rights conferred by international law as such (see above, p. 542), and this fact explains why in his conclusions Westlake emphasized this aspect of the question.

[2] The direct enforceability of *rights* given by international law was stressed by Westlake in his article referred to above (n .1). He said in his Conclusions: 'The English courts must enforce rights, given by international law as well as those given by the law of the land in its narrower sense, so far as they fall within their jurisdiction in respect of parties or places, subject to the rules that the King cannot divest or modify private rights by treaty (with the possible exception of treaties of peace or treaties equivalent to those of peace), and that the courts cannot question acts of State . . .' (*L.Q.R.*, 22 (1906), at p. 26).

of legal rules which do not owe their origin to the will of the individual State – although they owe to the willing acquiescence of the State their actual operation within the municipal sphere. The doctrine of incorporation thus conceived does not imply the supremacy of international law. For it is through the will of the State that the general act of incorporation has taken place. The State may, with an effect binding upon municipal courts, set aside the Law of Nations thus generally incorporated. The courts must apply Acts of Parliament which are clearly inconsistent with international law – although, as we have seen, the presumption, not lightly to be abandoned, is that no such overriding effect was intended. But so long as that overriding will has not been clearly manifested, the universal law of the *civitas maxima* is part and parcel of the law administered by the courts. So long as that voluntary submission lasts it has the effect of elevating to the authority of a legal rule the unity of international and municipal law. It results, to use the current terminology on the question, in an affirmation of the monistic and the rejection of the dualistic view of the relation of the two systems of law. Asserting as it does the ultimate identity of the subjects of rights and duties in both spheres of law, it shows that to describe by the term 'law' the rules applicable to the conduct both of individuals within the State and of individuals organized as States is not a misuse of language but a proper reference to a fundamental jurisprudential identity. That submission on the part of the State may – from the point of view of municipal law – be validly refused or withdrawn, but the sanction of such action might be, in Blackstone's words, that the State would 'cease to be a part of the civilized world'. It was largely on this ground that Sir Henry Maine, Westlake's predecessor in office, deplored the effect of the majority decision in *The Franconia* case as he understood it. If the State, he said, were to refuse to recognize international law as normally operating in its courts without a specific act of transformation, then 'it would probably be that the State which disclaims the authority of international law places herself outside the circle of civilized nations'.[1]

Practical advantages

Fourthly, by endowing at least some rules of international law with that high degree of enforceability which is common to the rules of municipal law administered by the State, the doctrine of adoption adds authority to the rules of international law in a world in which

[1] Maine, p. 38.

these rules are only imperfectly observed.[1] At the same time, the principle of adoption broadens the basis of interpretation and of application of international law by authorizing courts to rely on sources other than purely national jurisprudence. It is sufficient to mention the manner in which English and American courts have mutually relied on each other's decisions in matters involving international law.[2]

It is in these features of the doctrine of adoption that lies its progressive and beneficent quality. In fact, such is the esteem in which it is held in the world that nations desirous of giving expression to their attachment to international law and to their firm resolve to abide by its principles expressly incorporated into their constitutional law the rule that international law is part of their municipal system. Thus, for instance, when in 1919 Germany wished to manifest a new attitude to international law she enacted in Article 4 of her Constitution of 1919 the rule that 'the universally recognized rules of international law are valid as binding constituent parts of German Federal law'.[3] That example was followed by other countries. In view of this it is of interest to inquire into the reasons for the criticism which the classical rule has encountered in the last twenty years on the part of writers in the country of its origin.

[1] It is of some interest to note here the caustic passage in Blackstone's *Commentaries* in which, referring to the legal basis of the clergy's right to one-tenth of the produce of the harvest, he says: 'Considering the degenerate state of the world in general, it may be more beneficial to the English Clergy to found their title on the law of the land than upon any divine right whatsoever, unacknowledged and unsupported by temporal sanctions' (*Commentaries*, book II, ch. 3).

[2] See Dickinson, *The Interpretation and Application of International Law in Anglo-American Countries* (privately printed, 1932; also in *Hague Recueil*, 40 (1932) (ii), 328–49), ch. II, which contains a valuable discussion of the whole subject.

[3] When in 1919 the authors of the new Constitution discussed Article 4, they stated expressly that the intention was to adopt the Anglo-American rule on the subject, especially in the sense that the universally recognized rules of international law bind not only States but also their subjects (*Minutes* of Constitutional Committee, 3rd Meeting). There has recently been a tendency in Germany to interpret that Article restrictively, namely, as referring to such rules only as have received the specific consent of Germany: see Walz, in *Z.V.* 18 (1934), 150–1. Compare with this the much more comprehensive statement of Lord Alverstone in *West Rand Central Gold Mining Company* v. *The King*, [1905] 2 K. B. 391, in which he describes as directly enforceable, *inter alia*, any rule 'that . . . is of such a nature, and has been so widely and generally accepted, that it can hardly be supposed that any civilized State could repudiate it'. See also Walz, in *Z.V.* 18 (1934), 150–1, for the suggestion that the duty to interpret municipal law so as not to bring it into conflict with international law does not apply to the interpretation of the Treaty of Versailles, which was imposed upon Germany by force.

3. THE CRITICISMS OF THE DOCTRINE OF ADOPTION

The historical aspect

Lord Mansfield and Blackstone used language which created with some the impression that they were stating not only a sound principle of the mutual relation of international law and the law of England, but that in their view the relationship as formulated was one of great antiquity. They asserted repeatedly that the Act of Queen Anne on the subject of diplomatic immunity was only declaratory of the common law, of which the Law of Nations was part. These assumptions have recently been subjected to inquiry. As a result, the view has been put forward that diplomatic representatives did not in the seventeenth century enjoy exemption from civil and certainly not from criminal liability before courts; that such immunity as was undoubtedly enjoyed was one protected not by courts but by the royal prerogative; and that there is no evidence that in the seventeenth and the first half of the eighteenth century international law was regarded as part of the law of England.[1] Even if these criticisms were thoroughly justified, they would still be of limited relevance for answering the question whether, as a result of decisions regularly given for a period of more than 150 years, the doctrine of incorporation has not in any case become part of the law. It has been followed too consistently to be dependent for its continued validity on the results of historical researches.

A perusal of the judgments given by Lord Mansfield and others who adopted his terminology shows that what prompted them was not any desire to copy precedents of the past, but the conviction that it was fitting and proper that the courts of this country should give effect to a universally binding law. Prior to Blackstone and Lord Mansfield, the jurisprudential question of the relation of international law to the law of England was not a matter which was present to the minds of judges and writers. There is no mention of it in the writings of Gentilis[2] or Zouche, or in the Opinions of Sir Leoline Jenkins.

[1] See, in particular, Adair, *The Exterritoriality of Ambassadors in the Sixteenth and Seventeenth Centuries* (1929), pp. 238–43, and p. 88, where Lord Mansfield's *dictum* that the Law of Nations is part of the common law of England is described as 'all nonsense so far as the seventeenth and eighteenth centuries are concerned'. It is pointed out below that there is no justification for such vehement language in this connection. And see the same in *Cambridge Historical Journal*, 2, no. 3 (1929), 290–7. Sir William Holdsworth seems to have adopted some of Mr Adair's conclusions (see above, p. 546).

[2] In his *Hispanicæ Advocationis Libri Duo* (1661), Gentilis, in discussing the authority of Civil Law in the Court of Admiralty, says: 'Ut sic ego jura haec duo distinguo, non appello

Only occasionally was the substance of the question broached in support of an *ex parte* argument, as in 1654 when an attempt was made to justify the trial of the brother of the Portuguese Ambassador on a charge of murder,[1] or when, in 1693, a petition was made for the reprieve of John Golding, convicted of piracy in a trial in which the political element was not altogether absent.[2] The substance of most of the available evidence points to the fact that principles of international law, especially with regard to diplomatic immunities, were recognized and given effect by English law. There was no serious inaccuracy in the statement that the Act of Queen Anne was declaratory of the law of England. It is not unreasonable to assume that what Lord Mansfield and Blackstone had in mind was not that the Act of Queen Anne was declaratory of the details of the common law in its attitude to diplomatic privilege, but that it was declaratory of the general attitude of the common law in the matter, of that common law of which international law was a part – so much so that it made little difference whether it was said that the Act was declaratory of the common law of which international law was a part, or of international law which was part of the common law.[3] The avowed purpose of the Act was to introduce prohibitions and penalties calculated to secure respect for the general principle of diplomatic privilege. The prohibitions and penalties were new, but not the

alterum Anglicum, alterum autem Romanum. Nec enim in regno principe aliud jus sit, quam regni ipsius' (book I, ch. xxi, p. 95).

[1] Where it was argued that the *jus gentium* as practised by *other* nations is *not* part of English law. See *A Selection of the State Papers of John Thurlow* by Thomas Birch, II (1742), 428: 'A justification of the proceedings against the Portuguese for the murder of Mr Greenway, notwithstanding their relation to their ambassador... That the fact is murder, and so a sin against the law of God and man; such as by the Levitical law admitted neither pardon nor sanctuary... That the privilege of an ambassador cannot exempt him from trial by the law of this nation. It is a maxim in our law, that no foreign law, either civil or national, can take place in this nation, unless it be part of our law by Act of Parliament, or by a continued practice of the people time out of mind, if admitted here; and that supposeth an universal assent of the people; and then it goes for the law of the land. And therefore whatsoever the civil law is, or the *jus gentium* practised by other nations, it is not applicable to England.'

[2] The following passage in the petition is of interest: '... That the Law of Nations, to the judgment of which our case only belongs, is the great and imperial law of right and equity that judges of the rights of kings and nations, with respect to each other, and of the rights of war, and of the rights of peace; and all nations with respect to this law are considered as one great corporation, and each kingdom or nation but as a single member or part of this corporation. And therefore this law, or any rule of rights, or notion, cannot be altered, concluded or estopped by any notes, ordinances or statutes of any particular nation or kingdom' (12 How. St. Tr. 1278).

[3] See, e.g., *Heathfield* v. *Chilton* (1767), 4 Burr. 2016; *Magdelena Steam Navigation Co.* v. *Martin* (1859), 2 E. & E. 94; *Assurantie Compagnie Excelsior* v. *Smith* (1923), 40 *T.L.R.* 105 (*Annual Digest*, 2 (1923–4), 302). In *De Haber* v. *The Queen of Portugal* (1851), 17 Q.B. 171, the Act was described as declaratory both of the common law and of the Law of Nations.

principle to which they were intended to give effect. That principle was well established with regard to immunity from both civil and criminal jurisdiction. In the matter of criminal jurisdiction it was circumscribed by what appeared to be reasonable exceptions inherent in the nature of the privilege. Thus, it was held by some to be fitting that diplomatic immunity grounded in *jus gentium* should be forfeited as a result of heinous offences against *jus gentium* (as then understood) – for instance, in case of murder.[1] Plotting against the sovereign of the receiving State came within the same category. The immunity of servants – that perennial source of abuse of privilege[2] – for a long time prompted another exception. Remnants of these exceptions survived until the nineteenth century. But the principle of immunity was not denied. Neither did some of the asserted exceptions in the field of immunity from civil jurisdiction have the effect of nullifying the principle of diplomatic privilege. Some of these exceptions, like that relating to transactions of a private law nature, are even nowadays asserted and acted upon by various countries.

The part of international law relating to diplomatic immunities was not, it is true, administered in the sixteenth and seventeenth centuries by common law courts. It was part of the law within the province of the royal prerogative, as was indeed practically the whole field of foreign relations. Diplomatic privilege was enforced by the King, his Council, and the Court of Chancery.[3] But this does not

[1] In 1615, in the *Case of Marches*, a subject of the King of Morocco, who pretended to be ambassador to the United Provinces, the civilians expressed the view that an ambassador is, according to the Law of Nations and nature, immune from suit but that he loses his immunity if he commits an offence against the law of nature or reason (but not against the positive law) (1 Rolle 175; *Eng. Rep.* 81, p. 411). See also the Opinion of 16 January 1654 of Chief Justice Rolle and Justices Jermyn and Atkins of the common law, Drs Clerk and Godolphin, Judges of the Admiralty, and Drs Walker and Turner, on the demand of the Portuguese Ambassador for the return of his brother, Don Pantaleon [de Saa], committed for murder, on the ground that it is against the Law of Nations that 'one of his family should be tried by these laws'. The Opinion was that 'Where the offence is against the Law of Nations, the Ambassador and his followers forfeit privileges which they might otherwise claim. Having offended against the Law of Nations, they cannot pray the aid of those laws...' and that 'Murder is an offence against the Law of Nations, whilst an offence against the municipal law is only *crimen prohibitum*, and not *malum in se*' (*Calendar of State Papers. Domestic Series*, 1653–4, p. 360).

[2] In *Poitier* v. *Croza* (1749), 1 Black. Tr. 48 – an action by the plaintiff, who was a dancer, against the defendant, who was master at the Opera House and was at the same time retained by the Sardinian Envoy as his master of the horse – Foster, J. said: 'I remember a case where a person swore he was gardener to a public minister, who had no gardener; and a clergyman who swore he was chaplain to the Morocco Ambassador.'

[3] Examples of protection of diplomatic privilege by the King will be found in a Record Office volume entitled 'Precedents relating to satisfaction given Foreign Ministers', *State Papers* 100/66. For other examples see Adair, in *Cambridge Historical Journal*, 11 (1928), 290–7. And see Turner, *The Privy Council of England, 1603–1784*, 1 (1927), 178: '*At the Council in 1623*. This daye diuerse of the Justices of the peace of westminster & Middlesex

mean, as is suggested by some, that it was not part of the law. The law relating to the royal prerogative was and is part of the law of England. Any criticism of Blackstone's view by reference to the fact that the relevant portions of the Law of Nations were enforced by the royal prerogative and not by common law courts must be regarded as being based on a controversial technicality.

Association with the law of nature

The second reason for the weakening of the authority of the doctrine of adoption has been its initial association with the notion of an overriding law of nature. We find in the Judgments of Lord Mansfield statements to the effect that the Law of Nations is, like the law of nature, so much an integral part of the law of the land that it could not be changed even by an Act of Parliament.[1] This obsolete view can and must be rejected – as it has been abandoned elsewhere – without detriment to the authority of the principle of adoption as such. The latter has undergone an important modification in a similar direction without any substantial loss to its true meaning. In some of its early manifestations it failed, because of its close association with the law of nature, to take into account in a sufficient degree the fact that international law is based predominantly, although not exclusively, on the consent of States, and that such consent, in order to be a valid source of obligation, must have received the express or implied consent of this country. In the latter part of the nineteenth and at the beginning of the twentieth century judges began to stress that element of assent. Thus in *The Franconia* Lord Coleridge, one of the minority judges, emphasized the necessity for agreement, while holding that 'the English courts give effect, as part of English law, to such agreement'.[2] The necessity for assent was stressed by Lord Alverstone in the *West Rand Central Gold Mining Co.* case. He affirmed the direct applicability of rules of international law. But he insisted that the Law of Nations, in order to be applicable as part of English law, must 'be proved by satisfactory evidence, which must shew either that the particular proposition put forward has been recog-

were sent for before their Lps for the enquierie and order to bee taken, for the repressing of frequent insolencies and abuses informed to be offred unto Strangers, and many tymes to the offence of the Amb[rs] of forraine princes and Stats both in the streets of London and westminster . . .'

[1] See, e.g., Lord Mansfield in *Heathfield* v. *Chilton*, 4 Burr. 2016: 'The Act of Parliament of 7 Ann. c. 12, did not intend to alter, nor can alter the Law of Nations.' No such assertion seems to have been made by Blackstone. He said: 'But if the parliament will positively enact a thing to be done which is unreasonable, I know of no power than can control it' (*Commentaries*, I, 91).

[2] (1876), 2 Ex. D. 63, at p. 154.

nized or acted upon by our own country, or that it is of such a nature, and has been so widely and generally accepted, that it can hardly be supposed that any civilized State would repudiate it'[1] – the latter qualification constituting a not untimely reminder that in the matter of rules of international law of universal application no specific assent is required.

The positivist and dualist tendencies

The third, and most important, cause of the hesitation which has surrounded the doctrine of incorporation has been due to the fact that, at the beginning of the twentieth century, positivism and the insistence on State sovereignty in the international sphere gained practically unchallenged predominance in the science of international law. That tendency could not easily accommodate itself to a juridical doctrine by virtue of which international law is rendered automatically part of the municipal system. For a connection so intimate seemed to imply the subordination of the municipal law to a higher rule of law. Actually, there was no necessity, even from the positivist point of view, to question the doctrine of incorporation from that angle. There is nothing necessarily inconsistent between the principle that international law is *per se* part of municipal law and the positivist assertion that the will of the State is the sole source of the validity of international, as indeed of any other, law. For the doctrine of incorporation does owe its origin and its validity to the will of the State. It is not a principle imposed by an overriding will external to the State. The principle is valid only because it has been adopted.

In fact, it is not so much the positivist doctrine as such as its ramifications and corollaries which it was found impossible to square with a rule of broad generality laying down that international law is *per se* part of the law of the land. If the doctrine of incorporation accurately expresses an existing and working legal rule, then it constitutes an additional formidable argument against accepting the dualistic assertion which postulates that international law is essentially different from municipal law and that it is addressed not to individual human beings but to metaphysical entities called States. Confronted with that dilemma, positivist writers did not feel called upon to revise their theory; they assailed the doctrine of adoption for the reason that it was incompatible with the theory. Oppenheim's treatment of the subject is typical of that method. He pointed to what he believed to be the fundamental differences between the two systems of law with

[1] [1905] 2 K. B. 391, at p. 407.

regard to their sources, their subjects and their substance, and then proceeded to lay down that 'If the Law of Nations and municipal law differ as demonstrated the Law of Nations can neither as a body nor in parts be *per se* part of municipal law.'[1] Alternatively, attempts were made to devitalize the doctrine of adoption by suggesting that, as the result of a necessary logical implication, adoption of international law as part of the law of the land involved a complete transformation of the formal and material content of the law thus incorporated.[2] There was an air of artificiality about that attempt to fit a broad legal principle into the Procrustes-bed of a narrow theory.

Criticism based on existing law

(*a*) *Treaties and the requirement of legislative action*

The inadequacy of the purely theoretical approach prompted the critics of the doctrine of adoption to emphasize its limits and exceptions. These exceptions, and their relevance to the major issue, must now be considered. The first exception is the rule of British constitutional law according to which treaties finally concluded by Great Britain, although fully valid in the international sphere as part of international law, do not form part of the law of the land until they have been expressly incorporated into municipal law. In particular, treaties affecting private rights will not be enforced by the courts unless they have received the assent of the Legislature through an enabling Act of Parliament. The precise limits of that rule have never been authoritatively laid down by a court of law.[3] But the principle itself has not been seriously challenged. It was seized upon by Triepel, the first continental critic of the doctrine of adoption,[4] and his followers as yet another ground for maintaining that the doctrine that the Law of Nations is part of the law of England is a mere form of words. If a treaty ratified and internationally valid is without force within the State unless supplemented by legislative action, then, it is

[1] *International Law*, I (2nd ed. 1912), § 21. It is possible, however, that Oppenheim might have revised his views, for several years later we find him saying, on p. 10, in his Introduction to the monograph of Picciotto (referred to above, p. 546): '... It is possible for the municipal law of an individual State by custom or by statute to adopt rules of international law as part of the law of the land, and then the respective rules of international law become *ipso facto* rules of municipal law.' [2] See below, p. 567.

[3] They were not so laid down in *Walker* v. *Baird*, L. R. [1892] A. C. 491, although the major principle involved in the necessity for municipal legislation was admitted by the Crown. The final decision in *The Parlement Belge*, L. R. 5 P. D. 197, turned on a different point.

[4] In his *Völkerrecht und Landesrecht* (1899) he first attacked the doctrine of adoption as being juridically unsound on account of the fundamental differences between international and municipal law.

asserted, international law embodied in that treaty is not part of the law of the land. This is entirely true. The rule is obviously in the nature of an exception to the principle of incorporation. But the reasons for it lie not in any subtle intention of English courts to take away with one hand what they grant with the other, but only and exclusively in the exigencies of British constitutional law and the division of powers within the State. It is a rule of British constitutional law that the conclusion and ratification of treaties are a prerogative of the Executive. In other countries, such as the United States, the concurrence of the Legislature, or of a part thereof, is necessary for the valid ratification of a treaty. This is not the case in Great Britain. A treaty becomes binding for this country as soon as it has been finally ratified by the Crown. This being so, it might be possible for the Crown to impose burdens upon the subject, and to legislate for him, indirectly, without the concurrence of Parliament, by means of concluding a treaty.[1] The existing rule which requires in such cases an enabling Act of Parliament removes that possibility. It may be added that the likelihood of courts having to refuse to enforce a valid treaty because of the absence of an enabling Act is of a highly theoretical nature owing to the practice of passing the enabling Act *prior* to the ratification of the treaty.[2] Thus the Treaty of Versailles was signed on 28 June 1919; the enabling Act was passed on 31 July 1919; the formal act of ratification by the King took place on 10 October 1919; ratifications were exchanged and the Treaty entered into force on 10 January 1920. This practice of passing the enabling Act prior to the ratification of the treaty has now become the normal procedure. Moreover, it appears that, even apart from that practice, in certain matters, not clearly defined, ratified treaties are binding upon the courts and subjects without an enabling Act having been

[1] The case of *State of Missouri* v. *Holland, United States Game Warden*, decided in 1920 by the Supreme Court of the United States, is an interesting example of a Government arming itself, by means of a treaty, with powers which it did not apparently otherwise possess. In 1915 the Congress of the United States passed an Act concerning the protection of migratory birds. That Act was declared unconstitutional on the ground that it interfered with the rights reserved to the member States. Thereupon the United States concluded a treaty with Great Britain for the protection of migratory birds. The Supreme Court held that a statute providing for the enforcement of that Treaty was constitutional (252 U.S. 416; *Annual Digest*, 1 (1919–22), 4). The decision of the Judicial Committee of the Privy Council in *Att.-Gen. for Canada* v. *Att.-Gen. for Ontario and Others* (53 *T.L.R.* 325; *Annual Digest*, 8 (1935–7), 41) is also of interest in this connection. The question was, essentially, how far can Canada enact labour legislation, in pursuance of international labour conventions, in matters reserved by the Constitution to the Provinces?

[2] The only case, known to the writer, in which a court actually refused to apply a treaty because of the absence of enabling legislation is the judgment of the Supreme Court of Canada in *Re Arrow River and Tributaries Slide and Boom Co., Ltd.*, [1932] 2 D.L.R. 250 (*Annual Digest*, 6 (1931–2), 7).

passed.[1] Thus, probably, treaties modifying the belligerent rights of the Crown with regard to maritime warfare, or, possibly, treaties of peace or those akin to treaties of peace, or treaties conferring diplomatic or consular immunities,[2] will be acted upon by British courts without legislation. In the case of *Porter* v. *Freudenberg*,[3] decided during the World War, it apparently assumed that Article 23 (*h*) of Hague Convention no. IV respecting the Laws and Customs of War on Land was enforceable by British courts although that Convention had never received express legislative assent.

For these reasons the doctrine of adoption cannot be regarded as impaired in its value by the requirement of a municipal act of transformation in the case of treaties affecting[4] the private rights of the subject. In any case, the necessity for an explicit act of transformation in the matter of treaties does not detract from the validity or the vitality of the doctrine of adoption in its principal aspect, namely, in the matter of customary international law.

(*b*) *Overriding effect of Acts of Parliament*

Secondly, it has been argued that it is inaccurate to say that rules of international law are *per se* part of municipal law seeing that, so far as municipal courts are concerned, an Act of Parliament may modify or abolish any rule of international law. The answer must be that so long as there is no clearly conflicting statute, rules of international law are operative *per se* as part of the law of the land. The doctrine of

[1] See, for a lucid survey, McNair, in *B.Y.* 9 (1928), 59, and, in particular, his *The Law of Treaties* (1938), pp. 7–35.

[2] For a survey of authorities see McNair, *The Law of Treaties*, pp. 19 *et seq.*

[3] [1915] 1 K.B. 857.

[4] Perhaps it ought to be said 'affecting private rights *favourably or adversely*', seeing that it is equally clearly established that, in the absence of express municipal legislation to that effect, subjects cannot, as against the Crown, derive benefits directly under a treaty on the ground that the Crown acts as agent or trustee for the subject. See *Civilian War Claimants' Association* v. *The King*, L.R. [1932] A.C. 14 (*Annual Digest*, 6 (1931–2), 237); *Rustomjee* v. *The Queen*, L.R. (1876), 1 Q.B.D. 487; 2 Q.B.D. 69; *Baron de Bode* v. *The Queen*, L.R. (1848), 13 Q.B. at 383, where the question seems, in a sense, to have been left open. A possible reason for the established rule in the matter may be that, just as it is undesirable that the Crown should impose duties upon the subject, so it may also be fraught with danger if it were in a position to distribute benefits without the concurrence of Parliament. However, the reason usually given in decisions is that such matters are 'Acts of State' (as to which see below, p. 559). This being so, it may be difficult to see why in *Administrator of German Property* v. *Knoop*, L.R. [1933] ch. 439 (*Annual Digest*, 6 (1931–2), 240), Maugham, J. (as he then was) regarded as strictly applicable the rule in *Civilian War Claimaints' Association* v. *The King*, although in the former case the contention was that it was the German Government which acted as agent for German subjects. In *Mendizabel* v. *Machado*, 1 Sim. 67, it was held in the Vice-Chancellor's Court in 1826 that a Court of Equity was bound to uphold the provisions of a Treaty between France and Spain in which certain moneys were placed at the disposal of the Spanish Government for the satisfaction of private creditors.

adoption is not concerned with the question of the supremacy or otherwise of international law. Its essence is expressed in the fact of the direct operation of the Law of Nations. Statutes may override common law. It has not been asserted on this account that the common law is not part of the law of the land.[1] The paramount validity of Acts of Parliament signifies that the will of the Legislature is supreme within the municipal sphere; it is not relevant to the accuracy or otherwise of the doctrine of adoption. It will also be noted that, as suggested above,[2] the formal supremacy of Acts of Parliament is circumscribed – in practice, although not in strict legal theory – by the rule of construction which imputes to the Legislature the intention to observe the rules of international law.

(*c*) *Acts of State*

The doctrine of 'Acts of State', which has been applied especially to questions of State succession,[3] clearly limits the direct operation of international law before English courts.[4] That limitation has been narrowly circumscribed in a series of decisions and confined to executive acts in relation to aliens in foreign territory.[5] The recent practice of English courts[6] has been to reject the view, followed in earlier times in English common law courts[7] and to a somewhat alarming degree in the present-day practice in France, that the interpretation of treaties involving political questions is outside the jurisdiction of the courts.

In any case, it must be borne in mind that the doctrine of Act of

[1] This was clearly recognized by Holland who, while admitting that the Law of Nations 'is, no doubt, incorporated into the Common Law which binds the Courts of this country', said: 'If it can only claim obedience there through its incorporation into the Common Law of the Realm, we should expect to find that, like any other branch of the Common Law, it will be disregarded by our judges when it comes into conflict with an express enactment of the legislature' (*Studies in International Law* (1898), p. 195).

[2] See above, p. 542.

[3] See, e.g., *Elphinstone* v. *Bedreechund* (1830), 1 Knapp 316; *Secretary of State for India* v. *Kamachee Boye Sahaba* (1859), XIII Moore 23; *Cook* v. *Sprigg*, L.R. [1899] A.C. 572. See also Moore, *Act of State in English Law* (1906), p. 82, and the cases referred to in Westlake, *Papers*, pp. 21, 22.

[4] Possibly we may have to include here the rule which makes the determination of private rights in certain matters depend upon the statement of the Executive, as, for instance, in the matter of the status of foreign sovereigns. Even in these so-called political matters, governed by the principle of the conclusiveness of the statements of the Crown, international law is not eliminated altogether. On proper analysis, it is in these cases administered by the executive branch of Government as distinguished from the Judiciary.

[5] *Johnstone* v. *Pedlar*, L.R. [1921] 2 A.C. 262 (*Annual Digest*, 1 (1919–22), 231); *Buron* v. *Denman* (1848), 2 Ex. D. 157; *Sobhuza II* v. *Miller*, [1926] A.C. 518 (*Annual Digest*, 3 (1925–6), 40), where the territory in question was a British protectorate.

[6] See, e.g., *Stoeck* v. *Public Trustee*, [1921] 2 Ch. at p. 68 (*Annual Digest*, 1 (1919–22) 224).

[7] *Weymberg* v. *Touch* (1669), 1 Ch. Cas. 123, and other cases referred to in Moore, *Act of State in English Law*, pp. 24–8.

State – as well as the requirement of municipal legislation in the matter of treaties affecting private rights and the overriding validity of Acts of Parliament – constitute the limits of the direct operation of international law before English courts. They do not affect the nature and the significance of the doctrine of adoption in other spheres.

4. JUDICIAL HESITATION

The examination here undertaken of the various criticisms of the doctrine of adoption suggests, it is believed, that they lack foundation and that their force has now probably spent itself. But the challenge has been a vocal one. It has been expressed in leading text-books, with the result that we find a distinct echo of it in some recent judicial pronouncements. No more, it must be added, than an echo. For while the doctrine of adoption has occasionally been mentioned with some embarrassment and almost with a semblance of apology, it is still acted upon by judges with a thoroughness not surpassed by decisions given a hundred years ago. Some recent instances will illustrate this combination of full adherence to a well-established principle with a conciliatory reference pleasing to its critics.

One of these cases is the Opinion of the Judicial Committee of the Privy Council, given in December 1938, in the case of *Chung Chi Cheung* v. *The King*[1] – a case involving the jurisdiction of a British court with regard to a crime committed in British territorial waters on board a Chinese customs cruiser, an armed public ship of a foreign State. Lord Atkin, in giving judgment for the Board, did not rely on English precedent for the reason that there was probably no precedent directly applicable to the case. He relied on the Judgment of Chief Justice Marshall in *Schooner Exchange* v. *M'Faddon*,[2] and in particular on the views of international lawyers on the question of extraterritoriality of foreign public ships. He said, fully admitting – it would appear – the principle enunciated by Blackstone: 'The courts acknowledge the existence of a body of rules which nations accept among themselves. On any judicial issue they seek to ascertain what the relevant rule is, and, having found it, they will treat it as incorporated into the domestic law.'[3] There followed a qualification: 'so far as it is not inconsistent with rules enacted by statutes or finally declared by their tribunals'. With that qualification, which is in no way inconsistent with the principle of incorporation, few will quarrel

[1] [1939] A.C. 160 (*Annual Digest*, 9 (1938–40), 264). [2] 7 Cranch 116.
[3] At p. 168.

– so long as it is not suggested that a rule of international law thus applied must never be in derogation of any right or remedy granted by common law.[1] What is not so easy to follow, but what is indicative of the feeling of embarrassment with which the doctrine of adoption is now enunciated, are the two sentences immediately preceding the statement quoted above: 'It must be always remembered', said the learned Lord, 'that, so far, at any rate, as the courts of this country are concerned, International Law has no validity save in so far as its principles are accepted and adopted by our own domestic law. There is no external power that imposes its rules in our own code of substantive law or procedure.'[2] How does this warning and this assertion of the exclusive authority of municipal law compare with the statement, previously quoted, that the courts acknowledge the existence of international law and, after having ascertained its substance, treat it as incorporated into the domestic law? Probably what was meant was merely that English courts, and no external agency, are competent to assume responsibility for the laborious process of ascertaining what are the applicable rules of international law and how they must be interpreted in any given case. It is likely that the learned Lord did not intend to lay down that it is in any individual case open to courts to refuse to apply an undoubted rule of customary international law not inconsistent with a statute or with an absolutely binding judicial decision bearing on that particular rule of international law. Courts treat the relevant rules of international law as incorporated into the domestic law because they are bound to do so – not, indeed, by the fiat of any power external to the law of England, but by virtue of an established rule which bids them to act in that way. It is a rule of law – not a statement of fact or of policy – that the courts acknowledge the existence and the applicability of the relevant rules of international law. The courts themselves have engrafted that mandatory rule upon the common law. It is possible that at the beginning of the eighteenth century international law was not part of the common law; it is possible that Blackstone and Lord Mansfield in 1765 and Lord Talbot in 1737[3] were mistaken in assuming that

[1] For, clearly, when for instance a foreign State is granted jurisdictional immunities by virtue of a rule of international law which has not hitherto been applied by courts, the application of a rule of international law in that case *primae impressionis* results in the refusal of a remedy hitherto assumed to be granted by the law. Similarly, when in *Emperor of Austria* v. *Day and Kossuth* (see above, p. 541) the court granted an injunction on the ground that there was a right to an injunction by virtue of international law, it deprived the defendant of a right which, but for international law, he would have enjoyed by virtue of municipal law.

[2] At pp. 167, 168.

[3] There is no reason to assume that, as suggested by Mr Adair (*The Exterritoriality of Ambassadors*), Lord Mansfield's account in *Triquet* v. *Bath* and *Heathfield* v. *Chilton* of Lord

this was the position in the seventeenth and in the preceding centuries. But in the following 150 years that conviction has become part and parcel of the law. It is too late to question the general doctrine of incorporation – even if it were desirable to do so. The judgments in the various cases show that the generality of that doctrine does not in any way impair the importance of the judicial function in ascertaining the meaning and the scope of particular rules of international law, which they henceforth expressly declare to be incorporated into the law of the land in pursuance of the general rule that the law of nations is part of the law of the land. Thus in *Chung Chi Cheung* v. *The King* the learned Lord declined to base his judgment exclusively on the technical point of implied waiver of immunity on the part of the Chinese Government. He dealt at length and by reference to international law authorities with the substantive law of jurisdictional immunities of foreign vessels in a manner which makes this judgment a distinct contribution to the subject.

As the second example illustrating the same phenomenon we may take the case of *The Cristina*,[1] decided in the same year and affirming the jurisdictional immunity of a foreign State in respect of its property. There, too, the unanimous judgment of the House of Lords was based, in the words of Lord Atkin, on 'propositions of international law engrafted into our domestic law',[2] or, in Lord Wright's words, on 'a rule of international law, accepted among the community of nations',[3] a rule which 'is binding on the municipal courts of this country in the sense and to the extent that it has been received and enforced by these courts' (a qualification which lends itself to misunderstanding in so far as it denies the possibility of a customary rule of international law being binding on the courts of this country even if it had previously not been received and enforced by an English court). But it was in Lord Macmillan's speech that we find an interesting illustration of the matter here discussed. In answering the question whether foreign public ships not used for public purposes enjoy jurisdictional immunity in English courts, the learned Lord quoted what he regarded as the well-chosen words of Lord Dunedin in *Mortensen* v. *Peters*: 'It is a trite observation that there is no such thing as a standard of international law extraneous to the domestic law of a kingdom, to which appeal may be made.'[4] After quoting

Talbot's statements in *Barbuit*'s case was misleading and that the reporter of the latter case copied not the actual decision but Lord Mansfield's account of it.

1 [1938] A.C. 485 (*Annual Digest*, 9 (1938–40), 250).

2 At p. 490.

3 At p. 502.

4 As to which see above, p. 543. It is submitted that there may be two opinions on the

these words Lord Macmillan proceeded to elaborate the view that no immunity ought to be granted to public ships engaged in commerce as there was no consensus of opinion in international law that such immunity was due. He said:

I confess that I should hesitate to lay down that it is part of the law of England that an ordinary foreign trading vessel is immune from civil process within this realm by reason merely of the fact that it is owned by a foreign State, for such a principle must be an importation from international law, and there is no proved consensus of international opinion or practice to this effect.[1]

In a preceding passage he expressed the following view: 'It is manifestly of the highest importance that the courts of this country before they give the force of law within this realm to any doctrine of international law should be satisfied that it has the hall-marks of general assent and reciprocity.'[2] Thus, after starting from the proposition that 'there is no such thing as a standard of international law extraneous to the domestic law of a kingdom', the learned Lord proceeded in effect to ascertain what was the solution dictated by international standards. There ought to be no dissent from his reference to the courts of this country giving the force of law within the realm to any doctrine of international law so long as it is understood that in thus acting courts proceed in pursuance not of any law-creating capacity inherent in them or of a wide margin of discretion, but in conformity with the duty to ascertain and to give effect to the Law of Nations as part of the law of the land.

The case of *Commercial and Estates Co. of Egypt* v. *The Board of Trade*[3] is another striking illustration both of the vitality of the doctrine of incorporation and of the hesitation with which it has been recently expressed. The case arose out of the seizure of goods of a neutral brought into this country against his will. The question before the Court was one pertaining to the exercise of the right of angary. Both plaintiff and defendant agreed that the case was one of angary, but it was argued for the defendant that, as angary was a matter of international law, the adjustment of the rights and obligations in

question whether the frequently-cited passage referred to by the learned Lord was a felicitous one. It is possible that, given, as it was, in a Scottish court, the *dictum* could afford to disregard, in a somewhat drastic manner, the established English legal tradition on the matter. That tradition is that there *is* a, voluntarily accepted, standard of international law extraneous to municipal law.

[1] At p. 498.
[2] At p. 497.
[3] [1925] 1 K.B. 271 (*Annual Digest*, 2 (1923–4), 423).

question must be a matter to be settled between the State which had seized the goods and the State whose subject complained of the seizure. There was in fact, with the exception of a decision previously given in the same case,[1] no case decided by a common law court in the matter of angary. In *The Zamora*,[2] it is true, Lord Parker discussed the origins and the application of the right of angary, but he did so by reference to international practice and writings; and he did so in a court whose main business was to apply international law. But the majority of the Court in *Commercial and Estates Co. of Egypt* v. *The Board of Trade* had no hesitation in declaring the rules of international law on the matter to be part of the law of England. 'Is this right,' asked Bankes L.J., 'thus described by Lord Parker a branch of international law which constitutes part of the law of the land?'[3] In order to answer this question he quoted in full the passage cited above, from Lord Alverstone's judgment in the *West Rand Central Gold Mining Co.* case. He accepted that passage as a correct statement of the law. He held 'that the seizure of the claimant's goods can only be justified under, and must be attributed to, the right of angary, and that that right is so well established in international law that it forms part of the municipal law of this country'.[4] Atkin L.J. (as he then was) was substantially of the same opinion. The seizure, he said, could be justified only by the right of angary, which appeared to him 'to be well recognized by the conventions of civilized nations which constitute the body of international law'. After having gone so far, the learned Lord thought it necessary to utter the following warning. He said: 'International law as such can confer no rights cognisable in the municipal courts. It is only in so far as the rules of international law are recognized as included in the rules of municipal law that they are allowed in the municipal courts to give rise to rights and obligations.'[5] Judging from what preceded and followed this statement, it must be assumed that what Lord Atkin intended to convey was that any particular rule of international law, in order to have effect within the State, must be applied by the courts as part of municipal law – a proposition which, it is respectfully submitted, hardly called for a *caveat* of that somewhat alarming comprehensiveness. He may have meant that a rule incorporated from international law loses henceforth its quality as a rule of international law and becomes and is applied as a rule of municipal law –

[1] *Commercial and Estates Company of Egypt* v. *Ball*, 36 *T.L.R.* 526 (*Annual Digest*, 2 (1923–4), 421).

[2] [1916] 2 A.C. 77, 100.

[3] At p. 283.

[4] At p. 284.

[5] At p. 295.

a somewhat technical point. If he had meant that every rule of international law, in order to be applied by courts, must have previously, in some other case, have received the judicial imprimatur – then it may be difficult to assent to the proposition. The answer to these hypotheses is supplied by the fact that, after having insisted that international law cannot confer rights cognizable in the municipal courts, he curtly laid down: 'The right of angary therefore [*sic*] is a right recognized by English law.' Why 'therefore'? It clearly was not, prior to this case, a right recognized by an ordinary English court. The reasoning seems to have been that the right of angary could not be applied as international law; that the learned Lord therefore incorporated it as part of the law of the land; and that once incorporated, it was thereupon applied as municipal law. Having brought the matter so far, Lord Atkin went on to decide the case on the basis of international law. He said: 'It is plain that one of the conditions of the right of angary as recognized by international law is that full compensation shall be made to the neutral owner.'[1] The decision in this case, notwithstanding the reservations and disclaimers, will justly be regarded as ranking with some of the most outspoken judgments in which the doctrine of adoption has been acted upon.[2]

5. TERMINOLOGY AND PRINCIPLE

It has been shown that even in cases in which judges have deemed it advisable, in deference to a transient tendency in legal literature, to emphasize the independence of the standards of municipal law of those of international law, they have in fact acted upon the doctrine of incorporation, which has now acquired a definite place in the administration of the law in this country. At the same time, the fact that judges have succeeded in combining a measure of criticism of and caution in relation to the doctrine of adoption with its full application in substance raises the question whether the controversy is not to a large extent a matter of terminology or dialectics. On the face of it this is so to a substantial degree. How, it is argued, can it be said that international law is *per se* (or 'to its full extent') part of the law of the land if admittedly it is applied only because it has been adopted and only so long as the Legislature is content to tolerate it?

[1] *Ibid.*

[2] Recourse to international law was here had with the result, in the words of Professor Brierly, of defeating a particularly mean attempt on the part of the Executive to avoid its obligations (*L.Q.R.* 51 (1935), 28).

The answer turns largely on the meaning of the phrase '*per se*'. If '*per se*' means in this connection that international law is applicable by municipal courts *ipso facto*, by virtue of a rule of international law superior to and independent of the will of the State, then the doctrine of adoption is a theory and not a rule of existing law. If, on the other hand, its meaning is that international law as a whole has been incorporated by the State so that its individual rules and principles are applicable, so long as the State so wills, without any individual act of transformation, then the expression '*per se*' is not improperly used in this context. If this is so, then the difference of opinion on the matter is reduced to the distinction between a general and a specific act of adoption. The doctrine of adoption signifies that international law has been incorporated generally and is as such part of the law of the land. Once we realize the significance of this fact we shall be inclined to regard in their true perspective the terminological criticisms or suggestions on the matter.

Thus, for instance, we may feel hesitation in agreeing that it is more accurate to say that international law is a source of English law rather than a part of it. There is, in practice, no substantial difference between the two statements. A source of law is more than a potential part of the law; it is actually part of it. Acts of Parliament are both part of the law of the land and a source of it. The distinction between a 'source' of law and a 'part' of law is as artificial as the distinction between formal and material sources of the law. There is nothing illogical or misleading in the statement that international law is part of the law of England so long as we bear in mind the qualifying exceptions thereto (i.e. the necessity for municipal legislation in the matter of treaties and the rule as to Act of State) and so long as we do not impute to it a meaning which is alien to its true significance (namely, that it denies the supremacy of the Legislature).

Similarly, we shall be inclined to attach but little importance to dialectical niceties such as that international law once adopted by the municipal system is no longer international law but municipal law. For much will depend on our definition of municipal law. Is it the law enacted and created by the State and its organs or is it the law applied by the courts of the State regardless of its origin? The question has been discussed in a different connection by writers on private international law,[1] and the better opinion seems to be that there is no terminological looseness in asserting, for instance, that

[1] For a lucid discussion and survey of authorities, see Cheshire, *Private International Law* (2nd ed. 1938), pp. 11, 85–91.

English Courts apply French law in certain cases. For the same reason, there is no logical flaw in the statement that it is international law that is administered by municipal courts as part of the law of the land. Prize courts are municipal courts, but it has been repeatedly and authoritatively stated[1] and it is not seriously denied that they administer international law. The question would, even in this form, still remain essentially one of terminology, and would hardly warrant detailed consideration but for the fact that it has been treated by the Austinian and positivist critics of the doctrine of adoption as a means of reconciling their theory with a legal rule which it has proved difficult to ignore. Thus they have maintained that the process of adoption necessarily implies a complete transformation, both formal and substantive, of the law adopted.[2] The best that can be said of that assertion is that it begs the question. The essence of the matter is not the formal designation of the law applied by municipal tribunals subsequent to its incorporation, but the fact that courts are entitled and bound to apply rules of international law directly, i.e. without a specific act of transformation.

However, the issue is wider and its implications deeper than a purely terminological controversy would seem to suggest. In its broader aspect it is expressive of an attitude to the entire problem of international law. In a community in which the doctrine of adoption is part of the law, the courts, instead of proclaiming the exclusive authority of the national legal system, regard themselves, in addition to their normal function, as administering a law of a unit greater than the State. They recognize and are permitted to recognize that the substance of the international relation of States is not essentially and necessarily one of force, but that much of it can be organically woven into the structure of a fully developed and normally operating law of the State. It is arguable that the law of the State itself gains an accession of moral strength in consequence of the willing submission to the authority of a law only imperfectly endowed with temporal sanctions. There is, indeed, in that voluntary acquiescence no abandonment of the sovereignty of the State and of its legislative supremacy. From this point of view the doctrine of adoption is in the nature of a gesture.[3] With the passage of years and with the growth of the

[1] See, in particular, *The Zamora* [1916] 2 A.C. at p. 91.

[2] See, for instance, Anzilotti, p. 69. See also, for a spirited argument on the same lines, Sir James Stephen, *A History of the Criminal Law of England*, II (1883), 34–7.

[3] This circumstance explains to a certain extent the slight impatience of some foreign critics who have been tempted to see in the doctrine of adoption a political formula which, at a small cost, secured to the nation adhering to it a definite moral advantage.

field of judicial decisions in matters of international law, its symbolic character tends to become more pronounced inasmuch as questions once decided by reference to the doctrine of adoption are henceforth part of municipal case-law and are applicable as such.[1] But it would be a mistake to underrate its legal significance for the mere reason that its value lies also in other spheres. In the field of international legal theory, the doctrine of adoption has contributed to the successful challenge not only of a barren type of positivism, but – even more so – of the principal corollaries of the positivist doctrine. The positivist attack on the doctrine of adoption was bound to remain futile on the ground, even if there had been no others, that it assailed an established and workable legal rule. Its set-back is shared by the accompanying dogmas of the fundamental difference of the two systems of law and of their subjects – canons which, in the long run, cannot be maintained without a denial of the legal nature of the Law of Nations.

These are the reasons why, far from being a source of embarrassment, the doctrine of adoption ought to be looked at as a principle which, without subordinating one system of law to the other, adds to the authority both of municipal law and of the Law of Nations. In periods of crisis in the international sphere, whenever there reveal themselves tendencies to substitute for the authority of the Law of Nations an uneasy and precarious balance of physical forces, the task of municipal tribunals in administering and upholding at least some portions of international law, forming part of the municipal system and rendered real by the sanction of the State behind it, acquires special significance. There are no indications that courts are inclined to jettison or seriously to curtail, in the country of its origin, a beneficent and well-established legal doctrine which has now spread wide beyond its original confines, which has been fully adopted in

[1] A series of cases decided in connection with the conquest of Abyssinia and the Spanish Civil War of 1936–9 raised the question whether reliance on available case-law may not usefully be accompanied by a consideration of the relevant rules of international law and the international obligations of the country. In *Bank of Ethiopia* v. *National Bank of Egypt and Liguori*, [1937] Ch. 513 (*Annual Digest*, 8 (1935–7), 119), the Court relied on previous decisions laying down the principle of the validity of the internal acts of an authority recognized *de facto*. The decision was probably inevitable, but it would not have been improper if the Court had considered the relevance of the fact that the occupation of Abyssinia was effected in violation of a fundamental treaty – the Covenant of the League of Nations – to which Great Britain was a party. In *The Arantzazu Mendi*, [1938] 3 All E.R. 333; [1938] 4 All E.R. 267; [1939] 1 All E.R. 719 (*Annual Digest*, 9 (1938–40), 60), where the same principle was applied, it would have been fitting if the successive courts had considered the question to what extent the certificate of the Foreign Office on the matter must be interpreted in the light of the rule of international law relating to the recognition of a revolutionary Government *durante bello*.

the United States of America, and which other countries have justly regarded as a symbol of catholicity in matters international. It represents a legal principle which must in the future, as it has done in the past, constitute an object of emulation in times in which the external relations of States are allowed to pursue their course in the channels of the inevitable progression towards the political integration of mankind. That final development, when it comes to pass, will prescribe for municipal courts the supremacy of the Law of Nations over the law of the land – a consummation which will go much beyond the doctrine of adoption as now operative in this or any other country.[1]

[1] There may and probably will be intermediate stages in that development. At present the supremacy of the Legislature sets a definite limit to the doctrine of adoption. In the future, States so inclined and possessing written Constitutions may deprive themselves of the power to enact legislation contrary to the fundamental provision making international law an integral part of their system. They may also, in order to safeguard that part of the Constitution from the vicissitudes of internal changes, bind themselves reciprocally by treaty not to modify the fundamental law in that respect except by common consent. This might be a procedure suitable for States without a written Constitution. Such changes would imply a limitation of legislative power and the conferment upon courts, national or international, of the competence to invalidate legislation contrary to international law. As such, they would signify a radical innovation in the constitutional law of most countries in which judicial review of legislation is unknown.

INDEX

For EU product safety concerns, contact us at Calle de José Abascal, 56–1°,
28003 Madrid, Spain or eugpsr@cambridge.org.

www.ingramcontent.com/pod-product-compliance
Ingram Content Group UK Ltd.
Pitfield, Milton Keynes, MK11 3LW, UK
UKHW040229290926
15471UKWH00001B/83
* 9 7 8 0 5 2 1 1 0 7 4 1 9 *